Your Best Money Moves Now

By the Editors of MONEY Magazine

Edited by Junius Ellis

Contents

MONEY is a registered trademark of Time Inc.
Copyright © 1993 Time Inc.

Hardcover ISBN: 0-8487-1157-2
Manufactured in the United States of America
First Printing 1993

To order MONEY magazine, call Customer Service at 800-633-9970 or write to MONEY, P.O. Box 60001, Tampa, Florida 33660-0001.

Published by MONEY Books
Time Inc.
1271 Avenue of the Americas
New York, NY 10020

Your Best Money Moves Now

Editor: Junius Ellis
Art Director: Melissa Tardiff Design

New Business Development

Director: David Gitow
Assistant Director: Mary Warner McGrade
Operations Director: Deb Heilig
Production Director: John Calvano

Chapter 1

Where to Put Your Money in 1993

President Bill Clinton's victory was decisive. But now the voters who gave him a mandate to fix the economy are worrying that the task will overwhelm the former Democratic governor of the nation's fourth poorest state. Their hopes and fears can be summarized this way: will we get Kennedy or Carter? Can the new President rekindle the youthful idealism and sense of limitless possibility of the early 1960s, when Kennedy founded the Peace Corps and vowed that Americans would soon walk on the moon? Or will Clinton stand by as the country gives way to the helplessness that characterized the Carter years, when America was held hostage by runaway inflation at home and Third World thugs abroad?

The question is important for investors too. In Kennedy's first year, the Dow Jones industrial average rose a stunning 19%, and it went on to provide an average annual return of 13% over four years. Carter's first year was marked by a harrowing 17% price decline, and over his four years the Dow returned only 5% annually. The Carter term also hurt bondholders, who lost an average of 1.6% a year on long-term Treasuries, compared with annual gains of 3% in the four years following Kennedy's election.

Realistically, no one should expect the Clinton Administration to replicate Kennedy's Camelot. But that doesn't mean the alternative is Carter's fumbling and bumbling. The most likely scenario will be somewhere in between. Here's what many analysts foresee for the economy and the stock market:

The lid will stay on inflation. The 51 economists polled by Blue Chip Economic Indicators in Sedona, Arizona see an inflation rate of only 3.2% this year, a tad above the 3% rate estimated for 1992. MONEY thinks inflation could run a bit faster, about 3.5% or so, but still safely below the 4% to 5% range that would threaten investors.

Interest rates will remain in check. James Stack, editor of investment newsletter *InvesTech Market*

Will Clinton be a Kennedy or a Carter?

On average, the 30 Dow industrials have gained a modest 4.1% in the first year of presidential terms since World War II and 3.3% for the past eight terms shown at right.

Such subdued advances, however, mask some rather large variations. In John F. Kennedy's first year in office, the Dow rocketed up 18.7%, while in Jimmy Carter's first year, it suffered a 17.3% loss.

Analysts say that stock market behavior during a President's initial year reflects economic cycles more than political concerns. Since 1900, the Dow has had about the same chance of rising under both Republicans and Democrats. The swing factor was often whether stock prices had risen 15% or more in the year before the election year. Six of the eight times that happened, a bear market took hold within a year of the Inauguration.

Federal Reserve policies also have an effect. In the four years when the Fed aggressively pushed up short-term interest rates, the Dow fell (1969, 1973, 1977 and 1981). In the four years when rates went up only a little or declined, share prices rose (1961, 1965, 1985 and 1989).

Both those indicators are bad news for 1993. Since stocks rose 20% in 1991 and most economists think rates are likely to rise next year, the stock market in Clinton's first year may face hard going.

HOW THE DOW HAS FARED IN THE FIRST YEAR

61 KENNEDY — +18.7%

77 CARTER — -17.3%

65 JOHNSON — +10.9%

81 REAGAN — -9.2%

69 NIXON — -15.2%

85 REAGAN — +27.7%

73 NIXON — -16.6%

89 BUSH — +27.0%

Analyst in Whitefish, Montana, predicts that short-term rates will edge up from 3% to around 4% in 1993, though yields on long-term U.S. Tresuries, lately about 7.4%, could dip a little more. MONEY agrees with Stack on short-term rates but thinks a stronger economy could boost long-term rates above 8% by year-end.

Economic growth will pick up thanks in part to Clinton's policies. "An investment tax credit and acceleration in infrastructure spending would provide a small dose of budgetary stimulus," says Robert Barbera, Shearson Lehman's chief economist. He projects that even $20 billion of additional government spending—less than half what Clinton has proposed for the first year—could help push growth in real gross domestic product above a 3.5% annual rate in the first half of 1993.

Investors will soon realize how profitable U.S. companies are becoming. In the first half of 1992, corporate profits expanded at roughly a 25% annual rate, compared with a 4% decline in 1991, and are continuing to rebound, notes John Dessauer, publisher of *Dessauer's Journal of Financial Markets* in Orleans, Massachusetts. Says he: "Six months into 1993, analysts are likely to be talking about back-to-back years of double-digit earnings growth."

Stocks will move higher. "The market is likely to get off to a good start in 1993," says James Solloway, director of research at Argus Research in New York City. "You could see 10% appreciation in the first six months." That would translate into an all-time high with the Dow above 3500. Moreover, small-company shares could climb faster. Later in 1993, however, stocks could easily give back at least half their gains because of a slowing economy. Historically, the Dow has risen an average of 4% in the year following a presidential election. Unfortunately, this post-election year probably won't be that much better. We think both large- and small-company shares will be ahead by only 4% to 5% at year-end.

The problem for stocks is that the outlook for the economy beyond 1993 isn't encouraging. The main reasons: the sluggish growth in consumer incomes for the past 20 years and the relentless expansion of the national debt over the past 10 will curb basic growth. Any lasting stock boom would require a reversal of the long-established trends for corporate profitability as well as personal income. Prior to 1970, corporate pretax operating profits averaged around 12% of total national income. Since then, those profits fell to the 9% to 10% range in the 1970s and to less than 9% in the 1980s. Similarly, per capita GDP that rose 2.7% a year prior to 1973 has inched up only 1.2% on average since then.

To turn those trends around, some of Clinton's policies are targeted to boost profit growth and improve workers' skills. Reform of the health-care system, if done intelligently, could lighten one of the crushing loads corporations carry—the costs of medical benefits, which have doubled since 1986. In addition, money spent on public education and worker retraining would make U.S. labor more productive. But these programs could further burden corporations by increasing the costs of doing business.

Here's the bottom line for investors in 1993. The stock market could well rally 10% by this spring on a stronger economy and somewhat more buoyant consumer confidence. After that, however, stocks are likely to slip back to a 4% to 5% gain for the year as investors begin to focus on 1994 and beyond. "By the end of 1993, the market will be flat or up only nominally," says Michael Metz, chief investment strategist at Oppenheimer & Co. After 1993, the outlook for stocks could turn negative. "Following seven of the past eight presidential elections, a bear market has started within 18 months," says Stack of *InvesTech.* The exception was the 1985-86 period of Reagan's second term.

Therefore, your best strategy for 1993 is to invest cautiously with 35% to 50% of your money in blue chips and top-quality growth stocks. You may also be able to earn above-average gains on some select foreign investments that could outperform those in the U.S. But you should be willing to take profits on issues that run up 20% or more in the first half of 1993.

Stack advises investors to lighten up on stocks if the Federal Reserve begins to push up interest rates to slow the economy and ensure that inflation is not allowed to build up. One sign that the economy might be moving fast enough to alarm the Fed would be a sharp drop in the unemployment rate to 7% or less. Another would be the nation's factories running above 80% of capacity, compared with a recent rate of almost 79%. You can monitor the capacity utilization rate through monthly reports in your newspaper.

Our outlook for interest rates suggests that you should stick with intermediate bonds—those that have maturities of 10 years or fewer. Take a look at tax-exempt municipal bonds if you are in the relatively high 28% tax bracket or above ($35,800 for couples; $21,450 for singles). We don't foresee large price increases for tangible assets like gold and real estate. Returns on stocks and bonds in the 1990s may run 8% to 10%, well below those earned in the 1980s.

And even though the 3% offered on such cash investments as money-market funds seems pathetic, you should always keep money in cash for emergencies and buying opportunities. Back in 1980, when interest rates were 16%, an investor in the 54% tax bracket kept only 7.4% after taxes. With inflation at 12.5%, that was a 5.1% loss in real terms. In 1993, if money fund yields average around 3.5% for the year as a whole, an investor in the 31% bracket would keep at least 2.4% after taxes, and with inflation at 3.5%, would take a 1.1% real loss. That's not great, but cash investments are doing better today than they would have done in the glory days of double-digit certificates of deposit.

Most important, we recommend that investors lower their expectations. The fat annual returns of 17.5% on stocks and 12.6% on bonds during the 1980s were historical aberrations. You should consider yourself a winner in 1993 if you can simply match stocks' long-term average returns of 10%. With inflation at only 3.5%, a 10% return will provide 6.5% real profit after inflation. That's in line with what the typical stock investor has earned over the past 65 years.

Investing Safely for Steady Income

Many of these alternatives could double your savings account's anemic 3% return without exposing you to unreasonable risk.

If you're an income-oriented investor, 1993 could give you a case of *déjà vu* all over again, as Yogi Berra once put it. Like last year, you want to beat the paltry payouts of around 3% on formerly reliable cash cows like money funds and bank CDs. But even if short-term rates perk up by one percentage point during the year, as MONEY predicts, money-market funds and one-year CDs will yield only 4%—hardly cause for rejoicing.

Take heart! It's still possible to earn 7% or more without undue risk. Just accept that 1993 will be a trying year and chart your course accordingly. You should resist the impulse, for example, to load up your portfolio with 30-year Treasury bonds recommended by some advisers because of their relatively fat 7.4% yield. Reason: with the Clinton Administration determined to shake things up, there's no guarantee where interest rates are eventually headed. If Clinton fails to get the economy moving, long-term rates could slump another half point and add 6% to the value of your bonds. But it's equally plausible that his plans to spend $220 billion on new government programs by 1996 will renew fears of inflation, causing rates to rise by three-quarters of a point this year. That would knock 8% off your bonds' value and send your total return under water. Advises Richard Hoey, chief economist at Dreyfus Corp.: "Investors should keep their cool in 1993 and avoid making big bets on the direction of interest rates."

We agree. Besides the one-point rise in short-term rates, we expect long-term rates to tick up to about 8%. That is why we're advising income investors to stick mainly to intermediate- and even short-term instruments that are less susceptible than long-term ones to capital gains or losses on an interest-rate move.

The core of your holdings, say 50% of your income portfolio, should be in bonds or bond funds with maturities of five to 10 years. Yielding around 6%, these give you nearly as much income as a long-term bond with much less interest-rate risk. Even if intermediate rates climb by three-quarters of a point, for instance, a five-year Treasury bond would lose only 3% of its value—giving you a total return no worse than a money fund. And if rates stay level or fall, you'll earn twice what a money fund would pay—and possibly more.

For juicier yields, make tax-free municipal bonds or funds the centerpiece of this part of your income portfolio. Intermediate-term tax-exempt funds were recently yielding about 5.5%, equivalent to a taxable 7.6% for investors in the 28% federal tax bracket (singles making at least $21,450, couples $35,800). Another 30% to 40% of your income portfolio should go into money funds and short-term bond funds, despite their low 3% to 5% yields. They serve as a safety net and will benefit immediately from any hike in short-term rates. As for the other 10% to 20% of your holdings, consider putting it into funds that

hold riskier investments like high-dividend stocks (recently yielding 5% to 8%), Ginnie Maes (7% to 7.5%) or high-yield corporate bonds (9% to 10%), also known as junk bonds. These will bolster your earnings and lock in today's yields in case rates decline.

Should you buy individual bonds or funds? The short answer is choose funds if you have less than $25,000 to invest or if you simply don't want the bother of selecting bonds. A fund's diversified portfolio will insulate you against defaults. And the minimum investment, as low as $1,000, makes it easy to get in. If you decide to go with individual bonds, try laddering—that is, buying separate issues that mature in, say, two, four, six, eight and 10 years. That way, if rates rise, your longer-term bonds will suffer but you can reinvest the short-term ones at higher rates as they mature.

Given those rules, here are some of the income options available today, starting with money-market funds, then bond, stock and mortgage funds and, last, individual bonds.

Money-market funds. Their recent yield of 2.8% on average won't even keep you ahead of today's 3% inflation rate. You can squeeze out a bit more by going with tax-free funds like Strong Municipal (800-368-1030). The fund's 2.9% payout is equivalent to taxable yields of 4% and 4.2% for investors in the 28% and 31% (singles making $51,900 or more, couples $86,500) brackets respectively. But you're still losing money after taxes and inflation.

So why keep any money here at all? One reason is safety. Since money funds invest in securities with maturities of a year or less, the risk of loss is minuscule. Also, if long-term rates surprise the experts by spurting upward, you can move a portion of your money fund holdings into longer-term funds to lock in higher earnings. But choose a fund that is part of a family large enough to dip into its own pockets to make up any loss caused by defaults. Although such shortfalls are rare, John Nuveen, Evergreen and three other investment firms had to shore up their funds' share value last year after the failure of insurance company Mutual Benefit Life, which backed some of their holdings.

Short-term bond funds. By tiptoeing out to maturities of just one to three years, you can beat money funds' payout by two to three percentage points. An example is the T. Rowe Price Short-Term Bond fund (800-541-8832), which recently yielded 5.8% on its investments in government, corporate and mortgage-backed issues. But since its average weighted maturity is just 2.4 years, a one-point jump in rates would nick its share price only 2%. You can find even sweeter deals among tax-free funds. Flagship's Limited Term Tax-Exempt (800-227-4648) recently yielded nearly 4.8%, or the equivalent of a taxable 6.7% and 7%, respectively, for investors in the 28% and 31% tax brackets.

Intermediate-term bond funds. For yummy returns without stomach-wrenching risks, check out bond funds such as Fidelity Intermediate Corporate (800-544-8888), yielding 6.2%. Or choose a muni fund like Scudder Medium Term Tax-Free (800-225-2470), with a 5.6% yield that's the equivalent of a taxable 7.8% and 8.1% in the 28% and 31% brackets. To avoid defaults, buy only funds whose bonds average no less than Standard & Poor's second-highest grade of AA (or Moody's Aa). And since most bonds can be called (redeemed) early, ask about the fund's effective maturity—that is, the average of those dates on which its bonds are likely to be called. Steer clear of long-term bonds (those with maturities of 15 years or more) unless their rates move above 8%. If that happens, then consider shifting another 10% of your portfolio out of cash and into long bonds.

High-yield stock funds. Though they are generally more volatile than their bond brethren, high-dividend stock funds such as Franklin Income Series (800-342-5236) lately yielded upwards of 7.7%, beating long-term Treasuries. Such funds fall into two broad categories. So-called equity income funds, like the Franklin entry, invest in a mixture of bonds and high-dividend stocks. And utility funds like Fortress Utilities Fund (800-245-5051), recently returning around 5.5%, buy shares of electric-power, telephone and other such companies. True, their share price will fluctuate. But if you can afford to leave your money in them for, say, three or more years, you can probably ride out any market setbacks—and you may wind up with capital gains.

Ginnie Mae funds. These funds, which hold mortgage-backed securities issued by the Government National Mortgage Association, offer nearly the same protection against default risk as Treasuries but with yields that average as much as a percentage point higher. Be wary, however, of Ginnie Mae funds that yield in the 8% to 9% range. They probably own a lot of older, high-rate mortgages. As homeowners repay those loans early by refinancing, the fund manager has to reinvest the money in new, lower-rate mortgages, thus dragging down your yields. To avoid such unpleasant surprises, concentrate on funds like Benham GNMA Income Fund (800-472-3389) that pay 7.5% or so.

Also watch out for two other mortgage-backed investments: adjustable-rate mortgage (or ARM) funds and collateralized mortgage obligations (or CMOs). Though ARM funds share the prepayment risk of Ginnie Maes, they yield only about 5%—not enough of a premium to make them really worthwhile. CMOs, which recently yielded a tempting 8% to 8.5% at maturities of seven to 10 years, purport to reduce prepayment risk by dividing their loans into short-, intermediate- and long-term pools according to the likelihood of early repayment. Unfortunately, the issues that are sold to the public tend to be loan portfolios with relatively high risk whose yield may be most likely to dwindle.

Junk bond funds. After falling apart in 1990,

high-yield, low-quality junk bonds made a roaring comeback by delivering a total return of 50% since then (funds that specialize in them lately yielded 8% to 13%). But downgrades of Marriott Corp. bonds shook the junk market in October 1992, sending some funds tumbling nearly 4% in just three weeks. So if you dabble in junk, stick with funds like Vanguard High Yield Corporate (800-851-4999), yielding around 10%, that keep at least a quarter of their assets in bonds rated BB or better by S&P (Ba by Moody's).

U.S. Treasuries. Why go through the hassle of buying Treasuries on your own when no-load funds will buy them for you? First, unlike a fund, which never matures, individual Treasuries pay you back at face value at maturity. You get your principal plus earnings regardless of where interest rates happen to stand then. (In a fund, on the other hand, if interest rates are up, your share price will be down, and vice versa.) Second, if you have at least $1,000 to invest, you can buy Treasuries from the nearest office of the Federal Reserve. You will avoid the $50 or so you'd have to pay a broker or the 0.5% to 1% a fund would collect in annual management expenses.

Tax-exempt municipal bonds. If you have $25,000 or more to invest, you can buy individual munis usually sold in lots of $5,000 each. But if your stake is less than $50,000 or so, you should limit yourself to the very safest type— pre-refunded munis. These are typically older, high-interest-rate issues that have already been targeted for early redemption by the city or state that sold them. The municipality floats a second bond issue and invests the proceeds in Treasuries that will pay off the original bonds at the earliest possible date. Thus investors don't have to worry about defaults with pre-refunded bonds. And thanks to the recent wave of refinancings, some pre-refunded bonds are still attractively priced.

Finally, with $50,000 or more, you can create your own bond portfolio. Ideally, you should diversify your holdings among at least 10 issues with laddered maturities. Next to pre-refunded bonds, the safest ones are general-obligation bonds with S&P's top AAA rating (Moody's Aaa), since G.O.s are usually backed by the full taxing power of the issuer. But you can also sleep soundly with high-quality essential-services bonds—those that will be paid off with income from water, sewer or electric services.

Stocks to Buy, Sell or Hold

Even if this year's stock market proves to be difficult, some of these 50 new and true-blue chips seem destined for returns of 50% or more.

Although many pros expect the stock market to deliver ho-hum gains of about 5% in 1993, they're all on the lookout for issues that figure to shine in an otherwise lackluster year. MONEY has focused its search among blue chips. Reason: shares of large, high-quality firms can easily ride out the 5% or so market correction analysts anticipate in the second half of 1993. Many

volatile small stocks, on the other hand, are likely to get pounded down 10% or more during such a setback.

What qualifies as a genuine blue-chip stock these days? For answers, turn to page 14 and our exclusive ranking of 50 true-blue chips by their projected returns through 1993. To create our list, MONEY asked Waltham, Massachusetts consulting firm Mitchell & Co. to screen more than 4,000 companies for those that possessed these attributes: ample size (annual sales of at least $600 million), financial strength (debt equal to 50% or less of total capitalization) and consistent earnings growth (no more than three annual earnings declines from continuing operations during the past decade). In addition, all of the stocks paid a dividend yield of at least 1.4%. The consultants then applied proprietary techniques to identify the stocks on the list poised for significant price gains this year.

Our table contains several major surprises. For example, if you believe the 30 issues that make up the Dow Jones industrial average are as blue as they come, you'd better think again. Only four Dow shares made the cut for our lineup— General Electric, Merck, Minnesota Mining & Manufacturing (3M) and Procter & Gamble— and just one (Merck) is considered a buy for this year. Conspicuously absent from our 50-stock roster is IBM. Its shareholders, saddled with a 62% loss since 1987, might well agree with our unambiguous conclusion that Big Blue isn't blue chip anymore. Moreover, among the 50 stocks that did qualify as true blues, we discovered that some of the best-loved stocks on Wall Street, like 3M, could be losers in 1993. Meanwhile, the out-of-favor shares of financial services and publishing company McGraw-Hill—down 29% from its peak in 1989—are projected to surge to a nearly 46% gain for the year.

To arrive at its forecasts for 1993, Mitchell & Co. studied 15 years of trading history for each of the 50 selections, seeking the single variable— book value, cash flow, return on equity or sales, dividends, earnings or revenues—that had the greatest impact on each stock's price. Contrary to what you might expect, only 11 of the 50 companies' share prices moved in tandem with changes in the firms' earnings. The stocks of the remaining 39 companies responded mainly to one of the other six factors. For example, shares of food company H.J. Heinz, which attract income-oriented investors, typically fluctuate with dividend

growth. After isolating the crucial variables, the consultants used projected data for these factors from the *Value Line Investment Survey* to predict prices and total returns for each stock in 1993. Here's a rundown on selected blue chips within three winning categories:

Health-care providers. Although most of the 12 drug manufacturers in our lineup seem due to deliver tantalizing returns, analysts warn that President Clinton's aim to impose curbs on health-care costs could fundamentally change the outlook for many of these shares, leaving them short of their target share prices. So you might be wise to limit your drug-company holdings to Merck and Abbott Laboratories, which can develop new drugs to boost profits without raising prices. The stock price of Merck (projected 1993 return: 57%) mainly follows changes in the amount of cash the firm generates, which can be used to develop and promote new products. Analysts estimate that Merck's cash flow will rise 19% in 1993, driven by the strong performance of cholesterol-reducing Zocor as well as the 18 other major drugs it sells.

Historically, shares of Abbott Labs (projected return: 45%) have tracked the company's profits, which have grown 14% or more a year since 1981. While the firm derives only 40% of its earnings from pharmaceuticals, it has at least three major new drugs that should boost the division's earnings 20% annually during the next three to five years. Analysts also estimate that profits at Abbott's hospital and lab products division will climb 11% this year.

Makers of consumer goods. Among companies with popular consumer products, the highest rated in our analysis was Borden (projected return: 47%), the largest U.S. dairy company and the world's largest pastamaker. Borden's share price has typically tracked changes in cash flow, which could improve markedly in the next few years. Recent closings of scores of outdated facilities and a $650 million investment to build

50 True-Blue Chips for '93

You won't find faded blues like IBM—or, for that matter, 25 other of the 30 Dow industrials— in our exclusive ranking of 50 top blue chips compiled for MONEY by consulting firm Mitchell & Co. of Waltham, Massachusetts. Instead, our list is limited to companies with true blue-chip pedigrees—that is, firms that have the size, financial strength and earnings power to deliver solid returns to investors who buy them at the right price. Some shares that we have rated as buys may be surprising—and might make your broker cringe. Example: Borden, shunned by investors because of its three years of flat earnings, is projected to gain 47% in 1993. You should consider adding stocks rated as holds if their prices should decline sharply during the year.

One word of caution here. Though nine drug stocks on our roster are rated as buys, some could fall short of their projected returns in the event the Clinton Administration reins in health-care costs. So stick to Merck and Abbott Labs, whose promising pipelines of new drugs could boost earnings even if prices overall plateau.

Note: all stocks trade on the New York Stock Exchange except for McCormick and Reuters, which trade over the counter. Projected returns are for the period from November 9, 1992 through December 31, 1993. The price/earnings (P/E) ratios and yields reflect estimated 1993 earnings and dividends.

Rank	Stock	Projected capital gain (loss) through Dec. 31, 1993	Recent price	P/E ratio	Projected dividend yield	Projected 1993 revenues (in millions)
1	Syntex	84.3%	$25.25	9.7	4.7%	$2,400
2	Marion Merrell Dow	75.0	25.00	8.6	4.6	3,900
3	Eli Lilly	62.5	61.25	10.7	4.2	7,000
4	Merck	57.1	42.00	16.5	2.7	10,600
5	Warner-Lambert	49.9	66.75	12.5	3.5	6,015
6	Borden	47.4	27.25	11.1	4.8	7,575
7	McGraw-Hill	45.5	61.50	15.0	3.7	2,300
8	Abbott Laboratories	44.9	27.75	15.9	2.5	8,675
9	Bristol-Myers Squibb	36.6	64.75	13.2	4.6	13,000
10	H.J. Heinz	28.8	38.75	13.8	3.3	8,000
11	Rite Aid	26.9	23.00	12.4	2.6	4,500
12	General Motors E shares	26.4	28.25	17.7	1.4	9,200
13	Schering-Plough	26.2	61.25	14.4	2.9	4,500
14	British Telecom	26.0	58.00	10.3	6.5	23,500
15	Stanhome	23.8	33.00	10.6	3.0	865
16	Glaxo Holdings	23.4	24.75	18.3	3.6	8,200
17	Hubbell B shares	21.4	51.00	15.7	3.3	840

BUY

Rank	Stock	Projected capital gain (loss) through Dec. 31, 1993	Recent price	P/E ratio	Projected dividend yield	Projected 1993 revenues (in millions)
18	Deluxe	17.4%	$43.00	16.2	3.4%	$1,630
19	Bemis	15.4	23.00	17.0	2.3	1,290
20	Hershey Foods	14.3	46.50	15.8	2.5	3,450
21	Seagram	13.6	27.00	12.0	2.5	5,500
22	General Electric	12.6	77.50	12.6	3.4	44,800
23	Sherwin-Williams	11.8	29.00	15.7	1.7	2,985
24	Pfizer	9.2	74.00	19.0	2.4	8,400
25	American Home Products	8.8	65.25	11.9	4.6	8,600
26	Tambrands	8.0	68.00	18.9	2.2	770
27	Anheuser-Busch	7.8	57.25	14.3	2.2	12,000
28	H&R Block	7.1	38.75	20.4	2.8	1,650
29	McCormick	6.2	27.00	20.0	1.6	1,600
30	SmithKline Beecham	3.2	40.50	20.8	2.6	10,000
31	Clorox	1.9	43.50	14.5	3.9	1,840
32	Loctite	1.3	45.25	18.5	1.9	665

HOLD

Rank	Stock	Projected capital gain (loss) through Dec. 31, 1993	Recent price	P/E ratio	Projected dividend yield	Projected 1993 revenues (in millions)
33	Dun & Bradstreet	(1.6%)	$57.50	16.0	4.1%	$5,300
34	UST	(2.8)	33.25	20.2	2.9	1,230
35	Emerson Electric	(4.3)	51.75	15.9	2.8	8,700
36	International Flavors & Fragrances	(4.4)	113.25	20.6	2.6	1,265
37	Gannett	(4.6)	50.75	18.1	2.6	3,790
38	Potomac Electric Power	(4.7)	25.00	12.5	6.6	1,680
39	Kimberly-Clark	(5.3)	58.25	16.6	3.1	7,800
40	San Diego Gas & Electric	(5.6)	23.75	12.8	6.2	1,965
41	Kellogg	(5.7)	71.50	22.3	1.9	7,000
42	Polaroid	(7.6)	31.25	12.5	1.9	2,365
43	Interpublic Group	(7.8)	33.50	18.6	1.6	2,100
44	Minnesota Mining & Mfg.	(8.9)	104.75	16.5	3.2	14,815
45	K Mart	(13.1)	25.50	10.6	3.8	42,000
46	Procter & Gamble	(13.6)	53.25	18.4	2.1	32,000
47	Reuters	(14.3)	57.25	18.5	2.4	2,900
48	R.R. Donnelley	(16.5)	30.75	17.6	1.7	4,500
49	Wrigley	(17.4)	35.00	8.4	5.9	1,365
50	Sara Lee	(26.4)	58.50	20.9	1.9	14,000

SELL

10 giant plants worldwide could save $100 million by 1995. A $644 million restructuring announced in October 1992 could save another $100 million within two years. Portfolio manager David Katz of Matrix Asset Advisors in New York City figures that the amount of cash the firm generates will grow by 10% in 1993.

Or consider H.J. Heinz (projected return: 29%). Analyst Michael Mauboussin of First Boston in New York City thinks this maker of some 20 leading food brands, including Heinz ketchup and Star Kist tuna, will reward shareholders with an 11% dividend increase this year. Investors monitor that payout closely as an indicator of insiders' faith in the firm's long-term outlook, especially since the firm's earnings have been so volatile in recent years. The company's top managers have good reason to be confident. Chairman Anthony O'Reilly is reorganizing the firm's production process, which Mauboussin thinks will help generate $290 million in cash during the fiscal year ending April 30, a 26% increase.

Shares of Rite Aid (projected return: 27%), the country's largest drugstore chain, fluctuate with earnings. To improve profitability, the company will finish by early 1994 installing scanning systems that boost productivity in stores by speeding checkouts and keeping close tabs on inventory. Analyst Donald Hultgren of Raymond James & Associates expects earnings will rise 16% in 1993. Yet the shares trade at a below-average earnings multiple based on his 1993 estimate. By contrast, dividends drive the stock of Stanhome (projected return: 23.8%), which markets gifts and other products through retailers, in-home demonstrations and the mail. And for good reason: payouts have increased nine consecutive years and analysts foresee a 9% hike in 1993. The company also has $60 million in cash that can be used to fund additional dividend increases over the next few years.

Highly cyclical companies. A recovering economy should give a big lift to shares of strong companies whose prospects are closely linked to business conditions. Take McGraw-Hill (projected return: 46%), a publishing and information services giant. The firm's shares, which tend to trace its earnings, have fallen by 29% over the past three years, partly because of depressed results at its publishing division, which includes *Business Week* and 36 other publications. But corporate and muni bond offerings surged 76% last year, helping to lift profits 19% at the firm's financial services group, which rates the credit quality of such issues. Moreover, higher demand for advertising pages boosted publishing profits 9%. Analyst Douglas Arthur of Kidder Peabody figures earnings will rise 14% in 1993, even assuming the economy grows at only a modest 2% to 3% annual rate.

General Motors Class E shares (projected return: 26%) allow you to buy a stake in GM subsidiary EDS, provider of data processing and communications services to corporate and government clients, without investing in the loss-plagued parent company. Investors typically focus on changes in EDS' book value—a measure of underlying assets—and analysts project that figure will rise 18% in 1993 as the firm continues to profit from increasing worldwide demand for services that improve productivity.

Hubbell (projected return: 21%) is a manufacturer of electrical equipment for industrial customers. Analysts say a stronger economy and Hubbell's recent acquisition of Hipotronics, which makes equipment to test voltage, will help boost profits 7% in 1993. Almost all of that gain as well as earnings from upcoming acquisitions will flow to the firm's book value, boosting that figure nearly 10%. That's good news since Hubbell's share price rises in line with its increasing book value.

Our blue-chip list includes four foreign companies whose shares trade on the New York Stock Exchange or over the counter in the form of American Depositary Receipts (ADRs). The most promising is British Telecom (projected return: 26%), the leader in telephone service in the

United Kingdom. Dividends are the key factor driving this stock's price. The firm's shares recently yielded 5.7%, and the company's payout could increase 7% to $4 for each ADR this year. Analysts think the firm's earnings per ADR will rebound 20% during the fiscal year commencing March 1993 as the British economy recovers from its worst recession since World War II. The firm will help deliver that gain by slashing its work force 25% in two years. That figures to wire the company for profit increases of 7% annually over the next five years.

Add spice with growth stocks. Consider pepping up your blue-chip holdings with a few hot growth companies. To find the best buys, MONEY canvassed analysts and fund managers for picks with these traits: 1) estimated sales of at least $300 million this year; 2) solid balance sheets with debt no more than 40% of total capital; 3) likely profit growth of at least 15% in 1993 and beyond; and 4) projected price appreciation of 20% or more in 1993. Here are the pros' most promising recommendations, all of which trade on the New York Stock Exchange:

■ Gillette (lately $60). Fueled by the stunning success of the three-year-old Sensor shaving system, which now controls nearly one-fifth of the $3 billion wet-shaving market, Gillette's earnings have increased 22% annually since 1989. Analyst Gabe Lowy at Gruntal & Co. in New York City predicts that profits will stay on that track as the $5 billion company pushes its new Sensor for women and expands in such undeveloped markets as China, Russia and Turkey. Lowy adds that 70% or more of the company's revenues and earnings will come from international sales within five years. He also expects Gillette's shares to rise 21% to around $72 this year.

■ Franklin Resources ($37). Eaton Vance Special Equities fund manager Clifford Krauss in Boston believes this mutual fund operator with $85 billion under management should rack up a 15% to 20% profit gain this year. The main impetus, he argues, is that Franklin's stable of 36

municipal bond funds should benefit from a growing appetite for tax-free investments as Clinton raises taxes. Krauss' 1993 target price is around $46, a 26% gain.

■ Blockbuster Entertainment ($17). Despite its astronomic 13,788% sales growth since shifting from a dead-end computer software outfit to a videocassette rental business in 1985, investors are skeptical of $1.1 billion Blockbuster's prospects. Reason: the growing availability of pay-per-view movies on cable television. But Kidder Peabody analyst Gary Jacobson sees five-year earnings growth of 30% annually spurred by expansion overseas and a recent agreement with London's Virgin Retail Group to develop a chain of music megastores in the U.S., Australia and Europe. He also figures the stock can fast-forward 29% to about $22 in 1993.

■ CML Group ($31). The fitness craze could help this $500 million manufacturer and retailer of athletic gear and apparel pump hearty profits for the rest of the decade. Primed by its popular NordicTrack exercise machine and the introduction of two home exercise equipment systems, CML's earnings should sprint 30% or more annually over the next few years, says Fred Kobrick of State Street Research in Boston. His 1993 target price is $50 or so, a 64% gain.

■ Liz Claiborne ($41). Wall Street hemmed its expectations for this $2.2 billion apparel company, fearing it had little room to grow in the upscale department stores that provided 26% annual earnings gains since 1987. But Dick Weiss, co-manager of the Strong Common Stock Fund in Milwaukee, says Liz's purchase of the Russ Togs label last year gets the firm into moderate-priced retailers, such as Sears and J.C. Penney, which offer twice as big a potential market as more expensive stores. He sees the stock rising 45% to around $60 by early 1994.

■ Continental Medical Systems ($19). A Texas State commission inquiry into the medical rehabilitation industry last year hurt the stocks of many rehabbers, including shares of $659 million Continental. But the commission turned up no major wrongdoing at the firm, which is the nation's largest independent provider of occupational, speech and physical therapy. State Street Research's Kobrick says the stock could rebound 50% in 1993. Beyond that, he expects profits to double every three years as rehabilitation patients move from hospitals to Continental's more efficient—and much cheaper—centers.

Five Funds That Figure to Thrive

To succeed this year, fund managers must be independent-minded and vigilant against overpaying for stocks—just like these five exemplars.

If MONEY's economic and market forecasts are on target, the top stock funds in 1993 will be those whose managers can withstand market downturns and, at the same time, sniff out the values created by such slides. That's why, in nominating five funds that could handily outpace the competition this year, we chose veterans whose performance ranked in the top half of their categories in difficult markets in the past. We also stuck with disciplined value seekers. Such managers scour the markets for undiscovered bargains and eschew the most popular (and invariably overpriced) stocks. We start with funds that take the least amount of risk and then proceed to the modestly more daring ones that are investing in underappreciated sectors their managers believe will shine this year.

SoGen International. Despite $501 million SoGen International's name, manager Jean-Marie Eveillard usually keeps half of his shareholdings in U.S. stocks. Indeed, we classify SoGen (3.75% load; 800-628-0252) as a domestic growth fund, though many fund rating services variously list it as a global or as an asset-allocation fund. What is indisputable, however, is that Eveillard will invest anywhere in the world he can find securities that he thinks other investors have unwisely disdained. And when he can't find them, he has no hesitation about keeping the

fund's assets largely stashed in cash. "My first priority is not to lose any money," he says.

Because of Eveillard's aversion to risk, SoGen's price fluctuates only 30% as much as that of the average growth fund. But the fund's return hasn't suffered. As of mid-November 1992, its 335% gain for the past decade beat the average stock fund's 272% return by nearly 20%. For most of 1992, SoGen returned a solid 6.7% (vs. 3.5% for the typical growth portfolio) even though Eveillard was more than usually cautious. Only 43% of the fund was in stocks, 21% in bonds, 30% in cash and 6% in gold-related securities. "President Clinton is unlikely to engineer a sustained recovery in the U.S.," he explains, "and most markets overseas are still overvalued."

Eveillard, who has run SoGen International in New York City since 1979, nevertheless sees a few values in the U.S. and abroad. One typical pick is Manville Corp., the former asbestos company still stigmatized by its 1982 bankruptcy filing. Now reorganized, Manville generates revenues of $1 billion from producing beverage packaging materials. "With the stock trading at 30% below asset value," says Eveillard, "we could see big gains when Wall Street finally recognizes Manville's value." Among corporate bonds, he prefers below-investment-grade issues with above-average yields. Here too, Eveillard insists on minimizing risks. "We research each company's finances carefully," he says. "And we don't buy real junk." Thus the fund recently yielded a CD-beating 4.3%. That means SoGen shareholders will at least earn steady income while waiting for other investors to discover the treasures that Eveillard found first.

Dreyfus Strategic World Investing. Manager Fiona Biggs has shaped her $112 million Dreyfus Strategic World Investing (3% load; 800-782-6620) into an even more idiosyncratic portfolio than Eveillard's. Biggs, niece of Barton Biggs, chairman of Morgan Stanley Asset Management and a *Wall Street Week* regular, has run this global fund since 1988. To protect shareholders from losses, she uses short-term hedging tactics involving futures, options and short sales. These allowed her to keep a very cautious 75% of her assets in cash without condemning the fund to a 3% money-market return. Yet Strategic World's recent five-year return of 13.3% annually was almost double the average global fund's 7.8% gain, with less than half of the risk. "If my bets pay off, the fund will gain more than its cash position would indicate," she explains. "If not, the fund is less likely to do as badly as it would fully invested in stocks."

Biggs' conservative stance grows out of her bearish outlook for world stock markets. "Europe is going into a recession that could last two years, and the U.S. will go into a bear market this year," she predicts. Biggs recently had sold short some 15 stocks, worth about 16% of the portfolio, that she figures are particularly vulnerable to market declines. (Short selling involves borrowing shares and selling them, in the expectation that the price will drop and allow you to replace the borrowed shares at a lower price.) Among her short sales is software giant Microsoft, which she believes will report disappointing earnings this year because of Europe's recession.

Still, Biggs does see a few bright spots. She expects the U.S. economy to recover gradually over 1993. Thus she lately had 7% of Strategic World invested in companies that could do well despite slow growth, such as natural gas concerns. "Demand for natural gas has finally outstripped supply, which will lead to higher prices," she says. And Biggs is downright bullish on Southeast Asia companies, in which she plans to double her 8% holdings this year. "Because of the rapid pace of their economic growth, Southeast Asian nations will be the best investments in the world over the next five years," she says. Her favorite bet is Hong Kong because of its growing trade with China. Despite a 47% rise through mid-November 1992, the average Hong Kong stock carried a price of only 12 times earnings, compared with 25 in the U.S. Although the British colony's scheduled absorption into China in 1997 has scared many investors away, Biggs insists: "To maintain growth, China has to preserve Hong Kong's free market." Among her top holdings were C.P. Pokphand, a poultry producer, and Hopewell Holdings, a construction firm.

Mutual Beacon. Manager Michael Price is a bad-news bull who views corporate upheavals and earnings disappointments as opportunities to pick up stocks at cheap prices. "Wall Street overreacts to bad news," says Price, captain of $500 million Mutual Beacon (no load; 800-448-3863) for eight years. "That's when we often find our best buys." This strategy has netted his growth and income fund a 10-year return of 13.8% annually, with 40% less risk than the average stock fund. But don't let the low risk fool you. During economic recoveries, when value stocks often roar back into favor, this fund can zoom. In 1988 it gained 29%, double that of the average fund. And for most of 1992, Beacon was up 17.3%, compared with 4.6% for stock funds overall.

Better yet, in early 1992, Price lowered Beacon's minimum initial investment from $50,000 to $5,000. That made his expertise widely available to small investors for the first time since June 1989, when he closed his two best-known funds, $2.7 billion Mutual Shares and

$1.2 billion Mutual Qualified, to new investors.

Price specializes in distressed securities—typically from corporations in bankruptcy or liquidation—as well as companies undergoing mergers or those about to be acquired. All together, such stocks lately accounted for 15% of the fund's stockholdings. The other 85% was invested in traditional value stocks—going concerns shunned for some reason by most investors. The fund's largest stake was Sunbeam-Oster, a maker of household products that emerged from bankruptcy two years ago. Financial stocks made up the largest sector, accounting for 17% of assets. Top picks were Fund American, a mortgage servicing company, and Chemical Bank, which has forecast $280 million in cost savings from its 1992 merger with Manufacturers Hanover. And Price has been edging into health-care stocks, many of which slumped 20% or more last year. Recent buys were drug companies Warner-Lambert and SmithKline Beecham. "Both earn most of their profits from over-the-counter drugs," he contends, "so they can grow even if Clinton regulates prescription drug prices."

Price usually maintains a small stake in foreign stocks, about 9% of Beacon's assets. A major holding has been Thorn EMI, a British record and music publisher. Says Price: "The cash flows are tremendous, but they are not reflected in the stock price."

Lindner Dividend. Income, income, income. That's the chief goal of Eric Ryback, manager of $629 million Lindner Dividend (no load; 314-727-5305). Of our five managers, Ryback keeps by far the greatest proportion of his fund's assets (79%) in fixed-income bonds and preferred stock. This tilt served Lindner Dividend well for most of 1992. As long-term Treasury bond rates fell from 8.1% in March 1992, driving up bond prices, the equity-income fund returned an impressive 17.8% through mid-November. Although interest rates probably won't provide much capital-gains kick this year, Ryback figures that he can maintain Lindner Dividend's hefty

8% yield for shareholders who buy at the recent price of around $26 a share. During the past 10 years, the fund has returned 16.7% compounded annually, vs. 13% for the average stock fund, with barely a third as much risk.

Since taking over the fund in 1982, Ryback has followed the practice of founder Kurt Lindner, 70, of digging out bargains in down-trodden market sectors. Recently Ryback has been spotting buys among convertible preferred stocks—fixed-income securities that can be converted into shares of the issuer's common stock. "When the stock prices rebound, we get solid price gains," he says. "In the meantime, we collect the income." One top holding was Tosco Corp., a petroleum refiner whose convertible preferreds lately yielded about 8%.

While Lindner Dividend sometimes holds as many as 30 common stocks, it recently had just 14 concentrated in utility and energy companies yielding at least 5%. The largest holding was Centerior Energy, a Cleveland electric utility holding company that yielded 8.5%. "Regulators agreed to accounting changes that will boost Centerior's earnings," Ryback notes. He also favors Dallas-based Texas Utilities, yielding 7.3%, and United Illuminating, which provides electricity to southern Connecticut and yielded 6.5%. As the economy recovers this year, Ryback plans to move toward economically sensitive stocks. His picks include metals producer Asarco and Eastman Kodak, which has undergone a wave of cost cutting and restructuring. "Our goal is to hold our own against growth funds in bull markets," Ryback says, "and to outperform them in down markets."

Skyline Special Equities. Bill Dutton, the biggest risk-taker among our five managers, also has the best shot at chart-topping gains this year with his $98 million Skyline Special Equities (no load; 800-458-5222). Reason: the fund specializes in small-company stocks (mainly those with market values under $400 million), traditionally among the market's riskiest. But by sticking to issues that are selling for cheap prices, Dutton has been able to post a five-year return of 21.6% annually, nearly 26% more than his group overall, with 10% less price volatility. In 1992, Skyline was up 28.7% through mid-November, compared with a 6.5% gain for the typical small-company fund. "If you buy good growth stocks at low prices," says Dutton, "you'll see big returns when the markets recognize their value."

The case for keeping 25% or so of your money in small stocks this year is persuasive. After lagging large stocks since 1983 (with the exception of 1991), small-caps are relative bargains based on their earnings potential. Furthermore, since the New Deal, small stocks have returned 22.5% annually under Democratic Presidents. To control his portfolio's risk, Dutton looks for companies growing at a 10% or faster annual clip and trading for at least 20% less than comparable stocks in the market based on their P/Es. He keeps Skyline's portfolio well diversi-fied, with no holding exceeding 3% of the fund.

This by-the-numbers style of investing befits Dutton's C.P.A. training and his seven years as a money manager before taking over Skyline in 1987. Lately, the approach has led him to load up on consumer-products and retail companies, around 30% of the portfolio. Recent picks include furnituremaker Chromcraft Revington and Younkers, a Des Moines-based chain of department stores.

If Skyline Special Equities sounds appealing, invest soon. The fund plans to charge a 3.85% front-end load after March 31, 1993. And Dutton wants to close the fund to new investors when the total assets he manages, including private accounts, hit $300 million. "We want to stay small to maintain the flexibility needed to invest in small-cap stocks," Dutton says. That should help preserve Skyline's competitiveness with other small-stock funds—and is another reason to consider the fund a possible buy in 1993.

Your Best Bets Overseas

From Europe to the Pacific Rim, foreign stocks and funds offer a shot at double-digit gains that may not be matched in the U.S. this year.

From America's perch on the planet, the rest of the world's bourses and bolsas look like bargains now that many overseas markets have plunged to tempting lows. For example, by late 1992, stocks in Italy had dropped nearly 18% and in Spain almost 30% in dollar terms for the year. Japanese stocks were down 29% and off a whopping 58% from their 1989 peak. After such slides, price/earnings multiples on many foreign shares are 15% to 30% lower than the average 14 P/E of Standard & Poor's 500 stocks.

True, European economies are in a slow-down, and Japan is a case unto itself—some might say a basket case. But pressure in Europe to slash interest rates over the next one to two years could trigger dramatic stock rallies there, just as similar U.S. rate cuts in 1990 helped push 1991 returns here above 25%. And although Japan remains a quagmire for investors, the Pacific Rim's emerging markets combine low stock multiples with vigorous economic growth that could drive prices up 25% this year.

That's why financial advisers urge Americans to allocate at least 20% of their portfolios in 1993 to foreign holdings, focusing on Europe and Southeast Asia. "These regions offer better profit potential than the U.S., not only for 1993 but also for the longer term," says Ken Gregory, editor of the newsletter *L/G No-Load Fund Analyst* (415-989-8513). "The biggest financial story of the decade will be the opening of China to world markets and, to a lesser degree, the economic unification of Europe. Now is the time for investors to get in on these events."

No matter how sizzling the prospects in individual markets, though, prudence suggests keeping at least half your foreign dollars in a diversified international stock fund. Chosen wisely, such a fund will give you a big enough stake in the hottest markets to catch most of their gains. But it will also insulate you against losses through its geographic diversification and its ability to shift quickly into more profitable corners of the globe.

Stick with fund managers who choose companies with strong fundamentals. "Most international managers spend their time on macroeconomic analysis in order to pinpoint the promising markets. But when it comes to actual stock selection, they just load up on the local blue chips," says Lori Lucas, an analyst at *Morningstar Mutual Funds*, a Chicago fund rating service. "A more value-oriented investment approach helps steer the fund out of overly expensive markets and into fast-growing stocks in more moderately priced regions."

For a solid blend of the macro and micro approaches, Philadelphia financial planner Neil Kauffman likes Warburg Pincus International Equity (800-888-6878). Manager Richard King, who has handled international portfolios for 25 years, recently had nearly 30% of his assets in the emerging Southeast Asian markets, such as Hong Kong and Singapore, and another 38% in Europe. For a more Eurocentric approach, Lucas recommends Harbor International (800-422-1050). Its manager Hakan Castegren, a 34-year veteran of foreign investing, lately had about two-thirds of his money in Europe, where low P/E stocks are plentiful.

Once you've laid a diversified foundation for your foreign holdings, put the rest of your portfolio in markets with special promise. Top choices are the eight "tigers" of the Pacific Rim. Buoyed by trade with fast-growing China and strong demand from their own burgeoning middle classes, the markets of Hong Kong, Indonesia, Korea, Malaysia, the Philippines, Singapore, Taiwan and Thailand are likely to rise 6% to 8% a year on average for the next few years. Yet they carry a modest multiple of 14 times estimated 1993 profits. Projected collective gain this year: 15% to 25%.

Given the fact that pundits don't agree on precisely which tiger will lead the pack, your best investment may be a closed-end emerging markets fund. The closed-end format ensures that the manager won't have to sell profitable holdings if investors rush for the exits during a temporary downslide. And like the more broadly invested international funds, a diversified emerging markets portfolio can cushion against setbacks in the Pacific through holdings in other promising regions, such as Latin America.

Look for closed-end funds that trade either at a discount to their net asset value (the per-share worth of the underlying portfolio) or at a premium to NAV of no more than about 2% or 3%. One top buy, according to Ken Gregory, is Morgan Stanley Emerging Markets, which lately traded on the NYSE at a reasonable 1% premium. Another possibility down the road is Templeton Emerging Markets, which has had a stunning average annual return of 36.5% over the past five years. But don't buy it now, says Morningstar's closed-end fund analyst Catherine Gillis, because it has been trading on the Big Board at a lofty premium of 23%.

While the Pacific Rim may deliver 1993's greatest overall gain, money managers have been finding a lot of individual bargains in Europe. Shares there are trading at an average P/E of only 11, since investors are concerned that Europe's economic slowdown may be longer and harsher than government forecasts suggest. American investors must also contend with the dollar's anticipated 10% to 20% climb against many Continental currencies by the end of 1993. A stronger dollar reduces foreign-earned gains and magnifies losses.

Gregory and many other analysts contend that the risk of a more serious downturn is already reflected in European stock prices. Even if the slowdown deteriorates into full-blown recession, they say, that will only force the Bundesbank, Germany's equivalent of the Federal Reserve, to move quicker to cut short-term interest rates from the current 9.5% to 6% over the next year or two. Germany's neighbors, which have kept their rates high to guard their currencies, could then drop rates to revive economic growth. That could spark market gains of as much as 50% by the end of 1994. Still, depending on the rate of recovery, you might have to wait until then to collect your profits.

For most investors, the safest way to play any European rally is through a diversified overseas fund with a heavy bet on the region, such as Harbor International. If you can accept more risk, consider putting 15% to 25% of your foreign holdings in countries like France, Spain and Britain, where already weak local currencies stand to lose less from devaluations. One way to invest in these nations is through a mix of single-country closed-end funds, such as the France Growth Fund, which recently traded on the NYSE at an attractive 8.5% discount to its NAV.

Another way to play is through American Depositary Receipts, or ADRs, which represent stocks of foreign corporations but trade on U.S. exchanges. Look for companies that 1) derive part of their earnings here, so they'd profit from a stronger dollar; and 2) can thrive even if their home economies falter.

Among British companies, for example, Gene Walden, author of *The 100 Best Stocks to Own in the World* (Dearborn, $25), singles out Glaxo Holdings, the world's second largest drug company. Glaxo gets 42% of its revenues from North America. John Dessauer, publisher of *Dessauer's Journal of Financial Markets* (800-272-7550),

favors Cable & Wireless, a telecommunications firm that earns 66% of its revenues outside Europe. In France, Walden recommends L'Oreal, a world leader in cosmetics, and Madelynn Matlock, manager of Bartlett Value International Fund, names that country's Alcatel Alsthom, a global power in telecommunications and energy. In Spain, Dessauer is bullish on Endesa, an electric utility that is pursuing an aggressive expansion plan outside of its own borders. Walden prefers Telefónica de España, the Spanish Ma Bell that's cashing in on booming phone demand .

Analysts add one firm warning: don't sink so much as a dime into Europe's fixed-income markets. While the combination of high yields and interest-rate cuts seems appealing, a rising dollar is likely to devastate any gains you might make. And what about the most heavily marked down market of all—Japan? The majority of seasoned global investors advise staying away. "The knee-jerk reaction is, 'What a great buy!'" says Ken Gregory. "But even after its big drop, Japan is still one of the world's most expensive markets, with a P/E of at least 34 and possibly much higher."

MONEY HELPS

Q. Why do so few financial advisers recommend closed-end bond funds? My three funds pay 7%, 9% and 10%. Am I missing something?
— Stefanie Kranzler, Westport, Connecticut

A. We at MONEY like closed-end bond funds (which have a fixed number of shares and trade on exchanges like stocks) as much as their open-ended brethren. Our only concern is that you not buy them at the 5% to 10% premiums at which some were recently trading—meaning you had to pay that much more than the value of the underlying securities for each share of the fund. You, on the other hand, were wise enough to buy your closed-end shares a year or so ago, when many fund shares were trading at discounts of 5% to 6%. If the discounts return later this year, closed-end funds could be good buys again.

Chapter 2

Smart Tax Tactics for the Clinton Era

As hard as it is to digest, the fact is that the median American household pays 40% of its income—two of every five dollars it makes—in federal, state and local taxes. So says the Tax Foundation, a nonpartisan research group in Washington, D.C. And that family lives far below the $200,000-a-year level where President Clinton says he will start raising taxes. We're talking about working couples with two children and gross incomes averaging $53,984. As we endeavor to explain in this chapter, Clinton's agenda will demand higher taxes of upper-middle-income Americans. Eventually, even the median family's federal income tax, now 11% of earnings, will start moving back up toward 17%, where it stood in 1981. State and local taxes, up 93% since 1982, also will continue to rise. "In the absence of a tax revolt, families could be paying 45% to 50% of their incomes in taxes by the end of the 1990s," says Paul Merski, director of fiscal affairs at the Tax Foundation.

Such unsettling forecasts make your task all the more urgent, this year and in the future. Now is the time to roll up your sleeves and dig deeper into tax planning on all three levels—federal, state and local. Delay could mean that you'll enter the new millennium as an equal-opportunity taxpayer: half for you, half for them.

How Clinton Will Change Your Taxes

Increases won't be confined to households earning over $200,000 a year. And don't hold your breath in hopes of a middle-class tax cut.

President Clinton has promised a blaze of legislation that will end the Republican era of cut-your-tax tactics. Clinton's four-year plan calls for some $220 billion in spending, including $80 billion for public works and $60 billion for job training and education. He also intends to slash the estimated $327 billion federal deficit by as much as half by 1996.

To pay for all this, Clinton has pledged $140 billion in spending cuts, primarily aimed at defense and the federal bureaucracy, as well as $150 billion in tax hikes, mostly on the rich ($90 billion) and U.S. and foreign corporations ($60 billion). But both conservative and liberal analysts say that many of his spending cuts will prove elusive. For example, the $45 billion Clinton expects to squeeze from foreign corporations may crunch down to a mere $1 billion, according to calculations by Congress' Joint Tax Committee. Moreover, all that analysts know for sure about Clinton's plan for universal health coverage is that the spending involved could dwarf most of his other programs.

The glaring gap between the taxes coming in and the money going out will have to be filled by someone, and guess who'll get hit? Yes, despite Clinton's avowed intentions to tap only the 1% of all taxpayers making $150,000 or more, you're a likely target if you're married and earn $80,000 or more, or single and make above $50,000. This conclusion is drawn from an extensive analysis of Clinton's economic plan and interviews with economists, tax experts, policy analysts and congressional staffers. Our judgment rests on two assumptions. First, Clinton is serious about both his spending and deficit-shrinking plans. And second, he will keep his pledge not to raise taxes on the middle class.

Clinton, of course, has left himself ample wiggle room by vaguely defining "middle class."

The closest he came to it was in his proposal for a "middle-class tax cut." Even then he said only that the cut would apply to couples with less than $80,000 in adjusted gross income (AGI). Between that income level and the thresholds for his tax-the-rich hikes ($200,000 for couples and $150,000 for singles) grazes the cash cow that could be milked to feed his ambitions: the upper middle class.

To keep from crippling the crawling economy, the Clinton tax measures will probably take effect in stages. For openers, the new President will undoubtedly make good on his campaign pledge to slap a 10% surcharge on people making $1 million a year in addition to hiking the top federal income tax rate from 31% to 36% on couples with AGIs above $200,000 and individuals making more than $150,000. In all, however, fewer than a million taxpayers out of 114 million earn enough to be affected. Then, once the risk of renewed recession recedes, experts say Clinton will be compelled to extend his tax increases well below those cutoffs. Among his probable means are a rate hike, tightening deductions and extending taxes on Social Security benefits. Capital gains on assets held at least one year will likely continue to be taxed at 28%.

At the same time, taxpayers making as much as $80,000 will have a long wait for the middle-class tax cuts he promised: $300 per child or $200 for childless couples and $150 for singles. That's because those breaks would cost about $60 billion over four years. Thus, barring an economic miracle or an unexpected retreat, the Clinton Presidency will bring a range of specific tax changes. The most important ones are outlined below, along with advice from tax pros on what you can do now to ease the coming bite.

Alternative minimum tax. As the second leg of his tax-the-rich plan, Clinton promised to boost the AMT rate from 24% to 26% or 27%. Watch out: the AMT could catch a lot of taxpayers who make well under $200,000. Congress enacted this whammy in 1979 to force people who were tak-ing big write-offs to pay at least some tax. Since then, however, Congress has twice craftily raised the AMT while dropping the top regular rate. Reason: as the spread narrows between your normal top rate and the AMT rate, you're more likely to be snared by the AMT. Candidates include people who exercise hefty incentive stock options or take large write-offs for state and local taxes or for home-equity-loan interest.

What to do: when the AMT rate goes up, you should first consult a tax adviser before you make any major financial moves that might trigger this onerous tax. He or she may be able to suggest steps to eliminate the danger.

Cherished deductions. Taxpayers with income in even the low six figures will continue to lose some of their deductions. Currently, the total of most of your itemized write-offs is reduced by $30 for every $1,000 of AGI above $105,250. Similarly, your exemptions ($2,300 each for yourself, your spouse and any dependents in 1992) begin to phase out as AGIs exceed $157,900 if married, $105,250 if single. Those provisions, scheduled to expire in 1996 and 1997, respectively, seem likely to be extended. If you earn less than $100,000, your deductions look safe unless the deficit balloons further and Clinton feels forced to react. In that case, tax experts think his likeliest target would be your deduction for home mortgage interest. Together with Congress, he would consider these three main options: reduce the $1 million cap on mortgages for which interest is deductible; eliminate the interest deduction for mortgages on second homes; or lower the $100,000 cap on home-equity debt for which interest is deductible.

What to do: before you borrow, make sure you could afford your new mortgage or home-equity-loan payments if the interest weren't fully deductible. Also, preserve your deductions by keeping your AGI as low as possible. For example, you should contribute the maximum amount allowed to tax-favored savings plans at work, such as 401(k) retirement accounts.

Retirement plans. Chances are excellent that Individual Retirement Accounts will be liberalized soon despite the departure of Sen. Lloyd Bentsen, champion of IRAs on Capitol Hill, to become Treasury Secretary. The most likely 1993-94 IRA reforms would spur spending to help the economy without bloating the deficit immediately. They include allowing penalty-free withdrawals for new-home purchases, college costs, major medical bills and expenses while you're unemployed. You'll probably also be offered a so-called back-end IRA. With these accounts, your contributions won't be deductible, but you can withdraw the earnings tax-free after only five years. You'll probably have to wait until 1995 or later for passage of the heart of Bentsen's plan: a fully deductible IRA for couples with AGIs as high as $100,000 and singles making as much as $75,000.

What to do: lobby your representatives now for the liberalized IRA. Members of Congress who have supported previous IRA bills will be more inclined to do so again if they're aware of popular support for such measures.

Social Security and Medicare. Like any politician, Clinton will approach these so-called entitlements very carefully. Nonetheless, he'll probably press early for his plan to require retirees who make more than $125,000 to pay higher premiums for coverage of doctors' bills under Medicare. Under current law the government will pay around $110 of the monthly premium in 1993, and a retiree will pay $36.60 regardless of income. In addition, Clinton seems inclined to raise taxes on well-off Social Security recipients too. Currently, up to 50% of benefits are taxed for those whose income exceeds $32,000 if married or $25,000 if single. Taxing 85% of such benefits, as Ross Perot once proposed, might be the outer limit.

The self-employed. Chances are, Congress will agree to Clinton's proposal for an investment tax credit that would equal about 10% of the pur-

chase price of new business equipment, such as a computer, photocopy machine, car or truck. The self-employed also are likely to get a deduction for their health insurance premiums, though none of our experts knows whether Clinton's proposal to allow a 100% write-off will win out over Congress' 25% limit.

What to do: if possible, you should try your best to postpone the purchase of business equipment until it's clear when the ITC will become law. If the ITC is passed in 1993, it could well be retroactive to January 1.

Tax-favored investing. Clinton aides have pledged that he will not tamper with municipal bonds' tax-free status. He is also expected to favor extending the tax credit for investments in low-income housing for one year.

What to do: resist plunging blindly into munis. Before you buy, ask your tax adviser whether you would be better off with taxable bonds. As for low-income housing deals, they are complicated and best suited for investors who can take big risks.

If Clinton and Congress become frustrated in their search for new tax revenue, they could turn draconian down the road. Our sources don't count out such disturbing steps as:

■ Slashing the value of an estate you can leave to your heirs tax-free from $600,000 to, say, $300,000. Approximately 15% of estates would end up owing federal death taxes, up from the scant 2% that pay them today. The take: about $5 billion over five years.

■ Requiring that capital-gains tax be paid on assets you own at your death. The take: $17 billion over five years.

■ Eliminating the cap on wages subject to the Medicare tax (now 1.45% on amounts up to $130,200). The take: $28 billion over five years.

■ Taxing part of your employer-provided medical benefits. Taxing benefits above, say, $335 a month for families and $135 for individuals would bring in about $56 billion over five years.

■ Hiking the 14 cent federal tax on each gallon of gasoline. A 12 cent increase, small compared with Ross Perot's 50 cent proposal, would still bring in $55 billion over five years.

Even those tax shocks might not be enough, however. In an influential report sponsored by a bipartisan research organization, Sens. Sam Nunn (D-Ga.) and Pete Domenici (R-N.M.) recently endorsed a revolutionary plan favored by many budgetary experts inside and outside of government: a broad consumption tax that could be a far more prodigious and efficient money raiser than the personal income tax. After all, the government may need every cent it can raise.

Eleven Moves to Outflank the Feds

Clinton's agenda will require tax hikes to close the gap between federal income and outgo. Use these maneuvers to cut your bill in the 1990s.

In addition to an activist new President, your main tax nemeses this year are the covert hikes that Congress and George Bush began slipping into the law back in 1991. In 1993, for example, the total of your write-offs for mortgage interest, state and local taxes, moving and miscellaneous expenses will be reduced by 3% for every dollar that your AGI exceeds $108,450. Similarly, personal and dependent exemptions, worth $2,350 each in 1993, will be phased out for couples whose AGIs fall between $162,700 and $285,200, and for singles making between $108,450 and $230,950. What will those hidden cuts cost you? Let's say that you and your spouse have an AGI of $150,000 and deductions of $20,000. Your write-offs will be trimmed to $18,754.

Moreover, Social Security (FICA) taxes will continue to claim an ever-increasing chunk of your earnings. In 1993, employees will pay 6.2% of their gross wages up to $57,600 for retirement, disability and survivor benefits and 1.45% of wages up to $135,000 for Medicare hospital benefits. The maximum hit is $5,529, a $200 increase from last year and an astonishing $2,149 more than in 1988.

How can you cope? "You need strategies that combine a commitment to long-term tax-deferred savings with the flexibility to respond to change," says Kaycee Krysty of the accounting firm Moss Adams in Seattle. What follows is a rundown of such strategies tailored to the needs of employees, the self-employed and investors.

EMPLOYEES

Make retirement savings plans a priority. Beyond a doubt, your best single tax-slashing move is to contribute the maximum to a company-sponsored 401(k), up to the estimated legal limit of $9,000 this year. Your contributions, plus their earnings, escape federal and most state and local income taxes until withdrawn. If you can't afford the maximum, aim to put in at least enough to get your employer's full matching funds, typically 50 cents for every dollar that you invest up to 6% of your pretax pay. Another attraction is that you won't owe FICA tax on the money from your employer.

Contribute to flexible spending accounts. Next to 401(k)s, FSAs are an employee's most capacious shelter. They enable you to pay dependent-care costs and unreimbursed medical expenses with money deducted from your paycheck before federal income tax—and before FICA tax if you make below the $57,600 and $135,000 wage caps. (Money in FSAs is also free of state and local income taxes, except in New Jersey and Pennsylvania.) You and your spouse can each fund a medical-care FSA up to the limits set by your employers, generally $2,000 to $4,000. The tax law caps a couple's contribution to a dependent-care FSA at $5,000 (although your employer may set a lower limit). Thus, by paying $5,000 of bills from an FSA, you'd cut your tax bill by $1,783, assuming that you are in the 28% bracket and your gross wages are under the $57,600 FICA cap.

Coordinate your dependent-care FSA with the child-care credit. If your AGI is more than $24,000, you should use an FSA for dependent-care costs even though you'll lose all or part of your dependent-care credit as a result. Reason: the credit scales down as your AGI rises, while an FSA's tax-cutting power increases as your tax rate rises. In some instances, however, you can use the child-care credit and an FSA. Say, for example, your employer limits your FSA to $2,000 but you pay $4,800 to keep two children in day care. You could still claim a credit of $560. In addition, 22 states and the District of Columbia will grant you a dependent-care break if you claim a federal credit. Check your state tax instruction booklet for details.

Turn commuting into a tax break. Effective this year, the tax law lets employers give you as much as $720 a year—free of income and FICA tax— for mass transit commuting costs. The previous maximum was a modest $252. If your company offers the benefit, grab it. A $720 payment, made in the form of transportation vouchers or tokens, is equivalent to a before-tax raise of $1,120, assuming you're in the 28% bracket and pay FICA tax. If your company doesn't offer commuting assistance, lobby for it.

THE SELF-EMPLOYED
Maximize your deductions. Being your own

boss makes you eligible for a host of truly generous write-offs, such as those for work-related travel and entertainment expenses, dues to professional organizations, subscriptions to business publications and equipment depreciation. Equally important, the write-offs also reduce your self-employment tax (the sole proprietor's version of FICA), because you owe it only on income after deductions.

Fully fund a Keogh retirement plan. You can contribute and deduct a healthy chunk of your self-employment earnings to a Keogh account even if you're just a moonlighter and are covered by a pension plan at a full-time job. Entrepreneurs often are advised to start out with a so-called profit-sharing Keogh, which lets them contribute and deduct up to 13.04% of their net self-employment earnings each year. (That's net of allowable business expenses and half of your self-employment tax.) You can vary the contribution as your cash needs dictate or even not contribute anything at all. Once your business profits stabilize, you can add a second type of Keogh known as a money-purchase plan, which requires you to salt away annually a percentage of your income that you designate when you establish the plan. Since the combined percentage you can put in both a profit-sharing and a money-purchase Keogh works out to 20%, your best course is to contribute the 13.04% maximum to the flexible profit-sharing variety and commit 6.96% to the money-purchase plan. Also note that the total amount sheltered in all your retirement plans can't exceed $30,000 a year.

If you're at least 50 years old and haven't yet established a tax-deferred retirement plan, consider a defined-benefit Keogh. It lets you set aside annually whatever amount it takes to provide a retirement payout of as much as $112,221 a year at age 65 or older. You'll need an actuary's help to calculate the sum you must invest each year to reach your target.

Consider incorporating. By organizing yourself

Ten IRS Audit Traps to Sidestep

Every year the Internal Revenue Service decides on a short but explosive list of penalty and audit triggers—the tax-filing abuses it's gunning for after April 15. MONEY was given an exclusive look at the 10 most-wanted abuses for tax year 1992. When one shows up on a return, IRS enforcers will hit the taxpayer with a penalty of as much as 25% or summon him to a dreaded audit. So if you risk running afoul of one or more of these triggers, ranked below by how frequently they appeared on returns, follow our guidelines with care.

Fake dependents. To cut down on phony dependent exemptions, the IRS jumps on taxpayers who don't supply Social Security numbers or birth dates. It also checks your income against the number of exemptions you claim. "If someone lists income below $20,000 and 10 dependents, we'll question that person," says William Roth, IRS director of financial management and operations research.

Failing to pay self-employment taxes. "Many filers report income but don't pay Social Security taxes on it," says Roth. Other filers think that they don't have to pay the 2.9% Medicare tax on 1992 income above $55,500, the maximum on which taxpayers are required to pay Social Security tax. The Medicare tax on the self-employed, however, applies to salaries up to $130,200.

Early pension withdrawals. Generally, if you take money out of an IRA or pension plan before you reach 59.5 and don't roll over the cash into another such account within 60 days, you must pay a 10% penalty and report it on Form 5329. If you don't, you'll owe the penalty plus 7% interest.

Deducting miscellaneous expenses on Schedule C. You can write off tax-return preparation fees and unreimbursed employee business expenses on Schedule A to the extent that they exceed 2% of your adjusted gross income. To avoid that threshold, some taxpayers who aren't actually self-employed wrongly sneak such expenses onto Schedule C. If you are self-employed and use a tax preparer, be sure to deduct on Schedule C only the charges that are directly related to filling out that schedule; the rest must be claimed on Schedule A.

The off-the-books babysitter. If you don't list a babysitter's Social Security number on Form 2441, you can't claim the dependent-care credit of $480 for one child, $960 for two or more. The sitter is supposed to report the number to you on a W-10 (or face a $50 penalty). When these requirements became law in 1989, the number of taxpayers claiming the child-care credit plunged 31%, and the IRS rejected about $1.2 billion of the claimed credits.

The questionable hobby deduction. Many taxpayers wrongly consider their hobbies to be businesses and deduct all related expenses on Schedule C. To qualify as a for-profit business, however, a hobby generally must show a profit in three out of five years. Otherwise, you can deduct hobby expenses only up to the amount of your hobby income. You take the write-off on Schedule A, subject to the 2% threshold.

Excessive IRA deduction. You're entitled to deduct fully a $2,000 maximum IRA contribution ($2,250 if you also have an IRA for a nonworking spouse) only if you meet two tests. You or your spouse can't be covered by a pension plan at work, and your joint adjusted gross income must be less than $40,000 ($25,000 if you're single). But many taxpayers overlook the fact that above those income limits, the deduction gradually phases out if they are covered by a pension plan. In fact, the write-off disappears for couples who earn more than $50,000 a year ($35,000 for singles).

Unwarranted home-office deduction. About 4 million taxpayers annually write off home-office expenses on Form 8829. Many are denied the deduction, however, usually because they had regular places of business and therefore weren't entitled to the tax break. Many other taxpayers lose it by failing to report what space in their houses is used exclusively for business.

Filing late. If you can't file by April 15, you can get an automatic four-month extension by sending the IRS Form 4868. But enclose a check for the total tax due or you'll owe a maximum 25% delinquency penalty plus 7% interest.

Turning bad debts into business deductions. An unpaid loan to a friend can't be deducted as a bad business debt on Schedule C. Instead, you must write it off on Schedule D as a capital loss. And to prove the complete worthlessness of the debt to the IRS, you'll need, say, copies of the debtor's bankruptcy court filings.

as a so-called C corporation, you can arrange for your business to pay and deduct your family's health insurance premiums, deductibles and co-payments—plus premiums for life and disability insurance for you. Contributions to a qualified corporate profit-sharing plan also escape FICA tax. Be aware, however, that a C corporation could be a tax trap, especially if your business makes more money than you pay yourself in salary. One pitfall to watch out for is that accumulated earnings exceeding $250,000 get hit with a special 28% penalty and then are taxed a second time at your top rate when you eventually take the money as salary or dividends.

INVESTORS AND SAVERS

Look at low-income-housing investments. Clinton and Congress favor giving juicy tax credits to investors in complex new low-income-housing limited partnerships. (The old law granting such credits expired last year.) Clinton wants to make the credit permanent, while congressional leaders are willing at least to extend it year by year. With the top federal tax rate poised to increase, the timing couldn't be better. "Low-income housing is one of the last shelters left for investors," says Michael Marsh of accountant Grant Thornton in Kansas City, Missouri. "Unfortunately, the tax credits may entice investors who don't understand the risks."

In brief, here's how the deals work. By buying or building housing that is then one-fifth to two-fifths occupied by renters with household incomes 50% to 60% of the area's median, limited-partnership sponsors qualify for tax credits that they in turn parcel out to investors over 10 years. The credit on a minimum investment of $5,000 is typically $700 a year. (You would need to invest about $50,000 to qualify for the maximum credit of $7,750 a year if you're in the 31% bracket or $7,000 in the 28% bracket.) Prospective investors should bear in mind, however, that such deals rarely generate income or capital gains. "Stick with deals that project their returns solely on the value of the tax credits," says Marsh.

Here are some of the risks. If a project fails to meet strict federal rules each year, investors retroactively lose up to a third of the credits they've taken to date. If a deal goes bankrupt, both principal and credits are lost. Moreover, low-income deals are sometimes hyped, with financial planners spinning tales of big gains and rarely mentioning their commissions of as much as 10%. So don't invest unless you or a trusted adviser have the skills to evaluate a plan sponsor's prospectus and record.

Don't claim your child's investment income. As a convenience, many taxpayers report the unearned income of children under 14 on the parents' federal tax returns. The ploy could backfire on your state taxes, however. In 36 states and the District of Columbia, your state tax liability is pegged to the income or tax you report on your federal return. By adding your child's income to your own, you effectively boost your reported income or tax, thereby increasing your state tax liability. Moreover, if you file separately for your son or daughter, the child's standard deduction and exemption could wipe out his or her state tax liability.

Shift money into municipal bonds. This move could be particularly critical for retirees if Clinton and Congress agree to increase the federally taxable portion of Social Security benefits. At present, you owe tax when your AGI plus your tax-exempt interest and half your Social Security benefit exceed $32,000 (for joint filers) or $25,000 (for singles). Your challenge is to keep your income below those thresholds. Let's say your $50,000 nest egg is invested in taxable bonds paying 8%. Your annual interest of $4,000 would be included in your AGI, even though you'd pocket only $2,600 after taxes, assuming a combined federal and state tax bracket of 35%. But if you invested that $50,000 in comparable municipal bonds yielding 5.2%, you would be able to earn a tax-free $2,600, and only that amount would be counted toward the thresholds.

Check out Series EE savings bonds. You can shift as much as $15,000 a year into Series EE savings bonds ($30,000 for a married couple), which recently paid 4% for a bond held six months, vs. 3% on a six-month CD. The interest is not taxed until you cash in the bonds—up to 30 years after purchase. And the interest is free from state and local income tax. If you are a grandparent, or expect to become one before long, you may soon have a new reason to buy the bonds. Last year Congress passed a proposal— vetoed by President Bush—that would make income from EE bonds that are redeemed to pay college tuition tax-free, regardless of your income or relationship to the student. Currently, the interest is fully exempt only if your AGI is below $68,250 (for couples) or $45,500 (for individuals) and if you, your spouse or your dependent is the student. If the proposal is revived as expected and you were inclined to use the interest to help send your grandchild to college, you would be spreading the tax advantages across generations. And that's the ultimate accomplishment in the art of long-term tax planning.

Overlooked Ways to Cut State Taxes

Americans' state taxes have been climbing 11% faster than their federal bills. Lower yours by learning these little-known techniques.

Who would have guessed? Some of the best-kept secrets in tax planning are hidden in the dull and daunting instruction booklets published by state tax departments. There, amid jargon-jammed sentences, gems of write-offs can be found. For example, you can deduct all or some of your federal income tax in nine states— Alabama, Iowa, Louisiana, Missouri, Montana, North Dakota, Oklahoma, Oregon and Utah. By using this write-off, a couple earning $75,000 a year in Utah (the 13th highest in our state tax rankings beginning on page 32) could save $482. Another example: you can subtract some or all of your Social Security contributions from your state taxable income in Alabama, Massachusetts and Missouri. The savings are as much as $630 for a couple in Missouri's highest bracket (6% of taxable income above $9,000).

Finding these deductions has become more important as state and local taxes shot up 7% a year from 1982 to 1992, 11% faster than federal levies. After a brief election-year respite, the drumbeat of new or higher levies seems destined to resume in almost every state in 1993. "Over the next few years, virtually all states will see the cost of services far outpacing revenues," predicts Steven Gold of the Center for the Study of the States in Albany, New York. This forecast gets to the heart of why you must take steps now to trim your state taxes. Start by carefully planning your federal taxes. If a tax move is a good one federally, chances are it will cut your state taxes as well. That's because the amount you pay to your state is almost always based on your federal return. Next, read your state tax instruction booklet in search of nuggets such as these:

■ A retiree's Social Security benefits are exempt from local taxation in the District of Columbia and these 26 states: Alabama, Arizona, Arkansas, California, Delaware, Georgia, Hawaii, Idaho, Illinois, Indiana, Kentucky, Louisiana, Maine, Maryland, Massachusetts, Michigan, Mississippi, New Jersey, New York, North Carolina, Ohio, Oklahoma, Oregon, Pennsylvania, South Carolina and Virginia. And these 20 states are not allowed to tax your entire private pension income: Alabama, Arkansas, Colorado, Delaware, Georgia, Hawaii, Illinois, Louisiana, Maryland, Michigan, Mississippi, Montana, New Jersey, New Mexico, New York, North Carolina, Oregon, Pennsylvania, South Carolina and Utah.

■ You might be better off taking the standard deduction (even if you itemize on your federal return) in all states but Arizona, Georgia, Hawaii, Kentucky, Louisiana, Nebraska, New Mexico, Oklahoma and Rhode Island. Reason: if you itemize in 34 other states or the District of Columbia, you must add back to your taxable income the state taxes you write off your federal return. As a result, your taxable income will be higher, and your total deductions may fall below your state's standard deduction. For example, the standard deduction in Minnesota is $5,700 for a married couple. If their federal deductions totaled $10,000 but, say, $6,000 of that was from state taxes, they would be left with state itemized deductions of only $4,000.

■ You can take a more generous medical deduction than federal law permits in Alabama, New Jersey, Wisconsin and, in limited cases, North Dakota and Oregon. On your federal return, you can write off only expenses that top 7.5% of your adjusted gross income. But in New Jersey, for instance, medical expenses above 2% of your AGI are deductible.

■ You can write off some of the cost of sending a child to private or parochial school in Iowa and Minnesota. Deductible expenses include those for tuition, fees and textbooks for secular subjects (but not for religious instruction). The maximum deduction in Minnesota is $1,000 per child no matter what your income. In Iowa it's $1,000 for every dependent enrolled in a nonprofit school if you make $45,000 or less.

■ Renters, who normally miss out on real estate tax breaks, get some in Arizona, California, Hawaii, Indiana, Maine, Massachusetts, Michigan, Minnesota, New York, Vermont,

FROM $1,632 IN ALASKA TO $10,016 IN NEW YORK

What's the difference between living in Alaska and in New York? For a typical two-income family of four that subscribes to MONEY, as much as 17 feet of snow a year and $8,384 in state and local taxes—the widest gap in our fourth annual study of such taxes.

The table at right lists the tax load of a family that earned $72,385 in 1992, plus $2,782 in interest, $455 in dividends and $1,472 in capital gains. They spent $35,112 on food, clothing, prescription drugs, household goods, a new car ($12,456) and other items. Their two autos consumed 1,912 gallons of gas.

The first two columns show each state's rank and the family's combined bill for state and local income, sales, property and gas taxes. The third column grades each state on the likelihood of tax increases in 1993 or 1994, according to tax experts: A, no major tax hikes expected (seven states); B, moderate chance (16); C, strong probability (15); and D, best bet (13). Property taxes are estimates of this family's bill in each state. Tax rates in the comments column are for couples filing jointly in 1992.

All state income tax estimates were provided by the state and local tax group of Ernst & Young, the international accounting and management consulting firm.

Other sources: Vertex Inc.; *A Far Cry From Fair* by Citizens for Tax Justice and the Institute on Taxation and Economic Policy **Notes:** [1]Additional local income tax may also be assessed. [2]Local income tax calculated on state return. [3]"None" means state imposes no death tax; "0" means no tax applies to spouse or child heir.

	State
1	Alaska
2	Wyoming
3	Nevada
4	Florida
5	Tennessee
6	South Dakota
7	New Hampshire
8	Texas
9	Washington
10	North Dakota
11	Delaware[1]
12	Alabama[1]
13	Louisiana
14	Mississippi
15	New Mexico
16	West Virginia
17	Missouri[1]
18	South Carolina
19	Arizona
20	Indiana
21	Kentucky[1]
22	Montana
23	Oklahoma
24	Kansas
25	Pennsylvania
26	Iowa[1]
27	Arkansas
28	Illinois
29	Virginia
30	North Carolina
31	Colorado
32	Georgia
33	New Jersey
34	Michigan[1]
35	California
36	Idaho
37	Nebraska
38	Ohio
39	Utah
40	Vermont
41	Hawaii
42	Minnesota
43	Rhode Island
44	Connecticut
45	Oregon
46	Maryland[2]
47	Maine
48	Massachusetts
49	Wisconsin
50	District of Columbia
51	New York[1]

Total annual tax on typical house-hold	Grade for risk of future tax hikes	For singles earning $35,000	Tax on earned income			Sales tax		Property tax	Death tax on[3]		Comments
			For two-income married earning $50,000	For two-income married earning $75,000	For two-income married earning $100,000	State-wide rate	Highest combined state and local		$600,000 estate left to spouse	$600,000 estate left to child	
$1,632	A	None	None	None	None	0.000%	7.000%	$1,479	None	None	Most tax revenue from the oil and gas industry
2,945	B	None	None	None	None	3.000	5.000	1,451	None	None	Most tax revenue from oil company and sales taxes
3,539	B	None	None	None	None	6.500	7.000	1,161	None	None	Most tax revenue from sales, gambling and gas taxes
3,846	D	None	None	None	None	6.000	7.000	1,730	None	None	Most tax revenue from sales, use and admissions taxes
4,038	C	None	None	None	None	7.000	8.750	1,147	0	0	Certain interest and dividend income taxed at 6%
4,284	C	None	None	None	None	4.000	8.000	2,331	0	$41,250	Primary source of tax revenue: sales and gas taxes
4,591	D	None	None	None	None	0.000	0.000	4,023	0	0	Dividends and interest over $2,400 taxed at 5%
4,647	D	None	None	None	None	6.250	8.250	2,245	None	None	Revenue mainly from sales and oil company taxes
4,694	C	None	None	None	None	7.000	8.200	1,890	None	None	Revenue mostly from sales, property and corporate taxes
5,292	B	$751	$721	$1,547	$2,399	5.000	6.000	1,948	None	None	Top rate: 12% on taxable income over $50,000
5,354	C	1,812	1,822	3,351	4,950	0.000	0.000	1,234	0	31,250	Top rate: 7.7% on taxable income over $40,000
5,552	D	1,267	1,652	2,442	3,222	4.000	9.500	617	None	None	Top rate: 5% on taxable income over $6,000
5,752	D	895	1,195	1,829	2,456	4.000	10.000	925	0	17,050	Top rate: 6% on taxable income over $50,000
5,792	B	1,185	1,251	2,339	3,427	7.000	7.000	1,200	0	0	Top rate: 5% on taxable income over $10,000
5,948	B	1,329	1,489	3,038	4,824	5.125	6.875	902	None	None	Top rate: 8.5% on taxable income over $41,600
5,981	B	1,260	1,695	3,230	4,855	6.000	6.000	522	None	None	Top rate: 6.5% on taxable income over $60,000
6,047	C	1,265	1,660	2,612	3,552	4.225	7.725	1,154	None	None	Top rate: 6% on taxable income over $9,000
6,531	C	1,728	2,005	3,485	4,964	5.000	6.000	1,381	None	None	Top rate: 7% on taxable income over $10,600
6,637	B	1,271	1,402	2,436	3,578	5.000	8.500	1,781	None	None	Top rate: 7% on taxable income over $300,000
6,712	C	1,156	1,564	2,414	3,264	5.000	5.000	1,613	0	24,950	Rate: a flat 3.4% of federal AGI, with modifications
6,744	B	1,841	2,131	3,436	4,742	6.000	6.000	1,137	0	45,350	Top rate: 6% on taxable income over $8,000
6,781	D	1,552	2,199	3,776	5,393	0.000	0.000	2,301	0	0	Top rate: 11% on taxable income over $57,600
6,907	C	1,885	2,051	3,574	5,097	4.500	9.500	1,062	0	17,725	Top rate: 7% on taxable income over $21,000
6,935	A	1,630	1,395	2,755	4,153	4.900	6.900	1,923	0	21,750	Top rate: 6.45% on taxable income over $60,000
6,969	B	1,033	1,475	2,213	2,950	6.000	7.000	2,069	$35,880	36,000	Rate: a flat 2.8% on a broad base of taxable income
7,006	A	1,667	1,967	3,176	4,468	5.000	6.000	2,052	0	39,825	Top rate: 9.98% on taxable income over $47,700
7,074	B	1,690	2,289	3,812	5,335	4.500	7.500	902	None	None	Top rate: 7% on taxable income over $25,000
7,125	D	1,020	1,323	2,045	2,767	6.250	8.750	2,357	None	None	Rate: a flat 3% of modified federal AGI; 2.75% in 1993
7,217	B	1,537	2,061	3,312	4,563	4.500	4.500	2,159	None	None	Top rate: 5.75% on taxable income over $17,000
7,263	B	1,973	2,274	3,797	5,320	6.000	6.000	1,232	0	7,000	Top rate: 7.75% on taxable income over $100,000
7,268	A	1,455	1,716	2,804	3,892	3.000	9.000	1,884	None	None	Rate: a flat 5% of modified federal taxable income
7,301	C	1,682	1,991	3,296	4,602	4.000	6.000	1,637	None	None	Top rate: 6% on taxable income over $10,000
7,371	A	750	997	1,791	3,178	6.000	6.000	3,772	0	0	Top rate: 7% on taxable income over $150,000
7,493	B	1,513	1,914	3,064	4,214	4.000	4.000	2,866	0	34,300	Rate: a flat 4.6% of taxable income
7,605	C	1,512	1,159	2,897	4,920	7.250	8.500	1,998	None	None	Top rate: 11% on taxable income over $414,400
7,634	A	2,119	2,272	4,033	5,817	5.000	7.000	1,492	None	None	Top rate: 8.2% on taxable income over $40,000
7,728	D	1,371	1,545	2,961	4,466	5.000	6.500	2,703	0	5,850	Top rate: 6.92% on taxable income over $45,000
7,751	D	1,065	1,396	2,648	4,153	5.000	7.000	1,537	2,100	30,100	Top rate: 6.9% on taxable income over $100,000
7,892	A	1,839	2,242	3,596	4,943	6.000	7.250	1,751	None	None	Top rate: 7.2% on taxable income over $7,500
7,962	D	1,562	1,494	3,323	5,332	5.000	5.000	2,750	None	None	Top rate: 34% of federal income tax above $13,100
8,272	C	2,783	3,015	5,182	7,358	4.000	4.000	1,079	None	None	Top rate: 10% on taxable income over $41,000
8,311	C	2,041	2,326	4,067	5,807	6.500	7.500	2,027	None	None	Top rate: 8.5% on taxable income over $83,300
8,314	C	1,476	1,416	3,038	4,761	7.000	7.000	2,928	None	None	Rate: 27.5% of modified federal tax liability
8,389	C	1,377	1,071	3,037	4,500	6.000	6.000	3,245	0	37,895	Rate: a flat 4.5% of taxable income
8,390	D	2,469	2,930	4,889	6,847	0.000	0.000	2,910	None	None	Top rate: 9% on taxable income over $10,000
8,568	B	2,295	2,814	4,446	6,078	5.000	5.000	2,098	5,000	6,000	Top rate, with local surtax: 9% over $150,000
8,611	D	2,030	1,965	3,907	5,884	6.000	6.000	2,495	None	None	Top rate: 9.89% on taxable income over $75,000
8,764	B	1,952	2,594	4,082	5,569	5.000	5.000	2,732	23,500	55,500	Rate on earned income is 5.95%; unearned, 12%
8,770	B	2,113	2,474	3,985	5,554	5.000	5.500	2,813	None	None	Top rate: 6.93% on taxable income over $20,000
9,348	C	2,505	2,856	4,829	6,878	6.000	6.000	2,296	None	None	Top rate: 9.5% on taxable income over $20,000
10,016	D	1,846	2,157	4,108	5,821	4.000	8.500	3,255	0	25,500	Top rate: 7.875% on taxable income over $26,000

Wisconsin and the District of Columbia. In those places, renters may either deduct or take a credit for some of their rent. The benefit phases out in all of the states if your income tops certain levels ($45,000 for Vermont's credit of as much as $1,350, for example).

■ Like the federal government, 33 states and the District of Columbia let you deduct the cost of most work-related moving expenses. Check state rules before relocating. Connecticut, Pennsylvania and Wisconsin permit deductions only in limited circumstances (say, if you move into the state but not if you are leaving). Wisconsin allows a credit of 5% of your expenses above $8,900 if you move within the state or into it. And seven states (Illinois, Indiana, Massachusetts, Michigan, New Jersey, Ohio, and West Virginia) don't permit moving deductions for most taxpayers at all. One remedy: time your move so that you can deduct any unreimbursed expenses when you are in the state that permits it.

After exhausting the breaks in your state's instruction booklet, apply these general rules for still more tax savings:

Don't get unfairly zapped if you own two homes. If you work in a high-tax state but live in one with lower rates, don't do anything that might call your true domicile into question. That can happen if, for example, you own a second home in the high-tax state. Let's say your principal residence is in New Jersey (top bracket of 7%), but you own a pied-à-terre near your office in Manhattan (top combined state and local rate of 12.3%). In that case, you could risk having New York State and City insist that they are due taxes on your interest, dividends and capital gains as well as the income from your job. While New Jersey will give you a credit for the New York taxes, your final bill will be the same as if you lived in Manhattan.

It can be difficult to prove that you aren't actually a resident of the high-tax state even though you own a home there. For example, if you spend more than half the year in the high-

tax state, you meet the definition of resident used by many states. You can try to prove otherwise by, say, showing that you vote in the other state, register your car there, belong to local social clubs and send your kids to schools there. But fewer and fewer revenue-hungry states accept such evidence as conclusive. In the end, you may have to pay up or give up your second home.

If you're married, don't automatically file a standard joint state return. Ten states (Arkansas, Delaware, Iowa, Kentucky, Maryland, Mississippi, Missouri, Montana, Tennessee and Virginia) and the District of Columbia give a special break to married couples in which both spouses have income and file a joint federal return. These states let a couple calculate each spouse's state tax separately—at lower effective rates than if they filed jointly—and file a so-called joint-separate return. For example, a Virginia couple with one spouse earning $40,000 and the other $20,000, two children and $10,000 in deductions would pay 1992 state tax of $2,434 by filing jointly. With a joint-separate return, they would pay only $2,204, a $230 saving.

Look into triple-tax-exempt bonds. If you're in the 28% federal tax bracket or higher and live in a state with heavy income taxes, you might consider buying municipal bonds issued in your home state. Such bonds are triple-tax-free. Any income they generate is exempt from federal, state and local taxes. (Only Indiana, Utah and, in some cases, North Dakota exempt income from other states' munis.) For example, Fidelity's New York Tax-Free High-Yield Fund is 100% tax-exempt for residents of New York State. For top-bracket taxpayers, with a combined effective rate of 39.5% if they live in New York City, the fund's recent 5.4% yield is equivalent to 8.9% from a taxable investment.

Consider investing in Treasury securities. While income from Treasury bills, notes and bonds is taxed federally, it is free of all state and local taxes. You can buy Treasuries direct from the Federal Reserve (call 202-874-4000 for information) or by paying a $30 to $50 fee to a bank or brokerage. Or you can invest in a mutual fund such as Dreyfus 100% Treasury—Long Term Portfolio, recently yielding about 7.6%. Only Pennsylvania taxes the dividends. If you're a top-bracket resident of a high-tax state like New York or California, the break can add nearly a point to your after-tax yield.

Take any sales tax relief you can get. With the exceptions of Delaware, Montana, New Hampshire and Oregon, you face sales taxes up to 10% on an ever-growing number of purchases and services. In the majority of states, however, you can hold down the tax on the purchase of a car. (The exceptions are Alaska, California, Maryland, Michigan, Virginia and the District of Columbia). Simply ask the dealer to deduct the trade-in value of your old car before calculating

the state and local sales tax on the new one. If you sell your old car yourself, you lose the break. Also, look for this New Jersey sales tax break to spread to other states. Residents pay only 3%, half New Jersey's normal rate, on purchases in 10 state-designated enterprise zones, including economically depressed Newark.

Unhappily, most of the new state taxes you'll be seeing this year and in the future are true pests that are impervious to attempts to swat them. One such tax now being enforced with a vengeance is the use tax, which buzzes around in the District of Columbia and all 46 states that impose sales taxes. It's a sales tax on items you buy outside your state—overseas, in another state or through a catalogue. As yet, states have no way of forcing everyone to pay up, but that hasn't stopped them from trying. Auditors for California, Illinois and New York, for example, collect information at airports to help them tax goodies that travelers bring home from overseas.

Challenge Your Property Taxes Now

In many cities and towns, perhaps half the assessments are flat wrong. Simply by correcting the errors, you can cut your taxes 10% or more.

If you feel your property taxes are gnawing an ever-bigger hole in your wallet, you're not alone. In our latest Americans and Their MONEY poll of 300 subscribers, 60% said that their real estate taxes rose in 1992. According to the National League of Cities, property taxes went up an average of 5.5% in fiscal 1992. The hardest-hit region was the economically ailing Northeast, where a staggering 73% of cities and towns hiked their taxes. What's worse, as a result of common errors in appraising the value of property, approximately half the homeowners in some areas may be paying more taxes than they actually owe.

If you think you're among them, now's the time to appeal. About half the people who challenge their property tax bills wind up cutting them 10% or more, estimates Thomas Breecher of accountant Coopers & Lybrand. "Property taxes are more subject to whim and idiosyncrasy than other forms of taxation," says David Keating of the National Taxpayers Union, a Washington, D.C. lobbyist that offers an informative brochure, *How to Fight Property Taxes* (to order a copy, send $2 to 713 Maryland Avenue N.E., Washington, D.C. 20002).

Winning a tax fight on the picket-fence level

takes no special expertise—just a determination to be treated fairly by tax officials. Consider the case of Tom and Geri Kuchenberg, who pay about 36% of their $71,440 AGI in taxes, including $1,762 to Washington, D.C. for their three-bedroom, turn-of-the-century townhouse on Capitol Hill. Tom, a lawyer, has twice cut the couple's taxes by convincing the assessor that his house was overvalued. The first time, in 1988, he showed Polaroids of three comparable town-houses—all in better physical shape than the Kuchenbergs' but assessed for similar amounts. As a result, he lowered his assessment by 6% and his bill by about $100. That experience led Tom and a half-dozen neighbors to create the Capitol Hill Taxpayers Alliance. Each spring since 1990, the group has given local homeowners work-shops on cutting property taxes.

In 1991, the Kuchenbergs won another prop-erty tax reduction. Tom had invited the assessor to visit the couple's townhouse in the fall of 1990 because he knew an areawide revaluation was coming. The Kuchenbergs remembered that dur-ing a previous revaluation, tax officials had made what Tom calls "a windshield assessment" with-out ever entering the house. So Tom wanted to make sure that this time the assessor would see the water-stained living room ceiling from a 1978 fire, raw plaster in the upstairs hallway and an unfinished bathroom renovation. The assessor knocked $30,000 off the house's valuation, and the Kuchenbergs' tax bill plummeted by $288, a 19% saving.

The odds of winning such appeals seem to be getting better. One reason is that assessors, short-handed because of budget cuts, are making more mistakes. For example, Hibbing, Minnesota (population 18,000) taxes 10,000 properties but has only two assessors, down from four in 1982. State law requires assessors to view a property every four years, an unmanageable workload of 1,250 visits a year. Not surprisingly, appeals in Hibbing, where property tax bills on houses average around $400, doubled to about 150 last year. Two-thirds of the challenged bills were

revised. Typical savings were $50 to $100.

Fighting unfairly high property taxes is espe-cially worthwhile in places where tax bills amount to 3% or more of a house's assessed value and where property taxes rank among the highest. In these areas, tax rates can be inflated to compensate for out-of-date assessments that don't reflect current values. Or, their residents may pay steep bills because of duplication of ser-vices provided by their towns and counties. If you have reason to believe your taxes are high, follow these strategies to improve your chances of winning an appeal.

First, learn a few key terms and some simple math. Your correct assessed value is what you get when multiplying your home's fair market value (what the property would sell for) by its assess-ment ratio (the percentage of fair market value subject to tax). For an accurate property tax bill, officials must multiply the correct assessed value by the local tax rate, sometimes called the mill rate. The tax rate is set by law and can't be changed by appeal; your aim is to lower your property's assessment.

The assessment ratio often trips up home-owners. Some communities use full market value to compute tax bills (an assessment ratio of 100%), while others use a fraction of market value. In Connecticut, houses are typically assessed at 70% of value; in Louisiana it's 10%. "Fractional assessment can create a dangerous illusion," says Keating of the National Taxpayers Union. "People think they're making out like bandits when they're actually having their pock-ets picked." If your house is worth $200,000 and is assessed at $180,000, you may think you're get-ting a break. But if your town sets assessments at 75% of market value, you're actually being overassessed by 20% and are thus overtaxed.

To find out your municipality's assessment ratio, visit the assessor's office and ask. Also check your property record card for mistakes. The card (or computer printout) has descrip-tions of your home such as your lot size, the age of your house, the number of rooms, the type of heating and air-conditioning systems, and the property's most recent estimated market value. If you spot an error, tell a staffer in the assessor's office; someone will probably make a home visit to verify your claim. Even if the card seems in order, ask for a list of the property tax breaks available to homeowners. You may be entitled to one. Some 44 states exempt a portion of assessed value for certain owners (say, if they are elderly, disabled or veterans).

Most errors are readily corrected. But if the estimated market value on your card seems excessive, you'll have to show the assessor that at least three similar properties sold for less either six months before or three months after the valuation date of your home. You can stretch the time limit to a year or two if your real estate market is so sluggish that, say, houses take longer than six months to sell.

The assessor can often provide you with sales prices of properties comparable to yours. If not, ask a real estate agent for the figures. Or hire a real estate appraiser for a written valuation of your property (cost: $250 to $500). Choose a pro from the Appraisal Institute, the National Association of Independent Fee Appraisers or the American Society of Appraisers, all of which set professional standards for members.

Most tax jurisdictions have informal hearing processes that let you call the assessor for an appointment. Start that way and describe the inequities in a nice, conversational tone. Don't expect to get 100% of what you want; have a fall-back position in mind. If you reach agreement, ask the assessor for a letter of confirmation. Homeowners sometimes get no satisfaction from assessors, who can be tough and have the attitude that it's "us against the taxpayers." If you feel you didn't get a fair hearing, carry your case to the next level, usually a formal review board made up of public officials and others who are knowledgeable about the local real estate market.

At this point, you could hire a property tax consultant or real estate lawyer to fight the battle for you. Either will most likely charge 50% of the first year's tax savings if you win, nothing if you lose. If you pursue your case on your own, prepare to encounter annoying red tape. Read the official forms carefully because they'll note dates when written appraisals or other supporting documents must be submitted. If you miss one of these deadlines, your appeal could be summarily dismissed by the review board. Attend a hearing in advance of your own (most are open to the public) to learn the procedures and the kinds of questions that you may be asked.

Tax-Cutting Ways to Give to Your Kids

Astutely transferring assets to your children or grandchildren can generate sizable tax breaks that have miraculously remained untouched.

Just stop and think about the ways you'll be financing your child's future: college (for sure), a down payment on a house (increasingly likely), launching a professional practice ("anything for my daughter the doctor"), leaving a legacy (will it help them to remember?). Dissimilar as those

events may seem, they all require a tax-smart strategy for shifting assets to your children, maybe even one featuring a trust. And this isn't an exercise only for the rich. Minimizing taxes is a crucial element in keeping any middle-income family's hard-earned savings from being eroded as it shifts assets from generation to generation. The techniques may vary according to your motivation, but giving your property away with the least tax hit remains the common thread.

Your first antagonist is income taxes. To build up a child's college fund, for example, you must adjust both the timing and the choice of assets you give to tame the five-year-old kiddie tax, which requires a child under age 14 to pay at the parent's top rate on investment income over $1,100. Then comes the onslaught of gift and estate levies. These so-called transfer taxes are essentially one and the same. Gift tax is levied on transfers you make during your lifetime, while estate tax is imposed on property you leave at death. The rates kick in at 37% on taxable amounts above $600,000 and top out at 55% on sums above $3 million.

In general, the strategy that is right for you depends on your child's age, on when you want him or her to have the money, and on the amount. Following are your three best choices, beginning with the simplest.

Tax-free gifts. Thanks to a soft spot known as the gift-tax exclusion in the stonyhearted tax code, you can make tax-exempt gifts of as much as $10,000 a year ($20,000 if you give jointly with your spouse) to each of as many people as you wish. If your good-heartedness rises above those benchmarks, the excess is subject to gift tax. The taxable amount of each gift isn't due immediately but is subtracted from your $600,000 federal estate-tax exemption when your estate tax is figured at the time of your death.

Giving cash or other property outright is usually suitable only for children who have reached the age of majority (18 in most states). Because minors may be allowed to revoke otherwise legally binding contracts—to sell stock or real estate, for example—it is difficult to manage their property. Also, once you give an asset away, you legally have no say over what the recipient does with it.

One useful variation on simply ceding assets

to adult children is to combine the gift-tax exclusion with a loan. Say you'd like to present your son and daughter-in-law with a $50,000 down payment on a house. If you and your spouse give them that amount, $10,000 will be subject to gift tax ($50,000 minus the two $20,000 joint gift-tax exclusions). If you lend the amount, however, you sidestep the gift tax. Then, as payments of interest and principal come due, you can forgive the indebtedness. As long as what is forgiven is less than the gift-tax exclusion amount, no gift tax will be assessed. The IRS has lost court cases in the matter, yet it argues that if you intended to make a gift all along, you owe a gift tax. To bolster your case, be sure to charge a market interest rate and to record a lien against the house. Your son and daughter-in-law should also meet the minimum credit standards that would qualify them for such a loan from any lender. By setting up the loan as a commercial transaction, you're not making any tacit or implicit gift. You can simply forgive the loan later out of generosity.

Consider custodial accounts. For most parents or grandparents, the best way to give to young children is to open a no-fee custodial account at a bank, brokerage or mutual fund under the Uniform Transfers to Minors Act or, in some states, the Uniform Gifts to Minors Act. (UTMAs let you transfer a broad range of property, including cash, securities, life insurance, real estate and collectibles. UGMAs may be more restrictive, depending on your state law.) Your contributions to an UGMA or UTMA qualify for the annual gift-tax exclusion.

Custodial accounts have two drawbacks. One is avoidable: if you are both the donor and the custodian, the assets will be included in your estate if you die before the custodianship ends. For that reason, you should appoint a trustworthy and financially astute relative or friend as custodian. There is no defense against the other shortcoming: your child becomes the owner of the assets you place in the account. The custodian can spend the money for the benefit of the

Choosing the Right Tax Preparer

Taxpayers demanded $100 million in damages from certified public accountants in malpractice suits last year. That startling statistic comes from Crum & Forster, the chief insurance liability underwriter for the accounting field. The company won't disclose how many CPAs were sued. But one reason for the legal activity is clear: tax pros are making more errors on returns because they haven't stayed abreast of the major changes in tax law since 1980. "The average practitioner doesn't keep up to date," says Sidney Kess, an attorney and CPA who has taught tax law for more than 30 years. "Preparers just don't read tax law anymore."

In recent years one out of seven preparers, who haul in average annual fees of $179,000, has canceled subscriptions to tax information services that help accountants keep up with changes in tax law. Instead, according to a 1990 survey of 480 pros by New York City's Research Institute of America, these preparers routinely turn to other accountants on even simple questions or consult outdated tax publications. Why cut corners? Simply to save dollars, say tax experts and officials at the General Accounting Office, the congressional investigative agency. Commerce Clearing House's *Federal Tax Guide* , for example, costs $430 a year. Consequently, many tax preparers run a growing risk of committing errors that could leave you exposed to IRS deficiency notices, penalties and perhaps even audits.

To avoid such problems, first make sure to choose the right type of preparer. If your tax records consist only of a W-2 and a couple of 1099 forms, you could be well served at a tax chain, such as H&R Block or Jackson Hewitt. H&R Block keeps its preparers up to date with annual 15-week courses; Jackson Hewitt's run 12 weeks. A typical chain customer, with a few deductions and income of $30,000 or $40,000, will pay about $50 for federal and state returns.

If you can't use a chain, picking the right pro becomes more complicated. For example, our typical subscriber—annual income of about $72,385 and $21,000 in investments—probably needs the expertise of a CPA or an enrolled agent. Our subscriber might pay a CPA $350 to $700 for a federal and state return. The 310,000 CPAs enrolled in the American Institute of Certified Public Accountants (AICPA) are required to take 40-hour brushup courses on tax law every year. Societies offering client referrals operate in some 27 states. Call AICPA at 800-862-4272 for local phone numbers.

The 30,000 enrolled agents are as expert on taxes as CPAs but generally charge about a third less. Reason: most agents are self-employed and don't have the overhead of accounting firms, says Steven DeFilippis of the National Association of Enrolled Agents (NAEA). Agents' fees are based on the number of forms prepared, their time or a combination of the two. For a federal and state return, our subscriber would pay roughly $250. Enrolled agents meet rigorous requirements—for example,

passing grades on tough Treasury exams. The IRS also expects the agents to spend 72 hours over three years on tax refresher courses. You may want to confine your search to the roughly 7,500 agents who belong to NAEA. The organization requires members to take an additional 30 hours of classroom work a year. For the name of a local NAEA member, call the group's 24-hour referral service (800-424-4339).

Once you have decided on whether to use a chain, a CPA or an enrolled agent, interview at least three candidates to find one whose personality, experience and accounting philosophy suit you. Then weed out the underinformed by asking to see each prospect's tax library. Jack Porter of accountant BDO Seidman in Washington, D.C. says the "bare minimum" library should contain one weekly or monthly tax newsletter, such as the IRS's *Bulletin*, and either a looseleaf service like Commerce Clearing House's or the *Federal Tax Coordinator* from the Research Institute of America. Finally, make sure that the preparer you're considering owns the latest tax-return software.

Request an initial consultation with each of your three finalists. If it isn't free, don't go. At the meeting, review your past years' returns as well as the practitioner's fees. Answers to your questions should be clear and unequivocal. You should also ask how many 1040s the practitioner prepares annually. A very big number is bad news. Few can effectively complete more than 800 a year singlehanded.

child—say, for music lessons. But expenditures on items that are considered part of your parental-support obligation, such as food, clothing and shelter, are deemed to be taxable income to the parents. Once your child reaches the age of majority in most states, he or she will gain full control of the account. (In some states, like New York and Delaware, you can specify that the custodianship is to last until age 21. Review the rules in your state with a lawyer or tax adviser for further exceptions.)

Whatever the age at which custodianship ends, few kids abscond with their college funds. But that's nonetheless a possibility you must consider. Some parents also worry that a custodial account may disqualify their child for college financial aid, since students are expected to contribute as much as 35% of their assets toward college costs, compared with less than 6% for parents. The recommended solution: when your child begins high school, you should ask the college counselor to calculate whether your son or daughter is a potential candidate for aid. If so, restrict donations to the custodial account and save more in your own name as the time for college tuition approaches.

In the early years, when your child is under age 14 and therefore subject to the kiddie tax, you might limit his or her custodial account to just enough income-producing assets to generate a maximum of $1,100 a year in earnings. The first $550 will be tax-free because of the child's standard deduction; the next $550 will be taxed at your child's rate, typically 15%. All together, a child's tax bill on $1,100 of unearned income would come to $83, vs. $308 if the income was earned in your name and you and your spouse are in the 28% bracket. Assuming a 7% return on the investment, a child under age 14 can accumulate assets of $15,715 before triggering the kiddie tax.

If you put more assets than that into the account, consider growth stocks or growth mutual funds, particularly if your child has more than 10 years to go before college. Since such investments pay little or no dividends, you'll minimize or avoid income tax. Furthermore, by waiting until your child turns 14 to sell the growth investments, you will avoid kiddie tax on the capital gain. After your child turns 14 and the kiddie tax is no longer a problem, you can begin shifting money in the account to income investments. From that point on, all investment income is taxed at the child's rate, presumably 15%, compared with 28% or 31% for you. For more about investing for college, see "Meeting the High Cost of College" in Chapter 8.

The advantages of trusts. If you have already accumulated enough for your child's college education or you plan to give him or her at least $100,000 over a relatively short period of time, like five years, trusts offer significant advantages over custodial accounts. True, establishing a trust can cost you a bundle in legal fees ranging from $500 to $2,000, depending on its complexity, plus annual accounting fees of $250 to $500. But consider these merits of an irrevocable 2503(c) minor's trust, the best alternative for middle-income families.

A trust can cut your income taxes, no matter how old your child. The first $100 of trust income is tax-free. The next $3,450 is taxed at 15%; the next $6,900 at 28%. Amounts above that are taxed at 31%. Thus the tax on $10,450 of trust income is $2,450, vs. $3,240 if the money was taxed at the parents' 31% bracket. To get the most tax savings possible, distribute $1,100 (the kiddie-tax threshold) of trust earnings each year to the custodial account of a child under age 14. He or she will owe $83 of tax on the distribution. But the trust can still accumulate as much as $3,550 in income and pay tax on it at 15%. The result: a total tax bill of $600 on $4,650 of earnings, vs. $826 if the entire amount accumulated in the trust, or $1,442 if the money was earned in the names of parents in the 31% bracket. You can realize bigger tax savings by splitting trust income between the trust and a child over 14. If a trust earned $24,450 a year and retained $3,550, both that amount and the $20,900 that went to the child would be taxed at 15%.

Gifts to a trust also qualify for the annual gift-tax exclusion. Say your spouse and all four of your child's grandparents contribute the tax-free maximum to the trust. Thus $60,000 can be added to it tax-free each year. As long as none of you serves as trustee and you leave the trust agreement unchanged, any subsequent appreciation on the assets that the donors place in the trust will also be removed from your estates.

In addition, a trust gives parents some control over a child's access to the assets. Tax law stipulates that trust assets must be payable to the child at age 21. But you can add a provision to the trust document stating that if the child doesn't demand a payout, usually within 30 to 60 days of turning 21, the assets remain locked in the trust until a later date that you specify. Generally parents can persuade the child to leave the assets untouched, thus allowing the money to grow until the recipient is more mature.

Deciding Who Should Own What

Figuring out in whose name to hold major assets could prove to be one of the most important financial decisions that a couple makes.

If you're married, you and your spouse most likely hold your house and other major possessions in both your names. You figure, correctly, that when one of you dies, the other will become sole owner without having to go through a months-long probate proceeding. What could be more loving or more fair? Who could possibly lose in this situation?

Unfortunately, the answer is your children. The ways you and your spouse hold title to major assets can sock your heirs with all sorts of unnecessary taxes including estate tax, which can run as high as 55%. Those taxes can be avoided if you have a lawyer make sure your property is titled correctly (typical cost: about $1,000). This effort can also be important if you are single and share ownership, say, of a house with a friend.

There are three basic forms of co-ownership. With the most common, *joint tenancy with right of survivorship*, each person owns an equal share of the property and can dispose of it without the approval of the others. When one owner dies, his or her share is divided equally among the other owners. The second method, *tenancy by the entirety*, is similar to joint tenancy except that neither partner can sell his or her share without permission from the other. This alternative is available in only about 30 states. The third form, *tenancy in common*, permits co-owners to dispose of shares independently, like joint tenancy. When one owner dies, however, his or her share goes to the heirs named in a will rather than automatically to the co-owners.

A key caveat: if you live in one of the nine community property states (Arizona, California, Idaho, Louisiana, Nevada, New Mexico, Texas, Washington and Wisconsin) where assets acquired during a marriage are generally considered to be owned equally by both spouses, it would be wise to consult an estate lawyer about co-ownership.

Which form should you use? The answer ought to be based mostly on estate-tax considerations, not sentiment. Consider the case of an affluent couple who jointly own $800,000 in assets—a $315,000 house, $100,000 in life insurance on the wife and $80,000 on the husband, a $125,000 vacation retreat, $100,000 in investments, two cars worth a total of $50,000, and $30,000 in jewelry and antiques. After both die, they want the property to go to their two children. If this happily married couple own their property jointly, here's what will happen.

When the first spouse dies, his or her half of the property will pass to the survivor tax-free. But when the second one dies, federal estate taxes on the property, even assuming its value has remained flat at $800,000, will run a hefty $52,200. And that doesn't count state death taxes, which can take as much as 6%, or $23,000, in states such as New York. Those taxes can be avoided if our couple have their lawyer divide the ownership and draw up wills for each of them that include so-called bypass trusts. Then, when the first spouse dies, as much as $600,000 in property can go into his or her trust. The trustee will manage the property and pay out income to the surviving spouse. After the second spouse dies, the principal will go tax-free to the couple's children. Such wills cost about $1,000 each.

With that overall scenario in mind, here's a rundown of the best ways to share ownership of major assets, discussed in terms of the property held by our hypothetical couple:

■ Primary home. Experts say you should set sentiment aside and put the house in one spouse's name. Who should hold the title? Many lawyers say the spouse with the lower income and the least exposure to liability lawsuits. "Say the wife is a doctor who may get hit with a malpractice suit one day," says Edwin Baker, a senior estate attorney for Epstein Becker & Green in New York City. "If her husband owns title to the house, creditors won't be able to attach it."

■ Life insurance. When either of the spouses in our example dies, the proceeds of his or her life insurance policy will go tax-free to the survivor. But what happens when the second spouse dies and the $180,000 in total benefits is left to the children? You guessed it: the money will be hit with estate taxes. To avoid that, have your

lawyer set up an irrevocable life insurance trust. Such a trust cannot be changed after it has been created. When you die, the insurance money will go into the trust, and the trustee will pay income from it to the beneficiaries, including your spouse, for the rest of their lives. When the surviving spouse dies, the money will go to your children or other beneficiaries tax-free. Such a trust costs about $1,000 to establish.

■ Vacation house. The best solution here is for you and your spouse to hold the property jointly with right of survivorship. If one of you owns the retreat outright and it's in a state other than the one in which you reside, you could be complicating your estate unnecessarily. Reason: if the spouse who is sole owner of vacation property dies first, the property will have to go through probate in the state in which it is located. By contrast, if the property is owned jointly, the surviving spouse inherits it automatically and probate is delayed until that spouse dies. There is also a way that you can pass the property to your children while avoiding probate (although not escaping estate taxes). You should have your lawyer place the house in a revocable trust, which costs about $1,000 to set up .

■ Your portfolio. Assets in employee-benefit plans such as 401(k) accounts may be your largest investments, but the only decision you get to make is whom to name as the beneficiary to receive those assets when you die. For mutual funds, stocks and bonds that are held outside of such accounts, you can avoid taxes by splitting ownership. Separately titled assets can be readily transferred to a bypass trust to shelter them from estate taxes.

■ Valuables. Here's the best way to bequeath art, antiques, jewelry or collectibles to your heirs with minimum taxes and squabbles. Put each item in either your name or your spouse's. Then, insert letters of instruction in each of your wills and write letters to your executors specifying who should inherit what. The last thing you want is to have your children bickering over who is going to get which painting or diamond ring.

Chapter 3

Managing Your Portfolio Like a Pro

If there ever was a time for savers to brave the rite of passage to becoming investors, 1993 is it. True, a recovering economy may nudge the recent 2.8% to 5.4% yields on savings accounts and CDs up a full percentage point by year-end. But let's face it. Hunkering down in a 6% CD won't put you in the fast lane to achieving your financial goals. To make your money grow much faster than inflation, you must venture beyond the bank and own stocks, bonds and the mutual funds that invest in these securities.

Moreover, don't put off investing because of MONEY's forecast that stocks may rise a meager 5% or so in 1993 (see Chapter 1). Historically, stocks have averaged annual returns of about 10%. Here's what those high-powered gains could mean to you. Let's say you can afford to sock away $300 a month to help send your eight-year-old to college in 2002. With stocks, you could aim at accumulating about $52,150 by that time, after taxes. But stashing the same amount each month into CDs paying 5% a year would raise just $43,250, or 17% less.

Unfortunately, no one knows this math better than the slick financial pitchmen who prey on novice investors. In fact, with a new President in Washington, this is a time to be especially wary of unsolicited (or cold) calls from brokers urging people to "buy Clinton portfolios." Of course, the brokers don't point out that prices of the infrastructure or eco-play stocks they're promoting ran up in anticipation of Clinton's victory and are unlikely to keep rising at that pace. Thus the commission-earning broker, not you, will profit most from what could amount to self-serving advice.

To help you take the plunge without getting soaked, MONEY has assembled the following rules of successful investing. Our goal is to give you the realistic advice and strategies that you need to get started investing properly. Even if you think you already know the basics of investing, be sure to try your hand at our investing IQ test on the right. The test could serve as a quick check on just how much you really understand.

Choose the proper mix of assets to reach your financial goals before buying any investment. A truly savvy investor buys only securities that fit a well-thought-out portfolio divided among three basic asset categories: stocks (or stock funds), bonds (or bond funds) and cash investments such as money-market funds, savings accounts or CDs. That way, when one part of your holdings gets hammered, the other parts will keep chugging along. What's the right mix? Ignore advisers who say the correct combo depends mostly on your age. What really matters is how soon you will need the money. The longer that time period, the more you should favor stocks.

Roger Gibson, a Pittsburgh investment adviser and asset-allocation expert, recommends that if your goal is, for example, accumulating a down payment on a house in five years, divide your portfolio this way: 35% in stocks or stock funds, 20% in bonds or bond funds and 45% in cash. For a child's college tuition in 10 years, the proper blend would be 50% stocks, 20% bonds and 30% cash. And if your time horizon is 20 years or longer—say, you're investing for retirement—the mix would be 65% stocks, 20% bonds and 15% cash. After setting your mix, leave it alone except to re-balance once a year by switching profits from the parts of your portfolio that have done well to those that haven't.

Start out with mutual funds. Even if a novice is willing to spend the time to select and monitor individual securities, he or she is unlikely to do as well as a full-time mutual fund manager. A notable exception: if you want to invest in U.S. Treasury notes or bonds, you don't really need professional management. You can buy the securities directly from the Treasury for no fee (your bank can tell you how to get the right forms) or for $30 to $50 a bank or broker can purchase Treasuries for you.)

If you don't have the $10,000 or more necessary for a portfolio of funds, start by putting $1,000 or so into a conservative growth or growth and income stock fund. As you amass

What's Your Investing IQ?

Anyone who keeps up with financial matters should have no trouble fielding most of these queries. Score 10 points for each correct answer, explained below.

1 You can't lose money investing in a U.S. Treasury bond, because it is backed by the United States Government. True or false?

2 Investing in a mutual fund that holds a diversified portfolio of stocks protects your investment against market declines. True or false?

3 If a financial planner's business card says that he or she is a Registered Investment Adviser, the planner
a) meets rigorous standards set by the SEC
b) is recommended by the SEC
c) has simply paid a $150 registration fee to the SEC

4 You're considering investing in a mutual fund expected to distribute $1 a share in dividends. You should
a) buy now so you'll get the distribution
b) buy after the distribution is paid
c) buy either way, because it doesn't matter

5 Let's say the price/earnings ratio on Standard & Poor's 500-stock index is 23 and its dividend yield is 2.5%. This means that the stock market is relatively
a) undervalued by historical standards
b) overvalued
c) fairly valued

6 You invested $1,000 in a stock two years ago. The stock's trading price declined 40% the first year and rose 40% the next. As a result, you've
a) lost money
b) made money
c) broken even

7 A broker recommends a municipal bond that matures in 1999 but is likely to be called, or redeemed, as early as 1994. The best gauge of your expected return is its
a) current yield
b) yield to maturity
c) yield to call

8 You own shares in the Germany Fund. The value of your fund's investment in U.S. dollars would be higher if
a) the dollar weakens against the Deutsche mark
b) the dollar strengthens against it
c) neither; a change in the dollar's value doesn't matter in this case

9 The figure that best reflects a mutual fund's performance over a period of years is
a) its current yield
b) the total of dividends and capital gains it has paid
c) its total return

10 If interest rates climb one percentage point, which of these securities would be hurt the *least*?
a) a 20-year zero-coupon bond
b) a 20-year bond selling at its face value
c) a 20-year bond selling at a premium above its face value

ANSWERS: 1. False. If interest rates rise, the market value of all bonds falls. **2.** False. A portfolio holding stocks alone cushions you only against losses in specific stocks. **3.** c. Virtually anyone can register with the SEC as an investment adviser; no professional credentials are required. **4.** b. By waiting, you'll avoid taxes on the distribution. **5.** b. Stocks are generally considered overvalued when the market's P/E is higher than 20 and its dividend yield is lower than 3%. **6.** a. To make up your loss, you would need a 67% gain. **7.** c. The yield to call reflects both the shortened stream of interest payments and the faster principal repayment—sometimes more than the bond's face value—that occurs when a bond is redeemed early. **8.** a. The portfolio is valued in Deutsche marks. If it is converted to a dollar value, the stronger Deutsche mark will buy more dollars, thus increasing your return. **9.** c. Total return includes all income and capital-gains distributions plus the change in the fund's share price. **10.** c. In general, the lower a bond's coupon rate and the longer the maturity, the more its price fluctuates with interest rates. A zero has no coupon rate, and a premium bond has a higher coupon rate than one selling at face value. Thus the premium bond would be hurt least.

SCORING: 100: Congratulations! You could be the next Peter Lynch. **70 to 90:** You've mastered the basics. **50 to 60:** Bone up before making any big investments. **40 or lower:** It's time to start educating yourself about investing. In the meantime, don't take any unsolicited calls from brokers.

more money, you can gradually add other types of funds. Ultimately you should aim for five to seven, including stock funds from the growth, growth and income and equity income categories, as well as corporate or municipal bond funds and money-market funds. After you've assembled your basic portfolio, you might put 10% or so of your stock money in an international stock fund. If you want higher returns and can tolerate more risk, buy a small-company growth fund. (For our selections, refer to "Five Funds That Figure to Thrive" in Chapter 1.)

Adopt a Scrooge-like approach toward fund expenses. In the roaring '80s, when stocks gained 17% a year on average, few investors cared about surrendering 1% of their annual returns in management fees. But with stock prices likely to increase just 5% in 1993, giving up a percentage point is like trying to swim with a big weight around your neck. Be wary of any fund whose expense ratio (the cost of running the fund expressed as a percentage of assets) far exceeds that of similar funds. The average: 1.5% for stock funds and 0.9% for bond funds. In addition, the fund rankings that begin on page 187 list expense ratios and projections for the top-performing funds in their categories. And you can save a chunk of money by buying only no-loads or low-loads (funds with no initial sales fees or ones that are less than 4% of the amount you invest). The savings you'd reap on $10,000 that's invested in a no-load rather than a fund with an 8.5% initial sales fee is $850.

For personalized advice, find a trustworthy broker or financial planner. Ask your friends, your tax accountant or your lawyer for the names of brokers or planners they've worked with successfully for three or more years. This should eliminate rip-off artists. Interview at least three candidates to assure that their investment philosophies jibe with yours. Before signing on with your top choice, check whether he or she has a disciplinary record with your state securities regulator. You can get the phone number by calling the North American Securities Administrators Association (202-737-0900).

Never invest in things you don't understand. Tyros and veterans alike frequently throw money into faddish securities without knowing the risks. For example, in recent years shareholders have poured nearly $15 billion into global short-term bond funds that invest in the debt of foreign countries. In many cases these funds were touted as fairly safe CD alternatives that yielded a tempting 9% or more. But when the European currency markets unraveled in the fall of 1992, some of the funds lost as much as 10% of their value in a few weeks. Of course, no set of general guidelines can consistently guarantee gains or ensure that you won't make painful mistakes. If you follow our rules, however, at the very least you will tip the odds in your favor.

Stock Market Mistakes to Avoid

Even seasoned investors are susceptible to the mental blind spots and knee-jerk reactions that can result in diminishing returns.

You're smart. You don't buy stocks based on tips you hear at parties. You steer clear of hot mutual funds with crummy long-term records. You do your homework. You diversify. But every now and then one of your investments blows up in your face big. And the worst thing is that you're never sure what you did wrong. "I don't know how it happens," says John Hern, an attorney in Grosse Point Park, Michigan. Over a recent 12-month period, he and his wife Ann invested $12,500 in stock funds that lost about 4% overall, vs. the market's 7% gain. In fact, such missteps may stem from following familiar, time-honored investing principles that experts have been recommending to professional money managers and small investors for decades. Over the past several years, many of those cherished stock market ideas have been re-examined and revised by researchers ranging from scholars at the University of Chicago to management consultants like Mitchell & Co. based in Weston, Massachusetts, which advises companies on how to boost their stock price. The following questions will help you apply the latest findings to your own portfolio and hopefully increase this year's returns.

Which of these mutual funds is likely to deliver the best returns?
   A) A fund holding shares more volatile than the overall market.
   B) A fund invested in shares that are less volatile than the market.
   C) Neither; both funds have about the same profit outlook.

If you answered A, you made the common mistake of assuming that, over the long term, the investments that are most volatile relative to the stock market provide the best returns. The correct answer is C.

This would seem to contradict the 1960s research that helped Stanford professor William Sharpe win the Nobel Prize in economics. He concluded that in the long run, so-called high-beta investments (those that display above-average price swings) deliver higher gains than more stable assets. As a result, many financial advisers recommend investments such as aggressive mutual funds or volatile growth stocks for young investors on the theory that, in 10 years or longer, such high-beta holdings will provide the biggest possible gains.

More recent research, however, suggests that Sharpe's conclusion does not always hold true. Professors Eugene Fama and Kenneth French of the University of Chicago's Graduate School of Business studied the behavior of 5,000 stocks over the 50 years that ended in 1990. "Beta had nothing to do with the stocks' performance," says French. Sharpe counters that a single statistical study doesn't disprove his theory. Still, the new

research suggests that you should favor stable investments over volatile ones.

You own stock in a Fortune 500 company that plans to cut 12,000 jobs to slash annual costs by $500 million. What should you do?
   A) Sell your shares.
   B) Keep your shares.
   C) Buy more.

If you would buy more instead of selling or just hanging on to what you already own, you would be making the mistake of not knowing bad news when you hear it. Share prices often jump 10% or more immediately after companies announce restructurings. But consider this: in 1986, when Eastman Kodak announced the plan described in our question, its stock traded at $40 a share. Kodak's stock recently fetched around $41, up only a buck in almost seven years.

After studying 16 restructurings between 1982 and 1988, the consulting firm Mitchell & Co. found that the firms' shares trailed the market by an average of 24 percentage points three years after the shake-ups. Reason: restructurings are frequently a response to fundamental and invariably hard-to-solve problems such as increased competition or eroding markets.

Three days ago, a computer distributor reported strong quarterly earnings of 16 cents a share, vs. the 12 cents that many analysts had expected, and its shares shot up 14%. Should you still buy the stock now?

If you pass because the stock's price has already risen on the news, you are making the mistake of believing that the market quickly reflects all the news about a company. In fact, such news is often a sign of a long-term trend that will keep on rewarding shareholders for years. Melissa Brown, director of quantitative research at Prudential Securities, recently studied 50 stocks whose prices jumped 5% or more right after the companies reported quarterly earnings that topped analysts' estimates. She found that during the next 12 months, those shares outperformed the average stock by six percentage points. So what happened to investors in our example, Tech Data Corp. of Clearwater, Fla.? Its shares climbed another 285% in the 12 months after its November 1990 earnings report.

Wall Street analysts argue convincingly that profits of Company A will grow 240% over 15 years while Company B's profits will rise 144%, in line with the typical firm in the S&P 500 index. Do you buy Company A or Company B?

If you automatically bought shares in Company A, expecting to trounce the S&P 500, you made the mistake of thinking that rising earnings alone push up a stock's price. Take the former Beatrice Co. as an example. Despite spectacular earnings growth of 240% from 1968 to 1983, the company's share price rose only 57%, lagging the S&P 500 by two points. When Mitchell & Co. looked at how 11 different factors were related to the share prices of 75 large companies during the 10 years through 1988, the consultants discovered that earnings fully explained the share-price behavior of only two firms. The reason is that institutional investors often rely on other measures of a company's prosperity, such as growth in revenues or the amount of cash that a firm generates from its operations.

In 1987, this giant company announced plans to repurchase as much as $25 million of its shares. You invested in the stock assuming that the buyback would boost the shares' value over time. What happened?
A) Your stock outpaced the Dow.
B) Your stock trailed the Dow.
If you chose A, you made the mistake of believing that buybacks usually push up share prices because they automatically increase earnings per share—a firm's total profits divided by its number of shares. In fact, a Mitchell & Co. study of 16 major stocks found that 10 of them (63%) trailed the market during the three years after the companies announced large share

repurchases. Investors who bought Allied Signal stock in 1987, shortly before it announced the plan described above, have gained about 18%, while the average stock returned 38%.

This mutual fund specializes in owning stocks that are held by celebrated investors such as Warren Buffett, whose investments have earned more than 23% annually over the past 27 years. Are you interested?

If you are, you've succumbed to the fallacy of trying to follow the so-called smart money. The bogus theory holds that if you invest as the rich do, you'll eventually get rich too. The problem is that the rich are often wrong as investors. As evidence, take the Wealth Monitors Fund, started in 1986 to pursue just such a strategy. Lucky you, if you missed it. In four years, the fund lost more than a third of its value.

Last year you bought 100 shares of a $20 stock through a large brokerage. The stock pays no dividend, but it now trades at $22. If you sell, what is your total return?

If you say 10%, you're ignoring how commissions and taxes cut into your profits. Your gross return would indeed be 10% ($200 on a $2,000 investment). But round-trip brokerage commissions of as much as 4% could take more than a third of that. And federal taxes could reduce your net return to $83 or less if you are in the 28% bracket or above. So your actual total return will be approximately 4%. In order to minimize the bite of taxes, be sure to use tax-deferred savings plans such as IRAs, Keoghs and 401(k)s. You should pay special attention to commissions and fees, especially when you invest in fixed-income mutual funds, where such charges have the greatest impact on future returns.

In 1986 you invested $1,000 in a stock fund. Your investment is now worth $1,450. Should you be happy with your results?

If you are happy with that 6.4% compounded annual return, you have made the mistake of overlooking better opportunities. You would have boosted your return to 9.5%, compounded annually, and ended up with $1,730 if you had simply invested in an index fund that buys the stocks that make up the S&P 500. Similarly, Larry Siegel, director of research for the investment research firm Ibbotson Associates in Chicago, reckons that cautious souls who invested $10,000 entirely in Treasury bills instead of putting half the money in stocks 10 years ago would have missed out on profits that totaled a whopping $14,179. Economists have a fancy name for that gap: opportunity cost.

It's 1987. Seven investment newsletters are bullish on the same fund. Should you invest?
If you said no, you made the mistake of believing that conventional wisdom is usually wrong. The fund in question was Fidelity's mighty Magellan. Since the seven newsletters' endorsement, it has returned around 85%, more than double that for the S&P 500 index.

A Fund Family to Call Your Own

Our analysis of 25 full-service groups reveals that Financial/Invesco is tops in performance, Vanguard keeps costs low, and much more.

What are the best fund families—those one-stop-shopping conglomerations of stock, bond and money-market portfolios sponsored by a single investment company? It all depends on the attributes you value most. Above-average returns? Superior customer service? Low fees?

MONEY has the answers. Last year we evaluated the performance, service and expenses at 25 major full-service fund groups. Together these giants managed some $916 billion, about 64% of the mutual fund industry's total assets. To be included in our study, each family had to offer at least one entry from our data base of large, widely available funds in each of the following broad investment categories: aggressive growth, conservative total-return and overseas stock funds; taxable and tax-free bond funds; and money markets. Thus we excluded some sizable families such as Federated, which sells mainly to bank trust customers, and the Janus group, which had no tax-exempt fund. We also withheld an overall performance rating for two families—Franklin and Twentieth Century—because their overseas

stock funds were too new to have established meaningful track records. The winners:

Investment returns. Overall honors go to Denver's Financial/Invesco group, formerly known as Financial Programs. Strong results from the group's total-return funds—in particular, Industrial Income—helped it edge out larger competitors Vanguard, Scudder, Fidelity and the American Funds group.

Total fund expenses. Our comparison found that the no-load Vanguard Group offered far and away the most cost-efficient funds. The next closest competitors were Scudder for bond funds and Twentieth Century for stock funds.

Customer service. Since individual investors value specific services differently, we chose not to declare a champion for this category. But our table on pages 52-53 shows at a glance which of the 25 companies provided the amenities that most investors want and what they charged for them. And while it hardly constituted a scientific study, our informal sampling of shareholder phone lines will tell you what to expect when you call with a question about your accounts.

What conclusions can you draw from our ratings? First, do not assume that the families with the highest overall performance scores are necessarily the best places to keep all your money. Even top-ranked Financial/Invesco had a real nag in its stable—its Dynamics growth fund, which underperformed 80% of its competition in three of the five two-year time periods we studied. On the other hand, a middle-of-the-pack family such as 15th-ranked Kemper housed a thorough-

bred like Kemper Growth, which outperformed 70% of its competitors. Thus your first task is to find the individual funds that best match your goals and tolerance for risk—and no general rating of fund families can do that. (For comprehensive performance figures, see our fund rankings beginning on page 187.)

Our family evaluations should come into play once you've narrowed your choices to a few promising funds. We designed our ratings to give you a sense of each family's priorities: in what

How the Families Performed for Shareholders

FAMILY	Overall percentile score	PERFORMANCE GRADE (% of group assets in category)					BIGGEST FUNDS			
		Stock funds			Bond funds		Stock		Bond	
		Growth	Total return	Overseas	Taxable	Tax-exempt	NAME (category)	Five-year compound annual return	NAME (category)	Five-year compound annual return
Financial/Invesco	61.35	C(7%)	A(69%)	B(4%)	B(8%)	A(12%)	Industrial Income (TR)	14.2%	Tax-Free Income (TE)	9.4%
Vanguard	61.16	B(6)	B(49)	B(5)	A(23)	A(17)	Windsor (TR)	8.4	Fixed Income-GNMA (T)	10.6
Scudder	60.87	B(24)	C(11)	A(29)	C(16)	B(20)	Capital Growth (G)	11.5	Managed Municipals (TE)	9.5
Fidelity	60.31	A(43)	B(29)	C(4)	B(13)	B(10)	Magellan (G)	13.4	High-Yield Tax-Free (TE)	9.1
American Funds	60.04	A(19)	A(63)	A(8)	B(9)	C(2)	Investment Co. of America (TR)	11.2	Bond Fund of America (T)	9.5
John Hancock	56.24	D(5)	B(3)	C(5)	B(72)	B(15)	Sovereign Investors (TR)	12.0	Hancock Bond (T)	9.6
Oppenheimer	54.17	C(26)	B(29)	A(11)	A(30)	C(4)	Equity Income (TR)	8.1	High-Yield (T)	9.5
PaineWebber	54.01	B(3)	D(11)	B(6)	B(72)	C(8)	Dividend Growth A (TR)	10.4	Global Income B (T)	11.9
IDS	51.51	B(13)	A(26)	C(2)	B(28)	C(32)	New Dimensions (G)	14.1	High-Yield Tax-Exempt (TE)	8.7
Merrill Lynch	49.61	D(4)	D(32)	B(6)	B(32)	B(26)	Basic Value A (TR)	8.9	Federal Securities A (T)	9.8
United	48.02	C(26)	A(29)	C(4)	D(30)	A(11)	Income (TR)	12.5	High Income (T)	4.5
Colonial	47.93	B(2)	C(5)	D(0)²	B(66)	D(27)	Colonial Fund A (TR)	10.0	Tax-Exempt (TE)	8.1
Dean Witter	47.68	B(1)	C(20)	C(2)	C(71)	B(5)	Dividend Growth (TR)	11.5	U.S. Gov. Securities (T)	8.2
Alliance	47.57	C(25)	C(14)	C(8)	C(49)	B(5)	Alliance A (G)	9.8	Mortgage Income A (T)	9.7
Kemper	47.41	A(5)	B(8)	B(1)	C(76)	B(10)	Growth (G)	14.1	U.S. Gov. Securities (T)	9.6
Lord Abbett	43.62	D(7)	D(58)	C(0)²	A(30)	A(5)	Affiliated (TR)	8.0	U.S. Gov. Securities (T)	9.7
T. Rowe Price	43.24	C(29)	C(12)	A(10)	B(30)	D(19)	Growth Stock (G)	7.8	New Income (T)	9.3
Putnam	42.49	B(8)	C(23)	B(2)	C(58)	C(9)	Growth & Income (TR)	10.8	High-Income Gov. (T)	7.5
Dreyfus	41.88	B(15)	C(24)	B(0)²	C(19)	C(42)	Dreyfus Fund (TR)	9.2	Municipal Bond (TE)	8.5
Shearson	38.58	D(25)	B(8)	D(2)	C(50)	B(16)	Appreciation (G)	10.9	Managed Municipals (TE)	8.9
MFS	35.99	C(19)	B(19)	B(0)²	D(46)	C(15)	Mass. Investors Trust (TR)	10.6	Lifetime Gov. Income (T)	6.6
Prudential	33.57	C(11)	C(3)	D(5)	C(67)	D(15)	Equity B (G)	10.1	Government Plus B (T)	8.5
Keystone	26.36	B(21)	D(3)	D(2)	D(45)	D(28)	S-4 (G)	8.4	Tax-Free (TE)	8.1
Franklin	N.R.¹	C(2)	B(0)²	—	A(73)	B(24)	Growth (G)	11.6	U.S. Gov. Securities (T)	9.6
Twentieth Century	N.R.¹	A(91)	A(1)	—	D(8)	C(0)²	Select (G)	9.5	U.S. Governments (T)	7.8

Category abbreviations: G—Growth; TR—Total return; T—Taxable bond; TE—Tax-exempt bond. **Notes:** Percentages may not add up to 100% because of rounding. ¹ Not rated: International fund is less than three years old. ² Less than 1% **Source: Lipper Analytical Services**

categories of funds the group deploys its most talented managers; how concerned the family is about keeping shareholders informed; and how dedicated it is to minimizing shareholders' costs. That valuable information can be decisive for investors making close calls between equally attractive funds from different sponsors.

Overall family performance. First, a caveat: there's no definitive way to rate an entire fund family's returns. For example, in our first family ratings in November 1990, we averaged the performance scores of all the funds in each family, giving equal weight to all. In effect, we measured how well the group's average manager compared with his peers.

By contrast, our latest ratings, compiled with the help of fund authority Lipper Analytical Services, were designed to show how well the family's average shareholder fared. To do so, our methodology gave proportionately more weight to the return of a fund holding billions of dollars than to that of a smaller portfolio. Our reasoning is that, to some extent, a fund group can direct the flow of cash into individual portfolios by advertising particular funds or, in load families, by rewarding salespeople more generously

Ranking an entire family's performance is tricky business. We did it by following the money. Our asset-weighted performance ratings at left reward families for earning strong returns in categories where their shareholders had most of their money. As a result, a family's overall score—the average of its percentile rankings in five broad categories ranging from growth to tax-free bonds—was heavily influenced by the performance of its biggest funds. For example, Financial/Invesco emerged as the overall winner largely because of the A earned by its total-return funds, which account for 69% of the family's $5.5 billion in total assets. Keystone came in last of the 23 families rated overall because its taxable and tax-free bond funds, which account for 73% of the group's $8.8 billion in assets, both scored a D.

for selling some funds over others. Thus our system favored families in which the bulk of shareholders' money was managed by the group's most successful pros, and it penalized those in which an outsize share of assets languished in mediocre portfolios.

Shareholder services. At the minimum, a fund family owes you accurate execution of buy and sell orders, clear transaction records and, especially in no-load funds, knowledgeable telephone representatives. A family can go well beyond that, of course. Both Fidelity and Twentieth Century automatically execute college investing plans that you devise—for example, switching you into less risky funds as your children near college age. And T. Rowe Price sends out free copies of a widely acclaimed retirement planning kit that's designed to help investors determine exactly how much money they need to set aside and invest for the future.

The table on the next page gives you a guide to common (and not so common) shareholder services. The columns under the transactions heading cover your most basic dealings with a fund group: investing and withdrawing your money and moving it around within the fund complex. All 25 groups allowed you to transfer among funds within the family, though some, including Financial/Invesco and Vanguard, limited the number of switches you can make each year, and MFS and Keystone charged as much as $10 per switch. Most groups limited transactions roughly to business hours, though Fidelity and Dreyfus had phone reps on duty 24 hours a day.

All of our families except Shearson would, on your request, automatically deduct money from your bank account periodically and invest it in a fund of your choice. At Shearson, you could sluice money only from a company brokerage account. These automatic investment plans make it easy to build up assets through the prudent technique of dollar-cost averaging—that is, of investing a fixed amount of money in the fund at regular intervals. Seven families would even take money directly from your paycheck—with your employer's cooperation, of course.

The ability to write checks against your money fund gives you instant liquidity. Families typically refused checks under $500, but Colonial and Paine Webber honored any amount. Half our families automatically returned canceled checks, simplifying your record keeping.

With IRA funds invested for retirement goals, the annual fees subtracted from your account can retard your capital growth. Our table shows how much each family charged to maintain an IRA account and, equally important, whether you had to pay a separate custodial fee for each IRA fund you own. Once invested, your main source of information is your semiannual or quarterly shareholder report. The *Morningstar* shareholder report grade reflects the judgment of the Chicago fund-rating outfit on the quality of each family's reports, based on such factors as the reports' clarity and candor. "Quality shareholder reports are just another indicator of a fund family's concern for shareholders," says *Morningstar* editor John Rekenthaler. The top-ranked family for reports was Vanguard, followed by Merrill Lynch and T. Rowe Price.

A recently introduced service greatly simplifies a fundholder's relationship with the Internal Revenue Service. When you sell shares held outside an IRA or other tax-deferred account, you

What Your Fund Family Will do For You—and

FUND FAMILY	Total number of funds	Usual minimum initial investment	Free switches	Switching fee	Transaction hours (eastern time)	24-hour account information	Automatic investment from	Withdrawal by wire for all funds	Minimum amount of wire withdrawal
Alliance	36	$250	Unlimited	None	9 a.m.-4 p.m.	Yes	Bank	No[13]	$100
American Funds	25	250-2,500	Unlimited	None	8-8	Yes	Bank	No[13]	1,000
Colonial	30	1,000	None	$5	9-4	Yes	Bank	Yes	5,000
Dean Witter	45	1,000-5,000	Unlimited	None	9-4	Yes	Bank, payroll	Yes	1,000
Dreyfus	73	2,500	Unlimited	None	24 hours	Yes	Bank, payroll	Yes	1,000
Fidelity	180	2,500-5,000	4 per year[1]	$5[1]	24 hours	Yes	Bank, payroll	Yes	5,000
Financial/Invesco	25	250	4 per year[2]	None	9-8	Yes	Bank	No[13]	1,000
Franklin Funds	69	100	None	$5	9:30-9	Yes	Bank, payroll	Yes	1,000
John Hancock	18	1,000	Unlimited	None	8-8	Yes	Bank, payroll	Yes	No minimum
IDS	36	2,000	Unlimited	None	8-7	No	Bank	Yes	$1,000
Kemper	25	1,000	Unlimited	None	9-4	No	Bank[12]	Yes	10,000[15]
Keystone	33	1,000	None	$10[6]	9-6[7]	Yes	Bank, payroll	Yes	No minimum
Lord Abbett	21	250-1,000	Unlimited	None	8:30-4	No	Bank	No[13]	$1,000
MFS	36	1,000	None	$10	8-8	Yes	Bank	Yes	1,000
Merrill Lynch	65	250-5,000	None	None	8-4[8]	Yes	Bank	No[13]	100
Oppenheimer	29	1,000	None	$5	8:30-7	Yes	Bank	No[14]	2,500
PaineWebber	30	1,000	None	5	9-4	No	Bank	Yes	1 million
Prudential	60	1,000	Unlimited	None	8-6	Yes	Bank	No[13]	No minimum
Putnam	52	500-1,000	Unlimited	None	8:30-4	No	Bank	No[13]	$1,000
Scudder	28	1,000	Unlimited	None	8-6[9]	Yes	Bank	Yes	No minimum
Shearson	53	1,000	Unlimited	None	Broker only	No	Brokerage acct.	Yes	No minimum
T. Rowe Price	40	2,500	3 per year[3]	None	8-10[7]	Yes	Bank, payroll	Yes	$500
Twentieth Century	13	No minimum	Unlimited[4]	None	9-5:30[7]	Yes	Bank, payroll	Yes	No minimum
United	16	$500	Unlimited	None	N.A.[10]	No	Bank	No[13]	$1,000
Vanguard	60	3,000	2 per year[5]	None	8:30-5[7,11]	Yes	Bank	No[14]	1,000

Notes: [1]Except Select funds (unlimited switches for $7.50 each plus a 0.75% redemption charge if you hold it for less than 30 days), International funds (free, unlimited switches except the International Opportunitrip exchanges [4]Must own shares for 30 days, except in the Cash Reserve fund [5]Round-trip exchanges. Three round-trip exchanges allowed on sector funds. [6]$5 if switched by computer from Touch-Tone phone Friday [10]Must be a written request [11]All time zones [12]Payroll transfer to money market only [13]Money funds only [14]Money-market and selected other funds only [15]Money funds, $1,000 minimum [16]Except count [18]$1,000 minimum for money fund IRAs [19]Fees are waived for IRAs over $50,000.

owe capital-gains tax if your sale price was higher than your cost for the shares (your so-called tax basis). The problem is that calculating tax basis can be a five-aspirin headache, especially if you bought shares at a variety of prices. Eight of our 25 families said they did the dirty work for you, automatically calculating the tax basis on any shares you had sold and sending you that information along with your tax documents after the end of the year.

Fund fees and expenses. Figuring out exactly how much you pay to buy and own a fund has become more and more difficult in recent years. Of the 18 broker-sold families in our study, only

United still carried a traditional 8.5% initial load. The others hit you with initial charges ranging from zero to 6.5%, often backed up by a dizzying combination of withdrawal penalties and sales charges or "12b-1" fees of 0.75% to 1.25%. Some groups that sell funds directly to shareholders have also become harder to pin down. Most Fidelity stock funds, for example, carried initial loads of 2% to 3%, and Financial/Invesco had installed 12b-1 fees of 0.25%.

These amounts may seem trivial, particularly if you have grown accustomed to the 15% annual gains of the 1980s. But they can be a drag on your return. Costs matter the most in bond funds, where returns tend to be more uniform

What They'll Charge You for It

MONEY FUND CHECK WRITING		IRA COSTS AND SERVICES			OTHER SERVICES		
Minimum amount	Checks returned	IRA minimum initial investment	Annual custodial fee per fund	Maximum custodial fee per investor	Morningstar shareholder report rating	Will calculate tax basis	Telephone
$500	Yes	$250	$10	$10	B−	No	800-221-5672
250	Yes	250[18]	10	10	B	No	800-421-0180
No minimum	Yes	250	10	10	C	Yes	800-345-6611
$500	No	1,000	5	No maximum	D	No	800-869-3863
500	Yes	750	10	$25	D	No	800-782-6620
500[16]	No	500	10	30	C+	No	800-544-6666
500	No	250	10	10	C	No	800-525-8085
100	Yes	100	10	10	D	No	800-342-5236
250	Yes	500	15	No maximum	C+	No	800-225-5291
500	No	50	18	No maximum	C	Yes	800-328-8300
500	No	250	12	$24	C+	No	800-621-1048
500	No	No minimum	20	20	B	Yes	800-343-2898
500	Yes	$250	9	No maximum	B−	No	800-426-1130
500	Yes	250	15	No maximum	C	No	800-225-2606
500[17]	No	250	35	$100	A−	No	800-637-7455
100	No	250	10	10	B	Yes	800-525-7048
No minimum	Yes	No minimum	35	35	C+	Yes	800-647-1568
$500	Yes	No minimum	12	No maximum	C	No	800-648-7637
500	Yes	$1,000	10	$10	C+	Yes	800-225-1581
100	Yes	500	10[19]	No maximum	B−	No	800-225-2470
N.A.	N.A.	2,000	40	No maximum	C+	Yes	212-720-9218
$500	Yes	1,000	10	No maximum	A−	No	800-541-8832
500	No	No minimum	10	$30	C+	No	800-345-2021
250	No	$50	15	No maximum	C+	Yes	913-236-1303
250	Yes	500	10	No maximum	A	No	800-851-4999

ties Fund, which charges a 1.5% redemption fee if the shares are held less than 90 days), and Spartan funds (unlimited switches; $5 each) [2]Per fund [3]Round- [7]24-hour Touch-Tone transactions [8]24-hour Touch-Tone transactions available with money funds [9]24-hour Touch-Tone transactions, Monday through Spartan funds ($1,000 minimum) and Daily Income Trust and TaxExempt Money Market Trust (no minimums) [17]No minimum for Cash Management Ac-

You can use this rundown of shareholder amenities to help decide between otherwise equally promising funds in different families. For example, if you plan to trade often, you may want one of the 14 families that permit unlimited free switches among funds in the group; or you may prefer Fidelity or Dreyfus, where you can talk to a phone rep 24 hours a day. All investors should check out the two columns just before the phone numbers. In the first, fund rating service Morningstar grades each family's shareholder report. The second indicates whether the group calculates the average cost per share (or tax "basis") of shares you withdraw from the fund, a service that can save you hours of figuring at tax time—and possibly hundreds of dollars as well.

What You Will Pay to Play

No surprise here: the ultra-cost-conscious Vanguard Group of no-load funds had the lowest overall costs for both stock and bond funds of the 25 full-service families we surveyed. Our comparisons are based on a standard SEC formula, which projects expenses per $1,000 investment, assuming you earn 5% a year and redeem after three years. The formula takes into account any sales charges as well as total annual operating expenses. The most expensive group for both stock and bond funds: MFS Lifetime, a 12-fund offshoot of the MFS family with back-end sales loads as high as 6%.

	Stock funds				Bond funds	
FUND FAMILY	% maximum initial load	Three-year expense projection		FUND FAMILY	% maximum initial load	Three-year expense projection
Vanguard	None	$17.61		Vanguard	None	$10.99
Twentieth Century	None	32.18		Scudder	None	20.87
T. Rowe Price	None	32.98		Fidelity	None	22.27
Financial/Invesco	None	33.73		Dreyfus	None	26.78
Scudder	None	37.91		T. Rowe Price	None	27.46
Dreyfus	4.5%	45.50		Twentieth Century	None	32.00
Fidelity	3.0	50.52		Financial/Invesco	None	36.16
Franklin	4.0	59.13		Franklin	4.0%	56.71
Keystone	None[1]	73.21		Merrill Lynch	4.0	57.26
IDS	5.0%	79.05		Kemper	4.5	65.19
American Funds	5.75	79.82		Dean Witter	None[1]	69.60
Dean Witter	None[1]	80.91		IDS	5.0%	73.03
Kemper Invest Port.	None[1]	83.14		American Funds	4.75	73.35
Shearson	5.0%	84.24		Shearson	5.0	74.77
Merrill Lynch	6.5	84.30		Prudential	None[1]	75.97
Lord Abbett	5.75	86.92		Lord Abbett	4.75%	76.31
MFS	5.75	87.92		Kemper Invest Port.	None[1]	76.46
Putnam	5.75	90.19		Fidelity Advisor	4.75%	77.40
John Hancock	5.0	90.32		Oppenheimer	4.75	78.70
Kemper	5.75	91.31		Putnam	4.75	79.82
Colonial	5.75	91.51		Alliance	4.75	79.88
Alliance	5.5	91.57		MFS	4.75	80.09
Oppenheimer	5.75	92.62		Paine Webber	4.0	80.69
Paine Webber	4.5	94.66		Keystone	None[1]	81.96
Prudential	5.25	95.14		Keystone America	4.75%	84.38
Keystone America	4.75	95.86		John Hancock	4.5	85.61
Fidelity Advisor	4.75	97.52		Colonial	4.75	88.35
United	8.5	108.33		United	8.5	89.60
MFS Lifetime	None[1]	118.91		MFS Lifetime	None[1]	102.52

[1]Typically charges a back-end load on shares withdrawn within five years   **Source:** Morningstar Inc.

than in stock funds. Indeed, it's no coincidence that low-cost champ Vanguard also topped our performance rankings in both bond categories.

The fairest way to compare the total costs of investing in various funds is to add up all the charges, including sales loads and 12b-1 fees, levied over an established period under a uniform set of assumptions. That's the theory behind the expense projections in the table above. They are based on a standardized Securities and Exchange Commission formula that assumes you invest $1,000, earn a steady 5% return and withdraw the money in three years.

We asked *Morningstar* to average the expense figures for all the stock and bond funds in each of our families, giving proportionately more weight to funds with greater assets. Where organizations run subsidiary families with different cost structures from their main group (the case with Fidelity Advisor, Kemper Investment Portfolios, Keystone America and MFS Lifetime), the table ranks the main group and the mini-family separately.

Predictably, groups that sell directly to investors without sales charges had the lowest total expenses. The absence of a front-end load, however, does not necessarily translate into low total costs. The most expensive group in our study was MFS Lifetime, the 12-fund offshoot of MFS that carried no initial sales charge. The high totals came from stiff annual fees of 2.3% or so and a back-end sales load of 3% for withdrawals at the end of three years. As a result, the average MFS Lifetime bond fund would have needed to earn an extra 3.1% annually to break even with the typical Vanguard bond fund over three years. With numbers like that, it's not hard to decide which family would provide a better home for your money.

Rating telephone reps. Unlike most bank customers, fund shareholders can invest for decades without ever coming face to face with a representative of the firm that holds their money. Typically, the only direct human contact you establish with a fund company occurs over the phone. That's why no evaluation of a family's shareholder service can be complete without a survey of its telephone reps' skills.

In our survey, correspondents posing as potential investors made repeated calls to the families in our sample, asking a range of 10 basic and sophisticated questions about the family's funds. All 25 families answered the phone within 30 seconds. But there were distinct differences among the families in their ability to handle our questions.

Given the millions they've spent on telephone technology and staff training, it's no surprise that the largest no-load families, such as Fidelity, Vanguard and T. Rowe Price, were the best prepared. Only Fidelity and Vanguard reps, for example, knew how much their taxable bond funds would lose in value if interest rates rose by two percentage points. At our performance champ Financial/Invesco, however, reps seemed less sure of themselves. In one case, our caller had to be passed along to a superior merely to discover the average maturity of one of the family's four bond funds.

Phone reps at broker-sold funds tended to be somewhat less prepared to answer our inquiries. This is at least partially understandable, since most of these fund groups are set up primarily to handle questions from brokers, not shareholders. The most notable exception was Kemper. That firm's reps smoothly fielded questions that other groups often flubbed, including one about a fund's total expenses and a fairly technical inquiry about risk levels. Less helpful were reps at some house-brand brokerage funds, such as Shearson and Paine Webber, who answered tough questions by suggesting that the caller phone instead a broker within the system.

MONEY HELPS

Q. How do fund rating firms figure percentage gains? On January 1, 1991, I had 4,231 shares, worth $39,306, of the Neuberger & Berman Manhattan Fund. On May 22 of that year, I paid $46,000 for 4,196 more shares. On December 31, my 8,427 shares were worth $98,175 and I got a $4,297 dividend—a $102,472 total that is 20% more than the $85,306 (my initial $39,306 plus the extra $46,000) I had invested. Why did MONEY say my fund returned 31%?
— Laura Baker, Los Osos, California

A. The figure usually cited by us is total return—the change in a fund's share price plus any dividends. Your shares were worth $9.29 each on January 1. By year-end, they had risen to $11.65 and paid 51 cents per share in dividends, for a $12.16 total and a 31% gain. Your problem was the $46,000 that you added on May 22; it was invested for only part of the period (223 days, or 61% of the year). To calculate your percentage total return, use this simple formula: figure your earnings for the year ($102,472 minus $85,306 equals $17,166). Divide the $17,166 by the average amount you had invested each day, which is simply your initial balance ($39,306) plus a prorated share of any amounts added in midyear (in your case, $46,000 times 61%, or $28,106). Then multiply the answer by 100 to convert it to a percentage. Result: your total return was 25.5%.

Load Funds Well Worth the Burden

Buying funds through brokers usually means paying hefty sales charges. The returns of these standouts abundantly overcome that handicap.

Many independent-minded investors who shun load mutual funds—those with initial sales charges as high as 8.5%—may be in for a shock. Contrary to what you may think, there are a handful of stellar load funds, available only from brokers, insurance agents and financial planners, whose records are so extraordinary that they ought to appeal to every fund investor.

Before we tell you about them, however, be assured that the argument against load funds still holds true in most cases. For every one of the 1,800 load funds sold today, there is almost always a comparable no-load choice. That means you can usually make the same investment without paying a commission and starting off in the hole (or, in the case of back-end loads, without having to wait up to six years to withdraw your funds so as not to incur sales charges). Further, the evidence shows that load funds have no edge over no-loads. In our analysis of the five years to November 30, 1992, the average stock load fund provided the same 14% annual return as did the average no-load—before adjusting for commissions. When sales charges were factored in, the no-loads outperformed the load funds by a percentage point annually.

Nonetheless, 63% of total mutual fund assets is parked in load funds. Why? It's a testament to the persuasiveness of stockbrokers, financial planners and insurance agents who help direct investors to funds that, in theory at least, are right for them. "A load isn't paying to get you a better portfolio manager," sums up Don Phillips of Morningstar Mutual Funds, a Chicago rating service. "But it does pay for a broker or financial planner to help you make your choices." In rare cases, a load does get you a better portfolio. These are the only load funds you really need to know about. To find them, we asked Morningstar to screen the 1,575 load funds that it tracks. The funds were ranked by annualized five-year returns, adjusted for each fund's maximum initial commission or applicable back-end load. (The screen eliminated 625 funds because they have been around less than five years.) Then we examined those that beat the average no-load funds in the same categories. We accepted only load funds that received an A in MONEY's risk-adjusted grading system, which measures whether a portfolio's performance is in line with the risks the manager has taken. And we rejected funds that carry annual management and administrative expenses substantially above the norm of 1.5% of assets for stock funds, 1% for taxable bond funds and 0.7% for tax-free bond funds. In those instances where two or three similar funds passed our tests, we chose the one with the best performance.

Here are 14 load funds that are worth their fees. Our selections are spread among all the major fund types—growth, total return, international, taxable bond and tax exempt—and are ranked within their categories by five-year performance net of sales charges. (See the table on the right for additional information.)

GROWTH FUNDS

Alger Small Capitalization. This $207 million fund leads the five-year load-fund rankings in the growth category with a load-adjusted average return of nearly 30% annually. That's better than two-thirds more than the 17% annual return of no-load growth funds. (Alger has a back-end load of 5% if money is withdrawn in less than a year.) Manager David Alger has compiled his superb record by focusing on the shares of fast-growing companies. In 1992, profits for the 48 stocks in the portfolio zoomed more than 40%, on average. Lately, some 39% of the fund was invested in technology companies such as Wellfleet Communications, which makes products that link computer networks.

Pasadena Growth. While manager Roger Engemann's no-holds-barred bullishness isn't for skittish investors, his $604 million fund's results help soothe the nerves. Even adjusting for its 5.5% sales charge, the fund has returned 27% annually over the past five years. Though a perennial optimist, Engemann has been hedging his bets on the U.S. economy. Three of the fund's top holdings—drugmaker Pfizer, toiletries giant Gillette and Reuters, the British telecommunications company—generate the majority of their sales overseas.

New York Venture. Manager Shelby Davis fills his $500 million fund (4.75% load) with stocks that are out of favor with the majority of investors. One example is Salomon, the giant securities trading house whose shares sank 42% to $22 in 1991 after the firm admitted to rule violations in U.S. Treasury auctions. The fund recently owned 549,000 Salomon shares (average price: $32) that had rebounded to around $38 as the company solves its problems. With a load-adjusted return of 20% annually over five years, Davis' style is not only successful but also consistent. In fact, his fund has outpaced the S&P 500 index in 10 of the past 12 years running.

The Only Load Funds You Need to Know About

MONEY's rigorous search for the best load funds turned up these 14 gems: Each outperformed its no-load competitors—even after adjusting for sales charges—and rated an A in our fund grading system that compares return with risk.

Fund	Compound load-adjusted annual gain (or loss) to Nov. 30, 1992			Maximum sales charge	Telephone
	Five years	Three years	Since Jan. 1, 1992		
GROWTH					
Alger Small Capitalization	29.5%	16.7%	(6.5%)	5.00%[1]	800-992-3863
Pasadena Growth	26.8	15.6	(2.9)	5.50	800-882-2855
New York Venture	20.0	13.2	4.3	4.75	800-279-0279
TOTAL RETURN					
Vista Growth & Income	30.4	20.9	7.7	4.75	800-348-4782
Franklin Rising Dividends	16.0	13.1	4.8	4.00	800-342-5236
FPA Perennial	15.4	9.2	5.0	6.50	800-982-4372
Fortress Utility	14.3	11.9	5.5	2.00[2]	800-245-5051
INTERNATIONAL					
EuroPacific Growth	12.7	4.9	(5.8)	5.75	800-421-0180
Templeton Foreign	12.6	4.4	(7.1)	5.75	800-237-0738
Dreyfus Strategic World Investing	11.6	6.9	(5.8)	3.00	800-645-6561
TAXABLE BONDS					
Merrill Lynch Corporate High Income A	12.7	15.0	14.4	4.00	800-637-3863
Van Eck World Income	10.2	9.3	(8.7)	4.75	800-221-2220
TAX-EXEMPT BONDS					
Premier Municipal Bond	10.3	8.6	4.2	4.50	800-645-6561
Alliance Municipal Income–National	9.8	7.9	4.0	4.50	800-247-4154

Note: [1] Back-end sales charge on money withdrawn; it declines to zero over six years [2] 1% initial charge plus a 1% back-end load on withdrawals in four years or less **Source:** Morningstar Inc.

TOTAL RETURN FUNDS

Vista Growth & Income. Though this $170 million fund boasts a 3% dividend yield, manager Mark Tincher also aims for capital appreciation. Tincher starts with a stock-ranking model that he developed in the early 1980s with colleagues at Chase Manhattan Bank, the fund's adviser. He favors companies with better than average profit growth and below-market price/earnings ratios. One example is W.R. Grace, a chemical and health-care concern with a P/E of 13, vs. 15 for the S&P 500, and expected earnings growth of 14% annually, vs. 7% for the typical stock. Tincher's value orientation has enabled Vista (4.75% load) to beat the competition every year since it was founded in 1987 and to post a 30% load-adjusted annual return since then, compared with 13% for comparable no-load funds.

Franklin Rising Dividends. Despite its name, this $170 million fund pays only a 2% dividend yield. But Franklin delivers steady long-term capital appreciation. Over the past five years, co-managers William Lippman and Bruce Baughman have scored 16% annual returns, even factoring in a 4% up-front load. A stock must meet several tests before the pair will buy it. Among them are dividend increases in eight of the past 10 years, a debt level that is less than 30% of total capital and a profit-reinvestment rate of 35%—meaning at least that much of earnings is plowed back into the company's operations each year. That approach recently had 25% of fund assets invested in financial stocks such as life and health insurer Torchmark.

FPA Perennial. Despite this $70 million fund's 6.5% sales charge, manager Chris Linden has delivered a remarkable load-adjusted return of 15% annually over the past five years. His buy-and-hold approach zeros in on easy-to-understand businesses blessed with twice the profitability of the average stock. Typical of Linden's investments are two of the fund's largest holdings of late—Lubrizol, a producer of oil additives, and Melville, which operates more than 5,000 shoe, apparel, toy and drug stores across the nation.

Fortress Utility. Fund manager Chris Wiles knows that many shareholders in this $425 million fund are conservative investors who want high yield and low anxiety. And that's exactly what he gives them. For a paltry load of 1% (plus another 1% if funds are withdrawn before four years elapse), the fund provided a 5.7% payout and the second lowest risk rating of any fund graded by Morningstar. Wiles' approach mixes electric utilities stocks with other high-yield securities. The result was a load-adjusted annual return of 14% over the past five years.

INTERNATIONAL FUNDS

EuroPacific Growth. This $2.5 billion portfolio has compiled its star record with an unusual management approach. The fund is divided among six or more managers who often pursue different investment strategies. The results, however, add up to a five-year return of 13% annually, adjusted for the fund's 5.75% load. That's more than double the no-load international stock fund's average rise of about 6%.

Templeton Foreign. While international investing visionary Sir John Templeton no longer manages this $1.6 billion fund day to day, his successor Mark Holowesko continues the company's tradition of shrewd foreign stock picking. The fund's five-year return has averaged 13% annually, adjusted for its 5.75% load. His strategy consists of buying solid growth stocks when their shares have fallen out of favor with the majority of investors. One example: French telecommunications giant Alcatel Alsthom, which is depressed because of Europe's economic slowdown. At last count, the fund owned 187 stocks based in 26 countries and focused in 27 industries.

Dreyfus Strategic World Investing. Manager Fiona Biggs uses a number of complicated tactics to protect shareholders of her $112 million fund from losses while setting them up to benefit if her global bets pay off (for additional details, see our previous profile of Biggs on page 18). The fund's five-year return has averaged 12% annually, adjusted for its 3% load.

TAXABLE BOND FUNDS

Merrill Lynch Corporate High Income A. This category's best load entry invests in high-yielding junk bonds but steers clear of excessive risks. Moreover, smart bond picking by manager Vincent Lathbury has given this Merrill Lynch fund the oomph to outpace no-load competitors. This $1.5 billion behemoth's five-year return has averaged a fat 13% annually, adjusting for a 4% sales charge, vs. the corresponding 10% return of its no-load rivals as a group.

Van Eck World Income. Benefiting from higher interest rates overseas, this $290 million fund ranks near the top of all taxable bond load funds with a five-year return of 10% annually, adjusted for a 4.75% load. Co-manager David Kenerson lately had a fifth of assets in U.S. issues. But the biggest bang for his buck came from the 60% of the portfolio invested in Europe, where the German Bundesbank has been reluctant to cut that country's interest rates, keeping rates high across the continent. As a precaution against uncertain economics, he has more than a quarter

of the fund's assets in cash and has lowered its average maturity to 3.7 years, compared with 9.6 years for the typical world bond fund.

TAX-EXEMPT BOND FUNDS

Premier Municipal Bond. Over the past five years this $455 million fund (4.5% load) has bested 95% of its rivals, with an adjusted annual return of 10%, the highest among all national tax-exempt load funds. Manager Samuel Weinstock invests primarily in high-quality securities. He's especially fond of safe, high-paying bonds such as those issued by Parish of West Feliciana, Louisiana for Gulf States Utilities.

Alliance Municipal Income—National. Manager Susan Peabody is about as much of a gambler as you'll find running a muni fund. Her derring-do includes investments in issues such as the fund's big stake in Denver City & County Airport System Revenue bonds. These were far from popular when she began buying them in 1991, owing to investor fears that a $3 billion airport being built outside Denver would prove to be a boondoggle. But the project has stuck to its budget so far. As a consequence, the price of its bond has jumped about 46%. And the $275 million fund's five-year return has averaged an impressive 9.8%, adjusted for a 4.5% load, while its risk level is below that of the typical muni fund.

How Your Stockbroker Makes a Buck

Being knowledgeable about what products stockbrokers may push to earn the most can help you avoid biased investment advice.

Merrill Lynch calls them financial consultants. Paine Webber prefers investment executives. But whatever you call them, they're stockbrokers. And if you're like most of the 15 million

Americans who use full-service brokers, you may think the investment guidance you're getting is worth commissions totaling three or four times those levied by discount brokerages (which are analyzed in more detail later in this chapter).

Think again. These days, most full-service brokers bear little resemblance to the John Houseman stereotype that firms still advertise. No longer do brokers make most of their money from trading stocks and bonds. Instead, they typically generate over half their income from selling mutual funds, annuities and other products that carry commissions much higher than those on individual stocks and bonds.

Likewise, your broker's firm usually earns less than a fifth of its revenues from commissions paid by investors like you (vs. more than half only 20 years ago). The brokerage industry's focus has shifted to businesses like asset management and investment banking. Yet these lucrative operations may cut into your profits or at least create a conflict of interest for your broker. "There's a fundamental flaw in the whole full-service brokerage system," says John Markese, president of the American Association of Individual Investors in Chicago. "What's good for the broker is often bad for the customer."

To become a savvier investor—and save money on commissions—you need to understand how brokers make their money and whether that can adversely affect the advice they give you. Here are a few examples:

■ Brokerages are major mutual fund managers. At last count, they sponsored more than 630 mutual funds with assets totaling $307 billion, up from 232 funds with $140 billion in 1985. Many firms pay their salespeople extra to sell these house specials. One reason: in a recent study, funds owned by brokerages underperformed their competitors by an average of 20%.

■ Brokerages are their own most important customers. Each year firms trade an estimated $600 billion of stocks and bonds for their own accounts. When they make a mistake and end up holding securities they want to get rid of, they sometimes unload them on clients.

■ Brokerages are investment banks. They earn big fees for creating new financial products and bigger ones for selling them to customers, even though existing investments may be equally rewarding and less expensive for you.

The shift away from traditional brokerage services dates back to 1975, when the government abolished fixed commissions. That allowed discount brokers such as Charles Schwab and Quick & Reilly to slash their charges by as much as 75%. Today, for example, some discounters charge $56 on a $10,000 trade, vs. $218 at full-service firms. As a result, discounters now control about 25% of the small-investor market. Then, in the 1980s, droves of individual investors abandoned stocks for mutual funds. Since 1980, individuals have been net sellers of $872 billion of stocks and net buyers of $574 billion of funds.

To survive, full-service brokerages scrambled for new ways to make money. Some moved into such businesses as corporate finance and investment banking or created their own mutual funds. And almost every brokerage has raised the commissions and fees it charges investors like you. Consider the following:

Retail commissions. The fees you pay for buying or selling stocks, bonds, mutual funds and other products account for 15% of industry revenues today, about a quarter of the proportion of 20 years ago. Commissions typically are levied on top of the price of the investment you're trading. For example, if you buy 100 shares of XYZ Co. at $100 a share with a maximum commission of 2.5%, you'd pay $10,250—that's $10,000 for the stock plus $250 in sales charges. Full-service brokers, of course, can often discount commissions as much as 50% even if you trade as infrequently as six times a year. With many types of bonds, the commission is built into the price and is known as the spread. If you buy $10,000 of Sunny City bonds, you write your check for that amount. If you sold the same bonds, you'd get $9,800. The $200 difference is the spread.

Generally, the more complicated the investment, the higher the commission. So you'll pay less than 1% to buy a U.S. Treasury bond, one of the simplest investments, but 8% or more on limited partnerships that invest in such risky ventures as real estate or oil wells. The result: "There's a built-in incentive for brokers to sell more complicated and riskier products," explains Barry Alper, a former E.F. Hutton broker who runs Investors Arbitration Services, a Woodland Hills, California firm that helps investors recover losses caused by broker fraud or negligence. Since 1975, for example, investors have poured $140 billion into more than 15,000 limited partnerships. At least 25% of those investments have lost money since they were sold.

You should stay clear of any investment whose commission seems out of line. For example, commissions shouldn't be higher than 2% on actively traded stocks, or 5% on thinly traded issues. For bonds, spreads should never be above 5%, and limited partnerships should carry initial sales charges of no more than 8.5%. On mutual funds, the typical sales charge is 5.75% for stock funds and averages about 4.75% for bond funds.

Trading for a firm's own account. Nearly a third of industry revenues is generated by what Wall Street calls principal transactions. That's when a brokerage buys and sells securities for its own account. Like all investors, brokerages sometimes end up owning stocks or bonds that they don't want. But the firm has an out that you don't. It can encourage its brokers to unload those securities on customers. "The client doesn't know that the broker is just trying to get rid of the stock or bond," says Alan Hobart, a former broker at a major firm. In a typical case, the brokerage bought 50,000 shares of a stock offering at $15 a share, or 50 cents below the official price of $15.50. To encourage its salespeople to move the stock, the brokerage offered them an extra 50

Questions to Ask Before You Invest

Your broker's answers to these questions can tell you whether the investment that he or she is pushing really does serve your interest. The right question can also help you save as much as 50% on a broker's commissions and fees.

Just how much will you make from my investment? Commissions run from 1% to 3% on actively traded stocks to as much as 5% on thinly traded issues. For bonds and some stocks traded over the counter, instead of a commission you pay a spread—the difference between what the security costs the brokerage and what the firm charges you. Spreads range from one-half of 1% to 5%. Some mutual funds and limited partnerships carry initial sales charges as high as

8.5%. The broker keeps 35% to 45% of the commission or spread; the brokerage gets the rest.

Why are you recommending the investment? Some mutual fund companies pay brokerages $25,000 a year or more to give their funds extra promotion. In addition, firms often reward brokers with vacation trips or other incentives to sell a particular fund or limited partnership. And some brokers may suggest that you buy the shares of companies with which the brokerage has business ties, such as an investment banking relationship.

Is there a comparable investment that would cost less? You may be able to acquire an existing closed-end bond fund, for example, for a third of the commission and underwriting fees

that you could possibly pay on a new issue. Or there may be a no-load alternative to a load mutual fund recommended by your broker. Make sure that your broker gives you a persuasive reason to pay the higher price.

Can I get a discount on the commissions? Most firms authorize brokers to give discounts of as much as 20% on stocks. If you trade a minimum of six times a year, however, your broker may be able to give you up to 50% off.

How much must the investment rise before I break even? If 6% of your investment comes off the top to pay a commission, your remaining money has to earn 6.4% merely to earn back the fee. Many investors don't realize how much they have to gain just to get back to square one.

cents for every share they sold—or an additional $200 on a $6,200 trade. "The client doesn't pay any more than normal, but you have to wonder whether the extra money influences the broker," says Hobart.

When your broker recommends a stock, ask whether the firm has issued a public buy recommendation. If not, your broker could be trying to dump a loser on you. Also, inquire whether the broker is being paid extra to sell it. If the answer is yes, stay clear. If he or she won't answer, you may want to stay clear of the broker too.

Offerings of new securities. Underwriting, or buying newly issued securities from a company or government agency and reselling it to the public, accounts for about 9% of brokerage revenues, 30% more than in 1979. But in the rush to underwrite new issues, firms can steer customers into harm's way. Consider initial public offerings (IPOs), the sale of shares in private corporations to the general public. Brokerages keep about 7% of the money raised in an IPO, compared with 5% for stock offerings from companies with shares already trading and less than 1% for bond offerings. And investors? In a study at the University of Illinois at Urbana/Champaign, IPOs underperformed a group of similar but seasoned stocks by a stomach-churning 44%. So always be skeptical if your broker touts an IPO—and ask whether there's a comparable stock that you can buy instead.

Asset management. The major conflict here is that brokers are tempted to urge customers to buy house funds irrespective of whether they are the best investments. Often they aren't. In a recent ranking of the 31 largest mutual fund groups by the Institute for Econometric Research in Fort Lauderdale, all four of the worst performers were brokerages: Dean Witter, Merrill, Prudential and Shearson. Says Walter McGowan, a stockbroker who left Merrill Lynch in 1990 for Gruntal & Co., which doesn't have its own mutual funds: "Brokers at Merrill Lynch were under

constant pressure to put money into house funds regardless of how good they were." A Merrill spokesman disagrees, pointing out that the firm sells several hundred funds, of which only 60 are in-house. Still, many brokerages pay brokers a bonus to lure money into management accounts. A Paine Webber broker who recommends a $10,000 investment in a 6.25% load fund sponsored by the firm could earn $294, vs. $231 for a similar fund managed outside the company.

So be sure to ask your broker whether he or she collects more to sell a house-brand product. Again, if the answer is yes or the question is evaded, consider asking for a fund from another sponsor. Brokers can usually provide comparable products from independent fund groups, often at lower costs.

Lending to customers. Brokerage firms often let customers leverage their money by buying securities on margin. Typically, the customer puts up half the purchase price in cash and borrows the rest from the brokerage. Firms have two powerful incentives for encouraging margin buying. For one, brokerages charge customers several percentage points more on margin loans than the firm pays to borrow the money from banks. Second, clients on margin can buy twice as many securities. "That means double commissions," says Bruce Sankin, a former Prudential broker in Fort Lauderdale and author of *What Your Stockbroker Doesn't Want You to Know!* (Business Publishing, $22). But it also means twice the risk. Thus most investors should avoid buying on margin, period. But if you insist on doing it, negotiate for a lower interest rate. Just as with commissions, good customers can get more than 20% knocked off the going margin rate.

Finally, before deciding whether to pay for a full-service broker, you should make sure that the service you're getting is worth the price. And think about this: Thomas Saler, a former stockbroker and author of *Lies Your Broker Tells You* (Walker, $20), has calculated the performance of two people who began with $20,000 two decades ago. One used a full-service broker, and the other relied on a passive stock index fund. Even if the broker-led investor matched the market's 12% annual return during that period (no mean feat for even the best broker), Saler figures that the investor who used the index fund would have roughly $80,000 more today. For that kind of money, you should be getting brilliant investment recommendations from your full-service broker, plus personal service fit for royalty.

Sizing Up Discount Brokers

Switching to a cut-rate brokerage can dramatically reduce your commission costs. Here's how to find the firm that will save you the most.

After nearly two years as an active customer of full-service brokerage Prudential-Bache, neurologist Robert Ford of Birmingham finally got tired of paying top dollar for advice he didn't need. "Every day I watch CNBC and read *Investor's Business Daily*, the *Wall Street Journal* and *USA Today*," he says, a bit boastfully. "I find myself better informed than anyone I ever spoke to at Pru-Bache." So Ford transferred his $556,000 IRA to the discount broker Quick & Reilly. The move slashed his investing costs by approximately 70%. For example, he sold 6,655 shares of drugmaker Glaxo Holdings for $182,730 and bought 2,242 shares of Coca-Cola, paying Quick & Reilly $550 in commissions, 75% less than the $1,650 that he reckons he would have paid at Pru-Bache.

Ford thus joined the nearly 4 million investors who have been lured to discount brokerages by commissions much lower than those charged by traditional firms. Today, the 80 or so U.S. discounters account for roughly 25% of all brokerage trades of stocks. In recent years, as more and more investors re-entered the stock market, business has exploded at cut-rate firms like 10-year-old K. Aufhauser of New York City, where accounts doubled in 1991 to 10,000.

If you're considering a discounter, which one is best for you? That depends as much on the investments you tend to make as it does on how much a firm charges for its trades. Like full-service firms, discounters sell stocks, bonds, mutual funds and options. Customers' securities accounts, like those at traditional brokerages, are insured for at least $500,000 by the Securities Investor Protection Corporation, a nonprofit company established by Congress in 1970. Unlike full-service houses, however, discounters generally don't offer investment advice. "Full-service brokers' advice may not always be very good," says Perrin Long, the noted brokerage analyst at First of Michigan, "but at least it's hand-holding. And most of us like to have our hands held when we are investing."

Go-it-alone investors have two kinds of low-price brokerages to choose from: about 50 standard discounters and 30 deep discounters. The largest standard discounters are the big three, Charles Schwab (800-435-4000), Fidelity (800-544-8666) and Quick & Reilly (800-222-0439), plus Olde Discount (800-872-6533). These firms closely resemble full-service brokerages such as Merrill Lynch and Pru-Bache. They maintain walk-in offices around the country and offer company research reports to investors who ask for them. These discounters typically charge about 50% less than full-service firms do.

The no-frills deep discounters, which include

Waterhouse Securities (800-765-5185), Kennedy Cabot & Co. (800-252-0090) and Pacific Brokerage (800-421-8395), usually have no local storefront offices, so you must deal with them by phone. The payoff: deep discounters undercut the commissions normally charged by full-service brokerages by as much as 90% and the three biggest standard discounters by around 50%. Here's how to let your investment style determine which discounter is most suitable for you.

You want face-to-face service. If you insist on dealing in person with a broker, go with one of the big three or Olde. The largest, Schwab, recently had 2,300 brokers at 171 locations across the country; Fidelity had 1,000 brokers at 70 locations; Quick & Reilly had 325 at 156 offices; and Olde had 500 at 180 outlets. All four supply customers with research reports on request. Schwab's reports on 4,000 companies are a compilation of historical data, analyses by Standard

& Poor's and stories by Reuters news service (cost: $9.50 for the first report, $7.50 for each additional one). Fidelity and Quick & Reilly provide free S&P reports for the asking. Quick will also give you free *Value Line* write-ups. Alone among cut-rate brokerages, Olde has its own team of nine research analysts who regularly review 115 companies.

Quick & Reilly and Olde assign you to a broker with whom you work all the time. At Schwab and Fidelity, you must ask to be matched up with a specific broker; otherwise you'll get whoever is available when you make a trade.

You want to deal over the phone with the same broker. In this case, go with a deep discounter. Firms such as R.F. Lafferty (800-221-8514, 800-522-5653 in New York), Waterhouse and Thomas F. White (800-669-4483) routinely assign customers to account representatives. At others, you will get your own broker only if you

A Quick Guide to Choosing Among the Biggest

Following the guidelines in the accompanying text, you can scan this table to determine which of the major discounters, listed here by number of accounts, would best serve you. For example, Kennedy Cabot might suit an investor who needs to make a single small

	Number of accounts	Number of offices	Minimum fee for trade	Minimum account size	Check writing	Share-price quotes by telephone	Orders by tone telephone
Charles Schwab	1.8 million	171	$39.00	None	Yes	Yes	Yes
Fidelity	700,000	70	38.00	$5,000	Yes	Yes	Yes
Quick & Reilly	625,000	156	37.50	None	Yes	Yes	No
Waterhouse	200,000	38	35.00	None	No	No	No
Olde Discount	150,000 (est.)	180	20.00	$1,000	Yes	Yes	No
Kennedy Cabot	125,000	13	20.00	None	Yes	No	No
Pacific Brokerage	102,000	5	25.00	None	No	No	No
Brown & Co.	90,000 (est.)	6	25.00[1]	$10,000	No	Yes	Yes
Full service (average)	About 2 million[2]	400	50.00	None	Yes	No	No

Note: Margin loan rates are for small investors. [1] Plus 3¢ a share for listed stocks, 2¢ for over-the-counter stocks [2] Merrill Lynch has 7.9 million accounts.

request one. At all deep discounters, however, if your regular rep is busy when you call, you could be switched to a backup broker. Since most deep discounters don't provide research reports, you'll have to look up *Value Line* and S&P reports on your own—for example, at your local library.

You want to open an IRA. Most full-service and discount brokerage houses charge $20 to $40 a year for maintaining these accounts. Olde Discount, however, has no yearly fees. And Waterhouse Securities waives its $25 IRA maintenance fee for the first year for customers transferring accounts from other brokerages.

You want to buy mutual funds. Many discounters will buy or sell load mutual funds for you. And firms such as Aufhauser (800-368-3668), Fidelity and Schwab trade no-loads too. But if you buy a no-load from a discounter, you will usually be hit with a transaction fee. On a $5,000

purchase, you'll pay $35 to $50—the equivalent of 0.7% to 1% of your investment. Last year, however, Schwab dropped the fees on 84 funds of nine fund families, including Dreyfus and Janus. Schwab also publishes a useful free quarterly guide rating the performance of the roughly 600 stock and bond funds it offers, which include most of the large funds. Anyone can get the booklet by calling Schwab's 800 number. A benefit of trading fund shares through a discounter is that you get just one tax statement at the end of the year for all your funds.

You plan to trade stocks often. A few deep discounters cut their already low commissions for frequent traders. You'll get 10% off if your monthly commissions average at least $350 at Fidelity's deep-discount arm, Spartan (800-544-5115), $400 at Bull & Bear (800-847-4200) and $500 at StockCross (800-225-6196, 800-392-6104 in Massachusetts). Spartan accepts as customers

Discount Brokerage Houses Today

trade, since the firm charges among the lowest minimum transaction fees of all eight firms. But Kennedy Cabot doesn't permit trading by computer. In addition to these eight firms, you might want to consider the six smaller ones mentioned in the main text.

Trading by computer	Research reports	Recent margin loan rate	Special discounts	Comments
Yes	Yes	6.75%	10% off for computer trading	Just dropped transaction fees for 84 of the no-load mutual funds it offers
Yes	Yes	7.25	10% off for computer trading	High-tech speed in processing trades plus friendly service
Yes	No	7.25	None	Lowest rates of the biggest discounters
No	Yes	6.25	For good customers	Annual stock guide and monthly newsletter analyzing market trends
Yes	Yes	6.75	20% off for computer trading	MasterCard debit card with some accounts
No	Yes	5.75	None	Statements sometimes difficult to decipher
No	Yes	6.75	None	No-frills service at deep discounts
No	No	5.25	10% off for monthly commissions over $350	Accepts only experienced investors with net worths above $25,000
No	Yes	8.00	For good customers	Best for investors who want personal advice

only people who expect to make at least 50 trades a year and keep a minimum of $20,000 in securities and cash in their accounts.

You want to trade electronically. A number of discounters slice their commissions for investors who take faceless investing to the logical extreme by eliminating ever speaking to a human being. Fidelity and Schwab, for example, have tone services that let you punch in orders on your phone to receive an extra 10% discount. Fidelity's is called TouchTone Trader and Schwab's is TeleBroker. You can also get 10% off by trading via your IBM-compatible computer through Fidelity's On-Line Xpress system, known as FOX, or Schwab's Equalizer system. (Macintosh owners can use Schwab's GEnie service.) Schwab charges a one-time fee of $69 for its Equalizer software and $5 a month for GEnie. Fidelity charges $90 for its investment software, which provides price quotes, stock fundamentals such as price/earnings ratios and business news.

Hiring Your Own Money Manager

If you can put up at least $100,000, a pro can help you beat the market. But some charge so much you might be better off in a mutual fund.

Never mind that you don't have a spare million or two to invest. Investment firms are clamoring to sell you a perk once limited to the wealthy and famous—a personal money manager. Such a pro not only promises to create a portfolio of stocks and bonds that matches your particular investing style but also to beat the market over time. So-called managed accounts, formerly the preserve of pension funds and well-heeled investors with $500,000 or more, are now being hawked by brokerage firms to people with as little as $50,000 to invest. Even mutual fund companies have gotten into the act, among them the Fidelity, Franklin and Templeton fund groups.

Since 1987, individuals have poured an estimated $30 billion into these accounts. Some are managed by famed investors like contrarian David Dreman; others are overseen by neophytes with just a few years of experience. And cash continues to flow into them at the rate of more than $5 billion a year. Says Bert Meem, a Dean Witter broker in New York City who specializes in hooking up investors with money managers:

"Personal managed accounts are the product of the 1990s for Wall Street."

Ego gratification aside, there are good reasons to consider hiring a money manager instead of a mutual fund if you have at least $100,000 to invest. (Fees eat up far too much of smaller portfolios to make a manager worthwhile.) The first, of course, is profit. By signing on with an ace manager, you may earn higher returns than if you invested in the typical mutual fund or had the average investor's success in picking stocks on your own. Furthermore, you can keep better control over your money with a manager than with a mutual fund. You can stipulate that he or she (probably a he) not invest in certain stocks, such as the shares of tobacco, alcohol or weapons companies. Managed accounts also offer tax advantages over funds. If you're already facing a huge tax planning bill for the year, for instance, you can instruct your manager to delay selling your big winners until next year, thus deferring taxes on profits.

Before you get too revved up about having

your own money manager, though, let's strip away the hype. For one thing, you may not even get to meet your manager, let alone have a personal working relationship with him. Instead, your account will probably be one of hundreds and perhaps thousands that he oversees. What's more, if you're not careful, high fees can significantly drag down your account's performance. Many managed-account programs nick you annually for as much as 3% of your account. That's more than twice what you'd pay in the average stock fund. To recoup the difference, a money manager has to beat a fund by roughly 1.5 percentage points a year.

If you decide that you want a manager, finding a winner is difficult. The SEC estimates that roughly 8,000 of the nation's 17,500 registered investment advisers offer some type of portfolio-management service. With its tiny staff of about 150 examiners, the SEC can check up on only the very largest 500 or so firms that supervise more than $1 billion each—and even then only once every three years at best. Smaller managers may be inspected once a decade. Such lax oversight could leave you vulnerable to rip-offs.

The easiest way to choose a manager—asking a brokerage, financial planning or mutual fund company to recommend one from its managed-account program—is usually the worst. These programs offer a wide array of investing styles, from aggressive growth to conservative income, but they are the least likely to give you one-on-one contact with your manager. With such programs, you generally deal with your manager through an intermediary, typically the broker or planner who signed you up.

Worse yet, the prepackaged plans' prohibitive fees can turn your account into an underachiever even if it's handled by a market beater. The steep charges come in the guise of a so-called wrap fee. This means that instead of charging you 1% or 2% a year for the money manager's services, plus brokerage fees, the firm assesses an all-inclusive flat fee, typically 3%. "The 3% wrap is a horrible deal," says Robert Moseson of Performance

Analytics, a Chicago firm that tracks the returns of 1,500 managers. Though brokers rarely volunteer the information, you can often negotiate a wrap fee down to around 2%.

A better way of selecting a manager is to enlist the help of an independent specialist known as an investment management consultant. Such consultants are usually stockbrokers who search out money managers for clients and, in exchange, get the brokerage commissions generated by the manager for your account. These talent scouts will direct you to smaller independent money managers who can give you the individual attention you probably want from a pro. Moreover, since these brokers usually discount their commissions by 20% to 40%, your total annual cost generally will range from 1.5% to 2% of your portfolio. In the first year, you could pay 2.5% or so.

For help in finding talent scouts near you, phone the Institute for Investment Management Consultants (602-265-6114), which can recommend brokers with substantial work and educational experience. A consultant should have a stable of at least a dozen managers with different investing styles. Otherwise, he may simply steer you to a manager who funnels extra commissions his way in return for bringing in new clients. Before signing up with any manager, check that his investment style is compatible with your goals and risk tolerance. For example, if the stock market's periodic 100-point plunges make you queasy, you might prefer a balanced manager who invests in a conservative mix of stocks and bonds.

In picking a manager, you should examine the records of at least three. Once you've settled on one, ask for names and phone numbers of two or more current clients. Calling these customers will provide a true picture of the kind of attention the manager will give you. You will also learn whether the performance figures that the manager touts are realistic. To further increase your chances of winding up with an all-star rather than an also-ran, follow these guidelines:

Make sure the manager is registered with the SEC. Registration is no guarantee of quality, but it provides a way to check the adviser's background. Ask the broker or manager to show you Parts 1 and 2 of the manager's ADV (short for adviser) registration form. The annual statement, typically 12 or more pages, outlines the manager's investing experience, style and fee schedule. The statement also notes whether he has ever been disciplined by securities regulators.

MONEY HELPS

Q. My broker is recommending new securities called Trudy Pats that are supposed to yield 11.75% and be repaid in two years. They sound too good to be true. Are there risks?
— **Mukul Khurana, San Diego**

A. Trudy Pats (for trust deed participations from promoter National Investors Financial of Newport Beach, California) sound like Ginnie Maes, Freddie Macs and other cutely named government-backed mortgage securities. But if you read the whole boring offering circular, you realize that Trudy Pats are more like construction loans than mortgage-backed bonds. Our conclusion—and that of Galen Wells, a real estate attorney with the First Nationwide Bank—is that they could be very risky.

To see why, consider how your Trudy Pats would work. You and 5,999 other investors would lend at least $5,000 each for 11.75% a year to the Ved Corp., a Yorba Linda, California developer, so it could finish building an $83 million 329-home housing tract in nearby Oceanside. Ved would pay you back after it sold all the houses, which it hopes to do in about two years. Your investment would be backed only by a share in the pool of land mortgages and improvements, though. Result: if the deal collapsed, you probably would not get a piece of the land because you don't own the mortgages directly. Ved has pledged to repay its investors no matter what happens. But if its houses don't sell, or if they fetch less than the expected $220,000 and up, you could wind up in the Trudy Pits.

Look for managers with impressive records stretching back more than five years. This time period gives you an opportunity to see how each fared during the 1987 crash and the surprising recovery that followed. Compare the performance with a benchmark that reflects each manager's style—the Russell 2000 index, for example, in the case of one who specializes in small-company stocks, or the Russell Earnings-Growth index, for a manager who invests in growth stocks. The broker recommending the manager can provide such performance comparisons. Look specifically at the manager's record during the quarter including the 1987 crash. If you wouldn't be willing to incur such temporary losses in your account, you're probably better off with a more conservative manager who aims to preserve assets when stock prices drop.

Beware of tricks money managers use to inflate their performance figures. Unlike mutual funds, money managers don't publish their daily portfolio values in the newspaper. And managers are notorious for juicing up their stats. Two favorite ploys are deleting from their records clients who fared so poorly they pulled their money out and presenting the record of a top-performing account as a composite of the money they manage. To gauge a manager's prowess, demand the performance figures that represent all accounts invested the way you prefer.

Once you've chosen a manager, monitor his performance at least quarterly. The broker who found you the manager can give you a quarterly breakdown of the stocks or bonds in your portfolio, all securities bought and sold during the period and a comparison of your holdings' performance with one or more appropriate indexes. Don't fire a manager just because he doesn't beat the market for a quarter or two. But if his returns lag the market's and those of similar advisers for more than a year, you really should ask yourself whether it's a sign that he has strayed from his original strategy or otherwise lost his touch.

Chapter 4

Protecting Your Wealth Against Risks

Just How Vulnerable Are You? *Page 70*

The Problem With Financial Planners *Page 74*

The Importance of Disability Insurance *Page 78*

Your Life as a Tax Shelter *Page 79*

How to Save Big on Life Insurance *Page 81*

Strengthening Your Job Security *Page 84*

Jerold and Judith Starr didn't run with the borrow-and-buy crowd in the roaring '80s. "We practiced the conservative values that politicians say are good for our country," says Jerold, 50, a sociology professor at West Virginia University in Morgantown. "We scrimped, and we saved." Which makes it all the more cruel that the couple became casualties of the past decade's excesses when $2.5 billion Atlantic Financial Savings, once Pennsylvania's largest savings and loan association, collapsed in November 1991, taking $47,000 of the Starrs' $147,000 account with it. The moral of the couple's misfortune: never allow your savings balance to exceed the government's $100,000 deposit insurance limit.

As more and more people realize just how suddenly their financial underpinnings can be stripped away, as the Starrs' were, Americans are looking for ways to make their personal finances as secure as possible. As a result, the brash all-gain, no-pain mentality of the past decade is steadily giving way to the 1990s quest for safety. "The S&L mess, the bank failures, the insurance company collapses—all these things have made us less willing to take risks," says Bickley Townsend, editor of *Public Pulse*, a newsletter that tracks public opinion. "Today we're looking for safety in all aspects of our financial lives."

Just How Vulnerable Are You?

The quest for peace of mind begins with an unsentimental journey through your finances in search of major threats to your net worth.

Like the Starrs, most people harbor fears of financial disasters. But you can sidestep many potential pitfalls by taking a good hard look at what your family owns—and why. Start by carefully scrutinizing your savings and investments to determine your exposure not only to inherent market risks, such as rising inflation or interest rates, but also to the threat of inept or unethical financial advisers. Don't limit your inventory to investments kept in a brokerage account. Your future earning power probably is by far your most valuable asset, followed by the equity that you have built up in your home. Many people have also amassed substantial assets in tax-deferred company savings plans, like 401(k)s, or insurance policies with sizable cash values. Here's what you need to know and do to protect your net worth in each of these key areas:

Your savings accounts. Although the danger hasn't been highly publicized, a 1991 banking law, entitled the Federal Deposit Insurance Corporation Improvement Act, has actually increased your chances of losing money in a failed bank or S&L. The main reason is that the law requires the FDIC to shut down insolvent banks at the lowest possible cost to taxpayers. Therefore, rather than transferring both insured and uninsured deposits to another institution as the FDIC did 95% of the time in the past, the agency will increasingly transfer only the insured deposits, up to a $100,000 limit. That means individuals with more than $100,000 in a failed bank run the risk of getting burned. For maximum protection against potential losses from tottering banks and S&Ls, simply diversify your savings among several banks so that you never have more than $100,000 in any combination of accounts at any single institution.

Money-market funds, another popular stash

for savings, are more secure now that the SEC requires such funds to limit all but 5% of their holdings to the highest-rated securities. Tax-exempt money funds, however, remain exempt from this rule. The SEC is considering subjecting tax-exempts to the same regulations as taxable funds. But until that happens, tax-exempts will still carry risks for many investors. The best alternatives are taxable funds that invest solely in riskless short-term Treasury bills.

Your investment portfolio. Most people know that stocks, when compared with other types of investments, generally provide the highest returns over time—10% or so annually. So you may think that even if share prices temporarily retreat by 20%, your chances of being hurt in the long run are slim. Wrong. The fact is, you could lose out if you buy stocks at a peak.

A study of stock market returns over the past 65 years by the Leuthold Group, a Minneapolis investment firm, shows that investors who purchased stocks when price/earnings ratios were high (17 or above) or dividend yields were low (3.1% or less) received only a 4% to 6% average annual return during the following 10 years. With the S&P 500 recently carrying a 24 P/E and a 2.8% dividend yield, investors were clearly at risk of locking in substandard returns that can take a toll over the long term. For example, earning 6% rather than 10% on a $25,000 investment means that 10 years from now you will have $44,771 instead of $64,844. The best way to avoid such subpar returns is to employ dollar-cost averaging, in which you invest a fixed amount of money at regular intervals. Putting money into stocks periodically ensures that you don't invest everything at the top. Instead, the strategy forces you to buy more shares when stocks are cheap and to buy fewer shares when stocks rise.

A more sinister threat is the prospect of losing all or part of your money to a fraudulent or incompetent broker, financial planner or other adviser. Barbara Roper, a lobbyist for the activist group Consumer Federation of America, esti-

mates that customers lose $500 million a year to fraud and at least another $500 million annually because of advisers' poor counsel or self-dealing. Unfortunately, federal and state securities regulators lack the resources to safeguard your interests. For example, the SEC has a staff of only 46 examiners to monitor the activities of the 17,700 financial advisers registered with the agency.

Your most effective defense against a crooked or incompetent adviser is a thorough check into his or her background. Make sure the planner or adviser is registered with the SEC and your state securities commission. A broker should be enrolled with the National Association of Securities Dealers. Also check the adviser's disciplinary history by calling the North American Securities Administrators Association (202-737-0900), which can tell you how to get information from a data base of 410,000 brokers and advisers it maintains jointly with NASD. (The NASD can tap the same data base, but it deletes pending complaints.) If you're dealing with a financial planner or private portfolio manager, ask for a copy of Parts 1 and 2 of his ADV (short for adviser), a document filed with the SEC that discloses credentials, lists any disciplinary problems and reveals how the adviser is compensated. Says NASAA's investor education adviser, Scott Stapf: "More than 90% of the incidents of fraud and other abuse could be prevented if investors would check out the adviser."

Your retirement funds. The failures of several major insurance companies in recent years proved just how risky supposedly safe retirement investments can be. For example, when state regulators seized $10 billion Executive Life of California and $14 billion Mutual Benefit Life of Newark in 1991, an estimated 370,000 people found the cash value of their tax-deferred annuities frozen or their monthly pension benefits cut back as much as 30%. Another 300,000 people in 66 companies also faced potential losses when Executive Life defaulted on $1 billion of guaranteed investment contracts (GICs) held in 401(k) company savings plans. To insulate yourself from shaky insurers, look for companies that receive top safety rankings from major ratings firms (A.M. Best, Duff & Phelps, Moody's Investors Service and Standard & Poor's). Also be sure to diversify. Instead of buying a single $75,000 annuity, invest $25,000 with three firms. If you have a 401(k), check that it holds GICs of at least five different insurers.

Another menace facing your retirement money is the possibility that an unscrupulous trustee will steal or grossly mismanage your savings. One major danger is that half of the one million pension plans in the U.S. are subject only to so-called limited-scope audits by accountants because they keep a portion of their assets in federally regulated institutions such as banks or S&Ls. Some $774 billion of pension money is held in such institutions. What's more, with a skeleton staff of 300 investigators monitoring fraud—or only one per 3,333 plans—the U.S. Department of Labor's Pension and Welfare Benefits Administration (PWBA) isn't likely to detect problems the accountants miss. At greatest risk are the more than 7 million workers covered by the 800,000 or so pensions with fewer than 100 participants. Reason: the employer usually doubles as trustee in small pensions and, therefore, has easy access to employees' money.

To protect yourself, review your plan's documents, especially the summary annual report, which the company must give you each year. (If your plan has fewer than 100 people, you should get this report every three years and, in the intervening years, two pages of a document called Form 5500-C/R.) Possible signs of wrongdoing include loans to company officers or a default in payments owed to the plan. Examine your 401(k) statements as well, looking for sharp drops in your account balances or erratic investment performance. If you see anything suspicious, you should get in touch with one of the 15 regional PWBA offices (for the one that is nearest you, call the Labor Department's Division of Technical Assistance at 202-219-8784).

Your earning power. Although you probably don't think of it as an asset, your ability to earn a living and support your family over an average working life of roughly 40 years is the single most valuable resource you possess. Should your earning power be interrupted for any reason, you or your survivors could be left with mounting medical bills and other expenses. Thus your first line of defense is a long-term disability policy that replaces your income in the event that an accident or illness prevents you from working. If you work for a large corporation, chances are it offers a group disability plan that covers 60% of your salary, a level that's adequate. But about 70% of companies offer no disability coverage. If you work for such an outfit, are self-employed or if your employer's benefits fall below that 60% threshold, you need to look for an individual policy (discussed later in this chapter).

Of course, disability insurance doesn't pay up if you die. So if you have people depending on your income, you also need life insurance (explained in more detail later in this chapter). Consult at least two agents or a financial planner to figure how much you require. As to whether you should buy term insurance, which provides only a death benefit, or so-called cash-value policies like whole life that double as tax-deferred investments, remember that replacing your income is your primary goal. Thus you're better off buying the appropriate amount of term insurance than stinting on coverage to afford a whole life plan.

To prevent huge medical bills from creating debts that will soak up your income and deplete your savings, check out your medical insurance policy. You probably get this insurance through your employer. But if you are one of the nearly 19 million workers whose employers don't provide this benefit, you will have to seek out a private policy. Your biggest concern should be ensuring that a plan will handle large claims that could wipe out your resources. So look for policies with a lifetime benefit ceiling of at least $500,000 or, preferably, $1 million. And favor those with a so-called catastrophic or out-of-pocket limit that caps your share of medical bills at $2,500 a year.

Getting this coverage on your own is costly. Premiums can run $3,300 to $6,100 a year for a family of four. You can cut the premium by a third or so by raising your deductible—the amount you pay before the insurer kicks in—from the standard $250 to $1,000. If your household requires frequent medical care, consider becoming a member of a health maintenance organization, as 33.6 million Americans currently are. The toll can be stiff, with the average family premium running about $3,800 a year. But only minuscule out-of-pocket costs are required.

Your home and property. You can't insure your house against slumping real estate prices. But you can protect your biggest investment from uncovered losses resulting from disasters such as fire, hurricanes, earthquakes and floods by buying the right homeowners insurance. Moreover, ignoring this protection is foolhardy given the potential for sizable losses and the reasonable cost of coverage—annual premiums typically run $400 to $1,000 for a $150,000 home.

To guard your castle, base the amount of coverage on the replacement value of your home (what you'd pay to rebuild), not its market value, which could be higher or lower. The insurance company can help you determine the right figure. While some companies will write policies for as little as 80% of replacement value, you're better off paying an extra 10% or so on the annual premium and going to 100%. If you do, for a further nominal fee of $5 to $30 a year, most insurers will include in your policy a guaranteed replacement-value clause obligating them to pay the full cost of rebuilding, even if it exceeds the policy's face value. You should also insist on replacement-cost coverage for the personal contents of your home. To hold premiums down without compromising your protection, raise your deductible. By going from the standard $250 to a $500 deductible, you can cut your premiums by 5% to 10%, and by opting for a $1,000 deductible, you can save 15%.

To protect your income and assets against potentially devastating liability lawsuits, consider increasing the personal-liability segment of your homeowners and auto policies. This type of insurance protects you from lawsuits resulting, for example, from an auto accident or someone suffering serious injuries on your property. In today's litigious society you would be foolish not to spring for the extra $20 or so a year it takes to raise your homeowners liability protection from the standard $100,000 to $300,000—ample for most people. But if you have assets worth considerably more than that, you may also want to pay $100 to $200 a year for a $1 million umbrella liability policy that kicks in after your homeowners and auto liability coverage has been exhausted. That's because the more wealth you amass, the more likely you are to be hit with a big lawsuit.

MONEY HELPS

Q. Is my money as safe at a credit union as in a bank? And does anybody publish information on the strongest and weakest credit unions?
— Holly Hall, River Forest, Illinois

A. Your money is as safe—or safer—in a credit union as in a bank or savings and loan. For openers, most credit union deposits are backed by federal insurance of up to $100,000 per account, just as deposits in most banks and S&Ls are. So even if your credit union failed, you would have to worry only about when, not whether, you'd get your dough back. Many credit unions are actually healthier than banks and S&Ls because they don't make the kind of commercial and real estate loans that got those institutions into trouble. To get a reading on your credit union, you should request a report from a rating service, such as Veribanc ($10 for the first inquiry, $5 for each additional one; 800-442-2657) or Bauer Financial Reports ($10 for a report on one credit union, $29 for a statewide report; 800-388-6686).

The Problem With Financial Planners

Conflicts of interest, incompetence and outright fraud lurk in this booming field. Here's how you can keep from becoming a casualty.

A generation ago, few middle-class Americans saw any need for financial planning. Life insurance, bank savings accounts and secure jobs with dependable retirement benefits were enough for most people. But since then, as Americans have grown far more affluent and as their financial options have multiplied, a new class of professionals has emerged. Experts estimate that the number of advisers who call themselves financial planners has exploded from a negligible few in the 1960s to 250,000 or more today.

Despite this boom, there is still a disturbing shortage of advisers Americans can turn to with confidence. Many clients have found that the promise of financial planning—handing over your finances to a caring adviser who puts your interests first—is made to be broken. Regulators estimate that planners cause clients to lose at least $600 million every two years.

Some of these clients are victims of fraud. Far more often, though, people suffer because of planners' sloppiness, lack of training or conflicts of interest. Representatives of the three major financial planning organizations all note that professional standards have improved greatly over the past decade and say their groups have been working hard to raise standards further. Even regulators recognize the change. "There's no reason not to believe that the vast majority of planners today are honest and capable," says Marianne Smythe of the SEC's Investment Management Division. One reason for the field's improvement is the collapse of tax shelters in the late 1980s, which drove out many greedy practitioners by making it harder to earn big fees.

Still, would-be clients have reason to be wary. To take the measure of a cross section of the profession, MONEY interviewed 32 of the practitioners listed under "Financial Planners" in the Santa Rosa, California (population: 115,673) Yellow Pages. Our phone interviewers, who identified themselves as reporters, asked eight questions about professional practices and 12 questions designed to test knowledge. Highlights:

■ None of the planners answered all 12 knowledge questions correctly. More than half of them got at least one-third of the answers wrong.

■ Nearly one-third could not state within four percentage points the historic annual return of common stocks (10%), a crucial statistic for someone who provides advice on combining various investments to achieve long-term goals.

■ And more than two-thirds said they earned some or all of their income from commissions on the products they sell—an arrangement that creates conflicts of interest.

To be sure, there are outright crooks and con artists among planners. One who's going to prison for his crimes is John Pomerenke, 24, of Mesa, Arizona. He pleaded guilty last year to operating a Ponzi scheme from 1988 to 1991 that had bilked some 200 Phoenix-area investors out of $5.2 million. Pomerenke had promised naive clients incredible returns of 4% to 7% a month (60% to 125% a year) from investments in commodities futures and stocks. In fact, he used their money to pay off earlier investors, charter jets for junkets to the Cayman Islands and Australia and purchase a Jaguar, a Range Rover, two expensive homes and a $100,000 swimming pool.

The more common danger, however, comes from well-meaning planners who are poorly trained or otherwise not up to the job. "My bet is that competence issues cost consumers more money than fraud," says Ellyn Brown, a former securities commissioner of Maryland and the acting executive director of the North American Securities Administrators Association. In some states, it's easier to qualify as a planner than to get a driver's license. Thirty-eight of the 50 states require investment advisers to pass a licensing exam, which typically measures knowledge of securities law, not investment savvy. Yet advisers who sell as well as recommend securities are required by federal law to pass an exam on basic investment theory or to be affiliated with someone who has passed the exam.

Financial planners, however, do a lot more than just sell. A good planner provides advice on everything from insurance and investments to taxation, money management and retirement planning. Such a planner will review your total financial picture and suggest a strategy tailored to your resources, goals and attitudes toward risk. He or she will also help you implement the plan and update it periodically. "The actual selection of investments is probably planners' weakest area," says John Markese of the American Association of Individual Investors. "But I also hear a lot of dissatisfaction when it comes to tax advice and complicated estate-planning questions."

A case in point involves Raymond Oddi, a former chief financial officer for Baxter Travenol Laboratories. He was urged by a Chicago planner from Ayco Corp., a national organization, to take a lump-sum payment from his company's profit-sharing plan when he retired in 1986, rather than roll over the money into an IRA. Oddi questioned the planner's tax and investment projections. But the planner stuck to her advice, and Oddi took the lump sum. When he discovered later that the IRA option would eventually have saved his estate as much as $2 million, he sued Ayco. The court awarded Oddi $576,000 in damages inclusive of court costs and interest.

Aside from incompetent advice, clients often face conflicts of interest that stem from the way the vast majority of planners earn their compensation. They make their money by two basic methods. Fee-only planners charge a flat price, typically $1,500 to $5,000, or a $75 to $200 hourly rate. Commission-based planners, on the other hand, are paid fees built into the prices of the products they sell. Most planners, in fact, combine both approaches. They take a small up-front fee (say, anywhere from $200 to $1,000) and then collect commissions when they sell you products they recommend.

Not surprisingly, the risk of getting questionable advice is greatest when planners depend heavily on commissions to make their money. For example, a 1988 SEC survey found that of 69 planner firms that sold securities, only about half offered U.S. Government issues, some of the safest investments, while 81% sold real estate limited partnerships, a major source of small investor losses in the 1980s. In part, that may be because many investors need advice in choosing something as complex as a partnership, but there is another explanation as well. "If you put $100,000 in Treasury bonds, your adviser will get a $50 commission," notes Mary Calhoun, a securities arbitration consultant in Watertown, Massachusetts. "But if you buy $100,000 worth of limited partnerships, your adviser will get an $8,000 commission."

The lure of commissions can also lead some planners to recommend unnecessary transactions. For example, one North Carolina couple, who asked not to be identified, were urged by a planner to refinance their home in 1986 and boost their mortgage from $17,000 to $90,000, even though that forced them to pay nearly three percentage points more in interest and $3,000 in closing costs. The planner then convinced the couple to put the money raised by the refinancing, along with proceeds from the sale of five conservative stocks—about $81,500 in all—into four mutual funds with sales charges of 4.75% to

8% and four limited partnerships with 10% commissions built in. One partnership has since filed for bankruptcy; the other three aren't paying any dividends. The cost of this advice was a $400 fee plus $5,872 in commissions.

Although partnerships proved to be lousy investments in the 1980s, a recent survey by the trade journal *Financial Services Week* found that nearly a third of the planners polled continue to sell or recommend them. And experts say that some new products could present similar risks today. Chief among them: collateralized mortgage obligations (CMOs), bond-like securities that are peddled as alternatives to safe bank CDs. Because CMOs are backed by mortgages, their payouts are uncertain. "If interest rates drop and mortgages are refinanced, CMO investors could lose a lot of money," says Atlanta securities attorney Boyd Page.

You might think that government regulation would provide protection against bad planners— but you would be wrong. Denice Capitani can tell you just how toothless the government watchdogs often are. Capitani and her husband

William, the owners of a wallpaper and painting business in Unionville, Connecticut, consulted a planner from North Atlantic Planning in Farmington in 1988 for advice on investing a $30,000 inheritance. "We told him we wanted something that was very secure," says Capitani. "He suggested rare coins, which he said were fully insured and would appreciate 60% in five years." To be safe, Capitani called the Connecticut Department of Banking, which regulates investment advisers in her state. "They told me to proceed with caution," she recalls. What Capitani wasn't told was that North Atlantic president Thomas George had been denied a license to become an investment adviser in Connecticut two years earlier because he didn't have any securities training or experience.

Today, the coins purchased by Capitani and at least 80 other North Atlantic customers are worth a third or less of their original prices. In 1989, George was ordered by the Department of Banking to stop selling securities without a license, and he was indicted in 1991 in New York for defrauding consumers out of $64 million

Questions to Ask on Your First Interview

Any reputable financial planner should be willing to respond fully to the following questions. If you don't like what you hear move on immediately. But even if the planner seems friendly and competent, double-check the responses wherever that's possible.

Are you registered with the SEC and your state securities department?

Most financial planners are supposed to register with the SEC. In addition, all but seven states and the District of Columbia require that most planners register with the state's securities department. By

itself, registering doesn't guarantee that a planner is honest or competent, but it does show that the planner knows the law and obeys it. Says Barbara Roper of the Consumer Federation of America: "Registration is the absolute minimum to look for."

What is your educational and professional background? Unlike lawyers and accountants, planners typically are not legally required to have training or experience, so it is important to check credentials. Planners who have passed examinations in subjects such as investing, insurance and estate planning can

call themselves one of the following: certified financial planner, chartered financial consultant, chartered life underwriter or personal financial specialist. At the very least, such designations indicate some knowledge of planning basics.

What types of financial planning services do you provide? Some planners specialize in one or two areas, such as retirement planning, insurance or taxes. Make sure the planner you choose can address your particular concerns.

What types of products do you recommend? You want to find out whether a planner suggests good through rare-coin and condominium investments. In his defense, he says: "Nobody forced them to buy the coins. They knew the risks."

Beyond the licensing exams in 38 states, you can't be sure of government oversight. Most planners are required to register with the SEC, but "all it takes is a one-time fee of $150, a disclosure form, and no recent criminal record," says the SEC's Smythe. "Crooks can print up business cards saying they've registered and then steal. If they're little enough, we're not going to know until after the money's been stolen."

The SEC doesn't have nearly the resources needed to police the growing ranks of planners. And plenty of them escape even that scrutiny. A 1992 survey by the International Association for Financial Planning found that 47% of those surveyed were not registered with the SEC. The story is much the same at the state level. Alabama, for example, has one full-time examiner to monitor its more than 1,200 registered investment advisers and brokerage firms. Of the 46 states that responded to a U.S. Government Accounting Office survey in 1989, 21 plus the

District of Columbia do not routinely inspect investment advisers. Worse yet, the District of Columbia and seven states (Arizona, Colorado, Iowa, Massachusetts, Ohio, Vermont and Wyoming) don't have any financial planner regulation at all.

There may be some relief in sight, in the form of investment adviser legislation now being debated by Congress. Both the Senate and the House versions of the bill would raise registration fees to pay for more oversight by government regulators. But neither version would cover accountants, lawyers and others who do planning as a sideline. Moreover, the additional funds that would be raised by registration fees aren't likely to be enough to pay for all the scrutiny that's needed. So no matter what happens to the legislation, you must choose a planner with care. With money-market funds and certificates of deposit yielding as little as 3%, a burgeoning crop of customers is turning to planners in pursuit of safe, higher-paying alternatives. If you are among the searchers, be sure to study and ask the questions set forth in the box below.

old-fashioned investments such as government securities, municipal bonds, stocks and mutual funds in addition to products such as limited partnerships, unit trusts and insurance. You should also check whether your planner sells only products sponsored by his or her company. This can alert you to the potential for conflicts of interest.

Will you disclose in advance your total compensation—including the commissions you will get for selling particular products, as well as your general fees? The fact that a planner stands to earn commissions isn't necessarily a negative. But you should make sure that your needs—and not the commissions—determine which products you'll get

pitched. Duck if your planner tries to fill your portfolio with limited partnerships, which can carry commissions of 8% or more.

Have you been the subject of disciplinary actions by any federal or state agency or professional regulatory body, or been involved in arbitration proceedings with former clients? Be sure to verify the planner's answer with your state securities department and the SEC.

Will you provide me with a copy of your ADV? Discount the fancy brochures. The document you need is Part 2 of your planner's ADV form, which he or she must file with the state and the SEC and show on request. The form includes data about a planner's experience,

investment strategies and potential conflicts of interest.

Will you provide me with the names of three clients you've counseled for at least two years? Call these clients and ask whether they are satisfied, what types of returns they have been getting and whether they expect to stay with the planner in the future. Then, if you can, get more names from them to check with as well.

May I see three examples of plans and follow-up reports you've drawn up for other investors? The original plans will tell you whether advice was tailored to individual clients. Follow-ups will show how skillfully the planner made adjustments as events unfolded.

The Importance of Disability Insurance

Premiums are expensive. But the possible consequences of having no policy or skimpy coverage can be financially and emotionally devastating.

Contrary to what insurance agents may tell you, the coverage you need most isn't a big whole life policy. It's long-term disability insurance. This often overlooked protection pays you a monthly income if you are unable to work because of injury or illness. Statistics show that disability is far more probable than death, especially if you are young or middle-aged. At age 42, for example, you are about four times more likely to be disabled for at least three months before retirement than you are to die. In fact, disability is sometimes called "living death," since your family's financial needs continue but you can't meet them unless you have insurance.

Unfortunately, there are plenty of temptations to put off obtaining coverage. It's expensive: the premium on an individual policy offering a $2,200-a-month benefit for a 40-year-old, nonsmoking manager could run up to $1,950 a year. Also, you may mistakenly think you are fully protected by Social Security and possibly by your employer's group disability policy. But Social Security's disability criteria are so strict that only about 35% of those who apply for benefits actually qualify for them. And even if your employer offers insurance—as do 99% of large companies but less than 25% of businesses with fewer than 50 employees—there may still be holes in your coverage.

Some group policies don't cover you until you have worked for your employer for a year or two; others limit benefits to $2,000 a month. You can learn these details from the summary that federal law requires your employer's benefits administrator to make available. If your group plan seems skimpy, you can supplement it with an individual policy.

How much coverage do you need? In general, insurance experts recommend that disability insurance equal 60% to 70% of your before-tax earnings. Benefits should start 90 days after you become disabled (your savings presumably can carry you until then) and continue if necessary until you reach age 65. You probably cannot buy much more insurance than that anyway. To avoid attracting phony claims, most insurers will cover you only to the point at which your disability income from all sources, including Social Security and company benefits, would equal 70% of your current before-tax earnings. Still, that's better than it sounds. Benefits from a policy you buy with after-tax dollars are tax-free in contrast to income from a policy paid by your employer.

Equally important as the amount of coverage is the way your policy defines disability. Under the most generous definition, known as "own occ," insurers agree to pay full benefits if you can't work in your own occupation as long as you are under a physician's care. In contrast, a policy using the narrower "any occ" definition would pay only if you are unable to work in any occupation for which you are clearly suited. Under this specific rubric, for example, a practicing lawyer would not lose his benefits if he refused to work as, say, a taxi driver. But they would be cut off if he could teach law and declined, even if teaching would pay him an inadequate salary.

Insurers commonly compromise by splitting the definition and paying benefits under own-occ rules for the first one to five years of a disability and under any-occ rules thereafter. Not surprisingly, pure own-occ policies are 5% to 15% more expensive. The most expedient way to minimize the cost of your coverage is to prolong the so-called elimination period—the time you have to wait for benefits to begin after you become disabled. A 40-year-old nonsmoking manager would pay around $1,050 a year in additional premiums for a 30-day waiting period rather than the more usual 90-day wait. Savings are less dramatic for longer waits. Stretching from 90 days to 180 would typically cut premiums only about $100 a year.

Most financial advisers recommend that you choose a policy that stops paying benefits at age 65, because pension and Social Security retirement benefits kick in at that age. For premiums about 20% higher, you can select a benefit period that continues until you die. Such a policy would make sense if you are young and there is a possibility that a long-term disability would prevent you from building retirement benefits.

As with their other products, insurers tend to offer lots of options on disability policies. The most valuable (and often standard in a top-of-the-line policy) is a residual-benefits provision, which may add 20% to 25% to your premium. This option supplements your income if you are well enough to go back to work but not yet healthy enough to work at full capacity and earn full pay. Read your contract carefully. Some less generous policies pay so-called partial benefits (usually 50% of your full benefit) if you are partially disabled. Unlike residual benefits, which continue as long as needed, partial benefits typically terminate after three to six months.

Another valuable option is a cost-of-living adjustment (COLA), which will boost your premium 25% or so. With this rider, monthly benefits increase automatically to counter inflation, rising either at a specified rate or at the same rate as the consumer price index, up to a specified annual maximum. And you should insist on a policy that is at least guaranteed renewable. This arcane term means that the insurer cannot cancel your coverage as long as you pay your premiums or raise your premium unless it boosts premiums in general. A preferable alternative is a so-called noncancelable policy, which guarantees that your policy cannot be revoked and that your premium cannot be increased at all.

Your Life as a Tax Shelter

Here's the lowdown on cash-value life insurance, a catchall term for protection packaged with enticing tax-deferred investment accounts.

Once upon a time there was plain old whole life insurance on which you paid a fixed premium every year to provide for your family in the event of your untimely death. While you were still kicking, the policy offered a savings account, called the cash value, that grew tax-deferred at a slow but certain return. In a financial pinch you could retrieve your cash value and give up the policy.

Or you could borrow from it at low interest and never repay the loan (the balance due would be subtracted from the policy's death benefit). If you did not cash in your insurance, your beneficiary would get the policy's proceeds free of federal income taxes when you died.

Protection and savings in the same package—could anything be simpler or more comforting?

But times changed, as did the ways your cash value could be invested by insurers. In particular, tax reform made life insurance that doubles as an investment one of the most enticing shelters for your retirement stash. Yet many insurance shoppers remain wary, wondering whether they should instead buy low-cost term insurance, which provides a death benefit but no savings or investment account, and do their investing on their own. Do cash-value policies really deliver? The answer, according to many financial experts, is a cautious yes.

One reason is that term gets more expensive as you age. With cash-value policies, however, your premium dollars buy far less insurance than they do with a term policy. Suppose you need $250,000 of coverage but can't afford a cash-value policy that large (typical cost for universal life is around $1,750 a year for a 50-year-old male nonsmoker). You could buy term protection at around $425 for the first year, rising to $1,120 in the fifth year. Term is also the answer if your insurance need is temporary—say, for example, that you want coverage for 10 years until your children are educated.

One of the most popular forms of cash-value policies is universal life, which is essentially a combination of term insurance and a savings account that the insurer usually invests in fixed-income assets. Another possibility is variable life, which lets the policyholder choose among a broad range of investments, from Treasury bonds to stock and bond funds. A third choice is variable universal, a hybrid that combines the investment options of variable life with the flexible premium and death benefit of universal life.

Yet another option is single-premium life, which requires a buyer to pay the entire premium, from $5,000 on up, at the outset. Note, however, that Congress has axed single-premium's biggest attraction—tax-free loans against a policyholder's investment account—on policies bought after June 20, 1988. Now tax-free borrowing is permitted only from cash-value policies that require you to pay premiums over at

least seven years. Here are more detailed descriptions of the main varieties of cash-value policies:

Universal life. Policyholders can change both the premiums and the face amount of the policy from year to year. With universal life, money is deducted periodically from your investment account to pay for the company's administrative expenses and the cost of insurance on your life. As a result, this choice suits couples with fluctuating incomes or those who are not certain how much insurance coverage they will need.

Variable and variable universal. These policies make sense for people with reasonable risk tolerance and long time horizons. Generally, these policies offer all the conveniences of a large mutual fund family, including telephone switching among funds for free or at nominal cost. Thus policyholders can assume as much or as little investment risk as they desire, allocate their money among different kinds of funds and turn aggressive or defensive in anticipation of changing market conditions. The insurers' portfolios are often managed by well-known mutual fund firms such as Fidelity, Oppenheimer and Scudder Stevens & Clark.

Single premium. This option is recommended for people who need some insurance and want to park a lot of cash in a safe place. Single premium comes in as many forms as there are cash-value policies; the only difference is you pay all your premiums up front. Elimination of the tax-free borrowing benefit has caused these policies to more closely resemble single-premium annuities, which pay out periodic income for a certain number of years or for life but provide no death benefit. Single-premium insurance is probably the better buy if you plan to hold the contract until death. Single-premium annuities are better suited to a retirement fund. Reason: to pay for the protection, the life insurance policies typically offer returns that are one to 1.5 percentage points lower than those of the annuities.

Before deciding which cash-value insurance policy suits you best, be clear about two points. First, do not commit funds that you will need any time soon. Companies charge stiff surrender fees to discourage buyers from cashing in policies early. Anyone holding a cash-value policy for less than 10 years can expect to get an uncompetitive return. Second, determining whether a contract has inexpensive insurance and good investment returns is a tough assignment.

Diligent consumers can make use of two cost indexes in evaluating policies of the same type—for example, comparing one universal policy with another. Many states require companies to calculate these indexes for you. The interest-adjusted payment index is a measure of the average premium for $1,000 worth of coverage. The lower the number, the cheaper the policy. The interest-adjusted, surrender-cost index measures the current cost of cash-value policies if you were to cancel them in 10 or 20 years and take your money. This tells you your actual cost if you have to get out. Index amounts will vary with the size of a policy and the age of the policyholder, however, so a policy that represents good value for you may be a poor choice for your older sibling.

How to Save Big on Life Insurance

Don't expect your agent to tell you about rebates, blended policies and other nifty ways to chop the commissions you pay by up to 90%.

Y ou know about discount stockbrokers and no-load mutual funds. But how about the ways to slash life insurance commissions, which can equal 100% of your first year's premium? "Most life insurance companies really don't want people to know how to reduce their commissions," says Rick Nelson, an independent agent in Northbrook, Illinois. And no wonder: the right moves can slice as much as 90% from a policy's initial sales charge.

You pay the biggest commissions on whole life, universal life and variable life policies, which link insurance protection with savings accounts known as cash value. The commissions on these policies generally run five times higher than those on term policies, which provide insurance with no savings features. With a typical cash-value policy, your agent keeps 55% to 80% of the first year's premium; the company takes another 20% to 45% to cover its other selling expenses. In the second through 10th years, the agent usu-ally siphons off 5% or more of your premiums. You don't have to accept such exorbitant fees, though. Use these money-saving tactics instead.

Buy low-load insurance. Ten insurance companies, double the number in 1990, employ either salaried telephone representatives or financial consultants who collect only modest commissions or fees for selling policies. Generally, sales fees on these low-load policies amount to roughly 10% to 20% of your first year's premium and 2% or so of subsequent premiums. Most low-load companies are relatively small. The largest, Commonwealth Life, has $4.4 billion in assets, compared with $38.1 billion for a behemoth like John Hancock. And some aren't licensed to sell insurance in every state. Nevertheless, most of the 10 discount insurers earn high grades for financial soundness from major ratings companies A.M. Best, Moody's Investors Service and Standard & Poor's. Among the highest rated are

Ameritas, Commonwealth Life, Peoples Security Life, Southland and USAA. All get A+ grades from A.M. Best, for example.

Buying low-load coverage helps turbocharge your policy. Let's say that a 35-year-old non-smoking woman gets $350,000 of universal life coverage from Ameritas for a $2,000 annual premium. At the end of the first year, the policy's cash value will total $1,819. By contrast, after one year, a similar policy from Metropolitan Life, a highly regarded full-price insurer, would have zero cash value because of selling expenses. Furthermore, if Ameritas continues to pay 7.8% on its savings accounts—its rate after the first year—the cash value in our example will grow in 30 years to $192,800. Compare that to a sum of $148,821 for the MetLife policy, which pays only 7.2% chiefly because of annual marketing and administrative expenses.

If you know how much coverage and the type of policy you want, low-loads Ameritas (800-552-3553) and USAA (800-531-8000) will sell you insurance by telephone. Otherwise, you can get a financial planner or insurance consultant to determine how much insurance you should buy. This pro will charge a flat fee or a modest hourly rate. For example, 450 firms nationwide associated with Fee for Service, an insurance brokerage in Tampa, analyze a client's insurance needs for $100 to $150 an hour and then sell policies offered by cut-rate insurers. The planners charge $200 to $500 for selling $100,000 to $500,000 of whole or universal life coverage—7% to 15% of the typical agent's commission for a policy of the same size. (For the names of planners with Fee for Service, call 800-874-5662.)

Get a blended policy. This technique of combining different types of insurance into one policy can cost you 30% less than the premium for comparable whole life coverage. Blends have long been available to the wealthy. Lately, however, Guardian Life, Manufacturers Life, Prudential and other insurers have sold them to people who want as little as $300,000 of coverage.

With a blended policy, you buy a combination of whole life and term insurance. You also obtain paid-up additions, which are mini whole life policies (purchased with the earnings on your cash value) that gradually replace the term coverage. Many insurers require that whole life represent at least 25% of the blended coverage; other companies insist on a minimum dollar amount such as $200,000 of whole life. An agent generally collects 30% to 50% less in commission from a blended policy than from a regular whole life contract. Moreover, commissions on the paid-up additions you buy each year are a mere 5% or so of the whole life premium. Thus your agent will probably not recommend a blend; you may have to request it.

Here's how a typical blend works for a 45-year-old man looking for $350,000 of whole life coverage. He could buy, say, a Prudential whole life policy with an annual premium of $6,648. But sales commissions of roughly $5,000 and other expenses would vaporize the policy's cash value in the first year. On the other hand, if he bought a policy that blended $200,000 of whole life with $150,000 of term, his premium would drop by 36% to $4,287 (or $3,831 for the whole life and $456 for the term).

Blended policies have a few potential hitches. If interest rates fall, the whole life policy may not accumulate the dividends and the paid-up additions you expected. This could boost your premium since you would then have to pay for the paid-up additions or increasingly expensive term coverage to maintain the anticipated death benefit. To avoid getting stuck, plow some of your savings from commissions back into the policy through a paid-up-additions rider. In the process, you will also boost your cash value.

Another caveat is an IRS private ruling, concerning a universal life policy with a term rider, that could eliminate a valuable tax advantage of some blended policies. The break involves the option to withdraw money tax-free through policy loans. The IRS hasn't said how it would treat blends just yet. But if you want to be on the safe side, have your agent make certain that your blend doesn't run afoul of the IRS rules on maximum premiums for cash-value policies.

Use an agent who rebates. The premise behind rebating is simple. After you pay the policy premium, your agent refunds to you 50% or so of his or her commission. Unfortunately, rebating is legal only in California and Florida. And in Florida, insurance companies can refuse to allow their agents to rebate, which has effectively eliminated such discounting there. Moreover, even if you live in California, you may have trouble finding agents willing to rebate because many fear reprisals from insurers. In fact, the state's insurance department is investigating several big insurers for allegedly firing or refusing to do business with agents who want to offer rebates.

Nonetheless, at least one large agency, Direct Insurance Services in San Diego (800-622-3699), brazenly refunds 50% to 75% of all commissions on the whole, universal and term policies it sells for more than 80 insurers. "And we document the rebate percentage by sending the customer a copy of the commission statement from the insurer," says agency president Mark White.

You don't have to be a California resident to buy a rebated policy, but you do have to purchase the policy in person in that state. What if you don't live in California? If you need at least $300,000 or so of coverage, consider traveling there on vacation and picking up a policy as a souvenir. For example, a 50% rebate on a $350,000 Prudential whole life policy for a 45-year-old man would chop his first-year premium from $6,648 to $4,155, because he would get a $2,493 rebate, half of the $4,986 sales commission. In addition, he would get annual rebates of $332 for the next nine years, giving him total savings of $5,481. That's more than enough to cover the cost of taking the kids to Disneyland. Note, however, that the IRS considers insurance rebates to be a form of taxable income. So any refund you receive will effectively cut your savings by 31% if you're in the top federal tax bracket.

Want even bigger savings? Slash commissions to the max by combining a blended life policy with a rebate. For example, buying the $350,000 Prudential blend through Direct Insurance Services would net the 45-year-old man a $1,608 rebate in the first year, dropping the initial premium to $2,679, for a fetching 60% savings.

MONEY HELPS

Q. My wife and I work in the defense industry, and as the "defense drawdown" nears, we are looking for new jobs. We found an Illinois company that could hire us both. But my wife had breast cancer last year (she is now cured, thank goodness), and this firm's insurance does not cover pre-existing conditions. Though we are in our early thirties, we are afraid to move without insurance. Can she get coverage?
— Name withheld by request

A. Until our government agrees on some type of universal health coverage, your options are limited. You could ask the Illinois firm whether its insurer would give your wife partial coverage—meaning she'd be insured against every disease except cancer. Or you could extend your current coverage for as much as 18 months under federal COBRA rules by paying the premium your employer now pays (roughly $200 a month). If your policy has a so-called conversion feature, you could then convert it to an individual policy—albeit at a premium that is typically 50% to 150% higher. If your policy isn't convertible, or if that price is too expensive, you can enroll in the state health insurance pool known as the Comprehensive Health Insurance Plan (Illinois is among 27 states that have one). To join CHIP, your wife must prove that she's lived in Illinois for 30 days and can't find other coverage for less than CHIP's charges of about $201 a month for an individual policy with 80% reimbursement and $500 deductible. Apply as soon as you're eligible; there's a seven- to nine-month wait to get in, then a six-month delay before pre-existing conditions are covered. Good luck, and let's hope for a quick end to the health insurance crisis.

Strengthening Your Job Security

These winning strategies can help you make yourself more valuable—and less vulnerable—in today's increasingly treacherous employment market.

As announcements of mass layoffs pile up like a chain accident on a foggy freeway, it's a rare worker who isn't worried about what lies down the road. Don't look for the employment picture to improve soon. Companies typically wait a year after the economy picks up before restoring staff (as many as half the jobs will be lost forever). And while blue-collar workers have suffered the most, the proportion of laid-off professional and managerial staffers has risen steeply from 8.3% of all unemployed in the 1982-83 recession to 12.3% in the recent one.

Perhaps the scariest thing about the current payroll cuts is that many of them have little to do with the latest slump. "These result from companies making fundamental changes in their structure and in how they do business," says John Stewart of management consultants McKinsey & Co. in New York City. Facing global competition, automation and crippling debt, firm after firm has decided that a leaner and more flexible work force, rather than a fixed payroll, is the key to long-term profitability. To achieve that goal, they have trimmed middle managers, subcontracted for services that were once performed in-house and hired more temporary and part-time workers. The result: the undoing of the employment safety net that companies once tried to provide for loyal workers. "Employers now feel they need complete freedom to hire and fire at all levels—not just on the assembly line," says economist Martin Holdrich at consultant Woods & Poole in Washington, D.C.

The end of corporate caretaking doesn't mean there will be fewer jobs. Although employment growth stalled during the downturn, economists forecast a net gain of 15 million positions by the end of this decade—thanks mainly to gains in small and mid-size companies. But turnover will be swifter and competition stiffer for plum full-time corporate positions with all the benefits. This game of musical jobs means that to stay continuously employed in a position that matches your talents, you'll have to rethink your career strategically. Experts recommend that you consider the following steps even if your job seems secure:

Look for ways to add to your experience and repertoire of skills. Find a task that you can do better than it's being done and ask your employer for the challenge, including any training you need. "It's no longer enough to be either a generalist or a specialist," explains Neil Yeager of the Adult Career Transitions program at the University of Massachusetts. "You have to make yourself into a totalist—a person whose skills include not only general abilities like managing or marketing but also specific expertise, such as a thorough knowledge of your particular industry or profession."

Be alert to opportunities at other companies. "Otherwise, you're wasting the chance to scout while there is no pressure," says Joseph Duffy at outplacement specialist Drake Beam Morin in New York City. Even if you're happy in your present job, stay visible in your field by attending conferences and by talking to other professionals. Toot your horn a bit, swap cards and ask about business conditions, including who's hiring. Almost every successful person knows the value of keeping an eye on the horizon. One example of foresight is the fact that half the subscribers to *Exec-U-Net,* a job-leads newsletter (800-637-3126), were employed when they subscribed.

Step up your job search at the first sign of weakness at your firm or in your field. Believe what you read in the newspapers and what you hear on the grapevine about your company or division being in trouble. Watch for symptoms of personal trouble too, such as poorer performance ratings or low-priority assignments. They may indicate that you have lost interest in your job or, worse, that your employer has lost interest in you—either of which would be reason enough to start hunting for other work. Before you approach another employer, try to figure out what's been missing in your career so that you can fill in the blanks with your next job. If you're working for a big company, chances are you have the training and credentials you need but lack varied experience. If you've been in a small firm, it could be the other way around. Also ask about corporate cultures so that you can figure out where you might flourish. Only after you feel you have a handle on what you want from your next job is it time to schedule job interviews.

Find ways to apply your present skills in a new setting. Sometimes this is no problem. A bank personnel manager, for example, should find it easy to do the same job at a computer firm. But other times, you'll have to be more creative, like Henry Pochini. As a computer-aided design manager for Digital Equipment in Boxboro, Massachusetts, he was already in a field with long-term prospects. Still, when DEC phased out his group and offered the 51-year-old Pochini another job, he took a $60,000 severance package instead. Reason: he wanted to pursue a lifelong dream of working in a job—recruiting—that focused on people, not machines. So he and his wife Sue moved south to Charlotte, where he

How Secure Is Your Job?

Choose the answers that best fit you, then total your score. With 15 points or more, your job's rock solid; from one to five points, you could be on shaky ground; and at zero points or less, type out your resume tonight.

THE PROJECTS YOU ARE ASSIGNED TO ARE USUALLY:
high-priority (plus 3 points) .... **+3**
low-priority (plus 1 point) .... **+1**
changed in midstream (minus 1 point) .... **-1**

IN YOUR LAST PERFORMANCE REVIEW, YOUR WORK WAS:
rated as getting better (plus 1 point) .... **+1**
rated as unchanged (no points)............................... **0**
rated as somewhat worse (minus 1 point)............... **-1**
rated as a lot worse (minus 3 points) .... **+3**

YOU HAVE:
enemies above you (minus 3 points) .... **-3**
enemies below you (minus 1 point) .... **-1**
no enemies (no points) **0**

YOUR MENTOR:
is riding high (plus 3 points) .... **+3**
has fallen from favor (minus 1 point)...................... **-1**
doesn't exist; you don't have one (no points) **0**

YOUR BOSS
likes you (plus 3 points) .... **+3**
doesn't like you (minus 1 point)............................. **-1**
doesn't know who you are (no points) **0**

YOUR REPUTATION EXTENDS
beyond your firm to other companies (plus 3 p) .... **+3**
beyond your department to other parts of your firm **+2**
only within your department (minus 1 point)........ **-1**

THE LAST TIME YOU LEARNED A NEW SKILL WAS:
during the past year (plus 3 points)......................... **+3**
when you started your job (plus 1 point) .... **+1**
in college (minus 2 points) .... **-2**

HOW DO YOU FEEL ABOUT YOUR JOB?
excited (plus 3 points)... **+3**
indifferent (minus 1 point) .... **-1**
worried (minus 3 points) .... **-3**

WITHIN THE PAST 18 MONTHS, YOUR COMPANY
bought another company (minus 1 point)............. **-1**
was bought by another company (minus 3 points) . **-3**

THE PEOPLE WHO STARTED WORK WITH YOU ARE NOW:
in jobs better than yours (minus 3 points .... **-3**
in jobs on a par with yours (no points) **0**
in jobs worse than yours (plus 3 points) .... **+3**

TOTAL ____

began a new career with Management Recruiters, the largest executive-search firm in the country. "After 32 years in computers," he says, "I already know how to find talent in that field. Now I'm learning to recruit in other industries too." Working solely on commission, Pochini has yet to equal the $46,000 salary that he made at DEC. But he's not worried: "After the downturn is over, I expect to double my old pay."

Take steps to moderate any damage to your finances when you switch careers. Like Pochini, most career changers have to accept at least a temporary income setback. Rather than paying an expensive career counseling firm a fee of $3,500 or more, start your search informally at the library, through friends or with a community college career assessment course costing $200 to $300. If you have a computer, investigate software such as Career Design (800-346-8007; $99)

MONEY HELPS

Q. What rights does a surviving spouse have as beneficiary of an IRA or 401(k) plan? May he or she withdraw funds without penalty before age 59.5? Can you explain the rules?
— Harold Morehead, Akron

A. Planner Joel Isaacson at Clarfeld & Co. in New York City says the SS (our shorthand for surviving spouse) can tap the IRA or 401(k) of the NSS (nonsurviving spouse, of course) before turning 59.5 without paying the customary 10% penalty. But all the money must be withdrawn by the end of the fifth year following the NSS' untimely demise, or else be taken in annuity-like annual payments starting the year of the death. (In either case, the SS will owe ordinary income tax on the money, as with any withdrawal from tax-deferred savings plans.) The SS may also roll the funds into his or her own IRA but would then owe a 10% penalty on any subsequent early withdrawals. Bottom line: the longer you both stay SS's, the less complicated your lives will be.

and Career Navigator (800-345-5627; $199), which can help you figure out what job would make you happier. If your new career will require additional education, look for ways to cut your study costs. Georgia State University, for example, offers a master's in early-childhood education for those with undergraduate degrees in other fields. The $2,888 course runs one year, half the usual time needed to get certification.

If you're unemployed, don't try to hide it. Corporate restructurings have put so much first-rate talent on the streets that being out of work doesn't carry the stigma it once did. On the contrary, advertise your availability openly and aggressively. Contact your college alumni association; most schools extend placement services to all grads, not just new ones, and some schools offer special aid to older alumni. Place an ad in your trade or professional magazine. Call friends and professional acquaintances. To avoid putting them on the spot, start by asking for general advice rather than specific leads. And stay busy professionally by volunteering for work with your trade association, offering your services to a charity or contributing to a professional journal, even if it's just a thoughtful letter to the editor.

Consider a temporary job as a professional, not as a file clerk. *Executive Recruiter News* reports that at least 67 firms place professional temps in banking, electronics, engineering, manufacturing, marketing and dozens of other fields—up from just one or two such agencies four years ago. You can get a list of the agencies for $10 by calling the newsletter at 800-531-0007. Assignments typically last three to nine months and pay wages equal to those offered to full-time employees with similar duties. Often the temporary project will lead to something more lasting. At the Imcor agency with offices in Los Angeles, New York City and Stamford, Connecticut, 45% of placements eventually turn into permanent spots. In the job market of the 1990s, a growing number of employers like to try before they buy.

Financing a Secure Retirement

In contrast to previous generations of Americans, people in the third quarter of life today are more likely to view retirement as a time of renewal and adventure than a restful reward for a long career. Indeed, the evidence is overwhelming that we are now in the golden age of retirement. Social Security benefits and the number of company pensions and savings plans have never been higher. Innovations such as IRAs and Keoghs were unknown to retirees of earlier generations. Prospective pensioners not only stand a better chance of living better than they ever could, they also are freer to choose when to call it a career. Although the standard retirement age remains 65, both early retirement and late retirement are catching on.

Contributing to an early departure from work are attractive financial packages that growing numbers of companies offer to older employees. Working longer is on the upswing for quite different reasons. Since 1978, federal law has prohibited companies from making retirement mandatory for anyone except top executives. Career switching and part-time work late in life are more acceptable and available than before. Experts attribute the expanding job pool for older people to the national shift from a manufacturing economy to a service economy. The result is greater opportunities to start a new career in your sixties and to capitalize on your lifetime of experience and skills.

What's more, the generation nearing or in retirement is the wealthiest in U.S. history. These people bought houses cheap after World War II, prospered during the postwar economic boom, saw the value of their homes soar during the inflation-fanned 1970s and early 1980s and paid far less into pension plans and Social Security than they will take out. Much of their wealth is in real estate; nearly three-fourths of people over 65 own their own homes. Half of the couples retiring have a pension from a public or private employer. That can give you remarkable freedom to decide just how much you want to work, and when, and where. You can yield to passions and causes that you may have put off for years, from travel adventures to post-graduate study.

The goal behind both the acquisition of family wealth and saving for retirement is financial independence—and the opportunity to make the most of it. Alas, the price of this unprecedented opportunity is the increasingly complex planning required to build, protect and pass on your bundle to the next generation. And success is based on a premise that used to be unthinkable: Americans want to provide for their families and then retire with no significant reduction in their standard of living.

The purpose of this chapter is to help you pursue that lofty goal, regardless of your age. We will not beguile you with the notion that it is easily attained. Whenever you decide to retire, you are bound to encounter some sleepless nights. You have to worry about whether there will be enough money to live on until the end of your life and your spouse's. If you are to get a pension lump sum, you must suffer the anxieties that you might invest it poorly and live out the latter years of your life as a burden to your children. Even if you invest your funds wisely, you will have to contend with the nightmare of all retirees: no matter how smart and provident you are, inflation hurts you in the end. If you move too hastily to some putative paradise, you might wind up repenting your mistake at excruciating leisure. And you must wonder how you'll escape the paralyzing boredom that afflicts so many who no longer have jobs to go to.

Fortunately, the survival strategies for the future are at hand. Families that learn to talk to one another candidly about sensitive topics— Does Dad have a will? Should we ask the children about moving—will thrive. So will people who see retirement as a glorious mixture of work, play and learning. Growing old can be viewed as a kind of second adolescence. Like the first one, it is fraught with exhilaration and fear of the unknown. The difference is that this time around you are bringing wisdom with you, and the experience should be that much sweeter.

How to Reach Your Personal Goals

Your asset building should center around your house, your company benefits plans and some well-considered moves in the markets.

Having money in the family. What an idle dream it seemed when you started out in your first apartment with a few wedding presents and a batch of furniture the Salvation Army would not take. Your rent seemed bigger than the national debt and, to make ends meet, you drove an Own-a-Wreck and survived on a diet of meatless meat loaf.

Now that you have progressed in life and career, it's easy to see how your standard of living has advanced. If you are in your forties or fifties, you may be surprised to discover when you tot up your assets that you have accumulated a stunning sum. If you are younger, you may be equally amazed at your potential for doing so. Wealth, a term once reserved for the few, is beginning to touch the many. An estimated 1,500 families are worth at least $100 million, and several thousands more around $50 million. Surveys of estates by the IRS reveal that another 850,000 people had assets of at least $500,000, and half a million owned more than $250,000. Most people on their way to such wealth consider themselves solidly middle-income folks who will work, save and invest their way to a prosperous retirement. Yet with affluence comes responsibility. On the one hand, there is the risk of mismanagement and loss; on the other, the opportunity to enlarge your net worth, to secure your retirement nest egg and to pass some of it along to your heirs.

Start your asset-building program by making the most of what you have. You should pay close attention to your employee-benefits plans, particularly those to which you contribute. They have gained greatly in value because they allow you to stack up tax-deferred savings. Examine your investments; there may be sensible ways to invest that you have never thought of. Your house is probably the foundation of your family wealth because its value has likely ballooned over the past decade or so. Yet it may diminish in relative importance in the future even though it keeps pace with inflation. By coordinating these three elements, you can achieve both security and growth.

Your company benefits. The funds stored in your employee-benefits plans may well turn out to be the stars of your future personal finances. That is because these plans typically offer more opportunity for tax-free buildup and more choice of investments than you might otherwise have access to. While every company has its own wrinkles, employee-benefits plans fall into two major categories: defined benefit and defined contribution.

The first, which has been around for decades, is simply your pension plan. Defined benefit means that the company puts away money for you and decides what you get, based on a formula, when you retire. Spurred by tax breaks for themselves as well as their employees, more and more companies have added defined-contribution plans. These allow employees to put aside a portion of their salaries in a fund to which the company also adds. There are two types of such plans. In matching programs, a company contributes a specified percentage (usually 50%) of what you invest. In profit-sharing programs, your employer adds a portion of profits to your

QUIZ
Are You Really Ready to Retire?

	YES	NO
■ **Will you be able to cut back your hours at work gradually instead of all at once?**	+3	-3
Change may exact a toll if it's too abrupt. Making the transition slowly gives you time to adjust at your own pace.		
■ **Are you married?**	+4	-4
Being unmarried can reduce an individual's life expectancy more than smoking or being overweight.		
■ **If you're married, is the relationship satisfying?**	+2	-2
Retirement can put a strain on your marriage. If you don't get along before you retire, chances are things will get worse afterward.		
■ **If your spouse is working, will he or she retire at about the same time as you?**	+3	-3
An increasingly common problem occurs when the husband retires while his younger wife continues to work; it often reduces his self-esteem and creates confusion about household duties.		
■ **If you're not married, do you live with someone?**	+3	-3
Although being in a satisfying marriage is the best way to overcome feelings of isolation, living with someone is a close second.		
■ **If you live alone, do you have daily contact with family or friends?**	+2	-2
This is another substitute for a live-in companion.		
■ **Do you have at least one person outside of the office—for example, your spouse, a friend, even your banker or broker—in whom you can confide?**	+4	-4
Even if you rarely share intimacies, just the presence of a confidant is essential.		
■ **Do you have a place at home or outside of it where you can have total privacy?**	+2	-2
Together is fine up to a point. Everybody needs a retreat.		
■ **Do you try not to hang around the office after the workday is over?**	+3	-3
If you're spending too many hours at work, you may be dependent on the job for social life. Letting go will be hard for you.		

While you may be all set for a financially secure retirement, you may not realize how much life after work can draw on your emotional reserves. If you suddenly find yourself with 40 or more hours a week of free time that you haven't adequately prepared for, you could be headed for trouble. The following questions, based on the findings of gerontologists and psychologists, will help you determine how well prepared you are for the day when the alarm clock no longer rules. Answer each question that applies to you. Then tally the points assigned to each answer for your score. At the end, see what the specialists think.

	YES	NO
■ **Have you made any new friends outside of work this year?**	+3	-3
Don't make the mistake of assuming your work colleagues will still have time for you after you retire.		
■ **Are you involved with community, church or cultural groups?**	+4	-4
Such activities may prove to be the center of your post-work days. Don't wait until retirement to get involved outside your job.		
■ **Do you schedule activities—fishing trips, museum visits, picnics—to fill up your free time?**	+3	-3
Retirement may well be the first time in 40 years that you will control your own time. You should know how to plan your days without a boss looking over your shoulder.		
■ **Have you taken part in an intellectual pursuit, such as attending a class or lecture, or a physical one, such as a competitive sport, in the past month?**	+2	-2
Aim for a variety of activities. Just because you like fishing doesn't mean that after retirement you will enjoy it every day.		
■ **Have you learned something new—say, a foreign language or gourmet cooking—in the past five years?**	+2	-2
Taking on new challenges shows an openness to change.		
■ **Were you able to adjust easily when your children left home or during other periods of major change?**	+4	-4
If you have been able to weather most of life's changes, you'll almost surely adjust well to retirement.		
■ **Are you looking forward to retirement?**	+3	-3
Your attitude can cast a shadow over everything. A negative one could become a self-fulfilling prophecy.		

TOTAL

If you score 18 points or above, you are on solid footing.
Between zero and 18, you have some catching up to do.
Below zero, you need to work hard on improving your emotional preparation for retiring.

savings. Additionally, you may be offered an employee stock-ownership program (ESOP). In that case, your employer will typically match up to 50% of the amount you invest in shares of company stock.

In both types of plans, defined-benefit and defined-contribution, funds accrete quietly and inexorably until they total surprisingly large sums. At one company, a $55,000-a-year design engineer who left after 21 years of service took $314,000 from various plans. An ESOP would have added even more. The National Center for Employee Ownership found that employees who earned $35,000 a year at companies with ESOPs can generally leave their jobs after 20 years with proceeds from an ESOP of more than $200,000.

Defined-contribution plans offer far more opportunity for wealth building than do pension plans. If you leave your company, you can take all your contributions with you, and the company's contribution vests more quickly than in pension plans (usually after one to three years of employment). Furthermore, many companies let you contribute to these plans as part of 401(k) salary-reduction programs. That's the best deal because it puts you three giant steps ahead. First, you can stoke a 401(k) this year up to an estimated legal limit of $9,000 pretax—the amount increases annually with inflation—although most employers impose lower limits. Second, you get an immediate gain on your investment because your employer usually matches a portion of your contribution. Finally, the earnings are not taxed until you begin withdrawing them at age 59.5. If you change jobs, you can roll over the funds into an IRA that continues the tax-deferred buildup.

Perhaps even more important, defined-contribution plans usually give you more than one investment option. The choices may include your company's stock, diversified portfolios of stocks and bonds that operate much like mutual funds and guaranteed investment contracts—loans to large insurance companies that promise a fixed rate of return slightly higher than bank CDs. With most plans you can choose between two different types of investments, usually a growth fund and an income fund. If you are close to retirement and are leery of taking risks with your money, you will probably want to choose an income fund that pays steady dividends. If you have just started your career, you may prefer to invest for growth in stock funds. Although you may go for growth when the stock market is about to take a dive, such moves are at least partly offset by the company's matching contribution. The same holds true for your ESOP. Even if your employer's stock sags, the match will compensate for temporary drops in value.

When you retire, your company may offer you several payment options for your pension. The two most common choices are a monthly check or a lump sum, which is typically based on your length of service, final five years' pay and life expectancy. Deciding which to take requires detailed computations. If you believe you can invest the lump sum profitably enough to equal the pension you would otherwise get, you could leave behind a sizable legacy. And the tax bite on lump sums taken at retirement can be moderate. Almost everybody who retires after age 59.5 is eligible for five-year forward averaging, which lets you spread out the lump as though it were paid in equal installments over five years. While the entire tax bill must be paid the year you receive the lump sum, forward averaging will significantly lower your bracket.

Your personal investments. One factor you should take into account in designing your investment portfolio is the security of your income. That is because people's investment inclinations often mirror the way they earn their money. For example, a freelance writer, a musician, or a salesperson on commission might earn $35,000 one year, $60,000 the next, and $10,000 the third year. Yet these are the types of people who tend to invest in chancy emerging growth stocks, risky venture-capital deals and highly leveraged real estate projects. Such an individual might instead be better off hedging with safer vehicles—CDs, Treasury bills or mutual funds with holdings in stocks that pay dividends and promise some growth. By contrast, a corporate employee with a secure job who earns $50,000 a year and has a generous, diversified portfolio in his employee-benefits plans is often inclined to invest his spare cash in a safe but stodgy mutual fund. In this case, the person can obviously afford to look for a little more bang in his personal investments.

If your analysis of your income tells you that you should be investing some of your spare cash more aggressively, but you are the type of person who frets over every decision, you might adopt a strategy called dollar-cost averaging. With this technique, you merely pick a mutual fund that matches your investment goals and tolerance of risk and invest equal sums periodically. This way, you will be purchasing fewer of the fund's shares when securities prices are high and more when prices dip. To make dollar-cost averaging work, you have to have the discipline to keep writing those regular checks even when your investment plunges. No-load stock funds are ideal vehicles for this approach.

Another wealth-building avenue is to invest in mutual funds inside tax-deferring envelopes such as rollover IRAs. (If you are covered by a company pension plan and earn more than $25,000—$40,000 for a couple—you can no longer fully deduct your contribution to a standard IRA.) Single-premium deferred annuities, sold by insurance companies, operate in a similar fashion. You buy an annuity with after-tax dollars, but your gains accumulate tax-free. Some annuities promise a specified annual return; others may offer a choice among as many as 15 different investment funds and allow you to add small deposits monthly or quarterly so that you can dollar-cost average. You have to choose carefully, however, because many insurance companies extract hefty fees on annuities.

Your house. This remains the most valuable asset most families acquire. The Census Bureau has estimated that a house represents about 41% of a typical family's worth. Economists, however, aren't forecasting the heady gains for houses that they enjoyed in the inflationary late 1970s and early 1980s. Expect instead that single-family houses will track inflation over time. That means your home will more likely be a source of capital preservation than capital growth.

Owning an asset whose value keeps pace with inflation is just one of the reasons for pursuing the American Dream of home ownership. For example, making regular payments on the mortgage is a method of disciplined savings that works well for those who would normally spend every dollar they earn. Owning a house also qualifies you for one of the few tax shelters available to individuals: deductions for property taxes and mortgage interest. When you sell, you can defer taxes on the profits if you put them into a new house within two years. And at age 55, you can exclude $125,000 of your gain from taxation.

However impressive the fortune you ultimately create, you probably will have a harder time in the future ensuring that your family—and not the IRS or your state—is your prime beneficiary. Currently, estate taxes do not inhibit the passage of wealth within most families. The federal tax code exempts $600,000 for individuals ($1.2 million for a husband and wife). Above those limits, the IRS takes 40% to 55%. So if you and your spouse die at the same time and leave $1,200,001, the most the estate will owe in federal taxes is 40% of $1, or 40 cents.

Those generous limits are being scrutinized by an increasingly stingy Congress, which is threatening to toughen death taxes. Raising the percentage that the IRS can claim, scaling back the exemptions and taxing appreciated assets are all ways that Congress might choose to respond to the pressure to increase revenues and help reduce the budget deficit. Still, no matter how confiscatory estate taxes become in the future, it's better to have created a small family fortune than not. And who knows what your tidy bundle might grow to in another generation or two.

Figuring How Much You'll Need

The essentials are Social Security, a pension, company savings accounts and, most of all, a disciplined plan that you can live with.

Of all the major milestones in life—graduating from college, say, or getting married—leaving work may be the only one where the decisive consideration is whether you can afford to do it. Indeed, financial independence does not come cheap. It means being able to support your pre-retirement standard of living for as long as three decades in the face of an unpredictable economy and implacable inflation. Financial security in retirement isn't a birthright; to get it you have to plan for it.

The first step in setting your goals is to decide how much income you will require in retirement. If you are more than 10 years away from calling it quits, you obviously won't be able to predict your retirement expenses accurately. But the worksheet beginning on page 96 will help you form a reliable estimate. Then, you can compare this amount with figures on another worksheet, beginning on page 100, used by financial planners to determine how much you will need to maintain your standard of living later on. By measuring your income needs against the resources you will have in retirement, such as Social Security and your company pension, you can calculate how much capital you must accumulate. Equally important, you can use this information to implement a savings plan.

As you get closer to retirement and can estimate your budget more precisely, you are likely to find that you can get by on less. By the time you are ready to call it quits, for example, you may well have paid off your home mortgage and the bills for your children's education. With your kids finally grown and presumably self-sufficient, you may feel free to reduce your life insurance.

And if you move to a warmer climate, you can expect to save on heating bills. On the other hand, be sure to allow for larger discretionary expenditures such as travel and education. Be prepared also to spend about 30% more on medicine and health insurance.

What about Social Security? Despite persistent fears that the government's retirement program will fold, it's here for the long term. True, the program needed bolstering in the 1980s to ensure benefits for workers now nearing retirement. But the system will be on firm footing when today's 40- to 60-year-olds retire. Theoretically, Social Security could go bankrupt early in the next century when today's young workers retire; politically, there's little chance that such a debacle will occur. Instead, the rules will change in ways no one can now predict with absolute certainty.

So try to put aside the rhetoric and start analyzing the benefit you almost certainly will get. At last count, a 65-year-old could retire now and receive up to $13,536 a year—the amount increases annually with inflation. Generally, you must work 40 quarters or 10 years before Social Security will pay you a retirement benefit. Not everyone who works that long will get a check. If you are paid by a nonprofit organization, such as a museum or hospital, most of your working years probably won't count toward earning a Social Security benefit. Only employment since January 1, 1984 at a nonprofit institution will be used in the benefit formula, unless you've paid in Social Security taxes all along. About one-third of employees of state and local governments and all federal employees hired before January 1984 aren't covered by Social Security. Federal government workers hired since then are covered.

As do most companies, the Social Security Administration pays full benefits to employees who retire at 65 and cuts payouts for workers who quit earlier. You can't apply for your own retirement check until age 62, and it will be 80% of the amount you would get by waiting until age 65. Starting in the year 2000 and lasting through 2022, the early-retirement benefit for a 62-year-old will be nipped by about .8% a year. So by 2022, early-retirement checks from Social Security will be only 70% of full benefits.

Social Security rewards workers who put off their benefits past 65. Soon the lure will be more enticing. Today, Social Security enlarges your retirement check by 3% for each year you delay taking full benefits between age 65 and 70. That's in addition to the annual cost-of-living increase. The delayed retirement credit inches up a bit for anyone who turned 65 in 1990 or later. The credit increases by one-half of 1% every other year until it reaches 8% in 2008. But don't put off taking your Social Security benefit at 65 just to get a larger check later. The extra money you receive from the delayed retirement credit won't equal the Social Security income you could have been accepting starting at 65.

Social Security won't start sending you a check until you notify the local office that you're ready. File an application three months before you want the first monthly check to arrive and be sure to bring or send a certified copy of your birth certificate. If you expect a check for your spouse's benefit, you will need a certified copy of your marriage license. Divorcees filing for benefits have to present certified copies of marriage and divorce papers. In the January check, benefits automatically rise by the increase in the previous year's cost of living. If inflation is less than 3%, however, Congress must vote to raise Social Security checks by that amount.

If you're married but only one of you works, Social Security will send you one monthly check equal to 1.5 times the worker's entitlement, pro-vided the beneficiary doesn't start collecting until age 65. A nonworking spouse who collects Social Security at 62 will get only 37.5% of the worker's benefits. A working couple with only one spouse employed long enough to receive a full Social Security benefit at 65 will also get one monthly check of 150% of that spouse's entitlement. If the lower-earning spouse didn't earn enough to get a Social Security benefit equal to more than half the high-earning spouse's, the couple will also get a single check of 150% of the bigger benefit. Couples entitled to two full benefits are mailed separate checks, unless they request a single monthly payment. A divorced person can get the spouse's benefit at age 62, as long as the couple were married more than 10 years.

From Social Security's inception in 1937 through 1983, all benefits were free of federal, state and local taxes. Now up to half your benefits could be subject to federal income taxes if the total of your adjusted gross income, tax-exempt interest and half of your Social Security benefit exceeds $32,000 (for married couples filing jointly) or $25,000 (singles). You will be taxed on half of any excess or half of your Social Security benefit, whichever is smaller. Say your adjusted gross income is $25,000, and this year you will get $10,000 in Social Security benefits and $5,000 in tax-exempt interest. You add half your benefit, or $5,000, and all the interest to your income for a total of $35,000. So if you're married, you will exceed the $32,000 cutoff by $3,000, and you will add half that, or $1,500, to your taxable income. Many states tax Social Security benefits too. By the time baby boomers, born between 1946 and 1964, reach retirement, about half are likely to find their benefits taxed. Reason: the federal formula's thresholds aren't indexed to inflation, and in 30 years or so, many more retirees will have incomes exceeding $32,000.

The unpleasant surprise of retirement planning is that the combination of Social Security and pension benefits is unlikely to give you the income you need. Even if you spend a couple of decades with a fairly generous employer, you can

The Actual Costs of Your Retirement

While nearly everyone looks forward to retirement as a time of doing exactly as one pleases, there are as many ways to pursue your pleasures as there are people. That's an important retirement planning point, because the stuff of your post-working-life dreams—be it Caribbean cruises, relocating to the sunbelt or simply working on your golf score—helps determine how much money you should be putting toward those goals now. The rule of thumb among financial planners and benefit consultants is that you will need an annual retirement income amounting to roughly 70% to 80% of your current earnings.

Whatever the life style you envision, the best way to ensure that you can pay for it is to plan as far ahead as possible. The first step is to determine what your annual expenses are likely to be. The worksheet on the facing page is specifically designed to help you do that. Despite the diversity in retirement living, financial planners surveyed by MONEY note at least some similarities in spending patterns after age 65. For example, most retirees spend about the same amount on food, gifts, charitable contributions and personal care as they did while working. Medical and dental bills, on the other hand, are significantly higher, depending on how generous your company's retirement coverage is. Here are some general guidelines to help you fill out the worksheet.

Line 1: If you pay off your mortgage and take care of all necessary maintenance problems before you retire, housing costs should drop by as much as 25% to 30%. Count on even more shrinkage if you sell your house and buy a smaller one. Condominium owners and renters should factor in maintenance-fee and rent increases. And anyone who plans to spend more time at home should anticipate higher utilities charges.

Line 2: Financial planners estimate that if you are moving from business suits to jeans, you can expect to reduce clothing expenses by 20% to 35%.

Line 4: Scratch commuting costs. Other transportation expenses will increase if you intend to be very active. Planners recommend that two-car couples keep both autos during retirement, especially if both are fairly active.

Line 6: Most people keep giving the same amounts to charitable, political and educational institutions, as well as to family members outside the immediate household. But the overall figure drops, usually by the amount you used to give at the office.

Line 7: If your kids will be grown by the time you retire, you can eliminate education expenses, unless you plan to help pay your grandchildren's college bills. And if you intend to return to school yourself, check into reduced tuition costs for senior citizens.

Line 8: There will be little change in your payout for property, liability and auto insurance, but retirees can generally reduce their life insurance coverage by at least 50% or, if their spouses are fully provided for under their pension plan, eliminate it altogether.

Line 9: If you are currently covered by a company health plan, expect medical and dental costs to spurt by about 50% because of increased illnesses combined with reduced insurance coverage. Medicare pays only about one-fifth of doctors' fees and less than one-third of hospital bills. Check your company's coverage for retirees.

Line 10: You should plan to be debt-free by the time you retire, thereby eliminating loan repayment expenses.

Line 12: How much you spend for entertainment depends on how active you are. Expect such expenditures to rise an average of about 20% during your retirement.

Line 13: Budget for higher veterinary bills if you will have an aging dog, cat or other pet.

Line 14: While your contributions to pension plans cease at retirement, many financial planners encourage clients to continue setting aside about 10% of their income as a hedge against inflation.

Line 15: Unless you have some kind of job, it's farewell at last to Social Security (FICA) taxes. Also, check out laws in your state because some don't tax any income from retirement plans. The conventional wisdom that you will be in a lower tax bracket after retirement is no longer true for many high-income people. Moreover, married couples filing jointly whose total earnings exceed $32,000 ($25,000 for single retirees) could pay tax on up to 50% of their Social Security benefits.

Line 16: With more adult kids expecting financial help from Mom and Dad and Americans' increasing longevity, you could be contributing to the down payment on a child's first house while paying for a parent's nursing home.

Total current expenditures should equal 100% of your current before-tax income. By dividing your total expenditures at retirement by your current gross income, you will arrive at the percentage of your current income that you will need in retirement.

EXPENDITURES   At retirement   Current year

1. **Housing.** Rent, mortgage, property taxes, utilities (gas, oil, electricity and water), telephone, home furnishings, household services, maintenance, improvements _____ _____

2. **Clothing.** Purchases and cleaning _____ _____

3. **Food.** (including tobacco and alcohol) _____ _____

4. **Transportation.** Car repair and maintenance, installment payments, gas, commuting costs, other _____ _____

5. **Gifts.** _____ _____

6. **Contributions.** _____ _____

7. **Education.** _____ _____

8. **Insurance.** Life, medical, auto, property, liability _____ _____

9. **Medical and Dental Care.** Premiums, deductible and out-of-pocket costs _____ _____

10. **Loan-Repayment Costs.** _____ _____

11. **Personal Care.** Grooming, health club, other _____ _____

12. **Entertainment.** Vacations, dining out, movies, plays, concerts, sports events, cable TV, videocassettes, entertaining, sports, hobbies, other _____ _____

13. **Pet Expenses.** _____ _____

14. **Savings and Retirement.** Contribution to company plans, IRAs, Keoghs, SEPs, other savings, investments _____ _____

15. **Taxes.** Federal, FICA, state, local _____ _____

16. **Support of Relatives.** _____ _____

TOTAL EXPENDITURES. (add lines 1 through 16) _____ _____

TOTAL CURRENT EXPENDITURES DIVIDED BY CURRENT GROSS INCOME. _____

TOTAL EXPENDITURES AT RETIREMENT DIVIDED BY CURRENT GROSS INCOME. _____

generally expect the combination to replace no more than 40% to 60% of your salary in the first year you are retired. The rest will have to come from the capital you build up in your IRAs (and Keoghs for the self-employed), your personal investments and any tax-deferred savings plans offered by your employer, such as a profit-sharing or 401(k) account.

How much capital will it take to make up that gap? Consider this general guideline: a married couple retiring at age 65 should figure on about $179,000 of capital for each $10,000 that their pension and Social Security benefits fall short of their yearly income needs. Thus, if you need to replace $25,000 of annual income in retirement, the price of a worry-free retirement would be nearly $450,000.

Part of the reason you require so much capital is that the money has to last as long as you do. The median life expectancy is 20 years for a man at age 60 years and 25 for a woman. So you have a 50% chance of outliving the life expectancy

assigned to you when you retire. As a result, it's wise to base your planning on the assumption that you will live longer than 85% of the people your age. For example, a 60-year-old man could feel secure with savings sufficient to meet his income needs to age 90; a woman of the same age should lay in enough to reach 94. The other contingency that boosts the cost of financial independence is inflation. Because your Social Security benefits increase in step with the consumer price index, your benefits will continue to provide the same proportion of your retirement income in later years as in the year you left work. Almost no private employers' pensions are indexed to inflation, however. Consequently, your capital must be large enough so that it earns more than you need to live on, leaving you a surplus to reinvest. Later, as inflation pushes your expenses ahead of your investment earnings, you will have enough stashed away to meet the added need by dipping into your principal without having to worry about running out of money.

Why Your 401(k) Is So Crucial

Your financial security could depend on this awkwardly named retirement account. We offer these rules to help you make the most of it.

More and more employees, regardless of their age, are beginning to realize that a 401(k) may be the only pension plan they will ever have. That's because companies increasingly are scaling back or axing traditional defined-benefit pension plans in favor of defined-contribution 401(k)s (named for the tax code that created them in 1978). So the sooner you start one of these savings plans and the better you manage it, the more retirement security you'll get.

In fact, more than 42,000 employers terminated their defined-benefit plans from 1989 to

1991, three times as many as in the first three years of the 1980s. Meanwhile, the number of 401(k) plans zoomed from zero in 1980 to an estimated 100,000 recently. According to New York City benefits firm Buck Consultants, fully 95% of large and medium-size companies offer 401(k)s. In all, defined-contribution plans, including 401(k)s, constitute 81% of all retirement programs, and defined-benefit plans make up just 19%. Why? For most employers, 401(k) plans are cheaper to administer and fund than traditional pensions, because the company puts up money only if you put yours up first.

Even if your retirement doesn't depend on a 401(k), your returns from it still deserve close attention. Through payroll deductions, you make contributions that are exempt from income tax. Your company probably kicks in additional money, typically 50 cents for each dollar you contribute up to 6% of your salary. And the whole thing grows tax deferred until withdrawal. Bottom line: a 401(k) contribution invested in assets earning 9% a year will return a whopping 63.5% annually, after tax benefits and a 50% company match are taken into account.

For all the 401(k)'s unquestioned virtues, however, it's probably the investment approach that people understand the least. Generally, 401(k)s offer you from one to six or more investment options, usually mutual funds, into which you funnel your contributions. But most employers provide scant information on the importance of such plans and on the investment options available. Most give you no help at all on investment strategy. As a result, too few people take advantage of 401(k)s. Fully 28% of employees eligible to use the plans don't bother to do so. And, once employees enter the plans, they often make bad investment choices. For example, half of participants' own contributions are invested in guaranteed investment contracts (GICs) or money-market funds that don't beat inflation over time. A recent survey by insurer New York Life found that 27% of 401(k) participants admitted that they had no idea why they picked the investments in their plans. Our advice:

Strain to invest as much pretax salary as the plan allows. The IRS caps 401(k) contributions at 25% of your earnings or $30,000, whichever is less. Yet employer-imposed ceilings allow few people to go that high. You typically can kick in from 1% to 20% of your salary, with 11% to 15% the most common limit. Note, however, that any contributions over a ceiling set annually by the government (estimated to be about $9,000 in 1993) are subject to income tax. If the plan allows it, consider making additional contributions in after-tax dollars so that money can grow tax deferred. What if you can't afford to set aside the maximum your plan allows? At the very least, invest enough to qualify for 100% of whatever match the company is offering.

If you earn a plump salary, you may be restricted even further. Because it's easier for highly paid employees to contribute more than lower paid ones, the IRS imposes complex nondiscrimination rules to ensure that 401(k)s do not disproportionately benefit the fortunate (generally those who earn more than $62,345 and rank among the top 20% of a company's earners). To meet the IRS requirements, about half of medium-size and large plans must crimp their employees' contributions, typically at 6% or 7% of salary. So encourage your co-workers to invest in the plan, especially if you're highly paid. After Coors Brewing Co. began aggressively promoting its 401(k) a few years ago, workers in lower salary brackets increased their contributions from 4% to 6% of salary. That enabled the company to raise the limits of highly compensated employees from 9% to 15%.

Dig for information about investment options. By law, you are entitled to receive a booklet laying out the plan's rules and an annual statement of the assets you've built up in your account. Your employer isn't obliged to send your annual statement unless you request it, although many do it routinely. Most firms also provide a description of the objective of each option and the name of that investment's manager or issuer, usually a mutual fund or insurance company. Most plans give you three to five choices: fixed-income GICs issued by insurance companies (in 76% of plans); aggressive stock funds (48%); money-market funds (46%) and your employer's own stock (43%). Other common options include bond funds, stock funds tied to the performance of a given stock market index and balanced funds made up of an evenhanded mix of stocks and bonds. The larger the company, the greater the chance that you'll get detailed information about these investments (via a quarterly newsletter, for example).

You probably won't receive fund prospectuses that list current holdings, however. To get one, as well as to check on past performance of a mutual fund in your plan, call the toll-free number of the company that manages that fund. And because a portfolio of GICs is only as safe as the insurance companies issuing them, check the insurers' safety standing by calling Standard & Poor's (212-208-1527) for the ratings of as many as five insurers at no charge. Steer clear of any GIC offerings rated below AA by Standard & Poor's or of any GIC portfolio that is more than 20% invested with a single insurer.

Allocate assets wisely. According to a recent survey, only 21% of 401(k) participants' own contributions was invested in stocks (not counting the employer's shares). Some studies show the amount in GICs running as high as 70%. That's the wrong approach for many employees. "The biggest mistake people make is being too conservative," says Donna Winn, a specialist in company retirement plans at Merrill Lynch. "The only defense against inflation is stocks over the long term." During the past 40 years, she estimates, a fixed-income portfolio provided an average return of 5.5%, vs. 10.1% for one invested 75% in stocks and 25% in bonds. In general, the younger you are, the more aggressive you can afford to be because you can wait out market downturns.

Integrate your 401(k) into your portfolio. "If you hold securities outside your 401(k)," says Ethan Kra of benefits consultants William M. Mercer in New York City, "shuffle your stock and bond investments to take advantage of the tax-deferred power of your 401(k)." Let's say you have total assets of $100,000—half in your 401(k) and half outside—and have decided on an overall allocation of 70% in stocks and 30% in bonds. Because bonds throw off taxable income,

How Much Should You Try to Save Now?

The worksheet at right will tell you approximately how much you need to start saving now to hold on to your standard of living in retirement. The multipliers used in lines 7, 9 and 11 allow for inflation by assuming your investments will grow at three percentage points over the inflation rate, before and after retirement. This keeps all figures in today's dollars.

Line 3: If you and your spouse are over 60, call the Social Security Administration at 800-772-1213 for a projection of your benefit. Or use one of these rough estimates: $13,536 a year if you make over $57,600, or between $12,072 and $13,452 if your income is between $30,000 and $55,000.

Line 4: Your company benefits department may be able to estimate your pension. Make sure the estimate assumes that you continue working until your retirement age at your current salary. That will somewhat understate your likely eventual payout but will keep the figure in today's dollars.

Line 7: The multipliers in column A incorporate the cautious assumption that men will live to 90 and women to 94—longer than 85% of them do now. Single men should use the multiplier under "men." Women and couples should use the one under "women," since wives usually outlive husbands.

Line 8: Your personal retirement portfolio includes any investments you have specifically earmarked for retirement, aside from your IRA or Keogh. For your employer-sponsored savings plans, check the most recent statement from your 401(k), profit-sharing, thrift or stock ownership plan and total your vested balance in each.

Line 12: Consult the most recent annual statement from these plans to find the amount your company contributed on your behalf to each of the plans last year. Enter the total.

| AGE AT WHICH YOU | MULTIPLIER A | |
EXPECT TO RETIRE	men	women
55	22.1	23.5
56	21.8	23.2
57	21.4	22.8
58	21.0	22.5
59	20.6	22.1
60	20.2	21.8
61	19.8	21.4
62	19.3	21.0
63	18.9	20.6
64	18.4	20.2
65	17.9	19.8
66	17.4	19.3
67	16.9	18.9

TIME UNTIL YOU EXPECT TO RETIRE	MULTIPLIER B	MULTIPLIER C
1 year	1.03	1.000
3 years	1.09	.324
5 years	1.16	.188
7 years	1.23	.131
9 years	1.30	.098
11 years	1.38	.078
13 years	1.47	.064
15 years	1.56	.054
20 years	1.81	.037

1. Current gross income _____

2. Annual income needed in retirement, in today's dollars (70% of line 1) _____

3. Annual Social Security retirement benefits _____

4. Annual pension benefits _____

5. Guaranteed annual retirement income (line 3 plus line 4) _____

6. Additional retirement income needed (line 2 minus line 5) _____

7. Capital required to provide additional retirement income (line 6 times multiplier from column A at left) _____

8. Amount you have saved already

_____ + _____ + _____ = _____

| personal retirement portfolio | IRA/Keogh | employer-sponsored savings plans | total savings |

9. What your current investments will have grown to by the time you retire (total from line 8 times multiplier from Column B at left) _____

10. Additional retirement capital required (line 7 minus line 9) _____

11. Total annual savings still needed (line 10 times factor from column C at left) _____

12. Annual employer contributions to your company savings plans _____

13. Amount you need to set aside each year (line 11 minus line 12) _____

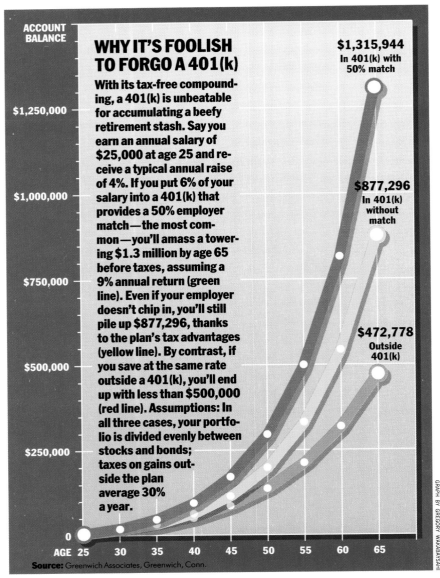

ACCOUNT BALANCE

WHY IT'S FOOLISH TO FORGO A 401(k)

With its tax-free compounding, a 401(k) is unbeatable for accumulating a beefy retirement stash. Say you earn an annual salary of $25,000 at age 25 and receive a typical annual raise of 4%. If you put 6% of your salary into a 401(k) that provides a 50% employer match—the most common—you'll amass a towering $1.3 million by age 65 before taxes, assuming a 9% annual return (green line). Even if your employer doesn't chip in, you'll still pile up $877,296, thanks to the plan's tax advantages (yellow line). By contrast, if you save at the same rate outside a 401(k), you'll end up with less than $500,000 (red line). Assumptions: In all three cases, your portfolio is divided evenly between stocks and bonds; taxes on gains outside the plan average 30% a year.

$1,315,944 In 401(k) with 50% match

$877,296 In 401(k) without match

$472,778 Outside 401(k)

$1,250,000

$1,000,000

$750,000

$500,000

$250,000

0

AGE 25   30   35   40   45   50   55   60   65

Source: Greenwich Associates, Greenwich, Conn.

GRAPH BY GREGORY WAKABAYSAHI

planned. Transfer assets to realign your balances with your original allocations. But resist the urge to time the market—that is, repeatedly alter your asset mix in hopes of anticipating short-term swings in investor sentiment. Almost half of plan administrators take four or more weeks to process a transfer of assets, thereby foiling even the most astute market timers.

Borrow, don't withdraw, from your plan prior to retirement. Most employers allow 401(k) withdrawals before age 59.5 if you face such hardships as high medical expenses. But the IRS will still sock you with income tax plus, in most cases, a hefty 10% penalty on the money you take out. A much smarter choice is to borrow against your plan's assets, an option offered in about two-thirds of 401(k)s. Companies typically require

do all of your bond investing inside your 401(k). Put $30,000 into the plan's bond fund. Then put the remaining $20,000 of your 401(k) money in the plan's stock fund and put the $50,000 you have outside the plan in stocks or stock funds. Why? Because a stock's capital gains can accumulate untaxed until you sell, some of a 401(k)'s tax shelter is wasted on stocks.

Rejigger balances once a year. When you get your annual statement, commonly in January or February, check on the performance of your funds. If the stock market zoomed, you could be more heavily weighted in stocks than you had

a minimum loan of $1,000 and will let you tap no more than half of your vested balance. Interest is commonly a percentage point above the prime rate, recently 6%. The IRS requires repayment within five years, though loans used to meet the down payment on a home can be repaid more slowly, usually in 10 to 20 years. In most plans, your loan entails no application fees or credit approvals, and you often get the money within four weeks.

Execute rollovers carefully. To avoid taxes and penalties when you leave your employer, you must roll your 401(k) distribution into an IRA or into your new company's plan within 60 days. But beware of a sneaky new IRS rule. Effective January 1, 1993, any departing employee who innocently requests a check for the contents of his or her 401(k) will be slapped with a 20% federal withholding tax. If such a Jane Doe has, say, $100,000 in her plan, she'll get a check for just $80,000. Here's the zinger: Jane still must roll over the full $100,000 to escape the 10% penalty, but she won't get the $20,000 back from the IRS until she files her taxes for the year. So unless she can scrape up $20,000 of her own money to add to the $80,000 within 60 days, the IRS could consider the $20,000 a distribution and hit her with the dreaded 10% penalty for early withdrawals.

The way to escape this withholding nightmare is to arrange what's known as a trustee-to-trustee transfer. That means the money goes directly from your old plan administrator to the new one, such as the mutual fund company you've selected for your IRA, without ever touching your hands. So if you plan to leave your job soon, be sure to ask your company benefits department to make such a transfer. Another option that's worth considering is to leave your 401(k) assets where they are, if your current employer allows it, until you're able to make all of the proper transfer arrangements.

The Squeeze on Health Benefits

More and more employers have reduced or plan to reduce health coverage promised to retirees. These steps can help you avoid costly surprises.

It's one of a worker's worst nightmares: after you retire, your old employer pulls the plug on your health benefits. That's exactly what happened to 93 former Massey-Ferguson employees. In 1988, they were informed that they no longer would receive any of their anticipated retiree health benefits from the farm-machinery manufacturer. "We had been told in a corporate memo, in effect, that we'd be receiving these benefits in retirement," says Jack Winslow, who retired in 1987 and has since had to purchase health insurance for himself and his wife Marian at a cost of $3,600 a year. Massey-Ferguson maintained that its benefits plan stipulated that it could be amended at any time.

In addition, the company said that since these employees had been transferred to a spin-off that was placed in receivership in 1988, it had no obligation to pay their health benefits. The group fought back with a lawsuit in the federal district court in Des Moines, where a jury awarded the retirees $8.3 million to cover their health-care needs, plus punitive damages. But hold your applause for now. None of the money has been paid out, nor is it clear whether it ever will be. Reason: Massey-Ferguson and its parent, Varity, are appealing the decision.

Even if the Massey-Ferguson retirees ultimately prevail, the rest of us still have plenty to worry about. Similar cases have been won recently by companies that cut benefits. What's more, everyone expects an increasing number of employers to cut back. "Many companies have made unlimited promises to retirees," says Edward Davey, a New York City executive with A. Foster Higgins, a national benefits consulting firm. "But health costs have gotten out of hand, and they have to make changes."

Indeed, 62% of the 2,000 employers surveyed by benefits consultant William M. Mercer said they had reduced or planned to reduce retiree health coverage. Chrysler, for example, asked each of its 15,000 salaried employees who retired before February 1988 to choose between these options: either begin paying annual deductibles of $200 to $1,500 on their health plan (depending on the coverage they chose) or forgo potential cost-of-living pension increases.

One impetus for these benefit rollbacks is a new rule that's been issued by the Financial Accounting Standards Board (FASB), an independent group that sets accounting policy for American corporations. FASB has ordered firms with more than 500 employees to account for future retiree health costs on their balance sheets beginning this year. Smaller companies will be affected as of 1995. In particular, if you are a white-collar employee at a big company in an economically depressed sector like the steel or automotive industry, watch out for deep cuts in your retirement health benefits. Such companies are especially desperate to shore up their finances by limiting expenses.

There are ways, however, that even the most vulnerable employees and retirees can protect themselves. Here's the outlook for your health benefits in retirement and the steps to take to avoid a nasty surprise:

If you are still working, the younger you are, the more you should fear cutbacks. Many employers are gradually phasing out health coverage entirely for their future retirees. Others now offer full coverage in retirement only to employees who have already worked at the company for at least 20 or 30 years. The best advice is to try to delay your retirement until age 65, when Medicare benefits kick in. If, however, you're weighing early retirement, scrutinize company literature describing your future health benefits. If your current benefits booklet includes what's known as a reservation clause, you probably have no legal entitlement to future health benefits. This clause notes that the employer reserves the right to amend, change or terminate your benefits at

any time. If that's your situation, start squirreling away all you can for your eventual health expenses by taking full advantage of company savings plans, such as 401(k)s.

If you're already retired and receiving health benefits from your former employer, there's little chance your company will eliminate your health coverage altogether. But you are likely to see your deductibles or co-payments rise in the next few years. You may also be asked to kick in a portion of the annual premium, say, 20% of the $3,000 it now costs your employer to cover a 60-year-old. Gordon Gould of benefits consultant Towers Perrin in Los Angeles estimates that about 10% to 15% of all companies will freeze the annual sum they spend for their health coverage, forcing retirees to pay for future premium increases.

So if you're 65 or over and paying to participate in your former employer's health plan, you should try to find less expensive coverage from either a similarly comprehensive Medigap insurance policy (about $500 to $1,400 annually) or a health maintenance organization (about $500 a year). Both of these options are less likely to slice your coverage than your employer is. If you retired before the mid-1980s and have lost your health coverage, consult a lawyer who specializes in employee benefits. You may have legal recourse, since most companies began inserting reservation clauses in company literature only in the past five years or so.

While the sums may seem imposing, the job of accumulating them needn't be if you start early. Assuming your investments grow at the conservative pace of three or four percentage points over inflation, you could build a retirement chest of $179,000 (in today's dollars) by saving only $6,600 a year for the next 20 years. The calculation includes the amounts your employer contributes to your tax-deferred savings plan at work, if you began 20 years before you retire. If, for example, you postpone saving until you are only 10 years from the finish line, you'd have to set aside more than $15,600 a year.

Chapter 6

The Consummate Consumer

At some point following the season of Cuisinart and the oat bran era, the predatory consumers of the abundant '80s began to chew their kills with notably less satisfaction. Perhaps it was the blizzard of pink slips that was precipitated by the 1990-91 recession and the rash of corporate restructurings financed by aptly named junk bonds. Or maybe it was glassy-eyed satiation after years of licentious spending. Whatever the reason, at a pace almost too gradual to be noticed, the pure high of the buy has faded for many consumers.

In addition to dismay with the economy's tepid recovery, there's dissatisfaction with the Faustian bargain that many consumers made over the past decade. To satisfy our appetite for the good life, the country ran up debt 162% to an eye-popping $3.4 trillion. Now, faced with the payments on those loans, we feel more emptied than fulfilled by the things we bought. Indeed, given today's economic uncertainty, many Americans are re-evaluating their roles as consumers. That means not only looking for ways to trim unnecessary expenditures but also rethinking ingrained spending habits and recalculating the benefits you derive from them. The often surprising result is cost savings that actually improve one's quality of life.

For anyone who is reassessing their spending and lifestyle, this chapter should provide fresh insights and practical advice. The emphasis is on longer-term strategies that will help you save on your largest expenditures. Take most families' biggest asset, their home. Now that mortgage rates have dropped to almost 8%, many homeowners are weighing whether it pays to refinance their house sooner, later or not at all. Others see temptingly low interest rates and generally flat home prices as a terrific opportunity to purchase a lot more house for only a little more money. And some families are thinking of trading down to smaller, less expensive digs to slash their housing costs. We provide advice for all three situations—and much more.

Great Ways to Cut Expenses 20%

Here are five no-nonsense strategies that should help you slash your spending and possibly improve the quality of your life.

The Olney family of Redmond, Washington demonstrates how a household can indeed live far better on much less. Three years ago Pam Olney quit her $30,000 job selling office furniture to devote more time to raising her three children. She and husband Guy figured they had to reduce spending by $4,000, the amount her wages (a third of the couple's total income) added to the family's bottom line after taxes, child care and Pam's work-related costs.

So the Olneys embarked on a disciplined but hardly draconian expense-cutting program.

Instead of blowing $150 on dinner at local restaurants each week, they cooked at home. Rather than buy clothes at upscale Nordstrom, they shopped J.C. Penney. Checking their progress after one year, the Olneys got a shock. "We cut our spending in half," says Guy. "We had trimmed $16,000, not $4,000." What's more, the couple insist that their quality of life is better than ever. Says Pam: "We enjoy our less stressful life far more than the things we used to buy."

Of course, going on a crash-spending diet isn't a practical solution for everyone. But you can slash your costs by 20% or more by reducing major expenses as you rethink the way you live. On the following pages we've laid out strategies that, alone or combined, can reclaim one of every five dollars you spend:

Trade down to a smaller, less expensive house. The strategy of buying the biggest house you could afford seemed a fail-safe idea a decade ago, when prices climbed as much as 20% a year. No more. Housing prices in most areas are flat or falling, and housing analysts expect average appreciation of 5% or so a year—barely ahead of inflation—in the 1990s. And as property taxes have zoomed 50% since 1985 in some communities, owning an oversize house could become even more onerous.

Trading down works especially well for families who overextended themselves on housing. For example, scaling down to even one less bedroom can reduce your annual housing costs by about 10% of the difference between what you get for your old house and what you pay for the new one. Say you sell a four-bedroom home for $175,000 and use the equity, including appreciation, if any, to buy a three-bedroom house for $40,000 less. You would save roughly $3,800 a year in mortgage payments, taxes and upkeep. "For many people, that's the difference between accumulating wealth and living on the edge," says financial planner Richard Dirksen in Southfield, Michigan.

If you reap a profit, you would owe taxes on the gain, unless you qualify for the one-time capital-gains exclusion. But if falling prices have wiped out your equity, trading down would be impractical since you'd have to dip into savings for the down payment on your new house. Another option that's worth considering is to put in sweat equity to lower your housing costs and gain space. For example, Dan Gagliardi and his then fiancée Robin Eisenson sold his $80,000 two-bedroom condo and purchased a dilapidated 100-year-old three-bedroom colonial in Ossining, New York for $70,000. As a result, their

monthly mortgage payment dropped 30% from $1,050 to $725. They used the $20,000 profit from the condo to cover rehab expenses and pay off more than $8,000 in credit-card debt. "We have everything we want," says Dan. "We're just paying less for it."

Relocate to an area with lower living costs. Such a move would be a major disruption for many families, but there's a persuasive argument for considering it. Although the cost of living varies as much as 90% from the most expensive parts of the country (California and the Northeast) to the least expensive (Florida and Texas), salaries seldom vary by more than 25%. According to the Economic Research Institute in Newport Beach, California, someone earning $48,000 in Los Angeles would typically take no more than a 13% pay cut by moving to Atlanta. Yet his cost of living would drop by more than half. "That 50% boost in buying power could be the difference between never owning a home in a high-cost city and buying one the minute you settle down in a more affordable area," says James Angelini of Right Choice, a Derry, New Hampshire company that analyzes the financial impact of relocating from one city to another (typical cost of service: $190; 800-872-2294).

It was savings like this, plus the allure of a less hectic lifestyle, that led Bonnie Hayman and Richard Meyer to relocate from San Diego to Canandaigua, a town of 15,000 in New York's scenic Finger Lakes region. A month after the couple moved east with their two daughters, Richard landed a $60,000 job as a computer programmer in a nearby town. Bonnie, meanwhile, expects to earn $50,000 this year as a freelance technical writer, boosting the couple's income $5,000 above what it was in San Diego. But the real gain comes from their 40% drop in expenses (about $2,250 a month in Canandaigua, compared with nearly $3,700 in San Diego). For half the price of their $300,000 four-bedroom on a quarter-acre in San Diego, they found a three-bedroom ranch on a rolling acre in Canandaigua.

The couple decided to rent rather than sell out-right the San Diego house, hoping for a higher price when the housing market improves. Fortunately, the cash freed up by their new lower expenses enables them to hold out. "I don't know if this qualifies as having it all," says Richard, "but it comes close."

Opt for a highly rated public college instead of a pricey private one. Choosing a top public institution over a private school is a painless way to save upwards of $30,000 in just four years without sacrificing quality of education. This year the average private college charged $14,403 for tuition, fees and room and board. Comparable costs at public schools came in at a much more modest $5,488. (To learn more about the cost and quality of higher education, consult Chapter 8, "The Best Colleges for Your Money," and the companion MONEY rankings of 1,000 schools.)

You might elect to forgo this big annual savings if a private college guaranteed a better education. But that's not always the case. Even in the face of cutbacks triggered by state budget deficits, top-drawer public schools offer as good an education as some of the best private schools, according to a growing number of experts. "During the 1980s, states poured money into public universities to attract better teachers, who in turn attracted better students," explains James Mingle of the State Higher Education Executive Officers Association. "The Universities of North Carolina, Texas and Virginia, for example, are now low-cost elites."

Unfortunately, many parents still equate reputation with quality. That's the reason Jerry and Barbara Mayer of Parsippany, New Jersey decided to send their daughter Beth to Brandeis despite the $21,000 annual cost. After Beth's freshman year, however, financial difficulties forced her to transfer to a school she'd rejected earlier, the State University of New York at Binghamton, costing around $10,000. In her senior year, Beth said she's convinced that her education was not compromised. "Both schools have the same cal-iber of students and teachers and the same size classes," she says, "plus the social life is much better at Binghamton."

Join a health maintenance organization. If you've got a traditional health policy, you probably pay a yearly deductible of $100 to $500, 20% of covered medical costs and 100% of uncovered ones, including bills for prescription drugs and preventive services. These costs can mount steeply if your family includes chronically ill or elderly members or small children in constant need of checkups, immunizations and minor emergency care. An HMO, however, provides virtually all your care for a flat fee, usually with no deductible, and co-payments that average just $5 per office visit. These lower out-of-pocket costs translate into big savings of as much as $1,000 a year for a family of four.

If your household has above-average medical bills, the savings can be even greater, as they were for Bill and Linda Sarkisian of Auburn, Massachusetts. The couple decided to switch to the Fallon Health Care HMO after spending more than $1,100 in nonreimbursed expenses to care for their daughter Megan's chronic ear infections and mild neurological problems and her older sister's routine childhood maladies. Although the Sarkisians paid $341 more in premiums since moving to the HMO, they avoided $4,184 in out-of-pocket costs for CAT scans and neurological tests. As a result, their bottom-line savings were $3,843 over two years.

Reconsider whether earning more money really improves your life. Once you've reached a certain level of comfort, the return on extra earnings begins to diminish, particularly if the extra work erodes your quality of life. When working couples take a hard look at where that second paycheck goes, as Pam and Guy Olney did, they find that additional expenses usually suck much of it away. So if one of you is working for money rather than fulfillment, you may be able to improve your life by reducing spending and quitting the lower-paying job. That's usually the case if one of you earns two or more times as much as the other and child care and taxes consume 50% or more of the smaller salary.

Living better by spending less is certainly the philosophy of Amy and Jim Dacyczyn (pronounced *decision*) in Leeds, Maine. The couple have six children, and Jim has never earned more than $32,000 annually in his job as a Navy communications technician. Yet their disciplined saving allowed them to buy their dream house: a pre-1900, four-bedroom farmhouse on seven acres for $125,000. "We saved nearly $50,000 in seven years," says Amy. "The kids got garage-sale toys and homemade Popsicles. But they have a seven-acre playground to show for it now."

Does It Still Pay to Refinance?

Set aside the conventional wisdom about when to swap the mortgage on your house for a lower-rate loan. Our rules are better.

Listen! Those thuds you've heard over the past year or so were mortgage interest rates falling. Lately, with the national average for a 30-year fixed-rate mortgage at 8.25%, it's time to decide whether to join the stampede of homeowners who are trading in their old high-rate loans for new lower-ticket ones.

It is tempting. For example, swapping a $100,000 mortgage at 11% for a new one at 8.25% will cut your monthly loan payment $201, from $952 to $751. But don't dally in your decision-making. While it's possible that mortgage interest rates could slip a bit more, many forecasters expect those rates to rise slowly as the economic recovery finally begins to pick up steam this year.

So should you refinance or not? Here's how to find the answer. First, forget the conventional wisdom on refinancing, sometimes called the two-two-two rule. This principle says it makes sense to trade loans only if you have been in your home longer than two years, you expect to stay there for at least two years more, and your new interest rate is two percentage points below your current rate. Let's take the "twos" in order:

■ You must have lived in your house two years. This is based on the natural tendency to think that, after paying thousands of dollars in closing costs, you should hang on to the note long enough to get your money's worth. That logic is faulty. You cannot recover money you have spent. Your only hope is to minimize future costs. If refinancing makes sense on other counts, don't wait unless you think interest rates will drop a lot more.

■ You must stay put at least two more years. Another cliché. In fact, if the difference between your new and your old loans' interest rates is big enough, you can recoup the costs of refinancing in 12 months or less.

■ Your new rate must be two percentage points lower. Not so if you plan to remain in your house for more than a couple of years (the average homeowner stays seven). If you don't move for five years, you can come out ahead refinancing for a one-point improvement in rate, even with closing costs as high as 3% of the loan.

Instead of relying on misleading rules of thumb, concentrate on your motives. Are you thinking of refinancing mainly to cut your monthly payment, or do you want to reduce the total lifetime cost of your mortgage? If your aim is to trim the payment, the decision is simple. Shop for the best loan terms, considering not only the interest rate but also the transaction cost—that is, the sum of all fees, closing costs and points (each point is 1% of the loan amount). "You can usually get a lower rate by paying more points, and vice versa," says Paul Havemann of HSH Associates, a Butler, New Jersey firm that tracks loan rates.

Then, for each loan you are considering, figure how long you would have to stay in your house before the total of your monthly savings would offset the closing costs. The calculation isn't difficult: divide the dollar amount you would save on payments each month into the total transaction cost to find the number of months until you break even. If you don't think you'll be in your house long enough to reach the break-even point, forget the whole deal.

If you'll be there only a year or so past that point, go for the loan that reaches break-even fastest (often the one with the lowest transaction cost) so as to maximize the number of months beyond that critical juncture when you'll reap savings. But if you plan to be in the house for, say, three to five years past break-even, choose the loan with the lowest monthly payment even if you have to pay a few extra points or higher closing costs to get it. That lower payment will usually give you greater savings over time.

If your overriding goal is to cut the lifetime cost of your loan, your decision is more complex. To see why, suppose you had a $100,000, 30-year fixed-rate mortgage that you took out 10 years ago at 10.5% (monthly payment: $915). Suppose further that you could refinance to a new 30-year loan at a fixed 8.25% (monthly payment: $688) with transaction costs totaling $1,780. Since you would save $227 a month in payments, you could break even in a scant nine months. But since you would also be extending your payments by 10 years, you will actually wind up spending $28,260 more for the lower-rate mortgage over its lifetime (ignoring, for the moment, the effect of inflation).

The surest way to reduce the overall cost of such a mortgage is to refinance to a shorter-term loan. In the case described above, for instance, if you switched instead to a 15-year mortgage at the national average of roughly 7.8%, your monthly payment would drop $50 to $865, but you would pay off the note five years sooner and save $63,830 altogether. This strategy makes sense if you can afford the payments and want to be debt-free faster because, for example, you plan to retire in a few years.

Regardless of whether you refinance for short- or long-term savings, look for ways to reduce your cost and hassle. If you live in one of the 36 major markets covered by HSH, you can zero in quickly on the best deals by ordering a weekly list of mortgage offers in your area ($20; 201-838-3330). Or you can let someone else's fingers do the walking by hiring a mortgage broker to find your loan for you. Some brokers do not charge you anything directly, since they collect a portion of the points paid to the bank. Others levy a finder's fee of as much as 1%. If you deal with the lender who wrote your original mortgage, you might be able to shave the cost of title insurance by 20% to 25% by updating your existing policy instead of taking out a new one. And if your old mortgage required private mortgage insurance because your down payment was less than 20%, you may be able to drop the PMI the second time around if your home has appreciated in value or if you have built up more than 20% equity in the house. The savings? The equivalent of a quarter-percentage-point cut in interest rate, or about $27 a month on a 30-year, $150,000 loan.

Even if you can't swap mortgages, you can pare your overall cost by taking advantage of the seldom used option—permitted with most home loans—of prepaying extra amounts of principal each month. For example, if you add just $23 to the $658 you pay monthly on a $75,000, 10% fixed-rate mortgage, you'll retire the 30-year loan in only 25 years and save $32,580. That's not bad for an investment of just $23 a month.

When Trading Up Makes Sense

With mortgage rates temptingly low and home prices flat, now's a terrific time to purchase a lot more house for only a little more money.

David and Jeanne Albaneze sure know how to take advantage of today's still squishy real estate market. The couple traded up from a $250,000 home to one worth nearly $400,000 on a country club golf course in Ponte Vedra Beach, Florida near Jacksonville. Their new 4,750-square-foot traditional stucco house has twice the space and a spectacular view overlooking the third fairway. With a mortgage payment that's 27% (or $600 a month) higher than what they were paying, the couple are getting 50% more house.

Here's where their trade-up cleverness comes in. They first squeezed for and got a $24,000 rebate on their one-acre lot's price from the development company, which also threw in the country club's $12,500 entry fee. Next they bargained with a hungry contractor to construct the home for $79.58 per square foot, 28% below the standard charge, for a savings of nearly $145,000. Then they snagged a 30-year adjustable mortgage whose rate is locked in at 8.25% for the first five years, keeping their monthly payments to a manageable $2,840. "All of these steps helped us to afford the home we always wanted," says David, a Jacksonville investment adviser.

The Albanezes' success shows how astute buyers are capitalizing on today's market conditions to trade up to houses they could only wish for a few years ago. Despite some signs of life in the housing market lately, prices in the $175,000 to $230,000 trade-up range have not risen since the late 1980s in many regions (see the table on page 112). Then too, 30-year fixed-rate mortgages remain temptingly low at around 8.25%. By ditching a double-digit mortgage on your old house for a single-digit adjustable loan on a new

one, you may even be able to trade up without increasing your monthly payments. Couple this with the fact that appealing prices and low rates have drawn thousands of renters into the market for smaller, so-called starter homes, and you've got a recipe for trade-up nirvana. "Trade-up buyers had been holding back because they couldn't find people to purchase their current houses," says economist John Tuccillo of the National Association of Realtors. "Now, first-time buyers are liberating them."

Anyone looking to trade up should seek out real estate agents, sellers, builders and lenders who truly want to move the goods. To find out how to identify them, and for the sharpest advice on trading up today, MONEY interviewed dozens of agents, builders, bankers and housing analysts. Here are their best strategies to help you decide whether to move up and, if so, how to handle the tricky transition.

Determine whether it really pays to trade up. "You probably shouldn't bother unless you expect to live in your new house for at least three to six years," says financial planner Bob Frater of Houston Asset Management. "Otherwise, it's unlikely that the house will appreciate in value enough to pay back for your closing costs, real estate agent's sales commission and moving expenses. The total outlay could easily exceed 7% of the home's price." You also need to determine whether you can afford the higher mortgage payments, property taxes and upkeep expenses that a trade-up is likely to require. The numbers don't always work in your favor. Moving up in the Washington, D.C. area from a three-bedroom

What Trade-up Buyers Pay and Get

The typical move-up house is 11% to 14% larger and better appointed than the starter home or condo that most first-time buyers choose. Despite that universal formula, costs vary widely from as little as $123,000 in St. Louis to as much as $396,000 in San Diego, according to this Century 21 survey of the 20 biggest metropolitan areas. Trade-ups range from a modest 1,500-square-foot house near Baltimore or St. Louis to a comparatively lavish 3,400-square-foot place in the New York City suburbs. Best buy: Houston.

Location/price	Description
Atlanta $170,000	4 bed/3 bath, 2,750 sq. ft., built-in bookshelves
Baltimore $125,000	3 bed/2 bath, 1,500 sq. ft., screened-in porch
Boston $340,000	5 bed/2 bath, 2,200 sq. ft., large eat-in kitchen
Chicago $280,000	4 bed/2.5 bath, 2,300 sq. ft., 2.5-car attached garage
Cleveland $205,000	4 bed/2 bath, 2,500 sq. ft., two fireplaces
Dallas/Fort Worth $157,000	4 bed/2 bath, 2,550 sq. ft., formal dining room
Detroit $150,000	3 bed/2 bath, 1,800 sq. ft., cathedral ceiling w/fans
Houston $128,000	4 bed/3.5 bath, 2,600 sq. ft., pool, palm trees
Los Angeles $390,000	3 bed/2.5 bath, 1,700 sq. ft., terrace, brick patio
Miami $126,000	4 bed/3 bath, 2,350 sq. ft., library, courtyard
Minneapolis $240,000	3 bed/1.5 bath, 1,800 sq. ft., adjacent to country club
New York City $280,000	4 bed/2.5 bath, 3,400 sq. ft., fireplace
Philadelphia $188,000	4 bed/2.5 bath, 2,400 sq. ft., large family room
Phoenix $170,000	3 bed/1.5 bath, 1,775 sq. ft., pool, patio, fireplace
Pittsburgh $176,000	4 bed/2.5 bath, 2,400 sq. ft., prof. landscaping, country kitchen
St. Louis $123,000	3 bed/1.5 bath, 1,500 sq. ft., custom kitchen w/Jenn-Air range
San Diego $396,000	4 bed/2.5 bath, 2,300 sq. ft., vaulted ceilings w/skylights
San Francisco $345,000	4 bed/2.5 bath, 2,000 sq. ft., garden, family room
Seattle $229,000	4 bed/2.5 bath, 2,650 sq. ft., cathedral ceiling, big backyard
Washington, D.C. $365,000	4 bed/2.5 bath, 2,800 sq. ft., Jacuzzi hot tub, patio

$225,000 condominium to a four-bedroom $375,000 house, for example, could give you only 35% more house but at 65% more cost, according to Century 21, the national real estate brokerage. In such a case, you may be better off staying put and remodeling.

Don't buy until you've sold the house you now live in. Otherwise, if you encounter trouble unloading your current house, you could be stuck making two monthly mortgage payments. You needn't wait until your current house has gone through closing to bid on a move-up. But insist on a lender's commitment letter from the buyer that shows he'll get financing. At that point, feel free to get serious about your trade-up. If you'll be selling and buying in the same area, use one real estate agent to list your current residence and to help you find the next one. By giving one agent the chance to make two sales, you can probably get him or her to shave one to two percentage points off the standard 6% to 7% commission on the sale of your house. You'll need to negotiate with the agent to get such a discount. Then be sure the agent puts the arrangement in writing for you.

If you want to trade up to a new home, bargain hard with a builder. You can still get many builders to reduce their construction charges by 5% to 15% and to upgrade things like carpeting, windows and heating systems at no extra cost. And many custom builders can be talked into slicing at least 10% off the price of their lots too. Be sure to investigate the builder's reputation; the best ones should still be available for a cut-rate price. Visit several homes that he or she has constructed and ask their owners if they've had such problems as leaky pipes or faulty wiring. To make sure that your house is ready on time (figure between four and six months from ground breaking to finish), you should insist that the contractor sign a completion-date guarantee specifying a penalty of, say, $500 a day for each day that you are delayed from moving in.

Get the mortgage that's right for you. If you plan to stay in the home for only three or four years, go for an adjustable mortgage whose interest rate cannot rise by more than six percentage points over the life of the loan. The typical first-year rate recently was about 5.3% on a one-year adjustable tied to Treasury bills. Even if mortgage interest rates go up by two points a year, you'll never owe more than 11.3%. And if you move in three years, you will pay less overall with an adjustable-rate mortgage than with a fixed loan.

By contrast, if you expect to live in the new house for five to 10 years, sign up for a 30-year or 15-year fixed-rate mortgage and avoid worrying about rising mortgage payments. Because you pay off the note sooner, a 15-year fixed mortgage will cost about 25% more a month than a comparably sized 30-year loan. On the other hand, you will cut your total interest costs by nearly 60% over the life of the loan. And the interest rate on 15-year fixed loans is also about half a percentage point less than on 30-year loans.

How to Hold Down Your Hospital Bills

Nine out of 10 have mistakes, estimate insurance company auditors. We note the most common ones and tell you how to get a refund.

In 1991, Karen Staving, a bank credit clerk in Tampa, had jaw surgery at Humana Hospital in nearby Brandon. It was her fourth operation in four years to repair severe injuries from a 1987 car crash. Because her employer's insurer would not cover the operation, Staving had to pay the hospital $5,600 in advance—80% of the $7,000 estimated maximum cost. Fortunately, the surgery to repair the cartilage in her jaw went smoothly. But three weeks later the hospital billed her for $3,093, or $1,693 above the promised charge. To make matters even worse, when she examined the bill, she realized that it was riddled with errors, including charges of $28 for four cans of liquid protein that she never received and $76.44 for two tubes of Neosporin (an antibiotic ointment that sells in drugstores for $5 each), even though she got only one.

Unlike most medical consumers who don't complain because their insurers pick up much of their hospital costs, Staving was determined to fight back. First she won a quick $420 just by speaking to the hospital's billing department.

Next she fired off a complaint to the Florida Health Care Cost Containment Board, the state agency that regulates hospital finances. At the board's prodding, the hospital president wrote to her a month later. In the letter, he didn't admit any errors but said her bill would be reduced as a "courtesy" by $1,271. All told, Staving's persistence saved her nearly $1,700.

Faulty bills like Staving's cost Americans billions of dollars in unwarranted charges every year. Auditors hired by insurance companies estimate that more than 90% of hospital bills have some kind of mistake, often inappropriate or duplicate charges. Hospital executives agree with that percentage but maintain that 60% of those mistakes are undercharges. Most auditors disagree. "Two-thirds of the mistakes are in the hospitals' favor," says Gary Gelman of American Claims Evaluation, a national health-claims auditing firm in Jericho, New York. For example, Blue Cross/Blue Shield of South Carolina last year made a random study of 9,360 bills from 72 hospitals in the state and found that "only two of

Reading a Hospital Bill for Costly Mistakes

This hypothetical bill includes common hospital billing errors. Each entry explains what's wrong and how to correct the mistake.

1. Make sure these dates and times are correct. Some hospitals tack on a late charge if you leave after 12 p.m., but don't pay it if the hospital is the cause of the delay.

2. Be sure the charge reflects the type of hospital room you had. Most health plans pay 100% for semiprivate rooms only.

3. These intravenous antibiotic solutions are ordered 24 hours or more in advance. You may not use all—or any—of them, especially on the day you checked into the hospital.

4. You know it as Tylenol. Pharmacies may send up a lot of tablets at once, but if you didn't use six in one day, don't let the hospital nick you for that many.

5. A catheter is commonly used during and after surgery. Chances are you needed only one. This type of equipment often shows up in duplicate because so many staffers are involved in the billing process that it's easy for two of them to unknowingly charge you for the same device.

ADMISSION DATE / TIME			DISCHARGE DATE / TIME		
1/12/92 11:30 a.m.			1/15/92 10:00 a.m.		

INVOICE DATE	DESCRIPTION	CHARGE CODE	QTY.	TOTAL AMOUNT	INSURANCE PORTION	PATIENT PORTION
1/12/92	MED-SURG/PRIVATE	101	1	$280.00	$250.00	$30.00
1/12/92	AMPICILLIN 1 GM INJ	252	4	128.40	128.40	
1/12/92	IV D5W 100 ML	259	4	84.20	84.20	
1/12/92	ACETAMINOPHEN	045	6	42.85	42.85	
1/12/92	CBC	592	2	65.75	65.75	
1/13/92	MULTILUMEN CATHETER 7FR	989	2	250.70	250.70	

Total amount	$17,453.60	
Your insurer will pay	$14,835.20	
Pay this amount		$2,618.40

Source: AccuCost

the South Carolina hospitals produced bills without some kind of overcharge," says Charles Higgins of the health insurer's corporate audit division.

Auditors routinely turn up overcharges of 5% to 7% on most bills, which translates into more than $10 billion in overpayments to hospitals each year. Or put another way: if a hospital sent you a typical bill of $10,000, chances are you or your insurer would overpay by $500 to $700. And even if you or a family member is never hospitalized, you still pay for overcharges because insurers routinely pass on the cost to all policyholders in the form of higher premiums. In 1991, overcharges helped raise the average family's medical insurance outlays by 17.4% to $1,212. Much of the increase, of course, was related to the 7.9% jump in health-care costs.

Despite the high probability of errors, you can't count on your insurer or anyone else to double-check your hospital bills. Federal and state regulators rarely monitor hospital billing practices. And health-claims auditors review less than 5% of the 300 million hospital claims

processed annually, focusing on a handful of those totaling $10,000 or more—the ones likely to save insurers the most money.

You have to protect yourself. Your defense against overcharges ought to start on the day you check into the hospital. Charles Inlander, author of *Getting the Most for Your Medical Dollar* (Pantheon, $16), recommends that you, a family member or a friend keep a daily log, describing each doctor's visit, dose of medicine, X-ray and any other service that you receive. If you don't know the name of a drug or procedure, don't hesitate to ask a doctor or nurse for an explanation. After you are discharged, you should request an itemized bill or a copy of the one that will be sent to your insurer. Some hospitals normally give patients summaries that don't contain details of actual services or prices.

Then read the bill line by line for errors. For example, are the admission and discharge times correct? Hospitals sometimes wrongly charge patients for additional days, at $300 each. Don't be intimidated by cryptic entries. A $16 "hydration kit," for instance, is simply the plastic water pitcher in your room. Ask the hospital's billing department to explain anything you don't understand. If your bill is for more than, say, $20,000 or seems particularly complicated, insist that a billing staffer decode the charges in person. Here are the most common billing errors to watch for:

Inaccurate charges. Typos by a computer data-entry clerk can create wild mistakes. For example, a bill may list $450 for an X-ray that actually cost only $45. Also be aware of errors in so-called charge codes or procedure codes, which some insurers use to process reimbursements electronically. One wrong digit could change your $1,200 appendectomy into a $2,000 gallbladder operation. You won't be able to decipher the codes on your own. But if the charge seems high or your insurance company rejects it, call the insurer's service number to make sure that you have not been a victim of miscoding.

High prices alone aren't necessarily mistakes. Faced with Medicare price caps and discounted rates for patients who have managed-care employee-benefit plans, many hospitals try to balance their budgets by jacking up charges for patients who either lack insurance or are covered by conventional fee-for-service policies. That's why it is not uncommon today for a hospital to bill $6 routinely for an aspirin tablet that costs 2 cents at a drugstore.

Duplicate charges. Here's where your log comes in handy. Doctors frequently order drugs and tests in advance. For example, a doctor typically will request three or four batches of intravenous antibiotic solutions at $100 or so each, and the hospital will immediately charge them to your account. If the doctor later cancels one or more of the batches, you should get a credit on your bill. Often, however, the credit never comes because some hospital departments, such as pharmacy and central supply, are notoriously forgetful about posting refunds for patients. Also, in some cases, two people in the same department will mistakenly charge you for the same procedure. For instance, your hospital bill might show two or more listings for SURGERY 8 HRS at the rate of $1,000 an hour.

Inappropriate charges. These are items that you're billed for but don't receive. Sometimes records simply get mixed up; charges for, say, your hospital roommate's $150 electrocardiogram might wind up on your medical chart and eventually on your bill. In other cases, the billing department may assume you underwent a standard package of procedures, not all of which were performed. Auditors note that new mothers who keep their babies in their hospital rooms are often wrongly billed for use of the nursery at about $250 a day. Some hospitals, however, maintain that this charge is not an error for the simple reason that their nursery staffs still provide services to the babies.

Don't delay before complaining. To correct any

Where to Get Help

PEOPLE'S MEDICAL SOCIETY
(462 Walnut Street, Allentown, Pennsylvania 18102). As part of its $15 annual membership fee, this consumer advocacy organization will decode your hospital bill. The society can also tell you where to file complaints about billing errors and overcharges.

AMERICAN ASSOCIATION OF RETIRED PERSONS
(601 E Street N.W., Washington, D.C. 20049; attention: Medicare/Medicaid Assistance Program). AARP provides free assistance, even to nonmembers, in deciphering hospital bills and dealing with both Medicare and private insurers.

STATE CONSUMER AFFAIRS OFFICES
In most cases, these agencies handle hospital bill complaints, or a staffer will direct you to the appropriate government office. If you were hospitalized out of state, write to the consumer agency in the state where the hospital is located.

mistakes, you should start by calling the hospital billing department and sending a follow-up letter with all relevant information. "In most cases, the hospital will correct the mistake right away," says Dr. John Renner of the Consumer Health Information Research Institute, a non-profit consumer group in Kansas City, Missouri. You should also notify your insurance company about the error; most insurers print their toll-free telephone numbers on claim forms. If the billing department does not get back to you within two weeks, call or write to the hospital's patient representative or administrator. If a month passes with no response, you should find out from your insurer which individual handles complaints and then write to him or her directly.

And don't forget to ask your employer's benefits department to inquire too.

When all your other options fail, complain in writing to your state or local consumer affairs department. A few states, such as Florida and New Jersey, have special agencies that handle hospital bill problems. For instance, Dave Wisniewski, a staff engineer for Exxon in Florham Park, New Jersey, protested to the state utilization review board over a $5,400 hospital bill for the delivery of his son. Wisniewski noted in his letter that the fee was excessive compared with the itemized charges on the bill. After a brief closed-door hearing, the state agency had the hospital cut his bill by $549. Says Wisniewski: "Not a bad reward for one afternoon."

Slash Your Dry Cleaning Bills to Shreds

Fed up with paying exorbitant prices? Knowing these four dirty facts about the business can prevent you from being taken to the cleaners.

So many customers have got sore at their dry cleaners that the industry zoomed from No. 11 to No. 7 on the Better Business Bureau's list of the top consumer complaints, beating out even auto repair shops. Top of the chart: bad service, followed by lost items, ruined fabrics, wrecked colors and stains that remained.

Moreover, the rising cost of dry cleaning is becoming one of life's most begrudged expenditures. Whole legions of folks are getting hot under the collar. According to a telephone survey of 300 MONEY subscribers conducted by the Gallup Organization, 49% found dry cleaning not worth the price (including 62% of women) and 44% of those who changed cleaners switched because of poor service. Even more telling: 63% decided to buy an item of clothing recently for the sole reason that it didn't require dry cleaning.

America's obsession with cleanliness has helped spawn the dry-cleaning industry's rapid growth, with revenues now up to $8.1 billion from only $5.5 billion in 1985. When you combine that out-damned-spot habit with the rise of two-career families, dry cleaning turns very profitable. Most cleaner shops today average revenues of $190,000 annually and chalk up hefty net profit margins of 13%, as compared with the measly 1.6% after-tax margins typically found at grocery stores. Profits like that support one of the largest service industries in the U.S., employing more than 140,000 personnel in about 37,000 shops nationwide (most of which actually clean clothing on-premises).

Until the 1950s, cleaners were relatively inefficient middle-men. They routinely shipped clothes to the outskirts of town to large processing plants where soiled garments were dipped first in kerosene, then in gasoline solvents that lifted off grease, oil and food spots. Furthermore, since pressing was done mostly by hand, it took about a week to get a freshly ironed suit back to a customer. Then by the 1960s, following the invention of smaller, self-contained machines and less flammable chemicals, cleaners were able to install their own time-saving and money-making units.

The technique works like a large washing machine. (Yes, your clothes do get wet at the dry cleaner's.) Instead of water and soap powder, however, the perforated drum is filled with fast-drying "perk," a compound of carbon and chlorine that belongs to a class of toxic chemicals linked to cancer. Bottom line: today, 50 gallons of perk, which costs around $200, can clean 35,000 pounds of clothes.

As you already know too well, the improved technology and cheap raw materials haven't resulted in lower bills for consumers. On the contrary, prices have marched steadily upward, outpacing inflation in most years. The cost of dry cleaning a man's two-piece suit now generally ranges from $5.50 to $8 across the country (big cities are more expensive), a woman's silk dress costs from $4 to $8 and a laundered man's shirt costs $1.10 to $3. Among the priciest places to clean togs are Los Angeles and New York City, where it is not uncommon to pay as much as $9.25 for a man's suit and more than $18 for a woman's silk dress. Then there are the elite shops that can really clean you out. At Effrey's on Melrose Avenue in West Hollywood, if Liz Taylor sends in a dress that chicken has free-ranged over, the price is likely to run more than five times the national average.

Many of you who spend, say, $300 to $600 a year on dry cleaning may feel that you have no choice. But you do. We've compiled four dirty facts about the dry-cleaning business that can prevent you from being taken to the cleaners.

Know your spotter. While perk does perform miracles on clothes, the real magician at cleaning shops is the spotter, an employee who uses a steam gun and tiny brushes to dab away stains with an arsenal of chemicals like ammonia, hydrogen peroxide and acetic acid. If your cleaner tends to miss your stains, get to know your spotter. The very best establishments send spotters to dry-cleaning school every year for refresher courses on the latest techniques and chemicals. Courses are offered at both the regional chapters and the Silver Spring, Maryland headquarters of the International Fabricare Institute, the national association for dry cleaners. Patronize only those cleaners with experienced spotters. And be sure the owners invest in keeping their spotters up to date.

Don't fall for French cleaning. Once upon a time, dry cleaning was indeed French. The process is credited to a Parisian tailor named Jolie Belin, a clumsy oaf who in 1840 supposedly knocked over his kerosene lamp, spilling the liquid on his none-too-clean tablecloth. When the fabric dried—*voila!*—civilization took a significant step forward.

Why do some U.S. cleaners still hide behind the facade of French cleaning? Marketing. They're betting that customers will buy into the notion that "French" will carry higher quality—and thus pay more for it. The only difference between French dry cleaning and regular dry cleaning is about 50 cents a garment. "One-Hour Martinizing" is another marketing moniker frequently sighted on street corners. But in fact, it's just a brand name emblazoned on 806 shop doors in 44 states, making it the only national dry-cleaning chain. It pioneered the process of on-premises cleaning, but Martinizing now just means the usual.

Women are charged more than men. "For the past 20 years, women have been taken advantage of at the dry cleaners," says an indignant Barbara Anthony, assistant attorney general of Massachusetts. "Women have to argue and create scenes with cleaners over a lousy shirt." What Anthony is steamed about is paying three times the amount a man shells out to launder and press one plain cotton Brooks Brothers shirt in Boston. As a result, the state attorney general Scott Harshbarger has warned dry cleaners that they now face fines of as much as $5,000 per violation if they charge women more than men for the same service.

Despite the spate of recent protests and lawsuits, it still costs more to clean women's clothes. "It's not sexist," insists Patsy Woodard, owner of Atlanta's Quick as a Wink. "Women's clothes are more labor-intensive to clean." In addition, cleaners argue, women's blouses and shirts are usually too small to fit on the industry's standard machine-pressing form, called a bosom, and must be ironed by hand, which adds to the cost.

Perhaps. But when confronted, many cleaners are quick to lower prices. Several years ago, a group of George Washington University law students filed a formal complaint with the Washington, D.C. Office of Human Rights and Minority Business Development alleging that 25 local cleaners charged women 200% more than they charged men for the same cleaning services. The department agreed that such practices were illegal. As a result, the two major Washington, D.C. trade groups—the Metropolitan Dry Cleaners Association and the Korean Dry Cleaners Association—were among the first in the nation to ban such sex discrimination and to agree to unisex pricing. Women's prices subsequently plummeted to the men's level.

When there's a probelm, dry cleaners are at fault 25% of the time. We've all been there: on the eve of an important meeting, you find that the cleaner has managed to lose the one suit you always feel good wearing. Or you slip the designer linen out of the plastic sheath and find that the slacks have shrunk to knickers. When you march back to the shop, you're vehemently told: "It was like that when you brought it in" or "The manufacturer's instructions were wrong" or even this

industry favorite, "We have no record of that suit." It's the old game of tag. Everyone blames the last guy who touched the garment.

Here are the averages. About half the time, the manufacturer did mislabel the clothes. Another 25% of the time, you caused the damage. For example, you might have tried a home remedy before enlisting the pros—and permanently set the stain (so don't try it). Even more likely, when you're surprised by the damage, you spilled some liquid like champagne or ginger ale that dried without leaving an obvious mark. Once heated in the cleaning process, however, the spot oxidized and popped out. The remaining 25% of the time, the ruined clothes are the cleaner's fault, usually because the shop used the wrong chemicals or the item was scrubbed too hard. Yet even when you can prove it, you usually can't collect more than a fraction of the garb's replacement value.

The best advice is to read all manufacturers' cleaning labels carefully and, if you have any questions about the fabric, ask your cleaner to run a test on a part that won't show. Don't experiment with cleaning solutions at home. Get the stained item to the cleaners as soon as you can. And remember to retain your receipts.

In addition, keep these tips in mind:

■ Buy clothes that you can wash at home. Several designers such as Carole Little and Kikit are successfully introducing washable fabrics to their lines. Stores like The Gap and Banana Republic are doing a dynamite business in cotton, ramie and rayon style. Even Sears and Giorgio Armani (with his new A/X Armani Exchange) are following their wash-and-wear lead. "Easy-care fabrics are now on the rise," says Max Weinstein of Leslie Fay Dress Group.

■ Think twice before buying silk. The most expensive fabric to dry-clean, silk must be washed in light loads—usually half the normal 80-pound wash—and the delicate fabric makes spotting harder. And by all means, you should stay away from bright silks at bargain prices. These are often made with cheaper dyes.

■ Learn to live without pleated skirts or dresses. Most cleaners today charge an additional 15 to 20 cents for each pleat they press. Some shops have even been known to charge 60 cents a pleat. Say your skirt has 30. That's an additional $6 to $18.

■ Don't take your favorite sweater to a new cleaner. Start with an item of clothing that you can afford to lose, just in case.

■ Ask your cleaner to cover brass, gold, pearl or other metallic buttons with aluminum foil to avoid scratches. Request that sleeves be stuffed with tissue after pressing so they won't get crushed when hung on the cleaner's rack. Most expert cleaners do this free of charge. Many will even remove shoulder pads and then sew them back in—the same with buttons. So be sure to ask about your cleaner's practices.

■ Get outside help. For troubles with clothes that have inaccurate cleaning instructions on the labels, write to the Federal Trade Commission (Correspondence Branch, Washington, D.C. 20508), and it will notify the manufacturer. For garment analysis, ask your cleaner or local Better Business Bureau to send damaged goods to the International Fabricare Institute (12251 Tech Road, Silver Spring, Maryland 20904; 301-622-1900). Or check your Yellow Pages for a regional or local dry cleaners association. The largest regional group is the Neighborhood Drycleaners Association (116 East 27th Street, New York, New York 10016; 212-684-0945).

How to Pick a Top Summer Camp

Some camps charge nearly $4,000 a season. To get your money's worth, you need to know the answers to eight key questions.

Chances are, you whiled away childhood summers in your own backyard, bored a lot of the time. But whether you loved your summers or not, you'll probably send your offspring to camp. For many busy parents, camp is considered a must. Besides providing professional day care and a much appreciated breather for mom and dad, sleepaway camp can build a child's confidence, self-awareness and sense of independence. There may be unexpected benefits too. During four weeks at Frost Valley, a 550-camper coed camp in New York's Catskill Mountains, 12-year-old Beth Lee-Herbert had an epiphany. Says Beth: "I realized how much I like my sister Lisa."

There are more than 5,500 camps in the U.S., accounting for 5 million campers and an estimated $1.9 billion in revenue each year. Camp can cost as little as $100 a week for some non-profit cabins-in-the-woods or as much as $800 a week for places that promise specialized training or such self-improvement as weight loss.

Finding a camp where your youngster will thrive and you'll feel your dollars were well spent is likely to take a bit of time. You'll need to assess your child's individual development and disposition, gather leads and narrow your choices to a possible half-dozen options. Then you must evaluate each camp's atmosphere, range of activities and staff quality. Here are answers to key questions about shopping for a camp:

How do I know my child is ready for camp? Camps generally set seven or eight as their minimum age, but behavior (not birth date) is your real guide. A youngster who makes friends easily, enjoys overnights away from home and looks forward to going has the best chance of enjoying himself at camp. While it's never wise to force a child to go, some camps are more suitable than others for a child who needs a supportive environment. Two such nurturing camps, both of which accept kids as young as four, are Gwynn Valley in Brevard, North Carolina ($880 for two weeks; coed; 180 campers; 704-885-2900) and Heart's Bend in Newfane, Vermont ($2,900 for six weeks; coed; 65 campers; 802-365-7797). Both camps maintain baby-animal farms; tending tiny creatures makes kids feel well-tended themselves. If you have any doubts about your child's readiness for camp, limit his or her stay to no more than two weeks rather than six or seven.

How do I match camps to my kid's personality? If a youngster's worried about getting lost in the crowd, being the last one picked at sports or finding the bathroom at night, start checking out small, noncompetitive places that offer toilets inside the cabins. Bear in mind that most special-interest camps put pressure on kids to perform, and competition can run high at more traditional camps as well. At camps such as Emendal in Willets, California ($1,650 for four weeks; coed; 50 campers; 707-459-5439), athletics simply isn't an issue. While swimming and water sports are available at Emendal, kids spend most of their time at farm chores, including raising chickens and churning butter.

Some camps make a specialty of "values enhancement," the current buzzword for building character. At Agawam in Raymond, Maine ($3,250 for seven weeks; 128 boys; 207-627-4780), for example, staffers give each camper a weekly goal to work toward, such as developing greater patience or making new friends. But any well-run camp should provide worthy role models and abundant opportunities to work with others. And in any case, parents shouldn't count on a camp to reshape their child's character. "Camp can be a great way to nudge your child toward your family's values, but it's a mistake to try to instill those that are not represented at home," says Bob Ditter, a social worker who trains camp personnel in child development.

Whom can I trust for advice? A quick way to cut through the thicket of camps is to consult a professional adviser. They are more common in the East, but you can locate one almost anywhere through parents' groups, such as the PTA, or find one at the well-advertised camp fairs frequently held midwinter in large cities. Most advisers charge no fee to parents but collect a 15% commission from camps for each kid who enrolls after referral. Others charge $400 or so but collect no commissions. You run the risk that commissioned advisers will steer you toward the most expensive camps to increase their fee. But there's no guarantee of quality with fee-only advisers either. The best way to avoid these hazards is to do much of the legwork yourself, using advisers merely to suggest possibilities that you may have overlooked.

All camps must meet health and safety standards set by their states. About 1,400 camps have also been vetted by the American Camping Association, which runs a voluntary accreditation program. Some camps, including many of the best, don't feel they need the ACA vote of confidence, but the rating does offer a degree of reassurance. A few local ACA offices can refer you to accredited camps in your area (call the national office at 317-342-8456 or, for $11, purchase the ACA's directory).

Is expensive always better? Almost always. In general, high-priced camps offer more physical comforts, more supervision and more activities and instruction. But lower-end camps, which are likely to be those sponsored by Scouts, YMCAs and other nonprofit organizations, will introduce your child to a wider array of cultures and economic classes. So if such diversity is important to you, a cheaper camp may be best. Don't forget to calculate the real bottom line. Figure how much it will cost to get your child to and from camp and whether there might be extra charges.

How can I tell how good the staff is? Find out the median age of the staffers, including the administrators and support staff. If it's under 22, there may be too many college kids and too few experienced adults. Then ask for the ratio of counselors to campers. For youngsters under 12, it ought to be at least 1 to 6; over 12, 1 to 8 is okay. Training, however, is more important than numbers. "Get a copy of the counselors' orientation sheet," suggests Bob Ditter. "See if it covers how to handle homesickness and bedwetting rather than just sing-alongs."

Inquire too about staff turnover. The two Wohelo camps for girls in South Casco, Maine ($3,350 for seven weeks; 200 girls; 207-655-4739) have been run by the same family since 1907, and 50% of last year's counselors had been Wohelo counselors before. Look for continuity among campers too. For nonspecialty camps, at least 50% should be repeat visitors.

How do I check on camps during the winter? A good way is simply to call parents of kids who have attended in the past. Naturally, the camp will provide only the names of satisfied customers, but you can ask those parents for names of other parents, including some who were not

satisfied. You might also have your prospective camper talk to previous campers for the kid's-eye view. For the past six summers, for example, Jon MacAlpine, 13, of Summit, N.J. has spent three weeks at the YMCA's Frost Valley. He also attends Boy Scout camp during other times of the year. "At Scout camp, they trust us to entertain ourselves," Jon remarked recently. "At Frost Valley, we're constantly supervised. It gets to be annoying at my age."

What common mistakes can I avoid? Two issues many parents overlook may loom large to a kid: what he eats and who sees him undressed. For instance, at many camps, nonnutritious snacks like soda and candy are banned, which may be too strict for your junk-food junkie. Similarly, if your daughter is unaccustomed to taking showers with other girls, she may be overwhelmed by the communal bathing experience at some camps. Another potential pitfall is communication with home while the kid's away. At most camps, letters are welcome, while phone calls are discouraged. Rules vary, however, so before signing up, you should find out exactly how a request to call home is handled, and make sure your child is comfortable with the policy.

Protecting Your Financial Privacy

Here's what today's insatiable data gatherers know about your finances, whom they are selling your secrets to and what you can do to stop them.

Kelly Gardner, an office manager who moved from Atlanta to Washington, D.C. six years ago, never dreamed she would have to take an apartment on a block with an open-air drug market because a credit bureau wouldn't listen to reason. But someone opened an Atlanta Gas Light account in Gardner's name three months after

she left Atlanta and then closed it in June 1990 without paying the $29 balance. Gardner quickly convinced Atlanta Gas that the bill wasn't hers. Yet for several months, Gardner couldn't get Equifax Credit Services to remove the debt from her credit report, where it labeled her an undesirable tenant. "I couldn't go to any apartment buildings run by management companies because they make you apply and pay for a credit check," says Gardner. She finally found a landlord with the apartment near the drug market who called her references directly. An Equifax spokesman responds that the credit bureau corrected the problem immediately after the utility sent the proper information. Police chased the drug dealers away, and Gardner's new landlord recently installed a security fence and a spotlight.

Gardner is just one of many Americans who've run afoul of the information industry, a vast network of companies that collect, massage and sell such personal financial secrets as roughly how much you earn, the size of your mortgage and whether you've ever bounced a check. "Most victims don't come forward because they're embarrassed," says David Linowes, former chairman of the U.S. Privacy Protection Study Commission. "But for every privacy-related problem that's visible, there are at least a thousand others out there."

Since the 1970s, increasingly sophisticated computer technology has made it possible for companies to strip away much of your financial privacy. Many of these companies are ones you do business with directly—retailers, banks, brokers, mutual funds—but others are firms you've probably never heard of. The invisible players include the $1 billion credit reporting business and the $1.3 billion industry that mixes, matches and markets consumer data.

This trend isn't all bad. Some of the biggest benefits arise when companies use data bases to find better ways to serve their customers. Your bank may remind you that your large savings balance entitles you to free checking—a perk you had overlooked. Or your long-distance phone company may note your frequent calls to Miami and offer discounted volume rates. Or an airline may send you coupons good for discounted flights. Also, by scanning for unusual volume or buying patterns, companies can alert you to fraud or scams. U.S. Sprint, for instance, puts computers to work finding illegal card users, thus

saving millions of dollars a year. You save too because Sprint catches fraudulent calls that you might have missed.

Still, as the collection and use of information have mushroomed, so have the opportunities for mistakes, misuse and abuse. Even at best, the information industry can be a nuisance, generating phone pitches just as you sit down to dinner and stuffing your mailbox with junk. Spiegel alone mails out some 65 different catalogues for its Spiegel, Honeybee and Eddie Bauer units each year. And the average American now receives 78 catalogues a year. Worse, some breaches of privacy have serious consequences. For instance:

■ Thousands of upstanding consumers have been denied house or apartment rentals, jobs,

MONEY HELPS

Q. Last year my purse and checkbook were stolen and the thief forged some checks. I notified the various credit reporting firms and filed affidavits with them saying the checks had been forged. But stores still won't take my new checks. Why is this happening?
— Linda Fernandes, La Mesa, California

A. Two of the companies involved—TeleCheck and Telecredit, a subsidiary of Equifax, the credit reporting bureau—were a bit sloppy. When either company receives an affidavit of fraud, they flag your driver's license number. Alas, that number, like your Social Security number, generally stays with you forever. Since you and the forger were using the same tainted driver's license for ID, your checks were being refused even though you opened a new checking account. TeleCheck merchants were supposed to give you a special telephone number to call if a check is refused so that you can clear up the problem right in the store, but apparently none of them did that. Telecredit was supposed to ask for a confidential password to distinguish you from the forger, but it didn't. Your luck may be changing, though. The forger was apprehended, and both firms have now dropped your driver's license from their hit lists.

mortgages or other loans because of erroneous or misleading information in their credit files. Eugene Wolfe, a retired Navy speechwriter from McLean, Virginia, paid 16% instead of the customary 12% interest on a new-car loan and was rejected for a $1,200 personal loan because information about another man with a similar name appeared on his credit report.

■ A growing number of workers are losing or being denied jobs because of leaks of medical or insurance data to employers. Robert "Poe," who asked that his real name not be used, says that he was fired from his job at a California computer dealer after his insurer told the company that Poe had tested positive for HIV, the AIDS virus.

■ Americans have been defrauded out of hundreds of millions of dollars by telemarketers who use personal financial data to identify people vulnerable to pitches for what turn out to be phony credit cards, loans or contest prizes. William Bennett, a retired Army officer in Mount Morris, Michigan, says that he received more than a dozen misleading credit-card and contest prize offers after telemarketers purchased his name, address and the fact that he was rejected for a Citibank Visa.

The erosion of privacy clearly angers many Americans. A recent telephone poll of 300 MONEY subscribers conducted by the Gallup Organization found that 68% object to the sale of even their name and address. More than 80% do not want their telephone number or estimated income sold. Over 70% would prefer that businesses be barred from selling personal data at all, even if that meant they wouldn't receive useful information. In order to lift the veil on the unseen market in personal information and to explain its dangers, MONEY interviewed some 200 privacy advocates, marketing experts, law enforcement officials and executives in 10 industries that make heavy use of consumer data. We also talked to dozens of victims of the system.

What emerged was a worrisome picture of how little privacy the average American actually enjoys. For just $400 or so, virtually anyone can

find out your age, hobby, estimated household income and whether you have children. Financial information is also plentiful, including the credit cards you hold, how much you spend on travel or eating out each year and what products you buy. Companies use these bits of information individually or combine them with other data to draw conclusions about you and your family. An insurer, for instance, might target you for a Medicare supplement if you're over 65, drive an upmarket car and play tennis. The car indicates you can afford the premiums, and the exercise suggests you won't file many claims. Such information is typically rented on a limited basis rather than sold.

Where do companies get these detailed data? Mostly from you. Sears, for instance, uses new account applications and customer transaction records to track the 70 million households that buy from its stores or subsidiaries. Among the people in the company's computers: Sears catalogue users, Discover credit-card holders, and clients of Sears' Allstate Insurance arm, its Dean Witter securities brokerage and Coldwell Banker real estate agency. "We know where these people live, how many are homeowners vs. renters, and what kind of car they own," notes Allstate's John Gragnola. Sears' computers can spew out, say, lists of Allstate customers who might be interested in stock tips from a Dean Witter broker.

Mail in a manufacturer's product-registration card for many products and you'll enter the data bank of a unit of the R.L. Polk organization in Detroit. Polk is one of three powerful companies that, among them, track the finances, interests and lifestyles of as many as 95% of the nation's 94 million households. The others are Donnelley Marketing in Stamford, Connecticut and Metromail in Lombard, Illinois. The registration cards, which Polk's National Demographics & Lifestyles unit collects for manufacturers, are just one of many sources Polk taps. From the cards, Polk learns respondents' hobbies and other interests and can sort people into one or more of about 60 categories, from hikers to real estate

THE 10 BIG BUSINESSES THAT HAVE YOUR NUMBERS

This table outlines the vast array of often confidential information that businesses may have compiled on you in addition to your name, address and phone number. You divulge a number of facts willingly. However, lots of personal details—shaded below—are purchased from data bases, public records or other sources without your knowledge. The information that changes hands is typically rented on a limited basis. Still, it's frequently used in ways you never intended. The specifics, of course, vary by company.

BUSINESS	WHAT THEY KNOW	WHAT THEY DO WITH IT	HOW YOU CAN STOP IT
Banks and thrifts	Your balances and transactions for all bank accounts, including loans and investments made through the bank; how profitable your account is Your age, your children's ages, estimated income, value of your home and car; how long you've lived in your home; how many credit cards you hold; how frequently you use them; estimate of your creditworthiness	They use it to identify additional services and products that they can sell you through statement stuffers and other mailings; they provide loan-payment information to credit bureaus; they share customer names with affiliated brokers, insurance agents or others who sell financial services.	Tell a customer service representative or bank officer to flag your file so you will no longer be solicited for bank and other financial products.
Credit bureaus	Age, Social Security number, balances on credit cards, mortgages and other personal loans; when you opened these accounts; your payment record and credit limits; any bankruptcies, judgments or liens; who requested your credit information within the past two years; your payment patterns. An Equifax unit collects information on your driving record. Your job, your spouse's name, number of children, previous addresses, estimated income, value of your car and home	They sell credit reports to lenders, utilities and employers; TRW and Trans Union identify credit-card holders, mail-order buyers, people who moved recently and prospects for financial service companies and other marketers; Equifax provides this type of information to financial institutions; its insurance division gives life and health insurers information about your lifestyle and driving record.	You can't stop a bureau from providing information without cutting off your access to credit. You can write any of the three major credit bureaus and request that your name not be used for marketing purposes. The three: Equifax Options (P.O. Box 740123, Atlanta, Ga. 30374); TransUnion Name Removal Option, TransMark Division (555 W. Adams St., Chicago, Ill. 60661); TRW Marketing Services (600 City Pkwy. West, Suite 1000, Orange, Calif. 92668, Attention: Mail Preference)
Credit-card issuers	What types of products, when and where you buy by credit card; your payment history and outstanding balances; how long you have had the card; your age and your estimated income Your hobbies; number of children; the value of your home and car	They use it to target people for specific credit offers or mail-order products; provide payment status and outstanding balances to credit bureaus; they rent lists of cardholders by age, sex and location; a few rent lists of customers based on types of purchases.	You can't stop the collection of credit-related information; to stop sales pitches, write your credit-card company or call its customer service 800 number.
Insurance companies	Life and health insurers: age, marital status, sex, medical history, driving record, other policies held with insurer, number and ages of your children, your spouse's age; for large policies, insurers may also investigate your lifestyle and financial status in depth. Auto and property insurers: the value and type of your home; make and model of your car; names and ages of the drivers in your family and their driving records. Estimated income, your level of education, when you married, divorced, bought a house or car; estimated value of your home; the likelihood of your buying certain insurance products; your hobbies and athletic interests	They use it to identify potential customers for insurance agents; lifestyle information also helps the insurer to determine policy premiums; some insurers rent lists of former customers as well as names of others who simply inquired about insurance products.	Write or telephone your insurance agent and tell the agent that you do not want any solicitations.

BUSINESS	WHAT THEY KNOW	WHAT THEY DO WITH IT	HOW YOU CAN STOP IT
Magazines	How you subscribed and for how long; whether you moved recently; other magazines, books and records you may have ordered from the same publisher. Some publishers poll subscribers to find out job titles, age and more. Age, estimated income, education, number of children, how long you've lived at your address, what publications you usually read, your leisure activities	They use it to sell you magazines and other products offered by the same publisher; they rent lists of subscribers to catalogues, other publications, charities, fund raisers, newsletters and companies interested in selling their related products to the magazine's subscribers.	Write to the publisher's customer service department.
Mail-order companies	What you buy, when you do it, and how much you spend; whether you buy by credit card; whether you order by phone or by mail; whether you buy on sale; what sizes you order Your age, occupation, whether you own a home, size of your home	They use it to identify other merchandise they can sell you; they rent or swap it with other catalogue companies, magazines and nonprofit groups.	Write to the company's name-removal service. Or write to Direct Marketing Association Mail Preference Service (P.O. Box 3861, 11 W. 42nd St., New York, N.Y. 10163) and request that you be dropped from lists.
Mutual funds and brokerage firms	Your investments with the company, how often you trade securities or switch funds; how much you typically invest and whether you use a systematic investment or withdrawal plan; which investment products you have requested information about Estimated income, your age, number of children and ages; whether you live in a high-income area with high tax rates; whether you own your home	They use it to pitch specific products to customers—single-state tax-free funds to high-income customers, for example; a few funds and discount brokers rent customer and prospect lists to financial publications, nonprofits and mail-order companies.	Ask your broker or fund service representative to delete your name from marketing lists.
Retail chains and department stores	Exactly what you buy; how much you spend per store visit and per year; how you pay Age, estimated income, type of home; whether you own certain models of cars	They use it to target you for discount coupons, sales and promotions; some stores swap or rent lists of customers to magazines, financial service companies and nonprofits.	Call the marketing department and ask that your name be removed from its lists.
Super-markets	If you are a member of a frequent-shopper program: how much you spend per visit, per week and per year; what types and brands of food and nonfood items you buy; they may also have personal information that was gleaned from your application Your age, estimated income, number of children, whether you work full or part time or are retired, and whether you are the family's primary grocery shopper	They use it to provide you with discounts and coupons tailored to your shopping patterns; determine what merchandise to carry; they may pass along information to, say, cereal or pet-food companies to help them determine whether their advertising is motivating the right customers.	Tell your store manager you don't want your personal information used for marketing purposes.
Telephone companies	What numbers you call and how often; whether you are a frequent caller of 800 or 900 lines; your payment history Estimated income; number and ages of children; interest in foreign travel; size of your home; marital status; occupation	They use it to sell you other services; some regional phone companies rent names, addresses and phone numbers to local merchants and national marketers; long-distance companies provide companies that buy 800 and 900 lines with phone numbers of 800 and 900 callers.	Write your local phone company's customer service department saying you don't want your name rented.

investors. Then, for anywhere from $10 to $100 per thousand names, it rents prospect lists to sporting goods merchandisers, magazine publishers, insurers and other marketers.

Various divisions of Time Warner, the company that publishes MONEY, among other magazines and books, also rent customer names. These names are made available only to buyers who adhere to strict conditions, such as agreeing not to telephone subscribers. Time Warner magazines take steps to protect you from deceptive offers. Before releasing a MONEY mailing list, for example, the magazine's marketing staff sees copies of the materials to be sent out. (Subscribers who prefer that their names not be rented can write to MONEY Customer Service, P.O. Box 60001, Tampa, Florida 33660.)

You don't have to buy a product or service to provide a firm with information about you. Mutual fund companies such as Value Line sell lists of people who merely inquire about services, while Fidelity and Vanguard, among others, use such information themselves. And data collection often becomes an end in itself, rather than the means to a sale. A Scottsdale, Arizona branch of the Circuit City electronics chain refused to sell a TV set to Kenneth Bates, a general contractor, unless he provided his name, address and phone number—even though he was paying cash. "I just couldn't believe it," says Bates, who finally made up the answers. A Circuit City spokesman says the firm requires personal data only for credit-card sales and deliveries, and just requests it on other sales. Requiring personal data for credit-card sales is illegal in California, Delaware, Georgia, Maryland, Minnesota, Nevada, New Jersey and New York.

What you don't divulge to the data gatherers can often be yanked from public records. You may think the "public record" is open only to someone who wants to spend the day poring over dusty ledgers in county courthouses. But many federal, state and local government agencies sell computerized data to commercial organizations. Available to anyone from local car

dealers to national marketers are property tax rolls, motor vehicle registrations, workers' compensation filings and police reports. Polk is one of 23 companies that pay the U.S. Postal Service $48,000 annually for a list of U.S. addresses that's updated twice a month. Marketers buy this information to update their mailing lists and, more important, to target people who have moved recently, because they are likely to spend on household goods and lawn care. Companies make heavy use of U.S. Census Bureau data too. Even though specific data are confidential, users can extrapolate information about you. For example, they can come close to figuring your earnings by using a Census Bureau neighborhood average.

Credit bureaus get their data, which include outstanding loans, credit-card balances and liens, from lenders and public records. They use the information primarily to verify a customer's creditworthiness. But two of the three largest credit bureaus, TRW and Trans Union, also sell information about credit-card ownership and other personal financial matters to cataloguers and other marketers. The third, Equifax, stopped selling data to direct marketers in 1991 but still offers this information to financial institutions.

Hundreds of small firms such as W.S. Ponton in Pittsburgh compile and rent specialized mailing lists such as newsletter subscribers or real estate investors. Bigger companies like Infobase Services in Conway, Arizona act as middlemen to resell information to marketers that was collected by bigger compilers. And more specialized data outfits track bounced checks, accident victims or troublesome tenants.

While usually benign, the information machine has grown so big and powerful that it can do serious harm when it malfunctions. The most publicized problems, of course, concern errors in credit reports. Credit reports are among the largest sources of consumer complaints received by the Federal Trade Commission. Because credit reports are used by lenders and employers, mistakes can cost you a loan, a job or a mortgage. Correcting errors hasn't been easy, either. Consumers who complained to the FTC about mistakes in their credit reports had already spent an average of 23 weeks trying to clean up the problems, according to an analysis of 155 consumer complaints by the U.S. Public Interest Research Group.

Credit bureaus have historically given short shrift to consumer complaints, refusing to settle disputes quickly and insisting that the creditor, not the customer, supply documents that prove an error. And because credit bureaus do not share corrections, consumers may have to communicate with all three to take care of each error. But public pressure is forcing some improvements. For example, TRW now has policies to verify, modify or delete disputed information within 30 days of a complaint; to accept documentary proof from consumers; and to make its reports easier to understand. TRW will also provide one free credit report each year to any consumer who requests it (phone 214-235-1200). The other bureaus charge as much as $20, though all consumers are entitled to a free report if they are denied credit.

Yet even correct data can do damage if it falls into the wrong hands. Many banks, for instance, allow customers to check account balances by punching their Social Security number and account number into a Touch-Tone phone. One San Francisco woman was disturbed to learn that her estranged husband was routinely tracking her checking and savings account transactions that way and then using that information in their divorce proceedings.

An innocent misstep can also cause big problems when it becomes part of computer records. Ben Kawamura, manager of minority outreach for the City of San Francisco, forgot to let a $54 check clear before he closed a Security Pacific checking account in January 1990. Kawamura was then turned down for a new checking account because the bounced check made him a bad credit risk in the eyes of ChexSystems, a computerized service used by banks for fraud

protection. A ChexSystems spokesman says it's the bank's responsibility to correct errors. Security Pacific says it reports losses or mismanagement on its accounts to ChexSystems.

You can be harassed at work or even lose your job if confidential information about large medical bills, pregnancy, mental illness or AIDS is passed on to your employer by its insurer or by administrators who handle claims. Privacy experts fear that such cases, though now infrequent, could become more common as rising health-care costs force companies to scrutinize employee medical bills.

Robert "Poe," mentioned earlier, injured his back by lifting a 90-pound computer monitor while working for Intelligent Electronics, a San Francisco computer dealer. When a doctor wanted to verify Poe's disability for the company's insurer, Poe explained to the doctor confidentially that he'd tested HIV positive. Poe returned to work after three months of recuperation from the back injury. "My new supervisor wouldn't come within five feet of me, and other people weren't friendly either," recalls Poe, who says he was fired soon thereafter. Poe is suing the insurer and the doctor, charging that his HIV status was included in a report to the insurer and eventually passed on to his employer. Poe has received $14,000 to settle his workers' compensation and wrongful discharge claims. But the company, doctor and insurer all refuse to comment.

On-the-job injuries can also prevent workers from finding future employment. John Lavergne, an oil roustabout, says he was fired by Mayronne Enterprises of Harvey, Louisiana after injuring his back by lifting drilling equipment. He was then told he would be blacklisted if he filed for workers' comp. Mayronne denies that it threatened Lavergne but admits to sending information to Employers' Information Service, one of several companies that sell workers' compensation data to employers.

Scam artists also use information from the data chain to target people for fraud. For example, you can be billed for goods or services you didn't order if someone buys a list that includes not only your name, address and phone number, but also your credit-card number. Lyle Woodruff, head of security for the Christmas Mountain Resort in Wisconsin Dells, bought two hand mixers advertised on TV from a company called Quantum Marketing. Woodruff says Quantum then sold his name, address and credit-card number to Discount Travel Club of Darien, Connecticut, which charged him $50, and also sold it to International Value Network of Des Moines, which billed Woodruff for $192 in merchandise. A lawyer for Discount Travel's parent firm says a mistake might have been made in Woodruff's case.

With research and ingenuity, con artists can buy enough information to credibly pose as someone else. In 1989, Robert Fine Jr. trolled property tax records to locate vacant land in Los Angeles and Orange counties. Fine then bought reports on the land's owners from a Burbank credit reporting agency. Using those data, Fine impersonated the owners and was approved for over $600,000 in loans against the land. Luckily the landowners weren't hurt. Fine pleaded guilty to mail fraud in May 1990 and is appealing his sentence.

You're especially vulnerable when scam artists know your specific interests, personal characteristics or weaknesses. Many telemarketers buy lists of Gold Card holders to pitch nonexistent vacations or contest prizes that actually cost money. Or senior citizens are targeted for unnecessary medical equipment based on their age or the fact that they live in a retirement community. "Lots of information sources can be merged to produce a fairly precise group that might be susceptible to a particular offer," says Laureen France, an FTC investigator in Seattle.

The FTC has cracked down on the largest of these operations. Listworld Inc., a Huntsville, Ala. mailing list broker that claimed to have files on 140 million Americans, allegedly offered one-stop shopping to telemarketer boiler rooms, selling not only lists of names and phone numbers

but also phone scripts used to pitch low-interest credit-card and loan packages. "All the boiler-room operator had to do was provide phones and bodies," says FTC attorney Charles Harwood. Listworld president Daniel Klibanoff signed a consent decree with the FTC not admitting guilt but agreeing to monitor the practices of client telemarketers.

One Listworld victim was Robert Wilson, a real estate leasing agent in Akron who had more than $5,000 in credit-card debt. Wilson paid $129 for a low-interest credit card but received only some worthless pamphlets and two bank-card applications. Wilson was rejected for one credit card because the application was phony and the second because he was overextended. Wilson wasn't alone. Listworld and the telemarketers with which it worked defrauded consumers out of roughly $250 million over two years, say sources familiar with the industry. Listworld bought the names of credit-card holders from major credit bureaus. And, sources say, Listworld obtained the names of rejected credit-card applicants that were sold by an employee of a major bank. Klibanoff denies using a list of rejected credit-card applicants and, he says, the telemarketers were responsible for any alleged fraud. He says he merely provided lists and completed the mailings.

The fact that Listworld settled with the FTC should not make you complacent, however. Many privacy experts say that another 10 to 15 companies are actively brokering this kind of information. Here are the steps you can take to protect your financial privacy:

■ Don't fill out surveys or product-registration cards if you don't want your answers marketed. You'll still qualify for all full and most limited warranties.

■ Request a personal identification number instead of your Social Security number for phone access to bank, brokerage or mutual fund accounts.

■ Don't buy products from companies you don't know that are sold on TV or by telephone.

■ Make sure your credit reports are accurate. Request a copy from each of the three main credit bureaus: Equifax Information Service Center (P.O. Box 740241, Atlanta, Georgia 30374; 800-685-1111); TRW Consumer Assistance Center (P.O. Box 749029, Dallas, Texas 75374; 214-235-1200); and Trans Union National Consumer Disclosure Center (25249 Country Club Boulevard, P.O. Box 7000, North Olmsted, Ohio 44070; 216-779-7200). Include your name and all the variations you have used in the past, your address and your Social Security number.

■ To get your name off mailing lists, write to the Direct Marketing Association (P.O. Box 3861, 11 West 42nd Street, New York, New York 10163) and request that you be dropped from lists.

Where to Find Free Financial Advice

From banking and credit to retirement planning, these publications provide information that's both accurate and reasonably unbiased.

Free advice is not always worth what you pay for it. The free or nearly free (top cost: $3) brochures, pamphlets and books listed here can provide valuable information on financial topics ranging from resolving credit-card billing disputes to planning your estate. The publications are useful if you do your own financial planning. But they can also save you time and money when dealing with professionals by suggesting the right questions to ask and teaching you enough financial jargon to understand the answers.

One of the most prolific purveyors of free facts is the federal government, which produces around 50 personal-finance brochures (we cite two of the best below). For a rundown of what's available from Uncle Sam, or to request the brochures themselves, write to the Consumer Information Center, Pueblo, Colorado 81002. Since most industry-sponsored handbooks are little more than thinly disguised sales pitches, we included only the publications we judged to be both accurate and reasonably unbiased. When requesting a publication, be sure to enclose a self-addressed, stamped envelope. When organizations appear more than once, we give the address or phone number at the first mention.

BANKING AND CREDIT

■ *Consumer Credit Handbook* (Consumer Information Center, Item No. 441Y; 50 cents). Tells you how to fix errors on your credit report and what you should do if you're turned down for a credit card.

■ *The Consumer's Almanac* (American Financial Services Association, Consumer Credit Education Foundation, 919 18th Street N.W., Suite 300, Washington, D.C. 20006; $2). Includes worksheets that can help you keep track of your monthly expenses. The association also publishes the brochure, *What You Should Know Before Declaring Bankruptcy*.

■ *How to Get Safety Information From Your Financial Institution* (Weiss Research, 2200 North Florida Mango Road, West Palm Beach, Florida 33409; $2). Contains questions to ask your bank, broker or insurer to gauge how much risk they are taking with your money.

■ *Managing Family Debt* and *Getting Out of Debt* (Bankcard Holders of America, 560 Herndon Parkway, Suite 120, Herndon, Virginia 22070; 703-481-1110; $1 each). Both of these informative brochures offer budgeting strategies and helpful tips on using your credit cards.

FINANCIAL PLANNING

■ *Estate Planning: A Guide for the Days After a Loved One Dies* (Aetna Public Service Library, RWAC, 151 Farmington Avenue, Hartford, Connecticut 06156; 203-273-2843).

■ *Money Matters* (AARP-Fulfillment, 60 E Street N.W., Washington, D.C. 20049). Helps you choose a tax preparer, lawyer, financial planner and real estate broker.

■ *Selecting a Qualified Financial Planning Professional* (The Institute of Certified Financial Planners, 7600 East Eastman Avenue, Suite 301, Denver, Colorado 80231; 800-282-7526).

FRAUD

■ *Avoiding Travel Problems* (The American Society of Travel Agents, The Fulfillment Center, 1101 King Street, Alexandria, Virginia 22314).

■ *Investment Swindles: How They Work and How to Avoid Them* (National Futures Association, 200 West Madison Street, Suite 1600, Chicago, Illinois 60606; 800-621-3570).

■ *Phone Fraud, We All Pay* (The National Association of Consumer Agency Administrators, 1010 Vermont Avenue N.W., Suite 514, Washington, D.C. 20005; 202-347-7395). Tells you how to guard against such rip-offs as calling-card abuse and phony third-party charges.

INSURANCE

■ *A Personal Property Inventory* (Aetna). Provides forms that guide you in listing and describing your valuables to make it easier for you to file insurance claims.

■ *Here Today, Gone Tomorrow* (The Insurance Information Institute, 110 William Street, New York, New York 10038; 212-669-9218). Includes a glossary of basic insurance terms and points to remember when you buy renter's insurance. Among the institute's other useful brochures: *Auto Insurance Basics, Tenants' Insurance Basics* and *How to File an Insurance Claim.*

■ *Shaping Your Financial Fitness* (National Association of Life Underwriters, 1922 F Street N.W., Washington, D.C. 20006). This helps to explain the ins and outs of annuities, Medigap insurance and other mystifying products.

■ *The Consumer's Guide to Health Insurance* (Health Insurance Association of America, P.O. Box 41455, Washington, D.C. 20018). Provides the basics of private health coverage.

INVESTING

■ *A Common Sense Guide to Taking Charge of Your Money* (Fidelity Investments; 800-544-4774). Explains how to handle a lump-sum pension distribution.

■ *Investors' Bill of Rights* (National Futures Association). Specifies, among other useful facts, the pertinent information a broker must disclose to you before selling you an investment.

■ *Nine Tax Tips for Mutual Fund Investors* (GIT Investment Funds, 1655 Fort Myer Drive, Arlington, Virginia 22209; 800-336-3063).

MORTGAGES

■ *Home Buyer's Vocabulary* (Consumer Information Center, Item No. 121Y; $1). Helps you master such mortgage jargon as escrow, earnest money and points.

■ *Refinance Kit* (HSH Associates; 1200 Route 23, Butler, New Jersey 07405; $3). Explains how to calculate the total cost of various mortgage refinancing deals.

■ *Your Money & Your Home* (Countrywide; 800-669-6064). Discusses all aspects of taking out a mortgage, from application to appraisal to closing.

RETIREMENT

■ *A Single Person's Guide to Retirement Planning* (AARP). Serves up guidance on investing, insurance and other financial topics as well as tips on nutrition, relationships and housing.

■ *Can You Afford to Retire?* Life Insurance Marketing and Research Association, P.O. Box 208, Hartford, Connecticut 06141; 800-235-4672; $1.50). Covers various sources of retirement income. Most helpful feature: worksheets to calculate your current and future net worth.

Chapter 7

How to Get Your Best Deal on Wheels

Putting a Price on Safety *Page 133*

A Survivor's Guide to Car Repair *Page 136*

The MONEY Car-Cost Ratings *Page 138*

There's something novel about the 1993 new-car season, and it's not just the stylish models in showrooms. Auto manufacturers at last seem to realize that they repel recession-weary buyers by boosting prices faster than inflation. Dealers, in turn, are trying to attract and keep customers with courtesy and service—qualities rarely before encountered outside Japanese luxury lines like Lexus and Infiniti.

To be sure, the industry still has its share of fast-talking sharpies in loud jackets. But the creeping evolution toward kinder, gentler car selling is already paying dividends for Detroit. Even as total auto sales plateaued during the past year at the lowest level in nearly a decade, domestic manufacturers increased their share of the U.S. car and truck market (from 70% in 1991 to 72% in 1992) for the first time since 1988. One reason for the improvement is sturdy sales in three sectors dominated by U.S. manufacturers: pickups, sport utility vehicles and minivans. The real winners, however, figure to be car buyers. Among the developments that make this a terrific time for savvy shoppers:

■ Pressure on prices. Japanese manufacturers, despite being squeezed by a weak yen, have held their average 1993 price increases to 2.7% against comparably equipped 1992s, about in line with inflation. Better yet, Ford, Chrysler and General Motors have raised prices an average of just 1.3%. And on a few models, including the $15,797 Ford Thunderbird LX and the $9,520 Chevrolet Cavalier RS, Detroit actually cut prices below 1992 levels.

■ One-price selling. Also known as the no-dicker sticker, this tactic has eliminated the haggling most car buyers detest at all 213 of GM's Saturn dealers and at least 500 of the 23,000 other new-car dealers nationwide. In addition, Chrysler and Ford have launched training programs for their dealers and salespeople, emphasizing polite, low-key selling. Some dealers have even taken it upon themselves to introduce special customer services such as day care for the children of shopping parents.

■ Declining auto-loan rates. They recently were at their lowest levels in 15 years, with bank loans running at about 9%. Some credit union deals are at about half that.

One basic principle of car shopping hasn't changed, however. The best-prepared buyer still gets the best deal. To that end, please consult our exclusive cost ratings of 527 foreign and domestic cars and light trucks beginning on page 138. The ratings are designed to help you identify the most cost-effective cars to buy and own, as well as to arm you with inside price information that will put you in control when you walk onto a dealer's lot.

Terry Casey and his wife Debbie used just that sort of data to get a great deal on their new Mazda Miata. Before buying, the Lake Elsinore, California couple researched the car's so-called invoice price—the dealer's wholesale cost—and checked out prices at a few traditional dealers. The Caseys then accepted the no-haggle sticker price of $16,055 offered at Campbell Mazda of Santa Ana, a mere 1.6% above the $15,804 invoice. Their experience illustrates how one-price dealers are changing the auto industry's modus operandi. GM's Saturn division has been the leader here, elevating one-price selling and attentive customer service from a concept to a corporate policy. Other dealers, representing most makes except luxury brands, have chosen independently to follow suit by abandoning haggling in favor of setting one firm low price.

To buy a car at the lowest possible cost, however, there is still no substitute for hard bargaining. "A price shopper will almost always get a better deal than someone who accepts a no-dicker price," says Bob Fitzharris, a consultant with the auto research firm J.D. Power & Associates of Agoura Hills, California. Though no-haggle prices tend to be $600 to $1,000 below the manufacturer's suggested retail, they are still $200 to $600 above the dealer's cost. At one-price seller Saturn, the gap can be even bigger. For example, the $9,995 Saturn SL1 (priced 12% more than its $8,896 invoice) may look like a bargain in com-

Putting A Price on Safety

Valerie Howard believes in air bags. Last year she was driving alone from her home near Fort Lauderdale to her mother's when another driver ran a red light and smashed into the left fender of her 1992 Dodge Caravan minivan. Her air bag burst open, protecting Howard's head as the van spun around and slammed into a tree. The vehicle was a total loss, but the 31-year-old mother of three walked away with cuts and bruises. "The police told me the air bag probably saved my life," she says. Not surprisingly, when the Howards went shopping for a new van, they insisted on a model with an air bag.

Fans of today's high-tech safety features aren't limited to drivers who've had a close call. In a survey of 400 buyers by the Insurance Institute for Highway Safety (IIHS), an industry research and public relations group, 67% of those polled called the availability of an air bag a very important factor. It may be that the real risks of driving have finally sunk in. According to the National Highway Traffic Safety Administration, two out of three motorists are involved in an accident at some time that injures someone in the car.

Manufacturers have responded by selling safety. Chrysler took the lead by installing driver's-side air bags as standard equipment in their minivans in early 1991—five years earlier than required by federal regulations—and then putting company chairman Lee Iacocca in commercials to promote them. For its part, Ford has added both driver and passenger air bags as standard equipment for 1993 on its top-selling model, the Taurus ($15,491 and up). And General Motors has put anti-lock braking systems in 95% of its 1993 cars and light trucks. They prevent a car from going into an uncontrollable skid during panic stops on slippery roads.

Assuming that safety is a high priority in your car shopping—and that you don't have unlimited money—how should you proceed? Brian O'Neill, president of the IIHS, suggests the following:

Get the largest car that fits your budget and taste. In collisions between larger and smaller vehicles, occupants of the larger one almost always fare better.

In setting safety priorities, pick an air bag over anti-lock brakes. Though there are no firm statistics on anti-lock brakes, most safety experts believe that, while desirable, they are not nearly as important as air bags in preventing injury. And finding safety-equipped passenger cars is getting easier. About two-thirds of all 1993 models come with at least a driver's air bag, and about half of them offer anti-lock brakes. (When passenger air bags are available as options, they cost $500 to $700; when anti-lock brakes are an option, they range from $500 to $1,000.) Such safety technology is still fairly rare among sports utility vehicles and pickup trucks, however. So far, the new Jeep Grand Cherokee—with list prices ranging from $19,700 to $28,440—is the only sports utility vehicle to offer driver's-side air bags (standard in all versions). No pickups have air bags even as an option.

Check into crashworthiness test results. The purest proof of a car's survivability—at least in relation to cars of the same size—is the National Highway Traffic Safety Administration crash tests. Each year NHTSA smashes a total of 30 to 35 of the most widely driven new and redesigned cars into a fixed barrier at 35 mph, roughly the force of two identical cars hitting head on at 35 mph. The agency then measures the probable head, chest and leg injuries that passengers would suffer, assuming that all available safety equipment was employed.

You'll find the clearest interpretation of the NHTSA crash results in the annual Car Book (HarperCollins, $11). Author Jack Gillis, a former NHTSA official and currently director of public affairs for the Consumer Federation of America, combines the data and gives each car either a good, moderate or poor rating in comparison with others of similar size. For safety ratings, check the Insurance Institute records of injury claims for 170 models. You should send a stamped, self-addressed envelope to Safer Cars, Box 1420, Arlington, Virginia 22210, for a summary of the results.

parison with the Honda Civic DX's $10,350 list price. But a hard bargainer should be able to get the Honda for 4% over its dealer cost of $8,694, or $9,041.

Unless you're in the market for a Saturn, whose dealers don't negotiate, the best way to leverage your shopping is to take a low bid from one dealership—whether a one-price or a traditional outfit—and ask another to beat it. That's how Chinnapan Kolandayan of La Crosse, Wisconsin managed to buy a new 1992 Nissan Maxima SE for $22,192, or $400 under the dealer's invoice cost. (The dealer still made a profit of around $275 thanks to the so-called holdback, a 3% fee that the manufacturer rebates to dealers.) Kolandayan, 32, decided on the car he wanted, then obtained the invoice price from a $135 pricing service called Car Bargains (800-475-7283) that also quoted best prices from six dealers in his area. Kolandayan visited the two low bidders and let both know that he was talking to the other. He wound up getting $500 off the original low offer.

Whether you consider yourself a candidate for the haggler's olympics or prefer the unbrave new world of one-price dealers, take these steps to assure you get the best price:

Pick your car before getting serious about shopping. Winnow your choices down to several models in the price range you have in mind by scanning our cost ratings and looking them over in low-pressure situations such as at an auto show. Go to a dealer for a test drive, but let the salespeople know that you do not intend to buy that day. If you wander into a showroom with only a vague idea of the car you want, the salespeople could easily hustle you into the highest-priced model on the floor. Also check to see whether the models are available as slightly used rental cars. While former rental cars obviously lack the cachet of a factory-fresh buggy, they often have less than 10,000 miles on the odometer, come loaded with desirable options and have been meticulously maintained by professionals.

Do your homework. It is essential to find out the dealer's cost or invoice price; that allows you to judge the fairness of any offer, either in negotiation or a no-dicker situation. The ratings beginning on page 138 provide actual or estimated invoice prices for each of the 527 models covered, a target purchase price and data to figure the dealer's markup on any options you desire. For the most part, it's reasonable to aim to pay 3% to 4% over invoice for cars costing less than $20,000 and 4% to 7% for more expensive models. But you should be prepared to pay close to the suggested retail price if you have your heart set on a hot seller that's in short supply, such as the $28,440 Jeep Grand Cherokee, $17,189 Dodge Intrepid ES, $41,400 Lexus SC 400 or $24,100 Volvo 850 GLT.

For more detailed quotations of dealer costs than you'll find in our tables, consult a pricing guide such as *Edmund's New Car Prices* or *Edmund's Import Car Prices* ($5 each on newsstands). You might also order an *Auto Cost Comparison*, a customized report published by Money in conjunction with the automotive research firm Intellichoice, the source of our cost ratings. The report gives retail and dealer costs for all options, plus an estimate of total five-year ownership costs ($20 for quotes on two cars; 800-777-1880).

Sell your old car before you deal for a new one. This will prevent a new-car dealer from muddying your price negotiation with talk of trade-in bonanzas—and will also boost your chance of getting a top price for your used car. To start, look up your car's value in a guide such as *Edmund's Used Car Prices*. Then consider selling the car yourself through the classifieds for close to the retail price quoted in *Edmund's*. If dealing with weekend tire kickers seems like too much trouble, spiff up your car and ask for bids at the used-car departments of dealers that sell the same make. Expect to be offered around trade-in value—or the wholesale price shown in *Edmund's*—some 20% less than you could get in a private sale. You are looking for a dealer willing to bid somewhat above trade-in. If you get such an offer, take it.

Shop around for financing. Like selling your used car, arranging financing is best done before you start shopping seriously for a new car. Many lenders, especially credit unions, will commit to lend a specified amount at a stated interest rate ahead of time. As always, the cheapest alternative is to pay cash. But if you're among the nearly two-thirds of auto buyers who finance part of the purchase price, be gratified that auto-loan rates are so deliciously low. Bank loans recently averaged around 9% when financing $13,000 over four years, according to the *Bank Rate Monitor,* though some go as low as 7.5%. Credit union car loans averaged an appealing 7.5%, and a few dangle rates as low as 5%.

Best of all, if you already have a loan, you don't have to negotiate with the dealer's F&I person—who sells financing and the insurance that goes with it. "Since finance is the most profitable part of the dealership, the F&I man will try to run up your total charge with life and accident policies attached to the loan," says Jeff Gutierrez of Baton Rouge, a onetime car salesman turned consumer advocate. The insurance, costing about $1,000, is promoted as a way for your family to pay off your car loan if you die or become disabled. If you already have disability and life insurance, as you should, you're probably amply covered. In addition, the F&I person typically adds the cost of your insurance to the price of the car. Thus you end up paying interest on your insurance premiums.

Take a look at leasing. Leasing is generally more expensive in the long run than buying. But leasing can make sense if manufacturers are subsidizing deals, as Ford has been for its Taurus, and Honda for its Accord LX. First ask yourself two questions. If you bought the car, would you trade it in by the time the typical lease expires in two to four years? If not, buying makes more sense.

Do you take good care of cars, and would you typically drive more than 15,000 miles a year? A dealer can charge you stiff penalties of 9 to 15 cents per mile if you return a leased car with mileage over a predetermined limit, usually 15,000 miles per year. The dealer can also levy penalties of $200 to $2,000 for what he decides is excessive wear. So forget about leasing if you plan to drive more than the deal's mileage limit. Leasing's main appeal is a monthly payment 10% to 20% lower than you would pay to finance a purchase over the same period. The payments are lower because in a lease you finance only the difference between the purchase price and the residual value—the car's projected worth at the end of the lease—rather than the whole value of the car. For the best deal, bargain to have the payments based on the lowest purchase price.

Don't squander your good deal with last-minute add-ons. In addition to insurance on your auto loan, many dealers (including one-price outfits) will try to run up your bill with items such as $100 to $500 rustproofing and $500 to $1,200 extended warranties. Both are unnecessary. Metal in today's cars is already rust-proof and, with most repairs covered by manufacturer warranties, a typical buyer might pay $800 for an extended-service contract and collect only $300 in claims.

If you really hate car shopping, employ an auto broker. As long as you already know exactly which model and options you want, using an auto broker generally lets you avoid haggling with a dealer. Because brokers typically buy through the dealers' fleet-sales department—and thus cut selling costs—a broker can usually get a price at least as low as the best individual negotiator. To find local brokers, start by checking the Yellow Pages or asking your credit union, which may have a buying service of its own or a broker tie-in. There are drawbacks to brokers, however. Because of political pressure from auto dealer lobbies, they don't operate in every state. Also, if a broker takes title to the new car and then resells it to you for a $300 to $500 markup, you will not be in the manufacturer's records as the initial owner. Thus notices of recalls or other such announcements will reach you only if the broker is responsible enough to pass them on.

Some national buying services avoid these problems by delivering cars to the customers through local dealers. One such buying firm, AutoAdvisor in Seattle (800-326-1976) will order the car you want from the factory for a $339 fee. If you need a car within four weeks, AutoAdvisor will track it down from a dealer near you for $437. Almost invariably, the price AutoAdvisor can get you will be so much lower than one you could get on your own that you'll come out ahead even after paying its brokerage fee.

Whether you use a broker, go to a one-price dealer or join in the trench warfare over price at an old-fashioned dealer, careful preparation is sure to pay off. Targeting the model you want, researching dealer cost and avoiding last-minute add-ons can easily save you as much as $2,000 on a car with a $20,000 list price. Considering the fact that banks now pay around 3%, a 10% cost saving turns out to be a handsome return.

A Survivor's Guide to Car Repair

If the scandals at Sears repair shops confirmed your worst fears, follow our advice for getting your buggy fixed without getting fleeced.

The news was dismaying, to say the least, last year when government authorities in California and New Jersey charged Sears Auto Centers—America's largest independent auto repair concern—with pushing unnecessary repairwork on customers. But it was hardly a surprise to the many consumers who hold auto repairers in as high esteem as, say, loan sharks. The Council of Better Business Bureaus reports that the $100 billion auto repair industry regularly ranks between third and sixth on its list of businesses that draw the most consumer complaints.

Believe it or not, the odds of getting satisfactory service are in your favor. Three-fourths of the 52,000 customers who were surveyed by the Washington, D.C. consumer advocacy group Center for the Study of Services said they were satisfied with the service they received. Follow the prescriptions below, and you'll lessen your chances of winding up in the disgruntled 25%.

The first decision to make when something goes wrong with your car is where to take it. If your car is still under the original warranty, take it to one of the car maker's authorized dealers. If not, and you're sure of the problem, go to one of the outfits that specialize in that kind of repair. They often do the work faster and cheaper than the corner garage.

If you're not certain what's wrong and the car is not under warranty, take it to an independent general repair shop for diagnosis. Surveys by consulting firm Booz Allen & Hamilton found that independents tend to do a better job satisfying customers than do service departments at car dealerships—and the independents charge 20% to 50% less. If your car's ailment is fairly straightforward—it needs new hoses or brakes, for instance—your best bet is to give the independent the job. By contrast, have the work done at a dealer if it calls for sophisticated equipment or knowledge that only a dealer is likely to have, such as repairs to an electronic dashboard.

Wherever you go, try to talk directly to the mechanic who will work on your car. Jim Mateyka, Booz Allen's vice president for the auto repair industry, says that a major reason for dealers' low satisfaction ratings is poor communication. Those who do the repairs usually work from an order written by a clerk in the repair shop's front office. "It's like that pass-the-message party game," says Mateyka. "What comes out at the end frequently bears no relationship to what went in." The Booz Allen survey found that return rates—that is, when a car has to be brought back because its problem wasn't fixed— drop by a third when the owner explains the problem to the mechanic one-on-one.

Of course, communication won't make any difference if the shop is more interested in hustling you than fixing your car. To protect against rip-offs, never give blanket authorization to make repairs. Stipulate in writing on the order form, if necessary, that any work beyond what's written must be approved in advance. Also remember that in most states you are entitled to receive any parts removed so that you can have them examined elsewhere. And go on alert if you are handed any of the following lines:

"I can't let you drive out of here without replacing these brakes. They're not safe." This scare tactic is one of the most common repair shop cons. Modern disk brakes don't wear out without warning. A piece of steel called a sensor is built into the brake pad and is designed to rub against the rotor and cause a squeak long before the asbestos pad wears out. If you haven't heard the squeal, your brakes are safe. You certainly have time to seek a second opinion.

"Our $49.95 tune-up (or front-end alignment, or whatever) will have your car running like new." When a general repair shop advertises a special offer like this, it's usually just a loss leader—a lure to get your car into the garage where mechanics can fish for something more expensive to fix. Tune-up come-ons tend to be especially dubious, since the fuel and ignition controls that needed periodic tuning on cars built before 1980 are now computerized. So a cut-rate tune-up these days probably involves simply replacing your air and fuel filters and checking your spark plugs and injectors. If there's a serious problem, that won't fix it.

"Look at this gunk in your transmission. You need the whole thing replaced." When your car is in for a periodic transmission check, sleazy mechanics often will point ominously to the guck at the bottom of the transmission oil pan and predict disaster if you don't agree to an overhaul. Forget it. The debris, which is made up of fibers scraped off the clutch and tiny particles of metal from the rest of the transmission, is normal and no cause for alarm. Sometimes the scam takes on an element of petty extortion. The mechanic might allow that you need less than a complete overhaul but that doing the minor work would take a week or more. The shop, however, happens to have on hand an overhaul kit that costs only $100—not including the $400 to $900 labor charge—and if you agree to the larger job, you can have the car back that afternoon. Instead, seek out a second opinion.

"This steering linkage is loose. Your front end needs an overhaul." Many of the parts in your car's front-axle system are spring-loaded, like the tie-rod end that connects the steering mechanism to the wheel. A mechanic can insert a screwdriver and push it around to make the part look loose, but it's meant to be that way. As with transmissions, if you're being pressured into major front-end work, get a second opinion.

In the end, your best defense against fraud is to develop a long-term relationship with a competent mechanic who knows you and your car. Ask for recommendations from friends, and when you first visit that garage, drop your friend's name. Let the mechanic know that if he stiffs you, he risks losing two customers.

THE MONEY
CAR-COST RATINGS

Whatever model you like among the 527 listed here, the column to check first is **total five-year ownership costs.** The San Jose research firm Intellichoice Inc. calculates this number for MONEY by combining the costs of financing, insurance, maintenance, repairs, registration fees, fuel and depreciation into a dollar amount that approximates the total costs of owning the car during the next five years. Comparing total costs proves that the car with the sweetest sale price isn't always the best value. "An inexpensive car to buy could turn out to be an expensive car to own," says Intellichoice president Peter Levy.

Compare two four-door imports aimed at the $10,000 to $15,000 buyer, the Nissan Sentra XE and the Honda Civic LX. The Nissan lists for $11,190, nearly $700 less than the Honda. But the Nissan is more expensive to own; it costs 30% more than the Honda to insure and will have a resale value in five years that's only 46% of its original price, compared with 58% for the Honda. The Nissan's total five-year ownership cost comes to $21,555, at least $2,000 more than the higher-priced Honda's $19,469.

To arrive at the total ownership cost estimate, Intellichoice assumes that you drive 14,000 miles annually, are an average insurance risk, pay $1.15 a gallon for regular gasoline and 10% interest on a car loan representing 80% of the car's target price. Our **five-year maintenance cost** figure is the estimated expense of performing all the car's scheduled maintenance plus additional routine tasks, such as replacing tires and the battery. The **five-year repair cost** is based on actual outlays for repairs not covered by the manufacturer's warranty, as reported by insurance companies that sponsor extended-warranty contracts. Since no information is yet available for the 1993s, our figures are data for last year's models.

Checking our ratings will help you to identify cars that are long-term values. You can then use the inside price information in the tables to make sure you get a great deal. The keys here are the **estimated dealer's cost** (the dealer's wholesale cost, or invoice) and **your target price.** The target prices reflect today's competitive market, in which a determined bargainer can usually get a price 3% to 4% above invoice on cars priced below $20,000 and 6% to 7% over invoice on the more expensive models.

Keep in mind that our prices include only standard equipment. If you want options on your car, you will have to add the cost of the option to your target price. Suppose you want a 1993 Pontiac Grand Am GT two-door with automatic transmission, a $555 option. To set your new target price, multiply $555 by the percentage in the table under **options price as a % of retail,** or 86%. The result, $477, is the dealer's cost for the automatic transmission. Since you should figure on paying about 4% over invoice on a Grand Am, you ought to aim to pay about $496 for the transmission ($477 times 1.04). Thus your total target price for the Grand Am with automatic rises to $13,601.

With a little arithmetic, you can figure out what auto dealers don't want you to know—your car's fair market value. Once you are armed with that information, you should be able to hold your own in any showroom negotiation.

MAKE AND MODEL	Suggested retail price	Estimated dealer's cost	Your target price	Options price as a % of retail[2]	Five-year resale as a % of original	Miles per gallon (city/hwy.)	Cost to insure[3]	Five-year costs Maintenance[4]	Repairs[5]	Total ownership costs[6]
Chevrolet Cavalier RS 2dr	$9,520	$8,901	$9,168	86%	39%	25/36	Average	$4,167	$288	$23,731
Chevrolet Cavalier VL 2dr	8,520	8,051	8,293	86	38	25/36	Average	4,167	288	23,348
Chevrolet Cavalier VL 4dr	8,620	8,146	8,390	86	39	25/36	Average	4,167	288	23,171
Chevrolet Cavalier VL 4dr wgn	9,735	9,200	9,476	86	38	23/31	Average	4,167	288	23,734
Dodge Colt 2dr hatch	7,806	7,488	7,713	86	43	27/34	High	3,652	145	19,357
Dodge Colt 4dr	9,448	9,001	9,271	86	N.A.	27/34	N.A.	N.A.	N.A.	N.A.
Dodge Colt GL 2dr hatch	8,705	8,309	8,558	86	41	27/34	High	3,652	145	20,333
Dodge Shadow 2dr hatch	8,397	7,888	8,125	85	44	27/32	High	3,658	197	20,135
Dodge Shadow 4dr hatch	8,797	8,255	8,503	85	44	27/32	Average	3,658	197	20,194
Dodge Shadow ES 2dr hatch	9,804	9,124	9,398	85	39	25/32	High	4,232	205	25,652
Eagle Summit DL 2dr	7,806	7,488	7,713	86	47	32/40	High	4,416	145	19,836
Eagle Summit ES 2dr	8,705	8,309	8,558	86	49	32/40	High	4,528	145	21,042
Ford Escort 2dr hatch	8,355	7,723	8,071	85	50	32/40	High	4,485	215	19,827
Ford Festiva GL 2dr hatch	7,869	7,378	7,599	85	46	35/42	High	3,605	129	19,141
Ford Festiva L 2dr hatch	6,941	6,515	6,710	85	46	35/42	High	3,541	129	18,269
Geo Metro 2dr hatch	6,710	6,254	6,442	89	55	46/50	Very high	4,378	223	18,584
Geo Metro 4dr hatch	7,199	6,709	6,910	89	50	46/50	High	4,378	223	18,589
Geo Metro LSi 2dr hatch	8,199	7,641	7,870	89	49	46/50	Very high	4,378	223	19,836
Geo Metro LSi 4dr hatch	8,599	8,014	8,254	89	49	46/50	High	4,378	223	19,520
Geo Metro LSi convert.	9,999	9,319	9,599	89	46	41/46	Very high	4,462	223	21,986
Geo Metro XFi 2dr hatch	6,710	6,254	6,442	90	55	53/58	Very high	4,378	223	18,335
Geo Prizm 4dr	9,995	9,395	9,677	86	45	27/34	Average	4,312	149	21,807
Honda Civic CX 2dr hatch	8,400	7,056	7,268	85	74	42/46	Average	4,444	137	15,876
Hyundai Elantra 4dr	8,999	8,123	8,367	88	N.A.	22/29	High	N.A.	377	N.A.
Hyundai Excel 2dr hatch	6,799	6,346	6,536	91	37	29/33	Very high	3,858	217	20,185
Hyundai Excel 4dr	7,699	7,185	7,401	91	41	29/33	Very high	3,858	217	20,709
Hyundai Excel GL 4dr	8,599	7,762	7,995	90	43	29/36	Very high	3,969	217	20,146
Hyundai Excel GS 2dr hatch	7,699	6,950	7,159	90	38	29/36	Very high	3,858	217	21,151
Hyundai Scoupe 2dr	9,069	8,187	8,433	90	27/35		High	3,864	170	N.A.
Isuzu Stylus S 4dr	9,700[1]	8,924	9,192	85	N.A.	30/36	High	4,795	345	N.A.
Mazda 323 2dr hatch	7,449	7,090	7,303	80	54	29/37	High	3,902	132	18,597
Mazda 323 SE 2dr hatch	9,129	8,412	8,664	80	50	29/37	High	3,902	132	19,549
Mitsubishi Mirage ES 2dr	8,939	8,042	8,283	82	N.A.	32/40	High	N.A.	N.A.	N.A.
Mitsubishi Mirage S 4dr	9,439	8,496	8,751	82	41	32/40	High	4,334	182	21,260
Nissan Sentra E 2dr	8,715	8,177	8,422	85	57	29/38	Very high	4,488	138	20,112
Plymouth Colt 2dr hatch	7,806	7,488	7,713	86	49	32/40	High	4,333	145	19,648
Plymouth Colt 4dr	9,448	9,001	9,271	86	N.A.	32/40	N.A.	N.A.	N.A.	N.A.
Plymouth Colt GL 2dr hatch	8,705	8,309	8,558	86	41	32/40	High	4,425	145	21,069
Plymouth Sundance 2dr hatch	8,397	7,888	8,125	85	44	27/32	High	4,100	197	20,618
Plymouth Sundance 4dr hatch	8,797	8,255	8,503	85	44	27/32	Average	4,100	197	20,634
Pontiac LeMans SE 4dr	9,854	9,184	9,460	86	38	31/41	High	3,885	334	23,720
Pontiac LeMans SE Aerocoupe 2dr hatch	9,054	8,438	8,691	86	39	28/37	Very high	4,175	334	23,451
Pontiac Sunbird LE 2dr	9,382	8,772	9,035	86	42	25/35	Average	4,170	320	22,724
Pontiac Sunbird LE 4dr	9,382	8,772	9,035	86	43	25/35	Average	4,170	320	22,396
Saturn SL 4dr	9,195	8,184	8,430	89	N.A.	28/37	Average	3,634	444	N.A.
Saturn SL1 4dr	9,995	8,896	9,163	89	N.A.	28/37	Average	3,687	444	N.A.
Subaru Justy 2dr hatch	7,338	6,824	7,029	90	46	33/37	High	4,546	182	19,029
Subaru Justy GL 2dr hatch	9,113	8,293	8,542	91	39	33/37	High	4,630	182	20,513
Subaru Justy GL 4WD 4dr hatch	9,478	8,625	8,884	90	39	28/32	Very high	4,630	188	22,476
Suzuki Swift GA 2dr hatch	7,299	6,569	6,766	88	57	39/43	Very high	5,009	225	18,255
Suzuki Swift GA 4dr	7,999	7,199	7,415	88	50	39/43	High	5,009	225	19,253
Suzuki Swift GS 4dr	9,399	8,271	8,519	88	46	39/43	High	4,893	225	20,153
Suzuki Swift GT 2dr hatch	9,999	8,699	8,960	88	54	28/35	Very high	5,193	225	20,519
Toyota Tercel 2dr	7,848	7,180	7,395	80	52	32/36	High	3,801	172	17,995
Toyota Tercel DX 2dr	9,678	8,710	8,971	80	47	28/34	High	3,801	172	19,670
Toyota Tercel DX 4dr	9,778	8,800	9,064	80	47	28/34	High	3,801	172	19,542

Notes: [1] Estimate [2] Dealer's average cost as a percentage of suggested retail price [3] Compared with other models in its class [4] Includes scheduled maintenance, as well as replacement of tires, brake pads, batteries and other parts [5] Average five-year repair costs not covered by warranty [6] Includes depreciation, financing, maintenance, repairs, state taxes and registration fees, insurance and fuel. Resale value, insurance, maintenance and repair costs are based on 1992 model history. [7] Includes a $375 destination charge [8] 1992 model; 1993s will be introduced early next year. N.A.: Not available **Sources:** Intellichoice Inc., AutoAdvisor Inc., Insurance Services Office and the manufacturers

MAKE AND MODEL	Suggested retail price	Estimated dealer's cost	Your target price	Options price as a % of retail[2]	Five-year resale as a % of original	Miles per gallon (city/hwy.)	Cost to insure[3]	Five-year costs Mainte-nance[4]	Repairs[5]	Total ownership costs[6]
Volkswagen Fox 2dr	$8,690	$7,995	$8,235	86%	51%	25/33	Very high	$4,320	$214	$20,777
Volkswagen Fox GL 4dr	9,520	8,663	8,923	86	48	25/33	High	4,342	214	21,151

$10,000 to $14,999

MAKE AND MODEL	Suggested retail price	Estimated dealer's cost	Your target price	Options price as a % of retail[2]	Five-year resale as a % of original	Miles per gallon (city/hwy.)	Cost to insure[3]	Mainte-nance[4]	Repairs[5]	Total ownership costs[6]
Acura Integra LS 2dr hatch	$14,835	$12,461	$12,959	84%	63%	25/31	High	$5,010	$190	$23,538
Acura Integra RS 2dr hatch	12,930	10,861	11,295	84	68	25/31	High	5,010	190	21,982
Acura Integra RS 4dr	13,855	11,638	12,104	84	57	25/31	Average	5,010	190	23,635
Buick Century Special 4dr	14,205	12,713	13,222	88	41	23/31	Low	4,361	356	26,146
Buick Century Special 4dr wgn	14,960	13,398	13,934	88	N.A.	21/29	Low	N.A.	N.A.	N.A.
Buick Skylark Custom 2dr	12,955	12,113	12,598	90	38	22/32	Average	4,334	300	26,272
Buick Skylark Limited 4dr	13,875	12,557	13,059	90	N.A.	22/32	Average	N.A.	N.A.	N.A.
Chevrolet Beretta 2dr	11,395	10,312	10,724	86	36	25/34	High	4,265	294	26,443
Chevrolet Beretta GT 2dr	12,995	11,760	12,230	86	38	19/28	High	4,376	294	28,055
Chevrolet Camaro RS 2dr [8]	12,075	10,964	11,403	86	39	17/27	Very high	4,184	270	30,459
Chevrolet Cavalier RS 4dr wgn	10,785	10,084	10,487	86	38	23/31	Average	4,357	288	25,775
Chevrolet Corsica LT 4dr	11,395	10,312	10,724	86	37	25/34	Average	4,293	294	25,588
Chevrolet Lumina 2dr	14,690	12,854	13,368	86	38	19/27	Average	4,930	314	27,652
Chevrolet Lumina 4dr	13,400	11,725	12,194	86	40	21/29	Low	4,930	314	27,230
Chrysler LeBaron 2dr	13,999	12,629	13,134	90	35	23/28	Average	4,152	277	26,233
Chrysler LeBaron 4dr	14,497	13,072	13,595	90	32	23/28	Low	4,424	270	28,861
Dodge Daytona 2dr hatch	10,874	10,028	10,429	85	30	25/32	Very high	3,807	276	28,933
Dodge Daytona ES 2dr hatch	12,018	11,046	11,488	85	29	25/32	Very high	3,910	276	30,440
Dodge Dynasty 4dr	14,736	12,956	13,474	85	39	21/27	Low	3,877	267	24,901
Dodge Shadow ES 4dr hatch	10,204	9,484	9,769	85	39	25/32	Average	4,232	205	25,273
Dodge Shadow ES convert.	14,167	13,050	13,572	85	39	25/32	High	4,232	205	28,989
Dodge Shadow convert.	14,028	12,925	13,442	85	40	25/32	High	3,870	205	27,586
Dodge Spirit ES 4dr	14,715	13,304	13,836	89	37	25/32	Low	4,044	251	26,317
Eagle Summit AWD 3dr	13,539	12,535	13,036	86	N.A.	22/26	Average	4,793	N.A.	N.A.
Eagle Summit DL 3dr	11,455	10,660	11,086	86	N.A.	23/29	Average	4,719	N.A.	N.A.
Eagle Talon DL 2dr	11,752	10,957	11,395	85	50	23/32	High	5,454	224	30,047
Ford Escort GT 2dr hatch	11,871	10,650	11,076	85	42	26/31	High	3,758	215	24,045
Ford Escort LX 2dr hatch	10,899[7]	9,809	10,899	85	43	30/37	High	3,330	215	20,683
Ford Escort LX 4dr	10,899[7]	9,809	10,899	85	42	30/37	High	3,450	215	21,465
Ford Escort LX 4dr hatch	10,899[7]	9,809	10,899	85	42	30/37	High	3,330	215	21,124
Ford Escort LX 4dr wgn	10,899[7]	9,809	10,899	85	41	29/36	High	3,330	215	21,390
Ford Mustang LX 2dr	10,719	9,670	9,960	85	46	22/30	Very high	3,800	209	26,541
Ford Mustang LX 2dr hatch	11,224	10,120	10,525	85	45	22/30	Very high	3,800	209	27,106
Ford Mustang LX 5.0L 2dr	13,929	12,564	12,941	85	42	17/24	Very high	4,675	286	31,731
Ford Mustang LX 5.0L 2dr hatch	14,710	13,222	13,751	85	43	17/24	Very high	4,675	286	32,221
Ford Probe 2dr hatch	12,845	11,557	12,019	85	49	26/33	High	4,546	238	27,977
Ford Tempo GL 2dr	10,267	9,228	9,505	85	36	24/33	Average	3,715	333	24,721
Ford Tempo GL 4dr	10,267	9,228	9,505	85	37	24/33	Low	3,715	333	24,481
Ford Tempo LX 4dr	12,135	10,890	11,326	85	34	24/33	Low	3,715	333	25,996
Geo Storm 2+2 2dr	11,530	10,608	11,032	86	49	29/35	Very high	4,666	160	23,293
Honda Accord DX 2dr	13,750	11,550	12,012	84	66	24/31	Average	4,876	171	21,341
Honda Accord DX 4dr	13,950	11,718	12,187	84	62	24/31	Average	4,883	171	21,635
Honda Civic del Sol S 2dr	13,200	11,220	11,669	85	N.A.	34/38	N.A.	N.A.	N.A.	N.A.
Honda Civic DX 2dr	10,350	8,901	9,257	85	N.A.	34/40	Average	N.A.	N.A.	N.A.
Honda Civic DX 4dr	11,055	9,397	9,679	85	62	34/40	Average	4,519	137	18,555
Honda Civic EX 2dr	12,400	10,416	10,833	85	N.A.	29/35	Average	N.A.	N.A.	N.A.
Honda Civic LX 4dr	11,885	10,102	10,506	85	58	34/40	Average	4,398	137	19,469
Honda Civic Si 2dr hatch	12,200	10,370	10,785	85	64	29/35	Average	4,872	137	19,724
Honda Civic VX 2dr hatch	10,800	9,072	9,344	85	74	48/55	Average	4,324	137	16,399

Notes: [1] Estimate [2] Dealer's average cost as a percentage of suggested retail price [3] Compared with other models in its class [4] Includes scheduled maintenance, as well as replacement of tires, brake pads, batteries and other parts [5] Average five-year repair costs not covered by warranty [6] Includes depreciation, financing, maintenance, repairs, state taxes and registration fees, insurance and fuel. Resale value, insurance, maintenance and repair costs are based on 1992 model history. [7] Includes a $375 destination charge [8] 1992 model; 1993s will be introduced early next year. N.A.: Not available **Sources:** Intellichoice Inc., AutoAdvisor Inc., Insurance Services Office and the manufacturers

MAKE AND MODEL	Suggested retail price	Estimated dealer's cost	Your target price	Options price as a % of retail[2]	Five-year resale as a % of original	Miles per gallon (city/hwy.)	Cost to insure[3]	Maintenance[4]	Repairs[5]	Total ownership costs[6]
Hyundai Elantra GLS 4dr	$10,299	$9,087	$9,360	88%	N.A.	21/28	High	N.A.	$377	N.A.
Hyundai Scoupe LS 2dr	10,199	8,999	9,269	88	N.A.	27/35	High	$4,263	170	N.A.
Hyundai Scoupe Turbo 2dr	10,999	9,704	9,995	90	N.A.	26/32	High	N.A.	N.A.	N.A.
Hyundai Sonata 4dr	12,399	11,061	11,503	88	43%	20/27	High	4,866	239	$24,889
Hyundai Sonata GLS 4dr	13,799	12,480	12,979	87	38	20/27	High	5,182	239	28,010
Mazda 626 DX 4dr	14,255	12,557	13,059	80	44	26/34	Average	4,616	160	25,885
Mazda MX3 2dr	11,875	10,701	11,129	80	N.A.	28/35	High	N.A.	377	N.A.
Mazda Protege DX 4dr	10,854	9,891	10,188	80	54	28/36	High	3,955	129	20,530
Mazda Protege LX 4dr	12,349	11,128	11,573	80	50	25/30	High	4,189	129	23,004
Mercury Capri convert.	14,452	12,429	12,926	84	45	25/31	High	4,437	155	28,997
Mercury Cougar XR7 2dr	14,855	13,351	13,885	85	36	19/26	Average	4,732	262	34,238
Mercury Topaz GS 2dr	10,801	9,703	9,994	85	35	24/33	Average	4,281	346	26,044
Mercury Topaz GS 4dr	10,801	9,703	9,994	85	36	24/33	Low	4,281	346	26,097
Mercury Tracer 4dr	11,665[7]	10,499	11,665	85	46	26/31	High	3,878	190	21,677
Mercury Tracer 4dr wgn	11,665[7]	10,499	11,665	85	46	29/36	High	3,998	190	22,348
Mitsubishi Eclipse 2dr hatch	11,719	10,252	10,662	82	56	23/32	High	4,101	231	24,434
Mitsubishi Eclipse GS 2dr	13,429	11,680	12,147	82	54	22/32	High	4,713	231	27,601
Mitsubishi Expo 4dr wgn	13,569	11,944	12,421	80	N.A.	21/28	Average	N.A.	N.A.	N.A.
Mitsubishi Expo LRV 3dr	11,429	10,289	10,701	80	N.A.	23/29	Average	N.A.	N.A.	N.A.
Mitsubishi Galant S 4dr	12,599	11,356	11,810	80	42	20/26	Average	4,757	439	25,732
Mitsubishi Mirage ES 4dr	10,479	9,430	9,713	82	44	32/40	High	4,765	182	23,713
Mitsubishi Mirage LS 2dr	10,299	9,266	9,544	82	N.A.	32/40	High	N.A.	N.A.	N.A.
Nissan 240SX 2dr	14,755	13,094	13,618	85	46	22/28	Very high	5,105	160	32,112
Nissan Altima GXE 4dr	14,024	12,231	12,720	85	36	24/30	N.A.	5,044	147	29,434
Nissan Altima XE 4dr	12,999	11,469	11,928	85	41	24/30	N.A.	5,044	147	26,978
Nissan NX 1600 2dr	11,635	10,444	10,862	85	N.A.	28/38	High	4,790	345	N.A.
Nissan NX 2000 2dr	14,720	13,062	13,584	85	N.A.	23/30	High	5,356	345	N.A.
Nissan Sentra E 4dr	10,165	9,020	9,291	85	55	29/38	High	4,491	138	19,945
Nissan Sentra GXE 4dr	14,145	12,481	12,980	85	43	29/38	High	4,602	138	23,738
Nissan Sentra SE 2dr	10,900	9,617	9,906	85	44	29/38	Very high	4,602	138	22,069
Nissan Sentra XE 4dr	11,190	9,930	10,228	85	46	29/38	High	4,614	138	21,555
Oldsmobile Achieva S 2dr	13,049	11,809	12,281	86	N.A.	22/32	Average	N.A.	N.A.	N.A.
Oldsmobile Achieva SL 4dr	14,949	13,529	14,070	86	N.A.	22/32	Average	N.A.	N.A.	N.A.
Oldsmobile Cutlass Cruiser S 4dr wgn	14,899	13,335	13,868	86	40	21/29	Low	4,117	321	27,856
Oldsmobile Cutlass Ciera S 4dr	14,199	12,708	13,216	86	36	23/31	Low	4,117	321	27,039
Plymouth Acclaim 4dr	11,941	10,863	11,298	91	39	23/28	Low	4,381	251	24,948
Plymouth Colt GL 4dr	10,423	9,846	10,141	86	N.A.	32/40	N.A.	N.A.	N.A.	N.A.
Plymouth Colt Vista 3dr	11,455	10,660	11,086	86	N.A.	27/34	Average	5,249	345	N.A.
Plymouth Colt Vista AWD 3dr	13,539	12,535	13,036	86	N.A.	27/34	Average	4,518	401	N.A.
Plymouth Laser 2dr hatch	11,406	10,687	11,114	85	56	23/32	High	4,438	224	25,631
Plymouth Laser RS 2dr hatch	13,749	12,739	13,249	85	52	22/29	High	5,232	224	29,320
Plymouth Sundance Duster 2dr hatch	10,498	9,748	10,040	85	N.A.	19/28	High	N.A.	N.A.	N.A.
Plymouth Sundance Duster 4dr hatch	10,898	10,108	10,512	84	N.A.	19/28	Average	N.A.	N.A.	N.A.
Pontiac Firebird 2dr [8]	12,505	11,355	11,809	86	38	18/27	Very high	4,241	299	31,328
Pontiac Grand Am GT 2dr	13,924	12,601	13,105	86	44	21/30	Average	4,641	260	28,925
Pontiac Grand Am GT 4dr	14,024	12,692	13,200	86	43	21/30	Average	4,641	260	28,930
Pontiac Grand Am SE 4dr	12,624	11,425	11,882	86	38	23/35	Average	4,020	260	25,764
Pontiac Grand Prix LE 4dr	14,890	13,327	13,860	86	40	19/27	Low	4,571	284	26,916
Pontiac Sunbird GT 2dr	12,820	11,602	12,066	86	33	19/28	Average	4,535	320	28,246
Pontiac Sunbird SE 2dr	10,380	9,394	9,676	86	38	25/35	Average	4,424	320	24,681
Pontiac Sunbird SE 4dr	10,380	9,394	9,676	86	43	25/35	Average	4,424	320	23,747
Saturn SC1 2dr	10,995	9,786	10,995	89	N.A.	28/37	High	4,087	444	N.A.
Saturn SC2 2dr	12,795	11,388	12,795	89	N.A.	28/37	High	N.A.	N.A.	N.A.
Saturn SL2 4dr	11,495	10,231	11,495	89	N.A.	24/35	Average	4,087	444	N.A.
Saturn SW1 4dr wgn	10,895	9,697	10,895	89	N.A.	28/37	Average	N.A.	N.A.	N.A.
Saturn SW2 4dr wgn	12,195	10,854	12,195	89	N.A.	24/35	Average	N.A.	N.A.	N.A.

Notes: [1] Estimate [2] Dealer's average cost as a percentage of suggested retail price [3] Compared with other models in its class [4] Includes scheduled maintenance, as well as replacement of tires, brake pads, batteries and other parts [5] Average five-year repair costs not covered by warranty [6] Includes depreciation, financing, maintenance, repairs, state taxes and registration fees, insurance and fuel. Resale value, insurance, maintenance and repair costs are based on 1992 model history. [7] Includes a $375 destination charge [8] 1992 model; 1993s will be introduced early next year. N.A.: Not available **Sources:** Intellichoice Inc., AutoAdvisor Inc., Insurance Services Office and the manufacturers

$10,000 to $14,999

MAKE AND MODEL	Suggested retail price	Estimated dealer's cost	Your target price	Options price as a % of retail[2]	Five-year resale as a % of original	Miles per gallon (city/hwy.)	Cost to insure[3]	Maintenance[4]	Repairs[5]	Total ownership costs[6]
Subaru Loyale 4dr	$10,478	$9,430	$9,807	90%	39%	25/32	Average	$4,375	$156	$21,867
Subaru Loyale 4dr wgn	11,328	10,195	10,603	90	40	25/30	Average	4,375	156	22,666
Subaru Loyale AWD 4dr wgn	12,828	11,545	12,007	90	40	21/27	Average	4,375	252	23,976
Toyota Celica ST 2dr	14,198	12,139	12,625	80	55	25/32	High	4,823	172	27,123
Toyota Corolla 4dr	11,198	9,966	10,265	80	53	27/34	Average	4,438	142	20,034
Toyota Corolla DX 4dr	12,298	10,575	10,998	80	50	27/34	Average	4,568	142	20,815
Toyota Corolla DX 4dr wgn	12,978	11,160	11,606	80	49	27/33	Average	4,568	142	21,276
Toyota Paseo 2dr	11,498	10,003	10,403	80	N.A.	28/34	High	N.A.	345	N.A.
Toyota Tercel LE 4dr	11,308	9,724	10,016	80	44	28/34	High	3,801	172	20,250
Volkswagen Golf GL III 2dr hatch	10,026[1]	9,023	9,384	86	55	24/32	Very high	4,243	197	21,579
Volkswagen Golf GL III 4dr hatch	10,149[1]	9,134	9,499	86	55	24/32	High	4,243	197	21,101
Volkswagen GTI III 2dr hatch	11,443[1]	10,299	10,711	86	59	24/32	Very high	4,727	194	22,412
Volkswagen Jetta III Carat 4dr	12,514[1]	11,012	11,452	86	63	23/30	Very high	4,736	187	23,760
Volkswagen Jetta III GL 4dr	11,484[1]	10,106	10,510	86	63	23/30	Very high	4,741	187	22,965

$15,000 to $19,999

MAKE AND MODEL	Suggested retail price	Estimated dealer's cost	Your target price	Options price as a % of retail[2]	Five-year resale as a % of original	Miles per gallon (city/hwy.)	Cost to insure[3]	Maintenance[4]	Repairs[5]	Total ownership costs[6]
Acura Integra GS 2dr hatch	$17,005	$14,284	$14,855	84%	62%	25/31	High	$5,093	$190	$25,343
Acura Integra GS 4dr	17,545	14,738	15,328	84	55	25/31	Average	5,010	190	26,630
Acura Integra GSR 2dr hatch	18,260	15,338	15,952	84	N.A.	24/29	High	N.A.	N.A.	N.A.
Acura Integra LS 4dr	15,585	13,091	13,615	84	55	25/31	Average	5,010	190	25,015
Acura Integra LS Special 2dr hatch	16,335	13,721	14,270	N.A.	N.A.	25/31	High	N.A.	N.A.	N.A.
Buick Century Custom 2dr	15,620	13,668	14,215	88	36	23/31	Average	4,361	356	27,634
Buick Century Custom 4dr	15,905	13,917	14,474	88	40	23/31	Low	4,361	356	26,800
Buick Century Custom 4dr wgn	17,250	15,094	15,698	88	37	21/29	Low	4,361	356	27,875
Buick Century Limited 4dr	16,865	14,757	15,347	88	37	23/31	Low	4,361	356	27,978
Buick LeSabre Custom 4dr	19,935	17,443	18,141	87	46	19/28	Low	4,953	235	28,791
Buick Regal Custom 2dr	16,610	14,534	15,115	86	38	19/30	Low	5,144	242	28,616
Buick Regal Custom 4dr	16,865	14,757	15,347	86	40	19/30	Low	5,144	242	28,486
Buick Regal GS 2dr	19,095	16,708	17,376	86	37	19/28	Low	5,268	242	30,994
Buick Regal GS 4dr	19,310	16,896	17,572	86	39	19/28	Low	5,268	242	31,466
Buick Regal Limited 2dr	18,260	15,978	16,617	86	37	19/30	Low	5,144	242	30,037
Buick Regal Limited 4dr	18,460	16,153	16,799	86	39	19/30	Low	5,144	242	29,994
Buick Skylark Gran Sport 2dr	15,760	14,263	14,834	90	34	20/29	Average	4,955	300	29,181
Buick Skylark Gran Sport 4dr	15,760	14,263	14,834	90	36	20/29	Average	4,955	300	28,784
Chevrolet Beretta GTZ 2dr	15,995	14,475	15,054	86	33	22/33	High	4,683	282	31,715
Chevrolet Camaro RS convert.[8]	18,055	16,394	17,050	86	44	17/27	Very high	4,184	270	36,473
Chevrolet Camaro Z28 2dr[8]	16,055	14,578	15,161	86	37	16/26	Very high	4,374	358	35,936
Chevrolet Caprice 4dr wgn	19,575	17,128	17,813	86	35	17/26	Low	4,090	273	30,549
Chevrolet Caprice Classic 4dr	17,995	15,746	16,376	87	37	17/26	Low	4,044	273	30,518
Chevrolet Caprice Classic LS 4dr	19,995	17,496	18,196	87	N.A.	17/26	Low	N.A.	N.A.	N.A.
Chevrolet Cavalier RS convert.	15,395	14,394	14,970	86	43	25/36	Average	4,357	288	29,889
Chevrolet Cavalier Z24 convert.	18,305	16,566	17,229	86	41	19/28	Average	4,196	288	31,365
Chevrolet Lumina Euro 2dr	15,600	13,650	14,196	86	37	19/30	Average	5,001	314	28,744
Chevrolet Lumina Euro 4dr	15,800	13,825	14,378	86	39	19/30	Low	5,001	314	28,468
Chevrolet Lumina Z34 2dr	18,400	16,100	16,744	86	N.A.	17/27	Average	N.A.	N.A.	N.A.
Chrysler Concorde 4dr	18,341	16,080	18,341	85	N.A.	20/28	N.A.	N.A.	N.A.	N.A.
Chrysler LeBaron convert.	17,399	15,607	16,231	90	40	23/28	Average	4,152	277	28,681
Chrysler LeBaron GTC 2dr	16,840	15,101	15,705	90	33	19/28	Average	4,123	270	29,360
Chrysler LeBaron GTC convert.	19,815	17,709	18,417	89	38	19/28	Average	4,123	270	31,383
Chrysler LeBaron Landau 4dr	17,119	15,353	15,967	90	32	21/28	Low	4,359	270	29,668
Chrysler New Yorker Salon 4dr	18,705	16,384	17,039	85	35	20/26	Very low	4,331	229	30,316
Dodge Daytona IROC R/T	19,185	17,425	17,948	85	30	19/27	Very high	4,622	347	31,650
Dodge Dynasty LE 4dr	16,267	14,257	14,827	85	42	21/28	Low	4,085	267	26,426

Notes: [1] Estimate [2] Dealer's average cost as a percentage of suggested retail price [3] Compared with other models in its class [4] Includes scheduled maintenance, as well as replacement of tires, brake pads, batteries and other parts [5] Average five-year repair costs not covered by warranty [6] Includes depreciation, financing, maintenance, repairs, state taxes and registration fees, insurance and fuel. Resale value, insurance, maintenance and repair costs are based on 1992 model history. [7] Includes a $375 destination charge [8] 1992 model; 1993s will be introduced early next year. N.A.: Not available **Sources:** Intellichoice Inc., AutoAdvisor Inc., Insurance Services Office and the manufacturers

MAKE AND MODEL	Suggested retail price	Estimated dealer's cost	Your target price	Options price as a % of retail[2]	Five-year resale as a % of original	Miles per gallon (city/hwy.)	Cost to insure[3]	Five-year costs		
								Mainte-nance[4]	Repairs[5]	Total ownership costs[6]
Dodge Intrepid 4dr	$15,930	$14,016	$15,930	85%	N.A.	20/28	N.A.	N.A.	N.A.	N.A.
Dodge Intrepid ES 4dr	17,189	15,086	17,189	85	N.A.	20/28	N.A.	N.A.	N.A.	N.A.
Dodge Stealth 2dr	18,506	16,900	17,576	86	N.A.	18/24	High	N.A.	$704	N.A.
Eagle Talon TSi Turbo 2dr	15,703	14,548	15,130	85	46%	22/29	High	$5,665	231	$32,289
Eagle Talon TSi Turbo AWD 2dr	17,772	16,435	17,092	85	43	20/25	High	5,631	231	35,265
Eagle Vision ESi 4dr	17,387	15,264	17,387	85	N.A.	20/28	N.A.	N.A.	N.A.	N.A.
Ford Crown Victoria 4dr	19,972	17,146	17,832	86	36	18/26	Low	3,600	219	30,192
Ford Mustang GT 2dr hatch	15,747	14,144	14,710	85	47	17/24	Very high	4,675	286	32,688
Ford Mustang LX convert.	17,548	15,747	16,377	85	48	22/30	Very high	3,800	209	32,494
Ford Probe GT 2dr hatch	15,174	13,630	14,175	85	43	21/26	High	5,304	267	33,005
Ford Taurus GL 4dr	15,491	13,308	13,840	85	40	21/30	Very low	4,141	336	27,096
Ford Taurus GL 4dr wgn	16,656	14,298	14,870	85	47	21/30	Very low	4,141	336	26,590
Ford Taurus LX 4dr	18,300	15,695	16,323	85	35	21/30	Very low	4,223	336	29,011
Ford Taurus LX 4dr wgn	19,989	17,131	17,816	85	44	19/27	Very low	4,219	336	28,951
Ford Thunderbird LX 2dr	15,797	14,189	14,757	85	37	19/27	Average	3,875	228	31,404
Honda Accord EX 2dr	18,770	15,767	16,398	84	54	24/31	Average	5,303	171	27,214
Honda Accord EX 4dr	18,970	15,935	16,572	84	52	24/31	Average	5,310	171	27,245
Honda Accord LX 2dr	16,350	13,734	14,283	84	55	24/31	Average	4,876	171	24,722
Honda Accord LX 4dr	16,550	13,902	14,458	84	53	24/31	Average	4,883	171	24,726
Honda Accord LX 4dr wgn	17,975	15,099	15,703	84	53	23/28	Average	5,182	171	25,971
Honda Civic del Sol Si 2dr	15,000	12,750	13,260	85	N.A.	29/33	N.A.	N.A.	N.A.	N.A.
Honda Civic EX 4dr	15,100	12,835	13,348	85	55	29/35	Average	4,677	137	21,865
Honda Prelude S 2dr	17,000	14,280	14,851	84	64	24/31	High	4,976	169	27,268
Infiniti G20 4dr	19,500	15,600	16,224	80	N.A.	24/32	Average	4,787	401	N.A.
Mazda 626 ES 4dr	18,725	16,305	16,957	80	N.A.	21/26	Average	N.A.	N.A.	N.A.
Mazda 626 LX 4dr	16,440	14,482	15,061	80	42	26/34	Average	4,616	160	26,908
Mazda MX5 Miata convert.	15,300	13,632	14,177	80	62	24/30	Average	4,613	155	26,296
Mazda MX6 2dr	16,300	14,358	14,932	80	44	26/34	High	4,596	172	27,295
Mazda MX6 LS 2dr	18,575	16,175	16,822	80	43	21/26	High	5,227	178	31,048
Mercury Capri XR2 convert.	17,250	14,835	15,428	84	43	23/28	High	4,895	161	33,168
Mercury Sable GS 4dr	17,349	14,891	15,487	86	40	21/30	Very low	4,611	330	27,584
Mercury Sable GS 4dr wgn	18,459	15,835	16,468	86	47	21/30	Very low	4,612	330	27,206
Mercury Sable LS 4dr	18,430	15,811	16,443	85	39	21/30	Very low	4,621	330	28,793
Mercury Sable LS 4dr wgn	19,457	16,684	17,351	85	49	21/30	Very low	4,623	330	27,766
Mitsubishi Eclipse GS Turbo 2dr hatch	18,049	15,700	16,328	82	55	21/28	High	4,101	231	25,503
Mitsubishi Expo SP 4dr wgn	15,669	13,473	14,012	80	N.A.	21/28	Average	N.A.	N.A.	N.A.
Mitsubishi Expo SP AWD 4dr wgn	17,019	14,641	15,227	80	N.A.	19/24	Average	N.A.	N.A.	N.A.
Mitsubishi Galant ES 4dr	15,509	13,182	13,709	80	42	20/26	Average	5,032	439	27,994
Mitsubishi Galant LS 4dr	16,539	14,060	14,622	80	42	20/26	Average	4,757	439	26,683
Nissan 240SX 2dr fastback	15,475	13,575	14,118	85	45	22/28	Very high	5,105	160	32,374
Nissan 240SX SE 2dr	17,220	15,105	15,709	85	42	22/28	Very high	5,105	160	34,269
Nissan 240SX SE 2dr fastback	17,675	15,505	16,125	85	42	22/28	Very high	5,105	160	34,431
Nissan Altima GLE 4dr	18,349	15,909	16,545	85	N.A.	24/30	N.A.	N.A.	N.A.	N.A.
Nissan Altima SE 4dr	16,524	14,326	14,899	85	36	24/30	N.A.	5,044	147	29,779
Oldsmobile Cutlass Cruiser SL 4dr wgn	18,399	16,099	16,743	86	38	21/29	Low	4,148	321	28,259
Oldsmobile Cutlass Ciera SL 4dr	17,899	15,662	16,288	86	36	23/31	Low	4,148	321	28,546
Oldsmobile Cutlass Supreme S 2dr	15,695	13,733	14,282	86	38	19/30	Low	4,899	242	28,108
Oldsmobile Cutlass Supreme S 4dr	15,795	13,821	14,374	86	40	19/30	Low	4,899	242	27,921
Oldsmobile EightyEight Royale 4dr	19,549	17,105	17,789	88	42	19/28	Low	4,793	256	29,285
Plymouth Laser RS Turbo 2dr hatch	15,267	14,105	14,669	85	48	21/28	High	5,606	231	31,598
Plymouth Laser RS Turbo AWD 2dr hatch	17,371	16,039	16,681	85	46	20/25	High	5,606	231	33,653
Pontiac Bonneville SE 4dr	19,444	17,014	17,695	88	37	19/28	Low	4,825	235	30,283
Pontiac Firebird Formula 2dr [8]	16,205	14,714	15,303	86	34	17/26	Very high	5,186	352	37,548
Pontiac Firebird Trans Am 2dr [8]	18,105	16,439	17,097	86	36	16/26	Very high	4,072	352	37,839
Pontiac Grand Prix SE 2dr	15,390	13,466	14,005	86	38	19/27	Low	4,571	284	27,383
Pontiac Grand Prix SE 4dr	16,190	14,166	14,733	86	40	19/27	Low	4,626	284	28,174

Notes: [1] Estimate [2] Dealer's average cost as a percentage of suggested retail price [3] Compared with other models in its class [4] Includes scheduled maintenance, as well as replacement of tires, brake pads, batteries and other parts [5] Average five-year repair costs not covered by warranty [6] Includes depreciation, financing, maintenance, repairs, state taxes and registration fees, insurance and fuel. Resale value, insurance, maintenance and repair costs are based on 1992 model history. [7] Includes a $375 destination charge [8] 1992 model; 1993s will be introduced early next year. N.A.: Not available **Sources:** Intellichoice Inc., AutoAdvisor Inc., Insurance Services Office and the manufacturers

$15,000 to $19,999

MAKE AND MODEL	Suggested retail price	Estimated dealer's cost	Your target price	Options price as a % of retail[2]	Five-year resale as a % of original	Miles per gallon (city/ hwy.)	Cost to insure[3]	Five-year costs Mainte-nance[4]	Repairs[5]	Total ownership costs[6]
Pontiac Sunbird SE convert.	$15,403	$13,940	$14,498	86%	39%	25/35	Average	$4,424	$320	$30,019
Subaru Legacy L 4dr	16,250	14,625	15,210	90	46	23/30	Average	5,813	289	26,167
Subaru Legacy L 4dr wgn	16,950	15,086	15,689	89	45	23/30	Average	5,813	289	27,308
Subaru Legacy L AWD 4dr	17,850	15,887	16,522	89	46	21/27	Average	5,591	253	28,017
Subaru Legacy L AWD 4dr wgn	18,550	16,510	17,170	89	39	21/27	Average	5,591	253	28,952
Subaru Legacy LS 4dr	19,150	16,852	17,526	88	38	23/30	Average	6,079	289	31,456
Subaru Legacy LS 4dr wgn	19,850	17,468	18,167	88	37	23/30	Average	6,079	289	32,018
Toyota Camry DX 4dr	15,158	12,809	13,321	81	52	22/30	Low	4,610	161	24,703
Toyota Camry DX 4dr wgn	17,288	14,608	15,192	81	N.A.	21/28	Low	N.A.	N.A.	N.A.
Toyota Camry DX V6 4dr	17,918	15,141	15,747	81	52	18/24	Low	4,950	172	26,632
Toyota Camry LE 4dr	17,908	15,132	15,737	81	51	22/30	Low	4,610	161	25,441
Toyota Camry LE 4dr wgn	19,228	16,248	16,898	81	N.A.	21/28	Low	N.A.	N.A.	N.A.
Toyota Camry LE V6 4dr	19,868	16,788	17,460	81	51	18/24	Low	4,950	172	27,308
Toyota Camry SE V6 4dr	19,138	16,172	16,819	81	N.A.	18/24	Low	N.A.	N.A.	N.A.
Toyota Camry XLE 4dr	19,878	16,698	17,366	81	51	22/30	Low	4,610	161	26,613
Toyota Celica GT 2dr	16,708	14,202	14,770	80	50	22/28	High	5,506	172	30,742
Toyota Celica GT 2dr lift	16,848	14,321	14,894	80	50	22/28	High	5,506	172	30,706
Toyota Celica GTS 2dr lift	18,428	15,572	16,195	80	46	22/28	High	5,751	172	33,038
Toyota Corolla LE 4dr	15,218	13,042	13,564	80	48	27/33	Average	4,822	142	23,016
Toyota MR2 2dr	18,368	15,521	16,142	80	35	21/28	Very high	5,449	243	34,105
Volkswagen Cabriolet Carat convert.	19,898[1]	17,709	18,417	86	52	24/30	Very high	4,585	163	30,655
Volkswagen Cabriolet convert.	18,380	16,358	17,012	86	54	24/30	Very high	4,585	163	28,783
Volkswagen Jetta III GLS 16V 4dr	16,254[1]	14,304	14,876	86	62	23/30	Very high	4,914	187	26,600
Volkswagen Passat GL 4dr	17,610	15,497	16,117	86	48	21/30	Average	5,352	163	29,042

$20,000 to $29,999

MAKE AND MODEL	Suggested retail price	Estimated dealer's cost	Your target price	Options price as a % of retail[2]	Five-year resale as a % of original	Miles per gallon (city/ hwy.)	Cost to insure[3]	Five-year costs Mainte-nance[4]	Repairs[5]	Total ownership costs[6]
Acura Legend 4dr	$29,200	$23,944	$25,381	82%	52%	18/25	Low	$6,280	$302	$34,550
Acura Vigor GS 4dr	26,750	22,203	23,535	83	N.A.	20/27	Average	N.A.	N.A.	N.A.
Alfa Romeo Spider convert.	21,764	18,064	18,787	83	33	22/30	High	5,089	519	38,991
Audi 90 CS 4dr	28,700	24,353	25,814	85	N.A.	20/26	N.A.	N.A.	N.A.	N.A.
Audi 90 S 4dr	25,850	21,959	23,277	85	N.A.	20/26	N.A.	N.A.	N.A.	N.A.
BMW 318 i 4dr	23,710	19,875	20,670	82	N.A.	22/30	High	N.A.	N.A.	N.A.
BMW 325 i 4dr	29,650	24,906	26,400	82	57	19/28	High	5,116	525	33,565
Buick LeSabre Limited 4dr	21,735	19,018	19,779	87	44	19/28	Low	4,953	235	30,806
Buick Park Avenue 4dr	26,040	22,525	23,877	86	44	19/27	Very low	4,987	574	33,605
Buick Park Avenue Ultra 4dr	29,395	25,427	26,953	86	42	17/27	Very low	5,040	574	38,007
Buick Roadmaster 4dr	22,555	19,736	20,525	88	N.A.	16/25	Low	4,415	273	N.A.
Buick Roadmaster Estate Wagon 4dr	23,850	20,869	22,121	88	29	16/25	Low	4,148	273	35,994
Buick Roadmaster Limited 4dr	24,920	21,805	23,113	88	N.A.	16/25	Low	4,415	273	N.A.
Chrysler Imperial 4dr	29,381	25,320	26,839	86	32	19/26	Very low	4,491	265	40,110
Chrysler New Yorker Fifth Avenue 4dr	21,948	19,261	20,031	85	31	20/26	Very low	4,546	265	34,488
Dodge Stealth ES 2dr	20,322	18,498	19,238	90	N.A.	18/24	High	N.A.	704	N.A.
Dodge Stealth R/T 2dr	27,366	24,697	26,179	90	N.A.	19/24	High	N.A.	704	N.A.
Eagle Vision TSi 4dr	21,104	18,458	21,104	85	N.A.	18/26	N.A.	N.A.	N.A.	N.A.
Ford Crown Victoria LX 4dr	21,559	18,495	19,235	86	37	18/26	Low	3,600	219	31,316
Ford Mustang LX 5.0L convert.	20,293	18,191	18,919	85	47	17/24	Very high	4,675	286	37,277
Ford Taurus SHO 4dr	24,829	21,245	22,520	85	37	18/26	Very low	4,451	336	36,633
Ford Thunderbird Super Coupe 2dr	22,030	18,856	19,610	85	41	17/24	Average	4,804	242	34,330
Honda Accord EX 4dr wgn	20,425	17,157	17,843	84	50	23/28	Average	5,303	171	28,751
Honda Accord SE 4dr	21,720	18,245	18,975	84	N.A.	22/28	Average	N.A.	N.A.	N.A.
Honda Prelude Si 2dr	20,000	16,800	17,472	84	57	22/26	High	5,644	169	32,462
Lexus ES 300 4dr	27,500	22,550	23,903	80	N.A.	18/24	Average	N.A.	401	N.A.
Mazda 929 4dr	29,200	24,835	26,325	82	41	19/24	Average	4,967	273	35,980

Notes: [1] Estimate [2] Dealer's average cost as a percentage of suggested retail price [3] Compared with other models in its class [4] Includes scheduled maintenance, as well as replacement of tires, brake pads, batteries and other parts [5] Average five-year repair costs not covered by warranty [6] Includes depreciation, financing, maintenance, repairs, state taxes and registration fees, insurance and fuel. Resale value, insurance, maintenance and repair costs are based on 1992 model history. [7] Includes a $375 destination charge [8] 1992 model; 1993s will be introduced early next year. N.A.: Not available **Sources:** Intellichoice Inc., AutoAdvisor Inc., Insurance Services Office and the manufacturers

MAKE AND MODEL	Suggested retail price	Estimated dealer's cost	Your target price	Options price as a % of retail[2]	Five-year resale as a % of original	Miles per gallon (city/hwy.)	Cost to insure[3]	Five-year costs		
								Mainte-nance[4]	Repairs[5]	Total ownership costs[6]
Mercedes Benz 190E 2.3 4dr	$28,950	$24,030	$25,472	80%	60%	20/29	Average	$5,128	$438	$32,702
Mercury Grand Marquis GS 4dr	21,973	18,857	19,611	86	40	18/26	Low	3,836	238	30,285
Mitsubishi 3000GT 2dr	23,659	20,111	21,318	81	N.A.	18/24	High	N.A.	491	N.A.
Mitsubishi Diamante ES 4dr	22,399	18,814	19,567	80	N.A.	18/24	Average	N.A.	491	N.A.
Mitsubishi Diamante LS 4dr	29,850	23,868	25,300	80	N.A.	18/25	Average	N.A.	491	N.A.
Nissan 240SX convert.	22,345	19,601	20,385	85	N.A.	22/28	Very high	N.A.	N.A.	N.A.
Nissan Maxima GXE 4dr	20,960	18,172	18,899	85	43	21/26	Average	6,279	281	31,721
Nissan Maxima SE 4dr	22,025	19,095	19,859	85	41	21/26	Average	6,191	281	33,569
Oldsmobile Cutlass Supreme convert.	22,699	19,862	20,656	86	40	19/30	Low	5,011	242	33,006
Oldsmobile Cutlass Supreme Intl. 4dr	22,899	20,037	21,239	86	38	17/27	Low	5,017	242	34,205
Oldsmobile 88 Royale LS 4dr	21,949	19,205	19,973	88	42	19/28	Low	4,793	256	31,424
Oldsmobile 98 Regency 4dr	24,999	21,874	23,186	86	40	19/27	Very low	4,939	441	35,031
Oldsmobile 98 Regency Elite 4dr	26,999	23,624	25,041	86	40	17/27	Very low	4,939	441	36,443
Pontiac Bonneville SSE 4dr	24,844	21,739	23,043	88	38	17/25	Low	4,863	235	35,203
Pontiac Grand Prix GT 2dr	20,340	17,798	18,510	86	38	19/30	Low	4,793	284	31,851
Saab 9000 CD 4dr	24,825	21,349	22,630	80	N.A.	19/27	Low	N.A.	N.A.	N.A.
Saab 9000 CS 4dr hatch	25,725	22,123	23,450	80	30	19/27	Low	5,360	425	39,781
Saab 900S 2dr hatch	20,345	17,192	17,880	80	37	20/26	High	4,559	342	36,507
Subaru Legacy LS AWD 4dr	20,750	18,260	19,356	88	38	21/27	Average	5,785	253	32,505
Subaru Legacy LS AWD 4dr wgn	21,450	18,876	20,009	88	37	21/27	Average	5,785	253	33,090
Subaru Legacy LSi 4dr	21,650	19,269	20,425	89	40	23/30	Average	6,079	289	32,063
Subaru Legacy Sport AWD 4dr	20,850	18,557	19,670	89	41	21/27	Average	6,100	253	32,843
Toyota Camry LE V6 4dr wgn	21,208	17,921	18,638	81	N.A.	18/24	Low	N.A.	N.A.	N.A.
Toyota Camry XLE V6 4dr	21,878	18,378	19,113	81	51	18/24	Low	4,950	172	28,522
Toyota Celica AllTrac Turbo 2dr lift 4WD	28,298	23,912	25,347	80	45	19/24	High	5,711	204	38,178
Toyota Celica GT convert.	21,768	18,503	19,243	80	54	22/28	High	4,987	172	33,450
Toyota MR2 Turbo 2dr	23,998	20,278	21,495	80	47	20/27	Very high	5,730	251	35,928
Volkswagen Corrado SLC 2dr	22,870	20,126	21,334	86	N.A.	18/25	Very high	N.A.	N.A.	N.A.
Volkswagen Passat GLX 4dr wgn	21,560	18,973	20,111	86	46	19/27	Average	5,352	163	29,892
Volvo 240 4dr	21,820	19,560	20,342	83	55	21/28	Very low	4,561	296	28,815
Volvo 240 4dr wgn	22,820	20,430	21,656	83	56	21/27	Very low	4,561	296	28,803
Volvo 850 GLT 4dr	24,100	21,115	24,100	82	N.A.	21/30	N.A.	N.A.	N.A.	N.A.
Volvo 940 4dr	24,995	22,070	23,394	83	36	19/27	Low	5,478	392	37,289

MAKE AND MODEL	Suggested retail price	Estimated dealer's cost	Your target price	Options price as a % of retail[2]	Five-year resale as a % of original	Miles per gallon (city/hwy.)	Cost to insure[3]	Mainte-nance[4]	Repairs[5]	Total ownership costs[6]
Acura Legend L 2dr[8]	$31,850	$26,117	$27,945	82%	56%	18/25	Average	$6,280	$302	$36,225
Acura Legend LS 4dr	35,700	29,274	31,030	82	53	18/25	Low	6,280	302	38,892
Acura NSX 2dr[8]	65,000	53,300	57,031	82	53	19/24	Average	9,716	638	72,934
Alfa Romeo 164 L 4dr	30,240	24,797	26,533	83	N.A.	18/27	Average	7,043	932	N.A.
Audi 100 CS Quattro 4dr 4WD	40,950	34,398	36,806	84	N.A.	18/23	Low	N.A.	N.A.	N.A.
Audi 100 CS Quattro 4dr wgn 4WD	44,250	37,170	39,772	84	N.A.	18/22	Low	N.A.	N.A.	N.A.
Audi S4 4dr	46,850	39,354	42,109	84	N.A.	18/23	Low	5,052	N.A.	N.A.
BMW 325 i convert.	36,320	30,395	32,523	82	61	17/24	High	4,290	525	38,979
BMW 525 i 4dr	37,100	31,095	33,272	82	53	19/28	Average	4,755	546	39,836
BMW 525 i Touring 4dr wgn	39,800	33,355	35,690	82	N.A.	18/25	Average	N.A.	546	N.A.
BMW 535 i 4dr	44,350	37,170	39,772	82	56	16/22	Average	5,575	546	46,825
BMW 740 i 4dr	54,000	44,150	54,000	82	51	16/22	Average	6,623	616	58,081
BMW 750 iL 4dr	80,900	66,145	70,775	80	N.A.	12/18	Average	8,437	616	N.A.
BMW 850 Ci 2dr	83,400	68,190	70,236	80	N.A.	12/19	Average	8,570	1,211	N.A.
BMW M5 4dr	60,700	50,988	54,557	82	N.A.	12/23	Average	7,160	N.A.	N.A.
Cadillac Allante convert.	59,975	51,459	55,061	86	33	14/21	Average	6,302	491	80,046
Cadillac DeVille Coupe 2dr	33,915	29,336	31,096	85	39	16/25	Low	5,212	363	42,892
Cadillac DeVille Sedan 4dr	32,990	28,536	30,248	85	43	16/25	Very low	5,212	363	41,130
Cadillac Eldorado 2dr	33,990	29,401	31,165	86	35	16/25	Low	5,941	434	45,997

Notes: [1] Estimate [2] Dealer's average cost as a percentage of suggested retail price [3] Compared with other models in its class [4] Includes scheduled maintenance, as well as replacement of tires, brake pads, batteries and other parts [5] Average five-year repair costs not covered by warranty [6] Includes depreciation, financing, maintenance, repairs, state taxes and registration fees, insurance and fuel. Resale value, insurance, maintenance and repair costs are based on 1992 model history. [7] Includes a $375 destination charge [8] 1992 model; 1993s will be introduced early next year. N.A.: Not available **Sources:** Intellichoice Inc., AutoAdvisor Inc., Insurance Services Office and the manufacturers

$30,000 and over

MAKE AND MODEL	Suggested retail price	Estimated dealer's cost	Your target price	Options price as a % of retail[2]	Five-year resale as a % of original	Miles per gallon (city/hwy.)	Cost to insure[3]	Five-year costs Mainte-nance[4]	Repairs[5]	Total ownership costs[6]
Cadillac Fleetwood 4dr	$33,990	$29,401	$31,165	85%	36%	16/25	Very low	$5,212	$402	$49,159
Cadillac Seville 4dr	36,990	31,996	34,236	85	39	16/25	Low	6,354	399	47,141
Cadillac Seville STS 4dr	41,990	36,321	38,863	85	40	16/25	Low	6,344	399	49,189
Chevrolet Corvette 2dr hatch	34,595	29,579	31,354	84	44	17/25	Average	7,215	356	50,576
Chevrolet Corvette convert.	41,195	35,222	37,688	84	46	17/25	Average	7,215	356	57,226
Dodge Viper convert.	50,000	43,625	46,679	N.A.	N.A.	N.A.	Average	N.A.	N.A.	N.A.
Infiniti J30 4dr	34,000	27,200	28,832	80	N.A.	18/23	N.A.	N.A.	N.A.	N.A.
Infiniti Q45 4dr	45,400	36,520	39,076	80	59	17/22	Low	6,013	401	44,449
Jaguar XJS 2dr	49,750	41,611	44,524	82	43	14/22	Average	8,404	1,079	75,685
Jaguar XJS convert.	56,750	47,466	50,789	82	53	14/21	Average	8,404	1,079	75,524
Jaguar XJ6 4dr	49,750	40,596	43,438	82	54	17/24	Average	7,118	1,079	49,333
Jaguar XJ6 Vanden Plas 4dr	56,750	46,308	49,550	82	50	17/24	Average	7,118	1,079	57,382
Lexus LS 400 4dr	46,600	37,280	39,890	80	58	18/23	Low	5,770	401	43,531
Lexus SC 300 2dr	34,700	28,454	30,161	80	N.A.	18/23	Average	N.A.	401	N.A.
Lexus SC 400 2dr	41,400	33,120	41,400	80	N.A.	18/23	Average	6,927	401	N.A.
Lincoln Continental Executive 4dr	33,328	28,256	29,951	84	32	17/26	Very low	6,502	455	45,153
Lincoln Mark VIII 2dr	36,640	31,144	33,324	84	35	17/24	Average	4,513	399	N.A.
Lincoln Town Car Executive 4dr	34,190	28,990	30,729	84	34	18/26	Very low	4,114	310	41,313
Mazda RX7 2dr	32,500	27,641	29,299	84	N.A.	17/25	N.A.	N.A.	N.A.	N.A.
Mercedes Benz 300 E 4dr	49,900	39,920	42,714	80	61	18/23	Low	5,157	416	43,812
Mercedes Benz 300 SD 4dr	69,900	58,020	62,081	80	N.A.	20/23	Low	N.A.	430	N.A.
Mercedes Benz 300 SE 4dr	69,900	58,020	62,081	80	61	15/19	Low	3,569	416	58,312
Mercedes Benz 300 SL convert.	83,300	66,640	71,305	80	69	16/23	Average	6,747	438	64,569
Mercedes Benz 300 TE 4dr wgn	54,400	43,520	46,566	80	62	17/21	Low	5,199	416	47,788
Mercedes Benz 400 E 4dr	56,400	45,120	48,278	80	N.A.	18/24	Low	5,273	294	N.A.
Mercedes Benz 500 SL convert.	98,500	78,800	98,500	80	69	14/18	Average	6,840	294	79,085
Mercedes Benz 600 SEL 4dr	127,800	102,240	127,800	80	N.A.	11/15	Low	4,913	N.A.	N.A.
Nissan 300ZX 2dr	30,095	25,786	27,333	86	42	18/24	Average	5,694	234	46,313
Nissan 300ZX convert.	36,570	31,333	33,526	86	N.A.	18/24	Average	N.A.	N.A.	N.A.
Porsche 911 Carrera 2 2dr	64,990	54,405	58,213	84	65	15/23	Average	5,968	294	63,576
Porsche 911 Carrera 2 Cabriolet convert.	77,340	62,070	66,415	84	69	15/23	Average	5,968	294	60,661
Porsche 928 GTS 2dr	82,260	68,030	72,792	83	N.A.	13/19	Average	N.A.	N.A.	N.A.
Saab 900 Turbo convert.	37,060	30,834	32,992	80	53	20/26	High	5,246	384	43,608
Saab 9000 CSE 4dr hatch	31,060	25,687	27,228	80	31	19/27	Low	5,360	425	41,155
Saab 900S convert.	32,160	27,175	28,806	80	53	20/26	High	4,559	342	39,349
Volvo 960 4dr	35,675	30,155	32,266	83	N.A.	17/25	Low	N.A.	638	N.A.
Volvo 960 4dr wgn	36,675	30,975	33,143	83	N.A.	17/25	Low	N.A.	638	N.A.

Minivans

MAKE AND MODEL	Suggested retail price	Estimated dealer's cost	Your target price	Options price as a % of retail[2]	Five-year resale as a % of original	Miles per gallon (city/hwy.)	Cost to insure[3]	Five-year costs Mainte-nance[4]	Repairs[5]	Total ownership costs[6]
Chevrolet Astro 3dr	$15,605	$14,123	$14,688	86%	71%	16/21	Very low	$4,446	$340	$23,803
Chevrolet Astro AWD 3dr	17,925	16,222	16,871	86	76	15/20	Very low	5,881	351	25,882
Chevrolet Astro Extended 3dr	16,295	14,747	15,337	86	67	16/21	Very low	5,881	351	27,769
Chevrolet Lumina APV 3dr	15,895	14,385	14,960	86	61	18/23	Low	4,557	321	25,631
Chevrolet Lumina APV LS 3dr	17,995	16,285	16,936	86	60	18/23	Low	4,530	321	26,500
Chrysler Town & Country 3dr	25,538	23,153	24,542	90	64	18/23	Very low	4,188	340	30,896
Chrysler Town & Country AWD 3dr	27,529	24,906	26,400	90	64	17/22	Very low	4,188	351	32,543
Dodge Caravan 3dr	14,073	12,869	13,384	85	74	20/30	Very low	4,002	325	21,935
Dodge Caravan LE 3dr	20,841	18,825	19,578	85	63	19/24	Very low	4,076	325	26,479
Dodge Caravan SE 3dr	16,101	14,654	15,240	85	73	20/26	Very low	4,002	325	22,901
Dodge Caravan SE AWD 3dr	19,285	17,481	18,180	85	72	17/22	Very low	3,720	336	24,888
Dodge Grand Caravan LE 3dr	21,784	19,680	20,467	86	69	18/23	Very low	3,831	340	25,903
Dodge Grand Caravan LE AWD 3dr	23,884	21,528	22,820	86	70	17/22	Very low	3,733	351	27,635
Dodge Grand Caravan SE 3dr	17,935	16,293	16,945	85	77	18/23	Very low	3,831	340	23,023

Notes: [1] Estimate [2] Dealer's average cost as a percentage of suggested retail price [3] Compared with other models in its class [4] Includes scheduled maintenance, as well as replacement of tires, brake pads, batteries and other parts [5] Average five-year repair costs not covered by warranty [6] Includes depreciation, financing, maintenance, repairs, state taxes and registration fees, insurance and fuel. Resale value, insurance, maintenance and repair costs are based on 1992 model history. [7] Includes a $375 destination charge [8] 1992 model; 1993s will be introduced early next year. N.A.: Not available **Sources:** Intellichoice Inc., AutoAdvisor Inc., Insurance Services Office and the manufacturers

Minivans

MAKE AND MODEL	Suggested retail price	Estimated dealer's cost	Your target price	Options price as a % of retail[2]	Five-year resale as a % of original	Miles per gallon (city/ hwy.)	Cost to insure[3]	Five-year costs		Total ownership costs[6]
								Mainte-nance[4]	Repairs[5]	
Dodge Grand Caravan SE AWD 3dr	$20,035	$18,141	$18,866	85%	79%	17/22	Very low	$3,733	$351	$24,035
Ford Aerostar Eddie Bauer 3dr	22,462	19,917	20,714	87	63	16/22	Low	4,081	495	27,363
Ford Aerostar Eddie Bauer 4WD 3dr	24,371	21,596	22,892	87	64	15/20	Low	4,021	350	29,739
Ford Aerostar XL 3dr	14,360	12,787	13,298	85	70	17/24	Low	4,081	495	23,227
Ford Aerostar XL 4WD 3dr	17,829	15,840	16,474	85	71	15/20	Low	4,021	350	24,831
Ford Aerostar XL Extended 3dr	15,759	14,018	14,579	85	70	17/24	Low	4,081	495	24,420
Ford Aerostar XL Extended 4WD 3dr	18,475	16,408	17,064	85	72	15/20	Low	4,021	350	25,540
Ford Aerostar XLT 3dr	19,585	17,385	18,080	87	69	17/24	Low	4,081	495	24,809
Ford Aerostar XLT 4WD 3dr	21,135	18,749	19,499	87	70	15/20	Low	4,021	350	25,894
Ford Aerostar XLT Extended 3dr	20,085	17,825	18,538	87	69	17/24	Low	4,081	495	25,953
GMC Safari SLX 3dr	15,824	14,321	14,894	86	69	16/21	Very low	3,771	340	23,404
GMC Safari SLX AWD 3dr	18,144	16,420	17,077	86	74	15/20	Very low	3,781	351	23,737
GMC Safari SLX XT 3dr	16,514	14,945	15,543	86	69	16/21	Very low	3,781	340	23,842
GMC Safari SLX XT AWD 3dr	18,784	17,000	17,680	86	72	15/20	Very low	3,781	351	24,413
Mazda MPV 3dr	16,555	14,750	15,340	82	56	18/24	Average	4,645	242	27,913
Mazda MPV 4WD 3dr	21,700	19,335	20,108	82	63	15/19	Average	4,659	280	28,996
Mercury Villager GS 3dr	16,504	14,688	15,276	85	N.A.	17/23	N.A.	N.A.	N.A.	N.A.
Mercury Villager LS 3dr	21,798	19,347	20,121	85	N.A.	17/23	N.A.	N.A.	N.A.	N.A.
Nissan Quest GXE 3dr	21,450	18,597	19,341	85	N.A.	17/23	N.A.	N.A.	N.A.	N.A.
Nissan Quest XE 3dr	17,545	14,865	15,460	85	N.A.	17/23	N.A.	N.A.	N.A.	N.A.
Oldsmobile Silhouette 3dr	19,499	17,647	18,353	83	51	18/23	Low	4,483	378	30,450
Plymouth Grand Voyager 3dr	17,555	15,958	16,596	85	77	19/24	Very low	4,200	340	22,524
Plymouth Grand Voyager LE 3dr	21,735	19,637	20,422	86	69	18/23	Very low	4,077	340	26,124
Plymouth Grand Voyager SE 3dr	17,935	16,293	16,945	85	77	18/23	Very low	4,077	340	23,145
Plymouth Grand Voyager SE AWD 3dr	20,035	18,141	18,867	86	79	17/22	Very low	3,959	351	24,113
Plymouth Voyager 3dr	14,073	12,869	13,384	85	74	20/30	Very low	4,142	323	21,794
Plymouth Voyager LE 3dr	20,703	18,704	19,452	85	63	19/24	Very low	4,216	323	26,545
Plymouth Voyager SE 3dr	16,101	14,654	15,240	85	72	20/30	Very low	4,142	323	23,056
Plymouth Voyager SE AWD 3dr	19,285	17,481	18,180	85	71	17/22	Very low	3,935	334	25,154
Pontiac Trans Sport SE 3dr	16,689	15,104	15,708	86	55	18/23	Low	4,446	346	27,442
Toyota Previa AllTrac DX 3dr 4WD	22,348	18,996	19,756	82	59	17/21	Average	4,855	228	29,199
Toyota Previa AllTrac LE 3dr 4WD	26,068	22,158	23,487	82	56	17/21	Average	4,833	228	31,986
Toyota Previa DX 3dr	18,498	15,816	16,449	82	57	18/22	Average	4,855	221	27,851
Toyota Previa LE 3dr	23,258	19,769	20,560	82	56	18/22	Average	4,833	221	29,221
Volkswagen Eurovan CL 3dr	16,640	15,099	15,703	88	N.A.	17/21	N.A.	N.A.	N.A.	N.A.
Volkswagen Eurovan GL 3dr	20,420	18,009	18,729	88	N.A.	17/21	N.A.	N.A.	N.A.	N.A.
Volkswagen Eurovan MV 3dr	21,850	19,268	20,039	88	N.A.	17/21	N.A.	N.A.	N.A.	N.A.

Utility vehicles

MAKE AND MODEL	Suggested retail price	Estimated dealer's cost	Your target price	Options price as a % of retail[2]	Five-year resale as a % of original	Miles per gallon (city/ hwy.)	Cost to insure[3]	Mainte-nance[4]	Repairs[5]	Total ownership costs[6]
Chevrolet S10 Blazer 2dr	$14,823	$13,489	$14,029	86%	61%	17/23	Average	$3,784	$294	$26,040
Chevrolet S10 Blazer 4dr	15,783	14,284	14,855	86	61	18/23	Average	3,784	294	26,526
Chevrolet S10 Blazer 4WD 2dr	16,583	15,008	15,608	86	58	16/21	Average	4,314	389	28,612
Chevrolet S10 Blazer 4WD 4dr	17,953	16,247	16,897	86	58	16/21	Average	4,314	389	29,427
Ford Explorer Eddie Bauer 4WD 4dr	24,066	21,353	22,634	85	54	17/22	Low	3,856	638	32,909
Ford Explorer Sport 2dr	17,649	15,706	16,334	85	60	18/23	Low	3,683	552	26,627
Ford Explorer Sport 4WD 2dr	19,380	17,229	17,918	85	59	17/22	Low	3,772	638	28,158
Ford Explorer XL 4WD 4dr	19,246	17,111	17,795	85	60	17/22	Low	3,772	638	28,120
Ford Explorer XLT 4WD 4dr	21,318	18,935	19,692	85	58	17/22	Low	3,772	638	29,556
Geo Tracker 4WD 2dr	11,750	11,186	11,633	89	52	25/27	High	5,065	210	24,857
Geo Tracker 4WD Soft Top 2dr	11,585	11,029	11,470	89	53	25/27	High	5,065	210	24,528
Geo Tracker LSi 4WD 2dr	12,950	12,328	12,821	89	50	25/27	High	5,065	210	26,022
GMC Jimmy 2dr	15,022	13,595	14,139	86	61	18/23	Average	3,488	242	24,205
GMC Jimmy 4WD 2dr	16,905	15,299	15,911	86	59	16/21	Average	3,488	330	26,321
GMC Jimmy 4WD 4dr	18,287	16,550	17,212	86	59	16/21	Average	3,488	330	27,003

Notes: [1] Estimate [2] Dealer's average cost as a percentage of suggested retail price [3] Compared with other models in its class [4] Includes scheduled maintenance, as well as replacement of tires, brake pads, batteries and other parts [5] Average five-year repair costs not covered by warranty [6] Includes depreciation, financing, maintenance, repairs, state taxes and registration fees, insurance and fuel. Resale value, insurance, maintenance and repair costs are based on 1992 model history. [7] Includes a $375 destination charge [8] 1992 model; 1993s will be introduced early next year. N.A.: Not available Sources: Intellichoice Inc., AutoAdvisor Inc., Insurance Services Office and the manufacturers

Utility vehicles

MAKE AND MODEL	Suggested retail price	Estimated dealer's cost	Your target price	Options price as a % of retail[2]	Five-year resale as a % of original	Miles per gallon (city/hwy.)	Cost to insure[3]	Five-year costs Mainte-nance[4]	Repairs[5]	Total ownership costs[6]
Isuzu Amigo XS 4WD 2dr	$15,733[1]	$14,160	$14,726	85%	64%	18/21	High	$4,602	$491	$25,853
Isuzu Rodeo LS 4WD 4dr	15,599[1]	13,727	14,276	85	52	18/21	Average	4,285	491	27,198
Isuzu Rodeo XS 4WD 4dr	18,500[1]	16,280	16,931	85	53	18/21	Average	4,285	561	29,166
Isuzu Trooper LS 4dr 4WD	24,856[1]	21,128	22,396	80	N.A.	15/17	Average	N.A.	N.A.	N.A.
Jeep Cherokee 2dr	12,137	11,490	11,949	85	67	20/23	Average	4,057	310	24,168
Jeep Cherokee 4WD 4dr	14,632	13,785	14,337	85	72	19/22	Average	4,400	368	25,601
Jeep Cherokee Country 4WD 4dr	18,533	16,779	17,450	85	63	16/20	Average	4,400	368	29,085
Jeep Cherokee Sport 4WD 4dr	16,845	15,294	15,905	85	63	16/20	Average	4,446	368	27,523
Jeep Grand Cherokee 4WD 4dr	19,700	17,951	19,700	85	N.A.	16/21	Average	N.A.	N.A.	N.A.
Jeep Grand Cherokee Laredo 4WD 4dr	20,884	18,993	20,884	85	N.A.	16/21	Average	N.A.	N.A.	N.A.
Jeep Grand Cherokee Limited 4WD 4dr	28,440	25,642	28,440	86	N.A.	16/21	Average	N.A.	N.A.	N.A.
Jeep Wrangler 2dr 4WD	13,343	12,127	12,612	85	67	18/20	Average	4,336	253	23,743
Mazda Navajo DX 4WD 2dr	17,595	15,308	15,920	87	56	17/22	Low	4,295	552	26,968
Mitsubishi Montero LS 4dr 4WD	24,650	20,820	22,070	80	53	15/18	Average	4,579	263	31,769
Nissan Pathfinder SEV6 4WD 4dr	23,230	20,378	21,601	86	78	15/18	High	4,909	214	26,836
Nissan Pathfinder XEV6 4dr	18,090	15,868	16,503	85	80	15/19	High	4,743	182	24,398
Oldsmobile Bravada 4dr 4WD	25,349	22,941	24,317	89	N.A.	16/21	Average	4,715	N.A.	N.A.
Range Rover County 4dr 4WD	44,500	38,270	40,949	86	64	12/15	High	7,152	932	46,522
Suzuki Samurai JL Soft Top 2dr 4WD	8,599	7,739	7,971	90	48	28/29	High	4,676	180	20,171
Suzuki Sidekick JLX Hardtop 4dr 4WD	14,199	12,353	12,847	87	47	24/26	High	5,520	213	25,778
Suzuki Sidekick JX Hardtop 4dr 4WD	12,999	11,309	11,761	87	N.A.	24/26	High	N.A.	N.A.	N.A.
Toyota 4Runner SR5 4WD 4dr	18,938	16,097	16,741	80	80	19/22	High	3,944	228	23,523
Toyota 4Runner SR5 V6 4WD 4dr	20,778	17,557	18,259	80	79	14/18	High	4,322	228	25,928
Toyota Land Cruiser 4dr 4WD	31,178	26,034	27,596	80	58	12/15	Average	4,319	230	34,145

Small pickups

MAKE AND MODEL	Suggested retail price	Estimated dealer's cost	Your target price	Options price as a % of retail[2]	Five-year resale as a % of original	Miles per gallon (city/hwy.)	Cost to insure[3]	Five-year costs Mainte-nance[4]	Repairs[5]	Total ownership costs[6]
Chevrolet S10 4WD reg. cab	$13,696	$12,395	$12,891	86%	48%	16/21	Average	$4,317	$311	$26,326
Chevrolet S10 Maxi Cab ext. cab	11,630	10,525	10,946	86	57	23/27	Average	3,760	221	21,754
Chevrolet S10 reg. cab	10,130	9,168	9,443	86	59	23/27	Average	3,687	221	20,185
Dodge Dakota 4WD reg. cab	14,751	13,376	13,911	85	50	15/19	Average	3,515	234	25,473
Dodge Dakota Club Cab ext. cab	12,414	11,279	11,730	85	54	22/27	Average	3,515	217	23,459
Dodge Dakota reg. cab	11,162	10,178	10,585	85	54	22/27	Average	3,515	217	22,401
Dodge Dakota Sport reg. cab	9,943	9,304	9,583	85	49	22/27	Average	3,515	217	22,145
Dodge Power Ram 50 reg. cab 4WD	11,956	11,149	11,595	86	57	19/22	High	4,113	184	23,026
Dodge Ram 50 reg. cab	8,865	8,475	8,729	86	58	19/24	High	3,973	120	20,565
Ford Ranger STX 4WD reg. cab	14,861	13,183	13,710	85	46	22/26	Average	3,563	209	26,374
Ford Ranger STX reg. cab	11,293	10,043	10,445	85	58	23/28	Average	3,731	209	22,873
Ford Ranger STX Supercab ext. cab	12,964	11,513	11,974	85	53	23/28	Average	3,563	209	24,426
Ford Ranger XL reg. cab	8,753	8,158	8,403	85	59	23/28	Average	3,657	153	19,867
Ford Ranger XLT Supercab ext. cab	12,147	10,794	11,226	85	N.A.	23/28	Average	N.A.	N.A.	N.A.
GMC Sonoma 4WD reg. cab	13,895	12,575	13,078	86	N.A.	16/21	Average	3,417	311	N.A.
GMC Sonoma Club Coupe ext. cab	11,829	10,705	11,133	86	N.A.	23/27	Average	3,295	221	N.A.
GMC Sonoma reg. cab	10,329	9,348	9,628	86	54	23/27	Average	3,295	221	21,217
Isuzu Pickup S 4WD reg. cab	12,535[1]	11,031	11,472	85	47	17/20	High	4,131	133	25,512
Isuzu Pickup S reg. cab	8,814[1]	7,933	8,171	85	53	22/24	High	3,998	128	21,156
Mazda B2200 reg. cab	8,775	8,086	8,329	81	70	21/26	High	3,736	113	18,577
Mazda B2600i 4WD reg. cab	11,835	10,906	11,342	81	64	18/20	High	3,943	121	22,208
Mitsubishi Mighty Max 4WD reg. cab	12,979	11,421	11,878	80	50	19/22	High	3,895	172	24,312
Mitsubishi Mighty Max reg. cab	8,539	7,714	7,945	80	54	19/24	High	3,705	132	20,173
Nissan Pickup 4WD reg. cab	12,830	11,647	12,113	85	67	18/22	High	4,205	157	22,894
Nissan Pickup reg. cab	8,995	8,441	8,694	85	67	23/27	High	3,839	127	19,557
Toyota Pickup DX 4WD reg. cab	13,518	11,828	12,301	82	64	19/22	High	4,272	157	24,917
Toyota Pickup reg. cab	9,188	8,269	8,517	82	67	23/28	High	3,836	119	19,246

Notes: [1] Estimate [2] Dealer's average cost as a percentage of suggested retail price [3] Compared with other models in its class [4] Includes scheduled maintenance, as well as replacement of tires, brake pads, batteries and other parts [5] Average five-year repair costs not covered by warranty [6] Includes depreciation, financing, maintenance, repairs, state taxes and registration fees, insurance and fuel. Resale value, insurance, maintenance and repair costs are based on 1992 model history. [7] Includes a $375 destination charge [8] 1992 model; 1993s will be introduced early next year. N.A.: Not available **Sources:** Intellichoice Inc., AutoAdvisor Inc., Insurance Services Office and the manufacturers

Chapter 8

The Best Colleges for Your Money

America's colleges and universities have entered an age of austerity. You may have thought that choosing a school for your child was all about books and professors, libraries and labs. Instead, as the campus budget squeeze gets tighter than ever, your search for the right school is really all about money. Overall, 57% of the nation's colleges and universities saw their operating budgets cut during the 1991–92 academic year, according to a survey of 411 schools by the American Council on Education. Public schools fared worse than private ones. That means students entering college this fall can expect higher tuition, fewer teachers and course offerings, increasingly crowded classrooms, diminished student services and sports programs, and less financial aid from the schools.

No wonder parents of today's college-bound children are asking themselves: how can we possibly afford college? And if we can manage to find the money, how can we be sure of getting value? This chapter will help you do both. Beginning on page 161, our exclusive value rankings highlight the 100 public and private schools that deliver the most for the dollar. We also advise you on saving and investing wisely for college expenses, whether your child is a toddler or a teen, and the best strategies for playing the financial aid game. Hundreds of colleges still provide topnotch educations. But you have to work harder to discover them. If that prospect seems daunting, you should just bear in mind that the more time you and your child spend investigating schools, the happier you are likely to be with your choice.

Meeting the High Cost of College

Whether your children are in diapers or driver's ed, these investing and savings strategies can help you pay their college bills.

College costs still look daunting, no matter how you crunch the numbers. If they continue to climb at the 7% annual average rate of the past 15 years, by 2010 you'll have to shell out more than $135,000 just to put today's newborn through the typical public university. Beget a genius destined for an ivy-clad campus and you're looking at a four-year bill close to $360,000. Now multiply the figures by the number of children you have. Sums that ugly are enough to make most parents throw up their hands in despair.

Don't get blue, get busy. The specific investments that will work best for your college fund depend primarily on how long you have before your first tuition bill. The following advice is divided into three sections tailored to your

child's age. (If you have more than one child, set up separate portfolios, gearing the investments in each account to that child's age.) But before you turn to the specific advice, review these universal rules that tend to apply to all families trying to build a college fund.

Make stocks the centerpiece of your plan. A half-century's experience demonstrates that only stocks can give you the growth you'll need to keep pace with college-cost inflation. According to data compiled by Ibbotson Associates, a Chicago investment research firm, since the end of World War II, stocks have gained an average of 12.3% a year, more than double the average annual returns of 5.7% for intermediate-term government bonds (whose yields are similar to those on U.S. Savings Bonds and long-term CDs) and just 4.8% for Treasury bills (similar to short-term CDs). And while stocks can suffer alarmingly big dips over short periods, they have not lost money in any of the 52 separate 10-year holding periods since 1931.

Invest an amount you can comfortably afford. "One of the biggest mistakes that families make is trying to save too much right away," says Raymond Loewe, president of Educational Planning Systems, a financial planning firm in Marlton, New Jersey. "They wreck their budgets, which forces them to chuck their investment plans, and they end up without a dime saved for college." The worksheet on page 153 will tell you how much you'll need to sock away each year. But don't be discouraged if the amount seems out of reach. Instead of setting lofty initial goals, begin with a modest sum that you can easily do without, say $50 or $100 a month. Then, as your income increases through raises and promotions, you can bump up the amount you save. A number of top mutual fund companies—including Dreyfus, Fidelity, Janus, T. Rowe Price and Vanguard—will lower or waive their minimum investments if you deposit a fixed amount each month or open a custodial account for a child.

Invest mostly in your name, not your children's. At best, the modest tax breaks accorded a child's investment income can save you a few hundred dollars a year. Under current law, the child's first $600 in investment income is tax-free and the next $600 is taxed at the child's rate, usually 15%. Any amount that he or she earns above $1,200 is taxed at your rate until the child turns 14. At worst, investing in a child's name can disqualify your family for financial aid or cost you several thousand dollars in assistance. Reason: the formula for determining aid requires a child to contribute as much as 35% of his or her savings, while parents are expected to ante up no more than 5.6% of their savings (see "The New Rules of Financial Aid" later in this chapter).

Don't neglect your retirement. "The parent who says 'I can't contribute to my 401(k) or IRA because all my money is going into the kids' college funds' is one sandwich short of a picnic," says Jonathan Pond, president of Financial Planning Information in Boston. "If you really can afford to invest in only one, the retirement account should be your choice." Why? Your dollars work harder in a retirement account because the earnings are not taxed until you withdraw them. Plus, with most 401(k)s, your employer makes matching contributions. And colleges rarely count retirement savings when determining your eligibility for financial aid.

With these rules in mind, you're ready to get started. Unless otherwise indicated, all mutual funds mentioned on the following pages do not charge sales commissions, or loads.

BIRTH THROUGH AGE EIGHT

For a running start, stash 65% to 90% of your savings in growth stocks. While stocks offer superior long-term returns, the market declines during one out of every four years, on average. Holding investments for a decade or more, however, should help to smooth out those bumps and grinds. That's why financial advisers recommend that parents of young children put 65% to 90% of their college savings into stocks. The greater your tolerance for risk, the higher your commitment can be.

You might make your first investment in a growth-stock fund that loads up on large and medium-size companies with histories of strong profit gains. While these stocks may return a few percentage points less over time than shares of tiny companies with more explosive profits, they're also likely to avoid the worst of the sharp drops that periodically plague smaller issues. For many parents, a steadier performance could make the difference between staying the course with stocks or fleeing back to safe but low-yielding CDs and savings bonds. "If you have 10 to 15 years to invest, you're a marathoner," says Don Phillips, publisher of *Morningstar Mutual Funds*, a fund rating service in Chicago. "If you start out with a fund that's a sprinter and it stumbles, you might quit the race before it's over."

To further reduce the chances of a severe loss, stick with growth funds that have consistently beaten the market while taking below-average risks. Phillips recommends Gabelli Growth ($1,000 minimum initial investment; 800-422-3554), which has earned 46% more than the average growth fund during the past three years with 20% less risk. Phoenix Growth ($500 minimum; 800-243-4361), a 4.75%-load fund favored by Raymond Loewe, keeps risks even lower by making adroit moves into cash when stocks look overpriced. Financial adviser Michael Kabarec of Palantine, Illinois suggests Financial Industrial Income ($250 minimum; 800-525-8085). Its substantial income from bonds and high-yielding stocks helps to cushion the price swings in its growth holdings and to keep its risk level at just 65% of that of the average stock fund.

Once your stake grows to, say, $3,000 or $5,000, you might begin to diversify among different types of funds, including a small-company holding and an international fund. Since 1926, Ibbotson calculates that small-company stocks have returned an average of 12% annually, vs. 10% for bigger companies. But small stocks' often dramatic price swings can give you a bad case of whiplash. That's why Kabarec urges parents to favor small-company funds with consistent records rather than the ones with the most eye-popping recent performances. "You want the fund that will have a warm decade as opposed to one hot year," he says.

Kabarec's top choice is Pennsylvania Mutual ($2,000 minimum; 800-221-4268), whose value-will-out approach makes it one of the least volatile small-company funds. Philadelphia financial planner Neil Kauffman is similarly impressed with Monetta ($100 minimum; 800-666-3882). Its manager's relatively quick sales of sinking stocks and willingness to hoard cash when the market looks too expensive have enabled the fund to make money in each of the

calendar years since its 1986 inception.

Kauffman suggests dipping your toes into international waters with Harbor International ($2,000 minimum; 800-422-1050), which consistently ranks in the top 10% of its category while taking 20% less risk than the average international fund. He also likes Scudder Global ($1,000 minimum; 800-225-2470), which is less risky than Harbor and only slightly less profitable.

For the 10% to 35% of your money that you don't put into stocks, financial advisers suggest government or high-quality corporate bonds with maturities of three to 10 years or funds that hold such issues. These bonds, recently yielding 4.8% to 6.7%, haven't suffered a calendar-year loss in more than two decades. Yet with annual returns averaging 10% over the past 15 years, they have bested more volatile longer-term bonds by half a percentage point.

The safest bonds over the long haul are Treasury securities. While their market value fluctuates with changing interest rates, their interest and principal payments are guaranteed by the federal government. As a bonus, you pay no state or local taxes on your interest. You can buy Treasuries direct from the Federal Reserve at no commission (call 202-452-3000 for information). Or you can invest through funds. Two solid choices worth considering, according to several advisers, are Fidelity Spartan Limited Maturity Government ($10,000 minimum; 800-544-8888), which holds such securities as short-term and intermediate-term Treasuries and mortgage-backed Ginnie Maes, and Harbor Bond ($2,000 minimum; 800-422-1050), whose portfolio is concentrated in government agency issues and corporate bonds of intermediate term.

Higher income families in the 28% federal tax bracket may do better in a tax-free municipal bond fund. One that delivers above-average returns with below-average risk, according to Jonathan Pond, is Vanguard Municipal Intermediate Term ($3,000 minimum; 800-662-7447). Its recent 6% tax-free yield is equivalent to a taxable 8.5% for investors in the 28% bracket.

AGES NINE THROUGH THIRTEEN

To keep your fund growing safely in these years, start to move toward a fifty-fifty mix of stocks and bonds. With five to 10 years before your first college bill, continue to steer at least half of your new investment dollars into stocks. During this period, you also might gradually bump up your holdings of fixed-income securities so that your assets will be about evenly split between stocks and bonds by the time your child enters high school. One easy way to achieve this redistribution is to direct roughly three-quarters of your new savings into balanced mutual funds, which typically keep 25% to 40% of their portfolios in bonds. The interest income generated by the bonds helps to cushion against big losses when stock prices fall.

Don Phillips of *Morningstar* suggests going with a "classic" balanced fund such as Vanguard's Wellington ($3,000 minimum; 800-662-7447). It keeps 60% to 70% of its assets firmly grounded in stalwart blue-chip stocks. For a bit more oomph, Phillips recommends Twentieth Century Balanced (no minimum investment; 800-366-5465). This fund looks for outsize gains by making a 60% commitment to growth stocks, but then tempers the risk with high-quality bonds of intermediate term. Over the past three years, Twentieth Century Balanced has returned 82% more than the typical balanced fund without assuming more risk.

Intermediate Treasuries and bond funds continue to be an excellent choice for the remaining 25% of your new savings dollars. If you earn less than $100,000 a year, you might also buy some Series EE savings bonds. As long as you use the money for your child's college tuition, interest on the bonds, which are guaranteed to yield a minimum of 6% if held for five years or more, will be at least partially free from federal taxes. (The full exemption starts to phase out for married couples filing jointly when their adjusted gross income reaches $66,200 and disappears completely at $96,200; those figures are adjusted upward every year with inflation.) Another plus:

How Much to Save

Use this worksheet to estimate the amount you must save to cover bills for a child who enters college at age 18. The worksheet makes these assumptions: costs will increase by 7% annually; your investments will earn 6.5% a year after taxes; and you will continue to save after your child begins college. Be sure that you recalculate line 4 each year.

1 Current annual costs (use $5,488 for public schools and $14,403 for private, or use the cost of a specific college) _____

2 Four-year cost in today's dollars (line 1 times 4) _____

3 Amount you must save at the beginning of the first year (line 2 times factor from column A) _____

4 Amount you must save at the beginning of each succeeding year (multiply line 3 by the appropriate factor from column B) _____

Age of child	A	Payment number	B
Newborn	0.0474	2	1.07
1	0.0495	3	1.14
2	0.0519	4	1.23
3	0.0545	5	1.31
4	0.0574	6	1.40
5	0.0606	7	1.50
6	0.0643	8	1.61
7	0.0684	9	1.72
8	0.0785	11	1.97
10	0.0849	12	2.10
11	0.0924	13	2.25
12	0.1014	14	2.41
13	0.1124	15	2.58
14	0.1262	16	2.76
15	0.1439	17	2.95
16	0.1675	18	3.16
17	0.2005	19	3.38
		20	3.62
		21	3.87

Source: Moss Adams, Seattle

A Guide to the Leading Loans

If you need to borrow money to help cover college expenses, you should consider the special loans described in this table. Made through financial institutions, they are available to any creditworthy family facing college bills. For more information, call the sponsor's 800 number, given below.

Name	Sponsor	Maximum amount	Rate equals . . .	Maximum term	Up-front fees	Repayment deferral[4]
Unsubsidized Stafford Loan[1]	U.S. Department of Education 800-562-6872	First- and second-year students: $2,625; third- and fourth-year students: $4,000[3]	91-day T-bill rate plus 3.1 percentage points, adjusted annually; 9% cap	10 years (extensions may be available)	Up to 6.5%	Yes
PLUS	U.S. Department of Education 800-562-6872	$4,000 a year per child[2]	One-year T-bill rate plus 3.1 percentage points, adjusted annually; 10% cap[3]	10 years	Up to 8%	Yes[5]
PLATO	University Support Services 800-767-5626	$25,000 a year per child	Greater of 30- or 90-day commercial paper rate plus 4.85 percentage points, adjusted monthly; no cap. Recent rate: 8.77%	15 years	4% plus $55	Yes
TERI	The Education Resources Institute 800-255-8347	$20,000 a year per child	Prime rate plus 1.5 to two percentage points, adjusted monthly; no cap. Recent rate: 7.5% to 8%	20 years	5%	Yes
EXCEL and SHARE	Nellie Mae 800-634-9308	$20,000 a year per child	Prime rate plus two percentage points, adjusted monthly; no cap. Recent rate: 8%. Also available: prime rate plus three to four percentage points, adjusted annually; no cap. Recent rate: 9.5%	20 years	5%	Yes
Knight Extended Repayment Plan	Knight Tuition Payment Plans 800-225-6783	Full cost of education	91-day T-bill rate plus 4.5 percentage points, adjusted quarterly; 18% cap. Recent rate: 8%	15 years	$55	No
ABLE	Knight Tuition Payment Plans 800-225-6783	Full cost of education	Prime rate plus 2.5 percentage points, adjusted quarterly; 18% cap. Recent rate: 9%	15 years	$55	No
Extra Credit	The College Board 800-874-9390	Full cost of education	First-year fixed rate: 7.5%. Thereafter: 91-day T-bill rate plus 4.5 percentage points, adjusted quarterly; 18% cap. Recent rate: 8.75%	15 years	$45	No

Notes: [1] Available Oct. 1, 1992 [2] Limits will rise on July 1, 1993. For the Stafford, they will be $3,500 for second-year students, $5,500 for third- and fourth-year students. For the PLUS, the limit will be the full cost of education. [3] Rate takes effect Oct. 1, 1992. [4] You pay only interest while student is in school; principal repayment begins six months after student leaves school with Stafford and PLUS and as soon as student leaves school with other loans. [5] After July 1, 1993, deferral available only under special circumstances

EE savings bonds pay a variable interest rate, making them one of the few fixed-income investments that actually benefit from rising rates.

AGES FOURTEEN AND OVER

Preserve your profits by gradually shifting from stocks to cash. As you get closer to the first college bill, you might divide as much as 80% of your new savings among Treasury notes that will mature when your child is in school, government money-market funds and short-term bond funds. Put the rest in low-risk balanced funds until your child's junior year of high school, when virtually all new savings should go into short-term fixed-income securities. Analysts recommend Scudder Short-Term Bond ($1,000 minimum; 800-225-2470) and United Services Government Securities ($1,000 minimum; 800-873-8637), a money-market fund, because they both have consistently paid above-average yields. When your college-bound son or daughter turns 14, you should begin selling your stock funds and putting the proceeds into your money-market and short-term bond funds.

Planners advise families who believe they may qualify for financial aid to sell securities on which they have capital gains by December 31 of their child's junior year in high school. Reason:

when you apply for financial aid, capital gains are added to your income, reducing your eligibility for aid. Parents who are sure they won't get a penny of help can stretch their profit taking over a longer period—perhaps selling the last stock investments in their college fund during their child's second year of college. Whenever parents do sell, however, they should first give appreciated assets to the child. (Married couples can make tax-free gifts of as much as $20,000 a year.) Then the parents can have the child sell the assets. As long as he or she is at least 14, the profits from the sale will be taxed at the child's rate.

What if your son or daughter is within a year of entering college and you haven't accumulated anywhere near the money you need to pay his or her way? A few judicious money-saving moves—for example, buying a used car instead of a new one—might help you squeeze a few thousand dollars for college out of your income. And your child may be able to contribute money earned from summer jobs or work/study programs. But in the end, you'll probably have to borrow. The table on the left describes low-cost loans that are specifically targeted for college costs. Homeowners can also tap some of the value of their houses by taking out home-equity loans; the interest charged is usually tax deductible.

The New Rules of Financial Aid

Here's what the Washington lawmakers have done to help you foot the tab for college, and what you can do to help yourself.

Middle-income parents of college-bound children finally got a break. Congress has voted to cut the rates on subsidized Stafford Loans and has made more families eligible for them. The changes will enable an estimated one million additional families to qualify for $3 billion in Stafford Loans. Financial aid rules are changing in other ways as well. Under pressure from the Justice Department's antitrust division, 23 elite colleges have stopped exchanging financial aid information with one another and offering similar financial aid packages to students accepted by more than one of the schools. And with the number of high school graduates shrinking, many schools are finding it harder to attract top students. As a result, many colleges are increasingly willing to sweeten financial aid packages for especially desirable students—generally those who have terrific high school records or will add to the student body's ethnic or geographical diversity—or for those students who make persuasive cases for receiving more assistance.

For most middle-income families the chief source of help will remain Washington, which in the 1991-92 academic year doled out $21 billion in grants, loans and work/study subsidies (about 75% of that year's total aid). The remainder came from colleges and independent sources (18%) and states (7%). By contrast, Uncle Sam's share was 86% of the total a decade ago.

About half of the federal aid comes in the form of subsidized Stafford Loans, which have always been good deals—and now are better. Congress lowered the rate on Staffords taken out after October 1, 1992 to 6.9%. The rate will be adjusted every July 1 to equal the rate on the 91-day Treasury bill as of the previous June 1, plus 3.1 percentage points. (Stafford Loans had formerly been fixed at 8% for the first four years and 10% thereafter.) Borrowers need not start to repay Staffords until six months after they leave school; the government covers the interest in the interim. In addition, the maximum students can borrow will rise on July 1, 1993 to $3,500 for sophomores and $5,500 for juniors and seniors. Freshman loans will remain capped at $2,625.

To open the Stafford program to more middle-income families, Congress directed that starting July 1, 1993, home equity will no longer be counted in calculating eligibility for loans. To gauge the possible benefit to your family, consider the following example of a family of four, prepared by the College Board, a higher education research group. The parents, both 45, have an adjusted gross income of $55,000, home equity of $80,000 and savings and investments of $50,000. Under the new rules the family could get government help for expenses above $7,900 of one child's college costs. Under the old rules, they would have been expected to pay $12,400 before qualifying for aid.

In addition, Congress mandated that beginning July 1, 1993, the financial aid formula will no longer count the assets of families with adjusted gross incomes of $50,000 or less who don't itemize deductions on their tax returns. This exemption previously covered only families with annual incomes of less than $15,000. (These changes apply just to federal aid. The schools may still consider home equity and other factors when handing out their own aid money.)

Congress also created an unsubsidized version of the Stafford that will be available to all families, whether or not they meet the government's qualifications for aid. The terms are similar to those of the regular Stafford, except that borrowers must begin paying interest immediately. Finally, Congress boosted the maximum amount parents can borrow from private lenders participating in the PLUS program sponsored by the U.S. Department of Education (800-562-6872). As of July 1, 1993, the limit will increase from $4,000 a year to the full cost of education (minus any financial aid).

Even with all the changes, your quest for aid will still begin with a trial by forms. And there's a new one you should pick up at your high school guidance office or at a local college. It's called the Free Application for Federal Student Aid and seeks details of your income and assets. Many colleges will also ask you to fill out supplemental aid applications. You should mail the completed forms to the appropriate processing firm (which is indicated on the application) on January 1, the earliest date permitted, or very shortly thereafter. Some schools may give tardy applicants less in grants, which are gifts, and more in loans, which must be repaid.

The processing firms will crunch your vital statistics according to the rules laid down by Congress to calculate your expected family contribution. (To estimate yours, fill out the worksheet on the right.) If your child's total college costs for tuition, room and board, books, transportation and miscellaneous expenses exceed your expected family contribution, he or she will get some combination of grants, loans and work/study. Typically, the total aid will fall somewhere between 65% and 100% of the amount you need, depending on the college.

To get more aid, take steps to reduce your expected family contribution. For example, you can put more money into a tax-deferred 401(k) retirement plan at work or an IRA account. The federal formula does not count the savings built up in such accounts as assets when figuring a family's eligibility for aid. Also, if you are planning to cash in profitable investments to pay college bills, do so by December 31 of your child's junior year in high school. Reason: the aid formula takes a bigger bite out of income, including capital gains, than assets. Finally, avoid saving a lot of money in your child's name; kids are expected to kick in a far higher proportion of their savings than you are of yours.

If you're not happy with the aid package offered to your child, you may be able to talk the school into a better deal. To have any chance of success, you'll need a bargaining chip. Perhaps the most effective one is a better offer from

Estimate Your Share of the Tab

This worksheet can help you estimate how much you will be expected to contribute toward your son's or daughter's college costs. It is based on the complicated formulas used in distributing federal financial aid, and it reflects changes enacted by Congress that take effect in 1993. The most important new rule: parents' home equity no longer is counted in calculating their assets. The worksheet assumes there are two parents in the family and that the older one is 45. Complete sections 1 and 2 to determine your income and assets. That total, entered on line C, is the parents' expected contribution. Then complete section 4 to calculate the student's share. The sum of the parents' contribution and the student's is called the expected family contribution. If that amount is greater than the college's total annual cost (including tuition, fees, room, board and an allowance for books and transportation), you will not qualify for aid. If it is less, you probably will be offered a package of grants, loans and work/study to help make up the difference.

1. PARENTS' INCOME

Enter your annual adjusted gross income from your tax return. _____

Add the sum of all nontaxable income. _____

Add back annual deductions for IRA and Keogh contributions. _____

Subtract annual federal, state and Social Security (FICA) taxes. _____

If both parents work, subtract employment expenses: $2,500 or 35% of the lower salary, whichever is less. _____

Subtract your income protection allowance (from Table I) and enter the total on line A. _____

A. $ _____

2. PARENTS' ASSETS

If your adjusted gross income is $50,000 or less and you do not itemize deductions on your tax return, enter zero on line B. Otherwise, enter here the total value of your investments, including stocks, bonds, and real estate other than your home. _____

Enter the sum of all cash, bank and money-market accounts. _____

Subtract $36,600. If result is negative, enter zero on line B; if it is positive, multiply by 0.12 and enter the result on line B. _____

B. $ _____

3. PARENTS' CONTRIBUTION

Enter the total of lines A and B. _____

Use this number to find the parents' expected contribution from Table II. Divide that figure by the number of family members attending college and enter the result on line C. _____

C. $ _____

4. STUDENT'S CONTRIBUTION

Enter the student's annual adjusted gross income as reported on his or her tax return. _____

Subtract annual federal, state and Social Security (FICA) taxes. _____

Subtract income protection of $1,750. If result is negative, enter zero; if positive, multiply by 0.5 and enter here. _____

Add 35% of the student's savings and investments and enter the total on line D. _____

D. $ _____

5. TOTAL FAMILY CONTRIBUTION

Enter the sum of lines C and D. **E. $ _____**

Table 1: Income protection allowance

Family size (including student)	Number of family members in college				
	1	2	3	4	5
2	$10,520	$8,720			
3	13,100	11,310	$9,510		
4	16,180	14,380	12,590	$10,790	
5	19,090	17,290	15,500	13,700	$11,910
6	22,330	20,530	18,740	16,940	15,150

Table II: Parents' contribution

If line A plus line B equals	Then the parents' contribution is
$3,408 or less	$750
$3,409 to $9,400	22% of line A plus line B
$9,401 to $11,800	$2,068 plus 25% of amount over $9,400
$11,801 to $14,200	$2,668 plus 29% of amount over $11,800
$14,201 to $16,600	$3,364 plus 34% of amount over $14,200
$16,601 to $19,000	$4,180 plus 40% of amount over $16,600
$19,001 or more	$5,140 plus 47% of amount over $19,000

Source: Higher Education Amendments of 1992—Conference Report, House of Representatives

MONEY HELPS

Q. My daughter, who has asthma, is covered under our health maintenance organization and receives treatment at a local HMO near the University of Vermont, where she's in graduate school. She "aged out" of our plan when she turned 22, however, and though we can continue her coverage until September '93 under federal rules, I don't know what to do then. The university health plan may not cover her asthma because she had it before enrolling. Will she qualify for affordable coverage?
—Maureen Gavin, Shady Side, Maryland

A. It was bad enough when many insurers refused to cover applicants suffering from cancer, heart disease and diabetes. Now they also exclude (or exact huge premiums from) those with high blood pressure, varicose veins, arthritis, asthma and other garden-variety ailments. In effect, the companies are turning their backs on as many as 81 million Americans, according to an estimate by Citizen Action, a Washington, D.C. health-care public interest group. Effective 1992, Vermont requires many carriers to accept applicants regardless of their health. But state regulators concede privately that some insurers may stop doing business in the state instead. Obviously, we need a federal solution. Blue Cross/Blue Shield of Vermont, which traditionally admits everyone, would take your daughter—and we do mean take her. She would have to pay $1,960 a year, and the policy wouldn't cover her asthma for the first 12 months. By contrast, the university's $351-a-year health plan doesn't look half bad. It will indeed treat her asthma, though up to only a $1,500 annual limit. But there is an even better alternative. The Community Health Plan of Vermont, where your daughter is now treated thanks to the arrangement with your HMO, will keep her on for only $99 a month. Although the plan won't pay for her $180 a month in prescription drugs or the first $500 of any hospital bill, it sets no other limits. After she leaves Vermont, though, her only hope of affordable protection will be to work for an employer with a generous group plan—or to marry a guy with same.

another school of equal or higher quality. When recently asked about dealmaking, Tom Gerety, president of Trinity College, insisted: "We don't bargain." But when pressed, Gerety, like many aid officials, admitted that Trinity will almost always take "another look" at a student who gets a better offer from a comparable school.

You might also win more aid if, like David Lang, an A+ student in high school, you can persuade colleges that special circumstances make it difficult for your family to come up with its expected contribution. Last year, soon after Lang submitted his financial aid applications to eight schools, he phoned the financial aid officers at each. He explained that his parents were divorced and that he did not believe his father would provide any money. That spring he was accepted by the three schools at the top of his wish list: Northwestern, which offered him $4,500 in grants and loans; Dartmouth, which pledged $5,825; and Stanford, which cited clerical snafus and said its offer would be forthcoming in a couple of weeks.

"I called the schools and told them that I wanted to attend but I had to choose the one that offered me the best financial aid deal," Lang says. A week later, Northwestern upped its offer with a $1,500 grant and a $500 loan, and Lang says Dartmouth promised to consider raising its award. He phoned Stanford's financial aid office three or four times, describing the other offers he had received and saying that Stanford was his first choice. A Stanford spokesman says the school would not be influenced by phone calls from a student. Nevertheless, Stanford came through with a $7,000 grant and a $5,500 loan, and Lang happily accepted the deal. And at Stanford's request, Lang's father readily agreed to chip in $6,026 toward his son's expenses.

Despite your best efforts, you may still find that an aid offer does not cut a first-choice college's cost to what you can afford. But that won't keep your child from going to college if he or she also applies to a financial safety school—one that you know you can afford even if you get no aid.

Scope Out Those Scholarships

Here's how to claim your share of the millions of dollars available from Uncle Sam, the states, corporations and the colleges themselves.

Colleges call them non-need-based awards, merit money or just plain scholarships. Whatever the name, they can sharply reduce a bright and ambitious student's college costs, or even eliminate them entirely.

Merit scholarships are awarded for academic achievement or other factors not related to a family's finances. (Funds given on the basis of financial need are usually called grants.) The amounts range from a token $500 to four full years of tuition, fees, room and board, which can be worth more than $80,000 at expensive schools. The chief sources of scholarships include Uncle Sam, the states, the colleges themselves and a growing number of corporations and private groups, including the National Merit Scholarship Corporation.

Despite these gains for brains, merit scholarships still represent a small sum when compared with the grants, loans and work/study jobs available to students who receive financial aid. Private colleges, for example, distribute about three times as much in need-based grants as they do in merit money, while state merit scholarships account for a mere 3% of total state aid for colleges. As a result, aid counselors recommend that you concentrate first on getting need-based aid, if you can qualify, as about half of all undergraduates do. "Once you've done that, you can fit a scholarship search into your financing strategy," says Anna Leider, author of *Don't Miss Out: The Ambitious Student's Guide to Financial Aid* (Octameron, $6).

If you qualify for financial aid, winning a scholarship from a source other than the college you plan to attend may not actually improve your financial position. Reason: many schools simply use an outside award to replace the grants they had planned to give you, leaving you no better off. Others, however, will use your outside scholarship to reduce or eliminate the loans and work/study opportunities that are part of most financial aid packages. That works out to be a net plus for you, because you won't have to pay the money back or spend time working rather than studying. Here's how to compete for major scholarships, listed below in order of the most widely available to the most specialized:

College scholarships. Public and private colleges alike are increasingly willing to use merit awards to attract top high schoolers. School-sponsored merit scholarships typically go to a handful of entering freshmen with outstanding high school grades and Scholastic Aptitude Test scores. For example, the Catholic University of America in Washington, D.C. annually promises full-tuition scholarships (recent tuition: $12,556 a year) to 31 high schoolers who have applied for admission. Those students usually have A averages and SAT scores of 1,200 or better. Similarly, Tulane University offers 125 scholarships for four years of tuition (lately $16,925 a year) to prospective freshmen with A averages, SAT scores of 1,250 or above and demonstrated leadership qualities. Tulane has also pioneered a scholarship aimed at students from middle-income families. It hands out $6,000-a-year merit-based awards for high-achieving students whose expected family contribution under financial aid formulas is between

$18,000 and a hypothetical $39,000 a year. The University of California's prestigious Regents Scholarship, offered to 488 exceptional high school seniors annually, is a hybrid. Winners who qualify for financial aid get a scholarship equal to the amount of aid they would have received; others get an annual $500 honorarium.

To learn about merit scholarships at schools you're considering, go to a library or guidance office to consult such references as *Peterson's 1992 College Money Handbook* (Peterson's Guides, $20), the *A's and B's of Academic Scholarships* (Octameron, $6) and *College Financial Aid, Fourth Edition* (Arco, $20). Then ask the schools' scholarship offices how to apply.

Federal scholarships. Army, Navy and Air Force Reserve Officers Training Corps scholarships are among Uncle Sam's most lucrative and coveted awards. Some 16,389 of the 58,464 men and women in ROTC are attending school on scholarships that cover 80% to 100% of their tuition, books and fees for up to four years, plus a stipend. (ROTC awards do not include room and board.) The trade-off: scholarship recipients, like all ROTC members, must serve at least eight years of active and reserve duty after graduation. To ask about applying for an ROTC scholarship, call the local recruiting office of the service branch that interests you or talk to your high school guidance counselor.

Winning an ROTC scholarship can also make you more attractive to colleges. For example, shortly after Erik Keeslar of San Mateo, California parlayed a 3.98 grade point average, a 1,250 on the SAT and credentials as an Eagle Scout into a three-year Navy ROTC scholarship, he heard from 11 universities to which he hadn't even applied. Seven offered to supplement his ROTC award by, say, picking up his room-and-board tab. The Navy ended up topping its own offer. To encourage Keeslar to attend the University of Washington, where the Navy funds research programs, it offered to cover a fourth year of tuition, fees and books. Keeslar accepted the deal. "My

parents could have paid my way if I went to a state school in California," he says. "But since I wanted to study out of state, to see a little more of the country, money became an issue that the scholarship quickly resolved."

State scholarships. Twenty-three states award scholarships to brainy residents willing to attend home-state public or private colleges. For example, Georgia high schoolers with certain outstanding academic credentials, such as a 3.75 grade point average and a score of 1,300 or better on the SAT, are eligible for Governor's Scholarships (up to $1,540 a year). Similarly, Wisconsin annually confers Academic Excellence Scholarships worth nearly $2,200 a year to about 600 outstanding high school students. And 20 states offer special merit scholarships to the children of veterans or deceased police officers or to students who agree to work in-state after graduation, often as teachers. Ask your high school guidance counselor about such programs or call your state's higher education agency.

Corporate and private scholarships. The nonprofit National Merit Scholarship Corporation runs the biggest private college award competition. To qualify, take the PSAT/NMSQT exam (a preliminary version of the SAT) early in your junior year of high school. Among a recent year's one million test takers, 8,572 won money from the National Merit Scholarship Corporation or one of the 205 colleges and 390 private companies that support it. In addition, 769 students who took the PSAT/NMSQT won National Achievement Scholarships for Outstanding Negro Students. In general, the awards in these programs are one-time payments of $2,000 or annual payments of $250 to $2,000 for four years, depending on the sponsor. Moreover, some sponsors may increase the awards for winners with financial need. For more information about National Merit Scholarships, ask your guidance counselor for the *Student Bulletin*, which can also be ordered free from the National

Merit Scholarship Corp. (1560 Sherman Avenue, No. 200, Evanston, Illinois 60201). Other private awards worth pursuing:

■ The Coca-Cola Scholars Foundation pledges $1.4 million to 150 outstanding college-bound seniors who are judged primarily on leadership qualities, along with academic accomplishment. Fifty winners receive $5,000 annually for four years; another 100 get $1,000 annually for four years. To enter this year's contest, request an application, due October 31, from your high school guidance counselor.

■ The Tylenol Scholarship Fund, sponsored by McNeil Consumer Products (part of Johnson & Johnson), pays $10,000 to each of 10 high school seniors who demonstrate leadership skills and community involvement, along with having solid academic records. Five hundred runners-up receive $1,000 each. Applications, which are due December 15, are available at stores where Tylenol is sold, or by writing to Tylenol Scholarship Fund, 1675 Broadway, 33rd Floor, New York, New York 10019.

■ The Westinghouse Science Talent Search awarded $205,000 to 40 science whizzes for projects in science, mathematics or engineering last year. The top 10 prizes range from $10,000 to $40,000; 30 students receive $1,000 each; all 300 semifinalists get college recommendations as gifted science students. Recent first-prize winner, Kurt Steven Thorn of Shoreham, New York, bested 1,700 other entrants with his study of the "Elemental Distributions in Marine Bivalves as Measured by Synchrotron X-Ray Fluorescence." For an application, due December 1, write to Science Service, 1719 N St. N.W., Washington, D.C. 20036, or call 202-785-2255.

Many other large corporations also award merit scholarships to employees' children; parents can get rules and applications from their benefits departments. Geico, the insurance company, gives 30 scholarships to employees' children through three different programs. One award, for example, worth $1,000 annually for two years, goes to two students who plan to major in arts-related fields. For information on other scholarships, consult *The College Blue Book: Scholarships, Fellowships, Grants and Loans* (Macmillan, $48). Don't waste money on expensive computerized scholarship search services. Most sell information that is already available from guidebooks. And don't overlook money from local churches and civic groups. You can learn about such scholarships from your school guidance office. While some groups provide as little as $100, every little bit obviously helps.

America's Top 100 College Values

Entries in our honor roll of four-year schools all sport prices that are bargains relative to the quality of education they provide students.

Almost every parent of a college-bound child asks: which colleges will deliver an education that's worth every penny I'll have to pay? To help answer that question, MONEY's college ranking team sifted through more than 100,000 pieces of information on 1,000 of America's four-year institutions of higher education. The results of that analysis begin on the following pages with our exclusive rankings of the 100 schools that deliver the most for your money.

We based our calculations on 16 factors, including the schools' official full prices. We didn't adjust them for financial aid, because such awards vary widely from student to student. For public schools, we used nonresident tuitions in our ranking of the top 100 to serve the needs of someone shopping nationwide. In addition to price, we employed the 15 factors described below, which were chosen after consultation with experts on educational statistics. The schools that did best were those that achieved higher scores on the 15 factors than the levels suggested by the prices they charge. For example, a college that costs $8,800 (about average for the schools we studied) would be expected to graduate between 55% and 56% of its freshmen within six years, which is typical. Thus, a higher-than-expected graduation rate would help a school rise in the rankings, while a disappointing one would tend to push it down.

We gathered our information from the colleges with the help of Orchard House of Concord, Massachusetts, a publisher of college directories for high school and private counselors. We also drew on data from the National Research Council, the Department of Education, Standard & Poor's and John Minter Associates of Boulder. Here's an explanation of the 15 factors we used in our analysis:

■ Faculty resources. We estimated the student/faculty ratio based on the number of full- and part-time undergraduate faculty and the number of full- and part-time students. Average for our sample: 14 to 1.

■ Faculty deployment. We used the ratio of full-time students to full-time faculty who actually taught courses in the fall of 1991. Average for our sample: 17 to 1.

■ Faculty strength. We counted the percentage of permanent faculty members holding the highest degrees available in their fields, usually doctorates. Average: 76%.

■ Library resources. We divided the total of all reference materials that were catalogued by the number of undergraduate and graduate students using the library.

■ Instructional budget. The figures are sup-plied annually to colleges by the government.

■ Student services budget. This is what a school spends on such things as counseling and student organizations.

■ Entrance examination results. We used the percentage of freshmen who scored above 500 on the verbal and math portions of the Scholastic Aptitude Test (average of those who did: verbal, 40%; math, 59%) or above 23 on the composite American College Test (average: 39%).

■ Class rank. We considered the percentage of freshmen who were in the top fifth or the top quarter of their high school classes. Average for our sample: from the top fifth, 43%; from the top quarter, 47%.

■ High school grade point average. This is the freshmen's average GPA on a four-point scale. Average: 3.0.

■ Freshman retention rate. This is the percentage of freshmen students who returned as sophomores. Average: 77%.

■ Graduation rate. We counted the percentage of students who earned degrees in six years or less. Average: 56%.

■ Percentage of graduates who go on to professional or graduate schools. This figure indicates how well a school prepares students for more difficult academic environments. Average who continued their educations: 23%.

■ Default ratio on student loans. The percentage of students who have defaulted on their student loans within two years of leaving college helps identify schools whose graduates have trouble using their educations as springboards to stable careers. Average: 6.3%.

■ Number of graduates who earn doctorates. We used data from the National Research Council, which compiles a list of the undergraduate colleges attended by all students who earned Ph.D.s between 1981 and 1990.

■ Business success. For this factor we relied on a tally of the schools that were attended by the 70,000 top corporate executives who were recently listed in *Standard & Poor's Register of Corporations, Directors and Executives.*

The Top 100 Colleges

Here is our dean's list of four-year colleges. Their prices are bargains
when measured against the quality of education they offer.

1. Rice University
2. New College, U. of S. Fla.
3. U. of Washington
4. Hanover College
5. Calif. Inst. of Tech.
6. Trenton State College
7. Ga. Inst. of Technology
8. Rutgers College
9. U. of N.C., Chapel Hill
10. New Mexico Tech
11. Ill., Urbana-Champaign
12. SUNY, Binghamton
13. Auburn University
14. U. of Texas, Austin
15. University of Kentucky
16. N.E. Mo. State College
17. Yale University
18. University of Virginia
19. Grove City College
20. Douglass College
21. Fisk University
22. Cook College
23. SUNY, Albany
24. St. Mary's of Maryland
25. University of Florida
26. Princeton University
27. Centenary College of La.
28. Spelman College
29. SUNY, Stony Brook
30. Mary Washington
31. University of Georgia
32. Wabash College
33. Texas A & M University
34. Livingston College

35. Baylor University
36. Harvard University
37. Pomona College
38. Trinity University
39. SUNY, Geneseo
40. Harvey Mudd College
41. Illinois College
42. SUNY, Buffalo
43. University of Iowa
44. U. of Wis., Madison
45. Ohio University
46. University of Tulsa
47. Samford University
48. Iowa State University
49. Clemson University
50. U. of South Carolina
51. Johns Hopkins University
52. Miami University (Ohio)
53. Washington and Lee
54. James Madison U.
55. Columbia University
56. Purdue University
57. U. of Mo., Columbia
58. Emory and Henry College
59. University of the South
60. Westminster College (Pa.)
61. UC, Berkeley
62. Swarthmore College
63. UCLA
64. Bellarmine College
65. Stanford University
66. Dartmouth College
67. Berry College
68. Centre College

69. Mich. Technological U.
70. N.C. State University
71. Furman University
72. Davidson College
73. Wake Forest University
74. MIT
75. Erskine College
76. Notre Dame (Md.)
77. William and Mary
78. Hillsdale College
79. Drury College
80. Agnes Scott College
81. St. Mary's (Texas)
82. Virginia Polytechnic Inst.
83. Ohio State University
84. U. of Missouri, Rolla
85. MacMurray College
86. Rosemont College
87. U. of Connecticut
88. Case Western Reserve
89. Indiana U., Bloomington
90. Grinnell College
91. Creighton University
92. Chestnut Hill College
93. Austin College
94. Millsaps College
95. Wofford College
96. Pennsylvania State
97. Claremont McKenna
98. Williams College
99. University of Chicago
100. Marquette University

MONEY'S GUIDE TO 1000 COLLEGES

The tables on the following pages deliver basic information you need to size up 1,000 public and private four-year colleges and universities that welcome students without regard to their religious backgrounds. Schools that placed in our top 100 are highlighted in blue with their ranks after their names. In ranking the top 100, we excluded schools where more than 45% of the students attend classes part time, specialized colleges that offer majors in only a few fields, the service academies, and schools that require students to work while attending classes. The data were gathered by MONEY and Orchard House of Concord, Massachusetts, a publisher of college directories, in surveys sent to colleges and in follow-up phone calls. Here is a description of the statistics that will help you understand the tables:

Tuition and fees. These prices apply to freshmen, unless otherwise noted. For public schools, we list the tuition for out-of-state residents. We also include the fees that are mandatory for all students; they typically cover the cost of student activities and health care.

Room and board. Schools generally offer a variety of room and meal plans. We decided to give the least expensive option among the most popular choices—usually a two-person dorm room and 14 meals a week.

Percent of students receiving aid. We count all undergraduates who received financial assistance from any source—federal and state governments, the college itself and private organizations. The figures include merit and athletic scholarships and other money that is distributed to students without regard for financial need.

Average gift aid per student. This number represents the total amount of outright grants (as opposed to loans or work/study programs) that the college dispensed out of its own assistance funds, which we then divided by the number of undergraduates on campus.

Student/faculty ratio. We list the figure that the schools reported for undergraduates and faculty members teaching them. (For our value rankings, we used two different student/faculty ratios that we calculated from our own data.) A student/faculty ratio is not a direct measure of class sizes, although schools with low ratios tend to have smaller classes.

Percent who graduate in five years. We give the average percentage of students who earn a bachelor's degree within five years of entering college; we do not include transfer students in this statistic.

Percent with high test scores. This number represents the portion of freshmen who scored above 500 on the verbal portion of the Scholastic Aptitude Test (indicated by the letter S), or 24 or above on the composite American College Test (indicated by an A). The average verbal SAT score nationwide was recently 424; the average composite ACT score was 20.6.

Percent from top fifth of class. We list the portion of freshmen who graduated in the top 20% of their high school classes.

Finally, we provide phone numbers for all schools—usually of the admissions offices—so that you can call to ask your own questions and request literature and applications from the colleges and universities that interest you the most.

College name and location	Tuition and fees	Room and board	% of students receiving financial aid	Average gift aid per student	Student/ faculty ratio	% who graduate in five years	% with high test scores	% from top fifth of class	Telephone
Adams State (Colo.)	$4,514	$2,754	42	$225	20:1	40	20(A)	35	719-589-7712
Adelphi (N.Y.)	12,100	5,530	63	1,500	13:1	54	18(S)	52	516-877-3050
Adrian (Mich.)	10,027	3,070	83	1,936	15:1	41	26(A)	12	800-877-2246
Agnes Scott (Ga.)[1] 80	11,625	4,825	75	4,325	8:1	47	N.A.	73	404-371-6285
Alabama A&M	3,100	2,350	70[2]	374	15:1	N.A.	N.A.	N.A.	205-851-5245
Alabama State	3,108	2,110	45[2]	345	16:1	15[2]	1(A)	29[3]	205-293-4291
Alaska Pacific	6,930	4,050	N.A.	551	12:1	24	10(A)	25	907-564-8248
Albany State (Ga.)	4,803	2,550	N.A.	147	20:1	35	51(S)[4]	3	912-430-4646
Albertson (Idaho)	11,002	2,850	N.A.	3,861	12:1	40	56(A)	52[3]	800-635-0434
Albertus Magnus (Conn.)	11,007	5,080	51	592	11:1	60	22(S)	23	203-773-8501
Albion (Mich.)	12,254	4,316	70	3,515	13:1	64	52(A)[5]	60	517-629-0321
Albright (Pa.)	13,960	4,135	88	2,399	11:1	71	54(S)	51	215-921-7512
Alcorn State (Miss.)	4,335	1,925	93	N.A.	20:1	38	N.A.	20	601-877-6147
Alderson-Broaddus (W.Va.)	8,666	2,860	95	2,494	13:1	45	19(A)	32	304-457-1700
Alfred (N.Y.)	14,998	4,735	69	3,070	12:1	N.A.	55(S)	63	607-871-2115
Alice Lloyd (Ky.)	3,770	2,480	N.A.	N.A.	18:1	38	38(A)	20	606-368-2101
Allegheny (Pa.)	15,750	4,210	N.A.	5,354	11:1	N.A.	51(S)	52	814-332-4351
Allentown–St. Francis de Sales (Pa.)	8,640	4,380	60	1,748	14:1	N.A.	34(S)	N.A.	215-282-1100
Alma (Mich.)	11,354	4,108	90	3,723	15:1	68	59(A)	63	800-321-2562
Alvernia (Pa.)	8,020	3,800	N.A.	169	14:1	41	10(S)	N.A.	215-777-5411
American (D.C.)	14,508	6,104	N.A.	2,763	15:1	56	74(S)	57	202-885-6000
American International (Mass.)	8,963	4,132	69	N.A.	16:1	78	32(S)	9	413-747-6201
Amherst (Mass.)	18,177	4,800	N.A.	5,031	10:1	97	92(S)	97	413-542-2328
Anna Maria (Mass.)	10,380	4,650	N.A.	1,621	16:1	71	9(S)	18	508-757-4586
Antioch (Ohio)	15,277	3,024	64	3,238	9:1	34	50(S)[11]	N.A.	513-767-6400
Appalachian State (N.C.)	6,345	2,370	N.A.	76	16:1	55	30(S)	48	704-262-2120
Aquinas (Mich.)	9,722	4,070	N.A.	1,592	15:1	51	29(A)	30	616-732-4460
Arizona State	6,996	4,000	28	446	16:1	38	30(S)	37	602-965-2604
Arkansas College	7,603	3,336	91	2,124	10:1	38	50(A)	56	800-423-2542
Arkansas State[6]	2,660	2,150	N.A.	56	19:1	40	22(A)	N.A.	501-972-3024
Arkansas Tech	3,060	2,270	N.A.	N.A.	18:1	40	19(A)	44[3]	501-968-0343
Ashland (Ohio)	10,563	4,367	85	2,639	16:1	50	20(A)	32[3]	419-289-5052
Assumption (Mass.)	10,470	5,240	N.A.	1,449	16:1	78	50(S)[7]	29	508-752-5615
Auburn (Ala.) 13	5,265	3,800	N.A.	N.A.	18:1	56	51(A)	49	205-844-4080
Auburn–Montgomery (Ala.)[6]	4,797	1,500[8]	N.A.	N.A.	22:1	28	N.A.	N.A.	205-244-3611
Augsburg (Minn.)	10,853	4,022	85	N.A.	15:1	35	25(A)	30	612-330-1001
Augustana (Ill.)	12,009	3,849	N.A.	2,633	14:1	53	65(A)	60	309-794-7341
Augustana (S.D.)	9,800	3,000	60[2]	2,371[2]	14:1	70	33(A)	58[3]	605-336-5516
Austin (Texas) 93	10,185	2,070	77	2,672	14:1	70	50(S)	67	903-813-2387
Austin Peay State (Tenn.)	5,230	2,630	40	N.A.	18:1	32	N.A.	52	615-648-7661
Averett (Va.)	9,090	3,900	75[2]	N.A.	16:1	41	34(S)	20	804-791-5660
Babson (Mass.)	15,666	6,458	34	2,710	14:1	87	44(S)	53	800-488-3696
Baker (Kans.)	7,566	3,800	92[9]	2,231	15:1	N.A.	N.A.	50[3]	800-873-4282
Ball State (Ind.)	5,877	3,168	15	N.A.	17:1	70	18(S)[7]	9	317-285-8300
Barat (Ill.)	9,320	3,800	70	693	12:1	60	30(A)	19[3]	708-234-3000
Bard (N.Y.)	18,265	5,830	66	N.A.	10:1	75	N.A.	65	914-758-7472
Barnard (N.Y.)[1]	16,854	7,010	N.A.	N.A.	12:1	92	N.A.	78	212-854-2014
Barton (N.C.)	6,720	2,997	N.A.	578	13:1	N.A.	7(S)	23	800-345-4973
Baruch College–City U. of N.Y.	5,150	No dorms	62	48	30:1	29	N.A.	37	212-447-3750
Bates (Maine)	22,850[10]	N.A.	37	3,196	11:1	88	98(S)	76	207-786-6000
Baylor (Texas) 35	6,590	3,805	N.A.	989	17:1	66	50(S)[11]	70[3]	817-755-1811
Beaver (Pa.)	11,710	4,900	56	2,093	13:1	63	28(S)	36	215-572-2910
Bellarmine (Ky.) 64	7,680	2,560	N.A.	958	15:1	71	57(S)	30	800-274-4723
Belmont Abbey (N.C.)	8,044	4,070	N.A.	837	17:1	37	17(S)	14	800-523-2355
Beloit (Wis.)	14,250	3,420	N.A.	4,151	12:1	69	60(S)	46	608-363-2500
Bemidji State (Minn.)	3,900	2,500	50[2]	36	19:1	34	47(A)[12]	36[3]	218-755-2040

Footnotes are on page 186

College name and location	Tuition and fees	Room and board	% of students receiving financial aid	Average gift aid per student	Student/ faculty ratio	% who graduate in five years	% with high test scores	% from top fifth of class	Telephone
Benedict (S.C.)[6,13]	$5,484	$2,892	N.A.	N.A.	19:1	46	N.A.	N.A.	803-253-5143
Bennett (N.C.)[1,13]	5,725	2,776	N.A.	$482	12:1	34	N.A.	N.A.	919-370-8624
Bennington (Vt.)	19,780	4,100	51	5,818	9:1	49	N.A.	56	802-447-0580
Bentley (Mass.)	13,000[14]	5,100	N.A.	1,729	20:1	76	23(S)	42	617-891-2244
Berea (Ky.)[15]	183	2,574	90	733	13:1	53	25(A)	47	800-326-5948
Berry (Ga.) 67	7,500	3,740	N.A.	1,365	15:1	52	N.A.	N.A.	706-236-2215
Bethany (Kans.)	7,444	3,225	96	1,769	12:1	40	N.A.	47[3]	913-227-3311
Bethany (W.Va.)	12,907	4,368	71	N.A.	13:1	N.A.	N.A.	15	304-829-7611
Bethel (Tenn.)	5,250	2,650	N.A.	N.A.	12:1	N.A.	45(A)[5]	N.A.	901-352-1000
Birmingham-Southern (Ala.)	10,306	3,840	N.A.	2,011	15:1	73	70(A)	55	205-226-4686
Blackburn (Ill.)[16]	7,750	1,000	N.A.	1,546	14:1	30	15(A)	34[3]	217-854-3231
Black Hills State (S.D.)	3,687	2,504	38	27	25:1	N.A.	12(A)	15	605-642-6343
Bloomsburg U. of Pennsylvania	5,232	2,754	N.A.	N.A.	19:1	64	31(S)	38	717-389-4316
Bluffton (Ohio)	8,100	3,324	90	1,557	12:1	48	45(A)	40	419-358-3257
Boise State (Idaho)	4,168	3,069	66[2]	48	19:1	N.A.	93(A)[12]	N.A.	208-385-1156
Boston College (Mass.)	14,580	6,470	N.A.	N.A.	15:1	88	82(S)	95	617-552-3100
Boston University (Mass.)	16,837	6,320	57	290	15:1	69	72(S)	68	617-353-2300
Bowdoin (Maine)	17,355	5,855	37	3,790	10:1	90	95(S)	55	207-725-3100
Bowie State (Md.)	4,785	3,606	41	N.A.	16:1	18	1(S)	N.A.	301-464-6570
Bowling Green State (Ohio)	7,308	2,900	N.A.	311	20:1	61	25(A)	39	419-372-2086
Bradford (Mass.)	12,635	5,950	67	3,639	12:1	40	N.A.	15	508-372-7161
Bradley (Ill.)	9,728	4,160	N.A.	1,542	15:1	58	79(A)[12]	50	309-677-1000
Brandeis (Mass.)	17,725	6,225	45	4,629	8:1	79	N.A.	70	617-736-3500
Brescia (Ky.)	6,320	2,790	N.A.	521	15:1	44	27(A)	7	800-264-1234
Briar Cliff (Iowa)	9,300	3,432	N.A.	1,565	13:1	43	25(A)	27	712-279-5200
Bridgewater (Va.)	10,135	4,355	98	2,891	14:1	55	N.A.	41	703-828-2501
Bridgewater State (Mass.)	6,840	3,790	N.A.	262	17:1	49	23(S)	N.A.	508-697-1237
Brooklyn College–City U. of N.Y.	5,203	No dorms	53	1	16:1	31	N.A.	20	718-780-5051
Brown (R.I.)	17,863	5,488	32[2]	2,912	9:1	92	95(S)	93[3]	401-863-2378
Bryant (R.I.)	11,653	6,079	48	1,777	19:1	74	23(S)	38	401-232-6100
Bryn Mawr (Pa.)	16,685	6,150	43[2]	N.A.	9:1	84	N.A.	76	215-526-5152
Bucknell (Pa.)	16,670	4,110	N.A.	2,547	14:1	87	76(S)	70	717-524-1101
Buena Vista (Iowa)	11,663	3,327	94	3,180	14:1	62	81(A)	48	712-749-2235
Butler (Ind.)	11,340	3,930	77	3,559	13:1	65	43(S)	58	317-283-9255
Cabrini (Pa.)	9,500	5,790	N.A.	613	19:1	55	4(S)[2]	19[2]	215-971-8552
California Institute of Technology 5	15,160	4,663	N.A.	6,417	3:1	73	100(S)	100	818-356-6341
California Lutheran	10,950	5,000	85	1,698	15:1	46	28(S)	29	805-493-3135
California Polytechnic–San Luis Obispo	9,115[7]	4,416	N.A.	61	17:1	58	N.A.	N.A.	805-756-2311
California State–Bakersfield	8,820[7]	3,635	13	N.A.	16:1	N.A.	N.A.	34	805-664-3036
California State–Chico	8,828[7]	4,274	36	N.A.	20:1	39	15(S)	N.A.	916-898-6323
California State–Fresno	8,734[7]	4,183	N.A.	93	18:1	38	13(S)[2]	39	209-278-6283
California State–Fullerton	8,860[7]	3,476[8]	17	N.A.	19:1	15	15(S)	N.A.	714-773-2370
California State–Hayward	8,803[7]	2,745[8]	N.A.	N.A.	19:1	N.A.	N.A.	N.A.	510-881-3817
California State–Long Beach	8,847[7]	3,753	N.A.	29	20:1	N.A.	10(S)[2]	N.A.	213-985-4141
California State–Northridge	8,880[7]	5,140	15	N.A.	19:1	16	11(S)	N.A.	818-885-3700
California State Polytechnic–Pomona	8,764[7]	4,527	20	43	N.A.	31	15(S)	33	714-869-2000
California State–Sacramento	8,812[7]	4,558	N.A.	178	18:1	26	N.A.	38	916-278-3901
California State–San Bernardino	8,820[7]	4,266	N.A.	123	18:1	N.A.	N.A.	N.A.	714-880-5200
California U. of Pennsylvania	6,778	3,460	52	N.A.	19:1	50	7(S)	16	412-938-4404
Camden College–Rutgers U. (N.J.)	7,227	4,200	43	71	17:1	52	49(S)	49	609-757-6104
Canisius (N.Y.)	9,502	4,900	76	1,546	17:1	60	35(S)	41	716-888-2200
Capital (Ohio)	11,935	3,840	N.A.	2,472	14:1	N.A.	39(A)	60	614-236-6101
Cardinal Stritch (Wis.)	7,384	3,350	61	283	14:1	50	26(A)	25	414-351-7504
Carleton (Minn.)	17,360	3,540	59	3,575	10:1	89	93(S)	76	507-663-4190
Carnegie Mellon (Pa.)	16,100	5,450	N.A.	4,242	9:1	69	71(S)	78	412-268-2082
Carroll (Mont.)	7,070	3,490	92	1,299	13:1	50	75(A)[12]	60[2,3,7]	406-442-3450

Footnotes are on page 186

stay-at-home
standouts

THE 20 TOP VALUES IN PUBLIC SCHOOLS WHEN WE USE IN-STATE TUITION AND FEES, NOT OUT-OF-STATE CHARGES, IN THE ANALYSIS

1. U. of N.C.–Chapel Hill	$1,296	11. Auburn University	$1,755
2. New College (Fla.)	1,855	12. New Mexico Tech	1,666
3. University of Texas–Austin	1,200	13. UCLA	2,886
4. North Carolina State	1,344	14. University of Arizona	1,590
5. University of Florida	1,580	15. U. of Wisconsin–Madison	2,344
6. U. of California–Berkeley	2,919	16. University of Iowa	2,228
7. Texas A&M	1,488	17. University of Kansas	1,796
8. Georgia Inst. of Tech.	2,196	18. Purdue University	2,520
9. University of Washington	2,274	19. University of Virginia	3,890
10. Florida State University	1,500	20. U. of N.C.–Charlotte	1,189

College name and location	Tuition and fees	Room and board	% of students receiving financial aid	Average gift aid per student	Student/ faculty ratio	% who graduate in five years	% with high test scores	% from top fifth of class	Telephone
Carroll (Wis.)	$11,432	$3,560	87	N.A.	15:1	74	43(A)	58[3]	414-524-7220
Carthage (Wis.)	11,525	3,470	78	$2,811	15:1	45	22(A)	29	414-551-6000
Case Western Reserve (Ohio) 88	14,650	5,140	70	4,991	8:1	68	77(S)	88	800-967-8898
Castleton State (Vt.)	7,538	4,500	N.A.	66	15:1	N.A.	N.A.	14	802-468-5611
Catawba (N.C.)	8,130	3,850	80	1,507	14:1	38	16(S)	25	800-228-2922
Catholic U. (D.C.)	12,986	5,870	40[2]	3,026	11:1	63	N.A.	25	202-319-5305
Centenary College of Louisiana 27	7,770	3,250	75	3,163	11:1	63	58(A)	22	318-869-5131
Central (Iowa)	9,850	3,552	97	N.A.	15:1	70	75(A)[12]	54	800-458-5503
Central Connecticut State	4,916	4,154	23	34	17:1	40	15(S)	17	203-827-7543
Central Methodist (Mo.)	7,050	3,370	25	935	13:1	45	21(A)	25	816-248-3391
Central Michigan	6,399	3,724	N.A.	215	20:1	48	46(A)[12]	51[2,3]	517-774-3076
Central Missouri State	3,990	2,986	27	219	19:1	40	19(A)	24	816-543-4290
Central Washington	6,372	3,300	58[2]	139	20:1	37	27(S)[2]	48[2]	509-963-1211
Centre (Ky.) 68	10,925	4,030	67	2,971	11:1	71	79(A)	83	606-238-5350
Chadron State (Neb.)[6]	2,505	2,456	N.A.	15	21:1	N.A.	24(A)	28[2]	308-432-6263
Chapman (Calif.)	14,916	5,346	N.A.	3,664	14:1	N.A.	17(S)	34[3]	714-997-6711
Chatham (Pa.)[1]	11,990	5,030	N.A.	3,056	9:1	48	N.A.	37[2]	412-365-1290
Chestnut Hill (Pa.)[1] 92	8,950	4,450	66	1,584	11:1	65	N.A.	57[3]	215-248-7001
Chicago State (Ill.)	5,368	No dorms	N.A.	44	20:1	N.A.	0(A)	N.A.	312-995-2513
Christ College (Calif.)	9,315	4,230	76	1,887	15:1	38	22(S)	N.A.	714-854-8002
Christian Brothers (Tenn.)	8,100	3,070	73	1,281	12:1	46	45(A)	42[2]	901-722-0205
Christopher Newport (Va.)	6,852	No dorms	N.A.	11	28:1	33[2]	31(S)	37[3]	804-594-7015
Citadel (S.C.)[17]	12,898[18]	2,683	70[2]	868	18:1	70	28(S)	9[3]	803-792-5230
City College–City U. of N.Y.	5,145	No dorms	72	N.A.	15:1	23	N.A.	8	212-650-6977
Claremont McKenna (Calif.) 97	15,620	5,480	50	3,829	8:1	82	91(S)	89	714-621-8088
Clarion U. of Pennsylvania	5,892	2,786	17	161	19:1	54	9(S)	19	814-226-2306
Clark (Mass.)	16,200	4,500	43	3,542	12:1	71	N.A.	56[2]	508-793-7431
Clarkson (N.Y.)	14,510	5,077	N.A.	129	16:1	75[2]	18(S)	71	315-268-6479
Clemson (S.C.) 49	7,394	3,474	34	N.A.	19:1	65	37(S)	61	803-656-2287
Cleveland State (Ohio)[6]	6,000	3,800	N.A.	141	23:1	26	4(A)[12]	18[9]	216-687-3755
Coe (Iowa)	11,535	4,090	58	2,721	12:1	65	60(A)	44	319-399-8500
Coker (S.C.)	8,369	4,076	85[2]	1,380	10:1	65	16(S)	57	803-383-8050
Colby (Maine)	17,610	5,480	41	3,280	10:1	87	N.A.	59[3]	207-872-3168
Colby-Sawyer (N.H.)	12,775	5,120	N.A.	3,488	11:1	75	19(S)	19[2]	603-526-2010
Colgate (N.Y.)	17,415	5,275	N.A.	N.A.	11:1	81[2]	N.A.	83[2]	315-824-7401
College of Charleston (S.C.)	4,650	3,000	10	N.A.	20:1	44	39(S)	42	803-792-5670
College of Mount St. Vincent (N.Y.)	10,800	4,900	N.A.	1,472	12:1	N.A.	4(S)	31	212-405-3267

Footnotes are on page 186

College name and location	Tuition and fees	Room and board	% of students receiving financial aid	Average gift aid per student	Student/ faculty ratio	% who graduate in five years	% with high test scores	% from top fifth of class	Telephone
College of New Rochelle (N.Y.)[1]	$10,240	$4,620	N.A.	N.A.	12:1	12	21(S)	N.A.	914-654-5452
College of Notre Dame (Calif.)	10,980	5,300	35	$949	10:1	34	25(A)[12]	53[3]	415-508-3607
College of Notre Dame of Maryland[1] 76	10,050	5,100	N.A.	N.A.	15:1	73	36(S)	26	800-435-0300
College of St. Benedict (Minn.)[1]	10,578	3,887	80	1,959	14:1	74	41(A)	51	612-363-5308
College of St. Catherine (Minn.)[1]	10,794	3,750	53	1,004	14:1	63	36(A)	38	612-690-6505
College of St. Francis (Ill.)	8,600	3,760	78	1,945	16:1	55	31(A)	40	815-740-3400
College of St. Scholastica (Minn.)	10,659	3,498	84	2,138	13:1	57	34(A)	49	218-723-6046
College of the Atlantic (Maine)	12,570	3,385	59	N.A.	10:1	12	63(S)	30	207-288-5015
College of the Holy Cross (Mass.)	16,635	6,000	41	3,148	14:1	92	85(S)[2]	68	508-793-2443
College of the Ozarks (Mo.)[15]	100	1,600	29	467	16:1	66	7(A)[19]	30[3,7]	417-334-6411
College of the Southwest (N.M.)	3,380	2,200	97	485	8:1	N.A.	17(A)[7,20]	10	505-392-6561
College of William and Mary (Va.) 77	11,426	3,190	21[2]	338	14:1	87	45(S)[2]	91	804-221-3999
College of Wooster (Ohio)	14,380	4,300	65	4,221	12:1	64	59(S)[9]	42	216-263-2270
Colorado College	14,880	3,820	54	7,476	13:1	79	78(S)	79	719-389-6344
Colorado School of Mines	11,200	3,865	65	1,304	13:1	55	75(A)	90[3]	303-273-3220
Colorado State	7,157	3,726	N.A.	N.A.	13:1	49	53(A)	48	303-491-6909
Columbia (Mo.)	7,166	3,236	38	1,031	12:1	58	N.A.	18	800-231-2391
Columbia (S.C.)[1]	9,190	3,460	53	1,227	14:1	51	N.A.	68[3]	803-786-3871
Columbia University (N.Y.) 55	16,970	6,510	N.A.	N.A.	7:1	93[2]	75(S)	94	212-854-2521
Columbus (Ga.)	4,227	2,760	N.A.	N.A.	14:1	N.A.	3(S)	N.A.	404-568-2035
Concord (W.Va.)	3,906	3,018	45	863	23:1	35	21(A)	32	304-384-5249
Concordia (Minn.)	9,200	2,900	N.A.	1,666	15:1	68	46(A)	49	218-299-3004
Connecticut	17,200	5,700	39	3,348	12:1	84	92(S)	95	203-439-2200
Converse (S.C.)[1]	11,350	3,500	N.A.	1,348	11:1	65	N.A.	N.A.	803-596-9040
Cook College–Rutgers U. (N.J.) 22	7,387	4,200	45	238	16:1	70	55(S)	62	908-932-3770
Cooper Union (N.Y.)[21]	300	4,100[8]	N.A.	414	7:1	60	75(S)	N.A.	212-353-4120
Coppin State (Md.)	4,343	4,500	85	510	17:1	N.A.	N.A.	10[9]	301-333-5990
Cornell (Iowa)	13,254	4,046	78	3,385	13:1	56	60(A)	52	800-747-1112
Cornell University (N.Y.)	17,276	5,676	41	N.A.	11:1	88	88(S)	95	607-255-5241
Cornish College of the Arts (Wash.)[21]	8,665	No dorms	59	491	7:1	55	N.A.	N.A.	206-323-1400
Creighton (Neb.) 91	9,670	4,000	N.A.	1,413	14:1	55	54(A)	25[22]	402-280-2703
Culver-Stockton (Mo.)	7,175	3,075	75	3,172	16:1	38	35(A)	48	314-288-5221
Cumberland (Ky.)	5,200	2,830	N.A.	682	14:1	N.A.	10(A)	N.A.	606-549-2200
Curry (Mass.)	12,945	4,900	42	972	15:1	52	5(S)	4[2]	617-333-0500
Dakota State (S.D.)	2,040	2,210	20	61	18:1	N.A.	11(A)	10	605-256-5139
Dakota Wesleyan (S.D.)	6,700	2,530	93	673	14:1	57	30(A)[12]	12	800-333-8506
Dana (Neb.)	8,050	2,930	N.A.	1,976	11:1	47	47(A)[12]	23	800-444-3262
Daniel Webster (N.H.)	11,160	4,454	68	2,037	14:1	64	17(S)	19	603-883-3556
Dartmouth (N.H.) 66	17,354	6,086	37	N.A.	12:1	94	94(S)	96	603-646-2875
Davidson (N.C.) 72	14,950	4,470	40	N.A.	12:1	88	83(S)	53	704-892-2230
Davis and Elkins (W.Va.)	8,160	3,930	65	956	14:1	39	9(S)	1	304-636-5850
Defiance (Ohio)	9,386	3,420	N.A.	N.A.	14:1	48	30(A)[12]	21	419-783-2330
Delaware State	3,840	3,210	20	N.A.	14:1	N.A.	N.A.	N.A.	302-739-4917
Delaware Valley (Pa.)	11,090	4,470	72	2,213	14:1	58	29(S)	19	215-345-1500
Delta State (Miss.)	3,802	1,690	70	343	18:1	34	37(A)[12]	N.A.	601-846-4656
Denison (Ohio)	15,640	4,220	50	3,487	11:1	78	46(S)	50	800-336-4766
DePaul (Ill.)	10,014	4,150	N.A.	632	17:1	59	77(A)[12]	62[3]	312-362-8300
DePauw (Ind.)	13,000	4,640	15	2,903	12:1	78	70(S)	65	800-447-2495
Dickinson (Pa.)	16,760	4,715	46	3,368	12:1	85	N.A.	73	717-245-1231
Dickinson State (N.D.)[6]	4,256	1,850	N.A.	150	16:1	33[24]	27(A)	15	701-227-2175
Doane (Neb.)	8,770	2,700	92	1,755	13:1	49	37(A)	33	402-826-8222
Dominican of San Rafael (Calif.)	11,280	5,410	59	3,531	12:1	37	27(S)	N.A.	415-485-3204
Douglass College–Rutgers U. (N.J.)[1] 20	7,348	3,940	49	159	17:1	76	51(S)	62	908-932-3770
Drake (Iowa)	11,780	4,215	75	2,801	16:1	72	63(A)	55	515-271-3181
Drew (N.J.)	17,294	5,094	50	4,200	12:1	77	78(S)	63	201-408-3739
Drexel (Pa.)[14]	13,035	5,300	N.A.	153	15:1	45	37(S)	42	215-895-2400

Footnotes are on page 186

College name and location	Tuition and fees	Room and board	% of students receiving financial aid	Average gift aid per student	Student/ faculty ratio	% who graduate in five years	% with high test scores	% from top fifth of class	Telephone
Drury (Mo.) 79	$8,450	$3,280	N.A.	$2,370	13:1	54	44(A)	44	417-865-8731
Duke (N.C.)	16,121	5,243	34	3,286	9:1	94	93(S)	96	919-684-3214
Duquesne (Pa.)	9,750	4,512	71	850	17:1	70	33(S)	77	412-434-6220
D'Youville (N.Y.)	8,320	3,940	80	576	14:1	44	17(S)	43	800-777-3921
Earlham (Ind.)	14,403	3,894	72	3,890	11:1	75	75(S)	50	800-327-5426
East Carolina (N.C.)	6,440[23]	2,900[23]	N.A.	190	15:1	43	12(S)	27	919-757-7640
East Central (Okla.)	3,255	2,068	N.A.	N.A.	25:1	N.A.	38(A)[12]	42[3]	405-332-8000
Eastern Connecticut State	4,916	3,464	N.A.	4	17:1	50	17(S)	26	203-456-5286
Eastern Illinois	5,901	2,856	N.A.	31	17:1	59	47(A)[20]	30	217-581-2223
Eastern Kentucky [6]	4,220	2,896	N.A.	126	23:1	29	N.A.	N.A.	606-622-2106
Eastern Michigan	5,570	3,670	28	169	27:1	N.A.	33(S)	N.A.	313-487-3060
Eastern Montana	3,881	2,260	41[2]	21	19:1	15	20(A)	10	406-657-2158
Eastern New Mexico	4,964	2,485	69	N.A.	20:1	46	12(A)	N.A.	505-562-2178
Eastern Oregon State	2,400	3,400	N.A.	N.A.	11:1	30	N.A.	N.A.	503-962-3393
Eastern Washington	6,297	3,618	N.A.	83	16:1	N.A.	15(S)	N.A.	509-359-2397
East Stroudsburg U. of Pennsylvania	5,860	3,075	N.A.	N.A.	20:1	43	17(S)	17	717-424-3542
East Tennessee State	4,890	2,808	39	126	23:1	29	38(A)[20]	33	615-929-4213
East Texas State	5,682	3,143	31[2]	N.A.	19:1	24	N.A.	N.A.	214-886-5081
Eckerd (Fla.)	13,825	3,500	80	3,947	14:1	70	57(S)	40	813-864-8331
Edinboro U. of Pennsylvania	6,555	3,460	62	N.A.	17:1	46	N.A.	20	800-626-2203
Elizabeth City State (N.C.)	5,686	2,648	89	114	13:1	35	4(S)	28	919-335-3305
Elizabethtown (Pa.)	12,550	4,100	57	1,856	14:1	62	41(S)	57	717-361-1400
Elmhurst (Ill.)	9,050	3,678	49	384	16:1	52	N.A.	27	708-617-3400
Elmira (N.Y.)	12,700	4,100	60	3,180	14:1	65	40(S)[25]	33	607-734-3911
Elms (Mass.) [1]	10,375	4,665	N.A.	890	14:1	87	N.A.	80	800-255-3567
Elon (N.C.)	8,110	3,485	57	759	17:1	51	21(S)	26	800-334-8448
Emerson (Mass.)	13,504	7,288	47	N.A.	15:1	60	48(S)	33	617-578-8600
Emmanuel (Mass.) [1]	11,153	5,528	76	1,680	12:1	54	16(S)	22[2]	617-735-9715
Emory (Ga.)	15,820	4,792	53	3,527	10:1	81	83(S)	N.A.	404-727-6036
Emory and Henry (Va.) 58	7,820	4,160	85[2]	971	14:1	57	32(S)	59	703-944-4121
Emporia State (Kans.) [6]	4,470	2,880	20	190	19:1	35	34(A)	N.A.	316-341-5465
Erskine (S.C.) 75	10,150	3,450	60	2,856	12:1	62	42(S)	71[3]	803-379-8838
Eureka (Ill.)	10,325	3,330	N.A.	2,569	11:1	N.A.	N.A.	37	800-322-3756
Evergreen State (Wash.)	6,297	4,000	34	169	20:1	43	59(S)	29	206-866-6000
Fairfield (Conn.)	13,720	5,650	N.A.	1,351	16:1	86	87(S)	53	203-254-4100
Fairleigh Dickinson (N.J.)	10,386	5,232	N.A.	1,967	14:1	49	17(S)	7	201-460-5267
Fairmont State (W.Va.)	4,006	3,040	57[2]	N.A.	24:1	45[2]	10(A)	5	304-367-4141
Fayetteville State (N.C.)	7,006	2,300	N.A.	384	15:1	17	N.A.	N.A.	919-486-1271
Ferris State (Mich.)	6,015	3,707	48	126	17:1	N.A.	22(A)[12]	N.A.	616-592-2100
Ferrum (Va.)	8,120	3,730	N.A.	N.A.	15:1	N.A.	6(S)[2]	14[2,3]	703-365-4290
Fisk (Tenn.) [13] 21	5,510	3,355	12	536	12:1	60	N.A.	40	615-329-8500
Fitchburg State (Mass.)	6,848	3,166	N.A.	66	16:1	49	13(S)	16	508-345-2151
Flagler (Fla.)	4,710	2,980	N.A.	396	20:1	47	37(S)	33	904-829-6481
Florida A&M	6,510	2,770	N.A.	392	13:1	31	9(A)	0	904-599-3796
Florida Atlantic [26]	6,493	3,454	36	N.A.	16:1	35	34(S)[20]	N.A.	407-367-3040
Florida Institute of Technology	11,850	3,723	57	152	15:1	25	50(S)	20	800-888-4348
Florida International [26]	5,688	5,624	25	104	14:1	64	39(S)	58	305-348-2363
Florida Southern	6,600[23]	3,660[23]	N.A.	1,143	19:1	N.A.	18(S)[2]	10[2]	813-680-4131
Florida State	5,630	3,880	31	262	N.A.	47	58(S)	0	904-644-6200
Fontbonne (Mo.)	7,750	3,600	N.A.	1,644	12:1	48	24(A)	18	314-889-1400
Fordham (N.Y.)	12,150	6,525	N.A.	N.A.	17:1	84	N.A.	62[3]	212-579-2133
Fort Hays State (Kans.) [6]	4,515	2,785	N.A.	N.A.	15:1	N.A.	25(A)[9]	N.A.	913-628-4222
Fort Lewis (Colo.)	6,073	2,960	40	43	20:1	30	10(A)	33[3]	303-247-7010
Framingham State (Mass.)	6,955	3,366	30	156	16:1	60	20(S)	20	508-626-4500
Francis Marion (S.C.)	4,920	3,078	29	43	19:1	N.A.	10(S)	32	803-661-1231
Franklin (Ind.)	9,590	3,650	96	3,207	12:1	56	41(S)	57[2,3]	317-738-8062

Footnotes are on page 186

tops for techies

SCIENCE AND TECHNOLOGY
SCHOOLS THAT SCORED HIGHEST
IN MONEY'S VALUE RANKINGS

California Institute of Technology

Georgia Institute of Technology

New Mexico Institute of Mining

Harvey Mudd College

Michigan Technological University

North Carolina State University

MIT

Virginia Polytechnic Institute

University of Missouri–Rolla

N.J. Institute of Technology

liberal arts havens

LIBERAL ARTS SCHOOLS WITH 1,600
STUDENTS OR LESS THAT SCORED
HIGHEST IN OUR VALUE RANKINGS

New College—U. of South Florida

Hanover College

Fisk University

Centenary College of Louisiana

Wabash College

Illinois College

Emory and Henry College

University of the South

Westminster College (Pa.)

Swarthmore College

College name and location	Tuition and fees	Room and board	% of students receiving financial aid	Average gift aid per student	Student/ faculty ratio	% who graduate in five years	% with high test scores	% from top fifth of class	Telephone
Franklin and Marshall (Pa.)	$18,350	$3,980	35	$2,979	12:1	83	79(S)	48	717-291-3951
Franklin Pierce (N.H.)	12,160	4,250	60	2,022	14:1	42	12(S)	5	800-437-0048
Frostburg State (Md.)	4,628	3,940	50	45	17:1	41	17(S)	N.A.	301-689-4201
Furman (S.C.) **71**	11,700	3,856	70	2,155	12:1	N.A.	100(S)	62	803-294-2034
Gannon (Pa.)	9,154	3,780	87	1,742	13:1	35	20(S)	43	800-426-6668
George Mason (Va.)	8,604	4,750	23	139	17:1	40	N.A.	28	703-993-2400
George Washington (D.C.)	16,370	6,310	48	3,712	14:1	68	74(S)	51	202-994-6040
Georgetown (D.C.)	16,589	6,018	44	3,129	13:1	91	86(S)	86	202-687-3600
Georgia College	4,314	2,490	N.A.	80	25:1	45	10(S)	N.A.	912-453-5004
Georgia Institute of Technology **7**	6,523	4,052	30	509	20:1	51	N.A.	90	404-894-4154
Georgia Southern	4,860	2,850	N.A.	53	22:1	30	N.A.	N.A.	912-681-5531
Georgia Southwestern	4,158	2,370	35[2]	N.A.	18:1	25	13(S)	N.A.	912-928-1273
Georgia State [26]	6,258	No dorms	N.A.	N.A.	30:1.	24[27]	30(S)[2]	N.A.	404-651-2365
Georgian Court (N.J.)	7,875	3,750	26	351	10:1	56	2(S)	27	908-367-4440
Gettysburg (Pa.)	17,650	3,815	42	N.A.	13:1	80	77(S)	72	717-337-6100
Glenville State (W.Va.)	3,820	2,928	56	115	18:1	42	16(A)	22[2,3]	304-462-4117
GMI Eng. and Mgt. Institute (Mich.) [21]	10,240	2,980	10	202	14:1	73	80(A)	87	313-762-7865
Goddard (Vt.)	13,000	4,380	N.A.	3,105	10:1	N.A.	N.A.	N.A.	802-454-8311
Gonzaga (Wash.)	11,240	3,900	60	2,026	14:1	51	37(S)	58	509-484-6484
Goucher (Md.)	13,646	5,873	36	2,735	9:1	75	66(S)	51	410-337-6100
Graceland (Iowa)	8,420	3,318	87	2,338	13:1	N.A.	62(A)[12]	42[3]	515-784-5196
Grambling State (La.)[6]	6,656[23]	2,612	N.A.	N.A.	21:1	N.A.	2(A)	N.A.	318-274-2435
Grand Valley State (Mich.)	5,860	3,800	N.A.	242	23:1	N.A.	88(A)	50[3]	616-895-2025
Grand View (Iowa)[6]	9,150	3,200	N.A.	1,338	15:1	40	26(A)	20	515-263-2810
Green Mountain (Vt.)	10,525	2,870	N.A.	844	14:1	65	23(S)[9]	14[9]	800-451-6116
Greensboro (N.C.)	7,240	3,504	62	N.A.	N.A.	39	31(S)	35	800-346-8226
Grinnell (Iowa) **90**	14,532	4,138	71	5,219	10:1	83	87(S)	81	515-269-3600
Grove City (Pa.) **19**	4,770	2,780	35	348	20:1	77	60(S)	76	412-458-2100
Guilford (N.C.)	11,610	4,784	96	2,551	14:1	60	58(S)	48	800-992-7759
Gustavus Adolphus (Minn.)	12,600	3,225	64	2,019	14:1	76	58(A)	61	507-933-7676
Hamilton (N.Y.)	17,650	4,750	44	4,051	11:1	85	77(S)	72	315-859-4421
Hamline (Minn.)	12,365	3,895	82	2,839	14:1	65	99(A)[12]	72[3]	612-641-2207
Hampden-Sydney (Va.)[17]	12,253	4,148	45	N.A.	13:1	65	47(S)	25	804-223-6120
Hampshire (Mass.)	18,665	4,875	51	4,972	13:1	53	N.A.	23	413-549-4600
Hampton (Va.)[13]	7,006	3,120	N.A.	309	18:1	63	N.A.	N.A.	703-727-5329
Hanover (Ind.) **4**	7,210	3,015	N.A.	1,489	14:1	63	N.A.	52	812-866-7021
Hartwick (N.Y.)	14,450	4,450	64	3,455	13:1	68	27(S)	37	607-431-4150

Footnotes are on page 186

top black colleges

HISTORICALLY BLACK SCHOOLS THAT SCORED HIGHEST IN MONEY'S VALUE RANKINGS

Fisk University
Spelman College
Howard University
Hampton University
Morehouse College
Clark Atlanta University
Benedict College
LeMoyne-Owen College

top values for women

WOMEN'S COLLEGES WITH THE HIGHEST SCORES IN OUR VALUE RANKINGS

Douglass College
Spelman College
Notre Dame of Maryland
Agnes Scott College
Chestnut Hill College
Wesleyan College (Ga.)
Elms College
Salem College
Wells College
Wellesley College

College name and location	Tuition and fees	Room and board	% of students receiving financial aid	Average gift aid per student	Student/ faculty ratio	% who graduate in five years	% with high test scores	% from top fifth of class	Telephone
Harvard (Mass.) 36	$17,674	$5,840	41	$4,606	8:1	96	N.A.	N.A.	617-495-1551
Harvey Mudd (Calif.) 40	15,920	6,160	55	3,172	8:1	75	94(S)	98	714-621-8011
Hastings (Neb.)	8,720	3,010	93	2,738	13:1	52	34(A)	32	402-461-7315
Haverford (Pa.)	17,125	5,700	36	3,755	11:1	90	90(S)	90	215-896-1350
Hawaii Loa	9,000	5,200	87	N.A.	12:1	N.A.	48(A)	20[2,3]	808-235-3641
Hawaii Pacific	5,150	6,300	20	139	20:1	N.A.	27(S)	10	808-544-0238
Heidelberg (Ohio)	12,380	3,960	82	3,017	14:1	50	42(A)	N.A.	419-448-2330
Henderson State (Ark.)	2,740	2,200	N.A.	N.A.	20:1	N.A.	N.A.	20[2]	501-246-5511
Hendrix (Ark.)	7,710	2,895	64[2]	N.A.	15:1	N.A.	71(A)	77	501-450-1362
High Point (N.C.)	7,250	3,460	58	412	17:1	40	21(S)	20	919-841-9216
Hillsdale (Mich.) 78	10,170	4,230	73	3,704	13:1	73	78(A)[12]	65[3]	517-437-7341
Hiram (Ohio)	12,897	4,047	N.A.	3,934	12:1	70	72(A)[12]	56	800-362-5280
Hobart and William Smith (N.Y.) [17]	17,291	5,358	42	3,640	13:1	80	75(A)	53	800-852-2256
Hofstra (N.Y.)	9,790	5,606	N.A.	849	17:1	62	40(S)	51	516-463-6700
Hollins (Va.) [1]	12,399	4,950	52	1,969	10:1	69	47(S)	48	703-362-6401
Hood (Md.)	12,228	5,675	95	2,770	12:1	66	49(S)	45	800-922-1599
Hope (Mich.)	10,792	3,926	65	1,989	12:1	73	52(A)	53	616-394-7850
Howard (D.C.) [13]	7,004	3,800	N.A.	180	7:1	34	N.A.	N.A.	202-636-6200
Humboldt State (Calif.)	7,540[23]	4,201[23]	N.A.	N.A.	18:1	N.A.	30(S)[2]	N.A.	707-826-4402
Hunter College–City U. of N.Y.	5,153	1,600[8]	75	6	17:1	24	N.A.	24	212-772-4490
Huntingdon (Ala.)	7,140	3,560	N.A.	1,969	13:1	50	48(A)	17[9]	205-834-3300
Huston-Tillotson (Texas)	4,650	3,304	N.A.	N.A.	19:1	N.A.	N.A.	N.A.	512-476-7421
Illinois Benedictine	9,400[23]	3,605[23]	98	1,263[2]	15:1	N.A.	N.A.	41[3]	708-960-1500
Illinois College 41	7,050	3,450	90	1,313	12:1	65	38(A)	43	217-245-3030
Illinois Institute of Technology	13,110	4,380	84	3,177	11:1	48	69(A)[12]	58	312-567-3025
Illinois State	7,227	2,900	N.A.	22	19:1	50	27(A)	34[3]	309-438-2181
Illinois Wesleyan	12,320	3,915	N.A.	2,468	13:1	78	N.A.	72	309-556-3031
Incarnate Word (Texas)	7,860	3,890	51[2]	N.A.	15:1	N.A.	N.A.	25[2]	512-829-6005
Indiana State	5,960	3,451	N.A.	N.A.	14:1	48[27]	10(S)	66	812-237-2121
Indiana U. at Bloomington 89	8,292	3,565	N.A.	165	19:1	63	38(S)	54	812-855-0661
Indiana U. of Pennsylvania	5,244	2,750	5	N.A.	19:1	N.A.	32(S)	49	412-357-2230
Indiana U.–Purdue U. at Indianapolis [26]	5,934	2,925	32	30	21:1	N.A.	11(S)	14	317-274-4591
Iona (N.Y.)	9,540	4,810	50	N.A.	17:1	N.A.	13(S)	21	914-633-2502
Iowa State 48	6,996	3,044	N.A.	478	19:1	55	56(A)	48	515-294-5836
Iowa Wesleyan	9,200	3,200	N.A.	1,380	16:1	27	N.A.	29[2,3]	319-385-8021
Ithaca (N.Y.)	12,870	5,512	40	2,015	13:1	68	46(S)	38	607-274-3124
Jackson State (Miss.)	4,190	2,606	N.A.	N.A.	17:1	N.A.	N.A.	N.A.	601-968-2100

Footnotes are on page 186

College name and location	Tuition and fees	Room and board	% of students receiving financial aid	Average gift aid per student	Student/ faculty ratio	% who graduate in five years	% with high test scores	% from top fifth of class	Telephone
Jacksonville (Fla.)	$9,320	$4,070	64	N.A.	18:1	43	28(S)	28	904-744-3950
Jacksonville State (Ala.)	2,240	2,330	41	N.A.	23:1	30	18(A)[20]	N.A.	205-782-5400
James Madison (Va.) **54**	7,240	4,284	40	$304	19:1	79	56(S)	62	703-568-6147
Jamestown (N.D.)	6,920	2,980	N.A.	N.A.	17:1	49	33(A)	22	701-252-3467
Jersey City State (N.J.)	3,533	4,650	37	16	16:1	26	11(S)	11	201-200-3234
John Carroll (Ohio)	10,440	5,450	70	1,790	14:1	70	45(A)	41	216-397-4294
Johns Hopkins (Md.) **51**	17,000	6,305	35	3,211	9:1	87	95(S)	89	410-516-8171
Johnson C. Smith (N.C.)[13]	6,138	2,331	N.A.	601	15:1	35	3(S)	11	800-782-7303
Juniata (Pa.)	13,250	4,010	75	790	14:1	N.A.	49(S)	55	814-643-4310
Kalamazoo (Mich.)	13,845	4,407	N.A.	3,458	12:1	68	75(A)	78[3]	616-383-8408
Kansas State[6]	6,012	2,640[23]	35	214	17:1	45[27]	57(A)[20]	57[2,3]	913-532-6250
Kean (N.J.)	3,165	3,275	N.A.	16	20:1	45	7(S)	17	908-527-2195
Keene State (N.H.)	7,345	3,772	36	63	19:1	53	19(S)	14	603-358-2276
Kent State (Ohio)	7,068	3,394	N.A.	226	23:1	35	20(A)	22	216-672-2444
Kentucky State	4,052	2,682	N.A.	598	12:1	19	N.A.	16[2]	502-227-6813
Kentucky Wesleyan	7,170	4,030	80	1,648	11:1	57	17(A)	55[3]	502-926-3111
Kenyon (Ohio)	17,610	3,570	31	3,331	13:1	86	37(S)[28]	40[28]	614-427-5776
Keuka (N.Y.)	8,760	4,170	N.A.	1,226	12:1	N.A.	16(S)	11	315-536-5254
King's (N.Y.)	8,310	3,920	N.A.	1,577	10:1	40	5(S)	37	914-944-5650
King's (Pa.)	9,650	4,500	17	1,223	17:1	68	24(S)	39	717-826-5858
Knox (Ill.)	13,842	3,858	79	4,404	11:1	76	N.A.	48	309-343-0112
Kutztown (Pa.)	5,868	2,840	25[2]	N.A.	18:1	N.A.	24(S)	29[3]	215-683-4060
Lafayette (Pa.)	16,795	5,190	39[2]	3,291	11:1	96	72(S)	61	215-250-5100
LaGrange (Ga.)	5,127	980	65	616	15:1	N.A.	N.A.	N.A.	800-476-4925
Lake Forest (Ill.)	15,085	3,535	57	4,025	11:1	74	75(A)[12]	64[2,3]	708-234-3100
Lake Superior State (Mich.)	5,250	No dorms	50	313	20:1	N.A.	38(A)[20]	25	906-635-2231
Lamar (Texas)	4,240	2,600	N.A.	151	25:1	19[27]	10(S)	N.A.	800-458-7558
Lambuth (Tenn.)	4,834	3,160	N.A.	1,057	14:1	40	N.A.	20	901-425-3223
Lander (S.C.)	4,218	2,880	8	220	15:1	N.A.	N.A.	N.A.	803-229-8307
LaSalle (Pa.)	10,970[35]	5,140	N.A.	1,250	15:1	65	60(S)	20	215-951-1500
Lawrence (Wis.)	15,342	3,429	79	5,457	11:1	75	77(A)	56	414-832-6500
Lebanon Valley (Pa.)	12,875	4,325	75[2]	1,879	11:1	68	36(S)	36	800-445-6181
Lehigh (Pa.)	16,700	5,240	35	3,208	12:1	88	63(S)	70	215-758-3100
Le Moyne (N.Y.)	9,885	4,260	65	1,275	15:1	73	32(S)	41	315-445-4300
LeMoyne-Owen (Tenn.)[6,13]	4,200	3,600	N.A.	N.A.	16:1	47	N.A.	55[2]	901-942-7302
Lenoir-Rhyne (N.C.)	9,500	3,665	N.A.	2,396	14:1	62	20(S)	36	704-328-7300
Lesley (Mass.)[1]	11,150	5,125	9	1,738	N.A.	60	13(S)	14	617-349-8800
Lewis (Ill.)	8,502	3,990	N.A.	1,054	16:1	41	19(A)	24	815-838-0500
Lewis and Clark (Ore.)	14,651	4,839	50	2,784	13:1	68	62(S)	67[3]	503-768-7040
Lewis-Clark State (Idaho)	3,558	2,900	N.A.	115	16:1	25	N.A.	N.A.	208-799-2210
Lincoln (Mo.)[6]	3,061	2,702	N.A.	113	19:1	N.A.	8(A)	8	314-681-5599
Lincoln (Pa.)[13]	8,000	2,800	N.A.	110	12:1	33	1(S)	11	215-932-8300
Lincoln Memorial (Tenn.)	5,250	2,570	55	592	19:1	43	78(A)[12]	44[3]	615-869-6280
Lindenwood (Mo.)	8,550	4,400	90	2,078	14:1	64	21(A)	21	314-949-4949
Lindsey Wilson (Ky.)	5,552	3,280	93	1,193	N.A.	25	10(A)	10	502-384-2126
Linfield (Ore.)	11,880	3,720	80	3,072	13:1	57	52(S)	58	503-472-4121
Livingston College–Rutgers U. (N.J.) **34**	7,425	3,940	43	253[2]	17:1	53	39(S)	41	908-932-3770
Lock Haven (Pa.)	5,396[23]	3,144[23]	N.A.	40	19:1	43	30(S)	42	717-893-2027
Long Island U.–Brooklyn (N.Y.)	9,600	4,090	N.A.	1,223	9:1	36[2]	N.A.	N.A.	718-488-1000
Long Island U.–C.W. Post (N.Y.)	10,810	5,280	65	971	15:1	40[27]	N.A.	32	516-299-2413
Long Island U.–Southampton (N.Y.)	10,850	5,480	N.A.	2,572	12:1	44	30(S)	38[3]	516-283-4000
Longwood (Va.)	7,990	3,586	40	163	14:1	50	28(S)	29	804-395-2600
Loras (Iowa)	9,900	3,470	70	1,772	13:1	60	44(A)	38	319-588-7235
Louisiana State and A&M	5,243[23]	2,710[23]	30	391	18:1	29	70(A)[12]	45	504-388-1175
Louisiana State–Shreveport[6]	3,790	No dorms	N.A.	24	21:1	20	N.A.	N.A.	318-797-5061
Louisiana Tech[6]	2,996	2,115	N.A.	N.A.	23:1	40	N.A.	45[3]	318-257-3036

Footnotes are on page 186

major money

SCHOOLS WITH THE HIGHEST
CHARGES FOR TUITION, FEES,
ROOM AND BOARD

Sarah Lawrence College	**$24,380**
Bard College	**24,095**
Brandeis University	**23,950**
Bennington College	**23,880**
Barnard College	**23,864**
Yale University	**23,700**
Tufts University	**23,594**
MIT	**23,565**
Hampshire College	**23,540**
Harvard University	**23,514**

rocketing rates

COLLEGES THAT IMPOSED THE
BIGGEST PERCENTAGE INCREASES
IN TUITION AND FEES THIS YEAR

Alcorn State University	**71%**
Western Montana College	**44**
Northern Montana College	**43**
Montana State University	**39**
Montana University	**39**
Alabama State University	**34**
Christopher Newport College	**33**
Salem-Teikyo University[1]	**30**
Millersville University (Pa.)	**28**
West Texas State	**28**

[1]Private school; for publics, we used nonresident charges

College name and location	Tuition and fees	Room and board	% of students receiving financial aid	Average gift aid per student	Student/ faculty ratio	% who graduate in five years	% with high test scores	% from top fifth of class	Telephone
Loyola (La.)	$9,720	$3,468	N.A.	$1,876	15:1	56	100(A)	42	504-865-3240
Loyola (Md.)	11,475	5,800	N.A.	1,698	15:1	73	57(S)	45	301-532-5012
Loyola Marymount (Calif.)	12,272	5,930	N.A.	193	15:1	60	N.A.	N.A.	310-338-2750
Loyola U. of Chicago (Ill.)	9,930	5,154	N.A.	1,095	N.A.	62[27]	41(S)	45	312-915-6500
Luther (Iowa)	11,600	3,300	70	1,859	14:1	73	83(A)[12]	58	319-387-1287
Lycoming (Pa.)	12,200	4,100	52	2,989	14:1	58	30(S)	35	717-321-4026
Lynchburg (Va.)	10,900	5,250	40	1,523	13:1	60	17(S)	16	804-522-8300
Lyndon State (Vt.)[6]	7,474	4,462	N.A.	59	17:1	38	N.A.	N.A.	802-626-9371
Lynn (Fla.)	12,200	No dorms	N.A.	N.A.	20:1	N.A.	N.A.	N.A.	407-994-0770
Macalester (Minn.)	14,125	4,208	70	3,910	12:1	70	88(S)	55	612-696-6357
MacMurray (Ill.) 85	8,620	3,480	90	1,258	12:1	45	41(A)[12]	24	217-479-7056
Manchester (Ind.)	8,960	3,440	N.A.	2,583	14:1	52	25(S)	42	219-982-5055
Manhattan (N.Y.)	12,000	6,250	60	2,125	15:1	69	41(S)	38	212-920-0200
Manhattanville (N.Y.)	13,435	5,900	95	N.A.	12:1	72	41(S)	44	914-694-2200
Mankato State (Minn.)	4,170	2,675	N.A.	N.A.	20:1	49	22(A)	22[2]	507-389-1822
Mansfield U. of Pennsylvania	5,327	2,638	35	61	18:1	73[2]	N.A.	21	717-662-4243
Marian (Ind.)	8,684	3,412	66	N.A.	12:1	N.A.	N.A.	5	317-929-0602
Marian of Fond du Lac (Wis.)	8,120	3,840	85	622	15:1	N.A.	14(S)	25	414-923-7650
Marietta (Ohio)	12,370	3,620	66	3,694	12:1	68	48(A)	41	614-374-4600
Marist (N.Y.)	9,730	6,283	N.A.	991	19:1	62	N.A.	21	914-575-3226
Marlboro (Vt.)	16,490	5,410	62	N.A.	8:1	50	N.A.	N.A.	802-257-4333
Marquette (Wis.) 100	9,934	4,150	60	741	14:1	74	65(A)	57	414-288-7302
Mars Hill (N.C.)	6,950	3,550	N.A.	1,101	13:1	48	N.A.	25	800-543-1514
Marshall (W.Va.)	4,600	3,600	N.A.	197	23:1	40	29(A)[20]	N.A.	304-696-3160
Mary Baldwin (Va.)[1]	16,565	6,495	70	3,282	11:1	60	29(S)[2]	N.A.	703-887-7019
Mary Washington (Va.) 30	6,752	4,552	40	96	17:1	66[2]	69(S)	69	703-899-4681
Marygrove (Mich.)	7,190	3,700	N.A.	409	17:1	30	N.A.	N.A.	313-862-5200
Marymount (N.Y.)	10,720	5,990	57	573	12:1	67	21(S)	40[3]	914-332-8295
Marymount (Va.)	10,192	4,882	N.A.	1,061	14:1	41	23(S)	17	703-284-1500
Marymount Manhattan (N.Y.)	9,645	4,500	N.A.	3,775	9:1	29	31(S)[9]	19[9]	212-517-0555
Maryville (Tenn.)	9,580	3,865	70	18	12:1	32	37(A)	55	615-981-8100
Marywood (Pa.)	9,350	4,400	65	1,279	16:1	63[2]	18(S)	25	717-348-6234
Massachusetts Inst. of Technology 74	18,000	5,565	N.A.	N.A.	4:1	N.A.	92(S)[2]	99[2]	617-253-4791
Mayville State (N.D.)[6]	4,305	2,196	N.A.	141	15:1	46	11(A)	13	701-786-4873
McKendree (Ill.)	7,076	3,350	83	221	15:1	45	19(A)	53[3]	800-232-7228
McMurry (Texas)	6,190	3,130	N.A.	924	15:1	26	23(A)	34	800-477-0077
Medaille (N.Y.)	7,750	4,100	N.A.	114	16:1	33[24]	N.A.	N.A.	716-884-3281

Footnotes are on page 186

College name and location	Tuition and fees	Room and board	% of students receiving financial aid	Average gift aid per student	Student/faculty ratio	% who graduate in five years	% with high test scores	% from top fifth of class	Telephone
Memphis State (Tenn.)	$5,350	$2,600	N.A.	$117	20:1	29	31(A)	N.A.	901-678-2101
Menlo (Calif.)	13,310	6,030	27[2]	N.A.	16:1	65[2]	9(S)[2]	N.A.	415-323-0406
Mercer (Ga.)	10,200	4,300	85[2]	N.A.	12:1	N.A.	34(A)[29]	53[3]	912-744-2650
Mercyhurst (Pa.)	9,288	3,543	N.A.	1,156	15:1	73	N.A.	19	814-824-2202
Meredith (N.C.)[1]	6,020	2,970	28	283	17:1	67	22(S)	51	919-829-8581
Merrimack (Mass.)	11,125	6,100	50	913	16:1	63	2(S)	25	508-837-5100
Mesa State (Colo.)	4,606	3,298	80[2]	82	19:1	33	N.A.[9]	32[9,30]	303-248-1376
Methodist (N.C.)	8,250	3,400	N.A.	387	14:1	62	8(S)	22	919-630-7027
Metropolitan State (Colo.)[26]	5,237	No dorms	49[2]	4	20:1	N.A.	17(S)	10	303-556-3058
Miami (Ohio) 52	8,686	3,620	32	292	21:1	75	75(A)	65	513-529-2531
Michigan State	9,520	3,375	50	323	12:1	62	79(A)[12]	85	517-355-8332
Michigan Technological 69	7,326	3,604	40	515	15:1	52	66(A)	61	906-487-2335
Middle Tennessee State	5,082	2,102	50[2]	N.A.	25:1	40[2]	31(A)[29]	33[3]	615-898-2111
Middlebury (Vt.)[10]	22,900[10]	N.A.	32	N.A.	11:1	89[24]	N.A.	85[3]	802-388-3711
Midland Lutheran (Neb.)	8,800	2,700	N.A.	2,463	15:1	55	N.A.	47[3]	402-721-6500
Midway (Ky.)[1]	6,240	3,550[2]	N.A.	597	11:1	38[2]	N.A.	N.A.	800-755-0031
Midwestern State (Texas)	4,692	2,918	N.A.	N.A.	22:1	71[2]	14(S)	48	817-692-6611
Miles (Ala.)[6,13]	3,800	2,400	N.A.	N.A.	22:1	70[24]	0(A)	89	205-923-2771
Millersville U. of Pennsylvania[26]	6,882	3,450	46	383	18:1	64	38(S)	46	717-872-3371
Millikin (Ill.)	10,681	3,956	87	2,988	15:1	64	46(A)	47	217-424-6210
Mills (Calif.)[1]	14,210	6,000	67	6,653	8:1	68	64(S)	64[3]	510-430-2135
Millsaps (Miss.) 94	10,280	3,980	67	2,448	14:1	65[2]	63(A)	51	601-974-1050
Milwaukee School of Engineering (Wis.)	9,960	3,000	80	2,166	15:1	46	59(A)	68[2,3]	414-277-7200
Minot State (N.D.)[6]	4,250	1,974	N.A.	71	12:1	37	N.A.	N.A.	701-857-3340
Misericordia (Pa.)	9,500	4,824	N.A.	702	13:1	N.A.	41(S)	30	717-675-4449
Mississippi State	3,685	3,030	N.A.	272	15:1	46	42(A)	46	601-325-2224
Mississippi U. for Women	5,010	2,042	68	446	18:1	47	47(A)	46	601-329-7106
Missouri Southern State	2,984	2,490	60	180	25:1	39[2]	25(A)[2]	28[2,3]	417-625-9300
Missouri Valley	8,200	4,850	99	6,442	N.A.	53[2]	6(A)	11	816-886-6925
Missouri Western State[6]	3,460	2,342	75	1,087	19:1	40[2]	12(A)	16	816-271-4263
Molloy (N.Y.)	8,340	No dorms	86[2]	485	11:1	60	16(S)	22	516-678-5000
Monmouth (Ill.)	13,000	3,610	N.A.	5,680	11:1	60	55(A)	60[3]	309-457-2131
Monmouth (N.J.)	11,160	4,680	65	1,065	15:1	48	3(S)	28[3]	908-571-3456
Montana Mineral Science and Technology	3,871	3,150	N.A.	812	16:1	100	N.A.	25	406-496-4178
Montana State	5,544	3,400	43	151	17:1	40	39(A)	27	406-994-2452
Montclair State (N.J.)	3,816	4,542	30	43	15:1	52	36(S)	44	800-331-9205
Moore of Art and Design (Pa.)[1,21]	12,804	4,864	N.A.	N.A.	10:1	80[24]	32(S)[2]	N.A.	215-568-4515
Moorhead State (Minn.)	4,256	2,712	48	41	20:1	40	31(A)	32	218-236-2161
Moravian (Pa.)	13,696	4,264	64	3,266	13:1	75	40(S)	40	215-861-1320
Morehead State (Ky.)	4,288	2,664	60	372	19:1	42	7(A)	N.A.	606-783-2000
Morehouse (Ga.)[13,17]	7,430	4,980	N.A.	912	18:1	N.A.	30(S)[2]	29[2]	404-681-2800
Morgan State (Md.)[6]	2,390	2,225	90	505	18:1	25	N.A.	N.A.	410-319-3000
Morningside (Iowa)	9,890	3,192	94	2,316	16:1	52	58(A)[12]	25	712-274-5111
Morris (S.C.)[6,13]	4,136	2,434	89[2]	42	15:1	44	N.A.	7	803-775-9371
Morris Brown (Ga.)[13]	7,032	4,146	25	N.A.	14:1	38[2]	2(S)	8	404-220-0152
Mount Holyoke (Mass.)[1]	16,995	5,180	N.A.	5,962	10:1	80	89(S)	70	413-538-2023
Mount Marty (S.D.)	6,718	2,870	91	2,189	12:1	65[24]	N.A.	27[2]	800-658-4552
Mount Mary (Wis.)[1]	7,300	2,796	60	449	13:1	60	N.A.	29[3]	414-259-9220
Mount Mercy (Iowa)	8,430	3,195	N.A.	821	15:1	53	25(A)[5]	49	319-363-8213
Mount St. Clare (Iowa)	8,400	3,400	81	1,197	10:1	N.A.	N.A.	10	319-242-4153
Mount St. Mary (N.Y.)	7,850	4,500	30	369	13:1	68[2]	30(S)	19	914-561-0800
Mount St. Mary's (Calif.)[1]	10,800	4,500	N.A.	N.A.	11:1	67[24]	46(S)[2]	90[3]	213-471-9516
Mount St. Mary's (Md.)	10,675	6,600	65[2]	422	16:1	77	31(S)	23	301-447-5214
Mount Senario (Wis.)	7,096	3,024	N.A.	711	12:1	46[2]	N.A.[2]	N.A.	715-532-5511
Mount Union (Ohio)	11,830	3,390	90	4,046	15:1	63	34(A)[31]	47	216-821-5320
Mount Vernon (D.C.)[1]	12,510	6,090	N.A.	N.A.	12:1	40[2]	N.A.	5[28]	202-331-3444

Footnotes are on page 186

helping hands

SCHOOLS GIVING THE MOST IN
NEED-BASED AID FROM THEIR OWN
MONEY, PER RECIPIENT

Mount Holyoke	$10,595
Bennington College	9,710
Reed College	9,677
Hampshire College	9,615
Mills College	9,511
Smith College	9,447
Amherst College	9,384
Williams College	9,276
Tulane University	9,223
Scripps College	9,115

St. Lawrence University	$9,005
Bates College	8,807
Brandeis University	8,654
Sarah Lawrence College	8,599
Connecticut College	8,495
Oberlin College	8,473
Haverford College	8,358
Trinity College (Conn.)	8,332
Brown University	8,113
Pine Manor College	8,057

College name and location	Tuition and fees	Room and board	% of students receiving financial aid	Average gift aid per student	Student/ faculty ratio	% who graduate in five years	% with high test scores	% from top fifth of class	Telephone
Muhlenberg (Pa.)	$15,740	$4,260	52	N.A.	13:1	81	54(S)	49	215-821-3200
Murray State (Ky.)	4,130	2,570	30	N.A.	18:1	40[27]	32(A)	55	800-272-4678
Muskingum (Ohio)	12,397	3,550	75	$4,196	14:1	62	26(A)[5]	44	614-826-8137
National-Louis (Ill.)	8,550	4,489	N.A.	213	12:1	45	4(A)	28	708-475-1100
Nazareth College of Rochester (N.Y.)	9,690	4,680	73	1,410	14:1	53	49(S)	36	800-462-3944
Nebraska Wesleyan	8,706	3,080	90	N.A.	13:1	59	73(A)[12]	42	402-465-2218
New College of the U. of South Florida 2	7,566	3,093	N.A.	416	11:1	47	75(S)[32]	80[3]	813-355-2963
New England (N.H.)	11,990	4,970	30	1,090	13:1	48	N.A.	16[2]	603-428-2223
New Jersey Institute of Technology	8,228	4,772	75	69	15:1	60	33(S)	37	201-596-3300
New Mexico Highlands[6]	4,940	2,050	70[2]	166	23:1	21	6(A)[2]	N.A.	505-454-3439
New Mexico Institute of Technology 10	5,366	3,022	N.A.	516	10:1	32	75(A)	N.A.	505-835-5424
New School for Social Research (N.Y.)	12,930	7,834	68	N.A.	9:1	70	73(S)	62[30]	212-229-5665
New York Institute of Technology	8,565	3,800	70	472	19:1	40[2]	11(S)	2	516-686-7520
New York University	16,650	6,700	70	N.A.	13:1	67	86(S)	85[3]	212-998-4500
Newberry (S.C.)	7,900	3,100	90	N.A.	13:1	48	14(S)	31	800-845-4955
Niagara (N.Y.)	9,548	4,346	73	1,232	17:1	54	25(A)	26	716-285-1212
Nicholls State (La.)[6]	3,449	2,450	31	92	23:1	29	9(A)	N.A.	504-448-4145
North Adams State (Mass.)	6,840	3,600	N.A.	N.A.	20:1	55	5(S)	3	413-664-4511
North Carolina A&T State	6,626	2,430	66	N.A.	14:1	28	5(S)	25	919-334-7946
North Carolina Central	5,586	2,603	N.A.	N.A.	15:1	11[2]	2(S)[2]	16[2]	919-560-6298
North Carolina State 70	7,902	3,250	30	232	14:1	49	43(S)	67	919-515-2434
North Carolina Wesleyan	7,660	3,790	78	N.A.	13:1	35	13(S)	8	919-985-5197
North Central (Ill.)	10,641	3,939	N.A.	1,733	14:1	58[27]	80(A)[12]	55	708-420-3414
North Dakota State[6]	5,141	2,394	N.A.	141	19:1	46[27]	25(A)	47	701-237-8643
North Georgia	4,266	2,364	N.A.	126	17:1	54	N.A.	N.A.	706-864-1800
North Park (Ill.)	11,295	4,140	N.A.	2,077	12:1	60	19(A)[2]	39[2,3]	312-583-2700
Northeast Louisiana[6]	3,210	2,410	N.A.	390	20:1	21	22(A)[20]	29[3]	318-342-5252
Northeast Missouri State 16	3,939	2,864	39	594	16:1	60	95(A)[12]	59	816-785-4114
Northeastern (Mass.)[26]	11,489	6,705	61	814	11:1	42	24(S)	20	617-437-2200
Northern Arizona	6,242	2,776	50	196	20:1	33	N.A.	N.A.	602-523-5511
Northern Illinois	6,732	2,956	55	N.A.	18:1	48	39(A)	29	815-753-0446
Northern Kentucky[6]	4,240	2,900	7[2]	84	15:1	36[2]	28(A)[12]	N.A.	606-572-5220
Northern Michigan	4,549	3,627	69	275	20:1	37	28(A)	36[3]	906-227-2650
Northern Montana	5,021	1,785	50	N.A.	17:1	N.A.	10(A)	5[28]	406-265-3704
Northern State (S.D.)[6]	3,008	1,874	50	32	19:1	N.A.	N.A.	N.A.	605-622-2544
Northland (Wis.)	9,190	3,620	80	2,092	16:1	46	44(A)	37	715-682-1224
Northwest Missouri State	3,542	2,818	N.A.	256	19:1	46	20(A)	19[2]	800-633-1175

Footnotes are on page 186

College name and location	Tuition and fees	Room and board	% of students receiving financial aid	Average gift aid per student	Student/ faculty ratio	% who graduate in five years	% with high test scores	% from top fifth of class	Telephone
Northwestern (Ill.)	$15,075	$5,079	54	N.A.	8:1	88	87(S)	89	708-491-7271
Northwestern Oklahoma State	3,467	1,784	30	N.A.	18:1	26	N.A.	N.A.	405-327-1700
Northwestern State U. of Louisiana[6]	3,570	2,154	69[2]	$72	33:1	37[24]	N.A.	N.A.	318-357-4503
Northwood Institute–Midland (Mich.)	8,410	4,000	N.A.	1,722	26:1	39	N.A.	N.A.	515-837-4273
Norwich (Vt.)	12,800	5,000	72[2]	2,318	14:1	54	27(S)[2]	21[2,3]	800-468-6679
Nova (Fla.)	7,750	4,700	20	233	11:1	N.A.	N.A.	N.A.	305-475-7360
Oakland (Mich.)	7,306	3,560	N.A.	175	19:1	50	50(A)	N.A.	313-370-3360
Oberlin (Ohio)	17,723	5,370	N.A.	4,247	13:1	80	88(S)[25]	78	216-775-8411
Occidental (Calif.)	15,381	5,121	N.A.	4,366	12:1	73	74(S)[9]	76	213-259-2700
Oglethorpe (Ga.)	11,287	3,900	76	N.A.	14:1	56	66(S)	76	404-364-8307
Ohio Dominican	7,370	3,930	N.A.	N.A.	15:1	47[2]	N.A.	N.A.	614-251-4500
Ohio Northern	13,455	3,615	90	3,359	13:1	57	76(A)[12]	61[3]	419-772-2260
Ohio State–Columbus 83	8,292	4,200	N.A.	145	14:1	45	72(A)[12]	48	614-292-3980
Ohio University 45	6,897	3,851	30	295	16:1	70	42(A)	42	614-593-4100
Ohio Wesleyan	14,644	5,130	65	N.A.	14:1	72	61(A)	51	614-368-3020
Oklahoma City	5,800	3,370	85[2]	1,371	21:1	N.A.	24(A)	46[3]	405-521-5050
Oklahoma State	5,000	3,100	N.A.	496	22:1	33	43(A)	49	405-744-6876
Old Dominion (Va.)	8,612	4,134	N.A.	68	18:1	34	N.A.	37	804-683-3637
Oregon Institute of Technology	6,452	3,350	N.A.	107[2]	15:1	40	N.A.	N.A.	503-885-1150
Oregon State	6,972	3,141	55[2]	99	17:1	44	N.A.	N.A.	503-737-4411
Ottawa (Kans.)	6,900	3,176	N.A.[2]	1,604	17:1	54	25(A)[7]	N.A.	913-242-5200
Otterbein (Ohio)	11,502	4,107	90	2,274	13:1	64	42(A)	N.A.	614-890-0004
Pace (N.Y.)[26]	9,976	4,680	N.A.	1,053[2]	22:1	55	20(S)	54	212-346-1323
Pacific (Ore.)	12,300	3,600	72	3,506	13:1	46	36(S)	60	800-635-0561
Pacific Lutheran (Wash.)	11,960	4,030	74	2,038	15:1	64	43(S)	68	206-535-7151
Park (Mo.)	7,160	3,600	95	491	12:1	30	20(A)	10	800-333-7276
Pembroke State (N.C.)	4,919	2,270	40	213	16:1	33	7(S)	26	919-521-9917
Pennsylvania State 96	9,644	1,940	64	472[2]	19:1	56	52(S)	71	814-865-5471
Pennsylvania State–The Behrend College	8,444	3,510	N.A.	N.A.	18:1	59[2]	22(S)	N.A.	814-898-6100
Pepperdine (Calif.)	16,260	6,030	70	N.A.	14:1	49[24]	51(S)	95[3]	310-456-4392
Peru State (Neb.)	1,964	2,740	N.A.	42	28:1	N.A.	N.A.	N.A.	402-872-2221
Pfeiffer (N.C.)	7,735	3,275	90	1,942	16:1	38	12(S)	25	704-463-1360
Philadelphia Textiles and Science (Pa.)[21]	10,344	4,798	61	1,004	16:1	N.A.	20(S)	24	215-951-2800
Phillips (Okla.)	8,524	2,820	90	2,144	13:1	34	31(A)	46[3]	405-237-4433
Pikeville (Ky.)[6]	4,000	2,350	61[2]	973	17:1	78	N.A.	N.A.	606-432-9322
Pine Manor (Mass.)[1]	15,000	6,100	32	2,591	13:1	58	14(S)	20	617-731-7104
Pittsburg State (Kans.)	3,964	2,704	48[2]	N.A.	17:1	47[27]	N.A.	26[3]	316-235-4250
Pitzer (Calif.)	17,380	5,090	N.A.	N.A.	10:1	74[24]	68(S)[2]	65	714-621-8129
Plymouth State (N.H.)	6,876	3,620	35	275	20:1	50[24]	N.A.	N.A.	603-535-2237
Polytechnic University (N.Y.)	13,880	3,000	100	3,753	14:1	N.A.	N.A.	N.A.	718-260-3100
Pomona (Calif.) 37	15,830	6,625	55	N.A.	9:1	90	90(S)	91	714-621-8134
Portland State (Ore.)	6,549	4,043	50	262	18:1	N.A.	21(S)	N.A.	503-725-3511
Prairie View A&M (Texas)	5,225	3,176	35	313	25:1	N.A.	13(S)[2]	37[3]	409-857-2618
Pratt Institute (N.Y.)	11,966	5,940	66	1,504	12:1	51	21(S)	36	718-636-3669
Presbyterian (S.C.)	11,114	3,280	70	2,279	14:1	77	61(S)	75[3]	803-833-8230
Prescott (Ariz.)	8,935	No dorms	50	740	10:1	N.A.	N.A.	N.A.	602-778-2090
Princeton (N.J.) 26	17,830	5,311	39	N.A.	6:1	95[24]	74(S)[2]	97	609-258-3060
Providence (R.I.)	12,925	5,600	N.A.	1,975	16:1	88	51(S)[2]	51[3]	401-865-2535
Purdue (Ind.) 56	8,190	3,650	25	290	18:1	68	31(S)[5]	59	317-494-1776
Queens (N.C.)	9,350	4,400	N.A.	1,871	12:1	51	26(A)[19]	56	704-337-2212
Queens College–City University of N.Y.	5,162	No dorms	44	14	14:1	37	N.A.	16	718-997-5600
Quincy (Ill.)	9,160	3,666	86	2,808	14:1	64	84(A)[12]	47	212-228-5215
Quinnipiac (Conn.)	11,070	5,340	49	1,141	14:1	66	41(S)	10	203-281-8600
Radford (Va.)	6,270	3,922	19	103	22:1	51	15(S)	N.A.	703-831-5371
Ramapo College of New Jersey	4,492	4,414	N.A.	98	15:1	29	20(S)	10	201-529-7600
Randolph-Macon (Va.)	11,400	4,700	N.A.	1,768	12:1	68	N.A.	31	804-752-7305

Footnotes are on page 186

meccas m.d.

COLLEGES WITH THE HIGHEST
PERCENTAGE OF GRADUATES
ENTERING MEDICAL SCHOOL

Davidson College	28%
Johns Hopkins University	25
Washington and Jefferson	21
Emory University	17
New York University	14
University of the South	13
Duke University	12
Illinois Benedictine	12
University of Chicago	11

holding court

COLLEGES WITH THE HIGHEST
PERCENTAGE OF GRADUATES
ENTERING LAW SCHOOL

Washington and Jefferson	18%
Brandeis University	17
Emory University	17
University of Chicago	16
Trinity College (D.C.)	15
University of the South	15
Davidson College	14
New York University	13
Transylvania University	12
Wabash College	12

College name and location	Tuition and fees	Room and board	% of students receiving financial aid	Average gift aid per student	Student/ faculty ratio	% who graduate in five years	% with high test scores	% from top fifth of class	Telephone
Randolph-Macon Woman's (Va.)[1]	$12,570	$5,500	78	N.A.	10:1	71	51(S)	51	804-846-9680
Reed (Ore.)	18,190	4,980	49	$4,474	11:1	58	93(S)	18	503-777-7511
Regis (Colo.)	11,540	4,800	N.A.	4,385	16:1	35	28(A)	N.A.	303-458-4900
Regis (Mass.)[1]	11,100	5,400	69[2]	N.A.	12:1	69[2]	N.A.	23	617-893-1820
Rensselaer Polytechnic Institute (N.Y.)	16,402	5,468	71	3,371	11:1	75	71(S)	81	518-276-6216
Rhode Island College	5,945	5,024	N.A.	N.A.	18:1	N.A.	19(S)[9]	31	401-456-8234
Rhode Island School of Design[21]	15,080	6,125	N.A.	N.A.	12:1	85	52(S)	35	401-454-6300
Rhodes (Tenn.)	13,950	4,709	66	4,594	12:1	74	87(S)	80	901-726-3700
Rice (Texas) 1	8,825	4,900	40[2]	N.A.	9:1	88	94(S)[2]	66	713-527-4036
Rider (N.J.)	12,075	4,962	70	1,504	16:1	60	16(S)	27	609-896-5042
Ripon (Wis.)	13,710	3,465	N.A.	5,281	11:1	64	N.A.	54[3]	800-242-0324
Roanoke (Va.)	12,000	4,150	68	N.A.	14:1	52	33(S)	36	703-375-2270
Robert Morris (Pa.)	5,610	3,808	60	224	23:1	59	8(S)	22	412-262-8206
Rochester Institute of Technology (N.Y.)	12,720	5,286	67	1,386	12:1	55	42(S)	43	716-475-6631
Rocky Mountain (Mont.)	8,050	3,327	70	1,563	15:1	N.A.	21(S)[2]	33	406-657-1026
Roger Williams (R.I.)	10,560	4,120	30	N.A.	19:1	60	N.A.	19	401-254-3500
Rollins (Fla.)	14,924	4,626	57	3,037	12:1	72	55(S)	46	407-646-2161
Rosary (Ill.)	9,990	4,236	80	1,252	11:1	65	33(A)[33]	44	708-366-2490
Rose-Hulman Inst. of Technology (Ind.)[17]	11,800	3,800	90	1,472	13:1	75	71(S)	94	213-877-1511
Rosemont (Pa.)[1] 86	10,200	5,620	40	968	10:1	72	N.A.	26	215-525-6420
Rowan State (N.J.)	3,783	4,700	10	N.A.	17:1	45	30(S)	30	609-863-5346
Russell Sage (N.Y.)[1]	11,270	4,240	72	2,200	9:1	55	36(S)	45[3]	800-999-3772
Rust (Miss.)[13]	4,100	1,948	90	N.A.	18:1	32	10(A)[12]	N.A.	601-252-8000
Rutgers College–Rutgers U. (N.J.) 8	7,399	3,940	60	228	17:1	77	70(S)	76	908-932-3770
St. Ambrose (Iowa)	9,170	3,650	90	1,877	11:1	67[27]	80(A)	20[2]	800-383-2627
St. Andrews Presbyterian (N.C.)	9,410	4,060	N.A.	1,323	11:1	55	37(S)	N.A.	800-763-0198
St. Anselm (N.H.)	11,170	5,200	49	1,985	16:1	76	40(S)	35	603-641-7500
St. Augustine's (N.C.)[13]	5,300	3,400	N.A.	N.A.	20:1	40	N.A.[2]	24[2]	919-828-4451
St. Bonaventure (N.Y.)	9,584	4,736	76[2]	2,245	14:1	61	28(S)	25	716-375-2400
St. Cloud State (Minn.)	3,965	2,600	43	54	22:1	35	43(A)[20]	25	612-255-2244
St. Edward's (Texas)	8,376	3,750	55	1,120	18:1	37	25(S)	51[3]	512-448-8500
St. Francis (Ind.)	8,010	3,630	N.A.	941	15:1	48[24]	N.A.	30[2]	219-434-3279
St. Francis (N.Y.)	6,150	No dorms	16	436	24:1	34	N.A.	N.A.	718-522-2300
St. Francis (Pa.)	10,384	4,490	N.A.	3,811	18:1	60[24]	25(S)	44	814-472-3000
St. John Fisher (N.Y.)	9,680	4,900	65	1,108	16:1	55	33(S)	44	716-385-8064
St. John's (Md.)	15,400	5,200	52	N.A.	17:1	60	N.A.	30	410-263-2371
St. John's (Minn.)	10,578	3,873	45	N.A.	14:1	67	45(A)	35	612-363-2196

Footnotes are on page 186

business bound

COLLEGES SENDING THE HIGHEST
PERCENTAGE OF GRADUATES TO
GRADUATE BUSINESS SCHOOLS

Ohio Wesleyan University	**33%**
Babson College	**30**
Hawaii Pacific University	**27**
Rutgers University	**25**
St. John's College (N.M.)	**20**
Incarnate Word College	**20**
St. Thomas Aquinas College	**19**
St. Joseph's College (Maine)	**18**
Wabash College	**15**
Furman College	**15**

melting pots

SCHOOLS FROM MONEY'S TOP 100
WITH THE HIGHEST PERCENTAGE
OF MINORITY ENROLLMENTS[1]

St. Mary's University	**67%**
UC–Berkeley	**61**
UCLA	**56**
SUNY–Stony Brook	**49**
California Inst. of Technology	**40**
Stanford University	**40**
MIT	**37**
Pomona College	**35**
Columbia University	**34**
Rutgers College	**34**

[1]Excluding historically black colleges

College name and location	Tuition and fees	Room and board	% of students receiving financial aid	Average gift aid per student	Student/faculty ratio	% who graduate in five years	% with high test scores	% from top fifth of class	Telephone
St. John's (N.M.)	$15,450	$5,200	N.A.	$4,468	8:1	64	87(S)	30	800-331-5232
St. John's (N.Y.)	8,230	No dorms	26	499	25:1	66	21(S)	39	718-990-6161
St. Joseph's (Ind.)	10,030	3,700	61	2,416	14:1	58	17(S)	30	800-447-8781
St. Joseph's (Maine)	9,025	4,550	73	1,739	13:1	78	11(S)	29	800-338-7057
St. Joseph's (Pa.)	11,200	4,850	53	1,505	16:1	72	N.A.	43	215-660-1300
St. Lawrence (N.Y.)	16,820	5,300	48	5,105[7]	12:1	80	49(S)	48	315-379-5261
St. Leo (Fla.)	8,990	3,880	65	937	17:1	19[24]	15(S)	N.A.	904-588-8283
St. Louis (Mo.)	9,880	2,055	40	1,265	15:1	72	80(A)[12]	43	314-658-2500
St. Mary's (Calif.)	12,066	5,764	N.A.	437	16:1	65	58(S)	66	512-631-4000
St. Mary's (Ind.)	11,762	4,244	39	1,781	11:1	78	45(S)	42	219-284-4587
St. Mary's (Texas) **81**	7,900	3,216	N.A.	901	17:1	58	28(S)	65[3]	512-436-3126
St. Mary's of Maryland **24**	5,980	4,300	32	370	14:1	58	86(S)	65	800-492-7181
St. Mary's of Minnesota	9,205	3,170	63	1,272	14:1	60	44(A)[12]	16	800-635-5987
St. Michael's (Vt.)	11,900	5,400	36	1,762	15:1	75	36(S)	26	802-654-3000
St. Norbert (Wis.)	10,805	4,010	85	2,923	15:1	56	52(A)	41	800-236-4878
St. Olaf (Minn.)	12,750	3,500	55	2,332	12:1	82	69(A)	65	507-646-3025
St. Paul's (Va.)[13]	4,556[23]	3,010[23]	N.A.	746	17:1	56	N.A.	N.A.	703-848-3984
St. Peter's (N.J.)	8,455	5,008	69	701	17:1	46	17(S)	29	201-915-9213
St. Thomas (Fla.)	8,300[23]	4,100[23]	88[2]	404	14:1	41[2]	N.A.	N.A.	305-628-6546
St. Thomas Aquinas (N.Y.)	7,350	4,500	8	260	17:1	57[24]	N.A.	11	914-359-9500
St. Vincent (Pa.)	9,610	3,652	75	2,572	15:1	55	30(S)	40	412-537-4540
Salem (N.C.)[1]	9,125[23]	5,600[23]	61	1,044	8:1	57	N.A.	24[2]	919-721-2621
Salem State (Mass.)	6,678	3,514	15	N.A.	18:1	50	N.A.	24	508-741-6200
Salem-Teikyo (W.Va.)	8,194	3,952	N.A.	N.A.	12:1	N.A.	6(A)[9]	11[9]	304-782-5336
Salisbury State (Md.)	5,148	4,290	40	25	16:1	49	41(S)	60[3]	410-543-6161
Salve Regina (R.I.)	13,000	5,960	53	1,285	12:1	86	N.A.	N.A.	401-847-6650
Sam Houston State (Texas)	3,960	2,800	N.A.	140	24:1	27	N.A.	0	409-294-1056
Samford (Ala.) **47**	7,064	3,741	75	1,986	15:1	48	N.A.	56	800-888-7218
San Diego State (Calif.)	7,022	4,436	N.A.	22	19:1	N.A.	16(S)	N.A.	619-594-6871
San Francisco State (Calif.)	8,804[7]	4,800[7]	N.A.	208	21:1	19	22(S)	N.A.	415-338-2017
San Jose State (Calif.)	8,932[7]	4,872	18	180	18:1	23	14(S)	N.A.	408-924-2000
Santa Clara (Calif.)	12,150	5,556	55	305	14:1	80	52(S)	64[3]	408-554-4700
Sarah Lawrence (N.Y.)	17,640	6,740	45	3,444	6:1	80[24]	81(S)	50	914-395-2510
Savannah College of Art and Design (Ga.)[21]	8,475	5,000	40	528	19:1	70	41(S)	60	912-238-2483
Savannah State (Ga.)	4,368[23]	2,205[23]	N.A.	N.A.	14:1	N.A.	N.A.	8[28]	912-356-2181
Schreiner (Texas)	8,015	5,620	N.A.	2,619	13:1	N.A.	N.A.	37[3]	800-343-4919
Scripps (Calif.)[1]	15,612	6,668	47	4,584	9:1	65	77(S)	70[3]	714-621-8149

Footnotes are on page 186

College name and location	Tuition and fees	Room and board	% of students receiving financial aid	Average gift aid per student	Student/ faculty ratio	% who graduate in five years	% with high test scores	% from top fifth of class	Telephone
Seattle (Wash.)	$11,520	$4,412	24	$1,855	14:1	N.A.	50(S)	30	206-296-5800
Seattle Pacific (Wash.)	11,376	4,263	59	2,725	15:1	39	37(S)	N.A.	206-281-2021
Seton Hall (N.J.)	10,960	6,068	N.A.	N.A.	17:1	N.A.	25(S)	40[3]	201-761-9332
Seton Hill (Pa.)	9,712	3,848	83	1,761	12:1	52	N.A.	31	412-838-4255
Sheldon Jackson (Ala.)[6]	7,012	4,635	N.A.	1,696	10:1	15[2]	N.A.	N.A.	907-747-5221
Shenandoah (Va.)	8,100	3,900	75	1,402	9:1	42	16(S)[2]	N.A.	703-665-4581
Shepherd (W.Va.)	4,500	3,500	39	139	18:1	55	71(S)	N.A.	304-876-2511
Shippensburg U. of Pennsylvania	6,782	3,206	15	83	20:1	62	26(S)	36	717-532-1231
Siena (N.Y.)	9,500	4,680	70[2]	967	16:1	82	44(S)	56[3]	518-783-2423
Siena Heights (Mich.)	8,100	3,550	80	640	15:1	40	11(A)	22	517-263-0731
Simmons (Mass.)[1]	14,924	6,360	57	3,399	9:1	70	40(S)	46	617-738-2107
Simpson (Iowa)	10,315	3,670	92	1,883	14:1	60	85(A)[12]	58	515-961-1624
Sioux Falls (S.D.)	7,996	3,084	70[2]	1,184	14:1	63[2]	18(A)[2,5]	43[3]	605-331-6600
Skidmore (N.Y.)	16,865	5,270	N.A.	2,406	11:1	80	75(S)[9]	38	518-587-7569
Slippery Rock (Pa.)	6,681	3,184	65	42	19:1	45	(S)	26	412-738-2015
Smith (Mass.)[13]	16,985	6,100	52	5,407	10:1	87	84(S)	80	413-585-2500
Sonoma State (Calif.)	8,476[23]	4,500	N.A.	31	23:1	22[2]	27(S)	N.A.	707-664-2778
South Carolina State	4,280	2,620	N.A.	N.A.	18:1	21[2]	1(S)[28]	22	803-536-7185
South Dakota State	4,020	1,946	43	405	17:1	55[2]	57(A)[12]	40[3]	605-688-4121
Southeast Missouri State	3,380	3,080	N.A.	271	24:1	34	21(A)	26	314-651-2255
Southeastern Louisiana[6]	2,540	2,210	N.A.	35	25:1	35[2]	17(A)[2]	N.A.	504-549-2123
Southeastern Oklahoma State	3,418	1,792	52	102	19:1	35[2]	14(A)	20	405-924-0121
Southern Arkansas[6]	2,120[23]	2,200[23]	31	243	19:1	42	28(A)[2]	11	501-235-4040
Southern College of Technology (Ga.)	4,230	3,211	21	N.A.	20:1	30[2]	17(S)	N.A.	404-528-7281
Southern Connecticut State	7,003	4,104	N.A.	140	19:1	40[2]	13(S)[2]	4	203-397-4450
Southern Illinois U. at Carbondale	6,156	3,024	N.A.	75	16:1	35	40(A)[20]	27	618-453-4381
Southern Illinois U. at Edwardsville	5,610	3,316	45	225	16:1	41	24(A)	26	618-692-3705
Southern Methodist (Texas)	12,688	4,832	51	N.A.	13:1	67	94(A)[2]	59	214-692-2058
Southern Oregon State	6,020	3,300	43	35	17:1	40	N.A.	N.A.	503-552-6411
Southern Utah[6]	3,786	2,505[23]	N.A.	66	18:1	48[2]	N.A.	N.A.	801-586-7740
Southwest Missouri State	3,384	2,630	30	341	27:1	31	27(A)	32	417-836-5517
Southwest State (Minn.)	4,321	2,600	67	160	19:1	35	11(A)	35[3]	507-537-6286
Southwest Texas State	6,232	4,286	30	72	22:1	24	12(S)	36[3]	512-245-2364
Southwestern (Kans.)	5,600	3,110	N.A.	1,244	12:1	51[2]	56(A)[12]	32[3]	316-221-4150
Southwestern University (Texas)	10,300	4,256	67	2,627	13:1	66	69(S)	70	512-863-1200
Spalding (Ky.)	7,828	3,600	60	N.A.	14:1	50[24]	12(A)[2,5]	40	502-585-9911
Spelman (Ga.)[1,13] [28]	7,327	5,000	N.A.	131	16:1	56	34(S)	N.A.	404-681-3643
Spring Hill (Ala.)	10,763	4,374	70	3,076	14:1	55	39(S)	37	205-460-2130
Springfield (Mass.)	9,870	4,300	40	N.A.	20:1	65	N.A.	19	413-748-3136
Stanford (Calif.) [65]	16,635	6,413	60	N.A.	10:1	90	95(S)	98[3]	415-723-2091
State U. of N.Y.–Albany [23]	6,783	3,654	N.A.	N.A.	18:1	61	63(S)	66	518-442-5435
State U. of N.Y.–Binghamton [12]	6,857	4,286	55[2]	66	18:1	76	72(S)[9]	96	607-777-2171
State U. of N.Y.–Brockport	6,765	4,060	51[2]	N.A.	21:1	45	19(S)	27	716-395-2751
State U. of N.Y.–Buffalo [42]	6,972	3,156	40	32	14:1	50	55(S)	81	716-831-2111
State U. of N.Y.–College at Buffalo	6,735	3,590	60	45	23:1	31	N.A.	24	716-878-4017
State U. of N.Y.–Cortland	6,797	4,040	N.A.	9	21:1	47	19(S)	27	607-753-4711
State U. of N.Y.–Fredonia	6,803	3,770	6	24	20:1	55	34(S)	41	716-673-3251
State U. of N.Y.–Geneseo [39]	6,855	3,554	N.A.	25	19:1	69	83(S)	99	716-245-5571
State U. of N.Y.–New Paltz	6,821	3,920	45	N.A.	18:1	46	36(S)	42	914-257-3200
State U. of N.Y.–Oneonta	6,780	4,200	N.A.	N.A.	20:1	55	N.A.	33[2,3]	607-431-2524
State U. of N.Y.–Oswego	6,830	4,080	40	2	19:1	55	40(S)	51	315-341-2250
State U. of N.Y.–Plattsburgh	6,765	3,616	40	64	20:1	55	31(S)	24	518-564-2040
State U. of N.Y.–Potsdam	6,798	3,690	44[2]	123	20:1	45	27(S)	51[3]	315-267-2180
State U. of N.Y.–Purchase	6,811	3,736	N.A.	33	18:1	32	N.A.	N.A.	914-251-6300
State U. of N.Y.–Stony Brook [29]	6,815	4,156	N.A.	5	15:1[2]	51	26(S)	64[3]	516-632-6868
Stephen F. Austin State (Texas)	5,528	3,276	N.A.	N.A.	21:1	40	18(A)	30[3]	409-568-2504

Footnotes are on page 186

mostly men

mostly women

College name and location	Tuition and fees	Room and board	% of students receiving financial aid	Average gift aid per student	Student/ faculty ratio	% who graduate in five years	% with high test scores	% from top fifth of class	Telephone
Stephens (Mo.) [1]	$12,400	$4,850	54	$1,472	11:1	57	29(A)	18	314-876-7207
Stetson (Fla.)	11,110	4,035	81[2]	1,833	12:1	57	43(S)	64	904-822-7100
Stevens Institute of Technology (N.J.)	15,675	5,050	N.A.	N.A.	10:1	72[2]	70(S)[9]	95	201-216-5194
Stockton State (N.J.)	3,096	4,332	N.A.	35	17:1	51	38(S)	44	609-652-4261
Stonehill (Mass.)	10,865	5,674	56	1,839	18:1	77	36(S)	45	508-230-1373
Suffolk (Mass.)	9,220	5,250[23]	42	827	20:1	56	28(S)	23	617-573-8460
Sul Ross State (Texas) [6]	5,461	2,620	N.A.	N.A.	20:1	18	2(A)	18	915-837-8052
Susquehanna (Pa.)	14,880	4,200	N.A.	2,468	14:1	70	N.A.	N.A.	717-372-4260
Swarthmore (Pa.) 62	17,646	5,844	60[2]	N.A.	9:1	92	95(S)[2]	92	215-328-8300
Sweet Briar (Va.) [1]	12,842	4,850	N.A.	2,749	8:1	57	50(S)	13	804-381-6142
Syracuse (N.Y.)	13,813	6,212	55	N.A.	9:1	66	68(S)	63	315-443-3611
Tabor (Kans.)	7,520	3,200	N.A.[2]	N.A.	16:1	42	34(A)	38[3]	800-822-6799
Talladega (Ala.) [13]	4,453	2,364	68	N.A.	13:1	29	6(A)	N.A.	800-633-2440
Tarleton State (Texas)	5,560	2,590	N.A.	72	22:1	16[2]	8(S)[2,5]	31[3]	817-968-9125
Teikyo Marycrest (Iowa)	9,116	3,280	N.A.	999	15:1	50	22(A)	N.A.	319-326-9225
Teikyo Westmar (Iowa)	9,280	3,350	99	1,605	14:1	44	N.A.	28[3]	712-546-2070
Temple (Pa.)	8,696	4,681	N.A.	319	12:1	27	N.A.	29	215-787-7200
Tennessee State	4,830	2,542	61	N.A.	N.A.	32	19(A)	N.A.	615-320-3420
Tennessee Technological	3,600	1,400	N.A.	311	20:1	34	28(A)	N.A.	615-372-3888
Texas A&I	4,590	1,924	70	N.A.	18:1	38	4(A)[5]	32[3]	512-595-2315
Texas A&M U.–College Station 33	5,628	2,894	37	469	20:1	59	40(S)	78[3]	409-845-1031
Texas Christian	8,570	3,128	50	1,653	17:1	62	N.A.	51	817-921-7490
Texas Lutheran	6,840	3,120	N.A.	1,627	14:1	35	32(S)	14	512-372-8050
Texas Southern	3,296[23]	3,250[23]	80[2]	323[2]	16:1[2]	38[2]	N.A.	N.A.	713-527-7070
Texas Tech	4,471	3,452	N.A.	N.A.	18:1	35	24(S)	46	806-742-1493
Texas Wesleyan	5,850	2,998	78	1,566	14:1	36	26(S)	41	817-531-4422
Thiel (Pa.)	9,983	4,505	N.A.	1,918	13:1	53	15(S)[9]	22	412-589-2345
Thomas Aquinas (Calif.)	12,200	4,800	70	7,854	10:1	86	78(S)	56[3]	800-634-9797
Thomas More (Ky.)	8,460	3,600	25	1,601	12:1	55	50(A)[12]	35	606-344-3332
Tougaloo (Miss.) [13]	5,090	1,840	17	549	17:1	33	14(A)[20]	27[3]	601-977-7770
Touro (N.Y.)	7,030	6,100[7]	N.A.	N.A.	14:1	60[2]	32(S)	N.A.	212-447-0700
Towson State (Md.)	5,072	4,290	30	125	20:1	57[2]	31(S)	N.A.	410-830-3333
Transylvania (Ky.)	10,000	4,140	47	3,105	12:1	65	74(A)	65	606-233-8242
Trenton State (N.J.) 6	5,289	4,750	N.A.	316	15:1	67	56(S)	92	609-771-2131
Tri-State (Ind.)	9,378	3,900	95	1,221	15:1	33	10(S)	33	219-665-4131
Trinity (Conn.)	17,830	5,160	36	3,333	10:1	87	83(S)	38	203-297-2180
Trinity University (Texas) 38	11,060	4,640	44	2,290	10:1	72	83(S)	86	512-736-7207

Footnotes are on page 186

College name and location	Tuition and fees	Room and board	% of students receiving financial aid	Average gift aid per student	Student/ faculty ratio	% who graduate in five years	% with high test scores	% from top fifth of class	Telephone
Troy State (Ala.)	$2,488	$2,120	N.A.	$259	32:1	55[2]	40(A)[2]	29	205-566-8112
Tufts (Mass.)	18,344	5,250	31	N.A.	13:1	90[2]	92(S)	86	617-628-5000
Tulane (La.)	18,185	5,190	48	5,274	13:1	75	72(S)	63	504-865-5731
Tusculum (Tenn.)	6,500	3,200	73	1,491	15:1	60	18(A)	26	615-636-7312
Tuskegee (Ala.)[13]	9,250	3,000	N.A.	352	14:1	41	N.A.	N.A.	205-727-8500
Union (Ky.)	6,200	2,710	69	1,295	14:1	51	26(A)	31	606-546-4223
Union (Neb.)[6]	8,100	2,510	77	1,040	12:1[2]	45	23(A)	N.A.	402-486-2504
Union (N.Y.)	16,748	5,722	37	3,082	11:1	85	86(A)	60	518-370-6112
U.S. Air Force Academy (Colo.)[34]	0	0	N.A.	N.A.	8:1	74[2]	0(A)[5]	92	719-472-2520
U.S. Coast Guard Academy (Conn.)[34]	0	0	N.A.	N.A.	9:1[2]	64	32(S)[2]	94	203-444-8501
U.S. Merchant Marine Academy (N.Y.)[34]	2,937	0	N.A.	N.A.	11:1	65	62(S)	54	516-773-5391
U.S. Military Academy (N.Y.)[34]	0	0	N.A.	N.A.	8:1	71	81(S)	85	914-938-4041
U.S. Naval Academy (Md.)[34]	0	0	N.A.	N.A.	7:1	76[2]	81(S)	81	410-267-4361
Unity (Maine)	8,700	4,525	N.A.	N.A.	14:1	52[2]	14(S)[2]	15	207-948-3131
U. of Akron (Ohio)[6]	7,207	3,486	N.A.	126	20:1	34	43(A)[12]	30[3]	216-972-7100
U. of Alabama–Tuscaloosa	5,016	3,288	30	397	20:1	60	5(S)	N.A.	205-348-5666
U. of Alaska–Anchorage[26]	4,017	4,820	N.A.	43	22:1	N.A.	N.A.	N.A.	907-786-1525
U. of Alaska–Fairbanks[26]	4,510	3,100	N.A.	71	14:1	N.A.	35(A)	4	907-474-7521
U. of Arizona	7,046	3,968	48	N.A.	20:1	44	36(S)	52	602-621-3237
U. of Arkansas–Fayetteville	4,868	3,175	32	710	12:1	32	28(A)	N.A.	501-575-5346
U. of Arkansas–Monticello[6]	3,324	2,200	60	215	20:1	24	24(A)[12]	5	501-460-1026
U. of Arkansas–Pine Bluff	3,334	2,060	N.A.	N.A.	20:1	33[2]	N.A.	N.A.	501-541-6542
U. of Bridgeport (Conn.)	12,485	5,920	65[2]	N.A.	13:1	50[2]	N.A.	10[9]	203-576-4552
U. of California–Berkeley 61	10,968[7]	5,730	38	503	17:1	71	74(S)	N.A.	510-642-2316
U. of California–Davis	10,679[7]	5,416	30	282[2]	19:1	65	49(S)	100	916-752-2971
U. of California–Irvine	10,774[7]	5,900	N.A.	499	20:1	N.A.	35(S)	N.A.	714-856-6703
U. of California–Los Angeles 63	10,585[7]	5,650	41	904	17:1	66	65(S)	100	310-825-3101
U. of California–Riverside	10,646[7]	5,045	N.A.	N.A.	15:1	60	33(S)	95	714-787-4531
U. of California–San Diego	10,712[7]	6,460	30	N.A.	18:1	59	65(S)	N.A.	619-534-3161
U. of California–Santa Barbara	10,667[7]	5,867	27	N.A.	19:1	30	47(S)	N.A.	805-893-2485
U. of California–Santa Cruz	10,828[7]	6,036	N.A.	525	19:1	50	59(S)	100	408-459-4008
U. of Central Florida	5,543	4,026	32	120	17:1	45	35(S)	55[2]	407-823-3000
U. of Central Oklahoma	3,362	2,150	45[2]	N.A.	24:1	N.A.	18(A)	6	405-341-2980
U. of Chicago (Ill.) 99	17,346	5,940	63	5,114	3:1	82	90(S)	90	312-702-8650
U. of Cincinnati (Ohio)	7,903	4,490	N.A.	N.A.	14:1	42	47(A)	47	513-556-1100
U. of Colorado–Boulder	11,272[35]	3,600	N.A.	N.A.	19:1	58	N.A.	52	303-492-6301
U. of Connecticut 87	10,374	4,878	7	506	15:1[36]	65	46(S)	67[3]	203-486-3137
U. of Dallas (Texas)	9,380	4,410	79	3,038	12:1	54	74(S)	67	214-721-5266
U. of Dayton (Ohio)	10,210	3,930	75	N.A.	17:1	N.A.	48(A)[5]	40	513-229-4411
U. of Delaware	9,382[23]	3,540[23]	N.A.	447	17:1	67	42(S)	68[3]	302-831-8123
U. of Denver (Colo.)	13,572	4,302	59	453[2]	13:1	63	33(S)	48	303-871-2036
U. of Dubuque (Iowa)	9,940	3,365	85	N.A.	15:1	10	23(A)	31[3]	319-589-3200
U. of Evansville (Ind.)	10,700	3,970	74	2,770	13:1	65	41(S)	55	812-479-2468
U. of Findlay (Ohio)	10,034	4,400	N.A.	1,115	14:1	44	N.A.	32[2,3]	800-548-0932
U. of Florida 25	6,030	3,950	20	285[2]	28:1	51	66(S)	N.A.	904-392-1365
U. of Georgia 31	5,757	3,105	N.A.	204	14:1	56	N.A.	55[3]	404-542-2112
U. of Hartford (Conn.)	14,228	5,598	45	313	12:1	49	6(S)	24	203-768-4296
U. of Hawaii–Hilo	2,680	2,400	N.A.	69	18:1	25	N.A.	N.A.	808-933-3414
U. of Hawaii–Manoa	4,168	3,505	N.A.	113	14:1[2]	41[2]	N.A.	N.A.	808-956-8975
U. of Houston (Texas)	5,425	3,770	22[2]	289	20:1	75	10(S)[2]	N.A.	713-749-2321
U. of Idaho	4,196	3,084	N.A.	269	17:1	37	68(A)[12]	36[2]	208-885-6325
U. of Illinois–Chicago	7,442	4,846	N.A.	555	12:1	22	15(A)	53[3]	312-996-0998
U. of Illinois–Urbana-Champaign 11	7,599	4,042	N.A.	585	10:1	76	83(A)	82	217-333-2033
U. of Iowa 43	7,192	3,206	53	393	16:1	51	57(A)	41	319-335-3847
U. of Kansas	5,968	3,080	33	N.A.	16:1	47	48(A)[9]	35	913-864-3911
U. of Kentucky 15	5,175	3,390	50	799	15:1	45	N.A.	N.A.	606-257-2000

Footnotes are on page 186

money for merit

SCHOOLS THAT GIVE OUT THE MOST IN NON-NEED-BASED SCHOLARSHIPS PER STUDENT

Viterbo College	**$4,204**
Wabash College	**2,982**
Transylvania University	**2,559**
Alma College	**2,519**
Polytechnic University	**2,345**
Rhodes College	**2,258**
Carthage College	**2,187**
Centenary of Louisiana	**2,107**
Regis College	**2,062**
Milwaukee School of Eng.	**1,896**

strangers welcome

PUBLIC SCHOOLS WITH THE HIGHEST PERCENTAGE OF STUDENTS FROM OUT OF STATE

University of Delaware	**61%**
Lincoln University (Pa.)	**53**
University of Vermont	**50**
West Virginia University	**50**
New College of U. of S. Florida	**48**
Northwest Missouri State	**45**
University of Rhode Island	**45**
Eastern Oregon State College	**42**
Moorhead State University	**42**
University of New Hampshire	**40**

College name and location	Tuition and fees	Room and board	% of students receiving financial aid	Average gift aid per student	Student/ faculty ratio	% who graduate in five years	% with high test scores	% from top fifth of class	Telephone
U. of LaVerne (Calif.)	$11,940	$4,550	63	N.A.	17:1	100	39(S)	45	714-593-3511
U. of Louisville (Ky.)	5,240	3,468	65	$450	21:1	22	31(A)	33	502-588-6531
U. of Maine	7,968	4,362	43	N.A.	16:1	55[24]	32(S)	42	207-581-1561
U. of Maine–Farmington	6,210	3,566	37	N.A.	20:1	60[2]	N.A.	50[3]	207-778-7050
U. of Maine–Fort Kent	6,200	3,545	N.A.	76	10:1	30	17(S)	18[2,3]	207-834-3162
U. of Maine–Machias	6,175	3,410	65	153	16:1	45	28(S)	N.A.	207-255-3313
U. of Maine–Presque Isle	6,090	3,344	66[2]	60	13:1	20	N.A.	8[2]	207-764-0311
U. of Mary (N.D.)	5,980	2,490	45	1,556	17:1	40[24]	19(A)	23	701-255-7500
U. of Maryland–Baltimore County	8,214	4,173	22	203	16:1	42[2]	39(S)	33	410-455-2291
U. of Maryland–College Park	8,555	4,650	N.A.	342	15:1	51	51(S)	54	301-314-8385
U. of Maryland–Eastern Shore	6,405	3,580	N.A.	533[2]	14:1	N.A.	22(S)[2]	N.A.	301-651-2200
U. of Massachusetts–Amherst	11,165	3,734	38	449	18:1	60	22(S)	27	413-545-0222
U. of Massachusetts–Dartmouth	7,747	4,200	N.A.	29	16:1	48	16(S)	29	508-999-8605
U. of Miami (Fla.)	15,050	5,910	N.A.	N.A.	8:1	52	N.A.	57	305-284-4323
U. of Michigan–Ann Arbor	14,069	4,285	N.A.	767	11:1	83	86(A)	88	313-764-7433
U. of Minnesota–Duluth	8,551	3,276	N.A.	151	13:1	34	27(A)	38	218-726-7171
U. of Minnesota–Morris	9,700	3,000	N.A.	302	15:1	59	68(A)	83	612-589-6035
U. of Minnesota–Twin Cities	8,177	3,255	N.A.	311[2]	N.A.	43[2]	43(A)[5]	48	612-625-2008
U. of Mississippi	4,608	1,430	N.A.	284	19:1	46	75(A)[12]	N.A.	601-232-7226
U. of Missouri–Columbia 57	7,170	3,035	47	77	10:1	50	58(A)	53	314-882-7651
U. of Missouri–Kansas City	7,650	4,200	34	363	12:1	31	56(A)	54	816-235-1111
U. of Missouri–Rolla 84	7,792	3,374	60[2]	747	12:1	53[2]	76(A)	67	314-341-4164
U. of Montana	5,355	3,100	N.A.	220[2]	19:1	26	N.A.	N.A.	406-243-4277
U. of Montevallo (Ala.)	4,130	2,820	N.A.	431	14:1	63	42(A)[20]	43[2,3]	205-665-6030
U. of Nebraska–Kearney	2,764	2,400	42[2]	1,111	22:1	N.A.	33(A)[20]	44[2,3]	308-234-8526
U. of Nebraska–Lincoln	4,362	2,915	N.A.	359	18:1	43	67(A)[12]	33	402-472-3620
U. of Nevada–Las Vegas [26]	5,740	4,650	N.A.	213[2]	25:1	79[2]	11(A)[2]	0	702-739-3443
U. of Nevada–Reno	5,500	3,700	25	N.A.	19:1	N.A.	17(A)[2]	26[2]	702-784-6865
U. of New England (Maine)	10,570	4,750	N.A.	N.A.	14:1	56	19(S)	48[3]	207-283-0171
U. of New Hampshire	10,299	3,728	N.A.	N.A.	18:1	63	44(S)	50	603-862-1360
U. of New Mexico	5,880	3,021	44	N.A.	15:1	N.A.	62(A)[12]	46	505-277-2446
U. of New Orleans (La.)	4,854	3,186	37	78	22:1	19[2]	23(A)	0	504-286-6595
U. of North Alabama	1,968	2,580	25	114	24:1	30	30(A)[20]	40[3]	205-760-4608
U. of North Carolina–Asheville	6,194[23]	3,210[23]	28	179	14:1	42	45(S)	62	704-251-6480
U. of North Carolina–Chapel Hill 9	7,880	3,950	N.A.	253	N.A.	79	64(S)	93	919-966-3621
U. of North Carolina–Charlotte	6,883	2,720[23]	30	124	16:1	43	22(S)	53	704-547-2213
U. of North Carolina–Greensboro	7,370[23]	3,266[23]	43[2]	N.A.	14:1	46	28(S)	41	919-334-5243

Footnotes are on page 186

posh pay

SCHOOLS THAT PAY THE HIGHEST AVERAGE SALARIES TO FULL PROFESSORS

Harvard University	$92,200
Calif. Inst. of Technology	90,900
Princeton University	88,200
Stanford University	86,500
Yale University	86,100
MIT	83,900
University of Chicago	83,300
Camden College	82,000
Columbia University	82,000
New York University	81,200

bottom dollar

SCHOOLS THAT PAY THE LOWEST AVERAGE SALARIES TO FULL PROFESSORS

Tougaloo College	$23,700
Bethel College (Tenn.)	27,500
MacMurray College	27,900
Union College (Ky.)	28,500
Concordia College (Mich.)	28,800
Tabor College	29,000
Ottawa University	29,200
Lambuth College	29,800
Dana College	30,000
Union College (Neb.)	30,700

College name and location	Tuition and fees	Room and board	% of students receiving financial aid	Average gift aid per student	Student/ faculty ratio	% who graduate in five years	% with high test scores	% from top fifth of class	Telephone
U. of North Carolina–Wilmington	$6,356[23]	$3,300[23]	N.A.	$95	16:1	41	16(S)	36	919-395-3243
U. of North Dakota [6]	5,254	2,500	59	97	19:1	40	N.A.	N.A.	701-777-3821
U. of North Texas	5,500	3,450	20	N.A.	19:1	24	N.A.	34	817-565-2681
U. of Northern Colorado	6,392	3,606	55	65	20:1	34	30(A)	25	303-351-2881
U. of Northern Iowa	5,570	2,450	60	236	17:1	49	74(A)[12]	41	319-273-2281
U. of Notre Dame (Ind.)	14,850	3,900	48	1,590	11:1	94	85(S)	93	219-239-7505
U. of Oklahoma	4,941	3,358	50	122	N.A.	35	45(A)	62[3]	405-325-2251
U. of Oregon	7,900	3,300	50	306	18:1	48	41(S)	N.A.	503-346-3201
U. of Pennsylvania	15,894	2,095	40[2]	N.A.	9:1	88	90(S)	93	215-898-7507
U. of Pittsburgh–Bradford (Pa.)	10,064	3,710	N.A.	457	14:1	22	N.A.	32	814-362-7555
U. of Pittsburgh–Johnstown (Pa.)	10,110	3,544	84	145	20:1	N.A.	N.A.	50	814-269-7050
U. of Pittsburgh–Pittsburgh (Pa.)	10,066	4,130	N.A.	365	16:1	53	N.A.	50	412-624-7488
U. of Portland (Ore.)	10,080	3,790	59	N.A.	15:1	58	29(S)	39	503-283-7147
U. of Puget Sound (Wash.)	13,910	4,160	65	1,606	13:1	56	57(S)	74[3]	206-756-3211
U. of Redlands (Calif.)	15,080	5,720	N.A.	5,151	12:1	N.A.	N.A.	65	714-335-4074
U. of Rhode Island	9,198	4,786	N.A.	130	16:1	59	25(S)	28	401-792-9800
U. of Richmond (Va.)	12,620	3,040	77	1,593	12:1	83	84(S)	N.A.	804-289-8640
U. of Rio Grande (Ohio) [6]	5,061	3,000	30	451	18:1	80	26(A)[20]	11	614-245-5353
U. of Rochester (N.Y.)	16,450	6,015	73	N.A.	12:1	74	65(S)	73	716-275-3221
U. of St. Thomas (Minn.)	10,568[23]	3,535[23]	N.A.	960	17:1	65	44(A)	45	612-647-5265
U. of St. Thomas (Texas)	7,436	3,330	N.A.	921	15:1	28[2]	33(S)	68[3]	713-522-7911
U. of San Diego (Calif.)	12,160	4,400	N.A.	2,211	18:1	61	35(S)	N.A.	619-260-4506
U. of San Francisco (Calif.)	11,816	5,480	42	N.A.	17:1	53	53(S)	19[2]	415-666-6563
U. of Science and Arts of Oklahoma	3,536	2,260	54[2]	N.A.	15:1	N.A.	24(A)[9]	N.A.	405-224-3140
U. of Scranton (Pa.)	10,715	5,122	46	1,028	17:1	84	56(S)	54	717-941-7540
U. of South Alabama	2,763	2,960	N.A.	N.A.	21:1	34[2]	32(A)	N.A.	205-460-6141
U. of South Carolina–Coastal Carolina	5,300	2,390[8]	N.A.	N.A.	17:1	20	12(S)	20	803-349-2026
U. of South Carolina–Columbia	7,046	3,210	N.A.	N.A.	16:1	56	28(S)	43	803-777-7700
U. of South Dakota–Vermillion	3,786	2,310	81	220	18:1	36	49(A)[2]	33	605-677-5434
U. of South Florida	5,000[23]	3,170[23]	N.A.	159	12:1	39[2]	42(S)	N.A.	813-974-3350
U. of Southern California	16,020	6,260	N.A.	N.A.	17:1	55[2]	N.A.	68	213-740-1111
U. of Southern Colorado	6,155	3,600	52	50	18:1	28	25(A)	25	719-549-2461
U. of Southern Indiana [6]	4,922	1,582[8]	18	180	20:1	20[7]	10(S)	11	800-467-1965
U. of Southern Maine [26]	7,704	4,038	75[2]	53	15:1	N.A.	N.A.	N.A.	207-780-4970
U. of Southern Mississippi	3,600	2,130	N.A.	N.A.	17:1	30	23(A)	N.A.	601-266-5555
U. of Southwestern Louisiana [6]	3,378	2,110	30	N.A.	25:1	34[2]	N.A.	N.A.	318-231-6841
U. of Tampa (Fla.)	11,690	4,237	65	N.A.	16:1	42	N.A.	N.A.	813-253-6228

Footnotes are on page 186

College name and location	Tuition and fees	Room and board	% of students receiving financial aid	Average gift aid per student	Student/ faculty ratio	% who graduate in five years	% with high test scores	% from top fifth of class	Telephone
U. of Tennessee–Chattanooga	$5,272	$2,720	N.A.	N.A.	17:1	35[2]	N.A.	N.A.	615-755-4662
U. of Tennessee–Knoxville	5,498	3,154	41	N.A.	17:1	48	44(A)	47	615-974-2184
U. of Tennessee–Martin	5,328	2,780	47	N.A.	20:1	32	33(A)[12]	N.A.	901-587-7020
U. of Texas–Arlington	4,394	3,960	25	$14	28:1	N.A.	22(S)	30[3]	817-273-2118
U. of Texas–Austin 14	4,100	3,400	40	547	20:1	58	57(S)	74	512-471-7601
U. of Texas–El Paso	5,458	3,850	45	N.A.	23:1	N.A.	N.A.	N.A.	915-747-5576
U. of the District of Columbia[26]	2,960	No dorms	7	N.A.	13:1	40	N.A.	N.A.	202-282-3200
U. of the Pacific (Calif.)	14,990	5,300	N.A.	N.A.	13:1	N.A.	36(S)	42	209-946-2211
U. of the South (Tenn.) 59	14,060	3,700	63	3,466	11:1	78	79(S)	67	615-598-1238
U. of Toledo (Ohio)[6]	6,750	3,015	N.A.	145	19:1	31[2,7]	21(A)[9]	0	419-537-2696
U. of Tulsa (Okla.) 46	9,405	3,775	70	2,831	12:1	68	81(A)[12]	46	918-631-2307
U. of Utah	6,075	4,136	35	N.A.	15:1	56[2]	45(A)	N.A.	801-581-7281
U. of Vermont	14,766	4,266	60	N.A.	15:1	78	51(S)	48	802-656-3370
U. of Virginia 18	10,826	3,470	30	724	11:1	91	83(S)	72	804-982-3200
U. of Virginia–Clinch Valley	4,610	3,200	44	N.A.	23:1	32	15(S)	18[3]	708-328-0102
U. of Washington 3	6,336	4,542	N.A.	77	8:1	55	41(S)	54	206-543-9686
U. of West Florida	6,722	4,100	N.A.	120	26:1	48	N.A.	32[3]	904-474-2230
U. of Wisconsin–Eau Claire	5,990	2,800	55	40	18:1	42	38(A)	45	715-836-5415
U. of Wisconsin–Green Bay	6,150	2,365	65	N.A.	22:1	32	25(A)	36	414-465-2111
U. of Wisconsin–LaCrosse	6,100	2,190	30	22	21:1	51[2]	76(A)[20]	33	608-785-8067
U. of Wisconsin–Madison 44	7,840	3,397	30	283	12:1	62	78(A)	60	608-262-3961
U. of Wisconsin–Milwaukee[26]	7,100	3,380	N.A.	9	19:1	N.A.	28(A)	28	414-229-3800
U. of Wisconsin–Oshkosh	5,924	2,176	40	3	20:1	58[2]	30(A)	41[3]	414-424-0202
U. of Wisconsin–Parkside	6,000	3,200	N.A.	N.A.	14:1	25[2]	44(A)[2]	68	414-553-2241
U. of Wisconsin–Platteville	6,270	2,170	48	N.A.	20:1	43	75(A)	33	608-342-1125
U. of Wisconsin–River Falls	6,097	2,060	N.A.	N.A.	17:1	45[2]	43(A)[20]	29	715-425-3500
U. of Wisconsin–Stevens Point	6,400	2,750	32	N.A.	19:1	35	28(A)	34	715-346-2441
U. of Wisconsin–Stout	6,000	2,420	37	10	20:1	42	11(A)	14	715-232-1411
U. of Wisconsin–Superior	5,660	2,362	N.A.	521	14:1	44	72(A)[2]	N.A.	715-394-8230
U. of Wisconsin–Whitewater	6,000	2,300	N.A.	N.A.	20:1	46	56(A)[12]	39[3]	414-472-1440
U. of Wyoming	4,502	3,313	42	529	17:1	34	39(A)	33	307-766-5160
Upper Iowa	8,840	3,060	N.A.	N.A.	15:1	N.A.	9(A)	5	800-632-5954
Upsala (N.J.)	11,500	4,580	75	N.A.	16:1	45	12(S)	20	201-266-7191
Urbana (Ohio)	7,841	4,140	98	781	10:1	36[2]	11(A)	71[3]	513-652-1301
Ursinus (Pa.)	13,340	4,800	N.A.	3,652	12:1	77	48(S)	62	215-489-4111
Utah State	4,983	2,790	70	N.A.	20:1	N.A.	50(A)	N.A.	801-750-1096
Utica College of Syracuse U. (N.Y.)	11,230	4,640	N.A.	1,433	14:1	55	52(S)	32	800-782-8884
Valley City State (N.D.)[6]	4,257	2,040	72	207	16:1	33	37(A)[2,12]	N.A.	701-845-7101
Valparaiso (Ind.)	10,840	2,940	64	1,799	14:1	73	48(S)	61	219-464-5011
Vanderbilt (Tenn.)	15,235	5,420	42	4,298	8:1	79	85(S)	56	615-322-2561
Vassar (N.Y.)	17,470	5,500	43	4,304	11:1	84	95(S)[2]	79	914-437-7300
Villanova (Pa.)	13,730	5,780	31	1,494	14:1	84	65(S)	62	215-645-4000
Virginia Commonwealth	9,625	3,860	10[2]	289	13:1	36	7(S)[2]	36	804-367-1222
Virginia Military Institute[17]	10,290	3,690	59	1,604	13:1	59	43(S)	25	703-464-7211
Virginia Polytechnic Institute & State 82	8,986	2,876	40	132	17:1	67	48(S)	59	703-231-6267
Virginia State	6,315	4,127	75[29]	N.A.	19:1	30[2]	2(S)[2]	N.A.	804-524-5902
Virginia Wesleyan	9,375	4,650	N.A.	1,051	16:1	5	63(S)	20	804-455-3208
Viterbo (Wis.)	8,360	3,240	75	4,706	12:1	54	22(A)[5]	31	608-791-0420
Wabash (Ind.)[17] 32	11,750	3,790	N.A.	6,336	11:1	78	59(S)	64	800-345-5385
Wagner (N.Y.)	11,250	5,000	70	2,122	12:1	52	46(S)	27	718-390-3411
Wake Forest (N.C.) 73	12,000	4,110	63	2,116	13:1	84	86(S)	65	919-759-5201
Walsh (Ohio)	7,072	3,600	30	478	19:1	65[24]	20(A)	25	216-499-7090
Warren Wilson (N.C.)[16]	10,627	2,852	79[2]	1,308	11:1	66[24]	31(S)[2]	15	704-298-3325
Wartburg (Iowa)	10,360	3,250	70	2,065	14:1	63[2]	56(A)[2]	59[3]	319-352-8264
Washburn U. of Topeka (Kans.)	3,872	3,000	N.A.	N.A.	17:1	N.A.	40(A)[12]	N.A.	913-231-1010
Washington (Md.)	13,226	5,128	50	2,854	12:1	65	45(S)[2]	49	410-778-7700

Footnotes are on page 186

cozy classes

COLORS WITH THE SMALLEST AVERAGE CLASS SIZE FOR FRESHMEN AND SOPHOMORES

Bennington College	7
Wilson College	10
Prescott College	11
Sweet Briar College	11
Centenary College of La.	12
Rosemont College	12
Wells College	12

book barns

SCHOOLS WITH THE MOST TITLES IN THEIR LIBRARIES, INCLUDING MICROFILM (IN MILLIONS)

Columbia University	15.1
Harvard University	14.1
Yale University	13.2
UC–Berkeley	12
UCLA	12
U. of Michigan–Ann Arbor	11
Cornell University	10.9
U. of Ill.–Urbana-Champaign	10.9
University of Washington	10.1
University of Texas–Austin	10

College name and location	Tuition and fees	Room and board	% of students receiving financial aid	Average gift aid per student	Student/ faculty ratio	% who graduate in five years	% with high test scores	% from top fifth of class	Telephone
Washington and Jefferson (Pa.)	$13,620	$3,490	15	$3,018	11:1	83	54(S)	55	412-223-6025
Washington and Lee (Va.) **53**	12,465	4,260	40	1,581	11:1	87	97(S)	81	703-463-8710
Washington State	7,448	3,730	35	319	16:1	50[2]	22(S)	N.A.	509-335-5586
Washington University (Mo.)	16,918	5,394	44	3,165	5:1	82	81(S)	87	314-935-6000
Waynesburg (Pa.)	8,120	3,060	85	1,783	16:1	45	N.A.	23	412-852-3248
Wayne State (Neb.)	2,415	2,340	N.A.	N.A.	22:1	40[2]	22(A)	19	402-375-7234
Wayne State University (Mich.)[6, 26]	2,694	2,700	N.A.	245	8:1	N.A.	25(A)	19	313-577-3577
Webber (Fla.)	5,390	2,720	56	540	15:1	40[2,7]	1(S)[9]	0	813-638-1431
Webb Inst. of Naval Architecture (N.Y.)[21]	0	4,800	N.A.	N.A.	8:1	75	100(S)	100	516-671-2213
Weber State (Utah)	4,332	2,430	32[2]	N.A.	25:1	N.A.	N.A.	N.A.	801-626-6743
Webster (Mo.)	8,000	3,850	54	791	13:1	45	62(A)[12]	27	314-968-7000
Wellesley (Mass.)[1]	16,281	5,657	55	N.A.	10:1	85[2]	89(S)	95	617-431-1183
Wells (N.Y.)[1]	14,100	5,100	80	5,060	8:1	69	68(S)	68	315-364-3264
Wentworth Inst. of Technology (Mass.)	8,755	5,200	29	N.A.	16:1	N.A.	11(S)	17	617-442-9010
Wesley (Del.)	8,755	4,000	N.A.	549	16:1	39	N.A.	15	302-736-2400
Wesleyan (Ga.)[1]	9,845	3,950	35	3,406	14:1	55	61(S)	58	800-447-6610
Wesleyan University (Conn.)	17,800	4,490	40	3,488	11:1	89	92(S)	88	203-347-9411
Westbrook (Maine)	10,200	4,650	97	1,265	10:1[2]	68[2]	N.A.	15	207-797-7261
West Chester (Pa.)	5,192	3,520	31	19	18:1	47	24(S)	33	215-436-3411
Western Carolina (N.C.)[6]	6,481	2,310	35	182	16:1	41	12(S)	24	704-227-7317
Western Connecticut State	7,021	3,562	N.A.	21	16:1	N.A.	16(S)[2]	23[3]	203-797-4298
Western Illinois	5,761	2,982	N.A.	N.A.	18:1	39	16(A)	25[3]	309-298-1891
Western Kentucky	4,160	3,070	25	372	19:1	39	21(A)	N.A.	502-745-2551
Western Maryland	13,130	5,150	62[2]	3,621	13:1	58	27(S)[2]	N.A.	410-857-2230
Western Michigan	6,490	3,830	51	181	19:1	45	34(A)	35	616-387-2000
Western New England (Mass.)	8,426	5,200	18	231	17:1	52	8(S)	17	413-782-1321
Western New Mexico	4,384	1,990	N.A.	N.A.	17:1	23[2]	5(A)	14	505-538-6106
Western Oregon State	5,979	3,262	42	N.A.	14:1	N.A.	20(S)[2]	N.A.	503-838-8211
Western State of Colorado	5,527	3,370	60	N.A.	20:1	43	8(A)	14	303-943-2119
Western Washington	6,417	3,990	54	183	19:1	47	33(S)	47	206-676-3440
Westfield State (Mass.)	6,536	3,903	31	N.A.	18:1	48	18(S)	36[3]	413-568-3311
West Georgia	4,749	2,514	40	83	22:1	35	8(S)	N.A.	404-836-6416
West Liberty State (W.Va.)	3,660	2,650	10	118	18:1	41	34(A)[12]	30[3]	304-336-8076
Westminster (Mo.)	8,900	3,500	75	2,443	14:1	68	68(A)[20]	N.A.	314-642-3365
Westminster (Pa.) **60**	11,210	3,125	83	3,080	15:1	64	34(S)	49	412-946-7100
West Virginia	5,300	4,038	34	383	19:1	49	31(A)	N.A.	800-344-9881
West Virginia Institute of Technology[16]	3,752	3,450	30	118	18:1	50[27]	19(A)	60	304-442-3167

Footnotes are on page 186

College name and location	Tuition and fees	Room and board	% of students receiving financial aid	Average gift aid per student	Student/ faculty ratio	% who graduate in five years	% with high test scores	% from top fifth of class	Telephone
West Virginia State	$7,588	$3,050	N.A.	$1	23:1	64[2]	17(A)[12]	N.A.	304-766-3221
West Virginia Wesleyan	12,605	3,350	70	3,573	15:1	53	28(S)	51	800-722-9933
Wheaton (Mass.)	16,770	5,830	54	4,412	13:1	63	44(S)	23	508-285-7722
Wheeling Jesuit (W.Va.)	9,130	4,150	77	1,474	13:1	60	25(A)	36	304-243-2359
Wheelock (Mass.)	11,776	5,224	54	N.A.	16:1	71	19(S)	65	617-734-5200
Whitman (Wash.)	14,504	4,560	60	4,368	11:1	68	69(S)	72	509-527-5176
Whittier (Calif.)	15,380	4,800[7]	N.A.	4,550	11:1	50	56(S)[2]	52	310-693-0771
Whitworth (Wash.)	11,095	4,075	88[2]	2,708	15:1	41[2]	36(S)[2]	53[3]	509-466-3212
Wichita State (Kans.)[26]	6,070	3,005	35	124	N.A.	N.A.	26(A)[5]	25	316-689-3085
Widener (Pa.)	11,120	4,860	58[9]	1,110	12:1	74	13(S)[9]	44	215-499-4126
Wiley (Texas)[6,13]	6,986	4,830	N.A.	N.A.	15:1	N.A.	N.A.	5	903-938-8341
Wilkes (Pa.)	9,864	4,500	75	1,143	14:1	52	24(S)	26	717-824-4651
Willamette (Ore.)	13,030	4,150	96	3,512	13:1	65	71(S)	47	503-370-6303
William Jewell (Mo.)	9,216	2,750	N.A.	2,147	14:1	51	76(A)[12]	62[3]	800-753-7009
William Paterson of New Jersey	3,135	4,170	26	N.A.	14:1	33	16(S)	38[3]	201-595-2125
William Penn (Iowa)	9,870	2,930	83	N.A.	13:1	45[2]	N.A.	26[3]	515-673-1012
Williams (Mass.) 98	17,790	5,410	35	3,434	11:1	95	94(S)	94	413-597-2211
William Woods (Mo.)[1]	9,085	3,920	85	2,620	13:1	57[2]	19(A)	N.A.	314-592-4221
Wilmington (Ohio)	9,280	3,650	N.A.	1,549	15:1	55	11(A)[5]	31	513-382-6661
Wilson (Pa.)	11,001	4,650	76	3,314	7:1	67	55(S)	41	800-421-8402
Winona State (Minn.)	4,300	2,700	15	32	20:1	55[2]	70(A)[2]	20	507-457-5100
Winston-Salem State (N.C.)	5,002[23]	2,762[23]	N.A.	187	15:1	N.A.	2(S)	13	919-750-2070
Winthrop (S.C.)	5,512	2,922	N.A.	419	17:1	44	N.A.	45	803-323-2191
Wittenberg (Ohio)	14,376	4,044	60	N.A.	14:1	70[2]	81(A)[12]	51	800-677-7558
Wofford (S.C.) 95	10,490	4,150	73[2]	2,723[2]	15:1	70	55(S)	55	803-597-4130
Worcester Polytechnic Institute (Mass.)	14,555	4,820	70	N.A.	11:1	79[2]	58(S)	82	508-831-5286
Worcester State (Mass.)	6,202	3,630	N.A.	N.A.	18:1	N.A.	22(S)[2]	12[3]	508-793-8040
Wright State (Ohio)[6]	5,766	3,600	N.A.	N.A.	20:1	N.A.	19(A)	26	513-873-2211
Xavier (Ohio)	10,450	4,330	75	N.A.	14:1	62	72(A)[12]	N.A.	513-745-3301
Xavier U. of Louisiana	6,225	3,400	59	459	14:1	36	18(A)	44	504-483-7577
Yale (Conn.) 17	17,500	6,200	35[2]	4,537	3:1[2]	93	50(S)[37]	100	203-432-1900
York College of Pennsylvania	4,715	3,160	29	194	19:1	62	29(S)	28	717-846-7788
Youngstown State (Ohio)[6]	4,389	3,555	55	174	19:1	N.A.	16(A)	25	216-742-3150

Notes and explanations:

[1] Women's college
[2] Data from the 1990 school year
[3] Percent from top quarter of high school class
[4] Percent with a combined SAT score above 1,000
[5] Percent scoring 25 or higher on the composite ACT
[6] Open admissions, in most cases for state residents only
[7] Estimate
[8] Room only; meals not included
[9] Data from the 1989 school year
[10] Comprehensive tuition price covers room and board.
[11] Percent scoring above 430
[12] Percent scoring 21 or higher on composite ACT
[13] Predominantly black college
[14] Computers required; tuition and fees include $1,000 computer rental fee
[15] Work/study college not included in MONEY's value study
[16] Work program required of all students
[17] Men's college
[18] Includes required freshman charges for uniforms, books and supplies

[19] Percent scoring 26 or higher on composite ACT
[20] Percent scoring 22 or higher on composite ACT
[21] Specialty school not included in MONEY's value study
[22] Percent from the top 10th of high school class
[23] 1991 tuition and fees
[24] Percent who graduate in four years
[25] Percent scoring above 510
[26] School with a large part-time student enrollment. Not included in MONEY value study
[27] Percent who graduate in six years
[28] Data from the 1987 school year
[29] Data from the 1988 school year
[30] Percent in the top third of high school class
[31] Percent scoring above 550 on the verbal SAT
[32] Percent scoring above 600 on the verbal SAT
[33] Percent scoring 23 or higher on composite ACT
[34] Service academy not included in MONEY value study
[35] Tuition is for arts and sciences; engineering and business students pay about $500 more
[36] Ratio includes graduate students.
[37] Percent scoring above 670 on the verbal SAT

THE TOP-PERFORMING
MUTUAL FUNDS

THE TOP FUNDS OF 1992

STOCKS

1 Fidelity Select Savings & Loan	**53.8%**
2 Oakmark	**47.3**
3 Fidelity Select Regional Banks	**46.5**
4 John Hancock Freedom Regional Bank B	**44.6**
5 Fidelity Select Financial	**40.6**

BONDS

1 Dean Witter High Yield	**32.9%**
2 Advantage High Yield	**26.5**
3 Fidelity Capital & Income	**26.1**
4 National Bond	**24.5**
5 Venture Income Plus	**23.1**

Note: Returns are to Dec. 24, 1992.

EQUITY

TAXABLE BOND

TAX-EXEMPT BOND

HOW TO USE OUR FUND TABLES

As is the case with financial assets in general, and mutual funds in particular, performance tends to run in cycles. Fund managers excel when the kinds of investments they favor are in fashion and languish when they're not. That truism is one reason that a top return is no guarantee of uninterrupted excellence in the future. This cardinal caveat applies whether the return was posted in the past year by the winners cited above—a group dominated by financial services funds and high-yield bond funds—or during the past five years by the 160 champs listed on the following eight pages.

So why bother poring over our performance rankings? Because the pages of comprehensive tables give you much more than a single return figure. We not only report on performance over a variety of different periods but also provide a wealth of data about each fund's investment approach. Here's how our rankings can help investors:

First, the columns headed **% compound annual gain** allow you to compare fund managers' results over one, three and five years (and for top performers, over 10 years as well). But be aware that sales loads could drag down your return. You can see the effect of such expenses under the column headed **value of $10,000**, which shows how much you would have now had you stashed 10 grand in the fund five years ago and paid any front-end sales charges.

You should also zero in on MONEY's exclusive **risk-adjusted grade**, which rates each fund's return in light of the risks it took over the past five years. The top 20% of funds in each category measured by this risk-adjusted yardstick receive an A, the next 20% a B and so on. To see how well a top-performing fund fares during market ups and downs, consult the column headed **% gain (or loss) during recent up and down markets**. Don't overlook our **portfolio analysis**, which reveals important facts about a manager's approach. For example, a stock fund with a low **P/E ratio**, a high **% cash** and generous **yield** is likely to hold up relatively well in a declining market but is less likely to take off in a rising one. Among bond funds, a low yield, a high cash level, a short **average maturity** and a high **% of assets rated at least AA** (a measure of the portfolio's credit quality) are signs of a conservative investment strategy.

The **Barra style analysis** gives further insight into the investment approach of our top growth and total-return funds. By comparing a fund's monthly returns over the past five years with those of various market indexes, the Berkeley, California investment consulting firm of Barra Inc. calculates what percentage of the fund's return can be attributed to its manager's bets on value, growth and small-company equities and other kinds of investments such as bonds or foreign stocks. That tells you to what degree a manager specializes in value, growth or small-cap stocks.

Finally, since a fund with high expenses must produce above-average returns just to keep up with its peers, focus on its **five-year expense projection**, a standardized calculation that estimates the total costs you would pay—including sales charges and annual fees—on a $1,000 investment that earns 5% annually and is eventually withdrawn in five years.

Ranked by five-year performance	Type	Money risk-adjusted grade	% compound annual gain (or loss) to Dec. 24, 1992				Value of $10,000 invested five years ago (net of sales charge)	% gain (or loss) during recent up and down markets		
			One year	Three years	Five years	10 years		Current rising market	Latest falling market	Prior rising market
GROWTH			**12.1**	**13.4**	**13.1**	**15.8**		**69.7**	**(22.4)**	**73.7**
1. Kaufmann Fund	SCG	A	14.5	22.9	33.2	—	$41,970	131.3	(32.1)	183.2
2. John Hancock Special Equities	SCG	A	32.0	28.8	26.1	—	30,646	181.7	(32.8)	89.1
3. Alger Small Capitalization Portfolio	SCG	A	6.1	18.9	26.0	—	31,867	90.6	(27.9)	177.0
4. Fidelity Contrafund	Gro	A	19.6	23.3	26.0	17.8	31,062	102.7	(17.8)	106.6
5. Fidelity Advisor Equity–Growth	Gro	A	13.4	25.1	26.0	—	32,093	131.6	(28.9)	135.0
6. Vista Capital Growth	Gro	A	18.6	21.6	25.9	—	30,242	120.5	(22.7)	85.9
7. Twentieth Century Ultra Investors	Max	A	4.3	27.1	25.4	17.0	31,203	141.6	(28.6)	117.7
8. Janus Twenty[1]	Max	A	5.6	20.7	25.0	—	31,135	92.4	(23.6)	122.5
9. Pasadena Growth	Gro	A	5.8	18.2	24.8	—	28,621	105.7	(31.3)	148.5
10. Delaware Group–Trend	Max	A	24.8	16.2	24.1	15.1	27,806	135.7	(36.6)	135.3
11. AIM Constellation	Max	A	18.0	23.1	23.9	18.3	27,897	134.5	(34.9)	135.3
12. Skyline Special Equities[1]	SCG	A	45.0	23.2	23.9	—	28,453	127.0	(25.9)	88.4
13. Thomson Opportunity B	Max	A	30.3	25.6	23.8	—	29,101	141.4	(26.2)	91.9
14. Hartwell Emerging Growth	SCG	A	6.1	21.1	23.3	13.2	27,407	112.8	(31.1)	144.4
15. Berger One Hundred	Gro	A	10.7	24.6	23.1	16.7	28,550	137.9	(28.0)	89.1
16. ABT Emerging Growth	Max	A	17.4	24.0	22.8	—	26,932	134.5	(28.1)	92.7
17. IDEX II– Growth	Gro	A	5.9	17.4	22.5	—	26,265	78.0	(23.6)	113.0
18. Columbia Special	Max	A	18.3	14.2	22.3	—	27,488	105.0	(35.5)	148.4
19. Founders Frontier	SCG	A	10.5	14.1	22.3	—	27,129	73.8	(22.0)	105.3
20. Oberweis Emerging Growth	SCG	A	16.0	28.6	22.1	—	27,279	162.2	(40.1)	115.8
21. IDEX Fund	Gro	A	4.3	17.5	22.0	—	25,018	77.1	(22.2)	105.0
22. MFS Lifetime–Emerging Growth	SCG	A	14.6	26.1	21.8	—	27,003	162.3	(36.3)	92.7
23. Fidelity Growth Company	Gro	A	10.6	18.5	21.7	—	26,115	95.2	(27.3)	125.1
24. Transamerica Spl.–Emerging Growth B	SCG	A	14.4	20.1	21.6	—	26,626	111.8	(31.4)	117.1
25. CGM Capital Development[1]	Gro	A	17.8	33.3	21.6	20.4	26,589	175.9	(31.3)	71.1
TOTAL RETURN			**11.5**	**10.4**	**12.9**	**13.5**		**51.6**	**(15.0)**	**55.6**
1. Vista Growth & Income	G&I	A	19.0	22.6	31.9	—	38,157	91.8	(17.5)	152.4
2. FAM Value	G&I	A	26.3	19.9	22.8	—	27,546	94.0	(18.6)	77.7
3. AIM Value[4]	G&I	A	17.8	19.3	21.2	—	25,069	94.2	(27.0)	112.0
4. Monetta Fund	G&I	A	6.0	21.9	20.3	—	25,215	91.6	(23.0)	101.0
5. Fidelity Convertible Securities	Conv	A	24.1	17.9	19.0	—	23,864	81.5	(14.6)	59.0
6. N&B Guardian	G&I	A	21.6	15.3	18.4	16.0	23,583	84.7	(20.6)	73.6
7. Fidelity Growth & Income	G&I	A	13.7	13.9	18.0	—	22,856	72.5	(18.5)	76.3
8. Flag Investors Telephone Income	Eql	B	15.2	9.1	17.8	—	21,959	46.7	(6.6)	71.0
9. Financial Industrial Income	Eql	A	3.0	14.5	17.3	17.0	22,541	61.7	(16.3)	81.4
10. IDS Managed Retirement	G&I	A	12.0	17.2	17.2	—	21,413	72.3	(20.4)	83.1
11. Pasadena Balanced Return	Bal	A	7.7	13.6	16.9	—	20,604	65.8	(19.8)	75.5
12. MainStay Value	G&I	A	22.8	16.7	16.9	—	22,134	80.8	(14.9)	53.6
13. Mutual Benefit	G&I	A	13.4	10.4	16.8	15.9	21,212	56.3	(16.4)	81.8
14. Pioneer Three	SCG	B	22.4	12.3	16.8	14.3	20,612	77.2	(22.1)	74.8
15. Value Line Fund	G&I	B	7.2	15.6	16.7	11.9	21,987	76.0	(21.2)	80.2
16. Shearson Income–Total Return B	G&I	A	13.7	14.1	16.4	—	21,756	67.8	(17.4)	72.7
17. Fidelity Advisor–Income & Growth	Bal	A	11.2	12.7	16.4	—	20,419	60.4	(11.0)	57.9
18. Selected American Shares	G&I	B	10.4	14.8	16.3	17.1	21,907	78.5	(19.3)	62.6
19. Alliance Counterpoint	G&I	B	8.6	10.6	16.3	—	20,341	60.9	(14.6)	69.1
20. AIM Charter	G&I	A	3.4	15.1	16.3	14.9	20,503	53.3	(11.2)	77.3
21. Franklin Managed Rising Dividend	G&I	A	12.6	14.9	16.3	—	20,457	75.5	(16.1)	51.3
22. Safeco Equity	G&I	C	12.2	8.6	15.9	14.4	21,496	53.8	(20.8)	91.9
23. Nationwide Fund	G&I	B	7.0	10.9	15.7	15.6	19,806	52.7	(15.1)	78.7
24. FPA Perennial	G&I	A	15.3	11.7	15.7	—	19,642	52.3	(14.2)	68.6
25. Vanguard Quantitative Portfolio	G&I	B	11.3	11.6	15.7	—	21,189	59.6	(18.2)	78.2
S&P 500-stock index			**7.6**	**10.8**	**15.9**	**16.2**	**20,913**			

Types: Bal-Balanced; Conv-Convertibles; Eql-Equity income; Flx-Flexible income; Gro-Growth; G&I-Growth and income; Max-Maximum capital gains; SCG-Small-company growth
[1] Currently closed to new investors   [2] Stocks with market values of $200 million or less   [3] Fund may impose back-end load or exit fee.   [4] Named Cigna Value until July 1   N.A.: Not available

| Net assets (millions) | Portfolio analysis | | | BARRA style analysis % of return attributable to ... | | | | Senior fund manager, age (years managing fund) | Expense analysis | | Minimum initial investment | Telephone |
	% yield	P/E ratio	% cash	Value stocks	Growth stocks	Small companies[2]	Other		% maximum initial sales charge	Five-year expense projection		
	1.0										◀ **CATEGORY AVERAGE**	
$193.8	0.0	29.1	0.0	0.0	80.8	19.2	0.0	Lawrence Auriana, 48 (6)	None[3]	$190	$1,500	800-237-0132
38.9	0.0	36.2	6.0	0.0	84.4	15.6	0.0	Michael DiCarlo, 36 (5)	5.0	188	1,000	800-225-5291
166.2	0.0	36.2	13.2	0.0	100.0	0.0	0.0	David Alger, 49 (6)	None[3]	136	None	800-992-3863
1,414.2	0.4	24.8	13.2	22.6	46.8	28.0	2.5	Will Danoff, 32 (2)	3.0	78	2,500	800-544-8888
151.9	0.1	28.7	13.0	0.0	100.0	0.0	0.0	Robert Stansky, N.A. (5)	4.75	139	2,500	800-522-7297
37.5	0.1	N.A.	19.0	0.0	80.4	19.6	0.0	Mark Tincher, 37 (1)	4.75	117	2,500	800-348-4782
4,012.8	0.0	30.5	0.7	0.0	100.0	0.0	0.0	Team management	None	55	None	800-345-2021
2,308.2	0.1	25.2	21.6	0.0	98.1	0.0	1.9	Thomas Marsico, 37 (4)	None	61	1,000	800-525-8983
524.5	0.0	28.3	0.5	0.0	100.0	0.0	0.0	Roger Engemann, 52 (6)	5.5	150	2,500	800-533-8636
130.3	0.0	29.1	9.0	0.0	74.6	25.4	0.0	Edward Antoian, 37 (8)	5.75	119	250	800-523-4640
890.0	0.0	29.0	4.0	0.0	100.0	0.0	0.0	Harry Hutzler, 69 (16)	5.5	125	500	800-347-4246
69.6	0.0	17.0	8.0	18.7	23.2	56.6	1.5	Bill Dutton, 39 (5)	None	120	1,000	800-458-5222
179.0	0.0	28.1	14.0	0.0	86.9	13.1	0.0	Don Chiboucas, 48 (6)	None[3]	113	1,000	800-227-7337
152.7	0.0	45.1	6.0	0.0	100.0	0.0	0.0	John Hartwell, 76 (14)	4.75	135	1,000	800-343-2898
384.1	0.0	34.1	18.0	0.0	82.4	0.0	17.6	William Berger, 67 (18)	None	107	250	800-333-1001
28.2	0.0	38.9	6.0	0.0	100.0	0.0	0.0	Harold Ireland, 53 (10)	4.75	130	1,000	800-553-7838
402.5	0.4	24.7	17.0	0.0	97.1	0.0	2.9	Thomas Marsico, 37 (7)	5.5	138	50	800-443-9975
315.2	0.0	26.1	4.3	0.0	95.6	4.4	0.0	Alan Folkman, 50 (7)	None	67	2,000	800-547-1707
104.0	0.0	23.7	13.0	3.5	75.3	11.5	9.7	Team management	None	92	1,000	800-525-2440
35.7	0.0	29.8	1.8	0.0	76.6	23.4	0.0	James Oberweis, 46 (6)	None	113	2,000	800-323-6166
290.2	0.6	24.3	9.0	0.0	95.7	0.0	4.3	Thomas Marsico, 37 (7)	8.5	155	50	800-443-9975
284.6	0.0	31.7	3.0	0.0	100.0	0.0	0.0	John Ballen, 33 (6)	None[3]	153	1,000	800-225-2606
1,448.8	0.4	28.9	16.1	0.0	100.0	0.0	0.0	Robert Stansky, 37 (5)	3.0	87	2,500	800-544-8888
77.5	0.0	25.8	8.0	0.0	63.1	36.9	0.0	Ed Larson, N.A. (5)	None[3]	170	1,000	800-472-3863
324.1	0.2	20.3	0.2	0.0	61.4	38.6	0.0	G. Kenneth Heebner, 52 (15)	None	49	2,500	800-345-4048
	3.1										◀ **CATEGORY AVERAGE**	
135.8	1.1	N.A.	20.0	18.7	35.8	44.4	1.1	Mark Tincher, 37 (1)	4.75	121	2,500	800-348-4782
25.8	0.4	N.A.	4.0	22.6	0.0	59.8	17.6	Thomas Putnam, 48 (5)	None	85	2,000	800-858-1415
187.5	0.7	25.9	10.3	1.6	75.9	10.8	11.7	Team management	5.5	117	500	800-347-4246
292.5	0.1	27.3	40.0	0.0	74.1	0.0	25.9	Robert Bacarella, 43 (7)	None	80	100	800-666-3882
332.5	4.1	N.A.	12.6	37.0	4.4	28.9	29.7	Andrew Offit, 31 (1)	None	64	2,500	800-544-8888
847.4	1.3	23.5	8.6	70.6	29.4	0.0	0.0	Kent Simons, 57 (10)	None	46	1,000	800-877-9700
4,290.8	1.8	23.1	20.0	60.9	14.7	18.9	5.5	Andrew Midler, 31 (6 mos.)	2.0	67	2,500	800-544-8888
285.0	3.9	23.1	2.0	42.0	17.8	0.0	40.2	Bruce Behrens, 48 (8)	4.5	95	2,000	800-767-3524
2,310.1	2.6	20.9	3.1	10.5	66.4	2.1	21.0	John Kaweske, 51 (8)	None	54	1,000	800-525-8085
1,307.0	1.8	24.5	4.9	0.0	89.4	0.0	10.6	Robert Healy, 57 (8 mos.)	5.0	100	2,000	800-328-8300
64.6	1.3	27.2	1.6	0.0	45.8	0.0	54.2	Roger Engemann, 52 (5)	5.5	180	2,500	800-533-8636
82.3	0.7	N.A.	13.2	49.9	7.8	29.9	12.4	Denis LaPlaige, 41 (6)	None[3]	149	500	800-522-4202
47.4	2.1	21.6	12.0	37.2	28.4	21.2	13.3	John Stone, 51 (12)	4.75	92	250	800-323-4726
779.6	1.8	21.7	2.2	28.6	31.3	38.4	1.7	Robert Benson, 45 (6)	5.75	104	1,000	800-225-6292
281.0	0.9	25.5	3.4	0.0	94.1	0.0	5.9	Team management	None	47	1,000	800-223-0818
641.2	7.8	18.9	17.6	47.3	26.4	8.3	18.0	John Fullerton, N.A. (7)	None[3]	102	1,000	800-451-2010
363.6	3.2	25.2	21.5	52.7	8.2	8.1	31.0	Robert Haber, 34 (6)	4.75	136	2,500	800-522-7297
566.6	0.6	23.0	7.0	37.1	55.7	0.0	7.2	Ted Kauss, 51 (7 mos.)	None	65	1,000	800-553-5533
71.5	0.8	22.4	1.1	43.2	55.2	0.0	1.6	Dutch Handke, 43 (7)	5.5	139	250	800-227-4618
1,204.8	1.9	22.1	5.0	0.0	84.1	0.0	15.9	Julian Lerner, 68 (24)	5.5	122	500	800-347-4246
137.5	1.9	16.2	20.0	53.3	11.4	5.5	29.8	William Lippman, 67 (5)	4.0	120	100	800-342-5236
70.8	1.3	23.1	2.0	36.8	35.3	27.9	0.0	Douglas Johnson, 38 (8)	None	54	1,000	800-426-6730
715.8	2.1	22.2	7.6	25.6	67.3	0.0	7.1	Charles Bath, 37 (8)	4.5	77	250	800-848-0920
67.2	2.4	19.1	20.0	39.4	10.6	18.2	31.8	Christopher Linden, 42 (8)	6.5	122	1,500	800-982-4372
375.7	2.8	20.5	2.6	46.0	54.0	0.0	0.0	John Nagorniak, 48 (6)	None	24	3,000	800-851-4999
	2.9	**24.4**										

Ranked by five-year performance	Type	MONEY risk-adjusted grade	% compound annual gain (or loss) to Dec. 24, 1992				Value of $10,000 invested five years ago (net of sales charge)	% gain (or loss) during recent up and down markets		
			One year	Three years	Five years	10 years		Current rising market	Latest falling market	Prior rising market
OVERSEAS			**(0.3)**	**(0.1)**	**7.1**	**13.8**		**9.7**	**(15.6)**	**16.5**
1. Scudder Global	Glo	A	6.7	4.6	13.5	—	$18,724	23.2	(12.6)	90.8
2. GAM Pacific Basin	Intl	A	2.1	2.0	13.5	—	17,814	12.9	(10.6)	93.8
3. Templeton Growth	Glo	A	6.4	7.6	13.3	15.1	17,672	43.0	(19.1)	73.3
4. Templeton Foreign	Intl	A	1.9	4.8	13.1	17.6	17,215	16.6	(12.5)	93.0
5. EuroPacific Growth	Intl	A	4.6	6.6	13.0	—	17,166	23.6	(12.6)	85.1
6. Oppenheimer Global	Glo	A	(12.0)	2.8	12.8	14.1	16,879	9.4	(16.5)	107.6
7. Templeton Smaller Companies Growth	Glo	A	5.0	6.6	12.8	13.4	17,257	52.6	(24.7)	68.1
8. Smith Barney World–Intl. Equity	Intl	A	3.5	7.0	11.8	—	16,633	38.4	(20.1)	69.6
9. New Perspective	Glo	A	7.1	7.9	11.6	15.4	16,396	34.5	(15.2)	65.9
10. G.T. Global–Worldwide	Glo	A	6.3	3.1	11.5	—	16,572	25.3	(18.1)	85.9
11. G.T. Global–Pacific	Intl	A	(6.1)	(2.9)	11.4	15.9	15,941	3.0	(15.9)	117.5
12. Ivy International	Intl	B	1.8	0.4	11.0	—	15,905	12.5	(16.9)	96.4
13. Dreyfus Strategic World Investing	Glo	A	(2.7)	6.6	10.6	—	16,347	14.1	(1.6)	59.0
14. Templeton World	Glo	B	5.6	4.2	10.3	14.0	15,478	39.3	(21.1)	61.7
15. GAM International	Intl	B	4.1	3.5	9.6	—	14,981	14.8	(11.6)	61.9
16. First Investors Global	Glo	B	(1.1)	(0.4)	9.4	13.9	14,664	11.7	(19.5)	90.6
17. Merrill Lynch Pacific A	Intl	B	(3.5)	0.1	9.1	20.0	14,234	9.0	(3.6)	52.5
18. Lexington Worldwide Emerging Growth	Intl	B	5.7	3.3	9.0	8.9	15,524	41.2	(23.9)	60.9
19. Merrill Lynch International A	Glo	B	6.9	3.6	8.7	—	14,145	22.4	(13.5)	54.8
20. G.T. Global–International	Intl	B	(2.9)	(2.7)	8.6	—	14,467	3.8	(14.1)	89.5
SECTORS			**12.2**	**13.2**	**16.1**	**13.4**		**63.0**	**(17.9)**	**68.4**
1. Fidelity Select–Biotechnology	Sec	A	(6.6)	37.0	30.1	—	36,640	106.6	(10.9)	138.6
2. Financial Strategic–Health Sciences	Sec	A	(12.2)	27.4	30.0	—	37,455	103.7	(19.5)	172.4
3. Fidelity Select–Retailing	Sec	A	26.8	24.7	28.3	—	33,341	145.0	(34.1)	139.2
4. Fidelity Select–Medical Delivery	Sec	A	(11.2)	21.6	26.5	—	30,986	95.8	(21.8)	143.2
5. Financial Strategic–Financial Services	Sec	A	27.5	26.6	26.2	—	32,149	155.2	(23.5)	76.3
6. Fidelity Select–Regional Banks	Sec	A	49.3	24.8	25.1	—	29,770	187.7	(23.9)	49.6
7. Financial Strategic–Technology	Sec	A	19.8	31.0	24.8	—	30,684	163.6	(36.4)	121.9
8. Financial Strategic–Leisure	Sec	A	26.4	18.7	24.0	—	29,303	121.0	(30.3)	115.1
9. T. Rowe Price Science & Technology	Sec	A	21.7	22.6	23.7	—	28,868	129.6	(34.5)	128.2
10. John Hancock Freedom Regnl. Bank B	Sec	A	46.5	23.7	23.3	—	28,683	153.0	(21.8)	52.4
11. Fidelity Select–Health Care	Sec	A	(14.1)	23.6	23.3	20.3	27,992	74.3	(10.8)	106.5
12. Vanguard Special. Port.–Health Care	Sec	A	1.4	19.1	23.1	—	28,537	67.1	(12.9)	113.3
13. Paine Webber Regional Fin. Growth	Sec	A	40.2	25.4	22.6	—	26,292	155.5	(20.4)	N.A.
14. Fidelity Select–Food & Agriculture	Sec	A	10.1	16.4	22.1	—	26,697	59.2	(12.0)	107.9
15. Fidelity Select–Savings & Loan	Sec	B	61.1	29.9	22.1	—	27,021	200.3	(28.1)	45.2
16. Century Shares Trust	Sec	B	30.4	15.9	20.0	17.8	25,132	109.7	(25.8)	68.1
17. Fidelity Select–Telecommunications	Sec	B	18.6	8.6	19.2	—	23,670	70.5	(20.3)	92.0
18. Putnam Health Sciences Trust	Sec	B	(7.4)	15.8	18.9	14.8	22,743	52.0	(13.5)	103.2
19. Fidelity Select–Software	Sec	B	37.5	25.7	18.6	—	23,043	153.9	(35.3)	71.2
20. Fidelity Select–Financial Services	Sec	C	44.3	20.2	17.7	17.5	22,302	167.7	(32.6)	38.3
GOLD AND PRECIOUS METALS			**(11.7)**	**(13.5)**	**(6.8)**	**(2.4)**		**(19.2)**	**(5.4)**	**(17.8)**
1. John Hancock Freedom Gold & Gov. B	Gold	E	3.7	5.0	6.7	—	13,800	20.5	(2.7)	17.7
2. Oppenheimer Gold & Special Minerals	Gold	D	(9.2)	(13.5)	(1.1)	—	8,885	(12.6)	(12.8)	37.0
3. Franklin Gold	Gold	E	(18.0)	(12.3)	(3.0)	2.2	8,177	(16.6)	(7.6)	8.2
4. United Gold & Government	Gold	E	(10.6)	(11.6)	(4.5)	—	7,205	(11.5)	(6.6)	(6.1)
5. Fidelity Select–American Gold	Gold	E	1.3	(9.3)	(4.5)	—	7,681	(11.4)	(6.1)	(5.6)
S&P 500-stock index			**7.6**	**10.8**	**15.9**	**16.2**	**20,913**			

Types: Glo-Global; Intl-International; Sec-Sector [1] Figure reflects borrowing to boost investments. [2] Fund may impose back-end load or exit fee. N.A.: Not available

Net assets (millions)	Portfolio analysis				Senior fund manager, age (years managing fund)	Expense analysis				Minimum initial investment	Telephone
	% yield	P/E ratio	% cash	Largest sector (% of assets)		% turnover	% maximum initial sales charge	Annual expenses (% of assets)	Five-year projection		
1.3										◀ CATEGORY AVERAGE	
$389.1	0.5	N.A.	4.0	Europe (40.0)	William Holzer, 43 (7)	45	None	1.59	$87	$1,000	800-225-2470
29.5	0.7	N.A.	15.0	N.A.	Michael Bunker, 42 (7)	43	5.0	2.20	100	10,000	212-888-4200
3,271.1	2.7	N.A.	12.8	United States (40.0)	Mark Holowesko, N.A. (5)	24	5.75	0.88	134	500	800-237-0738
1,678.4	2.8	N.A.	16.5	Europe (70.0)	Mark Holowesko, N.A. (5)	22	5.75	0.94	137	500	800-237-0738
2,424.1	1.7	N.A.	18.7	Europe (60.0)	Multiple portfolio counselors	64	5.75	1.24	122	250	800-421-0180
1,215.1	0.4	N.A.	4.3	Europe (65.0)	Bill Wilby, N.A. (1)	18	5.75	1.36	128	1,000	800-525-7048
932.6	2.0	N.A.	20.4	United States (36.0)	Mark Holowesko, N.A. (5)	49	5.75	1.33	146	500	800-237-0738
120.0	0.0	N.A.	0.8	Europe (48.0)	Committee management	12	4.5	1.60	128	3,000	800-544-7835
3,081.6	2.0	N.A.	17.4	Europe (45.0)	Multiple portfolio counselors	6	5.75	0.86	102	250	800-421-0180
136.5	1.1	N.A.	2.3	Europe (36.0)	Team management	85	4.75	2.01	156	500	800-824-1580
293.6	4.0	N.A.	12.2	Hong Kong (32.0)	Team management	42	4.75	2.01	156	500	800-824-1580
117.3	1.4	N.A.	10.0	Europe (70.0)	Hakan Castegren, N.A. (7)	27	5.75	1.70	144	1,000	800-456-5111
105.5	0.0	N.A.	(1.2)[1]	United States (45.0)	Fiona Biggs, 30 (4)	420	3.0	1.62	115	2,500	800-782-6620
4,021.4	2.9	N.A.	5.6	United States (40.0)	Mark Holowesko, N.A. (5)	27	5.75	0.86	106	500	800-237-0738
44.7	3.0	N.A.	3.7	Europe (45.0)	John Horseman, 34 (2)	38	5.0	2.00	90	10,000	212-888-4200
193.7	0.0	N.A.	2.4	Europe (42.0)	Jerry Mitchell, 53 (1)	64	6.9	1.95	167	1,000	800-423-4026
300.4	2.2	N.A.	8.9	Japan (63.0)	Steve Silverman, N.A. (9)	6	6.5	1.02	118	250	800-637-3863
28.3	1.2	N.A.	1.4	Pacific Rim (60.0)	Caesar Bryan, 37 (1)	112	None	1.97	106	1,000	800-526-0056
166.5	0.8	N.A.	9.3	United States (38.0)	Frederick Ives, 59 (8)	64	6.5	1.48	141	1,000	800-637-3863
425.1	1.3	N.A.	0.2	Europe (40.0)	Team management	71	4.75	1.88	145	500	800-824-1580
1.9										◀ CATEGORY AVERAGE	
719.6	0.0	38.9	24.9	Consumer goods (56.8)	Karen Firestone, 36 (4 mos.)	160	3.0[2]	1.50	117	2,500	800-544-8888
739.8	0.3	30.2	13.3	Consumer goods (71.7)	John Kaweske, 51 (8)	100	None	1.03	58	1,000	800-525-8085
48.4	0.0	26.9	28.0	Cyclicals (94.4)	Jennifer Uhrig, 31 (1)	205	3.0[2]	1.87	136	2,500	800-544-8888
113.3	0.0	24.2	3.2	Consumer goods (82.7)	Charles Mangum, 28 (2)	181	3.0[2]	1.69	127	2,500	800-544-8888
183.3	1.2	14.8	10.6	Finance (89.1)	Douglas Pratt, 27 (1)	249	None	1.13	64	1,000	800-525-8085
142.3	0.9	23.7	5.2	Finance (86.0)	Stephen Binder, 29 (2)	89	3.0[2]	1.77	131	2,500	800-544-8888
151.4	0.0	30.4	2.9	Capital goods (69.2)	Daniel Leonard, 56 (9)	307	None	1.19	67	1,000	800-525-8085
39.8	0.0	27.0	20.1	Cyclicals (59.8)	Tim Miller, 35 (1)	122	None	1.86	106	1,000	800-525-8085
196.2	0.0	26.8	4.8	Capital goods (68.7)	Charles Morris, 29 (2)	148	None	1.25	69	2,500	800-541-8832
53.6	1.5	16.1	6.0	Finance (71.3)	James Schmidt, 42 (8)	32	None[2]	2.04	130	1,000	800-225-5291
781.8	0.0	28.2	4.1	Consumer goods (82.3)	Charles Mangum, 28 (1)	154	3.0[2]	1.44	114	2,500	800-544-8888
577.1	1.5	30.6	3.2	Consumer goods (58.1)	Edward Owens, 46 (8)	7	None[2]	0.30	30	3,000	800-851-4999
46.8	0.7	N.A.	11.3	N.A.	Karen Finkel, N.A. (6)	31	4.5	1.72	134	1,000	800-950-5050
111.1	0.4	20.6	7.2	Consumer goods (73.7)	Deborah Wheeler, 35 (1)	63	3.0[2]	1.83	134	2,500	800-544-8888
91.4	1.1	12.2	13.2	Finance (80.8)	David Ellison, 34 (7)	134	3.0[2]	2.08	146	2,500	800-544-8888
204.8	1.6	14.1	16.5	Finance (106.9)[1]	Allan Fulkerson, 59 (21)	0	None	0.95	53	500	800-321-1928
87.8	1.1	24.7	6.2	Utilities (65.4)	Fergus Shiel, 33 (6 mos.)	20	3.0[2]	1.90	137	2,500	800-544-8888
942.6	0.9	30.0	13.6	Consumer goods (71.5)	Cheryl Alexander, N.A.	42	5.75	1.20	121	500	800-225-1581
70.1	0.0	22.7	20.9	Capital goods (52.8)	Arieh Coll, 29 (1)	348	3.0[2]	1.98	128	2,500	800-544-8888
95.4	0.9	20.5	8.8	Finance (87.6)	Bruce Herring, 27 (2)	164	3.0[2]	1.85	135	2,500	800-544-8888
1.7										◀ CATEGORY AVERAGE	
37.1	6.0	N.A.	4.2	U.S. Government bonds (85.7)	August Arace, 62 (9)	57	None[2]	1.82	119	1,000	800-225-5291
123.7	2.2	N.A.	4.1	Gold mines, N. America (78.0)	Bill Wilby, N.A. (1)	113	5.75	1.38	129	1,000	800-525-7048
235.2	4.1	N.A.	13.4	Gold mines, N. America (52.0)	Martin Wiskemann, 65 (20)	53	4.0	0.31	80	100	800-342-5236
31.2	1.2	N.A.	8.1	Gold mines, N. America (63.0)	John Olsen, 54 (7)	113	8.5	1.57	163	500	913-236-1303
171.3	0.0	N.A.	2.6	Gold mines, N. America (97.0)	Malcolm MacNaught, 55 (7)	40	3.0[2]	1.75	130	2,500	800-544-8888
	2.9	24.4									

ONEY's grades compare domestic equity, overseas and sector funds by five-year, risk-adjusted return. The top 20% in each category receive an A, the next 20% a B and so on.
Rankings by Lipper Analytical Services

Ranked by five-year performance	Type	MONEY risk-adjusted grade	% compound annual gain (or loss) to Dec. 24, 1992				Value of $10,000 invested five years ago (net of sales charge)	% gain (or loss) during recent up and down markets		
			One year	Three years	Five years	10 years		Current rising market	Latest falling market	Prior rising market
U.S. GOVERNMENTS			**6.9**	**9.8**	**10.0**	**10.5**				
1. Benham Target–2015	USG	C	11.1	8.7	14.7	—	$19,129	44.8	1.4	—
2. Benham Target–2010	USG	B	12.2	10.3	14.6	—	19,720	46.8	10.3	—
3. Benham Target–2005	USG	B	11.8	11.2	14.4	—	19,637	50.2	13.1	—
4. Benham Target–2000	USG	A	10.1	11.6	13.2	—	18,768	50.5	11.4	—
5. Scudder Trust–Zero Coupon 2000	USG	B	9.8	10.7	12.9	—	18,178	46.7	10.1	—
6. FPA New Income	USG	A	11.1	12.6	11.7	12.1	16,843	47.9	21.6	66.4
7. Dreyfus Premier GNMA	MBS	A	7.2	11.0	11.6	—	16,192	44.3	22.7	—
8. Vanguard Fixed Income–GNMA	MBS	A	7.6	11.4	11.5	11.4	17,236	47.4	15.3	61.9
9. Vanguard Fixed Income–Long-Term Treas.	USG	C	9.0	10.3	11.4	—	16,999	43.2	12.5	—
10. Benham Government–GNMA Income	MBS	A	8.2	11.2	11.4	—	16,948	45.7	15.8	—
HIGH-GRADE CORPORATES			**8.8**	**10.6**	**10.5**	**11.0**				
1. Vanguard Preferred	HGC	A	9.1	11.8	12.5	12.3	17,754	N.A.	N.A.	N.A.
2. Vanguard Fixed Income–Inv. Grade Corp.	HGC	A	10.9	12.3	12.4	11.7	17,740	48.6	14.5	67.8
3. Alliance Bond–Monthly Income Port.	HGC	B	14.5	12.3	11.6	12.1	16,191	49.6	11.6	73.4
4. UST Master Managed Income–Original	HGC	A	7.3	10.7	11.2	—	16,101	42.8	20.8	—
5. Putnam Income	HGC	A	10.0	10.7	11.1	11.5	16,061	42.6	14.7	65.1
6. Dreyfus A Bond Plus	HGC	B	9.3	10.5	11.0	11.1	16,803	42.7	11.7	69.3
7. Columbia Fixed Income Securities	HGC	A	8.4	11.1	11.0	—	16,712	44.8	13.2	57.1
8. Bond Fund of America	HGC	A	10.9	11.4	11.0	11.9	16,091	43.0	13.9	72.1
9. Shearson Inv.–Investment Grade B	HGC	B	9.8	11.3	11.0	11.8	16,915	45.6	7.6	85.4
10. Calvert Income	HGC	A	8.3	9.9	11.0	11.4	15,996	40.8	18.4	68.1
HIGH-YIELD CORPORATES			**17.2**	**12.7**	**9.9**	**10.8**				
1. Fidelity Advisor High Yield	HYC	A	25.1	21.5	16.9	—	20,666	75.3	18.1	—
2. Kemper Diversified Income	HYC	A	18.5	16.1	14.0	10.3	20,083	51.9	3.8	44.1
3. Merrill Lynch Corporate–High Income A	HYC	A	21.3	17.3	13.7	13.4	18,279	59.3	15.8	61.5
4. Liberty High Income Bond	HYC	B	17.4	17.9	13.5	12.6	17,755	55.1	14.3	61.7
5. AIM High Yield	HYC	A	18.6	15.3	12.8	13.2	17,182	47.2	17.9	68.5
6. Fidelity Capital & Income	HYC	B	27.4	16.8	12.3	13.1	17,227	46.4	11.0	78.3
7. Paine Webber High Income A	HYC	B	24.9	18.8	12.2	—	16,943	58.0	3.7	—
8. Lord Abbett Bond Debenture	HYC	A	16.8	14.2	12.2	11.5	16,892	44.9	14.3	57.8
9. Kemper Investment Portfolio–Diversified	HYC	A	17.5	14.1	12.1	—	19,384	46.2	0.5	—
10. Federated High Yield Trust	HYC	C	15.7	15.5	12.1	—	17,448	45.4	13.9	—
SHORT/INTERMEDIATE TAXABLES			**6.5**	**9.1**	**9.0**	**9.8**				
1. Benham Target–1995	STT	A	7.5	10.8	11.2	—	16,984	45.8	9.6	—
2. Vanguard Bond Market	STT	A	7.8	10.5	10.5	—	16,388	43.0	13.2	—
3. Merrill Lynch Corporate–Intermed. A	STT	A	8.0	10.5	10.2	10.9	15,868	41.8	11.6	61.8
4. Fidelity Advisor–Limited Term	STT	A	8.0	10.2	10.1	—	16,050	40.5	14.1	59.2
5. Dreyfus 100% U.S. Treasury Intermediate	STT	B	8.0	10.5	10.0	—	15,968	41.6	13.3	—
6. SteinRoe Intermediate Bond	STT	B	8.1	10.0	10.0	10.6	15,895	40.0	11.3	65.9
7. Eaton Vance Government Obligations	STT	A	5.8	9.8	9.9	—	15,208	40.4	15.2	—
8. Legg Mason Income–Gov. Intermediate	STT	B	7.0	10.1	9.9	—	15,836	40.5	—	—
9. Scudder Short-Term Bond	STT	A	5.9	10.0	9.9	—	15,984	42.3	9.7	59.4
10. Benham Government Treasury Note	STT	B	7.1	10.0	9.7	9.8	15,598	39.6	8.5	50.7
WORLD INCOME			**2.1**	**9.2**	**7.7**	**12.9**				
1. Putnam Global Governmental Income	WI	A	5.6	12.0	12.2	—	17,028	54.8	—	—
2. Van Eck World Income	WI	B	(2.8)	10.6	11.1	—	16,249	52.5	—	—
3. Merrill Lynch Global Bond B	WI	D	9.4	12.4	10.0	—	16,039	57.5	11.1	—
4. Paine Webber Global Income B	WI	D	0.9	9.5	9.8	—	15,983	44.2	24.8	—
5. MFS Worldwide Governments	WI	D	2.7	10.9	9.5	12.9	14,934	49.0	15.9	94.8
Lehman Bros. government/corp. bond index			7.6	10.6	10.7	11.5	16,624			

Types: HGC-High-grade corporates; HYC-High-yield corporates; MBS-Mortgage-backed securities; STT-Short/intermediate-term taxables; USG-U.S. Government bonds; WI-World inc
Value of $10,000 is to Dec. 1. [1] May impose back-end load or exit fee   N.A.: Not available

Net assets (millions)	% yield	Average maturity (years)	% cash	% of assets rated at least AA	% of assets rated at least BBB	Senior fund manager, age (years managing fund)	% turnover	% maximum initial sales charge	Annual expenses (% of assets)	Five-year projection	Minimum initial investment	Telephone
		7.0									◄CATEGORY AVERAGE	
$131.4	0.0	22.6	0.0	100.0	100.0	David Schroeder, 37 (2)	58	None	0.63	$35	$1,000	800-472-3389
55.7	0.0	17.5	0.0	100.0	100.0	David Schroeder, 37 (2)	39	None	0.70	39	1,000	800-472-3389
168.4	0.0	12.9	0.0	100.0	100.0	David Schroeder, 37 (2)	40	None	0.67	37	1,000	800-472-3389
190.1	0.0	8.0	0.0	100.0	100.0	David Schroeder, 37 (2)	41	None	0.68	38	1,000	800-472-3389
34.8	6.8	9.3	0.0	100.0	100.0	Ruth Heisler, N.A. (5)	91	None	1.00	55	1,000	800-225-2470
80.4	6.7	5.2	13.8	76.9	76.9	Robert Rodriguez, 44 (8)	22	4.5	0.78	91	1,500	800-982-4372
150.2	7.4	22.2	1.4	100.0	100.0	Garitt Kono, 52 (1 month)	37	4.5	0.64	106	1,000	800-346-8893
6,770.8	7.7	8.8	2.9	99.9	99.9	Paul Sullivan, 50 (12)	1	None	0.29	16	3,000	800-851-4999
908.5	7.3	21.4	3.6	100.0	100.0	Ian MacKinnon, 44 (6)	89	None	0.26	15	3,000	800-851-4999
936.3	7.7	10.0	0.5	100.0	100.0	Randall Merk, 38 (5)	97	None	0.57	32	1,000	800-472-3389
		7.6									◄CATEGORY AVERAGE	
203.6	7.8	N.A.	4.4	N.A.	N.A.	Earl McEvoy, 44 (9)	33	None	0.63	35	3,000	800-851-4999
2,625.0	7.7	17.7	3.3	43.3	97.3	Paul Sullivan, 50 (16)	72	None	0.31	18	3,000	800-851-4999
67.5	8.7	11.4	10.7	53.2	53.2	Wayne Lyski, N.A. (6)	610	4.75	1.48	124	250	800-227-4618
117.8	6.4	13.0	1.3	85.5	99.8	Henry Milkewicz, N.A. (5)	482	4.5	1.05	102	1,000	800-233-1136
638.9	8.7	12.3	1.1	28.6	71.0	John Geissinger, 33 (6)	84	4.75	0.91	102	500	800-225-1581
545.4	7.3	16.1	1.9	53.2	95.5	Barbara Kenworthy, 47 (7)	67	None	0.88	49	2,500	800-782-6620
266.5	7.1	6.5	3.8	82.8	100.0	Tom Thomsen, 48 (9)	159	None	0.69	38	1,000	800-547-1707
3,762.9	8.1	9.1	8.9	48.1	78.7	Mutiple portfolio counselors	56	4.75	0.77	88	1,000	800-421-0180
439.9	7.4	26.9	2.8	25.1	93.1	George Mueller Jr., N.A. (7)	82	None[1]	1.53	94	1,000	800-451-2010
43.5	7.5	16.0	1.0	59.0	98.0	Robert Gilkison, 57 (10)	27	4.75	1.08	104	2,000	800-368-2748
		10.2									◄CATEGORY AVERAGE	
132.8	10.4	7.6	7.1	3.7	3.7	Margaret Eagle, 43 (6)	103	4.75	1.10	105	2,500	800-522-7297
256.0	10.1	9.0	2.0	5.0	5.0	Mike McNamara, 46 (4)	20	4.5	1.23	110	1,000	800-621-1048
683.8	11.0	8.5	4.0	9.3	10.7	Vincent Lathbury, 52 (11)	41	4.0	0.59	72	1,000	800-637-3863
381.8	11.1	5.5	1.0	2.4	2.4	Mark Durbiano, 33 (3)	37	4.5[1]	1.02	99	500	800-245-4770
41.3	11.6	10.1	1.0	6.6	24.8	John Pessarra, N.A. (1)	119	4.75	1.53	145	500	800-347-4246
1,818.1	8.0	6.3	4.3	3.1	3.5	Dave Breazzano, 36 (2)	132	None[1]	0.80	45	2,500	800-544-8888
287.3	12.1	7.0	6.4	4.8	4.8	Evan Steen, N.A. (2)	181	4.0	0.98	100	1,000	800-950-5050
703.8	10.3	7.5	10.2	24.8	36.7	Morais Taylor, 40 (1)	209	4.75	0.85	92	1,000	800-426-1130
245.3	9.2	8.0	1.0	4.0	4.0	Mike McNamara, 46 (4)	50	None[1]	2.01	118	1,000	800-621-1048
304.3	10.8	5.5	3.5	6.7	6.7	Mark Durbiano, 33 (8)	61	None	0.76	42	25,000	800-245-2423
		6.4									◄CATEGORY AVERAGE	
94.6	0.0	3.0	0.0	100.0	100.0	David Schroeder, 37 (2)	70	None	0.65	36	1,000	800-472-3389
1,061.9	7.2	8.3	2.6	94.0	99.9	Kenneth Volpert, 33 (2 mos.)	31	None	0.16	59	3,000	800-851-4999
154.3	7.4	7.3	6.5	35.0	100.0	Jay Marbeck, N.A. (5 mos.)	95	2.0	0.62	54	1,000	800-637-3863
153.1	8.0	10.0	6.3	82.4	98.0	Michael Gray, 36 (5)	60	4.75	0.93	97	2,500	800-522-7297
237.6	7.8	7.0	0.2	100.0	100.0	Barbara Kenworthy, 47 (5)	22	None	0.62	53	2,500	800-782-6620
271.2	7.7	6.5	3.0	60.9	94.1	Michael Kennedy, 30 (4)	202	None	0.70	39	1,000	800-338-2550
467.6	9.0	N.A.	1.0	100.0	100.0	Mark Venezia, 43 (8)	25	4.75	1.18	148	1,000	800-225-6265
320.1	5.7	7.8	1.9	95.8	100.0	Stephen Walsh, 33 (2)	513	None	0.80	47	1,000	800-822-5544
2,848.7	8.2	2.9	12.0	69.0	86.0	Thomas Poor, 49 (4)	117	None	0.78	53	1,000	800-225-2470
370.6	5.7	4.0	0.0	N.A.	N.A.	David Schroeder, 37 (1)	152	None	0.54	30	1,000	800-472-3389
		7.8									◄CATEGORY AVERAGE	
428.5	7.7	6.6	0.0	34.9	34.9	Lawrence Daly, N.A. (3)	216	4.75	1.48	124	500	800-225-1581
287.3	8.9	5.8	24.6	100.0	100.0	Klaus Buescher, 63 (5)	109	4.75	1.39	120	25,000	800-221-2220
621.4	8.3	8.8	2.0	51.6	51.6	David Walter, N.A. (6)	68	None[1]	1.77	96	1,000	800-637-3863
1,559.1	7.0	N.A.	39.0	N.A.	N.A.	Stuart Waugh, N.A. (3)	92	None[1]	1.98	125	1,000	800-950-5050
347.6	5.9	10.3	20.0	15.5	15.5	Les Nanberg, 47 (8)	208	4.75	1.61	131	1,000	800-225-2606
		6.3										

MONEY's grades compare long-term and short/intermediate-term bond funds by five-year, risk-adjusted return. The top 20% in each group receive an A, the next 20% a B and so on.
Rankings by Lipper Analytical Services

Ranked by five-year performance	Type	MONEY risk-adjusted grade	% compound annual gain (or loss) to Dec. 1, 1992				Value of $10,000 invested five years ago (net of sales charge)	% gain (or loss) during recent up and down markets		
			One year	Three years	Five years	10 years		Current rising market	Latest falling market	Prior rising market
LONG-TERM TAX-EXEMPTS			**9.9**	**8.7**	**9.7**	**10.9**				
1. Fidelity Advisor–High Income Muni	HYT	A	11.0	11.1	11.8	–	$16,635	44.6	–	–
2. Dreyfus Premier Muni Bond	HGT	A	11.8	10.4	11.4	–	16,377	39.3	10.9	–
3. Dreyfus General Muni Bond	HGT	A	11.3	10.6	11.4	–	17,139	39.9	11.5	59.6
4. Financial Tax-Free Income Shares	HGT	A	9.9	9.0	11.2	11.3	17,027	35.3	14.4	72.5
5. Vanguard Municipal–High-Yield	HYT	A	11.2	9.8	11.1	11.7	16,950	37.7	15.4	66.8
6. Scudder High-Yield Tax Free	HYT	A	12.5	9.7	11.0	–	16,879	36.6	14.4	–
7. United Municipal Bond	HGT	B	11.2	9.2	11.0	12.0	16,158	36.0	16.3	73.9
8. Nuveen Insured Municipal	HGT	A	10.8	9.4	11.0	–	16,021	35.9	17.5	–
9. Alliance Muni–National Portfolio	HGT	A	11.4	9.8	11.0	–	16,058	37.6	17.0	–
10. Smith Barney Muni Bond–National Port.	HGT	A	10.8	9.8	10.9	–	16,098	38.2	14.4	–
11. UST Master Tax-Exempt–Long-Term	HGT	A	11.5	9.5	10.8	10.8	15,956	38.1	27.5	–
12. Vanguard Municipal–Long-Term	HGT	B	11.3	9.6	10.7	11.3	16,647	37.7	14.3	64.8
13. Alliance Muni–Insured National	HGT	A	10.4	9.1	10.7	–	15,890	35.2	14.1	–
14. Paine Webber Municipal High Income A	HYT	A	10.6	9.5	10.7	–	15,967	36.1	–	–
15. Eaton Vance Muni Bond	HGT	A	10.0	9.5	10.7	11.5	15,820	36.6	15.7	66.4
SHORT/INTERMEDIATE TAX-EXEMPTS			**8.3**	**7.8**	**7.7**	**7.6**				
1. Oppenheimer Tax-Exempt–Intermediate	ITT	A	10.9	9.1	10.4	–	15,841	34.9	17.4	–
2. Vanguard Municipal–Intermediate-Term	ITT	A	9.7	9.3	9.7	10.2	15,906	35.8	14.1	53.8
3. USAA Tax Exempt–Intermediate-Term	ITT	A	9.5	8.8	9.3	9.6	15,569	33.3	12.6	45.2
4. Dreyfus Intermediate Muni Bond	ITT	A	9.9	8.8	8.7	–	15,206	33.7	10.7	48.1
5. Fidelity Limited Term Municipals	ITT	A	9.1	8.6	8.5	9.7	15,055	32.7	9.8	52.5
Lehman Bros. muni bond index			**10.0**	**9.3**	**9.9**	**10.7**	**16,043**			

Types: HGT-High-grade tax-exempts; HYT-High-yield tax-exempts; ITT-Short/intermediate-term tax-exempts   [1]Reflects borrowing to boost investments   N.A.: Not available

Important Mutual Fund Terms That You Should Know

■ **Capital gains distribution.** The payout to a mutual fund's shareholders of the profits realized from the sale of stocks or bonds.

■ **Closed-end fund.** A mutual fund with a limited number of shares outstanding. Unlike conventional open-end funds, which continually sell and redeem their shares at net asset value, closed-end funds have a fixed number of shares that trade the way stocks do on exchanges or over the counter.

■ **Convertible fund.** One invested in corporate securities (usually preferred shares or bonds) that are exchangeable for a set number of common shares at a prestated price. Convertibles appeal to investors seeking higher income than is paid by common stock—

and greater appreciation potential than regular bonds offer.

■ **Dollar-cost averaging.** An installment technique that involves investing a fixed amount of money in funds at regular intervals (say, monthly or quarterly) rather than all at once. The goal is to buy fewer shares when prices are high and more shares when they are low.

■ **Dividend.** Distribution of income generated by stocks and bonds in a fund to its shareholders.

■ **Ex-dividend.** The interval between the announcement and the payment of a fund's next dividend. An investor who buys shares during that interval is not entitled to the dividend. A fund or stock that has gone ex-dividend is marked with an "x" in newspaper listings.

■ **Expense ratio.** Amount, expressed as percentage of total investment, that shareholders pay for fund operating expenses and management fees. This money is taken out of the fund's income.

■ **Ginnie Mae.** The federally backed debt securities issued by the Government National Mortgage Association. Ginnie Maes are a pool of mortgages; investors receive the homeowners' payments of interest and principal.

■ **Index fund.** One whose portfolio closely duplicates that of, say, Standard & Poor's 500-stock index and whose performance mirrors that of the market.

■ **Junk bond fund.** One invested in high-yield bonds with speculative credit ratings (say, BB or

Net assets (millions)	% yield	Average maturity (years)	% cash	% of assets rated at least		Senior fund manager, age (years managing fund)	% turnover	% maximum initial sales charge	Annual expenses (% of assets)	Five-year projection	Minimum initial investment	Telephone
				AA	BBB							
6.2											◄CATEGORY AVERAGE	
$148.0	6.5	20.6	6.9	13.9	35.8	Peter Allegrini, 40 (1)	10	4.75	0.90	$95	$2,500	800-522-7297
447.9	6.5	25.9	0.0	21.0	85.0	Samuel Weinstock, 34 (5)	51	4.5	0.54	95	1,000	800-346-8893
1,009.2	6.7	22.2	(4.8)[1]	29.0	91.0	Paul Disdier, 37 (4)	38	None	0.28	42	2,500	800-782-6620
284.4	5.6	26.0	1.9	50.0	99.7	William Veronda, 46 (9)	28	None	1.02	57	1,000	800-525-8085
1,528.1	6.6	14.0	0.0	35.9	92.2	Ian MacKinnon, 44 (11)	64	None	0.23	13	3,000	800-851-4999
185.8	6.0	13.6	3.5	29.0	99.0	Donald Carleton, N.A. (6)	79	None	1.02	57	1,000	800-225-2470
889.7	5.8	21.2	1.2	49.7	94.6	John Holliday, 57 (12)	125	4.25	0.57	73	500	913-236-1303
436.8	5.8	23.6	2.3	99.3	100.0	William Norris, 63 (6)	45	4.75	0.73	71	1,000	800-621-7227
258.7	6.2	24.0	0.0	66.0	97.0	Susan Peabody, 35 (6)	86	4.5	1.11	85	250	800-227-4618
323.8	6.7	25.6	0.0	62.1	100.0	Peter Coffey, 48 (6)	40	4.0	0.54	69	10,000	800-544-7835
77.6	4.9	16.2	6.3	73.1	99.8	Kenneth McAlley, N.A. (6)	276	4.5	0.85	91	1,000	800-233-1136
963.1	6.3	14.4	1.2	54.1	100.0	Ian MacKinnon, 44 (11)	63	None	0.23	13	3,000	800-851-4999
152.9	5.9	23.0	0.0	100.0	100.0	Susan Peabody, 35 (6)	105	4.5	1.12	83	250	800-227-4618
75.4	6.5	22.9	6.8	22.9	97.3	Gregory Serbe, N.A. (5)	46	4.0	0.75	106	1,000	800-950-5050
101.3	6.4	23.5	3.6	65.2	93.6	Thomas Fetter, 49 (6)	105	4.75	0.76	88	1,000	800-225-6265
5.4											◄CATEGORY AVERAGE	
29.3	5.7	10.5	4.3	N.A.	N.A.	Robert Patterson, N.A. (1)	93	4.75	1.16	108	1,000	800-525-7048
3,192.8	5.7	9.6	0.0	71.1	100.0	Ian MacKinnon, 44 (11)	32	None	0.23	13	3,000	800-851-4999
1,125.7	6.0	8.5	5.2	57.0	100.0	Kenneth Willmann, 46 (11)	67	None	0.44	25	3,000	800-531-8181
1,542.0	6.0	9.8	(4.9)[1]	55.0	95.0	Monica Wieboldt, 43 (7)	48	None	0.70	39	2,500	800-782-6620
922.5	6.0	10.8	9.5	56.7	88.4	David Murphy, 44 (3)	42	None	0.67	25	2,500	800-544-8888
5.4												

Money's grades compare long-term and short/intermediate-term tax-exempt bond funds by five-year, risk-adjusted return. The top 20% in each category receive an A, the next 20% a B and so on. **Rankings by Lipper Analytical Services**

lower by Standard & Poor's) reflecting doubts about the issuing company's credit strength.

■ **Load.** Commission for buying fund shares through a broker, financial planner or insurance agent. Some funds that sell directly to the public also charge loads. A charge when you sell shares is a back-end load or exit fee.

■ **Management fee.** Charge against investor assets for managing the portfolio of a fund. The fee is a fixed percentage of the fund's asset value, typically 1% or less per year, and is disclosed in the fund's prospectus.

■ **Net asset value (NAV).** The value of a share of a fund. It's computed daily by taking the closing prices of all securities in the portfolio, adding the value of all other assets, subtracting the fund's liabilities, and dividing the result by the number of fund shares outstanding.

■ **Prospectus.** The document that a fund supplies to all prospective shareholders, identifying its management company, outlining its investment objectives and assessing the risks involved. A corollary document, called Part B or the statement of additional information, generally describes in detail the fees that are charged and often lists the fund's holdings.

■ **Sector fund.** One that restricts its holdings to stocks of companies in a particular industry, service or region. Sector funds are often grouped into families, and investors switch among these funds as economic and market conditions warrant.

■ **Total return.** The dividends, interest and capital gains that a fund achieves in a given period. A total-return fund is one that pur-

sues both growth and income by investing in a mix of growth stocks, high-dividend stocks and bonds.

■ **Turnover rate.** Figure in a fund's prospectus that indicates how actively the fund traded securities in the past 12-month period. The higher the turnover, the greater the fund's brokerage costs. These costs, which are not included in a fund's expense ratio, can cut your return because they reduce the profits (or increase the losses) on securities trades. Most stock and bond funds have a turnover rate of 80% to 100% a year.

■ **12b-1 fees.** Cryptically named after a Securities and Exchange Commission rule that permits them, these assessments against shareholders' assets are levied by many funds to help pay for promotion expenses. The fees are included in a fund's expense ratio.

1,296 MUTUAL FUNDS

BENCHMARKS FOR INVESTORS

	% compound annual gain to Jan. 1, 1993				
	One year	Three years	Five years	10 years	% yield
S&P 500-stock index	7.6	10.8	15.9	16.2	2.9
Average equity fund	8.9	11.3	14.7	13.0	1.4
Russell 2000 small-company stock index	18.4	11.7	15.1	11.8	1.5
Average small-company growth fund	12.5	14.9	17.3	11.9	0.4
Lehman Bros. gov./corp. investment-grade index	7.6	10.6	10.7	11.5	6.3
Average taxable bond fund	7.9	10.1	9.7	10.6	6.9
Lehman Bros. municipal bond index[1]	10.0	9.3	9.9	10.7	5.4
Average tax-exempt bond fund[1]	9.6	8.5	9.3	10.3	6.0

Note: [1]Performance to Dec. 1, 1992

EQUITY

TAXABLE BOND

TAX-EXEMPT BOND

THE MONEY RANKINGS: EQUITY FUNDS

FUND NAME	Type	MONEY risk-adjusted grade	% compound annual gain (or loss) to Dec. 24, 1992			Value of $10,000 invested five years ago (net of sales charge)	Portfolio analysis			Net assets (millions)	Expense analysis	
			One year	Three years	Five years		% yield	P/E ratio	% cash		% maximum initial sales charge	Five-year projection
ABT Emerging Growth	Max	A	17.4	24.0	22.8	$26,932	0.0	38.9	6.0	$28.2	4.75	$130
ABT Growth & Income	G&I	E	5.7	6.8	10.5	15,853	2.2	25.3	12.0	83.1	4.75	114
ABT Utility Income	Sec	C	12.4	7.4	13.6	18,160	4.7	17.5	5.0	142.2	4.75	112
Acorn Fund[1]	SCG	A	28.1	14.4	18.4	19,775	1.6	31.8	4.2	1,243.8	None[2]	37
Advantage Growth	Gro	B	10.4	12.5	15.0	20,478	0.2	23.2	1.3	54.6	None[2]	119
Advantage Income	Flx	D	9.0	9.7	11.8	17,496	4.5	9.9	0.7	54.9	None[2]	109
AIM Charter	G&I	A	3.4	15.1	16.3	20,503	1.9	22.1	5.0	1,204.8	5.5	122
AIM Constellation	Max	A	18.0	23.1	23.9	27,897	0.0	29.0	4.0	890.0	5.5	125
AIM Growth	Gro	D	3.9	9.8	12.7	17,531	0.9	26.8	0.9	162.4	5.5	116
AIM Summit[7]	Gro	A	7.1	15.0	17.7	21,202	1.2	24.5	1.0	529.2	8.5	42
AIM Utilities	Sec	—	9.8	9.4	—	—	4.7	21.3	5.7	105.0	5.5	117
AIM Value	G&I	A	17.8	19.3	21.2	25,069	0.7	25.9	10.3	187.5	5.5	117
AIM Weingarten	Gro	A	2.5	15.7	18.0	21,911	0.4	26.6	4.0	4,977.3	5.5	116
Alger Small Capitalization Portfolio	SCG	A	6.1	18.9	26.0	31,867	0.0	36.2	13.2	166.2	None[2]	136
Alliance Balanced Shares A	Bal	E	9.0	8.4	10.5	15,844	3.3	25.5	4.2	144.7	5.5	129
Alliance Counterpoint	G&I	B	8.6	10.6	16.3	20,341	0.8	22.4	1.1	71.5	5.5	139
Alliance Fund A	Gro	C	18.0	14.1	15.9	19,992	0.8	21.8	4.1	734.6	5.5	99
Alliance Global Small Cap A	Glo	B	(2.3)	(3.9)	6.8	13,268	0.0	N.A.	0.3	58.5	5.5	171
Alliance Growth & Income A	G&I	C	6.6	9.7	13.4	18,089	2.3	24.3	3.1	417.1	5.5	130
Alliance International A	Intl	C	(2.7)	(6.7)	7.2	13,210	0.5	N.A.	4.7	153.7	5.5	148

MONEY's grades compare domestic equity, international equity and gold and sector funds by five-year, risk-adjusted return to Dec. 1. **Value of $10,000** is to Dec. 24. [1]Closed to new investors [2]May impose back-end load or exit fee [3]Three years [4]Performance from Dec. 31, 1987 [5]Reflects borrowing to boost investments [6]Manager absorbing expenses [7]Investment by contractual plan only N.A.: Not available

ABBREVIATIONS: AA Asset allocation; **Bal** Balanced; **Conv** Convertibles; **Eql** Equity income; **Flx** Flexible; **G&I** Growth & Income; **Glo** Global; **Gold** Gold/precious metals; **Gro** Growth; **HGC** High-grade corporates; **HGT** High-grade tax-exempts; **HYC** High-yield corporates; **HYT** High-yield tax-exempts; **Intl** International; **ITT** Short/intermediate tax-exempts; **Max** Maximum capital gains; **MBS** Mortgage-backed securities; **OpInc** Option income; **SCG** Small-company growth; **Sec** Sectors; **STT** Short/intermdiate-term taxables; **USG** U.S. Government bonds; **WI** World income

FUND NAME	Type	MONEY risk-adjusted grade	% compound annual gain (or loss) to Dec. 24, 1992			Value of $10,000 invested five years ago (net of sales charge)	Portfolio analysis			Net assets (millions)	Expense analysis	
			One year	Three years	Five years		% yield	P/E ratio	% cash		% maximum initial sales charge	Five-year projection
Alliance Multi-Market Income & Growth	Glo	—	3.0	—	—	—	4.6	1.2	22.0	$154.7	1.0	$120
Alliance New Europe A	Intl	—	2.6	—	—	—	1.7	N.A.	1.4	91.1	5.5	133
Alliance Quasar A	SCG	E	6.0	1.3	11.1	$16,102	0.0	20.0	1.6	252.5	5.5	139
Alliance Technology	Sec	D	16.1	19.5	12.0	16,921	0.0	24.4	11.6	152.5	5.5	143
AMCAP Fund	Gro	C	10.5	12.4	14.1	18,327	2.0	24.6	12.0	2,726.4	5.75	97
American Balanced	Bal	C	11.1	10.5	12.7	17,316	5.0	25.5	5.7	948.0	5.75	100
American Capital Comstock A	G&I	B	9.7	11.3	14.8	19,207	2.1	25.2	2.3	921.0	5.75	109
American Capital Emerging Growth A	SCG	B	13.0	21.1	18.2	22,012	0.1	32.5	8.9	324.0	5.75	112
American Capital Enterprise A	Gro	B	11.1	13.5	15.9	20,017	1.2	29.9	9.4	686.9	5.75	108
American Capital Equity Income A	Eql	C	13.1	10.5	12.5	17,272	4.2	23.0	9.3	114.0	5.75	111
American Capital Growth & Income	G&I	D	12.2	10.9	12.2	17,078	2.8	24.4	4.4	173.2	5.75	117
American Capital Harbor A	Conv	B	11.3	10.1	13.0	17,365	6.0	N.A.	3.4	382.1	5.75	110
American Capital Pace A	Gro	D	7.6	9.3	12.8	17,565	1.7	24.7	12.9	2,341.5	5.75	110
American Gas Index	Sec	—	13.6	1.2	—	—	4.0	23.4	0.5	175.4	None	48
American Growth	Gro	E	15.8	9.0	11.5	15,844	0.7	18.6	3.8	53.7	8.5	158
American Investors Growth	Gro	E	(10.1)	(2.7)	7.2	13,803	0.0	33.2	0.5	46.1	4.5	126
American Leaders	G&I	D	14.2	12.9	12.1	17,095	1.4	20.4	5.0	177.4	4.5[2]	99
American Mutual	G&I	C	10.6	9.3	12.5	17,244	4.1	31.5	4.9	4,597.1	5.75	91
American National Growth	Gro	E	1.1	9.8	11.0	15,916	1.2	20.0	6.3	115.9	6.25	138
American National Income	Eql	B	6.6	10.8	13.8	17,587	2.6	17.1	6.6	108.4	6.25	147
Analytic Optioned Equity	OpInc	D	8.1	7.2	10.5	16,635	2.4	18.6	8.2	91.0	None	61
Babson Enterprise	SCG	A	26.7	14.2	19.1	23,939	0.5	24.0	6.9	165.4	None	64
Babson Growth	Gro	E	13.2	8.1	11.8	17,467	1.6	19.8	4.3	236.3	None	48
Babson Shadow Stock	SCG	E	20.6	9.7	12.1	17,702	0.8	17.6	0.0	25.7	None	69
Babson Value	G&I	D	17.7	9.8	12.7	18,457	3.2	19.9	3.7	33.9	None	56
Baird Blue Chip	G&I	C	6.4	12.2	13.4	18,001	1.1	21.8	8.6	61.6	5.75	135
Baird Capital Development	Gro	B	16.9	15.5	16.8	20,818	0.5	20.0	16.5	37.9	5.75	143
Baron Asset	SCG	C	17.3	7.5	15.5	20,627	0.2	27.9	15.0	43.8	None	92
Bartlett Basic Value	G&I	E	12.8	8.0	11.7	17,612	2.4	25.3	5.0	92.6	None	66
Bartlett Cap—Value International	Intl	—	0.1	0.5	—	—	1.3	N.A.	5.0	26.9	None	108
Benham Equity—Growth	Gro	—	7.1	—	—	—	2.2	N.A.	0.0	58.4	None	40
Benham Equity—Income & Growth	G&I	—	10.8	—	—	—	3.6	N.A.	0.0	107.7	None	40
Benham Gold Equity Index	Gold	—	(3.0)	(13.4)	—	—	0.3	N.A.	1.0	163.3	None	40
Berger One Hundred	Gro	A	10.7	24.6	23.1	28,550	0.0	34.1	18.0	384.1	None	107
Berger One Hundred & One	G&I	C	6.0	15.7	13.9	19,358	1.3	22.2	22.0	32.9	None	145
Berwyn Fund	G&I	D	19.9	9.1	12.4	18,153	0.7	25.2	3.4	29.9	None	76
Blanchard Global Growth	AA	E	2.1	1.4	5.5	12,912	3.2	N.A.	5.0	104.1	$75	149
Boston Co. Asset Allocation	AA	—	11.8	11.9	—	—	2.1	18.7	24.2	28.6	None	79
Boston Co. Asset Manager Equity	G&I	—	8.8	—	—	—	2.9	N.A.	28.0	52.9	None	116
Boston Co. Capital Appreciation	Gro	E	7.2	3.6	10.1	16,452	1.8	25.3	3.7	434.8	None	66
Boston Co. Special Growth	Gro	C	29.3	15.2	16.5	21,841	1.1	30.4	9.9	48.8	None	92
Brandywine Fund	Gro	A	17.5	19.9	21.5	26,539	0.2	28.7	6.0	695.1	None	60
Bull & Bear Special Equities	Max	E	29.8	5.0	14.0	19,556	0.0	22.0	0.0	45.5	None	149
Burnham Fund	G&I	D	9.6	7.8	11.0	16,230	5.5	23.4	13.2	115.0	5.0	110
Calvert Ariel Growth [1]	SCG	B	17.4	7.6	16.9	20,537	4.1	20.2	2.0	236.2	4.75	113
Calvert Ariel Appreciation	SCG	—	15.5	13.6	—	—	1.2	23.7	12.0	146.2	4.75	125
Calvert Social Investment Fund—Equity	Gro	D	12.9	8.1	12.5	17,444	0.8	20.7	5.0	64.5	4.75	102
Calvert Social Invest. Managed Growth	Bal	D	9.8	9.0	10.9	16,104	3.6	N.A.	6.0	418.7	4.75	116
Capital Income Builder	Eql	A	12.1	12.9	14.2	18,218	4.7	22.5	6.5	1,132.4	5.75	109
Capstone U.S. Trend	Gro	C	4.5	10.2	13.8	18,519	1.4	28.7	10.0	97.3	4.75	116
Cardinal Fund	G&I	C	13.3	11.2	14.0	18,093	2.7	19.0	12.5	262.0	8.5	120
Century Shares Trust	Sec	B	30.4	15.9	20.0	25,132	1.6	14.1	16.5	204.8	None	53

MONEY's grades compare domestic equity, international equity and gold and sector funds by five-year, risk-adjusted return to Dec. 1. Value of $10,000 is to Dec. 24. [1]Closed to new investors [2]May impose back-end load or exit fee [3]Three years [4]Performance from Dec. 31, 1987 [5]Reflects borrowing to boost investments [6]Manager absorbing expenses [7]Investment by contractual plan only N.A.: Not available

FUND NAME	Type	MONEY risk-adjusted grade	% compound annual gain (or loss) to Dec. 24, 1992			Value of $10,000 invested five years ago (net of sales charge)	Portfolio analysis			Net assets (millions)	Expense analysis	
			One year	Three years	Five years		% yield	P/E ratio	% cash		% maximum initial sales charge	Five-year projection
CGM Capital Development [1]	Gro	A	17.8	33.3	21.6	$26,589	0.2	20.3	0.2	$324.1	None	$49
CGM Mutual	Bal	D	7.4	14.9	13.6	18,874	3.6	22.9	1.0	502.9	None	51
Clipper Fund	Gro	C	19.9	12.8	15.5	20,675	2.3	13.4	8.4	182.8	None	63
Colonial Fund A	G&I	C	17.6	10.5	13.7	18,023	2.3	21.8	8.5	406.1	5.75	113
Colonial Growth Shares A	Gro	B	14.0	10.0	16.1	20,166	1.1	19.2	0.1	146.7	5.75	119
Colonial U.S. Equity Index	G&I	C	10.2	9.8	13.8	18,403	1.6	25.9	1.3	50.7	4.75	138
Colonial Utilities A	Sec	B	23.5	13.8	14.3	18,577	5.7	17.0	0.1	200.8	4.75	106
Columbia Growth	Gro	B	15.5	13.4	15.3	20,614	1.4	27.8	3.4	443.0	None	50
Columbia Special	Max	A	18.3	14.2	22.3	27,488	0.0	26.1	4.3	315.2	None	67
Common Sense Growth	Gro	C	10.6	12.9	15.0	18,679	1.0	29.5	3.0	1,593.4	8.5	148
Common Sense—Growth & Income	G&I	C	10.6	11.4	13.6	17,672	1.8	26.0	2.1	576.6	8.5	142
Compass Capital—Equity Income	Eql	—	15.3	11.4	—	—	3.5	N.A.	6.9	153.5	3.75	89
Compass Capital—Growth	Gro	—	25.5	9.9	—	—	2.1	N.A.	7.0	119.1	3.75	91
Composite Bond & Stock	Bal	D	11.8	10.2	11.5	16,487	4.6	19.2	5.9	99.5	4.5	104
Composite Growth	G&I	D	13.8	9.8	11.8	16,807	2.7	18.0	4.7	81.2	4.5	103
Composite Northwest 50	Gro	A	5.1	13.6	19.0	23,389	0.4	20.6	0.7	158.9	4.5	109
Connecticut Mutual—Growth	Gro	B	14.7	12.3	16.0	20,457	1.5	15.7	10.0	41.7	5.0	112
Connecticut Mutual—Total Return	Bal	B	12.1	12.1	13.3	17,988	3.4	15.9	7.0	100.4	5.0	113
Convertible Securities & Income	Conv	B	10.7	10.9	15.3	20,377	5.5	N.A.	2.0	26.3	4.5[2]	100
Copley Fund	G&I	E	19.3	11.2	13.7	19,298	0.0	15.0	9.0	33.0	None	76
Cowen Income & Growth	Eql	D	15.2	9.5	13.4	18,063	3.8	20.7	0.6	32.3	4.85	117
Dean Witter American Value	Gro	B	5.6	16.8	16.6	21,901	0.2	30.3	4.3	381.9	None[2]	106
Dean Witter Capital Growth	Gro	—	2.9	—	—	—	0.0	22.3	0.5	951.0	None[2]	119
Dean Witter Convertible Securities	Conv	E	12.7	6.7	7.6	14,423	2.5	N.A.	8.80	217.8	None[2]	124
Dean Witter Developing Growth Securities	SCG	E	(1.6)	10.6	10.9	16,713	0.0	35.6	3.1	112.8	None[2]	123
Dean Witter Dividend Growth	G&I	C	8.9	9.1	14.5	20,133	2.7	25.8	2.70	4,667.3	None[2]	98
Dean Witter Equity Income	Eql	D	12.7	11.2	13.4	18,609	1.4	19.0	0.0	158.1	None[2]	133
Dean Witter European Growth	Intl	—	2.2	—	—	—	0.3	N.A.	0.0	315.6	None[2]	150
Dean Witter Managed Assets	AA	—	16.4	12.4	—	—	2.7	28.4	30.0	228.8	None[2]	113
Dean Witter Natural Resource Development	Sec	D	9.5	1.2	8.8	15,527	1.9	31.4	0.0	118.6	None[2]	124
Dean Witter Pacific Growth	Intl	—	5.3	—	—	—	0.1	N.A.	9.0	162.0	None[2]	150
Dean Witter Strategist	AA	—	15.7	15.8	—	—	1.6	25.5	1.4	474.7	None[2]	109
Dean Witter Utilities	Sec	—	11.7	9.6	—	—	5.0	18.3	4.9	2,689.8	None[2]	106
Dean Witter Value Added—Equity	G&I	D	17.1	10.0	13.4	19,023	0.9	21.2	1.2	202.5	None[2]	115
Dean Witter World Wide Investment	Glo	D	(3.1)	(0.4)	5.6	13,155	0.2	N.A.	0.8	233.9	None[2]	142
Delaware Fund	Bal	A	14.8	10.8	14.9	19,344	3.6	17.8	8.0	474.3	5.75	104
Delaware Group—Decatur I	Eql	E	11.3	5.2	10.6	15,523	4.7	28.3	2.0	1,517.8	8.5	121
Delaware Group—Decatur II	Eql	C	11.0	6.4	13.5	17,873	3.7	26.8	2.0	405.1	5.75	112
Delaware Group—Delcap	Max	B	3.9	11.4	16.4	20,318	0.1	21.4	10.0	989.8	5.75	129
Delaware Group—Trend	Max	A	24.8	16.2	24.1	27,806	0.0	29.1	9.0	130.3	5.75	119
Delaware Group—Value	Max	A	17.8	14.3	19.4	23,200	0.0	19.7	30.0	32.7	5.75	163
Dreyfus Appreciation	Max	B	8.8	13.6	16.0	21,373	1.3	N.A.	(1.6)[5]	160.4	None	71
Dreyfus Capital Growth	Max	E	8.5	11.7	11.2	16,476	2.1	21.4	4.5	516.9	3.0	91
Dreyfus Capital Value	Max	E	(10.3)	(2.2)	4.8	12,150	5.0	37.0	(1.7)[5]	538.2	4.5	132
Dreyfus Convertible Securities	Conv	E	4.7	4.8	10.2	16,252	3.2	N.A.	0.4	217.0	None	59
Dreyfus Fund	G&I	D	8.1	9.6	11.7	17,630	2.5	22.8	(5.6)[5]	2,987.4	None	43
Dreyfus Growth Opportunity	Gro	D	(1.8)	10.3	12.6	18,055	0.6	29.2	(2.1)[5]	580.6	None	53
Dreyfus New Leaders	SCG	A	11.0	11.5	17.1	22,026	0.7	27.2	(1.1)[5]	188.8	None	74
Dreyfus Peoples Index	G&I	—	11.3	—	—	—	2.4	25.7	0.9	89.1	None[2]	99
Dreyfus Peoples S&P Midcap Index	SCG	—	13.8	—	—	—	0.5	N.A.	0.1	45.1	None[2]	108[3]
Dreyfus Strategic Growth	Max	E	(13.5)	1.7	4.8	12,119	0.0	27.8	(3.2)[5]	49.8	3.0	113
Dreyfus Strategic Investing	Max	E	(2.6)	10.4	10.7	15,935	0.7	28.7	(9.2)[5]	239.1	4.5	144

MONEY's grades compare domestic equity, international equity and gold and sector funds by five-year, risk-adjusted return to Dec. 1. Value of $10,000 is to Dec. 24. [1]Closed to new investors [2]May impose back-end load or exit fee [3]Three years [4]Performance from Dec. 31, 1987 [5]Reflects borrowing to boost investments [6]Manager absorbing expenses [7]Investment by contractual plan only N.A.: Not available

FUND NAME	Type	MONEY risk-adjusted grade	% compound annual gain (or loss) to Dec. 24, 1992			Value of $10,000 invested five years ago (net of sales charge)	Portfolio analysis			Net assets (millions)	Expense analysis	
			One year	Three years	Five years		% yield	P/E ratio	% cash		% maximum initial sales charge	Five-year projection
Dreyfus Strategic World Investing	Glo	A	(2.7)	6.6	10.6	$16,347	0.0	N.A.	(1.2)5	$105.5	3.0	$115
Dreyfus Third Century	Gro	B	3.4	13.2	15.7	20,823	1.0	27.2	(2.1)5	463.1	None	60
Eaton Vance Equity Income	Eql	E	3.4	2.7	7.2	14,377	4.1	17.1	20.1	48.2	None2	141
Eaton Vance Growth	Gro	C	9.3	12.2	14.4	18,809	0.0	23.4	2.5	142.8	4.75	96
Eaton Vance Investors	Bal	D	8.6	9.7	11.6	16,694	4.8	18.8	4.8	212.8	4.75	93
Eaton Vance Special Equities	Gro	B	4.6	18.0	17.2	21,198	0.0	25.0	9.1	70.0	4.75	97
Eaton Vance Stock	G&I	C	11.2	9.9	13.7	18,572	2.2	21.4	0.3	89.8	4.75	97
Eaton Vance Total Return Trust	Sec	C	9.4	10.4	14.5	18,978	5.4	17.4	0.0	562.8	4.75	126
Eclipse Equity	SCG	E	21.1	10.2	11.7	17,385	0.7	18.4	3.9	142.5	None	65
Enterprise Capital Appreciation	Max	A	9.8	20.8	19.4	23,552	0.0	29.1	15.0	59.2	4.75	138
Enterprise Growth & Income	G&I	E	10.7	7.2	10.0	15,492	2.8	25.9	10.0	37.7	4.75	125
Enterprise Growth Portfolio	Gro	B	10.4	14.1	15.2	19,307	0.8	22.3	3.0	77.3	4.75	130
Equitable Balanced B	Bal	B	(1.4)	10.9	13.6	19,250	1.8	25.3	26.4	33.3	None2	125
Equitable Growth B	Gro	A	14.6	18.3	20.2	25,295	1.1	23.5	1.9	39.6	None2	125
EuroPacific Growth	Intl	A	4.6	6.6	13.0	17,166	1.7	N.A.	18.7	2,424.1	5.75	122
Evergreen Foundation	Bal	—	23.1	—	—	—	1.2	20.5	13.9	40.3	None	103
Evergreen Fund	SCG	D	10.9	10.2	13.2	18,713	1.2	19.5	12.1	713.5	None	63
Evergreen Limited Market	SCG	B	11.3	13.7	17.1	22,038	0.6	17.9	10.7	59.6	None	69
Evergreen Total Return	Eql	E	12.5	8.5	11.2	17,142	5.5	20.7	0.4	1,061.1	None	66
Evergreen Value Timing	Max	B	16.2	10.6	15.7	20,986	1.3	23.2	8.1	55.3	None	77
FAM Value	G&I	A	26.3	19.9	22.8	27,546	0.4	N.A.	4.0	25.8	None	85
FBL Series—Growth Common Stock	G&I	C	12.6	9.9	10.8	16,748	4.6	23.1	7.8	40.7	None2	112
Federated Growth Trust	Gro	A	8.5	10.8	17.4	22,471	1.5	18.9	4.0	394.0	None	56
Federated Index—Max-Cap	G&I	—	11.2	—	—	—	2.8	N.A.	0.0	287.5	None	17
Federated Stock & Bond	Bal	E	9.1	8.5	9.2	15,652	4.1	25.3	8.0	99.0	None	56
Federated Stock Trust	G&I	E	14.4	11.2	11.4	17,384	2.2	20.3	5.0	390.2	None	55
Fidelity Advisor Equity—Growth	Gro	A	13.4	25.1	26.0	32,093	0.1	28.7	13.0	151.9	4.75	139
Fidelity Advisor Equity—Income	Eql	D	17.0	9.5	12.8	18,538	3.7	24.8	7.3	133.0	4.75	124
Fidelity Advisor—Growth Opportunities	Gro	A	17.6	17.6	21.2	25,224	0.4	25.1	13.4	546.2	4.75	137
Fidelity Advisor—Income & Growth	Bal	A	11.2	12.7	16.4	20,419	3.2	25.2	21.5	363.6	4.75	136
Fidelity Asset Manager	AA	—	13.5	13.8	—	—	3.3	26.7	8.2	2,757.1	None	213
Fidelity Balanced	Bal	A	9.5	10.9	13.4	18,864	4.7	25.4	15.8	1,540.2	None	53
Fidelity Blue Chip Growth	Gro	—	9.9	20.0	—	—	0.4	27.9	7.5	490.7	3.0	97
Fidelity Capital Appreciation	Max	D	19.0	2.6	13.3	18,175	4.5	25.4	10.5	1,028.5	3.0	75
Fidelity Contrafund	Gro	A	19.6	23.3	26.0	31,062	0.4	24.8	13.2	1,414.2	3.0	78
Fidelity Convertible Securities	Conv	A	24.1	17.9	19.0	23,864	4.1	N.A.	12.6	332.5	None	64
Fidelity Destiny I 7	Gro	A	18.4	16.1	17.8	21,135	1.9	23.1	8.1	2,406.7	8.98	34
Fidelity Destiny II 7	Gro	A	18.1	17.0	19.3	22,382	1.4	24.9	6.0	505.2	8.98	49
Fidelity Disciplined Equity	Gro	—	16.0	15.4	—	—	1.3	N.A.	14.7	314.3	None2	65
Fidelity Emerging Growth	SCG	—	11.3	—	—	—	0.0	N.A.	14.2	505.4	3.0	100
Fidelity Equity-Income	Eql	D	16.6	8.5	12.7	18,056	3.9	24.9	11.9	4,650.8	2.0	57
Fidelity Equity-Income II	Eql	—	21.6	—	—	—	1.9	N.A.	15.5	1,602.1	None	83
Fidelity Europe	Intl	C	(0.5)	(0.7)	6.9	13,248	3.4	N.A.	9.0	456.3	3.0	100
Fidelity Fund	G&I	C	11.3	8.7	13.5	19,284	2.3	27.1	15.1	1,313.3	None	38
Fidelity Growth & Income	G&I	A	13.7	13.9	18.0	22,856	1.8	23.1	20.0	4,290.8	2.0	67
Fidelity Growth Company	Gro	A	10.6	18.5	21.7	26,115	0.4	28.9	16.1	1,448.8	3.0	87
Fidelity International Growth & Income	Intl	C	(1.0)	0.8	6.6	13,292	1.3	N.A.	5.6	64.3	2.0	120
Fidelity Low-Priced Stock	SCG	—	32.9	23.4	—	—	0.7	N.A.	34.2	1,042.9	None2	66
Fidelity Magellan	Gro	A	10.2	13.3	18.5	22,994	1.4	26.9	11.0	21,046.6	3.0	86
Fidelity Market Index	G&I	—	11.4	—	—	—	2.6	25.9	5.4	250.8	None2	75
Fidelity OTC	SCG	A	17.5	17.5	20.7	24,870	0.5	21.4	15.0	1,010.5	3.0	92
Fidelity Overseas	Intl	E	(9.2)	(3.2)	3.1	11,096	2.0	N.A.	2.2	881.5	3.0	111

MONEY's grades compare domestic equity, international equity and gold and sector funds by five-year, risk-adjusted return to Dec. 1. Value of $10,000 is to Dec. 24.
[1]Closed to new investors [2]May impose back-end load or exit fee [3]Three years [4]Performance from Dec. 31, 1987 [5]Reflects borrowing to boost investments [6]Manager absorbing expenses [7]Investment by contractual plan only N.A.: Not available

FUND NAME	Type	MONEY risk-adjusted grade	% compound annual gain (or loss) to Dec. 24, 1992 — One year	Three years	Five years	Value of $10,000 invested five years ago (net of sales charge)	Portfolio analysis — % yield	P/E ratio	% cash	Net assets (millions)	Expense analysis — % maximum initial sales charge	Five-year projection
Fidelity Pacific Basin	Intl	E	(5.5)	(9.0)	(1.2)	$9,012	0.0	N.A.	2.3	$122.8	3.0	$114
Fidelity Puritan	Eql	C	17.5	10.4	13.5	18,658	5.0	27.6	2.0	5,618.1	2.0	56
Fidelity Real Estate	Sec	C	21.7	14.3	13.1	18,677	3.4	N.A.	11.1	95.3	None	68
Fidelity Retirement Growth[8]	Max	B	13.3	12.9	16.1	21,463	1.0	24.9	1.9	1,992.4	None	46
Fidelity Select—American Gold	Gold	E	1.3	(9.3)	(4.5)	7,681	0.0	N.A.	2.6	171.3	3.0[2]	130
Fidelity Select—Automotive	Sec	B	45.7	21.6	17.0	21,691	0.1	19.5	8.6	72.1	3.0[2]	166
Fidelity Select—Biotechnology	Sec	A	(6.6)	37.0	30.1	36,640	0.0	38.9	24.9	719.6	3.0[2]	117
Fidelity Select—Chemicals	Sec	B	12.1	13.0	15.0	19,658	0.3	30.6	11.8	34.6	3.0[2]	150
Fidelity Select—Computers	Sec	D	23.0	23.7	13.2	18,314	0.0	32.1	2.4	28.0	3.0[2]	150
Fidelity Select—Electric Utilities	Sec	B	11.7	11.3	16.0	20,428	2.2	18.7	2.6	34.9	3.0[2]	134
Fidelity Select—Electronics	Sec	D	30.7	22.4	13.0	18,469	0.0	25.0	11.8	87.9	3.0[2]	150
Fidelity Select—Energy	Sec	D	(0.8)	(2.3)	8.9	14,866	1.3	31.1	6.7	79.8	3.0[2]	131
Fidelity Select—Energy Services	Sec	D	4.2	(7.5)	4.3	12,161	0.0	40.2	6.4	80.9	3.0[2]	146
Fidelity Select—Environment	Sec	—	(0.2)	0.7	—	—	0.0	24.9	9.6	56.7	3.0[2]	144
Fidelity Select—Financial Services	Sec	C	44.3	20.2	17.7	22,302	0.9	20.5	8.8	95.4	3.0[2]	135
Fidelity Select—Food & Agriculture	Sec	A	10.1	16.4	22.1	26,697	0.4	20.6	7.2	111.1	3.0[2]	134
Fidelity Select—Health Care	Sec	A	(14.1)	23.6	23.3	27,992	0.0	28.2	4.1	781.8	3.0[2]	114
Fidelity Select—Leisure	Sec	C	19.6	6.2	14.7	18,983	0.0	25.4	6.2	36.7	3.0[2]	152
Fidelity Select—Medical Delivery	Sec	A	(11.2)	21.6	26.5	30,986	0.0	24.2	3.2	113.3	3.0[2]	127
Fidelity Select—Precious Metals	Gold	E	(20.6)	(14.7)	(8.7)	6,056	1.4	N.A.	7.5	124.0	3.0[2]	133
Fidelity Select—Regional Banks	Sec	A	49.3	24.8	25.1	29.770	0.9	23.7	5.2	142.3	3.0[2]	131
Fidelity Select—Retailing	Sec	A	26.8	24.7	28.3	33,341	0.0	26.9	28.0	48.4	3.0[2]	136
Fidelity Select—Savings & Loan	Sec	B	61.1	29.9	22.1	27,021	0.7	12.2	13.2	91.4	3.0[2]	146
Fidelity Select—Software	Sec	B	37.5	25.7	18.6	23,043	0.0	22.7	20.9	70.1	3.0[2]	128
Fidelity Select—Technology	Sec	C	11.5	24.2	16.2	20,771	0.0	29.2	20.7	104.5	3.0[2]	128
Fidelity Select—Telecommunications	Sec	B	18.6	8.6	19.2	23,670	1.1	24.7	6.2	87.8	3.0[2]	137
Fidelity Select—Utilities	Sec	A	12.5	10.9	16.9	21,269	3.4	17.4	3.1	258.8	3.0[2]	117
Fidelity Special Situations—Advisor[1]	Max	B	15.0	9.1	15.7	19,870	3.0	25.4	1.8	194.7	4.75	100
Fidelity Stock Selector	Gro	—	18.1	—	—	—	0.5	N.A.	20.7	250.0	3.0	78
Fidelity Trend	Gro	B	19.5	11.6	17.2	22,418	0.9	25.4	5.3	949.1	None	30
Fidelity Utilities Income	Sec	B	12.7	11.5	14.7	19,866	4.3	19.5	11.3	881.1	None	53
Fidelity Value	Max	B	24.0	10.1	15.8	20,973	2.4	N.A.	19.3	316.8	None	54
Fidelity Worldwide	Glo	—	8.1	—	—	—	1.0	N.A.	17.5	106.7	None	92
Fiduciary Capital Growth	SCG	D	17.6	11.3	13.6	19,116	0.5	18.6	23.8	38.5	None	81
Financial Dynamics	Max	B	16.0	20.7	18.0	23,172	0.0	30.9	14.1	145.5	None	65
Financial Industrial	G&I	C	4.9	13.2	14.3	19,878	0.8	20.2	15.5	411.0	None	57
Financial Industrial Income	Eql	A	3.0	14.5	17.3	22,541	2.6	20.9	3.1	2,310.1	None	54
Financial Strategic—European	Intl	C	(4.9)	0.6	7.1	13,915	1.9	N.A.	2.7	125.7	None	80
Financial Strategic—Financial Services	Sec	A	27.5	26.6	26.2	32,149	1.2	14.8	10.8	183.3	None	64
Financial Strategic—Gold	Gold	E	(6.6)	(13.4)	(8.8)	6,234	0.0	N.A.	5.8	45.6	None	83
Financial Strategic—Health Sciences	Sec	A	(12.2)	27.4	30.0	37,455	0.3	30.2	13.3	739.8	None	58
Financial Strategic—Leisure	Sec	A	26.4	18.7	24.0	29,303	0.0	27.0	20.1	39.8	None	106
Financial Strategic—Pacific Basin	Sec	D	(11.3)	(9.7)	1.9	10,944	0.5	N.A.	11.2	27.9	None	70
Financial Strategic—Technology	Sec	A	19.8	31.0	24.8	30,684	0.0	30.4	2.9	151.4	None	67
Financial Strategic—Utilities Portfolio	Sec	C	12.3	8.7	13.7	19,130	2.3	14.4	1.6	106.0	None	68
Financial Trust—Equity	G&I	—	9.0	—	—	—	2.1	N.A.	2.6	69.0	None	54
Financial Trust—Flex	AA	—	12.3	—	—	—	3.9	N.A.	64.0	121.0	None	51
Financial Trust—International Growth	Intl	—	(8.5)	—	—	—	1.4	N.A.	8.5	36.2	None	81
First Eagle Fund of America	Max	D	27.4	7.2	13.9	19,024	0.6	24.9	19.6	74.1	None[2]	113
First Investors Blue Chip	G&I	—	9.9	10.1	—	—	0.6	N.A.	3.7	91.8	6.9	147
First Investors Global	Glo	B	(1.1)	(0.4)	9.4	14,664	0.0	N.A.	2.4	193.7	6.9	167
First Investors Total Return	AA	—	0.8	—	—	—	2.3	N.A.	5.0	64.8	6.9	152

MONEY's grades compare domestic equity, international equity and gold and sector funds by five-year, risk-adjusted return to Dec. 1. **Value of $10,000** is to Dec. 24. [1]Closed to new investors [2]May impose back-end load or exit fee [3]Three years [4]Performance from Dec. 31, 1987 [5]Reflects borrowing to boost investments [6]Manager absorbing expenses [7]Investment by contractual plan only [8]Open to retirement plans only N.A.: Not available

| FUND NAME | Type | MONEY risk-adjusted grade | % compound annual gain (or loss) to Dec. 24, 1992 | | | Value of $10,000 invested five years ago (net of sales charge) | Portfolio analysis | | | Net assets (millions) | Expense analysis | |
			One year	Three years	Five years		% yield	P/E ratio	% cash		% maximum initial sales charge	Five-year projection
Flag Investors Emerging Growth	SCG	—	(7.2)	2.0	—	—	0.0	35.3	27.6	$40.2	4.5	$126
Flag Investors Quality Growth	Gro	—	8.8	12.2	—	—	0.8	23.7	9.2	70.9	4.5	113
Flag Investors Telephone Income	Eql	B	15.2	9.1	17.8	$21,959	3.9	23.1	2.0	285.0	4.5	95
Flexfunds—Growth Portfolio	Gro	E	8.4	10.3	6.8	13,861	1.1	26.7	23.0	25.0	None	78
Flexfunds—Muirfield	Gro	—	10.0	12.4	—	—	1.0	N.A.	21.0	57.3	None	82
Fortis Advantage—Asset Allocation	AA	—	7.3	10.7	—	—	5.9	22.8	1.9	89.6	4.5	140
Fortis Advantage—Capital Appreciation	SCG	—	7.4	14.2	—	—	0.0	40.2	(1.9)[5]	39.7	4.5	139
Fortis Capital	G&I	C	8.4	12.8	15.1	19,659	0.5	28.4	0.1	232.4	4.75	114
Fortis Fiduciary	Gro	B	8.5	12.8	16.2	20,310	0.4	29.5	0.2	45.1	4.75	126
Fortis Growth	Max	B	3.2	16.5	19.0	22,778	0.1	36.1	1.6	481.4	4.75	110
Fortress Utility	Sec	B	9.9	11.6	15.0	19,622	5.6	17.3	0.5	362.5	1.0[2]	71
Founders Blue Chip	G&I	C	2.9	9.3	13.5	19,271	1.0	25.3	18.0	276.5	None	61
Founders Discovery	SCG	—	17.1	27.3	—	—	0.0	26.8	25.0	62.0	None	97
Founders Equity Income	Eql	E	7.7	7.5	11.4	17,152	3.5	24.4	15.0	29.0	None	95
Founders Frontier	SCG	A	10.5	14.1	22.3	27,129	0.0	23.7	13.0	104.0	None	92
Founders Growth	Gro	D	6.6	11.2	14.9	20,166	0.6	28.0	18.0	119.2	None	80
Founders Special	Max	A	11.0	16.4	19.7	24,535	0.5	25.5	20.0	274.8	None	64
Founders Worldwide Growth	Glo	—	3.4	12.9	—	—	0.2	N.A.	20.0	34.0	None	104
FPA Capital	Gro	B	27.9	19.7	19.7	23,608	0.4	28.9	3.4	101.2	6.5	121
FPA Paramount[1]	G&I	A	11.1	11.8	15.2	19,136	2.6	27.5	43.6	280.0	6.5	113
FPA Perennial	G&I	A	15.3	11.7	15.7	19,642	2.4	19.1	20.0	67.2	6.5	122
Franklin DynaTech Series	Sec	C	6.3	13.6	14.5	19,276	1.2	30.1	40.3	64.6	4.0	89
Franklin Equity	Gro	E	6.8	6.2	11.6	16,819	1.9	15.8	6.4	352.6	4.0	77
Franklin Gold	Gold	E	(18.0)	(12.3)	(3.0)	8,177	4.1	N.A.	13.4	235.2	4.0	80
Franklin Growth Series	Gro	D	5.3	10.1	12.0	17,189	2.5	23.8	29.8	532.9	4.0	77
Franklin Income Series	Flx	D	16.2	14.2	12.7	17,373	9.1	N.A.	0.0	2,483.5	4.0	70
Franklin Managed Rising Dividend	G&I	A	12.6	14.9	16.3	20,457	1.9	16.2	20.0	137.5	4.0	120
Franklin Utilities Series	Sec	C	10.9	11.3	14.0	18,510	5.9	14.4	10.0	2,191.1	4.0	72
FT International Equity	Intl	D	(3.7)	(3.7)	4.2	11,692	0.6	N.A.	17.2	107.8	4.5	124
Fundamental Investors	G&I	C	12.9	10.8	14.5	18,921	2.3	26.3	8.2	1,319.2	5.75	94
FundTrust—Aggressive Growth	Max	D	12.0	10.7	12.7	17,968	1.7	N.A.	1.8	29.0	1.5	114
FundTrust—Growth & Income	G&I	E	12.9	7.6	11.6	17,270	2.3	N.A.	1.1	36.5	1.5	114
Gabelli Asset	Gro	A	17.8	8.5	16.1	21,177	1.9	21.6	9.0	581.9	None	70
Gabelli Convertible Securities	Conv	—	13.0	10.4	—	—	5.8	N.A.	23.0	89.2	4.5	129
Gabelli Equity—Small-Cap Growth	SCG	—	20.1	—	—	—	0.1	N.A.	11.0	95.0	4.5	106
Gabelli Growth	Gro	A	8.3	11.6	21.5	26,718	0.7	27.5	12.0	545.2	None	74
Gabelli Value	Max	—	17.3	7.4	—	—	1.8	21.0	1.0	438.0	5.5	133
GAM Global	Glo	C	(4.0)	(2.1)	7.7	13,773	2.8	N.A.	5.0	30.0	5.0	100
GAM International	Intl	B	4.1	3.5	9.6	14,981	3.0	N.A.	3.7	44.7	5.0	90
GAM Pacific Basin	Intl	A	2.1	2.0	13.5	17,814	0.7	N.A.	15.0	29.5	5.0	100
Gateway Index Plus	G&I	A	5.5	11.3	14.2	19,571	1.9	30.8	4.4	189.4	None	64
General Securities	Max	B	6.7	12.9	14.1	18,676	9.2	20.1	70.0	26.7	5.0	65
Gintel ERISA[8]	G&I	D	14.4	7.0	11.3	17,135	2.4	18.2	4.8	53.6	None	80
Gintel Fund	Gro	C	24.6	10.0	15.9	21,189	1.8	14.3	13.3	156.5	None	74
GIT Equity Trust—Special Growth	SCG	D	7.0	3.7	11.6	17,265	0.9	18.5	10.0	43.6	None	76
Gradison-McDonald Established Value	Gro	E	13.8	7.5	10.2	16,475	1.6	16.6	30.0	177.6	None	72
Gradison-McDonald Opportunity	SCG	C	15.3	10.0	14.7	20,088	0.7	13.7	30.0	51.1	None	81
Growth Fund of America	Gro	B	10.2	11.8	16.3	20,096	1.4	25.0	15.2	3,776.1	5.75	99
Growth Fund of Washington	Gro	E	21.8	7.0	10.2	15,553	1.0	21.3	4.3	33.4	5.0	132
G.T. Global—America Growth	Gro	A	39.2	14.1	20.5	25,406	0.1	23.0	24.7	93.5	4.75	134
G.T. Global—Europe Growth	Intl	E	(8.3)	(7.4)	4.0	11,812	1.6	N.A.	6.7	880.5	4.75	143
G.T. Global Growth & Income A	Glo	—	3.9	—	—	—	5.2	N.A.	7.9	141.7	4.75	143

MONEY's grades compare domestic equity, international equity and gold and sector funds by five-year, risk-adjusted return to Dec. 1. **Value of $10,000** is to Dec. 24. [1]Closed to new investors [2]May impose back-end load or exit fee [3]Three years [4]Performance from Dec. 31, 1987 [5]Reflects borrowing to boost investments [6]Manager absorbing expenses [7]Investment by contractual plan only [8]Open to retirement plans only N.A.: Not available

FUND NAME	Type	MONEY risk-adjusted grade	% compound annual gain (or loss) to Dec. 24, 1992			Value of $10,000 invested five years ago (net of sales charge)	Portfolio analysis			Net assets (millions)	Expense analysis	
			One year	Three years	Five years		% yield	P/E ratio	% cash		% maximum initial sales charge	Five-year projection
G.T. Global Healthcare	Sec	—	(10.6)	15.5	—	—	0.0	32.8	7.1	$665.4	4.75	$151
G.T. Global—International	Intl	B	(2.9)	(2.7)	8.6	$14,467	1.3	N.A.	0.2	425.1	4.75	145
G.T. Global—Japan	Intl	D	(18.4)	(17.7)	1.6	10,310	0.0	N.A.	19.8	96.3	4.75	163
G.T. Global—Latin America	Intl	—	(1.9)	—	—	—	0.8	N.A.	4.5	92.5	4.75	119
G.T. Global Pacific	Intl	A	(6.1)	(2.9)	11.4	15,941	4.0	N.A.	12.2	293.6	4.75	157
G.T. Global Worldwide	Glo	A	6.3	3.1	11.5	16,572	1.1	N.A.	2.3	136.5	4.75	156
Guardian Park Avenue	Gro	B	22.6	12.5	16.1	20,073	2.0	16.2	4.5	292.4	4.5	81
Harbor Capital Appreciation	Gro	—	12.9	18.7	—	—	0.3	27.6	1.8	72.1	None	50
Harbor Growth	Gro	E	(3.4)	9.3	12.4	18,143	0.3	38.0	1.0	192.9	None	52
Harbor International	Intl	—	2.4	3.0	—	—	1.3	N.A.	12.2	715.5	None	76
Harbor Value	G&I	—	10.4	7.6	—	—	3.0	28.3	4.4	66.0	None	53
Hartwell Emerging Growth	SCG	A	6.1	21.1	23.3	27,407	0.0	45.1	6.0	152.7	4.75	135
Hartwell Growth	Max	D	4.2	11.8	14.0	18,306	0.0	27.2	1.0	25.7	4.75	169
Heartland Value	SCG	B	46.7	20.6	18.3	22,448	2.9	13.6	0.0	37.2	None	92
Heritage Capital Appreciation	Max	D	13.6	8.7	12.8	17,595	1.7	24.3	12.2	64.8	4.0	141
Heritage Income—Growth	Eql	D	13.5	10.3	12.6	17,386	3.1	22.4	11.7	26.6	4.0	135
IAI Emerging Growth	SCG	—	24.8	—	—	—	0.1	43.3	11.7	54.5	None	69
IAI International	Intl	D	(2.0)	(1.3)	6.2	13,444	1.1	N.A.	1.5	47.0	None	109
IAI Regional	Gro	A	6.4	12.0	16.6	21,600	1.1	19.8	15.8	576.8	None	69
IAI Stock	Max	E	7.1	7.7	11.4	17,296	0.8	26.2	3.9	122.9	None	69
IAI Value	Max	D	14.3	6.1	12.1	17,951	1.1	28.9	4.9	26.1	None	69
IDEX Fund	Gro	A	4.3	17.5	22.0	25,018	0.6	24.3	9.0	290.2	8.5	155
IDEX Fund 3[1]	Gro	A	4.0	17.0	21.3	24,326	0.4	24.0	10.0	194.5	8.5	154
IDEX II—Growth	Gro	A	5.9	17.4	22.5	26,265	0.4	24.7	17.0	402.5	5.5	138
IDS Blue Chip Advantage	G&I	—	11.1	—	—	—	1.6	N.A.	0.2	107.7	5.0	113
IDS Discovery	SCG	B	10.0	17.8	18.8	22,569	0.2	35.0	20.9	299.7	5.0	107
IDS Equity Plus	G&I	C	13.6	12.3	14.0	18,654	1.2	24.9	8.8	438.8	5.0	91
IDS Global Growth	Glo	—	(0.9)	—	—	—	0.7	N.A.	5.6	65.0	5.0	139
IDS Growth	Gro	A	11.2	18.0	18.7	22,654	0.9	30.4	7.7	846.9	5.0	98
IDS International	Intl	D	(2.0)	(0.1)	5.9	12,644	0.6	N.A.	9.1	227.2	5.0	125
IDS Managed Retirement	G&I	A	12.0	17.2	17.2	21,413	1.8	24.5	4.9	1,307.0	5.0	100
IDS Mutual	Bal	D	12.5	9.9	11.8	16,750	4.7	20.3	6.4	2,221.5	5.0	91
IDS New Dimensions	Gro	A	7.5	18.6	18.4	22,419	1.0	26.3	14.0	2,252.7	5.0	100
IDS Precious Metals	Gold	E	(5.4)	(12.8)	(7.5)	6,352	1.6	N.A.	4.6	49.7	5.0	140
IDS Progressive	Max	E	22.2	7.2	10.1	15,409	2.3	15.2	12.0	173.9	5.0	106
IDS Stock	G&I	B	8.8	11.6	14.1	18,725	3.0	22.5	3.5	1,648.1	5.0	88
IDS Strategy—Aggressive Equity	Max	C	1.5	14.2	15.6	21,053	0.1	26.0	21.9	478.9	None[2]	118
IDS Strategy—Equity Portfolio	G&I	B	15.0	10.9	15.1	20,440	2.2	N.A.	12.0	582.3	None[2]	118
IDS Strategy—Worldwide Growth	Intl	E	(2.9)	(3.6)	2.0	11,244	0.5	N.A.	12.8	43.3	None[2]	181
IDS Utilities Income	Sec	—	12.1	10.6	—	—	5.3	18.7	6.4	458.8	5.0	99
Income Fund of America	Eql	B	13.7	10.3	13.3	17,758	6.2	29.4	4.0	5,643.3	5.75	92
Investment Co. of America	G&I	B	9.5	11.3	14.5	18,842	2.4	25.2	7.8	14,025.4	5.75	89
Investors Research	Max	E	(6.1)	8.3	8.5	14,131	1.1	23.7	60.0	60.7	6.75	114
Ivy Growth	Gro	D	6.9	9.9	13.3	17,662	1.5	19.1	4.0	216.5	5.75	125
Ivy International	Intl	B	1.8	0.4	11.0	15,905	1.4	N.A.	10.0	117.3	5.75	144
Janus Flexible Income	Flx	E	12.3	10.5	9.3	15,599	8.9	N.A.	15.5	231.6	None	55
Janus Fund	Max	A	9.6	15.3	20.9	25,893	0.9	21.9	24.7	4,659.9	None	54
Janus Growth & Income	G&I	—	7.9	—	—	—	1.0	24.9	1.9	229.2	None	83
Janus Twenty[1]	Max	A	5.6	20.7	25.0	31,135	0.1	25.2	21.6	2,308.2	None	61
Janus Venture[1]	SCG	A	10.0	16.7	21.0	25,958	0.4	20.9	28.1	1,491.0	None	65
Janus Worldwide	Glo	—	10.9	—	—	—	0.0	N.A.	35.0	132.5	None	94
Japan Fund	Intl	E	(12.1)	(9.5)	(0.3)	9,839	0.0	N.A.	4.0	416.6	None	68

MONEY's grades compare domestic equity, international equity and gold and sector funds by five-year, risk-adjusted return to Dec. 1. **Value of $10,000** is to Dec. 24. [1]Closed to new investors [2]May impose back-end load or exit fee [3]Three years [4]Performance from Dec. 31, 1987 [5]Reflects borrowing to boost investments [6]Manager absorbing expenses [7]Investment by contractual plan only N.A.: Not available

FUND NAME	Type	MONEY risk-adjusted grade	% compound annual gain (or loss) to Dec. 24, 1992			Value of $10,000 invested five years ago (net of sales charge)	Portfolio analysis			Net assets (millions)	Expense analysis	
			One year	Three years	Five years		% yield	P/E ratio	% cash		% maximum initial sales charge	Five-year projection
John Hancock Asset Allocation	AA	—	8.6	10.0	—	—	1.2	33.3	19.0	$33.2	5.0	$164
John Hancock Discovery B	SCG	—	16.4	—	—	—	0.0	26.9	2.1	34.4	None[2]	110[3]
John Hancock Freedom Global Technology	Sec	D	6.0	4.2	7.3	$13,791	0.2	N.A.	5.0	28.0	5.0	168
John Hancock Freedom Gold & Government B	Gold	E	3.7	5.0	6.7	13,800	6.0	N.A.	4.2	37.1	None[2]	119
John Hancock Freedom—Natl. Aviation & Tech.	Sec	D	2.8	2.2	12.6	17,523	0.1	26.8	10.0	64.6	5.0	135
John Hancock Freedom Regional Bank B	Sec	A	46.5	23.7	23.3	28,683	1.5	16.1	6.0	53.6	None[2]	130
John Hancock Growth	Gro	C	9.1	11.2	14.2	18,735	0.2	31.8	4.0	141.1	5.0	125
John Hancock Sovereign Investors	G&I	A	9.5	13.9	15.1	19,426	3.2	18.5	9.0	674.9	5.0	112
John Hancock Special Equities	SCG	A	32.0	28.8	26.1	30,646	0.0	36.2	6.0	38.9	5.0	188
Kaufmann Fund	SCG	A	14.5	22.9	33.2	41,970	0.0	29.1	0.0	193.8	None[2]	190
Kemper Blue Chip	G&I	E	1.7	13.7	11.0	16,265	3.6	25.0	4.0	176.0	5.75	144
Kemper Environmental Services	Sec	—	(7.2)	—	—	—	0.0	27.9	1.0	49.4	5.75	137
Kemper Growth	Gro	A	2.6	19.7	19.2	23,153	0.4	26.4	4.0	1,417.8	5.75	115
Kemper International	Intl	C	(2.3)	(1.4)	6.1	12,593	0.0	N.A.	9.0	170.6	5.75	134
Kemper Investment Portfolio—Growth	Gro	B	1.4	14.7	16.1	23,646	0.4	N.A.	5.0	661.3	None[2]	118
Kemper Investment Port.—Total Return	Bal	B	7.1	14.4	14.4	19,594	2.3	N.A.	12.0	989.9	None[2]	116
Kemper Retirement Series I [1]	Bal	—	5.2	—	—	—	6.7	N.A.	1.0	120.4	5.0	79
Kemper Retirement Series II [1]	Bal	—	6.1	—	—	—	2.4	N.A.	1.0	195.7	5.0	80
Kemper Small Capitalization Equity	SCG	B	3.3	16.5	16.1	19,940	3.1	29.5	12.0	328.6	5.75	126
Kemper Technology	Sec	D	1.8	12.4	12.1	17,089	0.7	26.4	2.0	521.1	5.75	106
Kemper Total Return	Bal	B	4.9	14.5	13.7	18,244	2.8	25.9	5.0	1,183.9	5.75	113
Keystone America Omega	Max	A	6.8	15.9	18.2	22,198	0.0	31.7	6.0	64.8	4.75	123
Keystone International	Intl	E	5.2	(3.7)	1.7	10,877	0.7	N.A.	13.0	64.1	None[2]	164
Keystone K-1	Flx	D	5.5	8.2	10.1	16,848	4.3	N.A.	7.0	1,255.7	None[2]	107
Keystone K-2	Gro	D	10.9	12.3	13.6	19,261	0.4	26.7	7.0	327.7	None[2]	83
Keystone Precious Metals	Gold	E	(11.8)	(12.0)	(6.1)	7,178	0.9	N.A.	3.0	116.9	None[2]	143
Keystone S-1	G&I	E	3.4	7.3	11.0	17,188	1.6	28.4	6.0	216.9	None[2]	125
Keystone S-3	Gro	D	8.6	11.1	13.7	19,306	0.0	28.4	5.0	270.1	None[2]	85
Keystone S-4	SCG	B	12.4	20.5	18.7	23,806	0.0	30.2	1.0	772.9	None[2]	80
Kidder Peabody Equity Income	Eql	D	0.9	13.6	13.4	17,897	1.4	30.7	10.0	148.6	5.75	128
Kleinwort Benson International Equity	Intl	C	(1.0)	(2.6)	6.7	13,758	4.8	N.A.	2.6	65.1	None	101
Laurel Stock	G&I	—	11.0	13.5	—	—	1.5	23.1	5.0	45.0	None	50
Leeb Investment—Personal Finance	AA	—	7.3	—	—	—	1.0	17.7	68.5	34.3	None	47[3]
Legg Mason Special Investment	SCG	A	16.3	17.0	19.8	24,982	0.6	18.7	14.4	214.0	None	115
Legg Mason Total Return Trust	G&I	D	16.0	10.2	13.2	18,840	2.4	18.4	17.0	87.5	None	125
Legg Mason Value Trust	Gro	D	13.3	7.6	12.9	18,672	0.9	18.0	3.5	769.5	None	103
Lexington Global	Glo	C	(0.7)	(2.3)	6.3	13,529	0.9	N.A.	1.0	50.2	None	86
Lexington Goldfund	Gold	E	(18.6)	(16.2)	(9.0)	6,167	1.1	N.A.	0.1	85.5	None	91
Lexington Growth & Income	G&I	E	15.4	8.1	11.5	17,510	1.6	28.8	0.4	118.8	None	76
Lexington Worldwide Emerging Growth	Intl	B	5.7	3.3	9.0	15,524	1.2	N.A.	1.4	28.3	None	106
Liberty Financial—Utilities	Sec	—	11.3	—	—	—	5.8	N.A.	0.1	106.7	4.5	83[3]
Liberty Utility	Sec	—	10.3	12.2	—	19,010	5.0	17.4	3.0	578.4	4.5[2]	103
Lindner Dividend	Eql	A	21.9	12.9	14.8	19,943	8.0	17.8	4.8	545.1	None	48
Lindner Fund	Gro	D	14.7	7.1	12.2	17,776	2.8	19.1	8.2	998.2	None	44
Loomis-Sayles Small Cap	SCG	—	16.4	—	—	—	0.0	22.5	9.7	27.8	None	47[3]
Lord Abbett Affiliated	G&I	D	14.8	9.3	12.2	16,759	3.6	23.2	7.9	3,690.7	5.75	88
Lord Abbett Developing Growth	SCG	E	(1.4)	11.8	10.2	15,325	0.2	25.2	12.9	137.1	5.75	117
Lord Abbett—Fundamental Value	G&I	C	15.4	10.4	13.2	17,626	2.0	N.A.	7.8	26.3	5.75	140
Lord Abbett Global Equity	Glo	—	0.1	(0.1)	—	—	1.2	N.A.	6.0	33.2	5.75	140
Lord Abbett Value Appreciation	Gro	D	16.8	11.5	13.5	17,924	1.8	18.1	10.3	157.8	5.75	117
MacKenzie American	Gro	E	10.3	(0.2)	5.4	12,502	0.3	31.5	5.0	37.7	5.75	160
MacKenzie North American	AA	E	8.9	4.8	6.1	12,733	5.7	20.9	2.0	42.2	5.75	158

MONEY's grades compare domestic equity, international equity and gold and sector funds by five-year, risk-adjusted return to Dec. 1. **Value of $10,000** is to Dec. 24. [1]Closed to new investors [2]May impose back-end load or exit fee [3]Three years [4]Performance from Dec. 31, 1987 [5]Reflects borrowing to boost investments [6]Manager absorbing expenses [7]Investment by contractual plan only N.A.: Not available

FUND NAME	Type	MONEY risk-adjusted grade	% compound annual gain (or loss) to Dec. 24, 1992			Value of $10,000 invested five years ago (net of sales charge)	Portfolio analysis			Net assets (millions)	% maximum initial sales charge	Five-year projection
			One year	Three years	Five years		% yield	P/E ratio	% cash			
MainStay Capital Appreciation	Max	A	14.7	24.6	19.4	$24,626	0.0	N.A.	7.3	$135.2	None[2]	$155
MainStay Convertible	Conv	D	16.2	16.3	12.8	18,262	2.5	N.A.	7.3	30.4	None[2]	165
MainStay Equity Index	G&I	—	10.1	—	—	—	0.0	N.A.	1.3	43.2	5.5	128
MainStay Total Return	Bal	—	6.2	14.1	—	18,236	1.5	N.A.	6.7	304.3	None[2]	149
MainStay Value	G&I	A	22.8	16.7	16.9	22,134	0.7	N.A.	13.2	82.3	None[2]	149
Mass. Investors Growth Stock	Gro	D	9.9	14.1	15.4	19,510	0.0	31.8	2.0	953.1	5.75	98
Mass. Investors Trust	G&I	B	10.4	11.5	15.0	19,451	2.5	25.7	8.0	1,543.9	5.75	90
Mathers Fund	Gro	D	2.8	7.2	8.7	15,438	4.8	14.4	71.1	553.0	None	52
Mentor Growth	Gro	C	18.2	15.1	15.7	20,656	0.0	23.6	13.8	117.7	None[2]	127
Merrill Lynch Balanced B	Bal	E	6.0	7.8	9.5	15,778	2.4	N.A.	7.0	887.0	None[2]	103
Merrill Lynch Basic Value A	G&I	E	12.2	6.7	11.2	16,346	3.6	20.1	7.3	1,655.0	6.5	95
Merrill Lynch Capital A	G&I	B	6.5	9.7	13.4	17,760	5.0	20.2	5.0	1,760.5	6.5	94
Merrill Lynch Developing Capital Markets	Intl	—	3.7	5.7	—	—	5.2	N.A.	6.4	129.2	4.0[2]	132
Merrill Lynch Eurofund B	Intl	D	(4.4)	1.7	6.4	13,515	2.4	N.A.	10.0	472.2	None[2]	116
Merrill Lynch Fund for Tomorrow B	Gro	C	8.4	8.7	14.4	19,926	3.5	20.7	7.0	436.4	None[2]	107
Merrill Lynch Global Allocation B	AA	—	12.9	12.8	—	—	6.7	N.A.	18.2	881.0	None[2]	124
Merrill Lynch Global Utility B	Sec	—	10.1	—	—	—	3.6	15.2	14.4	184.1	None[2]	84
Merrill Lynch Growth B	G&I	D	11.6	9.5	14.6	19,847	0.1	31.8	2.1	740.9	None[2]	103
Merrill Lynch International A	Glo	B	6.9	3.6	8.7	14,145	0.8	N.A.	9.3	166.5	6.5	141
Merrill Lynch Latin America B	Intl	—	1.8	—	—	—	1.0	N.A.	12.6	121.1	None[2]	105
Merrill Lynch Natural Resources B	Sec	D	(4.9)	(1.5)	2.0	11,038	0.9	38.4	4.0	245.8	None[2]	108
Merrill Lynch Pacific A	Intl	B	(3.5)	0.1	9.1	14,234	2.2	N.A.	8.9	300.4	6.5	118
Merrill Lynch Phoenix A	G&I	D	27.4	10.3	14.9	18,963	8.6	26.4	4.0	135.9	6.5	134
Merrill Lynch Special Value A	Gro	E	17.0	8.9	8.7	14,061	0.6	21.4	24.0	52.6	6.5	144
Merriman Asset Allocation	AA	—	3.6	5.2	—	—	2.8	N.A.	70.0	26.6	None	83
Merriman Capital Appreciation	Gro	—	5.4	9.1	—	—	2.3	N.A.	50.0	43.8	None	81
MetLife—State Street Capital Appreciation	Max	B	12.4	17.1	20.2	24,200	0.0	31.7	7.8	133.0	4.5	123
MetLife—State Street Equity Income	Eql	D	14.1	5.8	11.3	16,388	3.7	22.7	1.6	55.4	4.5	123
MetLife—State Street Equity Investments	G&I	D	12.3	10.2	12.7	17,669	0.3	27.9	4.4	51.1	4.5	123
MetLife—State Street Managed Assets	AA	—	9.5	8.0	—	—	3.5	32.2	6.6	99.9	4.5	111
MFS Capital Development	Gro	D	11.7	8.3	11.7	16,633	1.2	27.2	3.0	671.3	5.75	112
MFS Emerging Growth	SCG	B	11.1	17.4	17.8	21,496	0.0	31.2	6.0	248.8	5.75	143
MFS Income & Opportunity	Flx	—	5.7	9.9	—	—	7.0	10.8	2.0	78.2	4.75	161
MFS Lifetime—Capital Growth	Max	B	11.1	11.6	15.3	20,561	0.0	21.0	5.0	404.6	None[2]	142
MFS Lifetime—Emerging Growth	SCG	A	14.6	26.1	21.8	27,003	0.0	31.7	3.0	284.6	None[2]	153
MFS Lifetime—Managed Sectors	Sec	C	9.7	13.0	15.6	20,973	0.0	35.6	5.0	225.8	None[2]	150
MFS Lifetime—Total Return	G&I	D	9.5	9.7	10.7	16,895	2.5	22.7	12.0	341.2	None[2]	143
MFS Lifetime—Worldwide Equity	Glo	C	5.0	1.4	6.4	13,376	0.0	N.A.	7.0	96.4	None[2]	172
MFS Managed Sectors Trust	Sec	B	10.4	14.0	16.4	20,442	0.0	35.1	3.0	134.4	5.75	144
MFS Research	G&I	C	14.4	11.2	13.8	17,903	0.0	26.6	5.0	240.3	5.75	115
MFS Special	Max	C	21.1	8.7	14.3	18,552	0.7	20.4	10.0	107.9	5.75	138
MFS Total Return Trust	Bal	C	11.5	9.4	13.0	17,542	5.2	24.3	8.0	1,184.0	4.75	93
MFS Worldwide Total Return	Glo	—	8.3	—	—	—	2.5	N.A.	14.0	43.2	4.75	180
Midwest Strategic—Utility Income	Sec	—	9.4	11.0	—	—	4.1	17.4	14.3	36.2	4.0	125
MIM Mutual—Stock Appreciation	Max	C	8.5	25.1	16.9	21,975	0.0	23.5	0.0	28.7	None	142
Mimlic Asset Allocation	AA	D	8.5	12.1	13.0	17,498	3.0	22.7	1.1	37.0	5.0	120
Monetta Fund	G&I	A	6.0	21.9	20.3	25,215	0.1	27.3	40.0	292.5	None	80
Montgomery Small Cap[1]	SCG	—	12.0	—	—	—	0.0	N.A.	5.0	180.0	None[2]	82
Mutual Beacon	G&I	A	24.9	9.7	14.7	19,851	1.7	21.4	16.5	478.4	None	48
Mutual Benefit	G&I	A	13.4	10.4	16.8	21,212	2.1	21.6	12.0	47.4	4.75	92
Mutual of Omaha Growth	Gro	C	4.8	14.2	19.1	22,933	0.2	38.1	6.3	103.1	4.75	111
Mutual of Omaha Income	Flx	C	8.2	9.7	11.4	16,307	6.4	N.A.	4.8	238.9	4.75	102

MONEY's grades compare domestic equity, international equity and gold and sector funds by five-year, risk-adjusted return to Dec. 1. **Value of $10,000** is to Dec. 24. [1]Closed to new investors [2]May impose back-end load or exit fee [3]Three years [4]Performance from Dec. 31, 1987 [5]Reflects borrowing to boost investments [6]Manager absorbing expenses [7]Investment by contractual plan only N.A.: Not available

FUND NAME	Type	MONEY risk-adjusted grade	One year	Three years	Five years	Value of $10,000 invested five years ago (net of sales charge)	% yield	P/E ratio	% cash	Net assets (millions)	% maximum initial sales charge	Five-year projection
Mutual Qualified [1]	G&I	B	24.6	10.0	14.6	$19,702	1.7	21.1	13.0	$1,170.7	None	$50
Mutual Shares [1]	G&I	B	23.1	9.6	14.5	19,685	1.6	22.1	16.0	2,729.1	None	47
N&B Genesis	SCG	—	18.4	10.6	—	—	0.1	15.1	2.9	72.5	None	90
N&B Guardian	G&I	A	21.6	15.3	18.4	23,583	1.3	23.5	8.6	847.4	None	46
N&B Manhattan	Max	B	19.4	12.2	15.9	21,302	0.8	25.9	1.8	414.3	None	59
N&B Partners	Gro	C	20.0	10.7	13.5	19,103	0.7	21.7	7.7	884.0	None	48
N&B Selected Sectors	Sec	B	24.8	12.7	16.0	21,378	1.3	24.4	4.5	439.2	None	50
National Income & Growth A	Bal	B	13.0	10.9	14.0	18,316	4.6	27.6	2.0	393.5	5.75	129
National Industries	G&I	C	2.3	10.9	13.4	18,955	1.4	20.5	31.5	33.4	None	88
National Stock	G&I	B	19.1	10.4	15.1	19,216	1.0	N.A.	0.0	202.8	5.75	130
National Total Return	Eql	C	12.1	10.2	13.6	18,071	2.6	21.9	0.0	263.4	5.75	129
National Worldwide Opportunities	Glo	D	6.4	0.1	4.0	11,467	0.1	N.A.	5.2	96.2	5.75	168
Nationwide Fund	G&I	B	7.0	10.9	15.7	19,806	2.1	22.2	7.6	715.8	4.5	77
Nationwide Growth	Gro	D	9.4	10.4	13.3	17,587	2.0	19.4	4.2	325.2	4.5	79
New Alternatives	Sec	C	6.3	6.7	13.6	17,672	1.4	20.1	11.0	25.6	5.66	117
New Beginning Growth	SCG	B	0.7	16.4	18.2	23,011	0.5	24.3	12.5	270.8	None	46
New Beginning Income & Growth	G&I	C	7.3	11.1	13.2	18,900	1.6	28.1	2.4	34.2	None	82
New Beginning International Growth	Intl	—	4.5	—	—	—	0.0	N.A.	5.2	26.2	None	101
New Economy	Gro	C	19.1	10.7	15.4	19,296	1.0	21.4	10.7	1,000.1	5.75	106
New Perspective	Glo	A	7.1	7.9	11.6	16,396	2.0	N.A.	17.4	3,081.6	5.75	102
New York Venture	Gro	A	16.4	15.9	20.1	23,892	1.8	23.1	0.9	511.8	4.75	95
Nicholas Fund	Gro	B	15.9	15.2	17.2	22,186	1.5	17.3	10.5	2,397.5	None	43
Nicholas Income	Flx	E	10.3	10.4	9.3	15,599	8.6	N.A.	7.9	116.0	None	42
Nicholas Limited Edition [1]	SCG	A	20.5	17.6	19.2	23,940	0.7	17.9	4.4	171.0	None	52
Nicholas II	SCG	C	11.6	12.5	14.4	19,594	0.9	17.9	8.8	674.0	None	39
Nomura Pacific Basin	Intl	D	(8.6)	(5.5)	3.6	12,049	2.2	N.A.	8.0	43.6	None	82
Northeast Investors Growth	Gro	C	2.8	11.9	15.4	20,826	0.0	25.5	0.9	38.0	None	82
Northeast Investors Trust	Flx	E	17.9	10.5	9.2	15,528	12.0	N.A.	0.0	452.0	None	49
Oakmark Fund	Gro	—	54.8	—	—	—	0.0	N.A.	2.7	78.1	None	78[3]
Oberweis Emerging Growth	SCG	A	16.0	28.6	22.1	27,279	0.0	29.8	1.8	35.7	None	113
Olympic Trust—Equity Income	Eql	E	15.3	7.7	13.0	18,591	2.9	21.8	6.0	70.3	None	57
Olympus Stock	Max	B	4.4	14.8	16.6	20,961	0.7	27.9	6.8	43.7	4.75	131
Oppenheimer Asset Allocation	AA	C	8.9	7.6	11.0	15,986	3.1	24.9	2.6	263.5	5.75	123
Oppenheimer Discovery	SCG	A	19.7	19.1	21.3	25,025	0.0	28.7	10.5	293.7	5.75	136
Oppenheimer Equity Income	Eql	D	9.0	7.5	10.5	15,720	5.2	30.2	2.6	1,588.4	5.75	100
Oppenheimer Fund	Gro	D	10.9	10.2	11.8	16,750	3.1	24.7	9.3	208.7	5.75	114
Oppenheimer Global	Glo	A	(12.0)	2.8	12.8	16,879	0.4	N.A.	4.3	1,215.1	5.75	128
Oppenheimer Global Bio-tech	Sec	—	(20.3)	23.8	—	—	0.0	65.7	13.8	129.5	5.75	129
Oppenheimer Global Environment	Sec	—	(9.5)	—	—	—	0.2	27.2	1.9	50.1	5.75	144
Oppenheimer Global Growth & Income	Glo	—	(5.4)	—	—	—	2.4	N.A.	7.1	49.7	5.75	146
Oppenheimer Gold & Special Minerals	Gold	D	(9.2)	(13.5)	(1.1)	8,885	2.2	N.A.	4.1	123.7	5.75	129
Oppenheimer Special	Gro	B	16.3	17.0	17.4	21,383	1.2	23.1	2.2	662.8	5.75	104
Oppenheimer Target	Max	A	12.7	15.2	18.6	22,390	0.7	24.6	2.0	358.2	5.75	120
Oppenheimer Time	Max	C	3.9	9.2	13.0	17,649	1.3	27.3	15.0	344.1	5.75	108
Oppenheimer Total Return	G&I	C	14.8	13.5	14.1	18,396	2.6	20.4	1.9	687.8	5.75	107
Oppenheimer Value Stock	G&I	C	12.9	10.9	13.5	17,967	2.2	23.4	11.8	55.6	5.75	123
Overland Express—Asset Allocation	AA	—	10.1	11.9	—	—	4.5	N.A.	1.9	42.5	4.5	111
Pacific Horizon Aggressive Growth	Max	C	1.2	20.3	18.6	22,494	0.0	31.3	2.5	137.3	4.5	120
Pacifica Balanced	Bal	—	10.7	—	—	—	3.8	N.A.	5.0	65.0	4.5	96
Pacifica Equity Value	Gro	—	13.6	—	—	—	1.9	N.A.	8.0	92.6	4.5	97
Paine Webber Asset Allocation B	AA	E	6.9	8.4	9.2	15,662	2.5	20.6	1.0	314.5	None[2]	129
Paine Webber Atlas Global Growth A	Glo	D	(6.6)	(2.7)	6.0	12,724	1.6	N.A.	16.1	141.6	4.5	134

MONEY's grades compare domestic equity, international equity and gold and sector funds by five-year, risk-adjusted return to Dec. 1. **Value of $10,000** is to Dec. 24. [1]Closed to new investors [2]May impose back-end load or exit fee [3]Three years [4]Performance from Dec. 31, 1987 [5]Reflects borrowing to boost investments [6]Manager absorbing expenses [7]Investment by contractual plan only N.A.: Not available

FUND NAME	Type	MONEY risk-adjusted grade	% compound annual gain (or loss) to Dec. 24, 1992			Value of $10,000 invested five years ago (net of sales charge)	Portfolio analysis			Net assets (millions)	Expense analysis	
			One year	Three years	Five years		% yield	P/E ratio	% cash		% maximum initial sales charge	Five-year projection
Paine Webber Blue Chip Growth B	Gro	D	8.9	7.6	13.1	$18,905	0.0	25.9	3.5	$68.5	None[2]	$137
Paine Webber Dividend Growth A	G&I	B	7.2	12.4	15.4	19,645	1.0	21.3	4.1	366.6	4.5	109
Paine Webber Europe Growth A	Intl	—	(8.6)	—	—	—	3.4	N.A.	14.0	85.1	4.5	137
Paine Webber Global Energy B	Sec	D	(2.5)	(0.0)	8.6	15,064	0.5	N.A.	9.0	102.5	None[2]	153
Paine Webber Global Growth & Income A	Gro	—	(2.2)	2.6	—	—	4.3	N.A.	4.6	62.8	4.5	145
Paine Webber Growth A	Gro	A	5.3	12.1	17.5	21,725	0.0	26.7	16.5	102.5	4.5	119
Paine Webber Income B	Flx	E	11.0	11.8	10.4	16,400	7.5	14.3	2.6	61.6	None[2]	129
Paine Webber Regional Financial Growth A	Sec	A	40.2	25.4	22.6	26,292	0.7	N.A.	11.3	46.8	4.5	134
Parnassus Fund	Gro	C	39.1	17.8	17.8	22,819	3.0	31.7	8.0	41.7	3.5	115
Pasadena Balanced Return	Bal	A	7.7	13.6	16.9	20,604	1.3	27.2	1.6	64.6	5	180
Pasadena Growth	Gro	A	5.8	18.2	24.8	28,621	0.0	28.3	0.5	52.5	5.5	150
Pasadena Nifty Fifty	Gro	—	7.4	—	—	—	0.6	30.4	0.7	179.1	5.5	170
Pax World	Bal	B	3.6	10.9	13.1	18,858	5.5	17.1	5.0	421.4	None	65
Penn Square Mutual	G&I	D	11.3	9.8	12.9	17,966	2.3	26.3	11.2	228.2	4.75	98
Pennsylvania Mutual	SCG	C	18.3	10.4	14.4	19,350	1.5	20.6	21.0	967.9	None	53
Permanent Portfolio	AA	E	3.2	2.1	2.7	11,424	6.0	N.A.	10.4	67.1	None	102
Philadelphia Fund	G&I	E	22.1	4.2	10.9	17,101	1.1	34.8	4.4	83.4	None	94
Phoenix Balanced Series	Bal	B	8.7	13.4	12.8	17,683	3.3	29.6	21.0	2,045.0	4.75	102
Phoenix Capital Appreciation	Gro	—	9.9	24.9	—	—	1.2	N.A.	18.0	210.6	4.75	112
Phoenix Convertible	Conv	D	13.7	9.8	10.5	16,781	3.8	N.A.	24.0	198.4	4.75	111
Phoenix Growth Series	Gro	B	7.3	12.8	13.8	18,446	2.1	25.5	34.0	2,104.4	4.75	111
Phoenix International	Intl	—	(10.0)	(2.8)	—	—	3.5	N.A.	1.0	29.6	4.75	155
Phoenix Stock Series	Max	E	10.1	9.9	10.5	15,882	1.8	25.5	6.0	124.8	4.75	116
Phoenix Total Return	G&I	C	13.1	14.3	12.1	17,253	1.4	19.5	42.0	52.1	4.75	129
Pilgrim MagnaCap	Gro	D	11.4	10.0	12.8	18,042	1.1	21.4	1.8	201.4	5.0	130
Pioneer Capital Growth	Gro	—	30.7	—	—	—	0.3	24.3	5.8	70.3	5.75	144
Pioneer Equity Income	Eql	—	22.5	—	—	—	3.7	19.5	1.5	34.2	5.75	147
Pioneer Europe	Intl	—	(0.4)	—	—	—	0.3	N.A.	7.5	37.7	5.75	117
Pioneer Fund	G&I	D	16.7	7.9	12.4	17,146	2.3	21.7	0.9	1,703.3	5.75	109
Pioneer II	G&I	D	12.3	6.7	11.9	16,934	2.4	18.9	5.7	3,974.2	5.75	109
Pioneer Three	G&I	B	22.4	12.3	16.8	20,612	1.8	21.7	2.2	779.6	5.75	104
Piper Jaffray Emerging Growth	SCG	—	10.3	—	—	—	0.0	25.8	4.7	110.1	4.0[2]	109
Piper Jaffray Value	Gro	A	6.4	15.7	18.6	22,984	0.9	23.8	6.0	199.6	4.0[2]	109
Portico—Equity Index	G&I	—	11.0	—	—	—	2.4	25.8	0.0	80.1	None	28
Portico—Income & Growth	Eql	—	7.2	—	—	—	3.1	N.A.	8.5	134.6	None	42
Portico—Special Growth	SCG	—	9.5	—	—	—	0.6	22.9	7.9	196.2	None	42
Primary Trend	G&I	E	3.0	5.8	8.0	15,138	3.2	42.2	25.0	31.7	None	61
Principal Preservation—S&P 100	G&I	D	9.1	9.9	13.1	18,255	1.7	30.7	2.0	28.5	4.5	107
Princor Capital Accumulation	G&I	E	14.8	10.6	11.4	16,597	2.1	24.9	0.8	188.1	5.0	159
Princor Emerging Growth	Max	—	16.4	17.8	18.2	21,799	0.7	23.5	25.9	27.2	5.0	140
Princor Growth	Gro	B	13.6	19.8	16.9	21,067	1.3	23.1	13.5	60.2	5.0	112
Princor Managed	AA	—	13.1	11.5	11.1	16,452	3.2	23.2	13.6	30.3	5.0	117
Princor World	Intl	C	1.9	1.5	7.1	13,619	1.2	N.A.	2.4	35.6	5.0	137
ProvidentMutual Growth	Gro	E	4.5	11.3	11.0	15,931	0.0	27.5	3.9	131.9	6.0	140
ProvidentMutual Investment Shares	G&I	E	4.4	0.1	7.1	13,470	1.7	21.0	2.6	153.1	6.0	133
ProvidentMutual Total Return	Bal	E	14.7	6.3	10.2	15,511	3.6	22.7	3.7	72.6	6.0	141
Prudential Equity B	Gro	C	15.2	10.1	14.4	19,953	1.2	23.4	11.0	1,089.0	None[2]	106
Prudential Equity Income B	Eql	C	10.9	8.8	12.9	18,587	3.0	26.4	6.0	187.9	None[2]	126
Prudential Flexifund—Conservative B	AA	E	7.9	10.0	10.4	16,359	3.1	N.A.	3.7	234.0	None[2]	122
Prudential Flexifund—Strategy B	AA	D	6.2	9.7	11.6	17,326	3.0	N.A.	2.7	323.3	None[2]	121
Prudential Global B	Glo	E	(2.1)	(3.9)	1.5	10,734	0.0	N.A.	5.3	180.7	None[2]	133
Prudential Global Genesis B	Glo	—	1.9	(1.8)	—	—	0.0	N.A.	6.4	31.5	None[2]	182

MONEY's grades compare domestic equity, international equity and gold and sector funds by five-year, risk-adjusted return to Dec. 1. **Value of $10,000** is to Dec. 24. [1]Closed to new investors [2]May impose back-end load or exit fee [3]Three years [4]Performance from Dec. 31, 1987 [5]Reflects borrowing to boost investments [6]Manager absorbing expenses [7]Investment by contractual plan only N.A.: Not available

FUND NAME	Type	MONEY risk-adjusted grade	% compound annual gain (or loss) to Dec. 24, 1992			Value of $10,000 invested five years ago (net of sales charge)	Portfolio analysis			Net assets (millions)	Expense analysis	
			One year	Three years	Five years		% yield	P/E ratio	% cash		% maximum initial sales charge	Five-year projection
Prudential Growth B	Gro	E	4.8	4.7	8.6	$15,435	0.8	N.A.	20.0	$234.6	None[2]	$125
Prudential Growth Opportunity B	SCG	B	23.4	13.1	16.4	21,491	0.0	22.2	8.0	173.3	None[2]	133
Prudential IncomeVertible B	Sec	D	9.0	6.7	10.1	16,243	5.3	N.A.	1.0	338.4	None[2]	124
Prudential Multi-Sector B	Max	—	3.5	—	—	—	1.1	N.A.	10.2	98.5	None[2]	124
Prudential Utility B	Sec	B	10.7	7.1	15.4	20,544	3.7	19.8	5.0	3,262.1	None[2]	101
Putnam Convertible Income & Growth	Conv	C	23.1	12.0	12.6	18,027	5.3	N.A.	6.8	590.0	5.75	117
Putnam Energy Resources	Sec	C	9.5	2.9	11.4	16,503	1.8	34.9	6.3	110.8	5.75	138
Putnam Fund for Growth & Income A	G&I	B	13.7	10.9	14.2	18,630	4.1	30.3	23.6	3,491.1	5.75	109
Putnam (George) Fund of Boston A	Bal	C	10.3	9.9	12.5	17,216	4.9	N.A.	2.0	628.4	5.75	107
Putnam Global Growth A	Glo	B	2.8	2.6	7.8	13,779	0.0	N.A.	8.6	643.7	5.75	136
Putnam Health Sciences Trust	Sec	B	(7.4)	15.8	18.9	22,743	0.9	30.0	13.6	942.6	5.75	121
Putnam Investors	Gro	D	10.9	10.8	13.8	18,228	1.3	27.8	8.1	709.5	5.75	104
Putnam Managed Income	OpInc	C	14.3	10.5	12.9	17.739	1.8	N.A.	26.8	635.9	5.75	117
Putnam New Opportunities	Gro	—	29.3	—	—	—	0.0	N.A.	6.8	154.2	5.75	142
Putnam OTC Emerging Growth	SCG	C	15.8	12.4	16.0	19,681	0.0	25.3	5.1	270.2	5.75	81
Putnam Strategic Income	EqI	E	6.3	6.6	10.7	16,021	5.2	N.A.	5.0	341.2	5.75	120
Putnam Vista	Gro	B	19.8	14.4	15.9	20,121	2.3	24.1	9.8	334.9	5.75	55
Putnam Voyager A	Max	A	12.9	16.8	18.8	22,313	0.2	29.1	7.1	1,585.0	5.75	119
Quest for Value	Max	C	21.3	13.4	14.8	19,234	0.6	19.0	13.0	139.7	5.5	149
Quest for Value—Global Equity	Glo	—	5.0	—	—	—	0.0	N.A.	0.0	118.4	5.5	145
Quest for Value—Opportunity	AA	—	21.3	17.2	—	—	0.2	20.9	30.0	38.1	5.5	174
Quest for Value—Small Cap	SCG	—	24.6	15.6	—	—	0.0	21.1	14.0	38.9	5.5	169
Rea-Graham Balanced	Bal	E	5.8	4.2	6.3	12,882	4.9	N.A.	46.6	26.6	4.75	153
Reich & Tang Equity	Gro	C	21.6	10.6	14.1	19,466	1.4	20.3	9.0	86.0	None	56
Rightime Blue Chip	G&I	E	8.0	9.7	9.3	15,282	1.0	25.7	1.0	210.5	4.75	163
Rightime Fund	G&I	E	7.5	11.3	8.1	15,057	0.5	N.A.	0.0	169.3	None	142
Rightime Growth	Gro	—	12.4	6.0	—	—	1.0	16.2	1.0	41.1	4.75	170
Robertson Stephens Emerging Growth	SCG	A	1.3	18.7	21.4	26,841	0.0	28.6	10.0	209.7	None	87
Rodney Square Multi-Manager—Growth	Gro	B	8.3	11.5	16.0	20,206	0.1	28.6	12.1	54.4	4.0	119
Royce Equity Income	EqI	—	20.6	—	—	—	4.0	20.8	5.3	47.7	None[2]	55
Royce Value	SCG	D	18.0	9.1	13.2	18,402	0.9	20.9	12.2	166.7	None[2]	137
Rushmore Nova	Max	—	2.7	1.8	—	—	4.6	25.4	75.7	102.9	None	64
Safeco Equity	G&I	C	12.2	8.6	15.9	21,496	1.3	23.1	2.0	70.8	None	54
Safeco Growth	Gro	D	(1.6)	9.5	13.5	18,879	0.0	17.3	3.0	121.4	None	50
Safeco Income	EqI	D	14.0	7.1	11.4	17,293	4.9	22.7	1.4	179.2	None	52
Safeco Northwest	Gro	—	15.9	—	—	—	0.5	20.4	8.3	33.9	None	70
Salomon Bros. Capital	Max	E	8.8	8.3	10.7	15,899	1.1	19.9	1.2	98.7	None	127
Salomon Bros. Investors	G&I	D	10.0	9.2	12.5	17,451	2.3	22.9	3.3	360.7	None	87
Salomon Bros. Opportunity	Max	D	16.8	7.9	13.0	18,590	1.7	17.1	7.3	105.9	None	71
SBSF Convertible Securities	Conv	—	12.8	10.5	—	—	7.5	N.A.	18.0	42.4	None	83
SBSF Growth	Gro	C	8.6	7.3	13.9	19,233	3.6	N.A.	17.4	105.7	None	64
Schroder International Equity	Intl	D	(0.6)	(3.7)	5.7	13,051	1.5	N.A.	3.0	158.6	None	60
Schwab Investment 1000	G&I	—	12.2	—	—	—	2.3	N.A.	1.2	300.4	None	26
Scudder Capital Growth	Gro	B	11.0	8.4	16.9	21,844	1.0	21.4	8.0	1,054.1	None	59
Scudder Development	SCG	B	0.4	19.0	17.6	22,660	0.0	26.8	8.0	715.8	None	70
Scudder Global	Glo	A	6.7	4.6	13.5	18,724	0.5	N.A.	4.0	389.1	None	87
Scudder Global Small Company	Glo	—	2.7	—	—	—	0.2	N.A.	8.0	55.2	None	47[3]
Scudder Gold	Gold	—	(6.5)	(11.1)	—	—	0.0	N.A.	6.0	31.8	None	135
Scudder Growth & Income	G&I	B	11.7	11.2	13.8	19,297	3.3	23.1	1.0	1,062.5	None	54
Scudder International	Intl	B	0.0	(0.0)	8.6	15,042	1.5	N.A.	4.0	1,044.4	None	71
Scudder Quality Growth	Gro	—	10.0	—	—	—	0.2	N.A.	3.0	93.9	None	40
Security Action [7]	Gro	E	9.3	8.6	11.3	15,800	6.9	24.4	10.5	297.4	8.5	44

MONEY's grades compare domestic equity, international equity and gold and sector funds by five-year, risk-adjusted return to Dec. 1. **Value of $10,000** is to Dec. 24. [1]Closed to new investors [2]May impose back-end load or exit fee [3]Three years [4]Performance from Dec. 31, 1987 [5]Reflects borrowing to boost investments [6]Manager absorbing expenses [7]Investment by contractual plan only N.A.: Not available

FUND NAME	Type	MONEY risk-adjusted grade	% compound annual gain (or loss) to Dec. 24, 1992 — One year	Three years	Five years	Value of $10,000 invested five years ago (net of sales charge)	Portfolio analysis — % yield	P/E ratio	% cash	Net assets (millions)	Expense analysis — % maximum initial sales charge	Five-year projection
Security Equity	Gro	A	13.4	13.0	16.9	$20,933	2.3	24.4	11.8	$313.6	5.75	$113
Security Investment	Flx	E	6.7	7.8	10.3	15,681	4.6	N.A.	1.7	75.5	5.75	123
Security Ultra	Max	E	9.4	7.0	10.8	15,740	0.6	20.4	3.5	57.1	5.75	126
Selected American Shares	G&I	B	10.4	14.8	16.3	21,907	0.6	23.0	7.0	566.6	None	65
Selected Special Shares	SCG	C	10.9	8.1	13.9	19,273	1.2	22.9	9.0	49.4	None	76
Seligman Capital	Max	A	15.2	21.0	18.5	22,487	0.0	26.8	5.6	176.3	4.75	103
Seligman Common Stock	G&I	C	13.5	11.8	13.8	18,389	3.0	26.2	3.2	496.7	4.75	88
Seligman Communications Information	Sec	C	20.9	17.5	17.3	21,199	0.0	29.7	5.2	46.3	4.75	135
Seligman Growth	Gro	C	15.2	13.9	15.5	19,892	0.5	24.5	5.8	565.1	4.75	90
Seligman Income	Flx	D	18.4	11.9	12.2	16,921	6.9	N.A.	3.3	197.5	4.75	94
Sentinel Balanced	Bal	C	8.4	10.4	11.7	16,049	4.8	25.2	11.4	117.8	8.5	111
Sentinel Common Stock	G&I	C	9.8	11.1	14.1	17,980	3.1	25.7	2.2	679.2	8.5	102
Sentinel Growth	Gro	D	9.2	10.6	11.4	16,665	0.9	27.1	5.7	58.7	5.25	123
Sentry Fund	Gro	A	9.3	13.8	15.8	21,191	2.2	22.8	33.4	68.5	None	51
Sequoia Fund [1]	Gro	B	13.0	13.8	15.8	20,740	2.2	33.3	23.4	1,339.2	None	56
Shearson Aggressive Growth A	Max	C	5.4	10.9	15.4	19,824	0.0	31.3	4.1	180.8	5.0	118
Shearson Appreciation A	Gro	B	9.5	10.8	14.2	18,876	3.3	27.2	7.6	1,798.5	5.0	105
Shearson Equity—Growth & Opportunity B	Gro	E	17.8	8.3	11.9	17,637	0.9	19.6	5.5	130.1	None [2]	125
Shearson Equity—Sector Analysis B	Max	E	10.8	9.8	6.8	13,958	0.7	31.2	0.8	183.1	None [2]	126
Shearson Equity—Strategic Investors B	AA	C	8.7	9.9	13.2	18,692	3.4	23.7	16.8	276.9	None [2]	121
Shearson Fundamental Value A	Gro	C	16.8	11.5	14.2	18,773	1.9	25.8	26.2	77.5	5.0	128
Shearson Global Opportunities A	Glo	E	(3.1)	(1.9)	4.1	11,528	0.0	N.A.	6.8	48.4	5.0	145
Shearson Income—Convertible B	Conv	E	14.4	8.9	10.2	16,252	4.7	N.A.	8.6	58.2	None [2]	112
Shearson Income—Total Return B	G&I	A	13.7	14.1	16.4	21,756	7.8	18.9	17.6	641.2	None [2]	102
Shearson Income—Utilities B	Sec	—	8.5	10.8	—	—	5.6	N.A.	7.4	1,935.7	None [2]	96
Shearson Investment—Directions Value B	Gro	E	19.0	10.0	12.3	17,861	0.4	21.2	9.9	195.5	None [2]	109
Shearson Investment—European B	Intl	D	(5.8)	(2.2)	5.5	12,941	1.5	N.A.	11.4	26.5	None [2]	151
Shearson Investment—Special Equities B	SCG	E	11.3	5.3	9.3	15,313	0.0	29.4	6.9	63.3	None [2]	133
Shearson 1990s A	Gro	—	(5.4)	—	—	—	0.0	28.3	1.4	43.1	5.0	133
Shearson Principal Return—1996 A	Bal	—	9.3	10.7	—	—	5.5	N.A.	0.1	111.0	5.0	45
Shearson Principal Return—1998 A	Bal	—	9.0	—	—	—	4.8	N.A.	0.0	172.8	5.0	105
Shearson Principal Return—2000 A	Bal	—	3.8	—	—	—	1.2	N.A.	0.0	130.7	5.0	86 [3]
Shearson Small Cap A	SCG	—	(8.5)	5.5	—	—	0.0	17.9	5.5	51.7	5.0	135
Sierra Emerging Growth	SCG	—	15.3	—	—	—	0.2	26.8	9.0	33.8	4.5	145
Sierra Growth & Income	G&I	—	5.5	8.4	—	—	1.3	28.0	5.5	89.0	4.5	123
Sierra International Growth	Intl	—	(6.6)	—	—	—	0.7	N.A.	7.0	28.0	4.5	160
Skyline Special Equities [1]	SCG	A	45.0	23.2	23.9	28,453	0.0	17.0	8.0	69.6	None	120
SmallCap World	Glo	—	8.4	—	—	—	1.0	N.A.	13.9	1,254.6	5.75	120
Smith Barney Equity	Gro	E	3.4	7.3	10.0	15,467	1.8	N.A.	7.4	86.5	4.5	97
Smith Barney Income & Growth A	G&I	D	8.2	6.8	11.9	17,021	5.6	N.A.	4.0	569.4	4.5	98
Smith Barney Utility A	Sec	—	8.5	—	—	—	7.3	N.A.	1.8	124.3	4.5	98
Smith Barney World—International Equity	Intl	A	3.5	7.0	11.8	16,633	0.0	N.A.	0.8	120.0	4.5	128
SoGen International	Gro	C	9.0	8.2	11.2	16,298	4.3	19.7	30.0	478.5	3.75	196
Sound Shore	Gro	B	23.9	13.1	16.0	21,149	1.4	17.5	15.0	35.4	None	71
Stagecoach Asset Allocation	AA	D	9.3	12.4	11.4	16,566	3.7	N.A.	2.0	476.4	4.5	96
Stagecoach Corporate Stock	G&I	C	10.6	10.3	14.1	19,835	1.5	N.A.	1.0	221.7	None	54
Stagecoach Growth & Income	G&I	—	15.6	—	—	—	1.5	N.A.	3.0	33.4	4.5	67
State Street Master Investment	G&I	C	9.4	11.1	14.0	18,747	1.6	23.8	0.8	692.9	4.5	72
SteinRoe Capital Opportunities	Max	E	4.1	5.4	8.6	15,220	0.8	28.5	8.6	118.8	None	65
SteinRoe Prime Equities	G&I	B	12.9	12.7	14.9	20,267	1.1	20.7	4.2	68.8	None	55
SteinRoe Special	Gro	A	16.2	12.8	18.6	23,447	1.6	20.9	9.9	626.1	None	57
SteinRoe Stock	Gro	B	11.2	17.1	16.5	21,643	0.5	26.8	10.5	372.5	None	53

MONEY's grades compare domestic equity, international equity and gold and sector funds by five-year, risk-adjusted return to Dec. 1. **Value of $10,000** is to Dec. 24. [1]Closed to new investors [2]May impose back-end load or exit fee [3]Three years [4]Performance from Dec. 31, 1987 [5]Reflects borrowing to boost investments [6]Manager absorbing expenses [7]Investment by contractual plan only N.A.: Not available

FUND NAME	Type	MONEY risk-adjusted grade	% compound annual gain (or loss) to Dec. 24, 1992			Value of $10,000 invested five years ago (net of sales charge)	Portfolio analysis			Net assets (millions)	Expense analysis	
			One year	Three years	Five years		% yield	P/E ratio	% cash		% maximum initial sales charge	Five-year projection
SteinRoe Total Return	Eql	D	9.8	11.3	12.1	$17,787	5.0	23.6	10.4	$173.5	None	$48
Stratton Monthly Dividend Shares	Sec	C	13.6	13.1	13.4	18,771	6.8	15.5	5.5	78.2	None	67
Strong Common Stock	Gro	—	24.6	—	—	—	6.5	24.7	16.0	105.9	None	124
Strong Discovery	Max	—	5.2	17.8	—	—	12.1	21.8	7.0	153.5	None	104
Strong Income	Flx	E	10.2	5.9	5.9	13,319	8.9	N.A.	21.0	103.5	None	84
Strong Investment	Bal	E	6.2	8.3	8.9	15,372	4.1	N.A.	2.0	212.5	None	80
Strong Opportunity	Gro	D	20.0	10.9	13.2	18,637	0.3	29.2	11.0	163.3	None	110
Strong Total Return	G&I	E	2.8	7.2	7.5	14,479	0.8	22.9	3.0	577.3	None	83
SunAmerica Balanced Assets	Bal	E	7.5	9.4	10.2	16,413	1.9	29.6	6.6	93.1	None[2]	114
SunAmerica Capital Appreciation	Gro	E	11.3	2.2	8.6	15,394	0.0	24.0	4.7	78.2	None[2]	146
SunAmerica Emerging Growth	SCG	—	17.7	12.3	11.2	17,360	0.0	N.A.	13.0	28.3	None[2]	125
SunAmerica Equity—Aggressive Growth	SCG	B	22.3	10.5	18.6	22,836	0.0	25.9	15.5	26.8	5.75	154
SunAmerica Equity—Growth	Gro	C	14.3	10.6	16.0	19,983	0.2	27.2	15.6	27.7	5.75	149
SunAmerica Multi-Asset—Total Return	AA	E	9.6	5.0	9.5	14,952	2.4	N.A.	0.0	25.5	5.75	153
Templeton Developing Markets	Intl	—	(10.7)	—	—	—	0.2	N.A.	14.8	165.3	5.75	139[3]
Templeton Foreign	Intl	A	1.9	4.8	13.1	17,215	2.8	N.A.	16.5	1,678.4	5.75	137
Templeton Global Opportunities	Glo	—	10.0	—	—	—	1.4	N.A.	17.3	234.4	5.75	147
Templeton Growth	Glo	A	6.4	7.6	13.3	17,672	2.7	N.A.	12.8	3,271.1	5.75	134
Templeton Real Estate Securities	Sec	—	6.5	6.4	—	—	3.1	N.A.	14.9	37.6	5.75	184
Templeton Smaller Companies Growth	Glo	A	5.0	6.6	12.8	17,257	2.0	N.A.	20.4	932.6	5.75	146
Templeton Value	Glo	—	(1.9)	—	—	—	1.7	N.A.	4.2	109.1	5.75	160
Templeton World	Glo	B	5.6	4.2	10.3	15,478	2.9	N.A.	5.6	4,021.4	5.75	106
Thomson Equity Income B	Eql	—	9.9	6.7	—	—	2.9	N.A.	25.0	45.1	None[2]	113
Thomson Growth B	Gro	B	5.3	13.7	16.5	21,888	0.1	31.3	6.0	853.0	None[2]	108
Thomson International B	Intl	C	(2.2)	(1.2)	6.3	13,644	0.0	N.A.	15.0	28.0	None[2]	128
Thomson Opportunity B	Max	A	30.3	25.6	23.8	29,101	0.0	28.1	14.0	179.0	None[2]	113
TNE Balanced	Bal	E	16.6	9.8	9.2	14,981	2.5	23.1	1.4	82.0	5.75	136
TNE Growth [1]	Gro	D	(5.0)	15.5	13.0	17,647	1.0	25.8	1.0	1,102.3	5.75	124
TNE Growth Opportunities	G&I	C	13.3	12.0	13.9	18,199	1.6	25.0	3.5	78.8	5.75	121
TNE Retirement Equity	G&I	E	20.2	8.9	8.5	14,429	1.7	26.3	1.0	150.5	5.75	124
Tower Capital Appreciation	Max	—	4.1	9.5	—	—	1.9	19.4	4.5	74.6	4.5	89
Transamerica Capital Appreciation	Max	E	6.9	10.1	14.1	18,216	0.0	38.7	1.0	80.1	4.75	134
Transamerica Growth & Income A	G&I	D	9.8	12.0	12.4	17,273	2.6	18.1	6.0	91.3	4.75	122
Transamerica Special—Blue Chip	Gro	E	5.8	11.1	10.4	16,650	0.0	26.6	9.0	41.6	None[2]	166
Transamerica Special—Emerging Growth B	SCG	A	14.4	20.1	21.6	26,626	0.0	25.8	8.0	77.5	None[2]	170
T. Rowe Price Balanced	Bal	—	10.5	12.1	12.9	13,556	4.0	N.A.	2.6	255.3	None	55
T. Rowe Price Capital Appreciation	Max	B	11.9	9.7	13.6	19,274	3.6	32.8	22.6	322.0	None	68
T. Rowe Price Equity Income	Eql	C	16.9	10.3	14.0	19,318	4.2	26.3	10.6	1,913.9	None	58
T. Rowe Price European Stock	Intl	—	(3.7)	—	—	—	0.9	N.A.	5.1	186.1	None	87
T. Rowe Price Growth & Income	G&I	C	17.8	10.7	14.6	19,999	4.0	29.8	7.1	760.4	None	51
T. Rowe Price Growth Stock	Gro	D	9.5	11.0	12.1	17,999	1.3	27.5	3.6	1,819.6	None	49
T. Rowe Price International Discovery	Intl	—	(7.6)	(4.2)	—	—	1.1	N.A.	8.3	178.4	None	82
T. Rowe Price International Stock	Intl	B	(0.2)	0.9	8.4	14,935	1.6	N.A.	9.8	1,924.9	None	61
T. Rowe Price New America Growth	Gro	A	13.8	15.8	20.0	25,012	0.0	24.9	6.2	376.5	None	69
T. Rowe Price New Asia	Intl	—	12.3	—	—	—	1.5	N.A.	5.8	272.5	None	95
T. Rowe Price New Era	Sec	D	5.7	2.4	7.7	14,629	2.7	38.9	7.4	720.0	None	47
T. Rowe Price New Horizons	SCG	C	13.4	14.6	16.2	21,304	0.3	27.3	7.7	1,250.5	None	53
T. Rowe Price OTC	SCG	E	15.4	7.4	13.4	18,562	0.5	21.4	13.5	165.4	None	78
T. Rowe Price Science & Technology	Sec	A	21.7	22.6	23.7	28,868	0.0	28.6	4.8	196.2	None	69
T. Rowe Price Small-Cap Value	SCG	—	23.4	13.1	—	—	1.0	16.5	18.1	162.0	None	69
T. Rowe Price Spectrum—Growth	G&I	—	10.2	—	—	—	1.9	N.A.	0.3	283.5	None	0
T. Rowe Price Spectrum—Income	Flx	—	8.7	—	—	—	7.2	N.A.	17.0	308.4	None	0

MONEY's grades compare domestic equity, international equity and gold and sector funds by five-year, risk-adjusted return to Dec. 1. **Value of $10,000** is to Dec. 24. [1]Closed to new investors [2]May impose back-end load or exit fee [3]Three years [4]Performance from Dec. 31, 1987 [5]Reflects borrowing to boost investments [6]Manager absorbing expenses [7]Investment by contractual plan only N.A.: Not available

FUND NAME	Type	MONEY risk-adjusted grade	% compound annual gain (or loss) to Dec. 24, 1992 One year	Three years	Five years	Value of $10,000 invested five years ago (net of sales charge)	% yield	P/E ratio	% cash	Net assets (millions)	% maximum initial sales charge	Five-year projection
Twentieth Century Balanced	Bal	—	(3.4)	12.3	—	—	2.1	30.3	3.9	$642.2	None	$55
Twentieth Century Growth Investors	Max	B	0.6	16.2	17.4	$22,824	0.1	28.8	2.3	4,396.4	None	55
Twentieth Century Heritage Investors	Gro	C	13.0	10.8	15.5	20,982	1.2	20.8	7.8	355.3	None	55
Twentieth Century Select Investors	Gro	D	(1.2)	8.5	12.7	18,594	1.6	20.8	0.4	4,469.2	None	55
Twentieth Century Ultra Investors	Max	A	4.3	27.1	25.4	31,203	0.0	30.5	0.7	4,012.8	None	55
Twentieth Century Vista Investors	Max	C	(0.8)	12.3	16.3	21,625	0.0	30.6	4.7	788.9	None	55
Twentieth Century World—International	Intl	—	7.3	—	—	—	0.1	N.A.	1.3	219.2	None	55
United Accumulative	Gro	D	15.5	8.3	13.0	17,216	2.4	21.3	24.0	905.6	8.5	117
United Continental Income	Bal	D	11.5	9.3	12.2	16,429	3.7	21.3	13.9	354.9	8.5	126
United Gold & Government	Gold	E	(10.6)	(11.6)	(4.5)	7,205	1.2	N.A.	8.1	31.2	8.5	163
United Income	Eql	B	14.6	11.4	15.3	19,140	2.1	26.2	4.9	2,336.2	8.5	119
United International Growth	Intl	E	1.9	0.7	4.5	11,636	0.4	N.A.	3.0	301.7	8.5	144
United New Concepts	SCG	B	7.6	26.2	16.7	20,345	0.2	33.8	30.5	155.5	8.5	143
United Retirement Shares	G&I	A	15.1	12.1	15.0	18,589	2.8	25.7	17.1	281.9	8.5	127
United Science & Energy	Sec	B	(2.3)	13.4	14.4	18,311	0.4	34.6	13.8	383.2	8.5	128
United Services Global Resources	Sec	E	1.6	(5.1)	(1.5)	9,169	1.3	N.A.	6.1	24.2	None	136
United Services Gold Shares	Gold	E	(51.7)	(35.3)	(21.7)	2,867	5.8	N.A.	22.3	147.5	None	101
United Services World Gold	Gold	E	(2.7)	(13.3)	(9.1)	6,144	0.0	N.A.	6.3	61.8	None	129
United Vanguard	Gro	D	4.8	8.3	10.4	15,506	1.3	29.7	16.1	844.1	8.5	134
USAA Investment Trust—Balanced	Bal	—	6.3	6.9	—	—	4.0	27.1	19.7	82.8	None	55
USAA Investment Trust—Cornerstone	AA	E	8.5	3.9	8.0	14,751	3.2	N.A.	1.0	567.5	None	65
USAA Investment Trust—Gold	Gold	E	(5.2)	(14.1)	(8.9)	6,198	1.2	N.A.	17.0	114.2	None	79
USAA Investment Trust—International	Intl	—	2.6	1.1	—	—	1.1	N.A.	7.5	42.8	None	99
USAA Mutual—Aggressive Growth	SCG	E	(5.8)	10.6	12.3	17,819	0.0	25.6	6.7	234.9	None	48
USAA Mutual—Growth	Gro	C	13.1	12.4	13.3	19,102	1.9	25.7	2.0	432.2	None	61
USAA Mutual—Income	Flx	B	9.3	11.9	12.6	17,709	7.5	N.A.	0.9	1,358.9	None	26
USAA Mutual—Income Stock	Eql	B	9.9	10.8	15.1	20,514	5.3	21.9	1.5	480.0	None	46
UST Master Equity	Max	B	19.2	11.3	15.1	19,699	0.5	26.5	3.0	87.9	4.5	107
UST Master—Income & Growth	G&I	D	23.1	7.6	13.0	17,717	2.9	25.9	6.6	27.2	4.5	111
UST Master International	Intl	E	(6.4)	(4.4)	4.2	11,659	0.1	N.A.	0.0	43.8	4.5	127
Value Line Convertible	Conv	C	15.2	11.9	12.1	19,471	5.0	N.A.	6.2	38.4	None	63
Value Line Fund	G&I	B	7.2	15.6	16.7	21,987	0.9	25.5	3.4	281.0	None	47
Value Line Income	Eql	C	4.0	10.3	12.6	18,333	3.2	20.5	3.1	163.5	None	51
Value Line Leveraged Growth	Max	D	1.7	12.4	13.9	19,608	0.9	22.6	9.3	267.3	None	51
Value Line Special Situations	Gro	E	(2.1)	7.5	8.9	15,378	0.3	29.6	20.5	85.4	None	57
Van Eck Gold Resources	Gold	E	(0.8)	(12.7)	(8.9)	5,844	0.3	N.A.	4.7	125.4	5.75	141
Van Eck International Investors	Gold	E	(27.8)	(19.1)	(9.0)	5,723	1.8	N.A.	2.3	430.5	8.5	144
Van Eck World Trends	Glo	E	(4.9)	(1.3)	2.9	10,901	0.5	N.A.	4.2	31.9	5.75	143
Vanguard Asset Allocation	AA	—	10.5	11.3	—	—	4.2	25.8	2.1	502.4	None	25
Vanguard Convertible	Conv	C	20.3	13.7	14.4	20,288	4.5	N.A.	11.8	87.3	None	45
Vanguard Equity Income	Eql	—	12.1	6.7	—	—	5.1	24.4	4.9	777.6	None	26
Vanguard Explorer	SCG	C	16.8	16.2	16.3	21,210	0.6	23.0	12.1	486.8	None	31
Vanguard Index Trust—Extended Market	SCG	—	14.7	10.9	14.7	19,992	1.4	25.0	2.6	480.4	None	70
Vanguard Index Trust—500 Portfolio	G&I	B	11.5	11.2	15.2	20,788	3.1	25.9	0.4	5,767.1	None	60
Vanguard Intl. Equity Index—Europe	Intl	—	(0.3)	—	—	—	2.8	N.A.	0.2	252.3	None	78
Vanguard Intl. Equity Index—Pacific	Intl	—	(12.4)	—	—	—	0.6	N.A.	0.6	197.6	None	77
Vanguard Morgan Growth	Gro	B	13.1	12.0	15.6	20,889	2.2	21.0	7.1	999.8	None	26
Vanguard PRIMECAP	Gro	D	10.4	12.3	14.2	19,474	0.9	24.2	5.9	566.6	None	38
Vanguard Quantitative Portfolio	G&I	B	11.3	11.6	15.7	21,189	2.8	20.5	2.6	375.7	None	24
Vanguard Small Capitalization Stock	SCG	D	19.9	11.5	13.6	18,858	1.3	23.6	3.9	201.8	1.0	72
Vanguard Special. Portfolio—Energy	Sec	C	8.4	1.5	12.4	18,042	3.3	45.3	8.6	170.4	None[2]	30
Vanguard Special. Portfolio—Gold & PM	Gold	E	(17.8)	(12.5)	(5.3)	7,489	3.4	N.A.	6.6	189.4	None[2]	32

MONEY's grades compare domestic equity, international equity and gold and sector funds by five-year, risk-adjusted return to Dec. 1. Value of $10,000 is to Dec. 24. [1]Closed to new investors [2]May impose back-end load or exit fee [3]Three years [4]Performance from Dec. 31, 1987 [5]Reflects borrowing to boost investments [6]Manager absorbing expenses [7]Investment by contractual plan only N.A.: Not available

FUND NAME	Type	MONEY risk-adjusted grade	% compound annual gain (or loss) to Dec. 24, 1992			Value of $10,000 invested five years ago (net of sales charge)	Portfolio analysis			Net assets (millions)	Expense analysis	
			One year	Three years	Five years		% yield	P/E ratio	% cash		% maximum initial sales charge	Five-year projection
Vanguard Special. Portfolio—Health Care	Sec	A	1.4	19.1	23.1	$28,537	1.5	30.6	3.2	$577.1	None[2]	$30
Vanguard Special. Portfolio—Technology	Sec	C	16.7	15.8	13.6	19,146	1.1	28.9	17.3	33.8	None[2]	33
Vanguard STAR	Bal	C	12.4	9.9	13.0	18,661	4.7	N.A.	12.0	2,214.5	None	22
Vanguard Trustees' Commingled—Intl.	Intl	C	(5.4)	(3.8)	6.0	13,306	2.7	N.A.	3.9	780.1	None	21
Vanguard Trustees' Commingled—U.S.	G&I	D	8.8	7.1	11.9	17,856	2.5	18.4	4.9	78.5	None	24
Vanguard Wellesley Income	Flx	B	10.4	11.3	13.5	18,865	6.9	N.A.	2.0	2,898.0	None	22
Vanguard Wellington	Bal	D	10.5	9.3	12.5	18,313	5.0	21.1	2.1	5,101.3	None	20
Vanguard Windsor [1]	G&I	E	16.8	7.7	12.5	18,395	4.4	31.1	2.6	8,229.3	None	17
Vanguard Windsor II	G&I	C	15.2	9.4	15.2	20,697	3.8	24.7	8.4	4,799.9	None	27
Vanguard World—International Growth	Intl	D	(2.7)	(4.4)	4.3	12,174	2.0	N.A.	2.5	902.2	None	32
Vanguard World—U.S. Growth	Gro	A	6.4	17.1	18.6	23,746	1.2	23.5	9.4	1,488.9	None	27
Van Kampen Merritt Growth & Income A	G&I	E	10.9	9.0	11.9	16,983	1.8	20.5	12.4	28.3	4.9	137
Vista Capital Growth	Gro	A	18.6	21.6	25.9	30,242	0.1	N.A.	19.0	37.5	4.75	117
Vista Growth & Income	G&I	A	19.0	22.6	31.9	38,157	1.1	N.A.	20.0	135.8	4.75	121
Warburg Pincus Capital Appreciation	Gro	C	11.2	8.8	14.3	19,634	0.5	N.A.	3.0	116.6	None	60
Warburg Pincus Emerging Growth	SCG	—	15.2	15.7	—	—	0.0	28.1	9.0	94.7	None	69
Warburg Pincus International Equity	Intl	—	(1.4)	3.2	—	—	1.3	N.A.	2.8	102.1	None	82
Washington Mutual Investors	G&I	C	12.3	9.5	14.1	18,603	3.4	28.6	4.3	9,479.3	5.75	96
Wayne Hummer Growth	Gro	B	13.9	14.5	14.1	19,739	1.5	N.A.	22.6	70.1	None	68
Westcore Midco Growth	Gro	—	8.4	22.4	—	—	1.9	27.1	9.7	178.3	4.5	80
William M. Blair Growth Shares	Gro	B	10.7	15.1	16.0	21,069	0.5	N.A.	10.6	99.6	None	50
Winthrop Focus Aggressive Growth	SCG	A	25.0	15.7	18.1	23,015	0.3	N.A.	2.4	38.6	None[2]	72[3]
Winthrop Focus Growth	Gro	E	6.3	7.0	11.3	17,384	1.4	33.3	0.1	49.3	None[2]	73
Winthrop Focus Growth & Income	G&I	D	8.9	8.4	12.5	18,353	2.5	30.6	2.0	47.1	None[2]	58[3]
World Funds—Newport Tiger	Intl	—	21.9	8.2	—	—	0.0	N.A.	8.0	80.7	5.0	143
World Funds—Vontobel EuroPacific	Intl	E	(0.4)	0.4	3.6	11,458	0.0	N.A.	20.0	41.2	5.0	148
World Funds—Vontobel U.S. Value	G&I	—	18.7	—	—	—	1.1	18.1	8.0	27.9	5.0	143
WPG Growth & Income	G&I	C	16.8	13.0	14.4	19,822	1.5	20.7	2.5	50.0	None	82
WPG Tudor	Max	C	8.0	12.8	15.0	20,366	0.6	31.0	0.6	248.2	None	70
Yamaichi Global	Glo	—	1.2	(3.2)	—	—	0.3	N.A.	1.0	52.1	4.75	147
Zweig Series—Appreciation A	SCG	—	11.8	—	—	—	0.3	N.A.	25.0	184.2	5.5	142
Zweig Series—Priority A	Max	D	(1.2)	8.2	13.2	17,912	0.6	24.0	40.0	56.4	5.5	151
Zweig Series—Strategy A	Gro	—	9.5	—	—	—	1.5	13.7	12.0	344.5	5.5	136

FUND NAME	Type	MONEY risk-adjusted grade	% compound annual gain (or loss) to Dec. 24, 1992			Value of $10,000 invested five years ago (net of sales charge)	Portfolio analysis			Net assets (millions)	Expense analysis	
			One year	Three years	Five years		% yield	Average maturity (years)	% cash		% maximum initial sales charge	Five-year projection
Advantage Government Securities	USG	D	10.4	11.4	9.6	$15,274	6.8	21.1	0.3	$136.5	None[2]	$77
Advantage High Yield	HYC	—	28.3	16.8	—	—	11.3	12.5	3.3	55.4	None[2]	80
AIM Government Securities	USG	C	6.5	9.5	9.3	14,779	7.4	3.0	6.1	122.4	4.75	100
AIM High Yield	HYC	A	18.6	15.3	12.8	17,182	11.6	10.1	5.0	301.4	4.75	110
AIM High-Yield Securities	HYC	E	15.4	4.4	3.3	11,165	8.8	10.4	1.0	41.3	4.75	145
AIM Income	HYC	C	8.6	9.7	10.3	15,407	7.7	17.3	2.5	229.8	4.75	100
Alliance Bond–High Yield Portfolio	HYC	E	17.0	9.8	4.9	11,805	11.1	11.5	10.9	117.1	4.75	133
Alliance Bond–Monthly Income Portfolio	HGC	B	14.5	12.3	11.6	16,191	8.7	11.4	10.7	67.5	4.75	124
Alliance Bond–U.S. Government Port. A	USG	D	6.8	9.9	9.8	15,206	8.3	7.5	0.0	520.5	3.0	87
Alliance Mortgage Income Securities A	MBS	A	8.5	11.5	10.8	15,967	9.3	5.0	0.0	752.3	3.0	92
Alliance Multi-Market Income	WI	—	1.4	—	—	—	4.6	0.2	92.9	64.2	None	93
Alliance Multi-Market Strategy A	WI	—	(1.8)	—	—	—	9.1	2.1	42.9	154.8	3.0	174

MONEY's grades compare long-term and short/intermediate-term bonds by five-year, risk-adjusted return to Dec. 1. The top 20% in each group receive an A, the next 20% a B and so on. **Value of $10,000** is to Dec. 1. [1]Currently closed to new investors [2]Fund may impose back-end load or exit fee. [3]Three years [4]Manager absorbing expenses [5]Performance from Dec. 31, 1987.

FUND NAME	Type	MONEY risk-adjusted grade	% compound annual gain (or loss) to Dec. 24, 1992 One year	Three years	Five years	Value of $10,000 invested five years ago (net of sales charge)	% yield	Average maturity (years)	% cash	Net assets (millions)	% maximum initial sales charge	Five-year projection
Alliance Short-Term Multi-Market A	WI	—	1.2	7.4	—	—	7.7	1.4	30.6	$1,711.1	3.0	$88
Alliance World Income	WI	—	2.2	—	—	—	4.9	0.4	100.0	351.6	None	80
American Capital Corporate Bond A	HGC	C	9.0	10.7	9.9	$15,091	8.1	18.4	4.2	192.0	4.75	100
American Capital Federal Mortgage A	STT	D	3.6	7.6	8.3	14,326	6.2	1.8	2.3	117.3	4.0	112
American Capital Government Securities A	USG	B	7.1	10.6	10.5	15,845	8.3	6.3	24.3	3,735.9	4.75	98
American Capital High Yield A	HYC	E	17.5	11.7	7.1	13,134	11.2	7.6	6.6	433.4	4.75	103
American High-Income Trust	HYC	—	14.8	14.6	—	—	9.1	6.9	3.4	437.7	4.75	97
Babson Bond Trust–Short-Term Portfolio	STT	—	7.7	10.0	—	—	7.3	4.5	N.A.	29.0	None	37
Babson Bond Trust–Long-Term Portfolio	HGC	B	8.6	10.3	10.0	16,225	7.6	8.0	1.2	145.4	None	54
Bartlett Fixed Income	HYC	C	7.7	9.1	9.6	15,863	6.2	8.6	3.0	142.2	None	55
Benham Government–GNMA Income	MBS	A	8.2	11.2	11.4	16,948	7.7	10.0	0.5	936.3	None	32
Benham Gov. Income–Adjustable Rate	MBS	—	5.4	—	—	—	6.3	4.5	0.0	1,485.8	None	36
Benham Government Treasury Note	STT	B	7.1	10.0	9.7	15,598	5.7	4.0	0.0	370.6	None	30
Benham Target–1995	STT	A	7.5	10.8	11.2	16,984	0.0	3.0	0.0	94.6	None	36
Benham Target–2000	USG	A	10.1	11.6	13.2	18,768	0.0	8.0	0.0	190.1	None	38
Benham Target–2005	USG	B	11.8	11.2	14.4	19,637	0.0	12.9	0.0	168.4	None	37
Benham Target–2010	USG	B	12.2	10.3	14.6	19,720	0.0	17.5	0.0	55.7	None	39
Benham Target–2015	USG	C	11.1	8.7	14.7	19,129	0.0	22.6	0.0	131.4	None	35
Benham Target–2020	USG	—	11.5	—	—	—	0.0	27.5	0.0	41.6	None	38
Blanchard Short-Term Global Income	WI	—	3.2	—	—	—	7.6	1.3	5.0	1,359.1	None	96
Bond Fund of America	HGC	A	10.9	11.4	11.0	16,091	8.1	9.1	8.9	3,762.9	4.75	88
Boston Co. Managed Income	STT	C	9.2	9.9	9.2	15,233	8.2	13.4	7.3	99.9	None	62
Bull & Bear Global Income	WI	E	12.7	9.0	5.6	12,778	8.5	16.0	0.0	46.6	None	104
Bull & Bear U.S. Government Securities	MBS	D	6.2	9.5	8.6	15,163	6.2	25.0	0.0	26.1	None	101
Calvert Income	HGC	A	8.3	9.9	11.0	15,996	7.5	16.0	1.0	43.5	4.75	104
Calvert Social Investment–Bond	HGC	B	7.6	10.3	10.4	15,473	6.8	15.0	7.0	50.3	4.75	88
Capital World Bond	WI	E	1.9	9.1	7.4	13,623	8.6	9.1	12.9	224.0	4.75	119
Capstone Government Income	STT	E	3.5	3.0	5.5	13,022	3.7	1.0	6.8	111.7	None	89
Cardinal Government Obligation	MBS	A	6.6	9.9	9.9	15,310	8.9	15.5	0.2	171.3	4.5	84
Colonial Federal Securities A	USG	C	7.1	9.5	10.0	15,408	7.9	21.7	0.0	1,851.6	4.75	111
Colonial High Yield Securities A	HYC	C	21.5	14.3	11.0	15,977	10.3	7.5	0.0	347.5	4.75	118
Colonial Income A	HGC	D	9.4	10.0	9.8	14,976	8.6	16.0	0.0	152.3	4.75	113
Colonial Strategic Income A	HYC	A	9.7	9.3	10.7	16,627	11.3	7.7	0.1	446.9	4.75	106
Colonial U.S. Government Fund A	MBS	D	5.4	8.7	8.7	14,471	8.4	16.9	(0.1)[6]	1,151.5	4.75	108
Columbia Fixed Income Securities	HGC	A	8.4	11.1	11.0	16,712	7.1	6.5	3.8	266.5	None	38
Columbia U.S. Government Securities	STT	D	5.9	9.4	8.6	14,967	4.7	2.7	2.0	38.5	None	42
Common Sense Government	USG	B	7.4	10.3	10.2	15,168	7.4	5.1	1.0	272.7	6.75	117
Compass Capital–Fixed Income	HGC	—	9.0	10.1	—	—	6.8	10.5	4.2	164.5	3.75	85
Compass Capital–Intl. Fixed Income	WI	—	3.8	—	—	—	0.5	6.0	1.3	33.8	3.75	108
Compass Capital–Short-Intermediate	STT	—	7.3	9.1	—	—	6.6	3.8	14.4	137.6	3.75	83
Composite Income	HGC	D	8.0	11.0	9.4	14,881	7.2	6.7	2.4	85.0	4.0	97
Composite U.S. Government Securities	USG	B	6.4	10.1	10.2	15,461	7.1	6.9	1.1	191.5	4.0	94
Connecticut Mutual–Government	MBS	B	6.6	10.2	10.5	15,625	7.2	7.1	23.0	68.4	4.0	97
Connecticut Mutual–Income Account	STT	D	7.0	9.1	8.6	14,822	8.3	3.6	6.0	35.8	2.0	71
Dean Witter Federal Securities	USG	C	7.2	9.3	9.6	15,901	7.1	13.6	3.0	1,195.9	None[2]	102
Dean Witter Global Short-Term	WI	—	2.9	—	—	—	7.5	2.6	5.7	454.9	None[2]	88
Dean Witter High Yield Securities	HYC	E	34.0	10.1	5.0	11,222	10.0	9.0	5.8	510.1	5.5	95
Dean Witter Intermediate Income	STT	—	6.7	8.3	—	—	7.0	3.8	6.7	194.2	None[2]	112
Dean Witter Premier Income	MBS	—	4.4	—	—	—	7.5	1.8	0.0	155.8	3.0	68[3]
Dean Witter Short-Term U.S. Treasury	STT	—	5.7	—	—	—	5.3	2.2	0.0	588.2	None	27[3]
Dean Witter U.S. Government Securities	MBS	D	6.3	8.6	8.7	15,081	8.1	5.0	0.0	12,686.1	None[2]	84
Dean Witter Worldwide Income	WI	—	3.8	6.8	—	—	6.9	5.7	6.1	338.7	None[2]	115

MONEY's grades compare long-term and short/intermediate-term bonds by five-year, risk-adjusted return to Dec. 1. The top 20% in each group receive an A, the next 20% a B and so on. **Value of $10,000** is to Dec. 1. [1]Currently closed to new investors [2]Fund may impose back-end load or exit fee. [3]Three years [4]Manager absorbing expenses [5]Performance from Dec. 31, 1987. [6]Reflects borrowing to boost investments

FUND NAME	Type	MONEY risk-adjusted grade	% compound annual gain (or loss) to Dec. 24, 1992			Value of $10,000 invested five years ago (net of sales charge)	Portfolio analysis			Net assets (millions)	Expense analysis	
			One year	Three years	Five years		% yield	Average maturity (years)	% cash		% maximum initial sales charge	Five-year projection
Delaware Group–Delchester	HYC	C	17.6	13.9	11.2	$16,114	11.5	6.3	0.0	$779.3	4.75	$104
Delaware Group–Treas. Rsvs. Intermed.	STT	C	5.9	9.4	8.8	14,709	7.5	3.1	1.7	625.9	3.0	78
Delaware Group–U.S. Government Income	USG	C	7.0	10.2	9.7	15,092	8.7	7.0	0.0	191.8	4.75	109
Dreyfus A Bond Plus	HGC	B	9.3	10.5	11.0	16,803	7.3	16.1	1.9	545.4	None	49
Dreyfus GNMA	MBS	C	6.9	10.2	9.8	15,852	7.6	22.5	0.6	1,862.8	None	53
Dreyfus Investors GNMA	MBS	C	8.0	9.7	9.6	15,707	7.7	20.9	0.5	45.1	None	82
Dreyfus 100% U.S. Treasury Intermediate	STT	B	8.0	10.5	10.0	15,968	7.8	7.0	0.2	237.6	None	53
Dreyfus 100% U.S. Treasury Long Term	USG	B	9.1	11.1	11.4	17,051	7.6	20.5	1.7	245.2	None	54
Dreyfus 100% U.S. Treasury Short Term	STT	B	7.1	8.7	9.2	15,660	8.6	2.9	2.1	137.0	None	82
Dreyfus Premier GNMA	MBS	A	7.2	11.0	11.6	16,192	7.4	22.2	1.4	150.2	4.5	106
Dreyfus Short-Intermediate Government	STT	B	9.2	10.3	9.5	15,630	7.1	3.2	1.4	322.2	None	44
Dreyfus Strategic Income	HYC	A	10.1	11.3	11.9	16,912	7.6	13.4	1.9	140.9	3.0	131
Eaton Vance Government Obligations	STT	A	5.8	9.8	9.9	15,208	9.0	N.A.	1.0	467.6	4.75	148
Eaton Vance High Income Trust	HYC	D	19.8	10.5	9.7	15,604	11.8	7.0	5.3	299.5	None[2]	137
Eaton Vance Income of Boston	HYC	C	19.1	12.6	11.3	16.328	11.8	7.0	1.9	85.0	4.75	108
Eaton Vance Short-Term Global	WI	—	(0.4)	—	—	—	7.2	N.A.	1.6	577.0	None[2]	113
Enterprise High Yield Bond	HYC	D	17.4	11.0	8.9	14,799	9.3	10.3	2.0	30.6	4.75	115
Enterprise U.S. Government Securities	USG	D	10.1	10.5	9.1	14,769	7.8	26.3	7.0	62.0	4.75	115
Federated ARMs	MBS	D	4.4	8.7	9.7	16,105	6.1	2.0	0.5	1,185.8	None	29
Federated Bond	HGC	D	9.5	10.4	10.1	15,727	6.4	21.0	5.0	36.7	None	48
Federated GNMA	MBS	A	7.0	10.8	11.1	16,868	8.1	5.8	0.2	1,656.3	None	29
Federated High Yield Trust	HYC	C	15.7	15.5	12.1	17,448	10.8	5.5	3.5	304.3	None	42
Federated Income	USG	A	6.3	10.2	10.1	16,014	7.7	4.9	0.4	1,471.6	None	28
Federated Intermediate Government	STT	B	6.8	9.9	9.4	15,538	5.7	3.1	0.8	813.0	None	28
Federated Short-Intermediate Government	STT	E	5.4	8.4	8.2	14,799	5.0	1.5	1.5	1,052.4	None	27
Federated Short-Term Income	STT	E	6.1	7.4	8.0	14,571	6.0	2.0	0.0	90.1	None	30
Fidelity Advisor–High Yield	HYC	A	25.1	21.5	16.9	20,666	10.4	7.6	7.1	132.8	4.75	105
Fidelity Advisor–Limited Term	STT	A	8.0	10.2	10.1	16,050	8.0	10.0	6.3	153.1	4.75	97
Fidelity Advisor–Short Fixed Income	STT	D	8.0	9.0	8.6	14,860	8.3	2.8	6.7	149.6	1.5	64
Fidelity Capital & Income	HYC	B	27.4	16.8	12.3	17,227	8.0	6.3	4.3	1,818.1	None[2]	45
Fidelity Global Bond	WI	E	4.2	9.6	8.7	15,192	10.1	8.0	9.7	348.3	None	55
Fidelity Government Securities	USG	B	9.0	11.4	10.6	16,267	7.2	13.8	0.7	581.4	None	37
Fidelity Income–GNMA Portfolio	MBS	A	7.1	10.3	10.4	16,344	6.9	7.1	7.0	951.2	None	46
Fidelity Income–Mortgage Securities	MBS	B	5.8	9.9	10.0	16,029	7.0	7.5	4.0	438.6	None	46
Fidelity Intermediate Bond	STT	B	6.8	9.5	9.5	15,546	7.3	9.6	17.1	1,444.1	None	36
Fidelity Investment Grade Bond	HGC	A	9.4	11.2	10.8	16,591	7.9	13.4	11.0	1,102.2	None	39
Fidelity Short-Intermediate Government	STT	—	6.7	—	—	—	6.6	4.0	0.8	173.8	None	13[3]
Fidelity Short-Term Bond Portfolio	STT	C	7.9	9.1	8.7	15,160	8.3	2.9	12.5	1,823.1	None	48
Fidelity Short-Term World Income	WI	—	5.3	—	—	—	7.5	2.6	5.0	672.6	None	55
Fidelity Spartan Ginnie Mae	MBS	—	6.8	—	—	—	7.5	7.8	0.1	840.1	None	19[4]
Fidelity Spartan Government Income	USG	—	8.1	10.7	—	—	7.0	9.7	7.7	520.6	None	41
Fidelity Spartan High Income	HYC	—	25.1	—	—	—	10.5	7.5	0.0	526.0	None[2]	27[3]
Fidelity Spartan Limited Maturity Gov.	STT	—	6.5	9.1	—	—	6.0	5.3	1.0	1,763.8	None	41
Fidelity Spartan Long-Term Government	USG	—	9.6	—	—	—	6.7	17.7	11.2	88.7	None	26[3]
Financial Bond Shares–High Yield	HYC	D	14.5	10.6	9.8	15,883	9.1	9.7	4.7	262.1	None	59
Financial Bond Shares–Select Income	HGC	A	10.8	11.2	10.6	16,371	8.0	10.6	1.8	150.2	None	64
Financial Bond–U.S. Government	USG	D	7.2	9.6	9.5	15,416	6.2	25.3	2.2	38.4	None	71
Financial Trust–Intermediate Government	STT	—	6.4	—	—	—	7.3	N.A.	1.7	30.1	None	52
First Investors Fund for Income	HYC	E	19.1	11.0	7.6	13,345	11.6	9.1	4.5	425.8	6.9	137
First Investors Government	USG	B	6.6	10.2	10.2	15,314	6.6	27.4	4.5	309.8	6.9	138
First Investors High Yield	HYC	E	19.5	9.9	6.7	12,824	9.3	8.9	4.9	200.5	6.9	156
Flag Investors Intermediate-Term Income	STT	—	6.0	—	—	—	6.9	13.9	5.1	79.8	1.5	54

MONEY's grades compare long-term and short/intermediate-term bonds by five-year, risk-adjusted return to Dec. 1. The top 20% in each group receive an A, the next 20% a B and so on. **Value of $10,000** is to Dec. 1. [1]Currently closed to new investors [2]Fund may impose back-end load or exit fee. [3]Three years [4]Manager absorbing expenses [5]Performance from Dec. 31, 1987.

FUND NAME	Type	MONEY risk-adjusted grade	% compound annual gain (or loss) to Dec. 24, 1992 — One year	Three years	Five years	Value of $10,000 invested five years ago (net of sales charge)	Portfolio analysis — % yield	Average maturity (years)	% cash	Net assets (millions)	Expense analysis — % maximum initial sales charge	Five-year projection
Flag Investors–Total Return Treasury	USG	—	6.9	9.0	—	—	7.6	11.1	15.0	$257.8	4.5	$92
Fortis Advantage–Gov. Total Return	USG	E	5.5	8.2	8.3	$14,125	8.4	14.4	11.9	97.6	4.5	112
Fortis Advantage–High Yield	HYC	—	16.0	13.5	—	—	11.0	9.0	3.6	48.2	4.5	124
Fortis U.S. Government Securities	USG	B	6.1	9.8	9.8	15,249	8.6	9.7	0.0	565.1	4.5	83
Fortress Adjustable Rate Government	MBS	—	4.7	—	—	—	5.8	2.0	0.5	1,225.0	1.0[2]	51[3]
Fortress Bond	HGC	D	16.6	14.6	10.9	16,341	8.1	14.0	3.5	47.7	1.0[2]	53[3]
Founders Government Securities	USG	—	6.1	8.1	—	—	4.9	5.5	2.0	43.3	None	65
FPA New Income	USG	A	11.1	12.6	11.7	16,350	6.7	5.2	13.8	80.4	4.5	91
Franklin AGE High Income	HYC	D	17.1	13.8	10.4	15,621	10.2	8.5	9.8	1,917.6	4.0	71
Franklin Inv. Trust–Adj. U.S. Gov. Sec.	MBS	E	4.0	7.4	7.8	14,140	5.6	27.0	0.0	3,496.3	4.0	78
Franklin Inv. Trust–Global Opportunity Income	WI	—	(0.3)	7.1	—	—	9.0	5.0	13.9	151.0	4.0	83
Franklin Inv. Trust–Short-Intermed. U.S.	STT	D	6.5	9.3	8.7	15,052	5.6	4.1	0.0	221.7	1.5	54
Franklin Managed–Investment Grade Income	HGC	D	6.5	9.9	9.1	14,793	7.0	4.3	2.6	28.3	4.0	106
Franklin U.S. Government Series	MBS	A	7.6	10.6	10.4	15,644	8.2	26.0	0.0	13,617.2	4.0	68
FT International Income	WI	—	(1.1)	—	—	—	7.3	9.8	4.4	91.9	4.5	83
Fund for U.S. Government Securities	MBS	B	5.6	9.8	9.9	15,259	8.3	3.9	1.5	1,621.3	4.5	93
FundTrust–Income	HYC	E	7.9	8.7	8.5	14,694	6.0	11.0	1.1	70.2	1.5	99
GNA Investors Trust–U.S. Government	USG	C	6.5	9.7	9.8	15,917	7.0	17.0	6.8	749.4	None[2]	99
Government Income Securities	USG	B	6.7	10.0	10.1	15,846	8.4	3.8	0.5	2,957.2	1.0[2]	60
Gradison-McDonald Government Income	USG	—	6.4	9.6	9.7	15,617	6.6	6.3	2.0	198.1	2.0	74
G.T. Global–Government Income A	WI	—	3.4	8.1	—	—	11.0	7.3	9.0	600.3	4.75	130
G.T. Global Strategic Income A	WI	—	2.8	8.3	—	—	7.5	8.4	1.8	84.5	4.75	143
Harbor Bond	STT	—	9.4	12.2	—	—	7.0	12.0	16.8	62.9	None	49
Heartland U.S. Government	USG	B	11.1	12.5	11.0	15,731	6.6	15.0	6.4	28.7	None	64
Heritage Income–Diversified	HYC	—	10.8	—	—	—	8.2	7.1	11.4	31.7	4.0	111
Heritage Income–Limited Maturity Gov.	STT	—	3.5	—	—	—	6.8	1.4	5.0	109.8	None	78
Huntington International–Hard Currency	WI	—	3.4	10.5	—	—	5.6	0.1	100.0	48.2	2.25	121
Huntington International–High Income	WI	—	(2.2)	9.3	—	—	8.3	0.1	100.0	44.6	2.25	119
Huntington Intl. Port.–Global Currency	WI	E	4.3	9.0	7.4	14,090	5.4	0.2	100.0	66.7	2.25	119
IAI Bond	HGC	C	7.7	10.4	10.7	16,303	6.5	12.2	23.6	111.7	None	61
IAI Government	USG	—	6.2	—	—	—	5.0	4.7	1.9	40.9	None	61
IAI Reserve	STT	E	3.4	6.5	7.0	14,072	4.2	0.2	82.9	122.2	None	47
IDS Bond	HYC	A	11.2	11.9	11.3	16,134	8.2	14.3	4.7	2,201.0	5.0	88
IDS Extra Income	HYC	D	20.8	14.1	10.1	15,208	10.6	8.4	2.1	1,315.1	5.0	94
IDS Federal Income	STT	A	6.8	9.3	9.5	14,899	6.7	7.7	6.6	913.8	5.0	91
IDS Global Bond	WI	—	9.6	12.3	—	—	7.9	11.7	24.5	86.0	5.0	122
IDS Selective	HGC	A	9.8	11.0	11.0	15,868	7.3	14.0	8.8	1,579.6	5.0	92
IDS Strategy–Income Portfolio	HYC	B	10.3	10.5	10.5	16,400	7.3	12.9	7.3	479.8	None[2]	120
IDS Strategy–Short-Term Income	STT	E	4.2	6.7	7.1[5]	14,142	5.2	3.9	11.0	170.7	None[2]	121
Intermediate Bond Fund of America	STT	—	6.8	9.3	—	—	7.7	5.1	6.4	1,294.9	4.75	95
Janus Intermediate Government Securities	STT	—	5.2	—	—	—	5.0	4.2	1.7	65.8	None	55
John Hancock Freedom Global Income B	WI	E	(1.8)	6.7	8.4	15,192	9.4	4.9	11.1	203.2	None[2]	103
John Hancock Freedom Short-Term World B	WI	—	3.2	—	—	—	7.8	1.4	10.2	242.2	None[2]	102
John Hancock Sovereign Bond	HGC	A	8.8	10.5	10.9	15,782	8.0	16.6	4.0	1,379.5	4.5	112
John Hancock Sovereign Government B	USG	C	5.7	9.3	9.8	16,160	7.4	6.8	1.5	197.8	None[2]	102
John Hancock Strategic Income	HYC	E	8.1	9.5	8.3	13,997	10.1	6.4	9.0	195.2	4.5	133
John Hancock–U.S. Gov. Securities	STT	D	5.0	8.2	8.5	14,252	6.3	3.7	2.7	259.5	4.5	120
Kemper Adjustable Rate U.S. Government	MBS	E	5.8	8.8	8.5	14,548	6.0	3.7	16.0	185.9	3.5	88
Kemper Diversified Income	HYC	A	18.5	16.1	14.0	20,083	10.1	9.0	2.0	256.0	4.5	110
Kemper Global Income	WI	—	(1.9)	10.0	—	—	8.6	4.6	5.0	76.4	4.5	125
Kemper High Yield	HYC	C	17.5	14.4	11.3	16,226	10.5	9.0	3.0	1,953.6	4.5	91
Kemper Income & Capital Preservation	HGC	C	8.6	10.8	10.3	15,298	7.9	13.0	9.0	486.7	4.5	89

MONEY's grades compare long-term and short/intermediate-term bonds by five-year, risk-adjusted return to Dec. 1. The top 20% in each group receive an A, the next 20% a B and so on. **Value of $10,000** is to Dec. 1. [1]Currently closed to new investors [2]Fund may impose back-end load or exit fee. [3]Three years [4]Manager absorbing expenses [5]Performance from Dec. 31, 1987.

FUND NAME	Type	Money risk-adjusted grade	% compound annual gain (or loss) to Dec. 24, 1992			Value of $10,000 invested five years ago (net of sales charge)	Portfolio analysis			Net assets (millions)	Expense analysis	
			One year	Three years	Five years		% yield	Average maturity (years)	% cash		% maximum initial sales charge	Five-year projection
Kemper Invest. Port.–Diversified Income	HYC	A	17.5	14.1	12.1	$19,384	9.2	8.0	1.0	$245.3	None[2]	$118
Kemper Investment Portfolio–Government	USG	D	5.0	9.4	8.9	15,217	8.0	4.2	23.0	5,289.2	None[2]	107
Kemper Investment Portfolio–High Yield	HYC	E	16.6	12.7	9.4	15,544	9.6	9.0	2.0	920.9	None[2]	109
Kemper Inv. Port.–Short-Intermed. Gov.	STT	—	5.7	7.9	—	—	6.2	3.5	27.0	213.0	None[2]	110
Kemper Investment Port.–Short-Term Global	WI	—	(7.8)	—	—	—	8.9	0.8	N.A.	273.9	None[2]	110
Kemper Short-Term Global Income	WI	—	(6.8)	—	—	—	9.5	0.8	N.A.	306.6	3.5	109
Kemper U.S. Government Securities	MBS	B	5.5	10.5	10.3	15,601	8.4	5.1	37.0	6,733.7	4.5	79
Keystone Amer. Cap. Preservation & Income	MBS	—	3.3	—	—	—	5.8	4.7	2.0	118.9	3.5	66[3]
Keystone America Government Securities	USG	D	8.6	10.4	9.5	15,380	6.8	13.0	8.4	50.5	2.0	122
Keystone America High Yield Bond	HYC	E	19.5	8.6	7.4	14,030	11.1	8.0	1.1	71.8	2.0	138
Keystone B-1	HGC	E	4.7	8.5	8.8	15,260	7.5	13.0	3.0	470.5	None[2]	110
Keystone B-2	HYC	E	10.5	8.5	8.4	14,871	8.5	14.0	4.0	911.1	None[2]	105
Keystone B-4	HYC	E	18.7	9.4	6.7	13,616	11.1	8.0	3.4	847.1	None[2]	112
Kidder Peabody Government Income	MBS	D	6.8	8.5	9.1	14,545	7.4	6.0	0.3	91.6	2.25	112
Legg Mason Income–Gov. Intermediate	STT	B	7.0	10.1	9.9	15,836	5.7	7.8	1.9	320.1	None	47
Legg Mason Income–Investment Grade	HGC	C	7.3	9.6	9.9	15,889	6.3	14.0	(2.6)[6]	49.9	None	47
Lexington GNMA Income	MBS	B	6.0	10.0	10.7	16,393	7.4	5.2	0.0	135.1	None	56
Liberty Financial–U.S. Government	MBS	C	6.5	10.2	9.4	15,005	7.8	19.7	0.0	831.9	4.5	92
Liberty High Income Bond	HYC	B	17.4	17.9	13.5	17,755	11.1	5.5	1.0	381.8	4.5[2]	99
Lord Abbett Bond Debenture	HYC	A	16.8	14.2	12.2	16,892	10.3	7.5	10.2	703.8	4.75	92
Lord Abbett Global Income	WI	—	6.8	11.0	—	—	9.4	8.6	7.3	144.6	4.75	115
Lord Abbett U.S. Government Securities	USG	B	7.8	11.4	11.0	15,803	9.0	8.0	4.6	3,216.3	4.75	97
MacKenzie Adjustable U.S. Government	MBS	—	4.2	—	—	—	5.7	23.0	7.3	29.9	3.0	76
MacKenzie Fixed Income	HGC	C	9.3	9.0	10.6	15,726	7.1	17.0	15.9	111.0	4.75	125
MainStay Government Plus	USG	E	4.4	8.1	8.6	14,982	8.2	11.7	8.5	984.3	None[2]	118
MainStay High Yield Corporate Bond	HYC	C	21.5	13.9	10.5	16,464	10.3	7.9	11.2	464.1	None[2]	134
Merrill Lynch Adjustable Rate Sec. B	MBS	—	—	3.2	—	—	5.5	3.2	4.3	955.2	None[2]	80
Merrill Lynch Corporate–High Income A	HYC	A	21.3	17.3	13.7	18,279	11.0	8.5	4.0	683.8	4.0	72
Merrill Lynch Corporate–High Quality A	HGC	B	8.4	10.6	10.7	15,873	7.3	9.2	6.8	362.1	4.0	71
Merrill Lynch Corporate–Intermed. Bond A	STT	A	8.0	10.5	10.2	15,686	7.4	7.3	6.5	154.3	2.0	54
Merrill Lynch Federal Securities A	MBS	A	5.7	10.1	10.4	15,626	7.0	7.4	3.0	2,048.1	4.0	83
Merrill Lynch Global Bond B	WI	D	9.4	12.4	10.0	16,039	8.3	8.8	2.0	621.4	None[2]	96
Merrill Lynch Short-Term Global B	WI	—	(3.0)	—	—	—	8.0	1.4	0.6	3,879.8	None[2]	58
Merrill Lynch World Income A	WI	—	7.1	12.6	—	—	11.0	5.7	10.3	490.4	4.0	92
MetLife–State Street Gov. Income	USG	C	7.6	10.6	10.2	16,109	7.4	11.4	4.7	813.0	None	58
MetLife–State Street Gov. Securities	USG	D	7.1	10.3	9.8	15,125	6.4	11.8	11.2	92.5	4.5	111
MetLife–State Street High Income	HYC	D	20.2	11.1	10.2	15,260	11.6	7.5	0.5	400.1	4.5	106
MFS Bond	HGC	A	7.0	10.8	10.9	15,777	8.0	8.7	6.0	478.9	4.75	95
MFS Government Income Plus	USG	E	6.9	7.6	9.1	14,400	6.4	N.A.	0.0	749.2	4.75	122
MFS Government Premium	STT	—	6.2	6.6	—	—	5.1	N.A.	23.0	316.4	3.75	108
MFS Government Securities Trust	USG	D	7.9	9.8	9.8	14,921	7.4	16.6	0.0	360.7	4.75	113
MFS High Income Trust	HYC	D	17.7	13.5	10.3	15,149	10.9	7.7	4.0	584.6	4.75	110
MFS Lifetime–Government Income Plus	USG	E	6.6	7.4	7.9	14,622	6.3	N.A.	0.0	2,570.1	None[2]	125
MFS Lifetime–Government Securities	USG	—	7.2	8.6	—	—	6.3	7.3	4.0	89.2	None[2]	134
MFS Lifetime–High Income	HYC	D	17.0	14.4	10.0	15,993	9.8	7.8	5.0	255.8	None[2]	147
MFS Lifetime–Intermediate Income	STT	—	3.1	7.0	—	—	6.6	5.0	8.0	343.1	None[2]	140
MFS Worldwide Governments Trust	WI	D	2.7	10.9	9.5	14,934	5.9	10.3	20.0	347.6	4.75	131
Midwest Income–Intermediate-Term Gov.	STT	D	7.3	9.6	8.8	14,937	6.3	7.6	4.5	59.1	1.0	65
Midwest Strategic–Gov. Long Maturity	USG	—	7.6	—	—	—	6.8	28.2	6.4	25.2	4.0	83
Midwest Strat.–U.S. Gov. Securities	MBS	D	6.6	9.1	9.1	14,655	6.9	27.8	1.0	42.0	4.0	103
Midwest Strat.–U.S. Treasury Allocation	USG	—	6.1	7.9	—	—	6.1	27.2	9.1	46.8	4.0	106
Mutual of Omaha America	USG	C	6.9	9.8	10.3	15,537	6.5	12.5	4.3	80.2	4.75	110

Money's grades compare long-term and short/intermediate-term bonds by five-year, risk-adjusted return to Dec. 1. The top 20% in each group receive an A, the next 20% a B and so on. **Value of $10,000** is to Dec. 1. [1]Currently closed to new investors [2]Fund may impose back-end load or exit fee. [3]Three years [4]Manager absorbing expenses [5]Performance from Dec. 31, 1987.

FUND NAME	Type	MONEY risk-adjusted grade	% compound annual gain (or loss) to Dec. 24, 1992			Value of $10,000 invested five years ago (net of sales charge)	Portfolio analysis			Net assets (millions)	% maximum initial sales charge	Five-year projection
			One year	Three years	Five years		% yield	Average maturity (years)	% cash			
N&B Limited Maturity Bond	STT	C	5.6	8.7	8.7	$15,171	6.0	2.8	5.9	$276.9	None	$36
N&B Ultra Short Bond	STT	E	4.0	6.7	7.1[5]	14,131	5.6	0.6	77.1	87.2	None	36
National Bond	HYC	E	24.5	17.3	8.9	14,327	12.4	8.3	4.9	552.5	4.75	123
National Federal Securities Trust	USG	D	8.4	10.6	10.0	15,267	7.6	12.5	0.3	336.9	4.75	96
National Multi-Sector Fixed Income A	HYC	—	13.0	14.8	—	—	9.1	10.1	3.8	143.2	4.75	140
Nationwide Bond	HGC	B	8.6	11.0	10.4	15,360	10.0	19.4	4.2	89.5	4.5	79
New Beginning U.S. Government Sec.	USG	C	6.1	9.8	9.7	15,798	6.7	13.3	2.6	36.8	None	55
North American Security U.S. Government	MBS	—	7.1	9.4	—	—	7.1	4.6	1.5	111.4	4.0	106
Oppenheimer Champion High Yield	HYC	—	16.6	15.9	—	—	11.4	7.6	19.9	47.0	4.75	118
Oppenheimer GNMA	MBS	C	5.4	9.7	9.6	14,944	6.9	2.1	1.2	99.8	4.75	120
Oppenheimer High Yield	HYC	C	14.5	12.2	10.7	15,592	12.2	7.6	13.1	956.8	4.75	96
Oppenheimer Investment Grade Bond	STT	B	7.7	10.0	9.8[5]	15,073	7.0	N.A.	16.2	109.4	4.75	112
Oppenheimer Strategic Income A	HYC	—	8.1	11.8	—	—	11.0	12.1	4.6	1,731.6	4.75	108
Oppenheimer U.S. Government Trust	USG	D	6.4	9.5	9.4	14,808	7.0	5.8	1.2	407.2	4.75	109
Overland Express–U.S. Government Income	USG	—	7.8	11.6	—	—	7.5	19.5	0.4	32.6	4.5	56
Pacifica Asset Preservation	STT	—	5.0	—	—	—	5.4	1.0	55.0	160.2	None	35
Pacifica Government Income	STT	—	6.3	—	—	—	7.1	5.3	7.0	137.2	4.5	82
Pacific Horizon U.S. Government Sec.	MBS	A	8.1	11.1	10.8	15,780	7.2	8.9	2.5	111.0	4.5	65
Paine Webber Global Income B	WI	D	0.9	9.5	9.8	15,983	7.0	N.A.	39.0	1,559.1	None[2]	125
Paine Webber High Income A	HYC	B	24.9	18.8	12.2	16,943	12.1	7.0	6.4	287.3	4.0	100
Paine Webber Investment Grade Income A	HGC	A	9.7	11.5	10.9	16,134	7.9	15.9	3.8	206.1	4.0	93
Paine Webber Short-Term Global A	WI	—	3.5	—	—	—	4.5	N.A.	80.6	317.9	3.0	66[3]
Paine Webber U.S. Government Income A	USG	B	6.8	10.5	10.2	15,595	7.6	26.1	7.9	719.4	4.0	90
Phoenix High Quality Bond	HGC	C	9.3	9.8	10.0	15,113	6.7	6.0	6.0	39.7	4.75	103
Phoenix High Yield Series	HYC	C	17.6	13.0	10.3	15,481	9.5	10.9	5.0	127.1	4.75	108
Phoenix U. S. Government	USG	C	8.5	10.2	9.8	15,175	6.6	6.5	14.0	39.6	4.75	102
Pilgrim Adjustable U.S. Government I	MBS	—	6.3	—	—	—	7.4	27.9	(0.5)[6]	790.8	None[2]	81[3]
Pilgrim GNMA	MBS	D	7.8	9.1	9.5	15,066	8.3	28.9	(30.7)[6]	92.9	3.0	89
Pilgrim Global Short-Term Multi-Market	WI	E	(14.7)	(10.4)	(7.1)	—	10.6	1.0	54.8	82.2	3.0	108
Pioneer Bond	HGC	B	8.1	10.2	10.0	15,268	7.8	9.6	2.4	107.7	4.5	102
Pioneer U.S. Government Trust	USG	—	7.0	9.4	—	—	7.4	8.2	0.3	82.1	5.75	98
Piper Jaffray Government Income	USG	D	5.1	10.6	9.7	15,066	9.6	N.A.	10.4	123.7	4.0[2]	102
Portico–Bond Immdex	STT	—	8.4	—	—	—	6.4	10.4	0.0	180.5	None	28
Portico–Short-Intermediate Income	STT	—	7.4	—	—	—	6.0	3.2	7.1	126.7	None	34
Principal Preservation Gov. Portfolio	USG	C	7.5	10.3	9.6	15,115	7.0	6.8	0.0	37.0	4.5	107
Princor Bond	HGC	—	8.9	10.1	10.6	15,722	7.8	10.6	4.3	60.4	5.0	96[4]
Princor Government Securities Income	MBS	B	6.7	10.7	11.2	15,988	7.0	26.1	1.4	160.0	5.0	100
ProvidentMutual U.S. Government Income	USG	E	6.0	8.1	7.7	13,776	7.1	11.5	2.8	66.2	4.5	119
Prudential GNMA B	MBS	E	6.3	8.9	8.7	15,117	7.4	4.8	3.6	319.9	None[2]	103
Prudential Government–Intermed. Term	STT	D	6.4	9.2	9.1	15,215	7.6	3.5	3.7	310.7	None	47
Prudential Government Plus B	USG	D	6.3	9.1	9.1	15,375	6.5	6.7	3.9	2,704.4	None[2]	125
Prudential High Yield B	HYC	D	16.3	12.0	9.2	$15,501	10.6	N.A.	5.0	$2,857.4	None[2]	$91
Prudential Short-Term Global Income B	WI	—	(0.8)	—	—	—	7.9	1.5	8.2	649.5	None[2]	101
Prudential Structured Maturity A	STT	—	7.8	9.7	—	—	7.2	3.2	0.4	109.4	3.25	84
Prudential U.S. Government B	USG	E	6.3	7.8	8.9	15,172	6.1	14.5	0.6	161.6	None[2]	122
Putnam Adjustable Rate U.S. Government A	MBS	—	3.8	6.4	—	—	6.5	10.7	0.0	380.2	3.25	105
Putnam American Government	USG	E	6.0	7.6	8.2	14,105	6.7	12.8	0.0	4,278.6	4.75	99
Putnam Diversified Income	HYC	—	12.9	13.5	—	—	7.8	8.4	0.0	364.7	4.75	126
Putnam Federal Income	USG	C	6.6	9.7	9.8	15,149	8.0	11.0	0.0	682.7	4.75	109
Putnam Global Governmental Income	WI	A	5.6	12.0	12.2	17,028	7.7	6.6	0.0	428.5	4.75	124
Putnam High Yield	HYC	B	20.0	16.1	11.7	16,460	12.3	7.8	3.7	2,523.9	4.75	105
Putnam High Yield Advantage	HYC	B	19.5	16.7	12.0	16,731	12.4	7.3	2.7	513.6	4.75	117

MONEY's grades compare long-term and short/intermediate-term bonds by five-year, risk-adjusted return to Dec. 1. The top 20% in each group receive an A, the next 20% a B and so on. **Value of $10,000** is to Dec. 1. [1]Currently closed to new investors [2]Fund may impose back-end load or exit fee. [3]Three years [4]Manager absorbing expenses [5]Performance from Dec. 31, 1987.

FUND NAME	Type	MONEY risk-adjusted grade	% compound annual gain (or loss) to Dec. 24, 1992			Value of $10,000 invested five years ago (net of sales charge)	Portfolio analysis			Net assets (millions)	Expense analysis	
			One year	Three years	Five years		% yield	Average maturity (years)	% cash		% maximum initial sales charge	Five-year projection
Putnam Income	HGC	A	10.0	10.7	11.1	$16,061	8.7	12.3	1.1	$638.9	4.75	$102
Putnam U.S. Government Income A	MBS	B	6.9	9.5	9.7	15,071	8.8	9.8	0.0	4,462.2	4.75	102
Quest for Value–Investment Quality Income	HGC	—	10.3	—	—	—	7.6	20.0	3.0	29.0	4.75	110
Quest for Value–U.S. Government Income	USG	—	6.8	10.0	—	—	6.4	5.0	2.0	154.0	4.75	108
Rightime Government Securities	USG	E	9.9	4.7	6.7	13,022	4.6	26.7	1.0	30.8	4.75	141
Safeco U.S. Government	MBS	B	7.2	10.2	10.2	16,140	7.5	9.5	2.2	56.1	None	54
Schwab Inv.–Short-Intermediate	STT	—	6.4	—	—	—	6.0	4.0	0.0	295.2	None	26
Scudder GNMA	MBS	B	7.3	10.7	10.4	16,211	8.5	6.2	0.3	471.9	None	55
Scudder Income	HGC	A	7.4	10.8	10.9	16,582	6.7	11.0	6.4	462.2	None	54
Scudder International Bond	WI	—	8.7	17.1	—	—	8.0	8.9	21.0	729.5	None	69
Scudder Short-Term Bond	STT	A	5.9	10.0	9.9	15,984	8.2	2.9	12.0	2,848.7	None	53
Scudder Short-Term Global Income	WI	—	5.3	—	—	—	9.1	1.3	36.4	1,358.4	None	32[3]
Scudder Trust–Zero Coupon 2000	USG	B	9.8	10.7	12.9	18,178	6.8	9.3	0.0	34.8	None	55
Security Income–Corporate Bond	HGC	D	9.2	10.5	9.6	14,949	8.1	24.8	3.1	99.1	4.75	102
Seligman High Income Bond	HYC	B	20.0	13.5	11.2	16,300	10.7	9.8	3.0	39.8	4.75	115
Seligman High Income–U.S. Government	USG	E	6.4	8.8	8.6	14,425	7.1	6.3	6.2	58.5	4.75	105
Sentinel Bond	HGC	A	8.4	10.9	10.8	15,763	7.0	8.4	12.7	57.7	5.25	99
Sentinel Government Securities	USG	B	7.9	10.6	10.3	15,336	6.9	6.6	4.8	68.1	5.0	101
Shearson Income–Diversified B	HYC	—	6.7	—	—	—	8.8	15.3	12.6	1,597.9	5.0	98
Shearson Income–Global Bond B	WI	D	4.3	10.1	8.9	14,627	6.6	7.1	2.3	55.8	None[2]	119
Shearson Income–High Income B	HYC	E	20.5	11.6	8.6	15,120	10.4	9.2	9.3	329.4	None[2]	100
Shearson Invest.–Gov. Securities B	USG	C	6.7	9.7	10.9	16,587	6.8	7.4	29.7	1,094.2	None[2]	90
Shearson Invest.–Investment Grade B	HGC	C	9.8	11.3	11.0	16,915	7.4	26.9	2.8	439.9	None[2]	94
Shearson Managed Governments A	MBS	C	7.2	10.9	9.9	15,169	7.7	7.3	17.6	494.4	4.5	101
Shearson Short-Term World Income A	WI	—	(1.9)	—	—	—	6.8	0.5	0.9	169.9	3.0	94
Shearson Worldwide Prime A	WI	—	(1.5)	—	—	—	5.2	0.2	4.7	283.9	None	95
Sierra–Corporate Income	HGC	—	10.4	—	—	—	8.2	23.7	4.0	217.3	4.5	96
Sierra–U.S. Government Securities	USG	—	6.8	10.0	—	—	7.6	24.3	4.0	604.7	4.5	83
Smith Barney Income Return A	STT	C	5.9	8.7	8.7	14,904	6.0	2.5	23.3	54.1	1.5	43
Smith Barney Monthly Government A	MBS	A	7.3	10.8	11.4	16,355	8.5	23.7	2.9	48.8	4.0	69
Smith Barney U.S. Gov. Securities A	MBS	A	7.5	11.0	11.4	16,395	8.3	23.9	1.8	459.9	4.0	68
Smith Barney World–Global Gov. Bond	WI	—	0.1	—	—	—	11.0	N.A.	7.5	112.2	4.0	114
Stagecoach GNMA	MBS	—	7.1	—	—	—	6.7	21.1	0.0	132.3	4.5	93
Stagecoach Government Allocation	STT	C	8.0	9.7	9.7	14,876	5.2	25.4	3.0	97.8	4.5	99
SteinRoe Government Income	USG	C	6.8	9.9	10.1	15,899	6.8	17.2	8.6	61.9	None	55
SteinRoe Income	HGC	B	10.0	11.0	10.4	16,256	8.1	10.2	7.9	121.3	None	50
SteinRoe Intermediate Bond	STT	B	8.1	10.0	10.0	15,895	7.7	6.5	3.0	271.2	None	39
Strong Advantage	STT	—	8.4	8.7	—	—	7.0	1.5	2.0	250.8	None	64
Strong Government Securities	USG	A	10.2	11.9	10.9	16,824	7.8	9.6	0.0	76.6	charge	75
Strong Short-Term Bond	STT	C	6.9	9.0	9.0	15,294	8.1	2.7	14.0	744.8	None	65
SunAmerica Federal Securities	MBS	C	5.2	9.5	9.7	15,695	6.5	20.3	5.9	131.5	None[2]	106
SunAmerica High Income	HYC	D	20.9	10.9	9.3	15,540	11.5	7.7	3.6	82.3	None	143
SunAmerica Income–Government Securities	USG	E	6.7	8.6	8.4	14,232	8.5	14.6	1.1	67.7	4.75	119
SunAmerica Income–High Yield	HYC	C	22.0	15.5	11.4	16,339	12.9	8.0	0.0	26.8	4.75	130
SunAmerica U.S. Government Securities	USG	E	5.1	8.2	8.1	14,727	7.7	12.7	(1.0)[6]	1,201.0	None[2]	114
Templeton Income	WI	D	4.6	9.5	9.1	14,703	8.5	10.9	6.7	178.9	4.5	100
Thomson Income B	HGC	E	8.1	6.9	7.6	14,243	8.5	6.0	2.2	242.0	None[2]	103
Thomson Short-Intermediate Government B	STT	—	2.3	—	—	—	5.5	2.0	4.0	136.0	None[2]	82
Thomson U.S. Government B	USG	E	3.4	8.1	8.7	15,064	7.4	5.2	23.0	531.0	None[2]	97
Thornburg Limited–U.S. Government	STT	C	7.7	9.7	9.1	14,923	6.5	4.6	5.0	102.4	2.25	76
TNE Adjustable Rate U.S. Government	MBS	—	5.2	—	—	—	5.6	3.0	9.3	258.7	3.0	62
TNE Bond Income	HGC	B	8.6	11.1	10.5	15,547	7.2	12.0	2.0	144.2	4.5	105

MONEY's grades compare long-term and short/intermediate-term bonds by five-year, risk-adjusted return to Dec. 1. The top 20% in each group receive an A, the next 20% a B and so on. **Value of $10,000** is to Dec. 1. [1]Currently closed to new investors [2]Fund may impose back-end load or exit fee. [3]Three years [4]Manager absorbing expenses [5]Performance from Dec. 31, 1987.

FUND NAME	Type	MONEY risk-adjusted grade	% compound annual gain (or loss) to Dec. 24, 1992 One year	Three years	Five years	Value of $10,000 invested five years ago (net of sales charge)	% yield	Average maturity (years)	% cash	Net assets (millions)	% maximum initial sales charge	Five-year projection
TNE Global Government	WI	—	4.2	8.1	—	—	7.5	8.0	0.0	$31.0	4.5	$146
TNE Government Securities	USG	D	8.2	9.1	9.3	$14,746	5.8	10.0	10.0	182.7	4.5	109
TNE Premium Income	STT	—	6.2	10.0	—	—	6.3	5.0	3.0	456.5	3.0	96
Tower U.S. Government Income	USG	—	5.2	9.8	—	—	7.4	6.1	0.5	63.7	4.5	82
Transamerica Bond–Government Securities	USG	D	6.7	10.4	9.7	14,925	8.7	8.0	0.0	753.6	4.75	111
Transamerica Invest. Quality Bond	HGC	D	6.3	10.4	9.7	15,110	8.8	8.0	1.0	112.7	4.75	118
Transamerica Spec.–Government Income	USG	—	5.6	8.9	—	—	8.0	8.0	4.0	224.6	None[2]	128
Transamerica Spec.–High Yield Bond	HYC	E	13.0	12.0	7.6	14,331	10.9	7.0	2.0	109.2	None[2]	140
T. Rowe Price Adjustable Rate	MBS	—	3.9	—	—	—	6.8	0.6	1.1	719.2	None	14[4]
T. Rowe Price Global Government Bond	WI	—	4.8	—	—	—	7.8	5.3	5.7	58.4	None	66
T. Rowe Price GNMA	MBS	B	7.0	10.6	10.3	16,154	7.8	6.8	(0.5)[6]	840.4	None	48
T. Rowe Price High Yield Bond	HYC	D	14.7	10.2	9.3	15,453	9.9	9.5	3.0	1,334.6	None	54
T. Rowe Price International Bond	WI	E	4.8	12.5	7.0	13,879	8.6	5.7	21.0	585.0	None	68
T. Rowe Price New Income	HGC	C	5.8	9.9	9.9	16,009	6.7	7.8	14.8	1,486.3	None	48
T. Rowe Price Short-Term Bond	STT	E	5.2	8.4	8.2	14,769	6.7	2.4	0.0	510.8	None	48
T. Rowe Price Treasury–Intermediate	STT	—	6.8	10.1	—	—	6.2	4.5	1.0	154.9	None	44
T. Rowe Price Treasury–Long Term	USG	—	7.0	9.6	—	—	6.9	14.7	0.0	60.9	None	44
Twentieth Century Long-Term Bond	HGC	C	6.2	9.7	10.3	16,439	6.3	4.9	7.7	162.6	None	55
Twentieth Century U.S. Governments	STT	E	4.5	8.0	7.8	14,561	4.5	1.6	16.0	580.9	None	55
United Bond	HGC	C	8.5	10.1	10.2	14,711	7.5	21.7	3.2	591.6	8.5	118
United Government Securities	USG	C	8.0	10.5	9.9	15,321	6.6	15.0	12.5	163.6	4.25	82
United High Income	HYC	E	16.9	10.8	7.1	12,778	9.8	9.5	10.2	960.9	8.5	125
United High Income II	HYC	D	16.0	12.9	9.6	14,367	9.5	9.2	11.3	345.1	8.5	130
USAA Investment–GNMA	MBS	—	6.6	—	—	—	7.9	6.1	0.0	216.8	None	12[3]
U.S. Government Securities	USG	B	8.3	10.5	10.1	15,315	8.1	8.8	5.7	1,365.4	4.75	93
UST Master Managed Income–Original	HGC	A	7.3	10.7	11.2	16,101	6.4	13.0	1.3	117.8	4.5	102
Value Line Aggressive Income	HYC	E	12.8	11.2	8.3	14,718	9.5	9.9	10.1	36.1	None	65
Value Line U.S. Government Securities	USG	A	7.1	11.0	10.6	16,439	6.9	23.7	2.1	428.8	None	36
Van Eck World Income	WI	B	(2.8)	10.6	11.1	16,249	8.9	5.8	24.6	287.3	4.75	120
Vanguard Bond Market	STT	A	7.8	10.5	10.5	16,388	7.2	8.3	2.6	1,061.9	None	59
Vanguard Fixed Income–GNMA	MBS	A	7.6	11.4	11.5	17,236	7.7	8.8	2.9	6,770.8	None	16
Vanguard Fixed Income–High Yield	HYC	C	14.7	11.7	10.3	16,180	10.0	10.1	6.0	2,365.1	None	19
Vanguard Fixed Income–Inv. Grade Corp.	HGC	A	10.9	12.3	12.4	17,740	7.7	17.7	3.3	2,625.0	None	18
Vanguard Fixed Income–Long-Term Treas.	USG	C	9.0	10.3	11.4	16,999	7.3	21.4	3.6	908.5	None	15
Vanguard Fixed Income–Short-Term Corp.	STT	A	6.7	9.7	9.5	15,656	6.6	2.7	2.1	2,737.8	None	15
Vanguard Fixed Income–Short-Term Federal	STT	—	6.5	9.4	—	—	6.1	2.5	0.9	1,593.4	None	15
Vanguard Fixed Income–Short-Term Treas.	STT	—	6.7	—	—	—	5.2	2.6	4.3	440.4	None	15
Vanguard Fixed–Intermediate Treasury	STT	—	8.8	—	—	—	6.5	7.8	2.4	584.4	None	15
Vanguard Preferred	HGC	A	9.1	11.8	12.5	17,754	7.8	N.A.	0.0	203.6	None	35
Van Kampen Merritt High Yield	HYC	E	18.0	12.2	7.9	13,743	11.4	8.1	17.3	227.3	4.9	123
Van Kampen Merritt Short-Term Global A	WI	—	6.0	—	—	—	9.1	1.7	52.2	204.9	3.0	100
Van Kampen Merritt U.S. Government A	MBS	A	6.5	10.7	10.7	15,756	8.8	6.9	7.6	3,559.1	4.9	91
Venture Income Plus	HYC	E	23.7	7.7	4.9	11,715	12.3	16.2	6.4	30.5	4.75	147
Venture Ret. Plan of America–Bond	USG	E	4.3	7.4	7.9	14,509	7.8	4.6	2.1	54.6	None[2]	134
Vista Government Income	USG	C	6.6	9.8	10.0	15,456	6.6	7.1	0.0	56.3	4.5	85
Voyageur U.S. Government Securities	USG	B	7.0	12.5	10.8	15,728	8.6	8.9	1.1	69.2	4.75	105
Warburg Pincus Fixed Income	STT	D	7.4	8.9	8.9	15,270	6.7	6.7	4.1	62.9	None	42
Warburg Pincus Intermediate–Government	STT	—	7.1	10.3	—	—	6.1	4.2	0.3	118.5	None	32
William M. Blair Income Shares	HGC	—	7.5	—	—	—	8.2	5.0	15.1	133.4	None	51
Winthrop Focus–Fixed Income	HGC	A	7.7	10.5	10.5	16,436	6.7	N.A.	7.2	30.7	None[2]	14[3]
WPG Government Securities	USG	A	8.4	10.4	10.6	16,429	7.4	6.0	0.4	264.5	None	48
Zweig Series–Government Securities A	USG	E	5.4	8.3	8.3	14,321	6.5	13.5	4.0	71.4	4.75	121

MONEY's grades compare long-term and short/intermediate-term bonds by five-year, risk-adjusted return to Dec. 1. The top 20% in each group receive an A, the next 20% a B and so on. **Value of $10,000** is to Dec. 1. [1]Currently closed to new investors [2]Fund may impose back-end load or exit fee. [3]Three years [4]Manager absorbing expenses [5]Performance from Dec. 31, 1987.

FUND NAME	Type	MONEY risk-adjusted grade	% compound annual gain (or loss) to Dec. 1, 1992			Value of $10,000 invested five years ago (net of sales charge)	Portfolio analysis			Net assets (millions)	Expense analysis	
			One year	Three years	Five years		% yield	Average maturity (years)	% cash		% maximum initial sales charge	Five-year projection
AIM Municipal Bond [1]	HGT	C	11.0	8.9	10.1	$15,393	6.2	21.2	5.3	$272.0	4.75	$96
Alliance Muni–Insured National	HGT	A	10.4	9.1	10.7	15,890	5.9	23.0	0.0	152.9	4.5	83
Alliance Muni–National Portfolio	HGT	A	11.4	9.8	11.0	16,058	6.2	24.0	0.0	258.7	4.5	85
American Capital Muni Bond A	HGT	B	10.0	8.6	10.2	15,463	6.3	21.0	6.6	291.5	4.75	95
American Capital Tax-Exempt High Yield A	HYT	E	9.8	8.3	8.7	14,441	7.7	19.6	3.2	299.5	4.75	103
American Capital Tax-Exempt Insured A	HGT	E	8.5	7.8	8.3	14,200	6.1	19.0	9.8	61.4	4.75	110
Babson Tax-Free Income–Long Term	HGT	D	9.9	8.6	9.6	15,815	5.4	19.0	0.7	31.2	None	55
Benham National Tax-Free–Intermediate	ITT	B	8.8	8.5	8.2	14,814	5.0	7.2	5.0	50.6	None	34
Benham National Tax-Free–Long-Term	HGT	C	10.9	9.2	9.9	16,043	5.6	20.9	3.0	46.6	None	34
Calvert Tax-Free Reserves–Limited-Term	ITT	E	5.2	6.0	6.5	13,410	4.8	0.8	46.0	524.4	2.0	59
Calvert Tax-Free Reserves–Long-Term	HGT	E	9.0	7.7	9.0	14,644	6.1	25.0	4.0	45.1	4.75	89
Colonial Tax-Exempt A	HGT	D	9.3	8.8	8.9	14,613	6.7	23.7	0.0	2,861.8	4.75	102
Colonial Tax-Exempt Insured A	HGT	D	8.9	8.4	9.1	14,687	5.9	23.3	0.0	216.2	4.75	104
Common Sense Municipal Bond	HGT	—	9.5	8.3	—	—	5.7	18.7	8.0	60.0	4.75	108
Composite Tax-Exempt Bond	HGT	E	9.9	8.7	9.1	14,818	5.5	11.5	4.5	173.9	4.0	81
Dean Witter Tax-Exempt Securities	HGT	B	10.1	9.0	10.5	15,792	6.7	19.0	0.0	1,284.9	4.0	68
Delaware Group Tax-Free–Insured	HGT	D	8.4	8.2	9.2	14,774	5.9	17.2	1.3	85.1	4.75	97
Delaware Group Tax-Free–USA	HGT	B	10.6	8.3	10.2	15,470	6.3	23.4	1.7	701.4	4.75	92
Dreyfus General Muni Bond	HGT	A	11.3	10.6	11.4	17,139	6.7	22.2	(4.8)[2]	1,009.2	None	42
Dreyfus Insured Muni Bond	HGT	E	9.1	8.4	9.1	15,451	5.9	23.3	(4.9)[2]	261.7	None	53
Dreyfus Intermediate Muni Bond	ITT	A	9.9	8.8	8.7	15,206	6.0	9.8	(4.9)[2]	1,542.0	None	39
Dreyfus Municipal Bond	HGT	C	9.5	8.8	9.7	15,894	6.4	22.0	(3.6)[2]	4,243.7	None	38
Dreyfus Premier Muni Bond	HGT	A	11.8	10.4	11.4	16,377	6.5	25.9	0.0	447.9	4.5	95
Dreyfus Short-Intermediate Tax-Exempt	ITT	D	7.6	7.2	6.9	13,952	5.1	2.9	(1.0)[2]	293.7	None	44
Eaton Vance Municipal Bond	HGT	A	10.0	9.5	10.7	15,820	6.4	23.5	3.6	101.3	4.75	88
Eaton Vance Municipal–National	HYT	E	11.9	8.2	8.7	15,199	6.9	25.1	1.5	1,490.5	None[3]	121
Equitable Tax Exempt B	HGT	E	8.4	7.3	7.3	14,239	4.8	14.5	7.0	35.0	None[3]	92
Federated Intermediate Muni	ITT	B	8.5	8.2	7.9	14,616	5.5	7.1	4.0	193.6	None	27
Federated Short-Intermediate Muni	ITT	E	5.7	6.2	6.3	13,539	4.7	1.8	3.0	228.9	None	26
Federated Tax-Free Income	HGT	B	9.6	8.8	10.0	15,375	5.9	26.2	5.0	651.5	4.5[3]	89
Fidelity Advisor–High Income Muni	HYT	A	11.0	11.1	11.8	16,635	6.5	20.6	6.9	148.0	4.75	95
Fidelity Aggressive Tax-Free	HYT	A	10.0	9.3	10.3	16,355	7.0	21.3	7.5	752.3	None[3]	25
Fidelity High Yield Tax-Free	HYT	B	8.2	8.9	10.2	16,277	6.4	20.2	7.0	2,082.0	None	25
Fidelity Insured Tax-Free	HGT	D	9.2	8.6	9.6	15,794	5.9	20.8	7.4	360.9	None	25
Fidelity Limited Term Municipals	ITT	A	9.1	8.6	8.5	15,055	6.0	10.8	9.5	922.5	None	25
Fidelity Municipal Bond	HGT	B	9.8	8.9	10.0	16,130	6.0	22.1	5.6	1,189.5	None	28
Fidelity Spartan Municipal Income	HGT	—	9.8	—	—	—	6.5	20.7	5.6	872.3	None[3]	29
Fidelity Spartan Short-Intermediate Muni	ITT	D	7.0	7.2	6.5	13,716	5.0	3.6	12.3	571.9	None	36
Financial Tax-Free Income Shares	HGT	A	9.9	9.0	11.2	17,027	5.6	26.0	1.9	284.4	None	57
First Investors Insured Tax-Exempt	HGT	E	8.8	8.0	9.0	14,317	6.6	18.0	0.8	1,319.4	6.9	131
Flagship All American Tax Exempt	HGT	—	11.8	10.1	—	—	6.4	23.0	0.5	140.9	4.2	90
Flagship Tax Exempt–Limited Term	ITT	C	9.3	8.4	7.9	14,255	5.6	5.0	0.2	385.1	2.5	63
Fortis Tax-Free–National	HGT	D	9.7	8.8	9.2	14,837	6.2	23.1	0.1	57.3	4.5	105
Fortress Municipal Income	HGT	B	9.4	8.5	9.9	15,840	6.0	26.0	1.9	256.9	1.0[3]	66
Franklin Federal Tax-Free Income	HGT	A	10.1	9.2	10.4	15,734	7.0	22.0	2.0	5,695.7	4.0	67
Franklin High Yield Tax-Free Income	HYT	A	9.6	8.5	10.0	15,482	7.6	21.0	0.0	2,464.4	4.0	68
Franklin Insured Tax-Free Income	HGT	B	9.9	8.8	10.0	15,473	6.3	21.0	0.0	1,360.0	4.0	68
GIT Tax Free Trust–High Yield	HYT	E	9.9	7.7	8.1	14,766	5.4	20.0	0.1	41.1	None	67
IDS High-Yield Tax-Exempt	HYT	C	9.9	8.5	9.7	15,062	6.8	21.1	5.8	5,958.1	5.0	85
IDS Insured Tax-Exempt	HGT	D	10.3	8.8	9.6	15,001	5.7	24.5	6.8	345.1	5.0	86
IDS Tax-Exempt Bond	HGT	E	8.6	7.7	9.0	14,588	5.6	17.5	9.8	1,254.3	5.0	84

MONEY's grades compare long-term and short/intermediate-term bond funds by five-year, risk-adjusted return to Dec. 1. **Value of $10,000** is to Dec. 1. [1]Formerly Cigna Municipal [2]Figure reflects borrowing to boost investments. [3]Fund may impose back-end load or exit fee. [4]Manager absorbing fund expenses [5]Three years

FUND NAME	Type	MONEY risk-adjusted grade	% compound annual gain (or loss) to Dec. 1, 1992			Value of $10,000 invested five years ago (net of sales charge)	Portfolio analysis			Net assets (millions)	Expense analysis	
			One year	Three years	Five years		% yield	Average maturity (years)	% cash		% maximum initial sales charge	Five-year projection
John Hancock Freedom Mgd. Tax-Exempt B	HGT	C	9.5	8.5	10.1	$16,199	5.5	24.0	2.5	$230.8	None[3]	$85
John Hancock Tax-Exempt Income	HGT	C	9.7	8.7	9.6	15,075	5.7	24.0	4.0	476.0	4.5	108
Kemper Municipal Bond	HGT	B	10.5	9.2	10.2	15,510	6.4	16.0	6.0	3,152.5	4.5	71
Keystone America Tax-Free Income	HGT	E	9.3	8.1	9.0	14,647	5.9	23.0	2.8	128.1	4.75	111
Keystone Tax-Exempt Trust	HGT	D	8.8	7.7	9.2	15,501	6.0	22.0	3.0	719.8	None[3]	103
Keystone Tax-Free	HGT	D	9.0	8.1	9.1	15,464	6.2	20.0	9.5	1,192.4	None[3]	95
Liberty Financial–Tax-Free Bond	HGT	C	9.9	8.7	9.6	15,090	5.7	19.1	0.0	165.8	4.5	74
Lord Abbett Tax-Free Income–National	HGT	B	10.0	9.3	10.3	15,533	6.1	24.5	1.0	546.8	4.75	93
MainStay Tax-Free Bond	HGT	E	9.5	7.8	8.2	14,830	5.8	22.3	2.7	304.5	None[3]	97
Merrill Lynch Municipal Income B	ITT	C	8.7	7.8	7.7	14,495	5.7	9.4	4.6	112.0	None[3]	65
Merrill Lynch Muni–Insured A	HGT	C	10.5	9.2	9.9	15,355	6.3	22.6	3.1	2,093.6	4.0	64
Merrill Lynch Muni–Limited Maturity A	ITT	E	6.3	6.4	6.5	13,588	4.6	1.8	12.5	682.2	0.75	30
Merrill Lynch Muni–National A	HGT	C	10.6	9.0	9.7	15,269	7.0	23.6	4.9	1,279.3	4.0	70
MetLife–State Street Tax-Exempt	HGT	C	11.0	8.5	9.9	15,321	5.4	21.0	2.8	177.0	4.5	111
MFS High Yield Municipal Bond	HYT	E	8.6	7.1	8.1	14,086	8.3	20.5	1.0	713.1	4.75	102
MFS Lifetime–Municipal Bond	HGT	E	8.8	7.4	9.0	15,358	5.5	22.5	4.0	441.4	None[3]	130
MFS Municipal Bond	HGT	C	10.5	9.2	10.1	15,391	6.0	19.9	3.0	1,925.1	4.75	79
Midwest Tax-Free–Intermediate-Term	ITT	D	8.0	7.5	7.2	14,014	5.5	8.4	10.6	44.6	1.0	68
Mutual of Omaha Tax-Free Income	HGT	B	9.8	9.2	10.3	15,531	5.9	20.8	2.2	453.1	4.75	93
National Securities Tax-Exempt	HGT	C	9.5	8.9	9.9	15,232	6.7	20.7	1.0	110.2	4.75	94
Nationwide Invest. II–Tax-Free Income	HGT	D	10.1	8.6	9.5	15,742	5.5	23.3	1.0	169.6	None[3]	63
New Beginning–Tax-Free	HGT	—	8.0	7.9	—		6.7	17.4	1.2	243.5	None	44
Nuveen Insured Municipal Bond	HGT	A	10.8	9.4	11.0	16,021	5.8	23.6	2.3	436.8	4.75	71
Nuveen Municipal Bond	HGT	B	9.5	8.7	9.9	15,253	6.0	20.4	0.2	2,091.4	4.75	80
Oppenheimer Tax-Exempt–Insured	HGT	B	10.5	8.8	10.2	15,484	5.5	20.9	1.3	32.7	4.75	118
Oppenheimer Tax-Exempt–Intermediate	ITT	A	10.9	9.1	10.4	15,841	5.7	10.5	4.3	29.3	4.75	108
Oppenheimer Tax-Free Bond	HGT	C	10.1	8.8	9.5	15,003	5.8	25.7	2.1	463.8	4.75	94
Paine Webber Municipal High Income A	HYT	A	10.6	9.5	10.7	15,967	6.5	22.9	6.8	75.4	4.0	106
Paine Webber National Tax-Free Income A	HGT	D	9.2	8.5	9.3	14,943	6.1	24.0	2.1	396.3	4.0	88
Pioneer Municipal Bond	HGT	C	10.0	8.6	10.0	15,388	5.7	17.3	7.6	53.6	4.5	90
Piper Jaffray National Tax-Exempt	HGT	—	10.0	9.1	—	—	6.0	12.0	0.6	59.4	4.0[3]	90
Principal Preservation–Tax-Exempt	HGT	E	9.2	8.4	8.1	14,118	5.8	16.9	2.0	61.1	4.5	92
Princor Tax-Exempt Bond	HGT	B	10.2	8.6	10.4	15,541	5.8	23.9	2.3	107.9	5.0	102
ProvidentMutual Tax-Free Bond	HGT	D	8.7	8.1	9.3	14,923	5.3	10.6	7.0	34.6	4.5	112
Prudential Muni–High Yield B	HYT	A	9.4	7.9	10.0	16,104	6.7	22.8	1.0	877.2	None[3]	72
Prudential Muni–Insured B	HGT	D	9.5	8.3	9.6	15,828	5.2	20.3	2.0	692.2	None[3]	72
Prudential Muni–Modified B	ITT	B	8.3	8.0	8.5	15,013	4.7	9.8	4.5	48.1	None[3]	100
Prudential National Municipal B	HGT	E	10.2	8.7	9.0	15,402	5.3	20.2	1.7	821.6	None[3]	73
Putnam Muni Income	HGT	—	12.2	10.1	—	—	7.3	23.4	1.8	411.5	4.75	110
Putnam Tax-Exempt Income	HGT	B	11.6	9.1	10.6	15,781	6.6	23.8	2.4	1,867.8	4.75	86
Putnam Tax-Free–High Yield	HYT	C	11.4	8.4	9.3	15,581	6.8	24.0	3.2	1,067.0	None[3]	103
Putnam Tax-Free Income–Insured	HGT	E	8.8	7.6	9.0	15,348	5.1	23.9	3.8	470.5	None[3]	120
Safeco Municipal Bond	HGT	B	10.3	9.3	10.6	16,556	6.0	22.0	0.0	508.4	None	30
Scudder High-Yield Tax Free	HYT	A	12.5	9.7	11.0	16,879	6.0	13.6	3.5	185.8	None	57
Scudder Managed Muni Bond	HGT	B	10.1	9.1	10.5	16,438	5.6	13.0	1.6	817.9	None	36
Scudder Medium-Term Tax-Free	ITT	C	10.1	8.9	7.7	14,467	6.0	6.7	2.3	568.5	None	0[4]
Seligman Tax-Exempt–National	HGT	D	8.6	7.9	9.6	15,076	5.9	25.3	0.0	132.1	4.75	90
Sentinel Tax-Free Income	HGT	—	10.0	—	—	—	5.8	12.8	4.2	52.7	5.25	99
Shearson Income–Tax-Exempt B	HGT	C	9.9	8.2	9.4	15,671	6.1	22.0	0.1	911.6	None[3]	90
Shearson Managed Municipals A	HGT	C	11.0	9.1	9.9	15,338	6.5	23.8	1.4	1,673.1	4.5	84
Sierra Trust–National Municipal	HGT	—	11.9	—	—	—	6.1	24.0	0.0	267.8	4.5	79

MONEY's grades compare long-term and short/intermediate-term bond funds by five-year, risk-adjusted return to Dec. 1. **Value of $10,000** is to Dec. 1. [1]Formerly Cigna Municipal [2]Figure reflects borrowing to boost investments. [3]Fund may impose back-end load or exit fee. [4]Manager absorbing fund expenses [5]Three years

FUND NAME	Type	MONEY risk-adjusted grade	% compound annual gain (or loss) to Dec. 1, 1992			Value of $10,000 invested five years ago (net of sales charge)	Portfolio analysis			Net assets (millions)	Expense analysis	
			One year	Three years	Five years		% yield	Average maturity (years)	% cash		% maximum initial sales charge	Five-year projection
Smith Barney Muni–Limited Term Port.	ITT	—	9.1	8.4	—	—	6.0	7.1	0.0	$216.8	2.0	$50
Smith Barney Muni Bond–National Port.	HGT	A	10.8	9.8	10.9	$16,098	6.7	25.6	0.0	323.8	4.0	69
SteinRoe High-Yield Municipals	HYT	C	5.3	7.3	9.6	15,780	6.6	21.0	7.8	393.1	None	38
SteinRoe Intermediate Municipals	ITT	B	8.7	8.5	8.1	14,728	5.0	7.7	6.8	185.5	None	44
SteinRoe Managed Municipals	HGT	C	9.2	8.8	9.8	15,960	5.9	17.5	7.6	740.6	None	36
Strong Municipal Bond	HGT	E	13.9	9.6	9.0	15,351	6.4	18.5	10.0	236.6	None	58
SunAmerica Tax-Free–Insured	HGT	E	6.9	7.1	8.2	14,105	6.3	23.6	6.7	110.6	4.75	118
Tax-Exempt Bond of America	HGT	D	10.0	8.5	9.2	14,813	6.0	10.0	6.9	945.1	4.75	85
Thomson Tax Exempt B	HGT	E	8.4	7.2	8.6	15,137	4.8	22.0	0.0	52.0	None[3]	103
Thornburg Intermediate Muni–National	ITT	—	10.4	—	—	—	6.2	9.8	0.0	60.7	3.5	66[5]
Thornburg Limited-Term Muni–National	ITT	C	8.3	7.6	7.8	14,147	5.7	4.9	0.4	496.7	2.75	83
TNE Tax-Exempt Income	HGT	D	10.2	8.5	9.6	15,104	6.1	22.0	1.0	179.4	4.5	95
Transamerica Spl.–High Yield Tax-Free	HYT	D	9.6	7.8	9.2	15,533	5.9	22.4	4.0	66.4	None[3]	146
Transamerica Tax-Free Bond A	HGT	—	11.5	—	—	—	6.3	23.3	1.0	95.0	4.75	87
T. Rowe Price Tax-Free–High Yield	HYT	A	10.4	9.3	9.9	16,062	6.6	20.7	6.0	723.9	None	46
T. Rowe Price Tax-Free Income	HGT	E	10.7	8.9	8.9	15,298	6.0	18.9	5.0	1,320.3	None	35
T. Rowe Price Tax-Free Short-Intermed.	ITT	E	6.7	6.7	6.4	13,649	4.7	3.3	13.0	400.4	None	36
Twentieth Century Tax-Exempt–Intermed.	ITT	C	8.5	7.8	7.3	14,230	4.6	6.0	6.0	76.8	None	55
Twentieth Century Tax-Exempt–Long Term	HGT	D	9.5	8.3	9.3	15,606	5.0	15.5	10.0	62.1	None	55
United Municipal Bond	HGT	B	11.2	9.2	11.0	16,158	5.8	21.2	1.2	889.7	4.25	73
United Municipal High Income	HYT	A	11.1	9.4	9.9	15,319	6.9	22.0	1.5	260.5	4.25	83
USAA Tax Exempt–Intermediate-Term	ITT	A	9.5	8.8	9.3	15,569	6.0	8.5	5.2	1,125.7	None	25
USAA Tax Exempt–Long-Term	HGT	A	9.8	9.0	10.5	16,494	6.5	20.6	3.8	1,782.4	None	22
USAA Tax Exempt–Short-Term	ITT	D	6.6	6.5	6.9	13,982	5.0	2.5	20.9	794.5	None	27
UST Master Tax-Exempt–Intermediate-Term	ITT	B	9.8	8.4	8.3	14,219	4.7	10.0	0.8	263.2	4.5	80
UST Master Tax-Exempt–Long-Term	HGT	A	11.5	9.5	10.8	15,956	4.9	16.2	6.3	77.6	4.5	91
Value Line Tax Exempt–High Yield	HGT	D	9.6	8.7	9.2	15,552	5.9	20.1	4.8	291.8	None	32
Vanguard Muni–High-Yield	HYT	A	11.2	9.8	11.1	16,950	6.6	14.0	0.0	1,528.1	None	13
Vanguard Muni–Insured Long-Term	HGT	B	10.9	9.2	10.4	16,368	6.2	14.9	0.0	1,958.6	None	13
Vanguard Muni–Intermediate-Term	ITT	A	9.7	9.3	9.7	15,906	5.7	9.6	0.0	3,192.8	None	13
Vanguard Muni–Limited-Term Portfolio	ITT	D	7.6	7.7	7.5	14,366	4.9	3.0	2.0	918.6	None	13
Vanguard Muni–Long-Term	HGT	B	11.3	9.6	10.7	16,647	6.3	14.4	1.2	963.1	None	13
Vanguard Muni–Short-Term	ITT	E	5.3	6.2	6.3	13,567	4.3	1.3	0.0	1,073.0	None	13
Van Kampen Merritt Ins. Tax-Free Income	HGT	C	10.4	9.0	9.9	15,267	6.0	21.5	10.2	953.6	4.9	95
Van Kampen Merritt Municipal Income A	HGT	—	10.4	—	—	—	6.8	25.4	4.5	426.7	4.9	103
Van Kampen Merritt Tax-Free High Income	HYT	E	0.8	4.0	6.6	13,116	8.1	21.4	9.6	593.5	4.9	106
Venture Muni Plus	HYT	D	8.9	7.6	9.0	15,348	7.4	17.0	3.8	127.2	None[3]	129

MONEY's grades compare long-term and short/intermediate-term bond funds by five-year, risk-adjusted return to Dec. 1. **Value of $10,000** is to Dec. 1. [1]Formerly Cigna Municipal [2]Figure reflects borrowing to boost investments. [3]Fund may impose back-end load or exit fee. [4]Manager absorbing fund expenses [5]Three years

Notes: To be ranked, a fund must be at least one year old, accept a minimum investment of $25,000 or less and have had assets of at least $25 million as of Sept. 30, 1992. Gain or loss figures include reinvestment of all dividends and capital-gains distributions. The MONEY risk-adjusted grade appears for funds with at least five-year records and covers the 60-month period to Dec. 1, 1992. The prospectuses of bond funds in the high-grade categories require them to invest primarily in issues rated BBB or better by Moody's or Standard and Poor's. Short/intermediate-term taxable and tax-exempt bond funds have average weighted maturities of up to 10 years. Stock and bond fund yields are the latest 12 months' dividends divided by the most recent share prices adjusted for capital gains-distribution. **Source: Lipper Analytical Services**

Index